D0160768

REACHING ADOLESCENTS: THE YOUNG ADULT BOOK AND THE SCHOOL

Arthea J. S. Reed

The University of North Carolina at Asheville

Merrill, an imprint of
Macmillan College Publishing Company
New York

Maxwell Macmillan Canada
Toronto

Maxwell Macmillan International
New York Oxford Singapore Sydney

Cover art: Tom Post
Editor: Linda James Scharp
Production Editor: Laura Messerly
Art Coordinator: Peter A. Robison
Photo Editor: Anne Vega
Text Design Coordinator: Jill E. Bonar
Cover Designer: Thomas Mack
Production Buyer: Patricia A. Tonneman

This book was set in Garamond by The Clarinda Company and was printed and bound by Book Press, Inc., a Quebecor America Book Group Company. The cover was printed by New England Book Components.

Macmillan College Publishing Company
866 Third Avenue
New York, NY 10022

Macmillan College Publishing Company is part of the
Maxwell Communication Group of Companies.

Maxwell Macmillan Canada, Inc.
1200 Eglinton Avenue East, Suite 200
Don Mills, Ontario M3C 3N1

Library of Congress Cataloging-in-Publication Data
Reed, Arthea J. S.
   Reaching adolescents : the young adult book and the school / by Arthea J. S. Reed.
     p.   cm.
   Includes bibliographical references and index.
   ISBN 0-02-398861-4
   1. Youth—United States—Books and reading. 2. Young adult literature, English—Study and teaching (Secondary)—United States. 3. Education, Secondary—United States. I. Title.
   Z1037.A1R43 1994
028.5'5—dc20   93-13543
                                    CIP

Printing: 1 2 3 4 5 6 7 8 9   Year: 4 5 6 7 8
Photo credits: Mary Jo Brezney: pp. 1, 47, 90, 154, 415; K. S. Studios/Macmillan: p. 247; Barbara Schwartz: pp. 416, 442; Anne Vega/Macmillan: pp. 2, 28, 47, 118, 178, 206, 248, 286, 330, 370, 398.

For text credits, see p. 527.

✦ **To M. Jerry Weiss, friend and mentor** ✦

Preface

The major goals of *Reaching Adolescents* are to provide scholarly information about young adult literature in a readable fashion and to offer a variety of methods for incorporating the literature into the curriculum. The focus of the text is inclusive rather than exclusive; suggesting teaching methods and approaches as well as a vast array of literature: literature written for children and young adults, popular adult literature, and classical literature. The text presents teaching methods that not only stimulate student response, but help students develop critical thinking skills. The literature discussed throughout the text is multicultural and multinational.

Audience

In addition to the holistic, inclusive approach to teaching suggested by the text, *Reaching Adolescents* is designed to be flexible. It is appropriate as a primary textbook in courses such as young adult (or adolescent) literature, English methods, and middle school language (or communication) arts. It is particularly appropriate in those courses which emphasize whole language and student-centered response techniques. It can be used as a supplemental text in children's literature, reading, and social studies or other middle school or secondary methods courses. Both teacher education and library science students will want to retain the text for their personal professional library. It is filled with teaching ideas that can be incorporated into the classroom immediately. For this reason, it is also an excellent resource for all in-service classroom teachers at the middle- and secondary-school level.

Organization

Reaching Adolescents is divided into four parts. The first, "A Rationale for Using Young Adult Literature," is based on the research of psychologists, learning theorists, educators (teacher researchers as well as university researchers), and parents. This section deals with why it is educationally and developmentally appropriate to incorporate young adult literature in the classroom and how young adult literature can be used to help develop literacy.

Part Two, "Literature for Young Adults," is a comprehensive examination of young adult literature by theme and genre. This section catalogs and annotates the world of literature for the young adult reader. It can be used as a reference as teachers plan to incorporate young adult books into the curriculum. Chapters on realistic fiction, coming-of-age literature, historical and multicultural literature, adventure and romance, fantasy and science fiction, and nonfiction and poetry introduce college and university students to highly regarded authors and their work.

Part Three, "The Young Adult Book in the School: Curriculum and Methodology," discusses techniques for incorporating young adult books into most middle and secondary school classrooms. The first two chapters present an inclusive, holistic approach which uses a wide range of literature to teach skills and concepts. In the two chapters on young adult literature in English and language arts (including reading) and across the curriculum, several unit plans that incorporate young adult books are featured. The subsequent three chapters deal with specific teaching methodology, including student-centered techniques for responding to and experiencing literature, using young adult books to teach important skills, and bridging the classics with the young adult book. These chapters contain numerous practical examples in several unit and lesson plans.

The final part of the book "Selection and the Classroom Library," gives the teacher, librarian, parent, and university professor a succinct and complete report of the bibliographic information and reviews available in the field. It discusses practical ways to build a classroom library. A final chapter is included that discusses the recent history of censorship in schools and libraries and suggests a positive approach to dealing with that problem.

Features

The various special features in *Reaching Adolescents* were designed to make it more teachable and readable as well as to provide additional information.

Focus Questions   Before each chapter are five or six focus questions to give students an overview of the material covered in the chapter.

Prologue   Each chapter begins with an anecdotal prologue, which are often written by well-known young adult authors or are comments from teachers or students.

Between the Covers: Authors at Work   Each chapter contains a biographical or autobiographical look at one or two authors, how they write, why they write, what they write, and what they think about the teaching of their books. Designed to give students a personal insight into some of the best authors in the field of young adult literature, each is selected to fit into the content of the particular chapter. All of the authors were selected based on the quality of their work; some are well-established with easily recognizable names, others are less well-known and many of their works remain under-utilized.

Unit or Lesson Plans   Throughout the chapters in section three, several unit and lesson plans appear. Some of the unit plans are examples of thematic or generic units in one subject area such as science, social studies, or English. One unit plan presents an interdisciplinary unit. These can be used as models as students develop their own plans or can be adapted for the classroom.

Case Studies   Case studies are cited to exemplify theory or methodology throughout the text. Some of these case studies are based on articles written by classroom teachers; others are from my own observations or teaching experiences.

Epilogue   The epilogues do more than summarize. They present concluding comments related to the important content of the chapter.

Writing Style

Reaching Adolescents was written with the professor and student in mind. As a professor who has taught young adult literature for more than fifteen years, I recognize the need to have a text that is teachable, interesting, practical, usable, and encourages further reading. Any young adult literature textbook must be used in conjunction with large numbers of young adult books; therefore, the tone of the book needs to be conversational. The content, however, must be well-researched and present current and field-tested approaches to incorporating and teaching the literature.

ACKNOWLEDGMENTS

Writing a textbook requires the work of many individuals without whom the book would never be published. First and foremost, thanks go to my students who have taught me much of what I know about adolescents and adolescent literature. The students who first passed on to me their enthusiasm for adolescent literature deserve special thanks. The students in my adolescent literature classes at the University of North Carolina at Asheville continue to introduce me to new books and authors that they, their adolescent children, and their students have come to love. Thanks go to the student assistants in the office of the UNCA Department of Education who helped type the manuscript, run errands, and do research: Susan Allman, Laura Bland, Melody Bock, Lara Koerber, Karen Shelton, and especially Michelle Fox who was able to find information that no one else could.

The experiences of hundreds of outstanding teachers fill the pages of this book. They have provided me with new insights and a renewed respect for the power of books and of teaching.

Of course, this book could not have been written if it were not for the wonderful writers of books for adolescents. Not only are these individuals gifted writers, but they care deeply about their readers. Thank you for letting me share your books and your thoughts on adolescence, on books for adolescents, and on the writing process. Your words enliven the pages of this book and make reading a joy for millions of young people. Thanks, too, to the publishers who sent books to me for review and possible inclusion in this text.

Thanks go to my colleagues who supported this project particularly Hugh Agee, University of Georgia; Verna E. Bergemann, UNCA; and M. Jerry Weiss, Jersey City State College. Without my trusted and talented assistant, Judy Carver, this book and much of my other work would never be completed. She keeps the office running smoothly while I am absorbed in the writing process. Also, thanks to the helpful staff at Ramsey Library who never hesitate to look up information; particular thanks to Nancy Hayes.

I would like to thank the reviewers of this text for their input: Leila Christenbury, Virginia Commonwealth University; James E. Davis, Ohio University; Peter J. Fisher, National-Louis University; Joanne M. Golden, University of Delaware; Patricia P. Kelly,

Virginia Polytechnic Institute and State University; Hollis Lowery-Moore, Sam Houston State University; Sue Mohrmann, Texas A & I University; Anne Sherrill, East Tennessee State University.

Every book needs one or more good editors. I have been blessed with three: Linda Scharp, who initiated the project; Martha Morss, who made my writing tighter; and Laura Messerly who saw the project through to completion.

It is difficult to imagine how any book could be completed without a supportive spouse. My husband Don supported me intellectually and emotionally as I struggled to complete the book. He read each chapter numerous times; he gently made suggestions for changes. And, he kept the household running when I was too busy to think about cooking or cleaning. Without his support this project would have been impossible.

Contents

PART THREE

Curriculum and Methodology   247

PART ONE

A RATIONALE FOR USING YOUNG ADULT LITERATURE

1 Young Adult Literature: A Bridge to Maturity

Focus Questions

1. How would you define young adult literature?
2. What are the characteristics of a young adult book?
3. How can young adult literature improve the reading skill of adolescents and increase the amount they read?
4. How does young adult literature make it possible for students to interact personally with books?
5. Why are the studies on reading development important if teachers hope to encourage their students to become readers?
6. How can young adult literature help students meet needs, develop more mature values, and become avid, aesthetic readers?

PROLOGUE

Of all the teachers I had through public school, three stand out with particular clarity. All happened to be English teachers. All were as different from one another as cheese from chocolate. . . .

The first of the three, my ninth grade English teacher, Mary Alice Foster, shines in my memory with the luster of a killing ice storm. Daily, with evangelistic fervor, she made our class a torment as she pressed upon us the vital importance for our future and for our moral and mental health of learning the rules of grammar and how to phrase sentences. We learned by rote, we learned by repetition, we learned by writing each rule ten times, then 25 times, if necessary, 50 times.

Not for Mary Alice the nonsense of reading or the equal nonsense of writing. She was teaching us *English*. In aid of this pursuit, her tough red lips enunciated certain sentences which have remained engraved in my mind to this day. "Class! A restrictive modifier, that is, a word or phrase *essential* to a correct understanding of the word it modifies, is *not* set off by commas. However, a nonrestrictive modifier . . . "

With relief I entered tenth grade and encountered Miss Coffin, a tall sweet woman *who required us to read*. I had been reading all my life. To be assigned this private pleasure as homework and then to discuss the novels and stories in class was nothing less than bliss. But life and teenagers being what they are, I argued with Miss Coffin over her choice of books. While I don't remember anything I said—doubtless, it was more cheeky than memorable—I do remember Miss Coffin's startled blushes, those pale rose blotches that spread over her cheeks, her chin and her forehead. . . .

Finally, in twelfth grade, there was Miss W., instantly recognizable by even the dimmest student as she sailed through the corridors of our high school in flowing grey garments, bestowing here a faint smile, there a royal nod. Queen of the English department, her steel grey hair always in perfect waves, her impressive, corseted bosom never revealing itself as anything so weak as flesh by the slightest quiver, Miss W. had charisma, long before any of us had ever heard the word. One had the impression that her lucid, grey-blue, appraising glance could cause presidents to quiver and dictators to reconsider their latest cruelty.

Long before I became one of the privileged allowed into Miss W.'s senior English group (it wasn't even called a class), I had heard her name uttered with equal amounts of fear and awe. She was considered the most demanding teacher in our school. A relentless marker and an arbitrary tyrant with no use for anyone who didn't follow her rules and give her and William Shakespeare their all.

For the fact of the matter was that for Miss W., English began and English ended with the great writer—the *greatest* writer, as she instructed us on the first day of her course. Thereafter, we read the sonnets and a good many of the plays. We were required to memorize speeches, to write them out on tests, and to recite them in class.

3

Public recitation was painful for me, but the memorization, which I could do alone at home, was deeply pleasurable. I was an obsessive but lazy reader, drawn to what quickly interested me. Left to my own devices, I might have missed Shakespeare altogether. . . .

Three English teachers: all women, all dedicated, each firm in the belief that her teaching method was The Way. Combined, the engineerlike mind of Mary Alice Foster, the emotion of Miss Coffin, and the arbitrary, impeccable taste of Miss W. might have made one Super Teach. Yet were I given a chance to play God . . . or even to do a Peggy Sue . . . and change the past in just that way, I doubt I would accept.

Each of these teachers was different, unique, individual. Each stamped her personality on her class: Mary Alice Foster could never have been confused with Miss W., nor Miss Coffin with Mary Alice, nor Miss W. with anyone else in the entire world.

How rare, how fine, how remarkable.   ◆

From: Norma Fox Mazer. "Three Teachers," *ALAN Review*. Fall, 1988, p. 52.

What Is Young Adult Literature?

Young adult literature can be defined most simply as "literature which adolescents read" (Carlsen, 1980, p. 1). It includes books written specifically for adolescents and books written for children, adults, or a general audience that relate to the young adult's needs and interests.

Characteristics of Young Adult Books

The common characteristics of books selected by young adults are simplicity, characters who are young or experience situations of the young, and modern themes that relate to the life of today's young adults (see Figure 1.1).

Cross-Over Literature

The definition of young adult literature as literature that adolescents read does not distinguish among books written for children, adults, or young adults. Most of the books mentioned in this text are written for the young adult audience about young adult characters. However, many are written for children, adults, or a general audience. The reason for the inclusion of books written and distributed to readers other than adolescents is that the young adult makes no distinction. The distinction is made by the publishing houses who market the books for a specified audience. Young adult readers distinguish only between books they like and books they dislike. As the popular young adult author of *The Cat Ate My Gymsuit*, Paula Danziger, says, "These books are not just for kids. They're for everybody!" (personal communication, April 1979)

Limiting the teaching of young adult literature to books specifically written for and marketed to the young adult audience would drastically reduce the world of reading possibilities for adolescents. Fay Blostein (1980), author of the wonderfully creative guide for librarians *Invitations, Celebrations*, agrees."I find it difficult to observe what often seems to me an arbitrary line of demarcation. . . . Admittedly, senior students are less self-conscious about reading a 'young-looking' book than 12–14-year-olds, and readers of fantasy cross all age barriers" (p. 174).

Figure 1.1
Characteristics of Books Selected by Young Adults

Character
Protagonist
- young (usually two years older than the reader)
- larger than life
- realistic
- readers can see themselves in the protagonist

Other Characters
- usually undeveloped
- parents are often undeveloped, out of the picture, or single-dimensional (seen only through the eyes of the protagonist)
- other adults may serve as mentor for the adolescent
- peers may serve as friends or antagonists

Plot
- usually a single plot line
- realistic
- fast-moving
- problems of interest to adolescent readers
- readers can place themselves in the plot
- plenty of dialogue

Point of View
- usually the protagonist's
- often in first person
- sometimes in third person, with an omniscient narrator

Voice
- usually the protagonist's
- sometimes the voice is of a more mature protagonist or second self
- often the voice is the author's
- the voice speaks directly to readers and is never condescending

Theme
- coming of age
- "you are not alone"
- "You can!"
- building self-esteem
- "Life is not so serious"
- "Know thyself"
- awareness
- acceptance
- developing relationships
- survival
- otherness and likeness
- heroism
- discovery/the quest

─────────── ❖ **Between the Covers:** *Authors at Work* ❖ ───────────

RICHARD PECK

Prolific and versatile young adult author Richard Peck says of writers of young adult books, "Our goal as writers for the very young is of course to make them inveterate, chronic readers whose tastes will keep pace with their maturity" (Peck, 1975). Richard Peck is a writer of nonfiction, fiction, and poetry. Born in Decatur, Illinois, in 1934, he is best known for his novels for young adults. He writes in many genres. His realistic fiction includes *Are You in the House Alone?*, a hard-hitting book about a young girl who is raped by a friend, and *Remembering the Good Times*, the story of a talented young man who commits suicide. He also writes realistic fantasies, such as *The Ghost Belonged to Me*, the first of his Blossom Culp books about a young, unattractive girl who has a supernatural ability, and humor and satire, such as *Those Summer Girls I Never Met,* about a brother and sister who must spend the summer on a cruise with their grandmother rather than roaming the shopping malls and taking driving tests. Peck, who graduated from DePauw University expecting to be a teacher, is a scholar of Latin and a lover of simple, straightforward English. His books speak to adolescents. His poetry for young adults (one collection is *Sounds and Silences: Poetry for Now*) often targets issues of special concern to teenagers, as in this example:

A Teenager's Prayer

Oh, Supreme Being, and I don't mean me:

Give me the vision to see my parents as human beings because if they aren't, what
*   does that make me?*
Give me vocabulary because the more I say you know, the less anyone does.
Give me freedom from television because I'm beginning to distrust happy endings.
Give me sex education to correct what I first heard from thirteen-year-olds.
Give me homework to keep me from flunking Free Time.

Give me a map of the world so I may see that this town and I are not the center of it.
Give me the knowledge that conformity is the enemy of friendship.
Give me the understanding that nobody ever grows up in a group, so that I may find
*   my own way.*
Give me limits so I will know I'm loved.
Give me nothing I haven't earned so that this adolescence doesn't last forever.   *AMEN*

The messages of this poem emerge from Richard Peck's young adult books. The messages are delivered by the adolescent characters themselves, as in this poem. And often, as in real life, the problems the young people face are unresolved and the endings are unhappy. ❖

Books Adolescents Read

As G. Robert Carlsen points out, "A book has a writer and reader within. Most writers in telling a story are telling it to someone; usually, they have an exact image of the audience they hope to reach" (1980, p. 2). However, the author's image and the audience to which the book is marketed are not always the same. Sue Ellen Bridgers, one of the most respected authors of young adult literature, does not consider herself an author of young adult books. She believes her books should have a wide appeal for a general audience. In fact, according to Bridgers, she didn't know that *Home Before Dark*, her first book, was a young adult book until her publisher told her it was. Julian Thompson, author of numerous young adult novels including *The Grounding of Group 6*, writes, "It was some time in 1981, I'm pretty sure, that I was first accused of having written a young adult novel. I'd never heard the term before" (1988, p. 7).

Most adolescents are willing to select a book for themselves that is written for someone older, but not younger. In fact, adolescents typically choose books with protagonists who are two or more years older than they are. Similarly, most young readers are not likely to be caught in the stacks of the children's room of the library, even though many libraries still house the young adult books in the children's section. It is likely that this reluctance to read books for younger readers has little to do with the books themselves and more to do with how they are labeled by libraries, bookstores, and publishers. Yet many books appropriate for young adults are in the children's stacks, just as many are in the adult reading room.

When given a stigma-free opportunity, young adults are likely to select and enjoy books written for both younger and older audiences. For example, one course on children's literature taught to high school juniors and seniors in Ohio has a record enrollment. The course, which examines literature from picture books for infants to books for young adolescents, attracts students of both high and low academic achievement. Students say they not only enjoy reading the books but are learning from them. Several of the students in the class are reading complete books for the first time in their lives. Others are able to use their mature reading ability to find new meaning in books like *Charlotte's Web* (White) and *Where the Wild Things Are* (Sendak).

Similarly, books written for adults in other generations are of interest to teenagers of this generation. Books such as *Gone with the Wind* and *Catcher in the Rye* have huge teenage audiences when they are placed on the bookshelves frequented by young adults.

There is little reason to doubt that children's books and adult books when written on themes of interest to young adults will be read by them if available in a stigma-free environment. G. Robert Carlsen points out in *Books and the Teenage Reader* that most adolescent novels (those written for or distributed to adolescents) are read by twelve to fifteen year olds. Only about 25 percent of the books read by high school seniors fall into the adolescent literature category. However, "there is some evidence that if the adolescent novel were more readily available to the late teenager, if teachers and librarians were more knowledgeable about the development of reading tastes, [the adolescent novel] would be more widely read by this older group" (p. 3). The experience of the B. Dalton bookstore chain tends to support this view. In 1980 the stores clustered some young adult titles in prominent floor locations and sales increased 65 percent. Similarly, the public library in Asheville, North Carolina, moved several hundred young adult paperback books from the children's room to a spiral rack in the adult room. The books began to circulate not only to adolescents but also to adults.

According to Carlsen, it has been well documented that reading interest peaks between the ages of twelve and fourteen. During this time young adults are interested in finding out about themselves and the world. However, young teenagers are usually unable to discover the world through direct experiences. They are limited by lack of transportation, money, and freedom. Therefore, many young adolescents read to learn more about themselves and the world. As mobility and freedom increase and money becomes more available, older adolescents are less likely to seek vicarious experiences through books.

Adolescents' interests in books change as they mature. Until the age of sixteen, most of the books selected by young adults relate to their intense interest in self and how they experience the world. After sixteen, adolescents are more likely to turn to books of greater variety. Books for young adults encompass a wide variety of topics, themes, and genres.

Why Is Young Adult Literature Important?

The reasons for using young adult literature in the classroom range from improving reading ability to developing interests, needs, and values. The books also help teachers create an inclusive curriculum that is appropriate for all students.

Reading Skills of Adolescents

In recent decades the public has become increasingly concerned with the lack of reading skills among students in secondary classrooms. Many people claim that teenagers today cannot read, at least not as well as the critics read when they attended school twenty or thirty years ago. Results of students tested on the National Assessment of Educational Progress (NAEP) reading tests since 1969 do not confirm these assumptions, but they do indicate that many of today's adolescents are not reading as well as they should be. For example, according to NAEP results, in 1971, 58 percent of all thirteen year olds tested could interrelate ideas and make generalizations in reading; in 1990, 59 percent could perform these skills. In 1971, only 10 percent of thirteen year olds could understand complicated information in reading; in 1990, 11 percent could perform at this level. Of seventeen year olds tested, 79 percent could interrelate ideas and make generalizations in 1971, 84 percent in 1990. However, among seventeen year olds only 41 percent could understand complicated information in reading in 1990 (Educational Testing Service, *Trends in Academic Progress*, September 1991, p. 15). NAEP test results indicate that by the time students graduate from high school significantly less than half are "adept" readers and only 7 percent are what the NAEP calls "advanced" readers.

Transaction with Texts

Educators must ask why adolescents are unable to understand complicated information they read. Louise Rosenblatt's research on the transaction between readers and texts may provide one of the answers to this question. According to Rosenblatt, "Meaning does not reside ready-made in the text or in the reader; it happens during the transaction between reader and text" (1989, p. 157). In other words, readers gain meaning from the text as they interact with it. A text, in this context, can be any work of writing: a novel, a picture book, a poem, a short story, an encyclopedia, or a textbook. Readers bring to their reading previously gained knowledge, experiences, interests, and values. All of us can think of examples from our own reading of how this transaction works. Most of us can remember reading a book, an essay, or a poem that moved us to tears or laughter.

We can also remember less positive transactions with the written word. I remember picking up a chemistry textbook while in college, reading for about an hour, and at the end of that hour not having the foggiest notion of what I had read. At the time I told myself, "You need to pay attention to what you are reading." I went back through the chapter again, rereading and underlining key information. Another hour passed, and I again realized I did not know what I had read. Why? I was a "good" reader and a "good" student.

I now know that there were many reasons why I was unable to associate meaning with words I clearly recognized. I had never studied chemistry before. So, not only was some of the vocabulary new to me, but the concepts were foreign. I had never looked at the world in this way; I had no idea of how a chemist thinks. Nor did I understand what I was expected to know after reading this chapter. I realized after my second hour of reading that I had highlighted nearly every word on every page. Before I had even opened this textbook, I had convinced myself that science was not my best subject and I was going to hate this required course.

According to Rosenblatt, the reader of any text must take a stance; sometimes the stance is conscious, at other times it is unconscious. I had certainly taken a stance toward the reading of my chemistry text. The stance the reader takes reflects the reader's purpose in reading the text. An *efferent* stance (from the Latin *efferre*, to carry away), focuses on what the reader retains after reading the text. I knew that I was expected to take something away from the text after reading it. In fact, I knew that a quiz was planned for the next class session. However, I had no idea what I was expected to understand after reading the chapter. Therefore, it was difficult for me to assume an efferent stance.

Rosenblatt uses the analogy of an iceberg to illustrate the stance of the reader. According to Rosenblatt, all reading requires both a public sense of a word or a shared understanding of meaning (the tip of the iceberg) and a private meaning or personal understanding (the large submerged part of the iceberg). In the case of reading my college chemistry text, I had no sense of private meaning, but I knew that if I was to pass the quiz, I must gain the public meaning, in this case the instructor's meaning, of the text. Unfortunately, I had little understanding of what that public meaning might be. There was no shared understanding between my instructor and me of the meaning of the text.

When a reader reads a text to gain a private, personal understanding, the reader is assuming what Rosenblatt calls an *aesthetic* stance. In this case the reader focuses attention on what is experienced during the reading act itself as opposed to what will be taken away from it. The base of the iceberg assumes more importance than the tip of the iceberg in aesthetic reading. Of course, this stance does not mean that the reader takes nothing away from reading the text. The public meaning may also be important, but more important is the reader's ability to experience and savor the work.

Rosenblatt suggests that the efferent and aesthetic stances toward a work form a continuum. Readers put themselves at a point along the continuum prior to reading a particular work. For example, when I read the essay by Rosenblatt to which I refer in this text, I placed myself somewhere between the efferent and aesthetic stances. I was reading her essay for what I could take away from it, but I was also reading for the personal satisfaction of better understanding my own reading process.

Rosenblatt makes the point that readers need to understand whether the reading they are doing requires an efferent or aesthetic stance. However, many adolescent readers do not understand this. *A Tale of Two Cities*, for example, could be read either way. If the book is being read so the student can write a paper about it or take a test on it, an efferent stance is likely to be assumed. If, on the other hand, it is being read to savor its literary qualities and personal meaningfulness, an aesthetic stance should be assumed. Few adolescents have the opportunity to read books aesthetically. Too often, in literature programs, we turn works of literature into efferent reading exercises. We rarely give adolescents the opportunity to read for pleasure and personal enhancement. If students only read for efferent purposes, are they likely to learn to enjoy the process of reading? If they read primarily to give back what they have learned to the teacher in the public sense, will they ever explore the much larger personal attributes of texts? Opportunities for aesthetic reading are important because it is through personal reading that students move to the higher levels of understanding. It is at the personal level that readers deal with the complexity of works.

We must provide our students with texts that they can read from an aesthetic stance. Textbooks, even well-written ones, are unlikely to be useful for this purpose. The classics, too, are not ideal for this use. A large percentage of adolescent readers are unable to read mature classic works aesthetically because they do not have the appropriate maturity, experience, or reading skills. The many excellent young adult novels written for adolescents, however, provide an opportunity to experience texts aesthetically. This experience will eventually carry over to more mature reading and will increase the likelihood that these adolescents will become avid adult readers.

Amount Read by Adolescents

In addition to those who worry about teenagers' skills in reading, other educators contend that teenagers do not read, at least not as much or not the same quality of material as students of previous generations read. Surveys done in conjunction with the NAEP tests indicate that the amount of reading students do for school is limited. Although teachers report giving ten hours of homework per week, high school seniors report doing only four to five hours per week (Educational Testing Service, 1991, p. 51). Researcher John Goodlad found that the amount of reading done during the school day is also limited. He found that in U.S. elementary schools (grades K–6), only 6 percent of the school day was spent reading; in junior high schools, only 3 percent of the day was spent actually reading; and in high schools, only 2 percent of the school day was spent reading (1984, p. 107).

Donald R. Gallo, on the other hand, looked at independent reading. In a study conducted in Connecticut in 1982, 3,399 students in grades four through twelve reported reading independently between three and five hours a week, in addition to school assignments. In fact, 9 percent of the boys and 13 percent of the girls surveyed indicated that they read more than ten hours per week for pleasure or information. Eighty-seven percent of students in grades seven through twelve reported reading at least one book per month that was not assigned for schoolwork; 43 percent indicated that they read three or more books per month. However, 23 percent of the boys responding to the survey and 10 percent of the girls reported that they did not read at all outside of school requirements. Gallo concludes that we cannot say whether today's students are reading more or less than students used to read, but only that the majority of students do read (1985, pp. 46–47). However, we can also conclude that they often do not read assigned texts and that they rarely read during the school day.

The Nonreading Curriculum

Perhaps the reason many teachers think today's students do not read as much as they used to is that students often do not complete reading that has been assigned, as the NAEP results confirm. Or the lack of student reading reported by teachers may be a result of not requiring students to read during the school day.

One reason many students do not complete school-required reading is related to Rosenblatt's studies above: either they are always required to take an efferent stance when reading school assignments, or they are unable to interact in a personal way with the material they are required to read. Frequently adolescents are required to read books and complete assignments that are not meaningful to them. As the NAEP survey of students and teachers indicates, students do far less homework than teachers assign. *Cliff Notes* and *Monarch Guides* to the classics are best-sellers. Often students read the synopsis and commentary about the book but fail to read the book.

Nancie Atwell in her wonderful book *In the Middle: Writing, Reading, and Learning with Adolescents*, about how she has turned middle school students into readers and writers, claims that all students can be good readers. A middle school teacher, Atwell contends that it is too often teachers who turn students into "aliterate" readers (those who can read but choose not to). Atwell says that we do this by demonstrating the following things about reading:

- Reading is difficult, serious business.
- Literature is even more difficult and serious.
- Reading is a performance for an audience of one: the teacher.
- There is one interpretation of a text: the teacher's.
- "Errors" in comprehension or interpretation will not be tolerated.
- Student readers aren't smart or trustworthy enough to choose their own texts.
- Reading requires memorization and mastery of information, terms, conventions, and theories.
- Reading is always followed by a test (and writing mostly serves to test reading— book reports, critical papers, essays, and multiple choice/fill-in-the-blank/short answer variations).
- Reading somehow involves drawing lines, filling in blanks, and circling.
- Readers break whole texts into separate pieces to be read and dissected one fragment at a time.
- It is wrong to become so interested in a text that you read more than the fragment the teacher assigned.
- Reading is a solitary activity you perform as a member of a group.
- Readers in a group may not collaborate; this is cheating.
- Re-reading a book is also cheating; so are skimming, skipping, and looking ahead.
- It's immoral to abandon a book you're not enjoying.
- You learn about literature by listening to teachers talk about it.

- Teachers talk a lot about literature, but teachers don't read.
- Teachers are often bored by the literature they want you to read.
- Reading is a waste of English class time.
- There's another kind of reading, a fun, satisfying kind you can do on your free time or outside of school.
- You can fail English yet still succeed at and love this other kind of reading. (Atwell, 1987, pp. 152–53)

Variety of Reasons to Read

As Rosenblatt's studies clearly illustrate and as Atwell's experience documents, there are many reasons to read. Typically our curriculum only addresses reading for efferent purposes, spitting back to the teacher what the student has learned from the reading. Is it any wonder, then, that a large proportion of today's students, like those in previous generations, do not read as much as we would like? Dan Jackson (1980), a junior and senior high school teacher in Spotswood, New Jersey, describes some of the readers he grew up with in the Bronx schools:

> The crowd I grew up with in the Bronx during the 1960's had plenty of style and color, no geniuses as far as I know, and not much class. But quite a few of us had the cheek or the need to do things our own way. That's how we played. That's how we partied. And that's how we read books. John, for example, went wild with Catullus one year for no apparent reason. He would recite romantic or sexy lyrics halfway through our beer blasts. Ten years down the line, he became probably the only IBM specialist whose first trip to Europe was highlighted by a visit to see the Catullus manuscripts in Venice. Fred liked Maugham. He read *The Moon and Sixpence*, *Of Human Bondage*, *Cakes and Ale*, and at least eight other works, while falling into and failing out of three high schools. And his vision of the world was shaped by those unrequired readings.
>
> The girls were no different. Lorraine hated the three high schools she attended, but read enough detective fiction to compile a bibliography for a dissertation. Marian was bookish and bright. She even stayed in the same school for four years. None of us were ever surprised when she showed up at Orchard Beach with *Siddhartha*, *Pere Goriot*, or *The Brothers Karmazov*.
>
> Sweeper and Razz liked only sports stories, which they weren't allowed to read in school. Bill's teacher thought this passion for Jules Verne was "just a stage." Ronny had a problem with his penchant for Sartre; what teacher would believe that a kid from the Bronx was really reading *Nausea* for the third time?
>
> So, along with the streets, the crowds and the noise, along with the ghosts, flowers and animals that filled our walks in Poe Park, the Botanical Gardens and the Bronx Zoo, we all had this other thing in common: our schools didn't recognize or exploit our enthusiasm for reading. (pp. 14–17)

Jackson's anecdote about students of an earlier generation illustrates what Gallo's study, Atwell's experience, and the NAEP test results confirm—that most students can and do read. However, many of today's schools are giving the message that reading is only for the purpose of giving back information to the teacher. Consequently, we have created curricula in which students have learned to avoid reading what is required. Therefore, if students transact aesthetically with books, they do so during their own time. This means that many students never experience the pleasure of developing a personal relationship with special books. Likewise, a large percentage of students, as shown by NAEP test results, will never read with sophisticated skill.

All of us who teach or have taught adolescents know that there are many capable readers who refuse to read what is assigned as well as numerous capable readers who read their assignments and also read for pleasure. At the same time, as the NAEP survey results reveal, there are large numbers of poor readers in secondary school classrooms. Gallo's survey confirms what most teachers already know, that most of these poor readers read neither in school nor at home. Last, there are some reluctant readers who can read but choose not to read, whether the reading is assigned or freely chosen. (See Chapter 2 for more information about capable, poor, and reluctant readers.) The task of the teacher is to turn all these students into readers, and, in the process, to open their minds to books and ideas they would not seek out themselves and to teach them how to recognize good writing. This is a demanding task, and there are many ways good teachers approach it. Regardless of approach, young adult books are an important element in developing students who are avid, capable, and mature readers.

How Readers Develop

Not all students become capable readers at the same rate. Some sixteen year olds read Shakespeare with such depth that they can capture the rhythm and power of his words in their own writing. Others find themselves totally lost in a morass of Elizabethan English. On the other hand, a sixteen year old who reads with the maturity of an adult may be unable to cope with the problems of adolescence, while a teenager who lacks simple interpretive skills may be well adjusted and comfortable. All young people, however, can enjoy and learn from their reading if they are directed to books that are appropriate for them. As Dan Jackson writes:

> As the world of our childhood crumbled, we turned more and more to books for answers. We searched frantically for characters who had done what we hoped to do: survive . . . feel joy . . . find love. It was important to look in books for people who could do what was rarely done by the train conductors and cops who worked with our fathers. It was important to consider the countless stories that have bittersweet endings in order to learn whatever sorrow teaches, and to better appreciate the joy that seemed so elusive to us at that age. It was important to do all this as it had been to make believe we were Yogi Berra or Whitey Ford or Mickey Mantle when, in earlier years, we played stickball outside Yankee Stadium. (1980, pp. 14–17)

Teachers are more likely to assist students in becoming avid, mature, and capable readers if we understand the three stages of reading growth, as outlined by Margaret Early in 1960 (see Table 1.1). According to Early, the primary stage of reading development, which begins before the child enters school and continues into late childhood or early adolescence, is characterized by unconscious enjoyment. The reader, or listener in the case of prereading children, displays delight for no apparent reason. Anyone who has read the same story to a three year old a dozen times has been witness to this first stage of reading development.

The second stage of development usually emerges, by the late elementary or early junior high school years, when the reader is willing to exert effort to increase pleasure

Table 1.1
Developmental Reading Stages

Estimated Beginning Age	Features of Stage
3–5 years	1. Unconscious enjoyment of language and books (reading fortifies child's learning to decode)
10–14 years	2. Egocentric interest in reading and books (exerts some effort to enhance delight in books; wants to become part of the story; story must be believable)
17+ years	3. Aesthetic interest in reading and books (exercises discriminating judgment; deeper feeling for mankind replaces concern for self)

NOTES:
a. Reader does not abandon one stage when entering another.
b. Most secondary school students are on stage 2, egocentric interest in books.
c. Most readers do not reach stage 3.
d. Most readers must progress through the stages in order; it is unusual for a reader to skip a stage.

Based on Margaret Early, "Stages in growth in literary appreciation," *English Journal*, March 1960, pp. 161–67.

in reading. This stage of reading development corresponds with the egocentric years of psychological development and is characterized by the reader wanting to see herself or himself in the characters or in the plot. The reader enjoys the book vicariously, becoming a part of the story. This is the stage that Dan Jackson and his friends entered when their "childhood crumbled." The second stage most often coincides with teenagers' search for self while needing to be accepted by others, particularly their peers.

Much required reading at school, however, does not engage students in this search for self. By fifth grade the curriculum begins to change. For many students the early years of elementary school, when students are learning to read, include the reading of imaginative children's stories. By fifth grade, students are required to read textbooks. Increasingly, the books contain what students may perceive as dry, dull facts that have no relation to their lives. Or, as in some literature anthologies, the books may contain stories about people to whom they cannot relate. By middle school or junior high school, much of the literature curriculum revolves around the classics, books selected by adults for their enduring literary quality (see Chapter 13). If Early's studies of reading development are correct, the majority of middle adolescents (ages 13 to 16) are not developmentally ready for what schools require them to read.

In the aesthetic, or third, stage of reading development, readers bring all their creative ability to a work of literature. Early says that most readers who advance to this stage reach it in their late teenage years, around age seventeen. However, according to Early, and NAEP tests, the majority of readers never reach this most advanced stage. In this stage readers use their past experiences, their previous reading, and their ideas and values to appreciate a written work. The reader now possesses a "deeper feeling for mankind" that replaces the "narrow concern for oneself" evidenced in the second, or egocentric, stage of reading development (Early, 1960).

Why do most readers never enter the aesthetic stage of reading development? Perhaps it is because the curriculum cuts them off at the passage between unconscious enjoyment and egocentric reading development. A *Weekly Reader* survey from the early 1990s seems to confirm this. In this survey, students reported that reading was their favorite activity up through fourth grade, but in fifth grade, when the curriculum changed, reading became one of the students' least favorite activities. According to Early, the egocentric stage of reading development cannot be bypassed if the reader is going to progress to the next stage. Incorporating books for young adults in the curriculum can help students progress through these stages and encourage them to keep reading.

Classrooms as Reading Workshops

Because an important goal of education is to develop mature, aesthetic, critical readers in all content areas, teachers must find ways to encourage students to read and respond to what they read. The first step is finding books that relate to students' egocentric needs and will help them develop beyond these needs. In addition, we must offer books that help students think critically about what they read, so they develop moral reasoning ability. Finally, the books we select and help adolescents select should include increasingly adult material. To make appropriate selections or recommendations, we must know the students as well as the books that are likely to appeal to them. As Dan Fader reported in *Hooked on Books*:

> How could I set up a school program when I know so little about the students it was meant to serve?
>
> I began again. This time I went to the students. What's wrong with your English class, I asked, that causes you to turn it off the way you do? You're out to lunch during your English class, I said, and I want to know why. They told my why: They told me that it didn't make any difference about them. That the teacher didn't like them so they didn't like the teacher. She didn't talk like she wanted you to understand. And never nothing to read that was any good, even if you wanted to read. What difference does it make anyway? (Fader and McNeil, 1966, p. 9)

Of course, this bleak picture of the secondary school English classroom is not true of most classrooms. Many classrooms reflect the exciting learning that happens within them. The walls are covered with student work; shelves and tables hold plenty of books, magazines, and newspapers; comfortable little nooks offer a place to read; and the teacher talks to students about the books they read with interest and enthusiasm.

Nancie Atwell's middle school classroom in Boothbay Harbor, Maine, is a good example of a classroom that encourages reading. Atwell has developed a reading workshop approach to teaching in which students select books, read them (often during class time), discuss them with peers and the teacher, and respond to them in writing.

How can we turn our classrooms into exciting centers of learning in which students read and respond to books? We must begin with the students. If the classroom is to become a place that interests and excites adolescents, the classroom must be theirs. If the curriculum is to meet their personal needs, help them develop new interests, and improve their reading ability, then it must be based on who students are. The students "must be met where they are before they can be led to where they should be (i.e., where we are)" (Fader and McNeil, pp. 9–10). Their reading must begin with books that relate to their egocentric stage of reading development.

An Inclusive Curriculum

Creating a curriculum in which students meet books as equals does not mean watering down the content of the curriculum; nor does it mean excluding the classics, eliminating the basics, or teaching only what interests students today. It does mean offering a variety of books that bridge the gap between childhood and adulthood and gradually teaching students how to examine ideas, issues, and situations in a more sophisticated way. An inclusive curriculum means that students read books like *Death Be Not Proud: A Memoir* (Gunther) and *My Brother Sam Is Dead* (Collier and Collier) so they can more easily understand and appreciate works such as *On Death and Dying* (Kübler-Ross) and *For Whom the Bell Tolls* (Hemingway) (bridging to the classics is discussed in Chapter 13). It means presenting vocabulary in the context of the book the student is reading rather than in isolation (teaching skills using young adult books is discussed in Chapter 12). It means broadening interests by beginning with a situation the student can understand, as in *Anne Frank: The Diary of a Young Girl*, and moving to a complete study of the Holocaust (using young adult books across the curriculum is discussed in Chapter 10). It means showing students how they can respond to books so that they can critically think about what they read rather than relying on crutches like *Cliff Notes* (responding to young adult books is discussed in Chapter 11). The reasons for using young adult literature in the classroom are summarized in Figure 1.2.

Figure 1.2
Why Young Adult Literature Is Important

1. Helps improve the reading skills of adolescents and allows all readers to read good books
2. Allows adolescent readers to interact with books as equals, thereby developing both reading skills and critical and creative thinking ability
3. Encourages adolescents to read more books, thereby improving their ability to read
4. Helps adolescents understand that there are many reasons to read, thereby encouraging them to keep reading
5. Allows readers to meet egocentric needs while developing aesthetic reading ability
6. Allows teachers to incorporate more books of interest to adolescents into the curriculum, thereby avoiding the nonreading curriculum or workbooks and lectures
7. Allows teachers to organize classrooms into reading workshops in which students respond to, experience, and share books
8. Allows for the development of an inclusive curriculum in which a variety of books on a variety of themes and in a variety of genres introduce students to themselves, their world, and the worlds of other cultures

Diversity of Today's Students

Before we can begin selecting books and developing methodologies, we must get to know our students. This is not as difficult as it sounds. We can still do advance planning before we meet our particular students, but we must be aware of similarities and differences among the adolescents we teach. Later, we can fine-tune our approach as we get to know the individuals in our classrooms.

Today's students are diverse. They have a broad range of beliefs, are raised with different ethical and religious values, live with different cultural influences, and have experienced different approaches to education. They come from a wide variety of backgrounds and face different problems. For example, over ten percent of public school students (4.5 million) are classified as either needing special education or having disabilities. In 1991, 26 percent of all children lived below the poverty level (Center for the Study of Social Policy, 1991). Nearly 25 percent of all children were in single-parent households in 1989. In 1988, 64 percent of all women with children between six and seventeen worked outside the home. According to the Bush Center in Child Development and Social Policy at Yale University, 65 percent of students now have working mothers, compared to 46 percent less than 15 years ago.

The school population today is ethnically varied. In 1987, 30 percent of the U.S. public school population was classified as minority (nonwhite). Today, according to the National Coalition of Advocates for Students, the number of school-age immigrant children has risen to between 2.1 and 2.7 million, or approximately 5 percent of the school population. The majority of these students come from Mexico, followed by Asia, Central and South America, and the Caribbean. In 1989, 1.6 million children had limited English proficiency and spoke English as their second language.

Students also vary in their social maturity. According to the Alan Guttmacher Institute, which studies reproductive issues, 38 percent of girls between fifteen and seventeen reported that they were sexually active. The 1988 Survey of Adolescent Males reported that a third of boys were sexually active at age fifteen, half at sixteen, and 86 percent at age nineteen.

Because students are diverse, it is essential that the books included in the curriculum value this diversity. As young adult author Richard Peck suggests, books can be used not only as mirrors but as windows for adolescents (p. 5). Through books students can read about situations that mirror their own worlds, and can learn about the world of others. The best young adult books help students see the similarities of age-mates who may come from different cultures or have different problems. Readers learn that we are all alike and we are all different. Good books can help adolescents celebrate these differences. Therefore, the variety of books used in the curriculum should be as diverse as the student population who reads them. (Chapter 5 examines literature across cultures and Chapter 10 presents methodologies for teaching multiculturalism through young adult books.)

Conflicting Needs of Adolescents

The second, or egocentric, stage of reading development as outlined by Early usually occurs during the early teenage years, when adolescents are seeking affirmation of the self through their peer group and possibly through personal, peer-group-acceptable accomplishments.

Psychologist Abraham Maslow contends that the egocentric nature of the adolescent fits the normal progression through the hierarchy of basic human needs. Normal human beings must meet the basic needs of belongingness, love, and self-esteem before they can become productive, self-actualized adults.

Hierarchy of Needs

Understanding the hierarchy of human needs can help us determine how to help adolescents progress in their reading development. According to Maslow, the basic human needs are these: (1) physiological needs (evident in homeostasis, the body's automatic efforts to maintain a constant, normal state of the bloodstream and appetites, and food preferences based on nutrient shortages); (2) safety needs (such as security; stability; dependency; protection; freedom from fear, anxiety, and chaos; need for structure, order, law, limits; strength in the protector; and so on); (3) social affection (belongingness or love); (4) self-esteem (a sense of strength, achievement, adequacy, mastery and competence, confidence, independence and freedom, and reputation or prestige); (5) understanding (the desire to know); (6) aesthetic needs (the desire for beauty); and (7) self-actualization (self-fulfillment, or reaching one's full potential).

Maslow tells us that generally each lower-level need must be met before the next-higher need becomes important, although there is a good bit of overlap and one need may be much stronger in some people. Further, he claims a person can become stuck on one need and therefore be unable to move to higher-level needs. This produces a great deal of frustration.

For many years I have conducted informal surveys of parents and teachers of adolescents. I have asked them to indicate the level of the needs hierarchy at which they find most teenagers. Most agree that adolescents, between the ages of ten and seventeen, usually are attempting to meet the third level of need, social affection. Some older adolescents, usually between the ages of fifteen and eighteen, are attempting to meet the fourth-level need of self-esteem. Adults who live or work closely with adolescents believe that most are attempting to meet the needs of social affection and self-esteem. Many of these adolescents' parents and teachers observe a struggle between these two needs.

Janet was an adolescent facing this struggle. When I first met Janet, she was a student in my ninth-grade English class. I remember the first paper she handed in; it was so well written. I wondered how I could possibly teach her anything. Her paper was so impressive I read it to the class. Of course I didn't use her name, but everyone knew whose paper it was. For Janet this was the worst kind of torture. She was one of those children who are not only intelligent but also talented, beautiful, athletic, and very popular. She was not about to give up that popularity. Overt intelligence in Janet's peer group was clearly unacceptable. Therefore, she stopped handing in papers in my English class. Janet's intelligence, however, caused a conflict for her. In order to be socially acceptable, Janet believed she should not exhibit her intelligence. On the other hand, her intelligence was part of her and her self-esteem required acknowledging it. Janet resolved her internal struggle in an antisocial way.

In the wee hours of a Sunday morning I received a phone call from a hysterical Janet. When she calmed down, she told me she was in a church and had taken the hymnals and thrown them through the windows. In her adolescent mind the community was to blame for her internal conflict between the need for social approval and for self-esteem. So she lashed out against the church, a visible symbol of her community.

The struggle to meet social affection and self-esteem needs is also evident in the developmental reading stage of adolescents. At this stage students tend to select books in which young characters face struggles similar to the ones they are facing. Janet, who was able to read and understand adult classics, was nonetheless fascinated by Bette Greene's young adult novel *Summer of My German Soldier* in which a young Jewish girl must face isolation in her rural, southern hometown where there are few Jews. Ironically when a young German prisoner of war smiles at Patty, she is an easy target for his attentions. She agrees to hide Anton as he attempts to escape from the prisoner-of-war camp in which he is incarcerated. Like Janet, Patty feels isolated from her community, and in her desire to belong she violates her family's moral principles and beliefs. Patty, in Bette Greene's novel, is struggling to meet the needs of social approval and self-esteem.

Needs Affect Reading

A study completed in 1977 by Lance Gentile and Merna McMillan, who attempted to determine why many teenagers won't read, helps show how a teenager's struggle to meet various needs may affect in-school reading. The study found ten factors that contribute to what the authors call the "reluctant reader syndrome."

1. Many students equate reading with ridicule, failure, or exclusively school-related tasks.
2. Many students are not excited by ideas but are driven to experience life directly rather that through reading.
3. Adolescents frequently do not want to sit, and in some cases are incapable of sitting for long periods.
4. Adolescence is a time of intense egocentrism.
5. Many teenagers insist on being entertained; they have little understanding or appreciation of intrinsic rewards.
6. Many students are pressured at home and at school to read. They may resist reading if they feel too much pressure.
7. Many young people grow up in an atmosphere where reading material is not available or not abundant.
8. Reading is considered an antisocial activity by some adolescents.
9. Many classroom texts and supplemental reading materials do not inspire by their content or appearance.
10. Some adolescents automatically reject reading because they see reading as part of the adult world. (Gentile, 1977, pp. 649–54)

The Adolescent's Values

According to psychologist Lawrence Kohlberg, values, like needs, are developed hierarchically. Kohlberg (1981) says that the ability to think and act in a moral way develops in an orderly pattern. When individuals are presented with conflicting views, they experience cognitive dissonance and how this dissonance is resolved depends on the individual's moral reasoning development. Kohlberg claims that the only way to develop one's maturity in moral reasoning is by confronting conflicts one level above the individual's current stage of moral reasoning. If the arguments are too advanced, the individual will not understand the conflict and will not gain in moral reasoning.

According to Kohlberg, the first level of moral reasoning, stage one, is preconventional moral reasoning. Young children, at this level, base moral reasoning on actual rewards or punishments. Rules are obeyed to avoid punishment. At stage two, conventional moral reasoning, older children comply with rules based on the expectation of reward. They base their judgments on the approval of family, traditional values, laws of society, and loyalty to country. At stage one, behavior is predicated on the concrete approval of others. At stage two, moral behavior is based on law and authority in the desire to avoid guilt and censure. Many individuals never move beyond the second stage of moral reason. The third, and final level of moral reasoning, stage three, is postconventional moral reasoning. At the earlier stages of moral reasoning good is based on socially agreed-upon standards of individual right and democratically determined laws. At this more mature stage of moral reasoning, "good and right are matters of individual conscience and involve abstract concepts of justice, human dignity, and equality" (Kohlberg, 1981, pp. 409–12). According to Kohlberg, this stage is reached by few people.

Kohlberg's studies suggest that individuals develop these stages at different times during their lives. Researcher Carol Gilligan further suggests that there are "two moral voices," male and female, that signal, "different ways of thinking about what constitutes a moral problem and how such problems can be addressed or solved" (1988, p. xvii). According to Gilligan, males focus primarily on justice and females on justice and care and concern for others. The teacher's goal is to move students from the early stages of moral reason to the more mature stages, and as Kohlberg suggests, we must do this by introducing students to moral dilemmas that are one stage above their current level of moral reason. The problems presented in young adult books when discussed in the classroom give us an excellent means for doing this.

Interests and Problems of Adolescents

Today's students have different interests, needs, and problems. At the same time, however, adolescents are surprisingly similar. According to a 1990 special edition of *Newsweek* ("The New Teens," 1990), U.S. teens are as similar as they are different. Their ages dictate many of their similar characteristics and interests.

Early adolescents, age ten through thirteen, are still relatively dependent on parents or other adults. However, as they develop physically, they begin to experience the desire for increased independence. In fact, according to University of Illinois researcher Reed Larson, between the ages of ten and fifteen the time adolescents spend with their families decreases by half ("The New Teens," 1990). Being with peers and belonging to a particular peer group become increasingly important. Although there is a new interest in the opposite sex, most peer groups of early adolescents are of the same sex.

At the same time, most preteenagers still need and want the guidance of adults. They are still interested in things of the home. Although they increasingly isolate themselves from their families and the bedroom door often becomes a line of demarcation, early adolescents spend four to six hours per day at home watching television and only one hour or less doing homework (Mernit, 1990). According to the Gallo (1985) study of adolescents' reading interests and habits, younger adolescents still indicate an interest in reading for pleasure. In addition, most early adolescents enjoy video games and music. They also participate in sports and enjoy watching them on television, and spend many hours on the telephone (girls particularly). They are interested in getting good grades (Girl Scouts of America, 1990) but are less interested in school than they were during the elementary grades.

By late middle school or early high school, adolescents are seeking increasing independence from parents. Most middle adolescents (ages thirteen to fifteen) spend an increasing amount of time hanging out with their peers, usually of the same sex but increasingly with the opposite sex. Adolescents of this age also spend a surprising amount of money on themselves. In 1989, teens between the ages of thirteen and nineteen spent $56 billion on themselves (The New Teens," 1990). Clothes and food topped the list of what they bought. According to the 1990 Rand Youth Poll, girls spend more on clothing, and boys spend more on food. Girls spend money on cosmetics and boys on grooming. Both boys and girls spend a good bit of money on entertainment (e.g., films, dates, video games) and on records and tapes. Nearly half of all teenagers own their own television set (47 percent), 28 percent have their own phones, and 60 percent own a calculator ("The New Teens," 1990).

Much of the money that middle adolescents spend on clothes, grooming, and entertainment helps them to be accepted by a peer group and attract the opposite sex. Adolescents of this age are increasingly interested in the opposite sex and are becoming more sexually active (particularly boys). They are also more likely than younger and older adolescents to be involved in extracurricular school activities and sports.

By late adolescence (age sixteen to nineteen), teenagers are becoming more independent. In 1989, 37.6 percent of sixteen and seventeen year olds worked for pay ("The New Teens," 1990). Older teens, according to a 1989 survey of high school seniors, were more interested in personal goals, such as getting good grades and good jobs, than in global concerns, such as hunger and poverty. According to a 1986 poll of high school seniors (Johnston, 1986), the top ten worries of older teenagers are, in order, (1) having a good marriage and family life, (2) choosing a career and finding steady work, (3) doing well in school, (4) being successful in their line of work, (5) having strong friendships, (6) paying for college, (7) the country going downhill, (8) making a lot of money, (9) finding purpose and meaning in life, and (10) contracting AIDS.

Older teens exert their independence in both positive and negative ways. One of the negative ways is by dropping out of school. In 1988, 71.1 percent of students who had entered ninth grade four years earlier graduated with their class (National Governors' Association, 1990); this translates to a nearly 30 percent dropout rate. Teenage boys and girls also show their independence by becoming more sexually active. By older adolescence more than a third of female students and over 80 percent of male students are sexually active (Alan Guttmacher Institute, 1987). In 1987, 473,000 teenage women gave birth, representing 12.4 percent of all births in the United States (U.S. Department of Commerce, 1990). According to Planned Parenthood Federation (1986), despite the fact that one-half of all U.S. teenagers are sexually active by age seventeen, only one-third use contraceptives consistently. Since 1956 the number of teens who contract syphilis and gonorrhea is up 300 percent. In 1991, AIDS was the seventh leading cause of death among people age fifteen to twenty-four. In 1986, 2,100 teenagers between 12 and 19 committed suicide, the largest number of these adolescents, 1,896, were between 15 and 19 (Gallup, 1991).

In a study of the interests of high school students, N.T. Gill (1980) found that these students "appear to express interests that reflect national values" and that "girls at this age level are still the more romantic of the species" (p. 166). He concludes that "the solution for preventing and correcting both disharmony in the classroom and general apathy toward education . . . may very well be nothing more complicated than simply to discover ways of making our schools into centers of interest rather than compounds of boredom" (p. 166).

Reading Interests of Adolescents

Other studies of teenage interests indicate that boys have a narrower range of reading interests than girls. After a ten-year study of young adult interests, Jo M. Stanchfield (1973) concluded that the narrower range of interests in male readers may account in part, for their greater difficulty in learning to read. Donald R. Gallo's 1985 study of adolescent reading interests confirmed that boys are more likely to read nothing than are girls.

As interest inventories of adolescents' reading show, girls are more likely to be interested in romance and love. When students were asked to select their favorite books in Gallo's study, romance outranked all the other twenty-four categories for adolescent girls. For the youngest adolescents, girls in grades four through six, however, romance ranked fourth with problems of growing up first followed by animals and then mystery and suspense. However, in grades seven through twelve, romance and love far outranked other genres; mystery and suspense was a distant second, followed closely by problems of growing up, and horror and supernatural. Following these came fantasy, true stories, animals, cartoons and humor, adventure and survival, famous classics, sexuality, and family life.

For male readers, the dominant choice of reading material at all ages was sports. Forty-one percent of the 1,647 boys surveyed indicated that sports was their favorite genre. The youngest male readers, grades four through six, had the largest gap between sports and the second-place genre for all males, science fiction. Males selected these genre in order as their favorites following sports and science fiction: horror and supernatural, adventure and survival, mystery and suspense, cartoons and humor, fantasy, science, animals, and history.

Determining Individual Interests

Knowing the general interests of adolescents is not enough for deciding which books to select for them. Teachers must learn the interests of the particular adolescents in their classroom. As I travel around the six public high schools in the county in which I live and work, I see many differences from school to school. The differences begin with dress. In one local school all the boys wear baseball caps. In another high school, not more than ten miles away, wearing a brimmed cap is grounds for instant ridicule.

Other differences are far less obvious. At one school nothing is more important than football—the team, the cheerleaders, pep rallies, and all the other hoopla that surrounds high school athletics. At another school football takes a back seat to cars, cycles, cruising, dragging, and the Friday-night races. At another school it is much more acceptable for a girl to play on the basketball team than to be a cheerleader. In a school six miles away, girl basketball players are socially unacceptable. However, within each school there are also differences among adolescents.

If we are to successfully instruct our students in our subject area, it is essential that we know them—what makes them cry, what makes them laugh, what makes them sing. If we know these things about our students, we can use their interests to turn them on to the subject we teach.

Many interest inventory techniques can be used to determine students' interests. Some are quite simple. A sentence-completion test, for example, can assess student reading, recreational, and content area interests (see Figure 1.3).

Teenagers today are interested in and excited by many things. If we can use their interests to design curricula, we can turn our classrooms into exciting centers of learning, and we can capture the enthusiasm with which the students read *Sassy*

Figure 1.3
A Sentence-Completion Test

1. The best book I have ever read is _____ .
2. The best movie I have ever seen is _____ .
3. I often read the magazine _____ .
4. In history I like studying _____ best.
5. On a free Saturday afternoon I am likely to be found _____
   _____ .
6. My favorite television show is _____ .
7. The neatest place I have ever visited is _____ .
8. I would like to visit _____ more than anywhere in the world.
9. Right now I'd rather be _____ .
10. If I could meet anyone in the world (living or dead), it would be _____ .

Magazine or tabulate baseball stats or write notes to friends. If we incorporate young adult literature into our classroom bibliographies, we can assist our students in learning new concepts by beginning where the students are, with the knowledge they already possess. We can create classrooms that are as Gill says, "centers of interest rather than compounds of boredom." We can make the learning that students do in school as meaningful as the learning they do outside of school.

There are young adult books appropriate for every subject area. For example, Christopher Collier's and James Lincoln Collier's *My Brother Sam Is Dead* is a gripping tale about a teenager who despite his father's loyalty to the British king goes off to fight with the patriots during the Revolutionary War. This is only one example of the hundreds of young adult books suitable for history classes.

Both fiction and nonfiction books are useful in science classrooms. The nature books of Jean Craighead George teach more than facts about our environment; they teach the necessity of maintaining an environmental balance that benefits all living creatures. George's fiction books, such as *Water Sky*, are marvelous tools for developing student interest in studies of animal life and nature. Nonfiction works written for adolescent readers can awaken scientific fervor. Titles such as *A Passion to Know: Twenty Profiles in Science* (Hammond) are interesting nonfiction companions to the fiction books on the science classroom shelf. The student who develops an interest in science through fiction could be directed to this informative book about being a scientist as well as many others about interesting scientific topics.

Our job as teachers is to find books that are useful in our classroom. We must determine which books are likely to be of interest to our students based on information that we have gathered from interest inventories and then encourage students to investigate these books. The reward is in watching a subject we love come to life for a previously unmotivated student.

The Teacher's Role

As teachers of young adults, not only do we have the responsibility to encourage reading, but also, as young adult author and sports broadcaster Robert Lipsyte once said, we have a "chance to change minds." We can encourage students to read books that will help move them from the egocentric stage of reading to the aesthetic, creative stage of reading appreciation. We can help adolescent readers understand the difference between reading for efferent and aesthetic purposes, thereby encouraging them to become critical and life-long readers. We can assist students in locating good literature that helps meet their needs and may even help them develop more mature moral reasoning skills.

For example, the adolescent who is struggling with the conflict between peer acceptance and feelings of self-worth might be directed to Robert Cormier's *The Chocolate War*, the story of a teenage boy who must decide whether being accepted by his peers is more important than doing what he believes is right. The conclusion of the book does not provide an easy answer nor does it prove that a person who chooses the ethical course is always the victor, but it does show struggling young adults that each is not fighting alone.

Young people who feel rejected by their parents can find a friend in the heroine of M. E. Kerr's *Dinky Hocker Shoots Smack!* Dinky, an overweight girl who feels hurt by her mother's apparent lack of concern for her as she pursues a career of social concern for others finds both solace and pain in overeating. In an attempt to gain her mother's attention, she scrawls the phrase of the book's title all over town.

Young adults who feel alone and rejected by their peers might enjoy a book such as Jean Little's *One to Grow on*. The heroine Janie is a quiet, plain girl who is convinced that no one could care about her for her own good qualities. Therefore, she often invents stories that make her life seem more exciting. In her loneliness, she falls prey to girls who use her in a variety of ways. Slowly, Janie learns to believe in herself, and this new confidence helps her find true friendship.

Before those of us who teach adolescents can recommend specific books to our students, we must first become familiar with the books written for and enjoyed by adolescents. Then we must find ways to incorporate this literature into the regular classroom curricula. We must help our students build a bridge from their childhood reading to the mature reading of an adult. We must help our students learn how to satisfy their needs for social acceptance and self-esteem as well as reach their full potential. We must help them develop the moral reasoning skills that will allow them to make decisions based on what is just and right rather than on punishment and rewards. Through young adult literature we can help our students become mature readers as they seek answers to the questions that all healthy adolescents ask.

EPILOGUE: BUILDING BRIDGES

The task of the teacher of young adults is to help students build bridges from childhood to emerging adulthood. To do this, teachers must understand that every student is different. No two people progress through the adolescent years at the same physiological pace, with the same needs, with identical interests, with equal intellectual maturity.

Literature written for young adults allows readers to see themselves in a book, to read a book with ease and interest, to respond to the book as an equal, and to gain new information that relates to the familiar world of young adulthood. Through young adult books readers meet characters who face problems and resolve conflicts similar to their own. However, as teachers, we want our students to move beyond the world of the young into the world of the adult, emotionally and intellectually. The literature of the young adult is not an end but a means. It allows the young reader to progress beyond the books read for childhood pleasures to the aesthetic, intellectual reading of the mature adult. Many young adult books are appropriate bridges to this world of mature adult reading.

The secondary school classroom should be a place where each student, like Jesse in Katherine Paterson's *Bridge to Terabithia*, "came to be knighted. After [he] stayed for a while and grew strong [he] had to move on." The teacher must discover materials and develop methods that allow each student to, like Jesse, "push back the walls of his mind and make him see beyond to the shining world—huge and terrible and beautiful and very fragile."

Suggested Readings

Alan Guttmacher Institute. Pregnancy, Birth and Abortion Rates in the United States and Other Countries. 1987.

Atwell, N. *In the Middle: Writing, Reading and Learning with Adolescents.* Boynton/Cook/Heinemann, 1987.

Blostein, F. *Invitations, Celebrations: A Handbook of Ideas and Techniques for Promoting Reading in Junior and Senior High Schools.* Ontario Library Association, 1990.

Carlsen, G. R. *Books and the Teenage Reader.* 2d rev. ed. Harper & Row, 1980. Bantam, 1980.

Center for the Study of Social Policy. *Kids Count Data Book: State Profiles of Child Well-Being.* 1991.

Early, M. "Stages in Growth in Literary Appreciation." *English Journal*, March 1960, pp. 161–67.

Educational Testing Service. *Trends in Academic Progress* (NCES 91-1264). U.S. Government Printing Office, 1991.

Endicott, A. Q. "Females Also Come of Age." *English Journal.* April 1992, pp. 42–47.

Fader, D., and E. B. McNeil. *Hooked on Books: Program and Proof.* Berkeley, 1966.

Gallo, D. R. "Are Kids Reading or Aren't They?" *ALAN Review*, Winter 1985, pp. 46–49.

Gallo, D. R. *Presenting Richard Peck.* Twayne, 1989.

Gallup Organization. *Teenage Suicide Study.* March 1991.

Gentile, L. M., and M. M. McMillan. "Why Won't Teenagers Read?" *Journal of Reading*, May 1977, pp. 649–54.

Gill, N. T. Comparison of High School Student Interests across Three Grade and Ability Levels." *High School Journal*, January 1980, pp. 160–66.

Gilligan, C. "Adolescent Development Reconsidered." In *Mapping the Moral Domain: A Contribution of Women's Thinking to Psychological Theory and Education*, ed. C. Gilligan, J. V. Ward, J. M. Taylor, and B. Bardige. Center for the Study of Gender Education and Human Development, 1988, pp. vii–xxxix.

Girl Scouts of America. *Beliefs and Moral Values of American Children.* 1990.

Goodlad, J. *A Place Called School.* McGraw-Hill, 1984.

Harbaugh, M. S. "Celebrating Diversity." *Instructor,* September 1990, pp. 45–48.

Jackson, D. "Books in the Bronx: A Personal Look at How Literature Shapes Our Lives." *Media and Methods*, March 1980, pp. 14–17.

Johnston, L. *Monitoring the Future Study: Questionnaire Responses from the Nation's High School Seniors.* University of Michigan, 1986.

Kohlberg, L. *Essays on Moral Development.* Vol. 1, *The Philosophy of Moral Development: Moral Stages and the Idea of Justice.* Harper & Row, 1981.

Maslow, A. *Motivation and Personality*, 2d ed. Harper & Row, 1970.

Mazer, N. F. "Three Teachers." *ALAN Review*, Fall 1988, p. 52.

Mernit, S. "Kids Today." *Instructor*, September 1990, pp. 35–43.

National Governors' Association. *Time for Results: The Governors' 1991 Report on Education.* 1986.

"The New Teens: What Makes Them Different?" *Newsweek* 115 (special issue), Summer/Fall, 1990.

Peck, R. "Some Thoughts on Adolescent Lit." *News from ALAN*, September–October 1975.

Planned Parenthood Federation. *Teenage Pregnancy.* 1986.

Reiff, G. 1985. The 1985 Fitness Study: Conducted for the President's Council on Physical Fitness. Washington, DC: U.S. Government Printing Office.

Rosenblatt, L. "Writing and Reading: The Transactional Theory." *Reading and Writing Connections*, ed. J. M. Mason. Allyn & Bacon, 1989, pp. 153–76.

Stanchfield, J. M. "The Reading Interests of Eighth-Grade Boys." *Journal of Developmental Reading*, Summer 1962, pp. 256–65.

———. *Sex Differences in Learning to Read.* Phi Delta Kappa, 1973.

Stanchfield, J. M., and S. R. Fraim. "Follow-up Study on the Reading Interest of Boys." *Journal of Reading*, May 1979, pp. 748–52.

Thompson, J. F. "Controversial Connecting: Surreal or Unbelievable? Meaningful or Meretricious? True or Twaddleful?" *ALAN Review*, Fall 1988, pp. 7–10.

U.S. Department of Commerce, Bureau of the Census. *Statistical Abstract of the United States*, 110th ed. U.S. Government Printing Office, 1990.

U.S. Department of Commerce, Bureau of the Census. *Statistical Abstract of the United States*, 111th ed. U.S. Government Printing Office, 1991.

2 The Young Adult Book As a Motivational Tool

Focus Questions

1. How can teachers motivate reluctant and poor readers to read?
2. Why is young adult literature important to capable readers?
3. Is it possible for all students to become good readers? How?
4. How does the amount a student reads affect reading motivation and ability to read?
5. Why is it important for teachers to learn about young adult books? And how can *you* learn more about them?

PROLOGUE

William Faulkner said, "No one can write who is not first a humanitarian." I'm not even sure I completely agree with that, but I do know this: No one can teach who is not first a humanitarian. I believe that the real reward of teaching lies in your audience, those students who look back at you every day. Those relationships are the true source of pleasure and fulfillment in our profession, and if you're not finding it there, then you probably won't find it at all.

To illustrate my point, I'm going to read you excerpts from two pieces of student writing. . . . The first excerpt was written by a girl I taught two years ago named Debbie. Like myself, Debbie was not a model student. During the year we spent together, she made several extended visits to the Alternative Education Center, I can recall at least one arrest, and I once broke up one of her fights in the hallway. She was mad because she was winning. But at the end of the year, she wrote me this:

> I want you to know that I never in my life picked up one book to read until this year when we read *To Kill a Mockingbird*. I cried when I read that book. I really enjoyed it. Now I am reading my second book (the one you wrote) and I am enjoying this too. In other words if it wasn't for you, Mr. M., I would be the same boring person I've always been.

Let's face it, we don't get paid very much, and we have a lot of hassles with our jobs. When it comes to rewards, a letter like that is as good as it gets. But I want to read another piece of student writing to you. This is by Ramon, a Hispanic boy who sits in the front row of my sixth period English class this year. Ramon has quite a life. I taught his pregnant girlfriend last year, and this year he works the late shift at the local Burger Chef every night. In fact, I can tell how well I'm doing on any particular day by how long it takes for Ramon's head to slump down to the desk. He wrote this in response to the topic "What scares me":

> Because it's weird when you have this feelin in that your scared and you don't even know what you're scared of. It gives you a real uneasy feeling in the pit of your stomach. And this feelin doesn't go away so easy, it keeps naggin you and doesn't let you rest easy. This feelin i'm talkin about is also something i'm scared of! And rite now i have this feelin, i have a feelin somethings gonna happen, and i won't be able to stop it. What i'm trying to say is that i'm scared of fightin, i try to ignore it and i hide it pretty good. Besides, if it shows, i read somewhere that blind teror in a fight can easily pass for courage. [S. E. Hinton, *Rumble Fish*]. What do you think?

What Ramon made me realize is how often I am unaware of what is actually going on in my classroom, and how important it is that I try to be aware. By the way, he probably will fail my class. He seldom does the work I assign, but he is working his way through my classroom bookshelf at an incredible rate, and I have hopes for the boy. ❖

From Dallin Malmgren, "Knowing Your Audience," *ALAN Review*, Fall 1989, p. 50.

A Profile of Today's Readers

One of the easiest and most enjoyable ways to motivate young adults to read is to introduce them to the wide world of young adult literature. The best thing about this reading world is that it has something for everyone, something for Dallin Malmgren's high school students in Texas, something for middle school students in Wisconsin, something for good readers in Maine, something for poor readers in Florida, and something for reluctant readers in South Dakota.

We recognize our students' differences and similarities and their wide range of abilities. The problem with the single-textbook approach to teaching is that it often assumes that all students are alike. A better approach is to capitalize on student differences, acknowledge that their differences will allow them to learn from one another, and utilize books that encourage all types of students to love to read.

One way to understand the differences among readers in the classroom is to group students into one of three categories: poor readers (students who read one or more years below grade level and usually prefer not to read), capable readers (students who read at or above grade level and enjoy reading), and reluctant readers (students who choose not to read).

This type of grouping, however, is designed to help us better understand the different kinds of readers in our classrooms, not to label students or to actually place them in reading groups. In fact, many students will fall into more than one category. Students, for example, might be both poor and reluctant readers or capable and reluctant readers. Our goal, of course, is to help all students become capable and willing readers.

Anyone Can Read Well

As Nancie Atwell points out in *In the Middle: Writing, Reading, and Learning with Adolescents*:

> Anyone can read well. Good readers begin to grow when teachers of reading level with ourselves about our processes as readers and begin to redefine what good readers do, revising the literature curriculum accordingly. Like writing, reading requires the creation of meaning, this time in collaboration with an author. Like writing, reading becomes meaningful only when it involves the particular response of the individual—one's own ways of perceiving reality through the prism of written language. And, like writing, reading generates its most significant meanings when the reader engages in a process of discovery, weaving and circling among the complex of behaviors that characterize genuine participation in written language. When we look at our own processes as readers and reflect on appropriate methods for teaching reading, it's hard to justify truncating reading into lecture-assign-evaluate lockstep. (1987, pp. 154–55)

Atwell suggests that when we look at our own reading process, we will discover what makes us good readers and will be able to teach reading more effectively.

As we look at the reading process, we can see that reading, like writing, is a process in which we first rehearse (plan and predict what we will read for what purpose and whether we will like it), then draft (discover meaning along the way), and finally revise (resee and reseek new meanings). All of this, Atwell suggests, takes time. Students need to have the time to read not only at home but also in the classroom. Those of us who are avid readers know that we must have time to read. Many of us resent that our busy lives take away from our reading time. Because our students also have busy lives, we must help them find the time to read at home and at school.

In addition, avid readers own what they have read. As they respond to it, it becomes theirs. Indeed, each text is different for each individual reader. You have probably had the experience of sharing a book that was meaningful to you with a friend or family member. Several years ago, after reading Gail Godwin's *A Mother and Two Daughters*, which I found to be an incredibly moving book, I recommended it to my mother. I gave her a copy of the book. After several months of her not mentioning it, I asked her, "Well, didn't you love it?" "Not particularly," she replied. I was crushed. I spoke sharply, "How could you not like it?" She looked at me strangely, and I ended the conversation. For a long time, I wondered why her not liking the book was so upsetting to me. Later, I realized that it was because I had assumed ownership of the book; the book had great meaning to me and had become mine.

Students cannot own texts to which they cannot relate, any more than my mother could own Godwin's book. Students need to be able to select their own books from the vast array of wonderful young adult books we recommend and make available to them. Atwell reports that her middle school students read more than thirty-five books per year. Over and over they report to her that having the freedom of choice turned them into readers. They are free to choose from "novels and short stories written expressly for young adults, adolescent literature of such breadth and depth no teacher need ever apologize for building a curriculum around kids' responses to their own books" (p. 161).

Finally, says Atwell, young readers, like all readers, need to have the opportunity to respond to the books they read. Avid adult readers have learned response techniques, often on their own. After finishing a particularly meaningful book, I often find myself simply sitting and thinking about it for a half hour or more. Young readers, however, usually do not know how to respond to books, so we must teach them. Atwell uses a dialogue journal to encourage responding to literature. She gives each student a folder with a sheaf of lined paper at the start of the year and a letter inviting the student to write to her about what they are reading. (Other techniques for responding to literature are discussed in Chapter 11.)

Understanding the reading process is important. But if we are to help all students become capable readers we must realize that students show significant differences in their reading ability, interests, and motivation. And, of course, there are also differences in how much they are encouraged to read at home and how much time they have for reading. After we recognize these differences, we can begin to provide all students with materials they are able and willing to read.

The Poor Reader

Many different terms have been used to describe poor readers. They are often called remedial readers, developmental readers, or disabled readers. Some educators differentiate between the terms; others do not. These students read at a level one or more years below grade. Table 2.1 lists some of the many reasons for poor reading ability, along with books that poor readers might enjoy. Other appropriate books can be found in the latest edition of *High Interest—Easy Reading* (National Council of Teachers of English) and *Easy-to-Read Books for Teenagers* (Young Adult Services of the New York Public Library), published yearly.

Of course, some reading-related problems are easier to deal with than others. Whatever the problem, if the student does not read, his or her ability to read will not improve. For those readers who are severely disabled, instructional or behavioral intervention is required. However, large numbers of poor readers either do not qualify for or do not receive special help in reading. This is particularly true in middle and secondary schools.

Classroom teachers in all subjects, however, can assist poor readers in developing important reading skills. One way is to introduce students to techniques that help

Table 2.1
Poor Readers

Characteristics	Recommended Books
Learning disability	*Freckle Juice,* Judy Blume (age 9–12)
Physical disability	*The Great Gilly Hopkins;* Katherine Paterson (age 12–14)
Lack of available and appropriate reading material	*The Outsiders,* S. E. Hinton (age 12–16)
Limited opportunity to develop preschool literacy skills	*The Last Mission,* Harry Mazer (age 12–17)
Economic deprivation	*The Cat Ate My Gymsuit,* Paula Danziger (age 12–15)
No interest in reading; would rather watch television or play video games	*The Contender,* Robert Lipsyte (age 13–17)
Behavior problems	*Figure of Speech,* Norma Fox Mazer (age 12–16)
Emotional problems	*Sounder,* William Armstrong (age 12–15)
Lack of parental supervision	*Those Summer Girls I Never Met,* Richard Peck (age 14–17)
Anxiety	*The Young Landlords,* Walter Dean Myers (age 12–16)
Poor self-esteem	
Speak English as second language	
Unable to decode words	
Poor vocabulary	
Speaking vocabulary differs from vocabulary found in books	
Did not learn reading-related skills in early schooling	
Difficulty in comprehending written language	
Lack of attention when reading	

Note: Books recommended for poor readers may also be appropriate for other readers.

them read the classroom text. Another way is to encourage them to read books written at a low reading level but a higher maturity and motivational level. A ninth-grade boy who has experienced great difficulty in gaining reading skills, for example, could be steered toward books that are written at a low reading level but are especially interesting to him in their content. Educational publishers call these books high-low books, easy-to-read books, or high-interest–easy-reading books. Their great value is that they address the needs of the adolescent in an interesting way without patronizing or insulting the reader.

Many poor readers are attracted to stories they can complete in one short sitting. Books like Michael Avallone's *Five-Minute Mysteries* or Alvin Schwartz's *Scary Stories to Tell in the Dark* are likely to fill the bill for the young reader who enjoys television suspense shows. If these short tales whet the teenage reader's appetite, the teacher could suggest longer mystery-suspense tales that are easy-reading fare, such as Jay Bennett's *The Birthday Murderer*, which is written on a fifth-grade reading level but has the ability to hold the interest of most teenage readers. This type of progression from short tales to longer, easy-to-read novels can be accomplished no matter what the reader's interest—animals, cars, sports, science fiction, romance, humor, and so on. Some examples of high-interest–low-reading-level books can be found in Table 2.1.

Reading aloud to poor readers is also another good technique for motivating them to read. Often students will seek out books that have previously been read to them. Many poor readers have not had the wonderful experience of listening to a story read out loud. (Reading-aloud techniques are described in Chapter 11.)

The Reluctant Reader

Many young adults fall into the category of reluctant readers. These readers may or may not possess the skills necessary to read on grade level, or may even read well above grade level, but for some reason they have become nonreaders. Sometimes these reluctant readers are called aliterate readers (people who can read but choose not to). After studying and analyzing a group of seventh-grade aliterate readers, G. Kylene Beers divided them into three groups:

1. Dormant readers—Students who like to read, identify themselves as readers, express positive feelings about others who enjoy reading, but do not presently make the time to read.
2. Uncommitted readers—Students who do not like to read, do not identify themselves as readers, express positive feeling about others who enjoy reading, and suggest they may read in the future.
3. Unmotivated readers—Readers who do not like to read, do not identify themselves as readers, express negative feelings about those who enjoy reading, and do not plan to read in the future. (1990)

We do not really know why students become aliterate readers, and often we confuse reluctance to read with inability to read. Table 2.2 shows some of the characteristics of aliterate, reluctant readers. One or more of these characteristics may be present in students who choose not to read even though they are able.

For reluctant readers there are thousands of young adult titles that will challenge their skills and keep them turning the pages. An important characteristic of most young adult books is a fast-paced start. By the end of the first chapter of Lois Duncan's *Killing Mr. Griffin* we know that "Griffin's the sort of guy you'd like to kill." When the end of each chapter leaves the reader hanging, as in Robert Cormier's *After the First Death*, putting the book down may be more difficult than punching the off button on the television set. According to educator Herbert Kohl in *Reading, How to*, "A lot of teachers complain that their students aren't motivated to read. That is like complaining that the students aren't motivated to walk or talk or run or dance or play" (1973). Students can be motivated to read if we help them find books that appeal to their interests and help them meet their needs.

Atwell's suggestion that students need time to read in school is certainly one way to encourage reluctant readers to read, particularly the dormant readers who see themselves as readers but do not take the time to read. Beers suggests some other strategies to use with aliterate readers. Her studies indicate that although choice of

Table 2.2
Reluctant Readers

Characteristics	Recommended Books
Read below, at, or above grade level	*Johnny Tremain*, Esther Forbes (age 10–15)
Equate reading with school, textbooks	*Tex*, S. E. Hinton (age 12–16)
Enjoy action more than words; would rather do it than read about it	*Hoops*, Walter Dean Myers (age 13–17)
	Tiger Eyes, Judy Blume (age 12–16)
Short attention span	*The Pigman*, Paul Zindel (age 13–17)
Find reading antisocial	*Spellbound*, Christopher Pike (age 15+)
Egocentric	*After the Bomb*, Gloria Miklowitz
Apathetic	(age 13–16)
Fear of ridicule from peers	*Killing Mr. Griffin*, Lois Duncan (age 14–17)
Demand to be entertained	*Abby, My Love*, Hadley Irwin (age 14–18)
Find books boring	*Are You in the House Alone?* Richard Peck
Opt for easier entertainment such as television, video games, movies	(age 13–17)
	This Place Has No Atmosphere, Paula
Think of books as part of the adult world	Danziger (age 11–13)
Pressured to read too much	
Rebel against parents and other adults	
Unenriched home environment	
Inability to find appropriate books	
Fear of failure	
Negative feelings about school	
Conflict with jobs, sports, etc.	

Note: Books recommended for reluctant readers may be appropriate for other readers.

books continues to be important to reluctant readers, choosing from a narrower field of books is helpful. Sometimes having a whole library of books from which to select can be intimidating to students who rarely read. She also suggests that aliterate readers are more interested in books with illustrations and are usually willing to listen to the teacher read an entire book aloud. Reading activities that allow the students to compare the book they are reading to a movie and art-related ways of responding to the book are likely to be perceived more positively by students who do not see themselves as readers.

Beers claims that uncommitted and unmotivated students approach all reading from an efferent stance (thinking about what they take away from reading the book) rather than an aesthetic stance (experiencing the book while reading it). Most of these students read nonfiction if they read at all. Since these students have difficulty shifting from an efferent to an aethetic stance, teachers should develop activities that allow students to begin responding personally to books of their choice. For some of these students, oral sharing activities may be most appropriate. According to Beers, the same motivational techniques do not work for all students, and the techniques selected must be adapted to individual readers.

❖ Between the Covers: *Authors at Work* ❖

KATHERINE PATERSON

Katherine Paterson, like most authors of books for young adults, travels to schools to discuss her books. In Gates of Excellence: On Reading and Writing Books for Children, *she reports on how one of her books and a classroom visit encouraged one reluctant reader to begin reading.*

Last spring I had been asked to speak in a junior high school, and I gave those in charge my usual speech about what I would do and what I expected them to do. For example: I do not sing, dance or do card tricks; therefore, I will not attempt to entertain an auditorium full of bored children. I will speak to a classroom-sized group of students who have read something that I have written and who want to talk with me about it. I don't care a bit if they liked what they read or not, simply that it aroused sufficient interest to make them want to discuss it.

When I was actually in the car on the way to the school, one of the ladies in charge of my appearance began to explain to me that they uh hadn't uh exactly been able to follow out my wishes and uh they hoped I wouldn't be too upset. Their original plan had been for me to speak to the gifted-and-talented ninth graders. (I gasped.) But they'd gotten fouled up. It seems that the special reading teacher had read *The Great Gilly Hopkins* out loud to her class and, when she heard that I was going to be at the school, had simply demanded that her class be allowed to horn in on the gifted-and-talenteds' special event. So there I was with about seventy junior high students to enthrall. Much to my surprise, not to say relief, the session went all right. I wasn't sure who was from the gifted program and who was from the special reading class; the questions were more or less of the ordinary variety. But I did notice a boy in a red sweatshirt sitting several feet away from everyone else in the room who was giving me more than ordinary attention. After the program was over, he came up and hung around until the other students had left, and then he began to ask me about Gilly. Who was she? Where was she? Then he wanted to know all the other stories—the things that had happened that somehow hadn't gotten into the book. It was one of those times when you know the real question is not being voiced, but I didn't understand what it was. Finally, a teacher persuaded the boy that he must return to class, and besides, she explained, I had to catch a plane shortly. When he had gone, the librarian told me that Eddie was a member of the special reading class who had heard Gilly read. Like Gilly, he was battling his way through a world of trouble. He had never shown any particular positive interest in books or school until his teacher had read Gilly to the class. And suddenly he had a passion. He was wild about a book—one of those reluctant readers, or even nonreaders, who had to this point seen words, not to mention books, as the deadliest of enemies.

I thought about Eddie for days. Here was a real-live Gilly who not only approved of but actually liked my fictional one. It was better than having a Japanese like *The Master Puppeteer* [a novel set in Japan that deals with the cultural tradition of puppetry]. Well, I decided, I'll just send him a copy. Even if he won't ever read it. At least he will own a book he likes. And that will be one for our side, now won't it?

Just before Gilly won the National Book Award, I got a letter from Eddie, and as some of you may remember, I read his letter with, I hasten to assure you, his permission, as part of my acceptance speech. But it feels so good to hear it that I'm going to repeat it.

Dear Mrs. Paterson,

Thank you for the book "The Great Gilly Hopkins." I love the book. I am on page 16.

Your friend always,
Eddie Young

And Eddie didn't stop on page 16. He's read the book four times. He's also read *Bridge to Terabithia*, and in his latest letter he said he was starting on *The Master Puppeteer*. I rushed off a "now don't be discouraged by all those long Japanese names" letter to him. I don't know as I write this if he finished it, or even if he's read any other books since he learned that books are not fearsome enemies. I hope he has. I believe he will. (1981, pp. 14–16) ❖

The Capable Reader

Even young adults who are capable, avid readers can profitably be introduced to titles written for adolescents. One of the characteristics of all mature readers is that they are able to read a variety of books, at the same time, for a variety of different purposes. If you think about the books you are currently reading, you will probably see this characteristic. It is rare, for example, for me to be reading fewer than four books at one time. Right now I am reading three travel guides on New Zealand, to help me plan for a trip there; Amanda Cross's latest mystery, for pleasure; a new edition of a textbook I use in my language arts class, so that I will be ready to teach the class in the fall semester; Shakespeare's *A Midsummer Night's Dream*, so that I can edit a teacher's guide on the play; and numerous professional articles, because I am interested in keeping up with what people in my field are studying. This list doesn't include the popular magazines I read, the newspapers I peruse with my morning coffee, or the numerous letters, reports, and student papers I read in my office. When I analyze what I am reading, I realize that I read to learn new information, meet my inner needs, explore my interests, perform my job, and escape from the day-to-day routine of my life. Such reading variety is important for the mature reader's personal and professional development.

By introducing young, capable readers to the wonderful world of young adult titles that challenge them, meet their personal needs, and appeal to their interests, we are encouraging them to develop reading versatility at an early age. We can also begin to teach them the difference between books that are read for pleasure, those read for personal development, and those read for educational or professional reasons. We can begin to help these young readers understand that each type of reading serves a purpose and helps in the reader's development. At the same time, we can show young readers that not all books are read at the same rate or for the same reason. According to young adult author Jeannette Eyerly, "The things young people want to read are related to their chronological age regardless of the level of their reading ability. Even if they have one foot in the world of adult literature, one foot will remain in the literature of childhood. I remember that one of my daughters, the summer before she reached sixteen, read not only *War and Peace*—at that time I had not read it—but also Maureen Daly's *Seventeenth Summer*."

Table 2.3 lists characteristics that may be present in students who are avid and mature readers. Good books for these readers are also listed.

The young adult classification includes an ever-growing number of challenging books. Younger and older adolescent readers will enjoy the thought-provoking books

Table 2.3
Capable Readers

Characteristics	Recommended Books
Read above grade level	*The Little Princess*, Frances Hodgson Burnett (age 10+)
Read a wide variety of books	
Have favorite authors	*A Wrinkle in Time*, Madeleine L'Engle (age 10+)
Have favorite genres	
Reading materials are accessible	*Bridge to Terabithia*, Katherine Paterson (10+)
Parents are readers	
Enriched environment	*Where the Lilies Bloom*, Bill and Vera Cleaver (age 10–14)
Were read to as preschoolers	*My Brother Sam Is Dead*, J. L. and C. Collier (age 10–14)
Have good vocabularies	
May or may not read school assignments	*A Solitary Blue*, Cynthia Voigt (age 12–16)
Have been successful students	*The Chocolate War*, Robert Cormier (age 12–17)
Write well	*In Summer Light*, Zibby Oneal (age 13–17)
Have many interests	
Independent	*Fallen Angels*, Walter Dean Myers (age 14–18)
Want to select books for themselves	
Enjoy age-appropriate books as well as more mature books	*Jabob Have I Loved*, Katherine Paterson (age 14–17)

Note: Books recommended for capable readers may be appropriate for other readers.

of Madeleine L'Engle, which can be read and reread on a variety of levels. Believable fantasies such as *A Wrinkle in Time*, *A Ring of Endless Light*, and *The Arm of the Starfish* will delight the "intelligent" young reader for whom L'Engle writes. Students who are not fantasy fans but who enjoy challenging books may be intrigued by Katherine Paterson's *Jacob Have I Loved* or Robert Cormier's *The Chocolate War*. The list of thought-provoking pleasure books for maturing readers is endless. The teacher who introduces students to such well-written books, as well as to textbooks and classic books, will be helping them develop skills and attitudes that will allow them to become lifelong readers. Young adult author Katherine Paterson explains how the engaging, challenging books of childhood can become the classic books of our adulthood. She says of her former college professor, "He began to speak about the powerful range of emotion that the book [*The Tombs of Atuan* by young adult author Ursula LeGuin] had evoked in him and wondered aloud if it was really suitable for children. . . . What I said to him rather inarticulately is the point I'm still fumbling to make. It was that what he had experienced in reading that book was not simply what the genius of the writer had put there (and I do not underestimate the genius), but the whole emotional history of a beautiful sixty-year-old life responding to that story. His creative genius had made a powerful book even more powerful" (1981, pp. 24–25).

As with poor and reluctant readers, teachers should use instructional methods that are specifically appropriate for capable readers. All of Atwell's suggestions work well with capable readers. However, there is another important consideration. Some of the most capable readers either choose to be or find themselves isolated from other students. In *Guiding Gifted Readers: From Preschool to High School*, Judith Wynn Halsted gives numerous examples of this problem:

> Now beginning junior high, Matthew has already learned that some of his ideas seem strange to his classmates and even to his parents and teachers. Entering a new school, he is determined not to mention thoughts that others might not understand; he tries, in fact, to stifle them in himself. At an age when he should be establishing his sense of identity, he is attempting to deny a part of it to himself as well as to others. . . .
>
> Sara loves to read, to play the piano, and to sew—all solitary activities. After a day crowded with people at school, she enjoys coming home to these quiet pursuits. Her parents are worried, however, because she seldom invites friends to come home with her. Although Sara is happy with her friends at school, and content with her activities at home, she senses her parents' concern and wonders whether there is something wrong with her. (1988, pp. 1–2)

As teachers we must help such students find their identity and communicate with their peers. Adolescent literature has the potential of allowing them to see that there are others just like them. When we guide them in their choice of books, we can help them find books with which they can identify. Likewise, in a program in which they are encouraged to read as much as they want, they are not held back by others in the class and there is no stigma for reading ahead.

At the same time it is important that they have the opportunity to share their thoughts, no matter how divergent, with their peers. Therefore, teachers should provide them with the opportunity to respond to books orally in small groups. If the students in the group are discussing a variety of books, perhaps on a single theme or genre, the capable readers may encourage others to want to read the same books.

(Chapters 9 and 10 provide many ideas for restructuring the curriculum to encourage different kinds of responding.) At the same time, we must allow students to utilize their abilities. Capable readers can read books in areas of interest, fiction or nonfiction, and report on these books in creative ways to the teacher, small groups, or the class (see Chapter 11). Or they might keep an ongoing dialogue journal which would give them an opportunity to respond to literature in ways they might avoid if sharing their response only with peers.

If a variety of books is available in the classroom, all students will have the opportunity to read books that interest and motivate them. Likewise, encouraging a wide variety of ways to respond to books, orally and in writing, allows all students to successfully share the books they have come to own. If we give students the time to read, we may convince them that reading is important, particulary if we read along with the class.

Reading Activity, Motivation, and Reading Achievement

In 1973 I surveyed 250 high school students as the beginning step in the development of an elective English program that was being designed to improve students' reading and communication skills. Through the survey I learned that the vast majority of the surveyed teenagers were not confident about their reading abilities. Many of them "hated" to read and read only when a course required it, and not even then if it could be avoided. More than 75 percent of the students indicated a strong dislike for reading and claimed they saw no purpose to it. These students were reluctant readers, and most of them were also poor readers. An examination of standardized reading test scores showed that over 60 percent of these reluctant readers scored below the 50th percentile (below grade placement). Because I was concerned about the large percentage of both reluctant and poor readers, I randomly analyzed previous standardized reading test scores for these students. The results of this analysis were not surprising. Nearly 80 percent of the reluctant readers' scores had declined since previous testing when compared to other students taking the tests.

Research indicates that the amount students read directly relates to their reading achievement as measured by standardized tests. As early as second grade a 60 to 70 percent variance in reading achievement is attributable to the amount of reading activity (Yap, 1977). National Assessment of Educational Progress reading test trends from 1971 to 1988 lead to a similar conclusion: the more students read, the better they read (Educational Testing Service, 1990). Thus, if reluctant readers give up reading, for whatever reason, their reading achievement in relationship to other readers is likely to decline. This is the nonreading cycle.

Reading is a skill, and like any other skill it needs practice. No one would suggest that an outstanding pianist, football player, or ballet dancer achieves success without practice. The same is true of the outstanding reader. The more readers practice the skill of reading, the more likely they are to become proficient at it.

The nonreading cycle, however, can be broken. For example, in one high school, a student teacher began reading *A Tale of Two Cities* aloud to a group of unmotivated seniors. When it became apparent that the students were bored, frustrated, and not listening, she closed the book and pursued another strategy. She borrowed multiple copies of five different young adult books from the high school library. *The Hard Life of the Teenager*, a nonfiction portrayal of teenage anxiety by James L. Collier, *The Chocolate War* (Cormier), *If I Love You, Am I Trapped Forever?* (Kerr), *Of Love and Death and Other Journeys* (Holland), and *I Heard a Scream in the Street: Poetry by Young People in the City* (Larrick, ed.). With these books she created a unit on teenage alienation. The unmotivated students not only read the books but enjoyed them. Another student teacher in the same high school had similar results when she created a unit on love and friendship for sophomore English classes using S. E. Hinton's first three books: *The Outsiders, That Was Then, This Is Now*, and *Rumble Fish*. One young man told her, after he had finished reading all three titles in two weeks, "These are the first books I've read all the way through!" He was as proud of his accomplishment as she was of hers. She should have been proud; she had broken the nonreading cycle.

One of the interesting discoveries these student teachers made was that once the students had completed reading a book, they demanded "another one just like the other one." The more they read, the more they wanted to read. Motivation to read was increasing as the amount of reading activity increased.

I have experienced similar results myself. In 1973 the unmotivated, poor readers I surveyed rarely read. By 1974, after the adoption of an English curriculum that encouraged the reading of a variety of books from different genres and cultures and at a range of reading and maturity levels, the students were reading a minimum of five paperbacks during every nine-week period. They were reading so much that the teacher had trouble keeping enough books in the classroom libraries to satisfy their needs.

Book sales in the local drugstore, the only purveyor of books, skyrocketed. Library circulation soared. Standardized reading test scores increased dramatically, and student writing improved. The percentage of the senior class electing to attend college increased from 4 percent to over 40 percent in three years. Discipline problems were practically nonexistent in the English classroom. The introduction of a wide variety of books including young adult literature was clearly turning nonreaders into avid readers, and producing other positive effects as well.

Nancie Atwell has documented similar results in her eighth-grade reading workshop program which encourages middle school students to read in school as well as at home. According to Atwell, in one year her students read "an average of thirty-five full-length works, from Blume to Brontë, Strasser to Steinbeck, Voigt to Verne. Their scores on standardized achievement tests averaged at the seventy-second percentile, up from an average at the fifty-fourth percentile when fully twenty-one percent scored in the bottom quartile; last year, that figure was just two percent" (1987, p. 158). More importantly, Atwell's students (92 percent) indicate that they regularly read at home for pleasure. When Atwell asked them in June how many books they owned, the average number was 98, up from 54 the previous September. Atwell concludes, "This is the kind of evidence that begins to convince doubting administrators and parents: Children read more, comprehend better, and value books to a greater degree when we let them read" (pp. 158–59).

Today in my university classes in adolescent literature, many students tell me that they rarely read for pleasure. It is not unusual to have future teachers say that the books they read in this university class were the first ones they read all the way through. It may seem difficult for you who are avid readers to believe that a significant population of adults, even college-educated adults, are nonreaders. However, studies of young adults today confirm that most are not capable readers. The National Assessment of Educational Progress (NAEP) has tested students' reading ability and surveyed students on reading-related questions. From 1971 to 1988 the test found that few students, even at age 17, read at the advanced level; only 7 percent of twelfth graders were capable readers. It also found, not surprisingly, that students who reported spending more time doing homework, read at higher levels than students who reported less time doing homework. Similarly, test results showed that students who read more per day are likely to read better. A negative relationship was found between test scores and the amount of television watched per day. Therefore, if we can motivate our students to read, they will not only read more, but they will be better readers.

Learning about Young Adult Literature

In our college courses, many of us did not learn about books written especially for adolescents. This book will help you identify a large number of young adult books and authors. Of course, the only way to really get to know these books is to begin reading as many as you possibly can. I challenge you to make a commitment to read one or two of these books per week. If you read only one a week, which is not difficult, you will have over fifty read in a single year, a good introduction to the fascinating world of adolescent literature.

A Brief History of Young Adult Literature

Young adult literature really became a separate field of literature in 1967 with the publication of S. E. Hinton's *The Outsiders*. When Viking published *The Outsiders*, they created a new publishing category independent of children's books and adult books, called young adult books.

The decade that followed changed the face of publishing and the nature of literature that was being read by adolescents. Prior to the late 1960s publishers believed that books published for children and adolescents were bought almost solely by schools and libraries. Therefore, they worried about things such as controlled vocabulary, reading level, and how the content of the books related to the curriculum. However, in the early 1970s the market shifted from schools and libraries, where teachers and librarians were purchasing books for adolescents, to bookstores where parents, children, and adolescents were buying books for reading at home. Consequently, publishers began to appeal to the adolescent. For the first time in the history of children's book publishing, pleasing adults was not prerequisite to selling books for adolescents. Suddenly writers could write and publishers could publish books that addressed the problems and concerns of the young. The genre of the problem novel, which had been introduced in late 1960s as schools focused more on understanding the personal and social problems of adolescents, came of age in the 1970s. Authors like Norma Klein, Richard Peck, and M. E. Kerr wrote books that adolescents themselves purchased and read. Many of the writers of books for young adults gained a following during the decade of the 1970s. Readers today still read the books of Katherine Paterson, Lois Duncan, Sandy Asher, Robert Lipsyte, Paula Danziger, to name just a few.

However, in the early 1980s, as author and publisher Patricia Lee Gauch reports, "The entire children's book industry seemed to have drawn a huge breath. After a decade of prosperity, there was a kind of momentary paralysis" (1990). What happened? First, the 1980s was the decade of education reform. Influenced by politicians such as William Bennett (*The Condition of Education*), commissions sponsored by interest groups (National Commission for Excellence in Education, *A Nation at Risk*), and educators such as Diane Ravitch (*The Schools We Deserve*), educators became less concerned with meeting the needs of the diverse student population and more concerned with ensuring that students were exposed to educational excellence. This shift in philosophy triggered a change in the secondary school curriculum from elective courses based on a variety of themes and topics to required courses emphasizing the study of texts and classic books. Therefore, schools were using their book budgets to purchase textbooks and multiple copies of classic titles rather than classroom sets and individual titles of young adult books. This change, of course, began to affect what was published.

About the same time, some other interesting events began to change the face of publishing. The Thor Inventory Tax Amendment taxed book inventories and made the former practice of keeping books in print for long periods of time obsolete. Therefore, many of the young adult titles teachers and librarians had come to believe would always be available went out of print. The 1980s was also a decade of corporate mergers. Many small publishing houses were merged into large corporate publishing conglomerates. If particular imprints were unprofitable (and changes in school purchasing patterns meant many young adult lines were not selling in their former numbers), corporate managers simply made the imprint inactive. In addition, the end of federal funding for Title I and Title II of the Elementary and Secondary Education Act signaled the end of purchasing single copies of multiple books for reading classrooms. School purchasing of young adult titles came to an almost complete halt. Hence, publishers slowed the publication of new young adult books, at the same time that they were taking older titles out of print. Teachers, librarians, and adolescents found it more and more difficult to find specific young adult books.

Since the only young adult books that were selling well were selling in bookstores, most often to adolescents, the types of books published were quick reads, primarily series and formula books. Ironically, the heyday of the problem novel may have ushered in the era of quick reads. Patricia Lee Gauch suggests that publishers became more interested in finding books that dealt with the right problems than in producing books of high quality. Instead of rich and literary romances by authors like Isabelle Holland, adolescents were buying formulaic series romances such as Sweet Valley High. Thus, if the 1970s was the golden era of the young adult novel, the 1980s represented the crash. Suddenly well-respected young adult authors like Sue Ellen Bridgers and Robert Cormier, who had been taught in the classrooms of the 1970s, were searching for new publishers.

Although the young adult literary novel may still be an endangered species, the early 1990s ushered in a new and exciting era in children's books that may signal future changes in the young adult field. Gauch suggests that this new era is the result of a new generation of parents, who want their children to have access to what she calls "up-market" books. They themselves love to read, and they want their children to have books worth reading and owning. As such books became more popular, a new type of bookstore emerged, specializing in books for children and young adults. Publishers in turn began to put more money in marketing high-quality books for children. This trend has not yet been realized in young adult books.

Another problem facing the young adult book market is that adolescents prefer to buy and read paperbacks. Unfortunately, paperbacks either come from successful hardbacks or are produced as paperback originals which often fall into the quick-read category. If schools, libraries, and adolescents are not buying hardback books, the best writers of young adult books may not be published.

Today there are many high-quality books for young adults, which we will discuss thoughout this text. (See Appendix A for a list of important young adult books.) The bulk of these books were published in the 1970s, but the authors who gained a following in those years are still writing marvelous books for adolescent readers. At the same time, new authors are being discovered. If adolescent book publishing receives the same shot in the arm in the late 1990s that children's books did in the 1980s, we can expect young adult books to flourish and improve.

The Controversial Nature of Young Adult Literature

Adolescent literature is controversial in part because it challenges the place of other books used in the curriculum. What books should we teach? After students have learned to read, should they be required to read textbooks and classic works? Or should they be allowed to select books that interest them? Some critics of using young adult books in the classroom feel that students' time would be better spent on other kinds of books.

Young adult books are also controversial because of their content. The protagonists of the books are adolescents, and the stories are told from the perspective of adolescent characters. Anyone who has studied the human life cycle understands that adolescence is a period of growth, change, and rebellion. The adolescent is attempting to develop a new independence, to seek an identity separate from parents and teachers. Often, in seeking this independence, adolescents experience problems and temptations; they may stray from the moral standards of their families and religions. Many adults wish to protect adolescents from these problems and temptations. Some of these adults believe that if the adolescents do not read about these problems, they are less likely to have them themselves.

The use of young adult books in the curriculum is likely to remain controversial; many books will continue to be the target of censors (see Chapter 15 for more on controversial books and the problems of censorship). Teachers cannot completely avoid the controversial nature of the young adult book; we may even have parents complain about the contents of the books. However, teachers can effectively use young adult books in their classrooms following the methodologies suggested in this text. They can also make a wide variety of books available to students, from easy-reads to the classics, so that the entire world of literature is open to them.

This text discusses many controversial books. If it didn't, there would be far fewer books to discuss. It also suggests methods for dealing with controversy and avoiding censorship. Before you select a book to be read by an entire class, read the book, know its content, be aware of potential controversy related to it, and write a clear rationale for why you are teaching it to the entire class (see Chapter 15 for more on writing rationales). Also, allow students to select from a variety of books on similar themes, genres, or topics within a single classroom. This lets students (and parents) preselect the books they will read based on their own needs, interests, abilities, maturity, and values. If we do not make a wide variety of potentially controversial books available to young readers, we may deprive them not only of the chance to improve their ability to read but of a more personal and sophisticated knowledge of the world in which they live. When we weigh the risk of using potentially controversial books against the risk of undereducating our students, conscientious teachers must choose the more challenging and more rewarding route of providing our students with the entire world of great books.

Epilogue: students as readers

The key to helping students become capable, avid readers is to get them reading. Studies of reading by today's adolescents indicate that they neither read as much as nor as well as they should and could. However, I know from experience, as do many other teachers, that every student can become a good reader if we provide reading time, engaging books, and the opportunity to respond to the books as equals. A knowledge of young adult books is the starting place for helping adolescents become lifelong readers. If you can pair the right young adult book with the right reader, it is very likely, no matter how reluctant or poor the reader, that this adolescent will read the book all the way through and will seek another book just like it. If you use the knowledge you gain in this book to select wonderful young adult books, begin a program of reading these books yourself, fill your classroom library with these books, and incorporate them in your teaching, you are well on your way to making your students good readers and exciting them about the subject you teach.

Suggested readings

Atwell, N. *In the Middle: Writing, Reading, and Learning with Adolescents*. Boynton/Cook/Heinemann, 1987.

Beers, G. K. *Choosing Not to Read: An Ethnographic Study of Seventh Grade Aliterate Readers*. Ph.D. dissertation, University of Houston, 1990.

Bend, W. *The Condition of Education*. U.S. Government Printing Office, 1985.

Donelson, K. "Fifty YA Books out of the Past Still Worth Reading; or, Enjoyment Is There If You Search for It." *ALAN Review*, Fall 1986, pp. 59–63.

Editor. *High Interest-Easy Reading: For Junior and Senior High School Students*. National Council of Teachers of English, published annually.

Educational Testing Service. The Reading Report Card, 1971–88: Trends from the Nation's Report Card. (Project of the Center for Educational Statistics, U.S. Department of Education). 1990.

Eyerly, J. H. "Writing for Today's Youth." *ALAN Review*, Winter 1981, pp. 1–3.

Fader, D., and E. B. McNeil. *Hooked on Books: Program and Proof*. Berkeley, 1966.

Gauch, P. L. "The Forest Will Always Be There: An Author/Editor Looks at Trends and Threats in Publishing." *ALAN Review*, Spring 1990, pp. 46–48.

Halsted, J. W. *Guiding Gifted Readers: From Preschool to High School*. Ohio Psychology, 1988.

Kohl, H. *Reading, How To*. Dutton, 1973. Bantam, 1974.

Malmgren, D. "Knowing Your Audience." *ALAN Review*, Fall 1989, p. 50.

National Commission for Excellence in Education. *A Nation at Risk: The Imperative for Educational Reform*. Washington, DC: U.S. Government Printing Office, 1983.

New York Public Library, Office of Young Adult Services. *Easy-to-Read Books for Teenagers*. Published annually.

Paterson, K. *Gates of Excellence: On Reading and Writing Books for Children*. Elsevier/Nelson, 1981.

Ravitch, D. *The Schools We Deserve*. New York: Basic Books, 1985.

Yap, K. O. "Relationships between Amount of Reading Activity and Reading Achievement." *Reading World*, October 1977, pp. 23–29.

PART TWO

LITERATURE FOR YOUNG ADULTS

3 Realistic Fiction

Focus Questions

1. Why do young adult books often mirror the lives of adolescents? How do authors provide young adult readers with windows on their world?
2. What is realistic fiction?
3. What is formula fiction and how is it unrealistic?
4. Why is humorous fiction important for young adults?
5. What are the characteristics of the young adult problem novel?
6. Why are relationships between the adolescents and other adolescents and adults so often the theme of realistic fiction for young adults?

PROLOGUE

As a kid I was clumsy, not over adept at games, a slow runner at best, and did not care too much for the chiding of other kids. So it became increasingly easy for me to choose the reality of books' plots and uncritical characters over the reality of my friends.

In junior high I did not particularly like myself and I was very much a loner. I read a great deal of fantasy and romantic love stories. I especially liked books in which there was a plain, shy girl who blossomed into beauty, inherited great wealth, and became the type of personality that made everyone want to be a close friend of hers.

Books were a haven. They didn't hurt my feelings. If I didn't like a book, I could stop reading whereas situations with flesh and blood people are sometimes hard to control.

Books to me in junior high were a way to escape the adjustment problems of eighth grade and to gain maturity for senior high school. They were my source of information for all the questions I couldn't put into words. They were like having an older brother or sister to show you what was going on and what was to come.

I grew up in an ethnic ghetto in Chicago. One of the reasons I was able to survive my childhood was to get lost in books.

When I was ten my mother died after a long illness and during the weeks before her death, life was anything but normal for us. The afternoon of the funeral I went straight to the library, perhaps as an escape from the house and its depression, but more likely as an attempt to reestablish a familiar pattern and security not present in the weeks of chaos. ❖

From "reading autobiographies" written by university students, in G. Robert Carlsen and Anne Sherrill, *Voices of Readers: How We Come to Love Books* (National Council of Teachers of English, 1988), pp. 81–82.

The Nature of Young Adult Books

Many writers of young adult fiction have written about the difficulty of writing realistic fiction for adolescents. As the students in the prologue remind us, books for adolescents often offer solace; they help them leave the real world and enter a world that is as they would like it to be, a world in which they are popular and in control. Can books for readers who seek escape be realistic?

Young Adult Books As Mirrors

Young adult author Richard Peck says of adolescent readers, they "choose books as they choose their friends—more as mirrors than as windows" (1975, p. 5). As Margaret Early's study of reading development confirms (see page 14), adolescent readers tend to choose books in which they can see their reflections. However, these same adolescents often want to escape the identities in which they find themselves trapped. This is the dilemma of authors of realistic fiction for young adults. As Peck says, the author of young adult realistic fiction must create a book in which "unreality [is] masked as realism. Setting, circumstances, dialogue had better reflect a familiar world. But the protagonist generally must be able to do something that most of the readers cannot. He must rise up independently from his tribe and assert himself. Or he must work his influence on others" (p. 5).

Young adult author Sandy Asher agrees with Peck and with the students writing in the prologue, reality is often too hard to take. "We would go stark, raving mad, I think, if we had to deal with reality exactly as it comes. It's too hard, too fast, too overwhelming, and far too complex. . . . Stories impose order on the otherwise unbearable chaos of our lives. Fiction is not a luxury. It's an absolute, rock-bottom, sanity-preserving necessity" (1985, p. 1). Realism in fiction, says Asher, is an "enriched reality that in turn enriches our lives." According to Peck, novels "must reach readers where they are. Bad novels leave them there. Worse ones promise unlikely escape in that ominous final line: 'And they got married and lived happily ever after.' Novels worth reading reach readers where they live in order to take them a step beyond themselves" (1990, p. 2).

Asher agrees and adds that where readers live is often normal and ordinary. According to Asher, a large proportion of the problem novels of the 1960s dealt with "relevant" issues facing teenagers: "death, divorce, alcoholism, child abuse and so on." However, these were not the problems of many teenagers who, if they read the novels of the era, might get "the distinct impression that if there were no dead, divorced, drunk child abusers in your family, you weren't normal somehow" (p. 2). Therefore, the problem of writing good realistic fiction for adolescents is writing fiction in which the normal young characters are realistic and are involved "in complex, sometimes humorous, sometimes unpleasant examinations of reality" (p. 2) that are typical of and yet different from everyday life.

Peck solves this problem by taking his realistic characters out of their everyday, complacent worlds of shopping centers, classrooms, and movie theaters. He places them in unusual situations. Blossom, the unattractive overweight teenager of many of his novels, escapes into a quasi-supernatural world of time travel (see *The Ghost Belonged to Me, Ghosts I Have Been, The Dreadful Future of Blossom Culp,* and *Blossom Culp and the Sleep of Death*). Blossom does not blossom into a slim femme fatale but, instead, learns more about who she is through her adventures. Peck's other books are also about personal growth. *Through a Brief Darkness* features an American girl at a British boarding school, and *Those Summer Girls I Never Met,* set on an ocean liner, is about two teenagers who travel with their grandmother in the Baltic Sea. In *Voices after Midnight* three typical California adolescents walk through a door and find themselves in the New York blizzard of 1888. Peck's characters are removed from their worlds, often against their will, and mature through their experiences before they return.

Asher solves the problems of taking real teenagers out of themselves by giving them complicated problems to address. She doesn't physically remove them from their everyday world but instead places new obstacles or situations in their way. In *Daughters of the Law* Denise helps her new friend Ruthie deal with her family's history as survivors of the Holocaust. *Missing Pieces* is the story of Heather and her mother who must develop their relationship after the death of Heather's father. In *Summer Begins* Terry, who does not like controversy, writes an article for her school newspaper that causes an uproar in spite of being on a safe topic. Terry's father defends her editorial against the principal's complaints and wants her to stand up for her rights; her mother disagrees. Terry is caught in the middle.

Asher and Peck are two of the many authors of young adult books whose characters mirror their young adult readers and at the same time, move beyond the day-to-day world of shopping centers, schoolrooms, and peer groups. As Peck says, "When I was still a teacher, I noticed that nobody truly grows up in a group. . . . They have to be removed a great distance much against their wills in order to take a step nearer their futures and their roots. Nobody grows up until he has to. In young adult novels somebody always has to" (p. 2). Throughout this chapter you'll read about other authors who help their characters grow (not always easily) by placing challenges before them.

Formula Fiction

Although young adult authors write thought-provoking books that offer readers windows onto their world, many adolescents often select books that are safe, that is, books that are just like books they have read before. Perhaps, in part, this explains the popularity of formula fiction with many young adult readers.

Formula fiction is fiction in which the plot and characters are familiar and predictable. Fiction that follows a particular formula is nothing new. The "dime novels" published in the mid-nineteenth century, precursors to the paperback, often followed a prescribed formula. Some of the favorite characters in these books were Seth Jones, Davy Crockett, "Old Sleuth," Nick Carter, and Deadwood Dick.

By the turn of the century, the Stratemeyer Syndicate produced numerous series books popular with young readers, including the Admiral Dewey books, the Rover boys books, and the most popular Nancy Drew series. Although each of these series had a named author, the name was a pseudonym for the many writers who produced a novel from an outline provided by the syndicate for a one-time fee. By the 1940s and 1950s romance series books, by Rosamund DuJardin, Betty Cavanna, and Anne Emory, and sports and car books, by John Tunis and Henry Gregor Felsen, were also being read by young readers.

In the early years of young adult literature, from the late 1960s through the early 1980s, few new series books were developed. Formula fiction took a back seat to realistic fiction, particularly the problem novel. As school purchases of these titles declined, however, publishers began to seek new markets for books for adolescents. Since the bookstores were already succeeding at selling books to adolescent buyers, the publishers moved to a long-tested, successful, inexpensive approach to producing and selling books—the formula novel.

Is today's formula novel realistic? The answer is yes and no. The formula novel tends to have characters that are not exactly like the adolescent readers but like the people adolescent readers would like to be. The plots do not reflect the actual lives of adolescent readers but rather an idealized version of their lives. As part of the newer trend toward formula books, many series books of the past, such as the Nancy Drew books, were updated with contemporary characters and plot lines. As in the past, the author of many of the formula books, such as Francine Pascal of the Sweet Valley High series, conceive basic plots and characters and then hire writers to produce the books from the provided guidelines. Each book, like a television soap opera, often ends at a climax that will be resolved in next month's book. Young readers become hooked, wanting to know what happens to the characters who have become their friends.

In addition to the romance books, other kinds of series have simple, predictable plots and one-dimensional characters. These include some teenage mystery books, solve-your-own adventure books (which work like many computer programs in which the plot progresses depending on the option selected by the reader), books about young adolescents who baby-sit, and sports series books. The mainstay of the market, however, is the series romance for young adolescent girls that follow the formula girl gets boy, girl loses boy, girl regains boy or finds an even better one. These books are no more realistic than the television soap operas watched by millions each weekday afternoon or the popular Harlequin romances.

Are formula books harmful? Unlikely. In fact, a large percentage of mature, aesthetic readers at some time in their lives read formula books by the dozen. The problem with formula books is that sooner or later the reader knows exactly what will happen after reading the first chapter. As young people mature as readers, many become bored with these books, they want something similar that provides a greater challenge and increased interest. If young readers do not find other books that whet their reading appetite, they may simply quit reading or move on to adult formula fiction. The goal of teachers, therefore, is to help young readers who tire of formula fiction find realistic fiction that does not provide pat, unrealistic answers to all life's problems, but instead portrays life with all its promise and with all its perils. In this chapter you will find many titles that will help move formula readers to more sophisticated and realistic fiction.

Humor

Adolescence is generally a period of change and struggle. However, it is also a time filled with humor. Humorous fiction allows adolescents to deal with the problems of their lives from a different perspective. However, understanding the humor of adolescence can be difficult for writers of young adult realistic fiction. As Jerry Spinelli, author of humorous books for young adults, writes, if adults attempt to determine why an adolescent takes the last drop of root beer from the bottle but leaves the bottle in the refrigerator, for example, "speculation may be exercising but is invariably fruitless, for this is the twilight zone where the adult, with all his superior powers of insight, begins to lose contact with the juvenile psyche" (1986, p. 15). The writer must also understand the humor perceived by adolescents themselves. He or she must enter the psyche of the adolescent in order to tell about events from the adolescent's perspective.

According to M. Kip Hartvigsen and Christen Borg Hartvigsen, adolescence is a period of time that "is like a house on moving day—everything is in a temporary mess" (1986, p. 25). The Hartvigsens suggest that one of the benefits of young adult literature is that it allows adolescent readers to gain "perspective on their lives at a time when objectivity is so hard to achieve . . . [and] it proffers this perspective with humor, helping the young to see what one critic [D. Carlson] has called the 'terrible hilarity of adolescence' " (p. 25). Another benefit is that adults who read the books of humorous authors can better understand and laugh at adolescent behavior we often find irksome. By showing young readers the humorous side of adolescence, writers, through their characters, can take readers outside of themselves and help them mature beyond adolescence.

Ellen Conford, an author of very funny books for adolescents, reminds would-be writers of humorous fiction for young adults that the books are not written to teach or to preach, but rather to entertain. If readers grow in the process of reading the books, as she hopes they will, so much the better. She quotes a letter she received from one of her readers: "Whenever something terrible happens to me, like, for instance, getting into a car accident on my first date, I try to think, 'Now, how would Ellen Conford turn this into a funny chapter?' " (1986, p. 21) Conford takes to heart the advice of an eleven-year-old reader who said there are three rules for good writing, "Don't bore me. Don't make me feel stupid. And don't treat me like a child" (p. 22). Good realistic humor for adolescents follows these rules. Figure 3.1 lists characteristics of high-quality humorous fiction for young adults.

The Hartvigsens claim that a wealth of humorous situations are tucked into the lives of typical teenagers. The comedy of adolescence, they say, is made up of "(1) the comedy of adolescent manners—life with the peer group, caught up in the intricacies of prescribed dress, speech, conduct and even humor; (2) the comedy of initiation—the bittersweet experience of the first everything: the first date, the first love, the first shaft, the first realization that parents are not perfect and do not have all the answers; and (3) the comedy of getting along with authority figures—the challenge of living with, understanding, and pleasing adults, most notably parents" (pp. 25–26). Spinelli agrees and claims there is no better source of humor than the adolescent: "What a repository [the adolescent is], what a garage sale, what a mother lode for the fiction writer stalking a story, looking for adventure, looking for suspense, conflict, looking for characters that aren't boring, looking for characters that are . . . 'characters' " (1986, pp. 17–18). However, Spinelli also reminds us that the best humor is not written to be humorous. He writes of his own books: "Certainly humor is there. But there is more. . . . I don't set out to write a funny book. I set out to write about kids as they really are (or as they appear to me), and sooner or later, is it not inevitable that most kids will lead you to humor?" (Jerry Spinelli, personal communication, 1993).

**Figure 3.1
Characteristics of Good
Humorous Fiction for Young
Adults**

Character
Protagonist
- young
- identifiable
- caught up in real situations
- realistic
- does things reader does or would like to do

Other Characters
- adults are often undeveloped; when developed, are portrayed as real people
- often an adult other than a parent acts as a mentor
- one or more characters act as foils to the protagonist

Plot
- situational
- wide-ranging
- humor found in situations which are not inately humorous
- novel may not be written to be humorous; however, a sense of humor helps the character mature
- often an element of suspense

Point of View
- protagonist's

Voice
- protagonist's

Theme
- "You can survive"
- "Life is not so serious"
- "There are other kids who share your problems"

─────── ❖ **Between the Covers:** *Authors at Work* ❖ ───────

JERRY SPINELLI

In a short period of time Jerry Spinelli went from being an unmarried businessman to a husband and stepfather of six children and the author of numerous novels for adolescents including the Newbery Award–winning *Maniac Magee* (1990). Spinelli remembers well how he became the author of young adult books.

> I remember when I started to pay attention [to adolescent humor]. On May 24, 1977, I went to sleep by myself in a third-floor efficiency in Norristown, Pennsylvania. On May 25, I went to sleep in a house in Havertown with a wife, six children and a hermit crab. Give me about a month to get over the shock, and figure by early July I was beginning to pay attention.
>
> And what did I find? I found six Huckleberry Finns, rafting, poling along, one near the headwaters, one near the gulf and the rest in-between, making their landfalls along the Mississippis of their kidhoods. (1986, p. 18)

Spinelli's children, now mostly grown, have provided him with models for the young adult characters and situations in his books. Spinelli says he began his first young adult book in the company cafeteria after he opened the container of fried chicken he had prepared for lunch the night before. He saw bones, ligaments, and some skin, but no chicken meat. And then he wrote about what he had found, not through his own eyes, but through the eyes of an adolescent who lived under the roof of his house:

> One by one my stepfather took the chicken bones out of the bag and laid them on the kitchen table. He laid them down real neat. In a row. Five of them. Two leg bones, two wing bones, one thigh bone.
> And bones is all they were. There wasn't a speck of meat on them.
> Was this really happening? Did my stepfather really drag me out of bed at seven o'clock in the morning on my summer vacation so I could stand in the kitchen in my underpants and stare down at a row of chicken bones? (1986, p. 16)

Spinelli didn't know it at the time, but writing about the bones that day instead of eating lunch launched him on his new career as a writer of humorous realistic fiction for young adults. His first book was *Space Station Seventh Grade* (1982). It was followed by *Who Put That Hair in My Toothbrush?* (1986) and five more books between 1990 and 1991 including *Maniac Magee*.

The heart of Spinelli's fiction for young adults is in his characters. They are real adolescents, and their situations are real. And in each situation Spinelli finds humor and a way to help readers learn more about themselves. Spinelli reports, "You know, it's nice. Every once in a while a kid will write to me saying, 'Thank you for showing me I'm a normal seventh grader'" (Murphy, 1991–1992, p. 342).

Spinelli writes of his own books: "A close check will show that each of my books runs the gamut, from funny to sad, coarse to tender. I try to suggest the totality of a kid's life, and the writer has to hit a lot of points because kids are not yet specialists. Their lives are varied and fractured; I try to reflect that in the books" (Jerry Spinelli, personal communication, 1993).

❖

Laughing at Oneself

Frequently authors of humorous young adult books feature characters who can laugh at themselves. Paula Danziger has written several books that young teens find very funny. According to Danziger, "Laughter helps us with being invincible. As long as we can laugh, we can survive."

She has discovered what makes young adults laugh by remembering what made her laugh as an adolescent, by discussing humor with young adults, by observing them, and by collecting "clean, good jokes" told by teenagers, such as "Did you hear about the rodent who almost drowned and his brother had to give him mouse-to-mouse resuscitation?" or "Did you hear the one about the guy who only works on Saturdays and Sundays because he's a candle trimmer and they only work on wick ends?" *(Can You Sue Your Parents for Malpractice?)*

Danziger's characters have the everyday experiences of young adults at school, at home, at the library, and they handle them with humor. In *The Cat Ate My Gymsuit*, for example, Marcy believes she's "too fat and ugly" to get into a gymsuit. She has hundreds of excuses for not taking gym, from "I had been mugged on the way to school by a syndicate specializing in stolen gymsuits" to "My little brother had misplaced his security blanket and was using my gymsuit instead" to "The cat ate my gymsuit." When Ms. Finney, the kids' favorite teacher and Marcy's adult mentor, is fired, Marcy and her friends come up with twenty-three ways to show everyone how they feel about the firing: "Clog up the faculty-room toilets with *The New York Times* school supplements, . . . steal all the chalk in the entire school, . . . go to the guidance counselors and ask for guidance, . . . steal the faculty room coffee pot, . . . call all the major TV networks and have them cover the story, . . . cut school and then forge notes saying that we were absent because of cases of acute acne." Incidents and responses like these are familiar to teenagers. Readers can see themselves in the situations, and they can laugh with Marcy and at Marcy. Another Danziger title, *There's a Bat in Bunk Five,* finds Marcy at summer camp with Ms. Finney as counselor.

The laughing-at-ourselves theme is found in many other humorous books for young adult readers. In *Can You Teach Me to Pick My Nose?* Martyn Godfrey tells the tale of Jordy Shepherd who moves to California from Montana. This social outcast still wears blue jeans and cowboy boots. Chris Williamson makes Jordy instantly popular by convincing everyone that Jordy is a skateboard champion. One problem—Jordy is challenged to show his stuff against Steve Powell, king of the ramp, but he has never been on a skateboard. Pamela Loseth, a social misfit herself, is a secret skateboard wizard and comes to Jordy's rescue. Teaching him not only how to pick his nose on the skateboard but also how to be a true friend.

The Heroic Life of Al Capsella by Australian writer J. Clarke is about another misfit. This one comes by it naturally. With good humor Clarke tells the story of Al Capsella, his eccentric parents, whom Al calls Mr. and Mrs. Capsella and hopes are not really his parents, and a cast of other oddball adults. In this book readers not only get to know Al, but they also become friends with the adults in Al's life. The wacky cast of characters helps Al understand that he is destined never to be normal.

Humor with a Message

Many young adult humorous books, including three by Judie Angell, have a message beyond the laughter. *Dear Lola, or How to Build Your Own Family* is the story of six refugees from an orphanage who band together to form their own family. *Secret Selves* is a warm story of two teenagers who are too shy to show their interest in each other. Finally, Julie calls Rusty on the phone under the pretense that she is trying to locate someone else. Rusty begins to play a similar game. The two become telephone friends, but remain aloof from each other during the school day. In *A Word from Our Sponsor, or My Friend Alfred,* a boy discovers that a drinking mug is made of poisonous materials. He decides to alert consumers to the problem. In the process he must challenge his father's advertising agency. The story allows the reader to laugh and at the same time consider the serious problem of keeping one's integrity.

Judy Blume has written many amusing and meaningful books for young adolescents. Margaret of *Are You There, God? It's Me, Margaret* is the new girl in town. It's bad enough to be new in town, but to be experiencing the onset of puberty at the same time can be agonizing. The story is told with great sensitivity and humor that allow the young reader who is experiencing the same problems to laugh at them along with Margaret and her friends. The heroine of *Blubber* is fifth grader Jill Brenner, whose classmates harass her. When another girl begins to show sympathy for Jill, the students persecute her as well. Like most Judy Blume books, *Blubber* is funny, but hidden behind the humor is a moral message.

Highly regarded young adult author M. E. Kerr also employs humor. *Dinky Hocker Shoots Smack* is about a girl whose mother is more concerned with serving others than with noticing Dinky, whose name does not reflect her girth. Dinky, in an attempt to deal with her own insecurities, becomes the queen of the put-down. Nearly every character in the book is a target. Although she directs her sarcasm at others, she more often directs it at herself. Like many adolescents, Dinky uses sarcasm as a means of making others feel as bad as she does. As author Richard Peck suggests, often "the laughter in a school room . . . is motivated either by nervousness or derision" (1975, p. 6). Dinky uses her humor in this way. By the end of the book the self-derisive Dinky spray-paints "Dinky Hocker shoots smack" all over the neighborhood in a desperate attempt to make her mother pay more attention to her than the drug addicts with whom she works. Kerr is a master of satire in young adult books. Reading the Fell series *(Fell, Fell Back,* and *Fell Down)* about a teenage sleuth and preppie gourmet who solves his mysteries by taking on the exclusive Gardner School, is an entertaining romp. However, as in all of Kerr's books, hidden beneath the humor and the well-crafted plot is an unobtrusive message, that adolescence may be difficult but each adolescent has his or her own gifts. John Fell is a delightful, realistic character who in each novel finds himself entwined in simultaneously realistic and unreal situations.

Outwitting Adults

Outwitting adults is a favorite humorous theme in young adult books. *From the Mixed-Up Files of Mrs. Basil E. Frankweiler* (Konigsburg), a Newbery Medal book, is about a brother and a sister who run away from home and hide out in New York's Metropolitan Museum of Art. Their escapades in avoiding guards and employees and the deal they make before they go home are very funny. *Secrets of the Shopping Mall* (Peck) has a similar premise. Two teenagers take refuge in a huge shopping mall and outwit suburban authorities.

Other good examples of humorous fiction in which kids take on adults include Gordon Korman's *A Semester in the Life of a Garbage Bag* and *The Zucchini Warriors* and Daniel Pinkwater's *The Snarkout Boys and the Baconburg Horror* and *The Snarkout Boys and the Avocado of Death*. Walter Dean Myers features inner city kids in his quasi-mysteries *Mojo and the Russians, The Young Landlords,* and *The Mouse Rap*.

Laughing at an Earlier Self

Many books allow teenage readers to look back on the days when they were younger. The Soup books by Robert Newton Peck are bad-boy stories that are particularly amusing to preteen or early teenage males. *How to Eat Fried Worms* by Thomas Rockwell is also funny to the same age group. Beverly Cleary's *Ramona, the Pest* is a laugh fest for young adolescent girls. This silly book recounts five-year-old Ramona's first few months in kindergarten. James Thurber said that "humor is emotional chaos remembered in tranquility," and this book allows the young adult reader to reflect on the emotional chaos of the first days in kindergarten in the relative tranquility of young adulthood. The problems of Ramona are far enough removed, but still close enough, that they can be laughed at and understood by the young reader.

School Humor

A number of hilarious books examine life in the classroom. Stanley Kiesel's *The War between the Pitiful Teachers and the Splendid Kids* and its sequel *Skinny Malinky Leads the War for Kidness* are about the "war" at Scratchland School. The students, led by Skinny Malinky, are clearly the "white hats" of the tale; the teachers are led by Mr. Foreclosure and have The Status Quo Solidifier on their side. Big Alice, the hyena girl, is the heroine of the students and the terror of the teachers; after all, she has eaten one of them! *Oompah* by William B. Crane looks at school life in a slightly softer way. The book is about a California high school band that is invaded by a very funny, very large tuba player from Texas. The reader can't help liking Fred, even though he is constantly teasing, playing practical jokes, arriving late to half-time, and getting other students in trouble. The author is a former high school bandmaster who captures the humor and fun of being in a high school band. A very funny how-to book that allows young readers to laugh at themselves is Delia Ephron's *Teenage Romance, or How to Die of Embarrassment.* From the book young readers can learn how to (or how not to) have a crush, hide a pimple, and talk to their mothers. M. E. Kerr's *Is That You Miss Blue?* and Paula Danziger's *Make Like a Tree and Leave* and *Earth to Matthew* also focus on school-based situations.

Two book by Louis Sachar explore the dangerous terrain of young adolescent relationships and the common feeling of being different from everyone else. Middle school and junior high school readers are likely to enjoy *There's a Boy in the Girl's Bathroom* and *Dogs Don't Tell Jokes.*

Jerry Spinelli enters the realm of school humor, in this case sports humor, in *There's a Girl in My Hammerlock.* In this book an eighth-grade girl, Maisie Potter, tries out for and makes the boys' wrestling team.

Bad-Boy and Bad-Girl Books

Walter Dean Myers writes bad-boy books using black dialect that depict life in modern Harlem. In a review of *Fast Sam, Cool Clyde, and Stuff,* a *Horn Book Magazine* reviewer commented, "The humorous and ironic elements of the book give it the flavor of a Harlem Tom Sawyer or Penrod." In *Mojo and the Russians* the action begins with a trumped-up bicycle accident in which the main character Dean runs into Drusilla, an old woman the boys fear: "Stupid child almost knock me clear out of this world! I walking along, minding not a soul's business in this whole world but my own, and along comes this child like a bat out of a dark place and send me flying in the middle of the street." Dean's friends convince him that he is in big trouble. Meanwhile, Willie, a janitor at the university where classified research is being conducted, is visited by a group of Russians. The boys imagine the worst. From these two early incidents the amusing narrative, filled with hyperbole, puns, and irony takes off. Two other humorous books by Myers are *It Ain't All for Nothin'* and *Mop, Moondance, and the Nagasaki Knights.*

Another bad-boy book for young adolescents, *The Best Christmas Pageant Ever* by Barbara Robinson, is one of the funniest Christmas books ever written. A group of children set about to destroy the school Christmas pageant but end up making it the best one ever.

The bad-boy books of Mark Twain are still very popular with young readers. According to a survey conducted by Ted Hipple and Bruce Bartholomew (1982), *The Adventures of Huckleberry Finn* (1884) is the book most widely read by today's college freshmen. The humorous misadventures of Huck and his raft-mate, the slave Jim, still provide some of the best belly laughs in print. *The Adventures of Tom Sawyer* (and Becky Thatcher) gives the young adult a look into the rural past and an understanding of the timeless nature of childhood antics. One of Mark Twain's funniest and shortest books is *Pudd'nhead Wilson.* Its length makes it particularly suitable for reluctant readers. The story revolves around two boys who are born on the same day in 1830, one to a prosperous landowner the other to his mulatto slave. In an attempt to advance her child, the slave arranges to switch the two infants. The witty story unfurls from that point.

Satire

Few authors have attempted to write pure satire for adolescents. Julian E. Thompson is a notable exception. In *Discontinued,* a satirical mystery, Duncan Banigan flees his home after his mother and brother have been murdered because he believes he is also a target. He joins up with a group of Nukismetic Humanists, who believe nuclear annihilation is inevitable and becomes romantically involved with Caitlin Fetish, whose father is a guru of the Nu-Hus. The Nu-Hus, however, have a food operation that is a cover for an illegal drug business. In *Simon Pure* Thompson writes of fifteen-year-old genius Simon Storm who goes to Riddle University, his father's alma mater. After Simon meets the president of Riddle, Henry "Gater" Portcullis, he finds himself involved in a cheating scandal, an encounter with a Washington group ordered to turn Riddle into a right-wing business school (or so Simon thinks), and an affair with President Portcullis's daughter. *A Band of Angels* is a book about a ragtag group of teenagers who decide to have every kid in the world sign a petition against nuclear war. The complicated plot involves an adult couple who are attempting to keep the super-virus they have discovered a secret from the federal government (and eventually commit suicide), a psychopathic federal agent, and a hippie college professor who sets out to sexually exploit teenage runaways. In *Herb Seasoning* Herb Herbzman is graduating from high school and doesn't know what he wants from life other than love and money. A guidance counselor recommends Castles in the Air, where Herb can test vocations while traveling in the Upwardlimobile. Herb sticks with wanting love and loses his virginity, but his heroine is part of a Health Care venture so he decides money is less important. In addition, Herb tries on careers in crime and politics. Like all of Thompson's books, this tongue-in-cheek, social satire is for mature readers.

Another good example of satire for adolescents is Sue Townsend's *The Secret Diary of Adrian Mole, Aged 13¾.* Adrian faces many typical teenage situations. The most humorous aspects of the book, however, involve Adrian's writing which he continuously sends off, in spite of its shallowness, to the BBC, only to have it rejected each time. In addition, Adrian breaks out in a terrible disease which is finally diagnosed by a doctor as "Acne Vulgaris," his mother runs off with the man next door, and his father loses his job and takes up with a woman with a small son whom Adrian baby-sits. Adrian finds true love in Pandora, who tells him she will not consummate their relationship because curing his acne and his frustrations is not worth her becoming a single parent.

Half Nelson, Full Nelson by Bruce Stone is a light-satire sports book for older adolescents about Nelson Gato, whose father is a second-rate wrestler who has neither the talent nor the breaks to make the circuit. He is known as the Gator Man both for his name and for losing his temper and wreaking homicidal mayhem on a geriatric alligator. Gator Man unwittingly runs off Nelson's mother and sister Venessa. This begins the search for Venessa by son and father across south Georgia and north Florida in an attempt to restore the family to what it was in the not-so-good days before the breakup.

Another good example of satire for older adolescents is the political satire *Burning Patience* by Antonio Sharmeta. In this book an unlikely friendship develops between Mario Jimenez, a poet-postman, and the Nobel–prizewinning Chilean poet Pablo Neruda. The story takes place during the Allende years in Chile. The plot turns on a love affair between Mario and Beatriz Gonzalez, which is assisted by Neruda and objected to by Beatriz's mother.

Humor in Science Fiction and Fantasy

Many of Daniel Pinkwater's books for young adolescents are extraordinarily funny fantasy or science fiction adventures. In *Lizard Music* the author mixes puns and absurdities in the fantastic tale of a child who attempts to track reality in a media-crazy environment. *Alan Mendelsohn, the Boy from Mars* is about Leonard, a short, fat, and wrinkled boy who feels he is doomed to a life as an outcast until he meets Alan Mendelsohn. The two friends then embark on a series of wild and hilarious adventures. In *The Dog Days of Arthur Cane,* by Ernesto T. Bethancourt, Arthur is magically turned into a stray dog who learns more about life than he has learned in his sixteen years as an upper-middle-class Long Islander. Another humorous book in the fantasy genre is the satire *The Kryptonite Kid* by Joseph Torchia. Jerry Chariot is the kryptonite kid, who writes letters to his hero Superman, and the story is told through his letters. Jerry dreams of being just like his hero and inspiring his classmates' jealousy and amazement when he performs his wondrous feats. Paula Danziger entered the science fiction realm with *This Place Has No Atmosphere.* In this humorous book Aurora Borealis Williams worries that Matthew, her dream boy, will not ask her out. She claims that is as likely to happen as her moving to the moon. However, the year is 2057 and both events occur. Matthew asks her out, and Aurora's father is transferred to the moon.

Many older adolescents also enjoy humor in fantasy and science fiction. *Tune in Yesterday* is a time-travel novel by Bethancourt which takes two teenage jazz fans back to the 1940s. This humorous novel allows the reader to see the jazz era from the vantage points of the 1970s. (Ernesto T. Bethancourt is the pseudonym of singer-guitarist Tom Pasley, whose knowledge of the music scene makes this novel informative as well as entertaining.) The classic George Orwell book *Animal Farm* is a satire that appeals to many older teens. In the book farmyard animals revolt against their human owners.

Humor in Mystery and Suspense

One of the funniest series to be published in some time is the Doris Fein series by Ernesto T. Bethancourt. Doris is a liberated Nancy Drew with a wonderful sense of humor. As Doris describes herself in *Doris Fein: The Mad Samurai:*

> I'm hardly a typical Southern Californian, even though I am a native. The standard of beauty here in SoCal is well known. The girls all look like Barbie dolls: tall, blond, beautiful and without ever having had a pimple in their lives. I, on the other hand, am five feet four inches tall and, depending on my discipline, a teensy bit, or a whole lot overweight.

M. E. Kerr's Fell series and Walter Dean Myers's Harlem series are two other excellent examples of recent humorous mysteries. Myers has also written *Tales of a Dead King,* a humorous mystery involving archaeologists in Egypt. Lynn Hall's *Murder in a Pig's Eye* is a wacky mystery with oddball characters. Sixteen-year-old sleuth Bodie Tureen seeks to discover if Bella Siler was murdered by her husband. He explores the Siler property from the cistern to manure pile to cellar in search of Bella's body.

Funny Books That Are Not Written Primarily to Be Funny

Numerous young adult books are not written to be primarily humorous, but reading them offers many good laughs. Paul Zindel's books are in this category. In *Confessions of a Teenage Baboon* fifteen-year-old Chris Boyd reveals the comical side of being a misfit as he moves with his mother, a practical nurse, from one live-in job to another. Some of Zindel's books combine grave and comical incidents. For example, Zindel's *Harry and Hortense at Hormone High,* about two teenagers who are intrigued by Jason Rohr, a young man who thinks he is the reincarnation of the demigod Icarus, is alternately tear-jerking and hysterically funny.

In Robbie Branscum's books the problems of her very realistic adolescent characters often seem insurmountable, but Toby and Johnny May tell stories of life and death, love, and hate in ways that only the young can tell them. Her regional books such as *Toby, Granny and George, To the Tune of the Hickory Stick,* and *Johnny May* have the language and the flavor of the rural South. Branscum says of her writing, "I love the things of childhood—slow-moving rivers, woods, fields and fishing poles, tall tales and mystery, long summer days and slipping away from the adult world into the world of children where the lines are boldly drawn."

One would not normally think of a book about a shoplifting mother as humorous. However, the mother of Lee Bennett Hopkins's book *Mama* is a very funny character who bamboozles train conductors, relatives, and employers. She justifies her shoplifting to her sons telling them she is patriotic for taking plastic flowers made in America rather than real African violets.

Madeleine L'Engle is not usually considered an author of humor. However, her books about the Austin family, particularly *Meet the Austins* and *The Moon by Night,* are often amusing. They recount the adventures of the Austin family as they take in orphaned Maggy Hamilton and go on a cross-country camping trip.

Books that offer social commentary can also be humorous. Byrd Baylor's *Yes Is Better Than No* is a story about three groups of people in Tucson, Arizona. The Papago tribe is attempting to understand and survive in the Anglo environment around them. The American social workers are trying to help them but make little effort to understand the Native Americans. And a group of militant Native Americans are opposed to all Anglos but do not understand their own people or their customs. The well-intentioned but wrong-headed actions of these three groups produce a funny commentary on the failure of people to understand each other. When one of the Papago, Mrs. Domingo, wins a swimming pool, for example, she uses it as a dwelling place for herself and her daughter, who has a mental disorder. The empty pool also provides the address needed by a neighbor to collect welfare checks. With all good intentions, the community bands together to fill the pool. As the pool is filled, the home and the address are lost.

The Problem Novel

When you think of the term *young adult literature,* what comes to mind? For many it is the problem novel, the novel that mirrors the difficult predicaments of adolescence. Indeed, the problem novel is the largest genre within the young adult field and predominated during the 1970s. No similar genre exists in adult literature. In fact, the concept of a problem novel is almost redundant since all novels with plots involve a problem.

Today, however, young adult problem novels are less likely to be published, and when they are, they are considerably different from many of the earlier problem novels. There was a time when the plots of most young adult novels focused on a single problem. As in many television dramas that resolve problems in thirty or sixty minutes, the problem was usually solved by the end of the book. The problems ranged from the physical signs of puberty to sexuality, from pregnancy to parenthood, from rape to drugs. These problems are still addressed in young adult books, and new problems such as eating disorders, AIDS, and incest have been added to the list. Although a problem is still central to today's problem novels, most are likely to use the problem as a means of exploring the growth of the adolescent character. A large proportion of today's problem novels may end with a resolution that is not a neat solution to the problem or is not the solution anticipated by the protagonist. The best books in the genre attempt to help young readers see beyond their problems. They have well-rounded characters who mature by learning how to understand or cope with a problem that may never be solved. These novels do not provide pat answers for adolescent readers nor do they guarantee happiness ever after. See Figure 3.2 for a list of characteristics of good problem novels for young adults.

Following an interview with Paul Zindel, one of the most respected writers of young adult problem novels, interviewer Michael Angelotti summarized Zindel's approach to writing novels:

1. Writing is problem solving.
2. The problem is perceived in the milieu of life.
3. The problem is one that must engage the writer's emotionality.

4. The problem is thoroughly researched.
5. The problem is two dimensional, including:
   a. the *apparent problem* which serves to provoke the writer's response
   b. the *true problem* which reveals itself during or as a consequence of the writing process.
6. Writing is a function of research and personal experience.
7. Writing is storytelling.
8. Writing is exciting. (1991, pp. 37–38)

Zindel's approach to writing produces thought-provoking young adult novels. The novel leaves the reader wondering what the true problem really is.

Figure 3.2
Characteristics of Good Problem Novels for Young Adults

Character
Protagonist
- matures as he or she deals with the problem
- experiences an epiphany; often surprised at the nature of the problem
- loses innocence
- experiences catharsis, often not related to solving the problem
Antagonist
- sometimes the problem itself
- person who causes the problem
- often unknown or unrecognized by protagonist
Other Characters
- someone who helps the protagonist deal with the problem; often a peer, a mentor adult, or a family member, although not often a parent
Plot
- problem of the protagonist is central to the plot
- individuals and relationships are affected by the problem
- problem gets worse before it gets better
- the suspected problem is often not the real problem
- ends with a resolution, not necessarily a solution or resolution the protagonist predicted or desired
Point of View
- usually protagonist's
- sometimes that of the person who helps the protagonist
Voice
- often second self or more mature protagonist
- sometimes the person who helps or attempts to help the protagonist
Theme
- "You are not alone"
- "Although the problem may not be solved, you can learn to deal with it"
- "You grow as a person because of trying to deal with the problem"
- "You can!"

Physical Appearance

Being too fat is dealt with in such novels as *One Fat Summer* by Robert Lipsyte, *I Was a Fifteen Year Old Blimp* by Patti Stren, Paula Danziger's *The Cat Ate My Gymsuit, The Fat Girl* by Marilyn Sachs, and M. E. Kerr's *Dinky Hocker Shoots Smack! The Fat Girl,* puts a different twist on the problems of being fat. In this beauty and the beast tale, Ellen weighs 200 pounds, is clumsy, and can't keep her eyes off the handsome narrator of the story Jeff. Jeff and his girlfriend Norma are in the same art class with Ellen, and when she breaks a ceramic teapot he makes, Jeff is at first repulsed and later fascinated. He sets about to transform Ellen by helping her diet and change her clothing and hairstyle. What makes this story interesting is the turnabout that happens between Jeff and Ellen during the transformation.

Judy Blume helps boys understand the problems of approaching puberty in *Then Again, Maybe I Won't;* she does the same for girls in *Deenie* and *Are You There, God? It's Me, Margaret.* The central character in *C. C. Poindexter* by Carolyn Meyer has to face the problems of being sixteen, over six feet tall, and female. Being thirteen is very difficult for many girls, and they can share their problems with the protagonist in Betty Miles's *The Trouble with Thirteen.* Fifteen and a half may not be much better for some girls. Many readers can relate to the experiences of the protagonist in Richard Peck's *Don't Look and It Won't Hurt.* Acne is a traumatic and often not-spoken-of problem for many teenagers. *I Was a Ninety-Eight Pound Duckling* by Jean Van Leeuwen and *Do Black Patent Leather Shoes Really Reflect Up?* by John R. Powers show that acne need not ruin a life. Stuttering is a difficult problem for some teenagers. Tuck Faraday in Mildred Lee's *The Skating Rink* withdraws into his own shell because of his stuttering. Some days he is so embarrassed that he walks a long distance home from school rather than take the bus and face his peers. When a skating rink is built near his home, he discovers that stuttering does not keep him from being successful. He becomes a skilled skater and a small-town hero.

Handicaps and Injuries

Mental and emotional handicaps are dealt with in a number of young adult problem novels. *A Boy Called Hopeless* (Melton) is about a boy with brain damage. Learning disabilities, a common problem of many adolescents, are dealt with sensitively in *Just One Friend* (Hall). *Hey, Dummy* (Platt), *Yesterday's Child* (Brown), *All Together Now* (Bridgers), *Melissa Comes Home* (Krentel), *But I'm Ready to Go* (Albert), and *The War on Villa Street* (H. Mazer) focus on mental retardation. Emotional and mental illness in teens is handled in *The Language of Goldfish* (Oneal), *Passing Through* (Gerson) and *Ordinary People* (Guest). Emotional illness of parents is a part of the plot in *Notes for Another Life* (Bridgers), *The Keeper* (Naylor), and *The Big Way Out* (Silsbee). The protagonists of *The Best Little Girl in the World* (Levenkron), *Second Star to the Right* (Hautzig), *Nell's Quilt* (Terris), and *The Bigger Book of Lydia* (Willey) are victims of anorexia nervosa, an emotional disorder related to excessive dieting and weight loss. Hannah Green (who also writes under the name Joanne Greenberg) depicted recovery from mental illness in *I Never Promised You a Rose Garden,* which has become a classic young adult book.

It is difficult to think of giftedness as a handicap, but for some adolescents it is a problem. High school junior Jennie Quint, in Caroline Cooney's *Among Friends,* sums up the problem this way: "I like to be good. Wrong. I like to be terrific. Wrong. I *have* to be terrific. And *that's* wrong. I can feel I am going to pay. Some awful price is waiting for me, like a monster in the dark" (1987, p. 15). Well-written books that deal with the difficulties of being gifted include *Been Clever Forever* (Stone), *In Summer Light* (Oneal), *Come Sing, Jimmy Jo* (Paterson), and *Sons from Afar* (Voigt). In each of these books, the problem is not what it seems to be at first. For example, in Zibby Oneal's *In Summer Light* Kate attempts to deny her artistic talent because it makes her different. She doesn't realize until the end of the novel that her denial was caused by feeling intimidated by her famous artist father. She began suppressing her gift four years earlier when her father did not respond to an award-winning painting she had done in the way she had hoped.

Other young adult books focus on physical handicaps that begin at birth or during childhood. *On the Move* (Savitz) is about wheelchair patients and sports. *Only Love* (Sallis) recounts the love story of two handicapped people confined to wheelchairs. *In Nueva York* by Nicholasa Mohr and M. E. Kerr's *Little, Little* are about growing up as a little person. In *Of Such Small Differences* (Greenberg), 26-year-old John was born blind and lost his hearing in early childhood. Deafness is also examined in *A Single Light* (Wojciechowska) and *In This Sign* (Greenberg). Lynn Hall examines the problems of epilepsy in *Halsey's Pride*. In *Change of Heart* (Mandel) Sharlie has a congenital heart defect. Her love for a young lawyer encourages her to undergo a heart transplant which is her last hope for a normal life.

A physical disability does not always occur early in life; it can happen when least expected. A high school athlete in Robin Brancato's *Winning* is completely paralyzed during the first game of the season. With the help of a teacher, his girlfriend, a friend he didn't know was a friend, and others who are disabled, he gains the courage to face life in a wheelchair. Ben, who is blinded in an accident, in *The World of Ben Lighthart* (Haar), must fight himself and his family to begin a new life. Another novel about an adolescent blinded in a car accident is *The Unfrightened Dark* (Holland). *Head over Wheels* (Kingman) is the story of twins, one of whom is paralyzed in a car accident. *Izzy, Willy-nilly* (Voigt) deals with not only the physical changes in Izzy after she is disabled in a car accident but the emotional and psychological changes. Gradually she develops a new image of herself and through her inner strength and self-knowledge is able to deal with tragedy and help others do so as well.

Conflicts with Adults

In *The Great Gilly Hopkins* (Paterson), Gilly is a rebellious foster child who has been moved from home to home. Two other stories about young adults in foster homes are *Toby Lived Here* (Wolitzer) and *Broken Promise* (Hayes and Lazzarino). Buddy in *Gentlehands* (Kerr) discovers that his beloved grandfather is a Nazi war criminal. *Nice Girl from Good Home* (Arrick) is about how different family members react to their father's firing and inability to find a job. Franny in *Something Beyond Paradise* (Slepian) is torn between what she believes to be her responsibilities to herself and her obligations to her mother and senile grandmother.

In *The Masquerade* (Shreve), seventeen-year-old Rebecca's father is arrested for embezzlement and her mother suffers a nervous breakdown. *What Daddy Did* (Shusterman) looks at an unthinkable crime: a boy's father killed his wife. The story is not so much about the murder but about how Preston, who goes from age nine to fifteen in the novel, deals with the horror of his father's crime.

In *Taking Terri Mueller* (Mazer), Terri believes her mother is dead. When Terri learns that she was kidnapped by her father after her parents' divorce, she begins a search for her mother and her family roots. Lois Lowry in *Find a Stranger, Say Goodbye* writes of seventeen-year-old Natalie Armstrong who searches for her birth mother with the blessing of her adoptive parents. Her search is more about who she is than about finding her mother. Successful in her search, she begins to understand why she was given up for adoption and eventually returns home to her adoptive parents.

Abusive parents figure in a number of young adult novels. In *The Question Box* (Hughey) Anne must learn to deal with her psychotically rigid father who will not allow her to wear jeans or makeup, go on dates or school trips, or continue to see her best friend. Physical abuse occurs in such moving books as *Center Line* (Sweeney) and *Running Before the Wind* (Wolverton). A very difficult but beautifully written book on the topic of incest is *Abby, My Love* (Irwin). In this book it becomes clear that sexual abuse occurs in even the "best" families. The end of the book provides no simple answers, but concludes that incest is "a secret that must never be kept."

To Be a Killer (Bennett) is a horrifying tale about a high school senior who plans to kill his chemistry teacher because his low grades will keep him from being accepted in a university. In a similar story Rachel Gilbert in *Final Grades* (Heyman) battles her senior English teacher who requires her to use a textual analysis approach to literature. She uses this as an excuse for not doing well in school, not applying to college, and rejecting her mother's dreams for her.

Unanticipated Roles

In several young adult books the protagonist is a child totally in charge of other children. Books that place young adult characters in charge of siblings or other children include *Where the Lilies Bloom* and *Trial Valley* (Cleaver and Cleaver), *Mountain Laurel* (Emery), *Fike's Point* (Britton), *When the Phone Rang* (H. Mazer) *The Night Swimmers* (Byars), and *Edith Jackson* (Guy). The protagonists in these books fight for their independence; some are successful, some not. In Isabelle Holland's *Alan and the Animal Kingdom*, Alan is left alone to care for his animals and the house. He keeps his lonely situation a secret in an attempt to remain independent.

Several books have been written about teens who are runaways. In *The Boll Weevil Express* (Petersen) fifteen-year-old Lars runs away with Doug, a delinquent of the same age from San Francisco. Doug's sister tags along with the boys. Although this book takes place in 1957, it does not gloss over the problems of running away. *If I Asked You, Would You Stay?* (Bunting) is the story of two teenage runaways who find each other when their mutual friend Valentine attempts to commit suicide in the ocean. The book is filled with interesting symbolism and paints a vivid picture of runaways.

Sexuality

Emerging adults must discover and nurture their sexuality. Sexuality has been a topic of young adult novels only since the 1970s. Even today books that deal honestly and explicitly with teenage sex are quite controversial and are often banned from schools and libraries. These are some of the most popular books with young adult readers, however, perhaps because there has been a dearth of such books available to young adult readers. One of the early books dealing with sex remains popular and controversial today. Judy Blume's *Forever* is a narrative about a first love that the heroine believes will last "forever," and a first sexual encounter. Told from the point of view of Katherine, *Forever* ends like most first loves, at a new beginning, as Katherine begins college and a new romance.

Emerging sexuality is interesting to both sexes. A book that is told from both the male and female viewpoints is *Up in Seth's Room* by Norma Fox Mazer. This popular book for older teens centers on the first serious romance of fifteen-year-old Finn. Seth, who is nineteen, is ready for a sexual relationship but Finn is not. Finn's conflicting feelings about Seth and her virginity, and Finn's parents' objections to her dating the older Seth are the major conflicts in the narrative.

Many other young adult books deal with developing sexuality from the male viewpoint. While some are more explicit than others, all give the teenage male the opportunity to explore his sexual identity. Books that may be appropriate for your students include *The Sum and Total of Now* (Robertson), *The Terrible Love Life of Dudley Cornflower* (Platt), *The Running Back* (McKay), *Hey Kid! Does She Love Me* (H. Mazer), *Hard Feelings* (Bredes), *Very Far Away from Anywhere Else* (LeGuin), *Stop-time* (Conroy), *Vision Quest* (Davis), and *If I Love You, Am I Trapped Forever?* (Kerr).

Developing sexuality is described from the female viewpoint in books such as *Morning Is a Long Time Coming* (Greene), *Home Before Dark* (Bridgers), *Loveletters* (Shreve), *Dear Bill, Remember Me?* (short stories by Mazer), *Cruisin' for a Bruisin'* (Rosen), *A Little Demonstration of Affection* (Winthrop), *Love Is One of the Choices* (Klein), *The Green of Me* (Gauch), and *A Love, or a Season* (Stolz). *Marcia* (Steptoe) is told from the perspective of a fourteen-year-old African American girl who talks to her best girlfriend, her boyfriend, the reader, and, finally, her mother about the confusion she is feeling about her emerging womanhood. The conversation with her mother about her boyfriend, her fears, babies, love, abortion, contraception, economics, and self-respect is frank and sensitive. In Barbara Corcoran's *Me and You and a Dog Named Blue*, Maggie Clarke explores her developing sexuality in a personal atlas she keeps.

Young adult literature also provides students with narratives about homosexuality. Most of these accounts are handled sensitively and honestly. Isabelle Holland's *Man Without a Face* is the story of a teenage boy Chuck who feels rejected by his family and inferior to his bright, beautiful sister. While studying for prep school entrance exams, Chuck meets the "man without a face," a disfigured, lonely man who tutors him. The two not only become friends, but are naturally attracted to each other, and the attraction leads to a brief, sensitive homosexual encounter. The book ends not with the encounter, however, but with Chuck's developing understanding of the meaning of love and affection. Other books dealing with homosexuality from the male point of view include *Good Times/Bad Times* (Kirkwood), *Trying Hard to Hear You* (Scoppettone), *I'll Get There. It Better Be Worth the Trip* (Donovan), *Sticks and Stones* (Hall), *Those Other People* (Childress), and *Cages* (Covert).

Books that deal with homosexuality from the female viewpoint include *Hey, Dollface* (Hautzig), *Happy Endings Are All Alike* (Scoppettone), and *Ruby* (Guy). In recent years some books that deal with homosexuality also deal with AIDS. Most often these books are not so much about the protagonist's developing AIDS but about others' awareness of his homosexuality because of AIDS. A very sensitive, well-written book on this topic is M. E. Kerr's *Night Kites. Rumors and Whispers* (Levy) is another good book dealing with this difficult subject.

A ground-breaking book about adolescents' perceptions of homosexuality is Bette Greene's *The Drowning of Stephan Jones.* Sixteen-year-old Carla wants nothing more from her life than to be the girlfriend of the handsome Andy and be a part of his group of friends. The daughter of a librarian in Rachetville, Arkansas, Carla wonders why her single-parent mother must take on every cause. When the values Carla has been taught come face to face with the bigotry and homophobia of Andy, his friends, and much of the community, however, she must decide whether she will act to protect the two young men who seem to be hurting no one. As the title suggests, the climax of the book is tragic, and as in many young adult problem novels the book ends without a solution.

Pregnancy, Abortion, and Parenthood

The problems of teenage pregnancy, abortion, and parenthood are addressed in a number of young adult novels, although such books are less common than they were in the early 1970s. Earlier books on teenage pregnancy are still worth reading, such as *Too Bad About the Haines Girl* (Sherburne), *It Could Happen to Anyone* (Craig), *You Would If You Loved Me* (Stirling), *Phoebe* (Dizenzo), *Arriving at a Place You Never Left* (Ruby), and *Growing Up in a Hurry* (Madison). Two more recent books that discuss teenage pregnancy and include more character development and drama than the earlier books are *If Not For You* (Willey) and *The Dear One* (Woodson).

The struggle to keep and support an illegitimate child is examined in *The Girls of Huntington House* (Elfman), *A House for Jonnie O.* (Elfman), and *Diving for Roses* (Windsor). The alternative of abortion is raised in young adult novels such as *My Darling, My Hamburger* (Zindel), *Bonnie Jo, Go Home* (Eyerly), *It's Not What You Expect* (Klein), *Love Is One of the Choices* (Klein), and *Mia Alone* (Beckman). It's the rare book that deals with the male's perspective in cases of teenage pregnancy, abortion, and parenthood. In *He's My Baby Now* by Jeannette Eyerly, however, Charles, after his casual affair, discovers he has surprising feelings for the baby and objects to the mother's insistence on putting the baby up for adoption. The male's perspective is also explored in Norma Klein's *That's My Baby.*

Rape

Rape is the basis for the plot of many fine young adult books. Janet, in Sandra Scoppettone's *Happy Endings Are All Alike*, is raped by a disturbed boy. The rape leads to the discovery of her lesbian relationship with Peggy. Other books that deal with rape in a more traditional manner are *Why Me? The Story of Jenny* (Dizenzo) and *Are You in the House Alone?* (Peck). A recent concern of adolescents is date rape. Marilyn Levy's *Putting Heather Together Again* deals with this difficult topic in a thoughtful and sensitive manner. Heather is raped by a boy she has dated a few times. She experiences feelings of guilt and is unsure what part she has played in the rape, but is reluctant to tell her parents, friends, and boyfriend her true feelings.

Teenage Prostitution

The topic of *Steffie Can't Come Out to Play* by Fran Arrick, who writes books for younger teens under the name of Judie Angell, is teenage prostitution. Steffie is a fourteen-year-old runaway who dreams of becoming a model. Her dreams are shattered, however, when she meets a man named Favor and becomes one of his prostitutes.

Drugs and Alcohol

Drugs and drug addiction are the topics of *Go Ask Alice* (anonymous), *Richie* (Thompson), *That Was Then, This Is Now* (Hinton), *A Hero Ain't Nothin' but a Sandwich* (Childress), *The Angel Dust Blues* (Strasser), *Cool Cat* (Bonham), *Tuned Out* (Wojciechowska), *Crack in the Heart* (Orgel), and *Can't Hear You Listening* (Irwin).

One interesting young adult book that deals with drug dependence in an unusual way is Isabelle Holland's *Heads You Win, Tails I Lose*. Caught in the middle of her parents' fighting, fifteen-year-old Melissa feels fat and ugly. When her drama coach suggests she try out for a play, she steals diet pills from her mother. She loses weight, gets a part in the play, and in the process nearly loses her life. Her experience with the pills and the knowledge of her mother's pill and alcohol dependence bring her closer to her father. In the end Mel doesn't lose. She overcomes her problems, gains a new friendship with her father, and develops an understanding for her mother.

Alcoholism is also a topic developed in young adult literature. Books like *Sarah T.—Portrait of a Teenage Alcoholic* (Wagner), *The Boy Who Drank Too Much* (Greene), *The Late Great Me* (Scoppettone), and *I Can Stop Anytime I Want* (Trivers and Davis) frankly discuss the problem that has become epidemic among teenagers. The books clearly show that both popular and lonely teenagers may become alcoholics. In Linnea A. Due's *High and Outside* the star pitcher of the girl's softball team, Niki, has a drinking problem she won't admit. Alcoholism of parents is discussed in *Touching* (Levy). For Eve the situation at home is so bad that she carries a duffle bag filled with necessities so she can move out at any time.

Young adult books have also dealt with the topic of drunk driving. In Kevin Major's *Hold Fast* fourteen-year-old Michael and his seven-year-old brother are orphaned when their parents are killed by a drunk driver. The story is not so much about the accident but about how it tears apart the family and teaches the boys they must "hold fast." Another book about drunk driving is Marc Talbert's *Dead Birds Singing*. Matt also must go through the stages of anger, hatred, confusion, and acceptance as he copes with the deaths of his mother and sister due to car accident caused by a drunk driver.

Suicide

Suicide was for many years a taboo in young adult literature. However, as the suicide rate among adolescents has grown, so has the number of young adult novels that focus on the topic. Several are exceptional in their sensitivity, truthfulness, and lack of sensationalism. Chris Crutcher's *Chinese Handcuffs* is a well-written novel about extreme athletic competition and suicide. Triathlon athlete Dillon Hemingway decides not to participate in school sports because he can't tolerate the high school principal. Throughout the story, Dillon writes letters to his dead brother Preston in an attempt to understand Preston's suicide. In *So Long at the Fair* by Hadley Irwin, Joel Wendell Logan III has all the material things of life plus a rich girlfriend. After his friend Ashley commits suicide at the fair, Joel runs away to join the traveling amusement company that put on the fair, becoming Joe Logan, in an attempt to understand her suicide and himself. Other good books about suicide include *Blindfold* (McCuaig), *Remembering the Good Times* (Peck), *How Could You Do It, Diane?* (Pevsner), and *About David* (Pfeffer). Lynn's plight in *About David* is more difficult than most in that she is not only attempting to understand why her apparently normal friend David killed himself but why he killed his parents first. She blames herself for not anticipating the tragedy and averting it.

Developing Relationships

Relationships are of prime importance to young adults, and are frequently the subject of young adult realistic fiction. As psychologist Abraham Maslow has pointed out, one of the primary needs people have is to belong. For adolescents this means belonging to a peer group. Richard Peck says of adolescents' friendships, "Many young friendships are painfully inarticulate, and yet those friendships are emotional to a degree rarely known in later life. In all their relationships—including family ties—most of the young are emotionally frozen. Novels in which characters actually express themselves by word and deed are very satisfying and necessary" (1975, p. 6). Young adult author Alden R. Carter agrees, "We remember best those novels that contain characters that arouse our empathy and sympathy. This is particularly so when we are young, uncertain, and eager to know how others deal with the problems of growing up" (1988, p. 4). The emotional impact of relationships is portrayed in almost all young adult literature. Friendships between young adults, sibling relationships, parent-teenager relationships, the changing family circle, the ending of relationships, and the friendships between teenagers and nonparental adults are all important in the young adult novel.

Self-Concept

Before an adolescent can begin to develop real relationships, relationships that go beyond doing things together, she or he must have a sense of self. In some ways, the first relationship we develop is a relationship with ourselves. Many young adult novels depict this process. The best writers of young adult fiction are in touch with how adolescents feel about themselves and how they develop into who they are. In *Pardon Me, You're Stepping on My Eyeball* Paul Zindel reflects on how a young person's physical appearance, and how his peers perceive his looks, is central to developing a positive self-concept. Marsh Mellow writes about Edna, "That was one thing that always burned Edna up. Only the good-looking ones seemed to be the most popular ones. They were the ones that got everything out of school" (p. 36). In *My Darling, My*

Hamburger Zindel returns to the same theme. When Maggie breaks a date with Dennis without any real excuse, Dennis thinks, "Ugly. I'm sick. I'm ashamed. My clothes are ugly. My face is ugly. My body is ugly. What am I doing alive? I always come back to this point. It's always there. This ugliness. I can't fight it" (p. 114). Zindel and other authors of young adult books recognize that until adolescents become comfortable with their individual appearance they will not develop a very positive self-concept. This idea is explored in many other young adult novels including M. E. Kerr's *Dinky Hocker Shoots Smack!* and *I'll Love You When You're More Like Me*, Paula Danziger's *The Cat Ate My Gymsuit* and *The Pistachio Prescription*, Patricia McKillip's *The Night Gift*, and Judy Blume's *Blubber*.

Often the adolescent's self-concept is related to how she sees her place in the family unit. In Katherine Paterson's *Jacob Have I Loved* Louise sees herself as the less attractive, less talented, and less loved twin. Often she misinterprets the comments of her family. As Jan Allen remarks about Paterson's book: "[The twins'] mother once recalls, when Louise prods her with questions about babyhood, that Louise never gave them a minute's worry. The remark is intended to be reassuring, but it only injures the lonely twin more, as she feels it is the worry that makes a child's life special. Therefore, she is not special" (1984, p. 15). Until Louise comes to terms with her relationship with her twin and other members of her family, she cannot develop a strong sense of self.

Best Friends Novels

In adolescence the most important developing relationships are often those between two young adults. The best friend plays an essential role in the life of the teenager and, consequently, in young adult fiction. The development of friendship is important in all literary genres read by young adults. In the historical novel *The Witch of Blackbird Pond* (Speare), for example, the friendships between Kit and Mercy, Kit and Hannah, and Kit and Prudence are central to the development of plot and theme. In the genre of fantasy the relationship of the young adult to other young adults is equally important. In *Hangin' Out with Cici* (Pascal) thirteen-year-old Victoria goes back in time and becomes best friends with Cici, who turns out to be Victoria's mother as a teenager. Mysteries too provide many examples of the importance of best-friend relationships. How would Nancy Drew ever make her discoveries without her friend George? Some specific books involving strong friendships are

- *Moon and Me* (Irwin)
- *Something Left to Lose* (Brancato)
- *The Better Angel* (Bograd)
- *Sheila's Dying* (Carter)
- *Nobody Told Me What I Need to Know* (Colman)
- *N.I.K.—Now I Know* (Chambers)
- *Beneath the Surface* (Hamlin)
- *Be Still My Heart* (Hermes)
- *The Boy in the Moon* (Koertge)
- *Say Goodnight, Gracie* (Deaver)
- *The Year Summer Died* (Gauch)

- *Three Friends* (Levoy)
- *Just Friends* (Macguire)
- *Just for the Summer* (Mango)
- *Babyface* (Mazer)
- *Silver* (Mazer)
- *Libby on Wednesday* (Snyder)
- *Something's Rotten in the State of Maryland* (Sonnenmark)
- *Night of the Whale* (Spinelli)
- *Corey's Fire* (Wardlaw)
- *Finding David Dolores* (Willey)

Sometimes the friendships that develop in young adult novels are not positive. For example, *A Sinless Season* by Damon Galgut (who was a teenager when he wrote the book) is about four boys in a reformatory who are caught up in a wave of destructive incidents. In Robert Cormier's *The Chocolate War* Jerry attempts to join a vigilante group called the Vigils. This book examines how the need for peer approval can be very destructive to the young adult. Jerry refuses to sell the fifty boxes of candy required by Brother Leon for Trinity High School. For the first several days of the candy campaign, he follows the orders of the Vigils, the powerful school "fraternity," in an attempt to gain recognition and membership. However, when their requests become too demanding and demeaning, Jerry balks and refuses to implement them. Because of his refusal to participate, Jerry becomes a hero to his peers, but his hero status threatens Archie, the leader of the Vigils, and Archie uses his power to turn the school against Jerry. The book ends with an arranged boxing match between Jerry and a bully who is trying to be accepted by the Vigils. Jerry learns that trying to become a member of a peer group can cause both emotional and physical pain. He tells his friend Goober at the end of the novel: "They don't want you to do your thing, not unless it happens to be their thing too. It's a laugh, Goober, a fake. Don't disturb the universe, no matter what the posters say."

Cormier acknowledges that all young adult books are about relationships: "I feel the novels must work first as stories with real people who have meaning for the reader. Otherwise, the novel would be an empty tract. So I emphasize story and character, knowing if they work, the themes will emerge as strong and forceful" (Robert Cormier, personal communication, 1979).

Siblings

Young adult literature reflects the difficult nature of sibling relationships. In some young adult novels a sibling relationship is the central element in the narrative. In *And You Give Me a Pain, Elaine* (Pevsner), thirteen-year-old Andrea resents her older sister, whose behavior is tearing the family apart. In Judy Blume's *Tales of a Fourth Grade Nothing*, Peter is convinced he must be a "nothing" because his baby brother Fudge gets all the family attention. The central character in *The Loner* (Bradbury) is twelve-year-old Jay Sharp. His brother, the "Great Mal," who is fourteen, seems to have everything Jay lacks: Mal is good-looking, athletic, popular, and outgoing. The story is about how Jay resolves his resentment. In another book about a difficult sibling relationship, the flashback technique is used to relate the story of eighteen-year-old

Rion and his older brother Doug. In *Count Me Gone* (Johnson), Rion tells his story to a sympathetic lawyer after he has been seriously injured and charged with assaulting an officer and resisting arrest. Everyone, including his parents, believes Rion is mentally unstable, but Rion describes how his difficult relationship with his brother, including Doug's unasked-for advice and the bizarre behavior of Doug's fiancee, caused his problems.

Even though most of the sibling relationships portrayed in young adult books have difficult moments, they are often beneficial to the young protagonists. The siblings in S. E. Hinton's *The Outsiders* and *Tex* are left on their own most of the time. As children alone, they experience many problems, but their life is bearable because they have each other. Eleven-year-old Claudia and her nine-year-old brother Jamie, run away from home in Elaine Konigsburg's *From the Mixed-Up Files of Mrs. Basil E. Frankweiler*. They make a home in the Metropolitan Museum of Art and develop methods for eluding the guards and museum workers. During their escape, which ends when the children agree to return home in exchange for the name of the sculptor of a "mystery statue," Jamie and Claudia become friends. A boy's attempt to save the life of his brother is a central part of the action in Sharon Mathis's *Teacup Full of Roses*. This stark story is a narrative about three brothers trying to survive life in the ghetto. One escapes through drugs, one relies on his academic talents, and the other joins the Navy and helps his younger brother reach his dream. Other good books about sibling relationships include Jerry Spinelli's *Who Put That Hair in My Toothbrush?* and Cynthia Voigt's *Homecoming, Dicey's Song,* and *Sons from Afar*.

Parents

Many relationships, other than those with other young people, are important in the young adult's life. The bond that exists between parents and young adults is a changing one. Young adults moving toward independence seek to redefine their relationship with their parents. Often this redefinition causes pain for both child and parent. Young adult author Ouida Sebestyen says that she writes about parent-child relationships because she knows them:

> I've spent my life being either a daughter or a mother, and nearly twenty years being both at once, hands-on. Maybe, as an only child with an only child, I've been more aware of the parent-child ties and stresses than more thickly-branched, sibling-rich families are. While I was struggling with the technical aspects of plot, character, dialogue and all the rest . . . I may instinctively have chosen families as the subject matter I could feel—well, *familiar* with. (1984, p. 1)

The mother-daughter relationship plays an important role in many young adult books. In *Mom, the Wolfman, and Me* (Klein), Brett has enjoyed her closeness with her mother, who has never married, wears jeans, and works odd hours. Then the Wolfman enters their lives, proposes marriage to her mother, and threatens to change Brett's relationship with her mother. In *Anne Frank: The Diary of a Young Girl*, Anne describes her mother as always criticizing, as liking her older sister better, and as condemning her friendship with Peter. Even in the extreme, life-threatening situation of a Jewish family hiding from the Nazis, the difficulties of the mother-daughter relationship retain their poignancy.

In the teen years many girls are just beginning to realize that their mothers are not perfect, that they too have problems. Iris in *A Midsummer Night's Death* (Peyton) believes her mother lacks the "prerequisite of ninety-nine percent of the mother race: a natural concern for its young." In *Can't Hear You Listening* (Irwin) Tracy's mother is a successful author who is unable to communicate with her daughter. *Someone's Mother Is Missing* (Mazer) is about a mother who leaves her two daughters when the death of her wealthy and successful husband leaves them penniless. Jessica in *Unfinished Portrait of Jessica* (Peck) blames her mother for the divorce of her parents until her mother sends her to Mexico to visit the father she thinks is perfect. She soon learns he is manipulative and immature and returns home to rebuild her relationship with her mother.

Often female protagonists must deal with their mothers' problems as well as their own. In *The Sister Act* (Elfman), Molly is torn between making her own life or staying home with her neurotic mother to help support the family. In *Beloved Benjamin Is Waiting* (Karl), Cherry's mother cares about her children but has so many of her own problems that she "had to keep running to stay ahead of them and didn't have time for much else." In *Rabble Starkey* (Lowry) twelve-year-old Rabble lives with her mother, Sweet Hosanna, and the Bigelow family for whom she works. Sweet Hosanna holds both families together while Veronica Bigelow recuperates from a mental breakdown. Rabble learns that even though her mother was only fourteen and unwed when she was born, she is a very special person. The changing relationship between mother and daughter is exemplified by Rachel and her mother in *Hey, That's My Soul You're Stomping On* (Corcoran):

> When her mother wasn't throwing an emotional tantrum or trying to possess her family's lives, she was nice and she was fun. As a little girl Rachel had thought she had the best mother in the world. But when you got to be sixteen and your mother expected to know not only everything you did, but everything you thought and felt, that was more than a person could stand. Rachel knew exactly how her father felt. Smothered. Her mother was like a big, squashy quilt that came down over your head and smothered you.

The relationship between sons and fathers can also be difficult. In Barbara Wersba's *Run Softly, Go Fast*, Dave and his father have a love-hate relationship. The death of his father forces Dave to reexamine this relationship, his own life, his values, and his beliefs. In *The Boy Who Could Make Himself Disappear* (Platt), Roger's father is so wrapped up in his career that he has little time for his son. In response, Roger, who is afflicted with a speech impediment, withdraws into schizophrenia. In *Father Figure* (Peck), seventeen-year-old Jim accepts the role of surrogate father for his younger brother Byron after his parents' breakup. Jim's role is threatened when Byron and Jim are forced to move in with their father.

A difficult father-son relationship is examined by Suzanne Newton in *I Will Call It Georgie's Blues*. Fifteen-year-old Neal is a jazz musician; his father is a preacher. The family has a near-perfect public image, but beneath the veneer is a self-righteous father who dominates Neal, his sister Aileen, and his emotionally disturbed little brother Georgie.

Relationships between fathers and daughters and between sons and mothers also are important in young adult literature. In Isabelle Holland's *Of Love and Death and*

Other Journeys, Peg must learn to accept her long-absent father after the death of her beloved mother. Isabelle Holland says of the parent-child relationships in her books:

> It is that struggle between the child and the adult in the creating of that self-portrait, that often preoccupies my writing. The lucky children are the ones who are taught to believe, as they go through life, that, whatever their faults, they themselves are lovable and estimable human beings. Most parents do not mean to convey a different message, but they often do. And if my books are about wounds given in that message, they are also about the healing that can take place given the right adult at the right time.

In *RoboDad* Alden Carter examines an exceedingly difficult father-daughter relationship. Shar's father becomes emotionally distant when an artery bursts in his brain. She is determined to help her father become a loving dad once again. His violent outbursts after hours of hypnotic television viewing raise horrifying fears for Shar and the rest of the family. Other excellent books about father-daughter relationships include *Midnight Hour Encores* (Brooks), *In Summer Light* (Oneal), *Celine* (Cole), *Just the Two of Us* (Colman), and *The Moonlight Man* (Fox).

In Lee Bennett Hopkins's *Mama*, a mother loves her two sons a great deal, but the sons are disconcerted when they learn that she steals to buy them things. Bruce Brooks's *No Kidding* is set in the middle of the twenty-first century. It is the story of fourteen-year-old Sam who has his alcoholic mother institutionalized and learns how much she truly cares for him and his religious-fanatic, alcoholic-hating brother. *Changes in Latitudes* (Hobbs) is another good book about a mother-son relationship.

Not all relationships between parents and children in young adult literature are beset with problems. Even in *Mama* (Hopkins) the boys learn to accept their mother and her love. In *Bridge to Terabithia* (Paterson), Jesse is embarrassed by his parents' lack of education. He believes that because he is not the oldest and is a boy, he must do too many things around the house. On the other hand, he is jealous and envious of the good relationship Leslie has with her parents. However, after Leslie's death, the concern and support he receives from his father show him the power of his father's love. Rob in *A Day No Pigs Would Die* (Peck) does not always understand his father, but he always respects him. Papa is poor, but he is proud and works hard for his family. Rob learns of his father's humanity and becomes an adult when he is forced to slaughter his pet pig to provide food for the family:

> "Oh, Papa. My heart's broke."
> "So is mine," said Papa, "but I'm thankful you're a man."
> I just broke down, and Papa let me cry it all out. I just sobbed and sobbed with my head up toward the sky and my eyes closed, hoping God would hear it.
> "That's what being a man is all about, boy. It's just doing what's got to be done."

In *Home Before Dark* (Bridgers), Stella must form a new relationship with her father after her mother's death. At first the relationship is strained. However, he gives her space and time, and at the end of the novel the continuing relationship between father and daughter is ensured. In Cynthia Voigt's *A Solitary Blue* Jeff, an only child, idolizes his free-spirited mother who abandoned him and finds his college professor father intellectual and boring. As he grows up alone along a sea island marsh, however, he begins to understand that his mother, though beautiful and exciting, is also irresponsible and selfish. At the same time he begins to appreciate and build a relationship with his caring father.

Grandparents

Touching relationships between young adults and their grandparents or great-grandparents are popular in the young adult novel. Salty in Ouida Sebestyen's *Far from Home* searches for his long-lost father. He finds, instead, the love and friendship of family with his elderly grandmother in the Buckley Arms Hotel. Other relationships with grandparents are found in Madeleine L'Engle's *The Summer of the Great-Grandmother* and M. E. Kerr's *Gentlehands*. In Newbery Honor book *After the Rain* Norma Fox Mazer explores the relationship between fifteen-year-old Rachel and her grandfather Izzy. At first Rachel resents Izzy, believing him to be predictable and not very thoughtful. However, when she discovers he has cancer, she begins to take walks with him and get to know him. Perhaps the novel is so poignant because it is a story exploring the death of Mazer's own father. Mazer explains:

> Faith is how I got through writing *After the Rain*. It took me years to get that story out. A dozen years ago, my father died of asbestosis, one of the killers of our modern world. Years before, he had worked in a factory and was unpacking asbestos for perhaps a month. Thirty years later it killed him. After he died, he came back to me quite often in dreams. In one dream I remember, he looked healthy. I said, "Excuse me, Dad, but you're supposed to be dead."
>
> Around that time I thought of a story I wanted to write about a girl and her grandfather. I wanted it to be about his death. I thought it should be very short, very plain, very simple. A book about death that would not be frightening, but would not be false either. It would look at death openly and calmly, as part of life. (1991, p. 3)

An extremely difficult relationship with a grandparent is experienced by the twins Caroline and Louise in Katherine Paterson's *Jacob Have I Loved*. In Hadley Irwin's book *What about Grandma?* the relationships between mother, daughter, and grandmother are interestingly contrasted.

Changing Family Relationships

Changes in familial relationships are the basis for many realistic young adult novels because they are a part of so many young adult lives. A family who learns it is not what it thought it was is the subject of Susan Shreve's *The Masquerade*. Seventeen-year-old Rebecca must face the changes in her family after her father is arrested for embezzlement and her mother suffers a nervous breakdown. In *Unlived Affections* George Shannon explores problems that have remained in a family's closet for many years. When Willie's grandmother dies he is responsible for cleaning out her belongings. In the process he discovers letters written between his parents, of whom his grandmother refused to talk. Through these very moving letters he gets to know and understand his family: his homosexual father, his grandmother with her attachment to the past, and his loving mother.

Separation and Divorce

The family that changes from a two-parent household to a one-parent household because of separation or divorce faces many problems. Tensions often develop between the young adult and the parent, and the teenager may feel isolated. In Bianca Bradbury's *The Blue Year*, seventeen-year-old Jill stays with the family of her friend while her mother is in Nevada getting a divorce. Jill is convinced she is the cause of the divorce, although she does not know what she has done. When her mother returns, she becomes dependent on Jill. Jill attempts to reunite her parents, but learns that her father, whom she sees once a week, is dating another woman. Jill has no one to talk to and is very confused. Like Jill, Katie in Hadley Irwin's *Bring to a Boil and Separate* has no one to talk to about her parent's divorce. Her younger brother refuses to talk about it, and her best friend is away at camp until the end of the summer. The feeling of aloneness after the separation of a family is also experienced by Jimmie in *Leap Before You Look* (Stolz). Jimmie, at fourteen, feels alienated from her mother and can't talk to her father about the physical and emotional changes she is facing. Joanna Douglas lives through a crisis in *A Family Failing* (Arundel) when her father loses his job and must rely on her mother for support of the family. When Joanna's father finds a temporary job, he encourages his family to move with him. Mark, Joanna's brother, who has withdrawn from the family since the start of the crisis, refuses. Joanna's mother says she has too many business responsibilities to consider moving. Joanna agrees to go, but spends most of her time traveling between family members. She, like many young adults, hopes the family will be reunited. Eventually, Joanna understands that reunion is impossible and she must live her own life.

In Norma Klein's *Taking Sides*, Nell feels she must choose sides in her parents' divorce. When she is living with her mother, she believes she wants to be with her father, but when she is with him she is distressed by his relationship with another woman and the fact that she and her young brother must share a room. Like Joanna, Nell begins to understand that the divorce is final and nothing will be the same again. Finally, she realizes that she need not choose between her parents, but can love and be loved by both of them. In *Guy Lenny* (Mazer), Guy has enjoyed his life with his father. However, things start to change when his father begins to date Emily. Guy's mother asks him to move in with her and her new husband, but Guy, who resents his mother for leaving the family, refuses. However, he learns that his father had asked his mother to take him. He runs away but eventually returns to face both parents. Deciding which parent to live with is also the theme of Marc Talbert's *Pillow of Clouds* in which Chester must decide between living with his mother, an alcoholic businesswoman in Iowa, or his father, a quiet bookstore owner in New Mexico. Although Dinah's parents in *Risking Love* (Orgel) allowed her to choose which one to live with, six years after the divorce she is still wrestling with why her mother did not insist she live with her.

Some family divorces lead to the total separation of the young adult from the parents. In Vera Cleaver's and Bill Cleaver's *Ellen Grae*, for example, Ellen Grae is sent to Florida to live with Mr. and Mrs. McGruder. In the sequel, *Lady Ellen Grae*, Ellen Grae is again sent away, this time to Seattle to live with her aunt Eleanor, who is to teach her to be a lady. In *This Is a Recording* (Corcoran), Marianne lives with her grandmother while her parents travel in Europe. She does not know that the trip will end in divorce. When word of the divorce reaches Marianne, she begs to stay with her grandmother, convinced that she is a burden to her parents and the cause of their problems. In *Notes for Another Life* (Bridgers), Wren and Kevin attempt to understand why their mother chose to leave them with their grandparents while she pursued a career. The stress caused by the mental illness of their father (Tom), who is institutionalized through much of the book, the divorce of their parents, and their mother's move to a faraway city leads Kevin to a suicide attempt. Through the teenagers' love for music and for each other, the book ends on an upbeat note: "He took a deep breath and croaked out a little noise. It sounded better than he'd expected. And so they went the distance, covering the miles between themselves and Tom, singing as they went." The problems arising when one parent gains custody of the child, and the way the custody affects the child's relationship with the other parent, are discussed in Judy Blume's *It's Not the End of the World* and John Neufeld's *Sunday Father*.

Relationships between parents and teenagers are complicated when two families become one through remarriage. Hila Colman explores the situation of the melded family in *Weekend Sisters*. In Betty Bates's *Bugs in Your Ears*, Carrie objects to her mother's remarriage. She believes that no one is listening to her. Even her new brothers and sisters pay no attention to her. When her stepfather wants to adopt her, she rebels and causes an unpleasant scene in the courtroom. Chloris of *Chloris and the Creeps* (Platt) attempts to turn her eight-year-old sister Jenny against their mother's new husband, Fidel. When he offers to adopt the girls, Chloris refuses. Fidel accepts her decision, hoping that she will eventually change her mind. Chloris, like Carrie, unrealistically glamorizes her real father. The saga of Chloris and Jenny continues in two sequels, *Chloris and the Freaks* and *Chloris and the Weirdos*, which recounts the divorce of Fidel and their mother and the effects of this divorce on Jenny, who begins to wonder if all adults act irrationally, particularly after Fidel defines "mature behavior": "It means to have a genuine concern for other individuals, and very little concern for oneself."

Illness or Death in the Family

Familial relationships change for young adults when a parent becomes critically ill or dies. The death of a father is examined in a number of young adult novels. In *Swift Water* (Annixter), Bucky has a good relationship with Cam, his father. They share the dream of setting up a wildlife sanctuary in northern Maine. Cam, an idealist, is killed on a hunting trip while trying to stop the duck hunters from shooting at geese. Grief-stricken, Bucky believes the dream of the sanctuary is lost. He takes his new role as developer of the sanctuary seriously, though, and word of the dream spreads through the publicity gained when a newsman investigates the story. In *Big Doc's Girl* (Medearis) an adolescent must assume responsibility for the family after the death of her father and the institutionalization of her mother. In *Red Sky at Morning* (Bradford), Josh's father leaves in 1944 to enlist in the navy, and Josh and his mother move to New Mexico. Josh adjusts quite well to his new life, but his overprotected mother has many difficulties. He learns he must accept responsibility for the family.

This new role becomes more important after his father is killed and his mother suffers a nervous breakdown. In *Ronnie and Rosey* (Angell), Ronnie plays a new role as companion to her mother after her father's death. At first she resents her mother's dependence on her, but she learns to adapt to their new relationship.

The grief, guilt, and sense of loss that young adults experience with the death or serious illness of a father is exemplified in *The Ups and Downs of Jorie Jenkins* (Bates). Jorie has always been close to her handsome, strong father. When he suffers a heart attack, she feel he has let her down. He is not the man he used to be, and she can no longer relate to him in the same way. In *Run Softly, Go Fast* (Wersba), nineteen-year-old David Marks returns from his father's funeral and begins a journal about their relationship. At first he catalogues the hate he feels for his father. However, as the journal unfolds he realizes he has made an error in his recollections of his father, and he reexamines them. When Birdie McShane is told of her father's death in *A Sound of Chariots* (Hunter), she automatically carries on with her life as usual, pedaling through the village on her paper route. But she is plagued by nightmares of death, and soon she is devastated by grief. Several years later her teacher tells her she can't come to terms with his death by continuing her grief; she must begin to live her own life to the fullest. In *Fog* (Lee), Luke suffers two tragedies: the death of his father and the death of a friend in a fire for which Luke assumes responsibility. The book explores Luke's feelings of grief and guilt, and his great sense of loss.

The changing roles within the family after the death of the mother is central in *The Rock and the Willow* (Lee). Enie had always taken on the helping role in her poor household, but she sustained herself with her love of learning and the knowledge that one day she will go to college. Her mother shared her dream. The dream appears to be shattered after her mother's death when Enie is needed at home to maintain the household. Ingrid in *The Pigeon Pair* (Ogilvie) must take on the responsibility of homemaker after the death of her pregnant mother and the withdrawal of her father. Barbara Girion's *A Tangle of Roots* deals with Beth's reaction to her mother's sudden death. She must adjust to the fact that her assumption that her parents would always be there is untrue. In *The Night Swimmers* (Byars), Retta must care for her siblings after their mother's death. Their father, a country singer, is never home. The children are resourceful and cope with their problem successfully. The title comes from the recreation the children find for themselves by swimming in the neighborhood pools as the neighbors sleep. In *The Blanket Word* (Arundel), Jan feels grief over the death of her mother even though she did not love her. Through her friendship with Thomas she explores her feelings about love and comes to terms with her mother's death. Grover knows his mother is ill in *Grover* (Cleaver and Cleaver), but he assumes all will be well when she returns from the hospital. Once she is home he notices that she wants to talk to him more than usual. One day while Grover is outside playing, she commits suicide. Grover feels utterly alone after his mother's death because his father withdraws and he has no one to confide in. In *A Matter of Time* (Schotter), Lisl witnesses her mother's slow deterioration from cancer. Through her mother's illness and death Lisl struggles to find the meaning of her own life.

The death of both parents often leads to the breakup of a family or the struggle to keep it together. The relationship of all the siblings and their roles within the family change dramatically. In *Break a Leg, Betsy Maybe!* (Kingman), Betsy ends up living in the suburbs with her rich aunt and uncle. Throughout the book she is desperately seeking a role for herself in her new life. In *Where the Lilies Bloom* and its sequel *Trial Valley*, by Bill Cleaver and Vera Cleaver, fourteen-year-old Mary desperately attempts to keep the family together as a promise to her dead father. To do so she must conceal his death from the authorities, who will attempt to send the children to the county home.

The death of a grandparent can greatly change the role of the young adult within the family unit. In *A Figure of Speech* (Mazer), Jenny's grandfather has lived with her family since she was an infant. Jenny does not communicate with her parents but she does develop a special relationship with Grandpa. When she learns her family plans to move him to a nursing home, she tries to help Grandpa move back to his boyhood farm. They stay in the unoccupied farmhouse. One night Jenny "dreams" she hears Grandpa say, "No use, Jenny." The next morning he is dead. Jenny returns home, but knows life will not be the same. Other books that focus on a young adult's relationship with a grandparent and the changes after a grandparent's death are *Toby Alone* (Branscum), *Duffy's Rocks* (Fenton), *The Loners* (Garden), and *The Changes* (Rabin).

A Ring of Endless Light by Madeleine L'Engle is a beautiful book in which the author relates the thoughts and feelings of sixteen-year-old Vicky Austin as she deals with the death of a family friend and her beloved grandfather. Throughout the narrative Vicky struggles with the question of mortality. Vicky learns to live with the death of her grandfather and family friend, as well as that of a small girl who dies in her arms, by remembering the light that her grandfather had urged her to seek: "You have to give the darkness permission. It cannot take over otherwise. . . . You are to be a lightbearer. You are to choose the light."

The death of a sibling is sensitively portrayed in many young adult books. Pudge in *Uncle Mike's Boy* (Brooks) blames himself for his sister's death. He turns to Uncle Mike, who is a steadying influence on the grief-stricken, guilt-ridden boy. *The Year of the Three-Legged Deer* (Clifford) is a story of guilt, responsibility, and prejudice. Takawsu, who is fourteen, and his younger sister, Chilili, live with their white father and Native American mother. When Chilili's pet deer escapes and Chilili is killed in the search for it, the family's life changes drastically. Takawsu feels guilty because he didn't help his sister look for the deer, his father feels responsible for not fixing the pen, and his mother takes Takawsu and moves back to her tribe, which is forced to move farther west. Perhaps no character is more influenced by the death of a sibling than Karana in *Island of the Blue Dolphins* (O'Dell). After most of the men in the village are killed, a boat comes to rescue the women and children of the island. When Karana realizes her brother Ramo is not aboard, she leaves the boat to search for him. The two children are left alone on the island, and Ramo is killed the next morning by a pack of wild dogs. Karana survives on her own until a boat finally comes to the island eighteen years later. *The Magic Moth* (Lee) is a book written for younger readers, but its sensitivity on the subject of death makes it appropriate for all ages. Maryanne, who has incurable heart disease, is one of five children in the Foss family. The story depicts the confusion and wonder the family members feel as they stand at the deathbed of Maryanne and watch a moth emerge from a cocoon she has kept through the winter. Just as the life leaves Maryanne's body, the moth "flutters to life."

Adoption

The adoption of a new family member can cause confusion in family relationships. *Edgar Allan* (Neufeld) is the story of a white family's love for and eventual rejection of the three-year-old African American child they have adopted. As Edgar Allan enters nursery school in the all-white community, the family experiences prejudice for the first time. When a cross is burned on the family's lawn, sixteen-year-old Mary Nell delivers an ultimatum: "if he stays . . . I'll just leave." Succumbing to the pressure and fear for the lives of the other children, the parents return Edgar Allan to the adoption agency. The two youngest children are shaken when their little brother is "given away." Michael, who tells the story, and his mother feel the injustice done to Edgar Allan. In the end the rest of the community turns on the family for giving way under pressure. Other books tell of the phenomenon of adopted children searching for their natural parents. In *Tell Me No Lies* (Colman), an adolescent searches for her real parents. In *Find a Stranger, Say Goodbye* (Lowry), Natalie is planning a medical career, but before she can pursue it she feels compelled to find her biological parents. Although her home life has been happy and her adoptive parents disapprove, she begins her search. In *Molly by Any Other Name* (Okimoto), Molly is required to fill out an application that asks questions about family history. The story is told in three parts that describe Molly and her Anglo adoptive parents, her Japanese birthmother, and the reunion of two families and cultures.

Relationships with Nonfamily Adults

Numerous young adult novels deal with the relationship between a teenager and a nonfamily adult. One of the best known of such narratives is *The Pigman* (Zindel), in which John and Lorraine befriend an eccentric old man called the Pigman. They take advantage of the friendship, however. While the Pigman is in the hospital, they use his house for a party and invade his privacy by removing his dead wife's clothes from the closet where he has kept them for years. *The Pigman's Legacy* is the sequel. John and Lorraine befriend another man who has been hiding from the Internal Revenue Service in the Pigman's house. They share many poignant experiences with him, and through these experiences discover the legacy the Pigman left for them.

A more recent Zindel book on a similar theme is *A Begonia for Miss Applebaum*. This book, like the Pigman books, has dual narrators. This time the elderly adult is the teenagers' favorite high school teacher Alice Applebaum. Henry and Zelda befriend Miss Applebaum when they learn she is dying and participate in many adventures in Central Park and the Metropolitan Museum of Art. The lessons she teaches the adolescents about death are really lessons about living. In *Better Than Laughter* (Aaron), a book with a similar theme, two boys befriend an eccentric junkman. In *Lilith Summer* (Irwin), a young girl is hired to take care of elderly Lilith, or so she thinks. Lilith, on the other hand, believes she has been hired to baby-sit the girl. Even though the deception is discovered, a relationship grows. In *Remove the Protective Coating a Little at a Time* (Donovan), fourteen-year-old Harry, who has a difficult home life, meets Amelia, an elderly beggar.

Most of the relationships between adolescents and adults in young adult books are built on mutual need and caring. This is particularly true in Isabelle Holland's *Man without a Face* and Francina Glass's *Marvin and Tige*. Tige is an orphaned street-wise

African American boy who meets Marvin, a white, alcoholic, dropout executive. A friendship is established based on their mutual need.

In Theodore Taylor's *The Cay* caring develops between a boy who is white and racially prejudiced and an old man:

> I was thinking that it was very strange for me, a boy from Virginia, to be lying beside this giant Negro out on the ocean. And I guess maybe Timothy was thinking the same thing.
>
> Once, our bodies touched. We both drew back, but I drew back faster. In Virginia, I knew they'd always lived in their sections of town, and us in ours.

Phillip, a survivor of a shipwreck, is rescued by Timothy, a kind West Indian. Injured in the wreck, Phillip goes blind and must rely totally on Timothy. Timothy encourages Phillip by telling him the blindness will go away: "Once, ovah 'round Barbados, a mahn 'ad an outrageous crack on d'ead when a salin' boom shift. Dis mahn was blin' too. Tree whole day 'e saw d'night. Den it true went away." Phillip's blindness does not go away, but the old man teaches the boy so well that even after Timothy's death Phillip is able to survive on the island by remembering the things Timothy told him. Finally he is rescued from the island, discovers his parents are alive, and after several operations regains his sight. He vows to return to the cay:

> Someday, I'll charter a schooner out of Panama and explore the Evil's Mouth. I hope to find the lonely little island where Timothy is buried.
>
> Maybe I won't know it by sight, but when I go ashore and close my eyes, I'll know this was our own cay. I'll walk along east beach and out to the reef. I'll go up the hill to the row of palm trees and stand by his grave.
>
> I'll say, "Dis b'day outrageous cay, eh, Timothy?"

Perhaps because adult mentors for adolescents are so needed and often missing, many young adult books describe how an unlikely adult becomes the mentor of an adolescent, often through chance encounter. Some excellent examples of such books are *Mighty Close to Heaven* (Gibbons), *The Truth Trap* (Miller), *The Foxman* (Paulsen), *The Old Man* (Ruby), *Agnes the Sheep* (Taylor), and *The Great Man's Secret* (Van Raven).

The "Good Cry" Novel

Adolescents are very emotional, and many of them enjoy certain young adult books that can be called "good cry" novels. These novels, read particularly by girls, may be about death, broken relationships, handicaps, or young adults making it despite the odds against them, and they appeal to the sentimentality of the young adult reader. Many problem novels fall into this category. As young adult author Richard Peck says, "To oversimplify, after a reassuring outcome in a story, I suspect . . . [young adults] like best a good cry" (Peck, 1975, p. 6). The teacher who gives book talks on the theme of attitudes toward death by reading sections of the books *Bridge to Terabithia* (Paterson), *A Ring of Endless Light* (L'Engle), *The Magic Moth* (Lee), *Our Eddie* (Ish-kishor), and *The Edge of Next Year* (Stolz) will need to have a box of tissues on hand, for even the least sentimental student is likely to be moved to tears. Here's a sample from Katherine Paterson's *Bridge to Terabithia* in which eleven-year-old Jesse must deal with the death of his best friend Leslie:

> "Jess." Bill came over to him and put his arm around him. He could feel Bill's body shaking, and he was afraid that if he looked up he would see Bill crying, too. He didn't want to see Bill crying. He wanted to get out of this house. It was smothering him. Why wasn't Leslie here to help him out? Why didn't she come running in and make everyone laugh? You think it's so great to die and make everyone cry and carry on. Well it ain't. (p. 113)

Young adult author Bette Greene says of writing for young adults, "We are obligated to write about what makes us break out into tears or into song." The characteristics of "good cry" novels are listed in Figure 3.3.

Figure 3.3
Characteristics of Good "Good Cry" Novels for Young Adults

Character
Protagonist
- realistic
- vulnerable but also strong
- at the mercy of circumstances
- humorous side
- normal and usually happy
- loses innocence

Antagonist
- often not a recognizable person; may be society, a disease, an unforeseen death, the law, and so on
- not always recognized by the protagonist

Other Characters
- often a mentor adult
- often a close friend

Plot
- provides the background or point of reference for the character and reader
- emphasizes emotions of characters
- development of the protagonist is central

Point of View
- the protagonist's
- that of a close friend or peer

Voice
- older more experienced protagonist or second self
- close friend or peer

Theme
- metamorphosis
- maturation
- epiphany
- "In spite of trials you can survive"

A Relationship Ends

The ending of relationships, through death, war, departure, or family opposition, is touching to the young adult, who is spending a large amount of energy building relationships. Saying good-bye to a loved one who is about to die is a tearful episode in a number of young adult books. *Love Story* (Segal), though not written as a young adult book, was read by an entire generation of young adult women. In Patricia Windsor's *The Summer Before*, the young protagonist must put her life back together again after the death of her love, Bradley, the summer before.

Many young adults experience the departure of a girlfriend or boyfriend to a distant college campus or the military. Although not many young adults today have sent their lovers into the unknown world of war, all young adults sympathize with the great loss experienced by Patty in *Summer of My German Soldier* (Greene) when she sends her German soldier off to his likely capture. When Patty receives word of his death, young female readers understand her torment.

Having to choose between family ties and the love of another person is not unusual for young adults. In *The Beethoven Medal* (Peyton), when Ruth becomes infatuated with Pat, a truck driver who is always in trouble, her mother attempts to force a breakup. Ruth is pleased to learn that Pat is an accomplished musician, but he is also sentenced to nine months in jail for his criminal acts. Unsure of her feelings, Ruth does not know whether to succumb to her emotions and wait for his return, or to use her common sense and leave him.

Friendships that endure despite all the reasons for ending them provide many sentimental moments in young adult novels. In *First of Midnight* (Darke), set against a backdrop of slavery, Jess, an auctioned white chattel, befriends Midnight, an African American boxer. Their relationship continues to grow despite their differences.

Young adult literature of today often has a "star-crossed lovers" theme. In *Kathleen, Please Come Home* (O'Dell), Kathleen's love for a deported alien, Ramon, leads her to a life in Mexico with Ramon's family, a pregnancy and miscarriage, a car accident, and, finally, a return to her home, now owned by strangers. *Circle of Love* (Leahy) is the story of Anton and Anna, who fall in love while bicycling through Germany in search of Anna's parents after World War II. They are separated after each emigrates to America, but eventually their tale has a happy ending. *Across the Barricades* (Lingard) is the story of two lovers torn by war, one a Belfast Protestant, the other an Irish Catholic. In *Masks: A Love Story* (Bennett), Peter Yeng, a college freshman and son of a Chinese immigrant, falls in love with sixteen-year-old Jennifer. He resents his father for not having accompanied his mother to China, where she died, but when Peter's father forbids him to see Jennifer, he complies despite his love for her. He would rather leave Jennifer than destroy his relationship with his father.

Relationships with Handicapped Young Adults

The portrayal of relationships between young adults who are handicapped and young adults who are not is less sugarcoated in today's young adult fiction than it was in the past. *The War on Villa Street* (Mazer) is the story of thirteen-year-old Willis who escapes from an unhappy home life and meets and coaches a retarded boy in athletics. The relationship begins as a business venture, and Willis resents the extra time he must spend coaching Richard. Both boys, however, experience satisfaction when

Richard makes his best jump at Field Day. In *It's Too Late for Sorry* (Hanlon), Kenny becomes friends with Harold, a mentally handicapped teenager. When Kenny's friend Phil bullies Harold, Kenny tries to compensate by being especially nice to Harold. Then Kenny meets Rachel, who has a retarded sister. He tries to use his friendship with Harold to impress Rachel, but when he senses that his friendship with Harold is infringing on his relationship with Rachel, he begins mistreating Harold. Later he is remorseful and tries to patch up the friendship, but finds that "it's too late for sorry."

The difficulty of maintaining relationships with friends who become handicapped is vividly portrayed in Robin Brancato's *Winning*. When Gary is paralyzed, his best friend visits him in the hospital, but Gary notices that their usual comfortable banter is missing. The friendship ends as the visits become less and less frequent. However, Gary discovers new relationships, with an African American teammate, a teacher, and other handicapped young adults.

Making It Despite the Odds

Young adult characters who succeed despite the great odds against them appeal to teenagers. In *Tell Me That You Love Me, Junie Moon* (Kellogg) three grotesquely injured people live together as normally as possible by defying the regulations of normal society. Sentimental young adults will be moved to tears by *Only Love* (Sallis), in which two young people conduct a love affair despite their confinement to wheelchairs and their knowledge that one of them will die soon.

Poverty cannot keep some young adults from triumphing. A family of orphaned children survive the difficult life of Appalachia by wildcrafting, collecting plants for medicinal purposes, in Vera Cleaver's and Bill Cleaver's *Where the Lilies Bloom* and *Trial Valley*. The children in *Broken Promise* (Hayes and Lazzarino) cling together to fight the juvenile court system. Five children abandoned by their parents spend many months struggling to stay together. Another book about children fighting to remain together is Adrienne Jones's *So Nothing Is Forever*, about the children of an interracial marriage who are suddenly orphaned. In the autobiographical fiction narrative *A Sound of Chariots* (Hunter), a Scottish girl overcomes poverty and a series of family tragedies to accomplish her dream of becoming a writer.

Realistic Novels about the Arts

Adolescents are beginning to discover their talents and seek outlets for them, and some adult novels are about young people pursuing artistic interests. Dance is the topic of *Thursday's Children* (Godden). Doone Penny struggles against almost insurmountable odds to become a ballet dancer. From his early childhood to his first appearance on stage at London's Royal Theatre at age thirteen he must fight against family rivalry, jealousy, and rejection.

Gary Paulsen's *The Monument* is a very powerful novel about art. Rachel has been rejected because she is an orphan with caramel-colored skin and a bad leg until artist Mick Strum comes to town to do a war memorial. He immerses himself in the town's history, sketching everything in sight. Rachel is fascinated by how Mick sees things from the inside out, and she learns about the artist's vision as he commands her to

"Draw!" Through her friendship and work with Mick, Rachel sees herself and her life with an artist's perspective. Zibby Oneal has also written a perceptive book about artists. *In Summer Light* is the story of Kate Brewer who during the summer between high school and college is writing an analysis of Prospero in *The Tempest* because a case of mono kept her out of school the previous spring. She sees a parallel between Shakespeare's character and her father because both do as they please without regard for others. Kate's father is the famous painter Marcus Brewer. During the summer a graduate student is on their island cataloging Brewer's work. She learns through him and through her analysis of *The Tempest* that her father, like Prospero, is becoming an old man whose magic powers are nearly gone. According to Kate's paper, "[Shakespeare] means us to see that if we refuse to forgive, then we will never free ourselves, but will be trapped, like Prospero—exiles on islands." This insight allows her to return to her own art which she had abandoned after her father gave only luke-warm approval of a prize-winning painting she did as a high school freshman.

Although not directly about art, Katherine Paterson's *Bridge to Terabithia* presents Jesse, a young boy who is almost embarrassed by his artistic ability. His friend Leslie and his music teacher convince him that what he loves to do is important and not at all sissyish.

Music is the theme of numerous young adult novels including *Midnight Hour Encores* (Brooks), which is also a fine coming-of-age novel. Sixteen-year-old prodigy Sibilance T. Spooner is an internationally renowned cellist. She was raised by Taxi, her father, after being abandoned by her mother. Supported by her father's belief in her, she is worldly, independent, and self-confident bordering on arrogant. She believes that her musical ability is due to her own talent, determination, and effort. As she sets out to meet her mother, her self-concept matures, and she becomes aware that her father has provided her with the support and love she needs to succeed.

Neal Slone in *I Will Call It Georgie's Blues* (Newton) is a gifted jazz pianist, although his preacher father objects to his interest in jazz. Neal learns, in part through his music, more about himself and the other members of his family.

Come Sing, Jimmy Jo (Paterson) is about country music singer Jimmy Jo who is eleven years old. James, as he is called before he becomes famous, is at first afraid to sing in public. He doesn't want to leave his mountain home and his grandma to sing on television, but she convinces him to do so. He is a success, but doesn't want his school friends to know of it because he doesn't want to be different. At the same time, the other members of his family singing group are jealous of his popularity.

There are a number of young adult books about rock and roll. Three by Todd Strasser (*Rock 'n' Roll Nights*, *Turn It Up*, and *Wildlife*) are probably the best known. All of these novels focus on Gary Spector a talented musician who organizes a rock group. In the first novel the group becomes a reality; the second catalogs their pursuit of stardom through a would-be rock group manager; and the third deals with the breakup of the group after they have completed a successful tour. *Song for a Shadow* (MacKinnon) is another good novel about a rock star. This one shows that even famous stars have private lives and problems that make life difficult.

Author! Author! (Terris) is a novel about Valerie who has had her first children's book published with the help of her father's friend, poet Tekla Reis. Valerie struggles for independence from her parents, questions her own writing, fights for an understanding of her need to write, and dreams that she is really Tekla's daughter. Gary Paulsen's *The Foxman* is a book about storytelling and reality. On cold winter's nights in Minnesota a family tells stories, many about war. When the Foxman appears, the fifteen-year-old narrator of the novel wonders how the entertaining stories could be about the war that claimed Foxman as a victim. Through the stories and through Foxman the boy learns about truth. Another Paulsen story *The Winter Room* uses storytelling to convey the seasons of Minnesota.

Sports Novels

Adolescent males are often interested in sports more than any other topic. Therefore, the sports novel is an important type of realistic young adult fiction. Sports novels for young adult males have been popular for years. In the 1950s and 1960s boys read sports fiction by John Tunis and Henry Gregor Felsen. Many of these books were often trite, with the protagonists showing superhuman characteristics. In recent years, however, sports novels have become much more realistic. The athlete not only experiences the physical challenges of her or his sport but must deal with balancing sport and life. Problems do not disappear because the athlete is successful in his or her sport. In addition, sports novels have expanded to sports not written about in earlier decades, such as swimming, tennis, wrestling, and gymnastics. Moreover, many contemporary sports novels focus on female athletes.

The change in sports literature for young adults began with *The Contender* by Robert Lipsyte, published in the late 1960s. The protagonist is a young boxer who is not perfect. Alfred fights the odds to become the champion. He never becomes one, but he learns that being a contender is just as important.

Protagonists of sports in fiction for today's teens include a handicapped hero, in *Winning* (Brancato); a wrestler who lives with his girlfriend, in *Vision Quest* (Davis); a wrestler who attempts to get to know the father he has never known through the sport they share, in *Takedown* (Christopher); a hero who does not always come in first, in *Brogg's Brain* (Platt); a hero with an alcohol problem, in *The Boy Who Drank Too Much* (Greene); a Native American boxer who is unable to control the monster within himself, in *The Brave* (Lipsyte); a basketball player who sees the game as his way off the streets of Harlem, in *Hoops* (Myers); a baseball player whose brother is killed in a car accident, in *My Brother Stealing Second* (Naughton); a student just out of reform school, in *The Running Back* (McKay); a boy who fulfills his father's dreams, in *Football Dreams* (Guy); a teen who plays all life as a game, in *The Game Player* (Yglesias); swimmers who accept the challenge not to seek the crowd's applause but strengthen their inner selves, in *Stotan* (Crutcher); and heroes who are not great athletes, in *Quarterback Walk-on* (Dygard). These characters are not superhuman, not beyond reproach. They face real problems and real frustrations, and resolving their problems makes the characters winners in life, even if they are not champions in sports.

The protagonists of many young adult books for females are involved in sports. For example, Katherine in Judy Blume's *Forever* is a champion tennis player. However, the woman athlete has only recently become the central character in books that focus on sports and the personal development of the athlete. In *The Magic Box*

(Cossi), Mara Bennetti is caught smoking before the state championship basketball tournament and is about to be benched. The book not only details the excitement of competition but also depicts the tensions in a realistic mother-daughter relationship. *In Lane Three, Alex Archer* is written by New Zealand swimmer Tessa Duder. The book explores the competition, sacrifice, and parental pressure involved in trying to become an Olympic swimmer. *High and Outside* by Linnea A. Due portrays a female softball star with a drinking problem. Jenny is a fifteen-year-old British girl who is entrusted with the care of a tempestuous thoroughbred in *Darkling* by K. M. Peyton. Kristen is ostracized, and even rejected by her best friend, when she decides to quit the basketball team in her senior year to concentrate on academics in *These Are the Best Years?* by Nadine Roberts. Maisie in Jerry Spinelli's *There's a Girl in My Hammerlock* plans to continue wrestling despite teasing, aches, and bruises. The relationship between Graham and Leslie, whose fathers are trainers of racehorses, begins to change during their thirteenth year in *Mariposa Blues* by Ron Koertge. *When No One Was Looking* by Rosemary Wells centers on a champion tennis player who thrives on pressure until the death (possibly murder) of a competitor. Her reexamination of the sport, her values, and her motives provides an interesting view into competitive athletics among women.

EPILOGUE: YOUNG ADULT BOOKS AS WINDOWS

Today's young adult realistic novel is far more realistic than adolescent books of the past. The young protagonists, who mirror young adult readers, experience real problems and deal with them in realistic ways. The characters and their relationships are three-dimensional. Thus readers can learn from the problems the characters face and grow because of them. Realistic novels provide windows through which young readers can see and understand the world around them. For young adults a good realistic novel is like a good friend who, like Leslie in Katherine Paterson's *Bridge to Terabithia*, helps the young reader "push back the walls of his mind and make him see beyond to the shining world—huge and terrible and beautiful and very fragile."

SUGGESTED READINGS

Allen, J. B. "How Do I Know Who I Am?" *ALAN Review*, Spring 1984, pp. 14–17, 44.

Andrews, M. "Music in the young adult novels of Sue Ellen Bridgers." *ALAN Review*, Fall 1990, pp. 14–16.

Angelotti, M. "Zindel on Writing and the Writing Process: An Interview." *ALAN Review*, Winter 1991, pp. 37–40.

Asher, S. The problem with realism. *ALAN Review*, Spring 1985, pp. 1–3.

Carlsen, G. R., and A. Sherrill. *Voices of Readers: How We Come to Love Books*. National Council of Teachers of English, 1988.

Carlson, D. "Smack." *New York Times Book Review*, February, 1973, p. 8.

Carter, A. R. "Characters That Connect." *ALAN Review*, Fall 1988, pp. 4–6.

Conford, E. "I Want to Make Them Laugh." *ALAN Review*, Fall 1986, pp. 21–24.

Hansen, K. "Something Wonderful, Something Beautiful: Adolescent Relationships through the Eyes of Paul Zindel." *ALAN Review*, Winter 1991, pp. 41–43.

Hartvigsen, M. K., and C. B. Hartvigsen. "The Terrible Hilarity of Adolescence in *Dinky Hocker Shoots Smack!*," *ALAN Review*, Fall 1986, pp. 25–29.

Hipple, T., and B. Bartholomew. "The Novels College Freshmen Have Read." *ALAN Review*, Winter 1982, pp. 8–10.

Mazer, N. F. "Words on a Ketchup Bottle." *ALAN Review*, Fall 1991, pp. 2–5.

Murphy, S. "Stories That Reach the Kids: An Interview with Jerry Spinelli." *Journal of Reading*, December 1991–January 1992, pp. 342–345.

Pantanizopoulos, J. "I'll Be Happy When I'm Thin Enough: The Treatment of Anorexia Nervosa in Adolescent Literature." *ALAN Review*, Fall 1989, pp. 9–10.

Peck, R. "Some Thoughts on Adolescent Literature." *News from ALAN*, September–October 1975, pp. 4–7.

Peck, R. "Traveling in Time." *ALAN Review*, Winter 1990, pp. 1–3.

Riley, K. L. "The Gift and the Price: The Gifted Adolescent in Current YA Literature." *ALAN Review*, Winter 1990, pp. 37–38, 40.

Sebestyen, O. "Family Matters." *ALAN Review*, Spring 1984, pp. 1–4.

Spinelli, J. "Before the Immaculate Cuticles." *ALAN Review*, Fall 1986, pp. 15–18.

Strickland, R. W. "Themes of Death and Dying in Adolescent Literature." *ALAN Review*, Fall 1987, pp. 18, 37–39.

4 Coming-of-Age Novels

Focus Questions

1. What is meant by coming of age?
2. How is the traditional rite of passage related to coming of age in adolescents?
3. How is coming of age dealt with in literature, and why is this type of literature important for young adults?
4. What are the characteristics of good coming-of-age novels for young adults?
5. What are the three phases of the coming-of-age period, and how is each explored in literature for adolescent males and females?
6. What are some of the symbols found in coming-of-age novels?

PROLOGUE

Looking back I can see that Wychwood was, as my sister had judged, a very kindly school. The classes were small, the teaching pretty good, particularly that of English, the staff were intelligent and friendly; but I came there too late. I had had those seven years of living on my own, with adults, in a gracious environment; I could never be reconciled to the world of school. My reports said that I was self-centered, went my own way, was antisocial; as I got higher up the school they began to be critical of my friendships. I had a friend called Evelyn, two years older, two forms higher; she was witty, intelligent, entertaining; I liked her because she reminded me of home. Authority disapproved of this friendship because of the age gap, because we used to break rules and go off to wander about the Oxford colleges, whose beauty we had just noticed. At Wychwood there was a tradition of "pashes," younger girls having raves on older ones, or on the staff; there was nothing of this in my relations with Evelyn, we simply enjoyed each other's conversation and liked walking about Oxford. Our particular enemy was the games mistress (neither of us showed the least aptitude for any form of athletics); later there was a lesbian scandal and that same games mistress left abruptly; it is to be presumed that she had viewed our friendship from her own angle. ❖

From "Joan Aiken," *Something about the Author: Autobiography Series*, vol. 1, ed. A. Sarkissian (Gale Research, 1986), p. 27.

Most of us were not prepared to go to jail. Doris Erskine, a student from Jackson State, and I had to take over a workshop the following day. Some of the ministers were in charge of the mass rally that night. But if we had dispersed, we would have been torn to bits by the mob. The whites standing out there had murder in their eyes. They were ready to do us in and all fourteen of us knew that. We had no other choice but to be arrested.

We had no plan of action. Reverend King and some of the ministers who were kneeling refused to move; they just kept on praying. Some of the others also attempted to kneel. The rest of us just walked to the paddy wagon. . . .

When Doris and I got to the cell where we would spend the next four days, we found a lot of our friends there. There were twelve girls altogether. The jail was segregated. I felt sorry for Jeanette King, Lois Chaffee, and Joan Trumpauer. Just because they were white they were missing out on all the fun we planned to have. Here we were going to school together, sleeping in the same dorm, worshipping together, playing together, even demonstrating together. It all ended in jail. They were rushed off by themselves to some cell designated for whites.

. . . . All of the girls in my cell were college students. We had a lot to talk about, so we didn't get bored. We made cards out of toilet tissue and played Gin Rummy almost all day. Some of us even learned new dance steps from each other.   ❖

From Anne Moody, *Coming of Age in Mississippi*, (Dial, 1968; Dell, 1980). Reprinted by permission of Bantam, Doubleday, Dell Publishing Group, Inc.

Coming of Age and Rites of Passage

Coming of age, rite of passage, initiation, and *transition* are all terms used to describe the passage from childhood to adulthood. The literary term for a work that deals with this passage is *Bildungsroman,* meaning a "novel of education." In such books "the central character learns about the world as he or she grows into it" (Peck, 1989, p. xi).

In this text we will use *coming of age* to describe the entire period of becoming an adult and *rite of passage* or *initiation* to identify a key event that marks the passage to adulthood. The *transition* denotes the central, pivotal phase of the period, the phase in which the rite of passage usually occurs. Rites of passage have been well documented across cultures by anthropologists. In early societies the rite of passage was often a specific ritual. Anthropologist Arnold van Gennep described the typical rite, or ceremony, of passage for young men in primitive societies as having three phases: separation, margin, and aggregation. According to van Gennep, during the separation stage young men, either alone or in a group of their peers, were separated from the community. During the margin stage the boys, remaining separate, took part in the rite. If they successfully met the requirements of the rite, the young men moved to the third stage, in which they were accepted into the adult society. Often, a celebration marked their new status.

Although an actual rite or ceremony marking a young male's acceptance into adult society is not as common today, something like it can still be observed in some religious ceremonies such as the bar mitzvah which in Judaism marks the boy's arrival at the age of responsibility (age 13). The bar mitzvah follows the boy's study of Hebrew to read the Torah, the body of Jewish religious literature. In some forms of Judaism young women are recognized in a bas mitzvah. First Holy Communion, in the Roman Catholic church, confirmation in many protestant churches, and believers' baptism in several other Christian faiths also mark the attainment of religious responsibility.

Many rite-of-passage events today do not involve ceremonies, such as going away to school, going to camp, attending the prom, or getting a driver's license. Perhaps the most ceremonial rite of passage for the majority of adolescents is attending high school graduation. Sweet-sixteen parties, debutante balls, and scout award ceremonies are also rite-of-passage events.

All of the above events are not only condoned by adult society but are usually structured by adults. Many young people today rebel against participating in some of these activities. Indeed, rebellion against adults has itself become a kind of rite of passage and is a hallmark of adolescence. Anne Moody's rebellion in the prologue was along political lines. Other young people may express their independence in other ways, often by embracing values or beliefs that differ from those of their parents. In contemporary society rites of passage are more likely to be informal than formal. They occur throughout adolescence, the period in which teens come of age as adult human beings.

The Rite of Passage in Literature

According to David Peck in *Novels of Initiation*, much of American literature focuses on adolescence and thus much of it deals with the themes of coming of age, loss of innocence, and rebellion. He claims that, America being a young country, American literature is "essentially an adolescent literature—which is one of the reasons many of the classics of American literature can be taught in high school literature, and are" (1989, p. xx). To support his argument he cites authors such as J. D. Salinger, Mark Twain, Sylvia Plath, F. Scott Fitzgerald, Stephen Crane, Harper Lee, Carson McCullers, and John Steinbeck. Peck suggests that young adult literature, literature written specifically for an adolescent audience, has a very comfortable niche in American literature.

All young adult literature could be called coming-of-age literature because all of it focuses on adolescent protagonists. A distinguishing feature of the young adult novel, according to Richard Peck, is that "it needs to end at a beginning" (1975, p. 6). The fifteen-year-old has not yet begun to live life; the best and worst still lie ahead. The events of the young adult novel, therefore, must prepare the reader and the book's protagonist for a life yet to be lived.

There is, however, a specific genre of young adult literature that focuses on the growth of the adolescent from carefree childhood to responsible adulthood, usually emphasizing psychological and sexual growth. During adolescence young adults experience isolation, socialization, confusion, and rebellion. They desire to return to dependence on the family and at the same time to forge ahead into the unknown. Teenagers seek the support of a peer group and at the same time are fiercely individualistic and independent. These conflicts give rise to many of the plots of young adult coming-of-age or rite-of-passage books.

In our discussion of these books we will examine them in three categories which roughly parallel the phases of the rite of passage formulated by anthropologists. These categories also correspond roughly to the stages of early, middle, and late adolescence. Although the boundaries between phases are vague. Following terms used by educator Hugh Agee we will look at the separation from childhood, the transition, and incorporation into the adult community. For the young adult these three stages, taken together, denote an ending of one life and the beginning of a new life.

Traditionally, most coming-of-age books have focused on male protagonists. This is probably the result of society's traditional concern with the maturation of males to become the dominant figures in the family and community. Although more female protagonists have been featured in contemporary coming-of-age literature, the preponderance of books about the adolescent male's maturation is evident in the books discussed in this chapter.

Literature is one means by which the adolescent can explore the passage from childhood to adulthood. (See Figure 4.1 for a list of the characteristics of good

Figure 4.1
Characteristics of Good Coming-of-Age Novels for Young Adults

---

Character

Protagonist

- maturing from one phase of development to the next
- confused
- often unsure about physical changes
- is developing sexually
- exhibits psychological growth, and changing emotions and values
- rebellious
- seeking independence and fearful of independence
- afraid but puts up a good front
- loses innocence but gains experience

Antagonist

- often the situation in which the adolescent finds himself rather than a character
- often the perceived antagonist is not the real antagonist
- adult (parent, teacher, or other)
- former friend
- self
- society or culture (family, school, community)

Other Characters

- individual who allows growth to occur
- often initially assumed to be the antagonist
- mentor adult
- best friend

Plot

- situations that impede the development
- situations that encourage development (often unrecognized by protagonist)
- separation from society (through peer association, a journey, etc.)
- some things remain the same as others change dramatically
- initiation may be social, religious, political
- reversal common
- values change
- protagonist may choose to remain outside of society

Setting

- more important than in other young adult novels
- often physically and symbolically isolated from society (on an island, boat, etc.)
- often associated with peer group (at school, camp, hangout, etc.)

Point of View

- protagonist's
- sometimes alternate points of view are interspersed with protagonist's

Voice

- protagonist
- second self
- omniscient

**Figure 4.1
Continued**

Theme
- often not explicitly stated
- developing a values system
- self-knowledge
- deeper meaning of life

Style and Language
- protagonist often takes a real or symbolic journey
- humor interspersed
- language reflects theme
- characters speak in vernacular

---

coming-of-age novels for young adults.) As David Peck writes, "The adolescent in America . . . is often in a kind of social and psychological limbo, someone with limited economic power but no real status, treated as a child by parents and teachers, but with social, sexual, and cultural sophistication that sometimes belies this position. . . . Reading literature about themselves helps teenagers to define their own identity and to develop their own values" (p. xxi). The characters in young adult books face many of the problems that readers do, and young adults can view the book's protagonist as a model. According to young adult author Lloyd Alexander, "A [good young adult] book should speak to readers not only where they are . . . but where they will be."

Separation from Childhood

Separation from childhood is a phase that most young adolescents enter between ages ten and twelve when, for the first time, they question the values and decisions of their parents. Young adolescents often exert their new-found independence by rebelling against the rules and mores of the home and the school. They often think about running away from home. Many get in trouble in school. Some adolescents experience their first extended stay away from home at this time.

Relationships are changing too. Interest in the opposite sex develops. Increasingly preteens and young teens are concerned with themselves: their physical appearance, their friends, their homes. They worry about the opinions of others, usually the peers with whom they want to associate. They become more involved in activities outside the family.

For adolescents who are developing a positive self-image and who have the unwavering support of caring adults who set limits for them, these years can be ones of pleasure. For others, who do not have these advantages, the years of early adolescence can be exceedingly difficult. Even those young adults who appear to have every advantage often find these years traumatic. An alarming number of young girls, for example, feel pressure to succeed at everything and become anorexic during this period. Disturbing too is the increasing number of young men who appear to be progressing successfully toward young adulthood but who commit suicide. The adolescent protagonists in young adult novels progress through this period with varying degrees of difficulty and assistance. To help you select novels appropriate for particular adolescents, each coming-of-age section has been subdivided by gender and topic.

Preadolescent Boys

The challenges boys face in growing up are dealt with in Judy Blume's *Then Again, Maybe I Won't*, Ray Bradbury's *Dandelion Wine*, Robert Lipsyte's *One Fat Summer*, Paula Fox's *One-Eyed Cat*, Robert Newton Peck's *A Day No Pigs Would Die*, Wilson Rawls' *Where the Red Fern Grows*, Bill Wallace's *Shadow on the Snow*, and Bill Brittain's *The Fantastic Freshman*. These books deal with everything from wet dreams, first drinks, girls, lies, friendship, acne, and being overweight to accepting responsibility for one's actions, caring for animals, and assuming a new more active role in the family or community. All of them reflect on problems related to physical and emotional growth.

Physical and Emotional Change   In *Then Again, Maybe I Won't* (Blume), Tony, thirteen, has moved to a new neighborhood. He is thrown together with the boy next door, Joel, who introduces him to pornographic books and booze. Tony is not sure what he thinks about his new friend. He worries about his new life and his physical maturation. He is concerned about the erections and wet dreams he cannot control. He likes to think about girls but dislikes himself for looking into Joel's sister's window while she undresses. He is upset that his mother believes Joel is a gentleman because of his good manners. All these concerns give Tony a nervous stomach. When his brother decides to leave his teaching job to take a high-paying job with his father, Tony is upset. His stomach pains grow worse, and he finally ends up in the hospital. During his stay the physician recommends that he see a psychiatrist, who will help him understand and cope with his normal problems.

An unusual coming-of-age book, *Downwind* by Louise Moeri, places Ephraim in a terrifying adult situation after a possible meltdown at a local nuclear power plant. The Dearborn family who lives downwind from the plant attempts to escape to the west hills with thousands of other families. Ephraim is only twelve but the oldest of four children. He is forced to help his father with two injured children and his mother who breaks down under the stress. He learns about human nature as he observes both violence and self-sacrifice as people attempt to help others or take advantage of the situation.

Animals and Growth   Animal stories are a subgroup of coming-of-age books for preadolescent males. In the Newbery Honor book *One-Eyed Cat* (Fox), Ned, the son of a minister, fires a forbidden air rifle and accidently wounds a wild cat. At first he denies and hides his action, then he atones for it, and finally he confesses it. By the end of the book he is attempting to understand why he did it. Some other books, that place young adult males in responsible positions with animals and families include *A Day No Pigs Would Die* (Peck), *Alan and the Animal Kingdom* (Holland), and *Where the Red Fern Grows* (Rawls).

─────────── ◆ **Between the Covers:** *Authors at Work* ◆ ───────────

ROBERT NEWTON PECK

Robert Newton Peck's *A Day No Pigs Would Die* is considered by many to be the classic coming-of-age novel. It deals in a poignant way with a boy's separation from childhood. The main character Rob grows up in the Shaker way on a Vermont farm and is forced to deal with concerns of his family over his love for animals. One can't help noticing the parallels between the protagonist and the author. The autobiographical nature of Peck's books can also be seen in his bad-boy, coming-of-age books about the character Soup, who was Robert Newton Peck's best friend in the one-room schoolhouse they attended in rural Vermont.

Peck was the son of poor, illiterate farmers. He reminisces about his childhood: "Sometimes, at home, a learned scholar would stop by, and he was always asked, following supper, to read to our family. There was one book in our mountain home. It was black and large, yet we never referred to it as our Bible. It was known only as The Book" (1986, pp. 235–36). Neither Peck's parents nor his six older brothers and sisters had gone to school. His parents had opposed his going. However, Peck reports that when his father met Miss Kelly, the teacher he credits with his love of literature, he initially said nothing until Miss Kelly told him, "Thank you for giving me Robert. I shall try to be deserving of your trust." Peck's father took off his hat and said to her, "We hope he's got manners . . . and whatever he breaks, we'll pay for" (p. 236).

And so Robert was the first in his family to attend school. At school Miss Kelly had a shelf, just a board, on which she kept the precious few books she could afford, (*Tom Sawyer, The Wind in the Willows, Ivanhoe*). She read from those books to the children and required them to wash their hands before they were permitted to touch them. Peck remembers many things about Miss Kelly. He remembers her telling her charges, "Teachers and farmers . . . are alike. But I'm luckier, because a farmer has to go to his garden. My garden comes to me" (p. 236). In spite of the fact that Robert and his friend Soup Vinson were often in trouble and Robert caught the blame and often Miss Kelly's ruler, he reports, "She liked *me* best. Every kid thought the same" (p. 236).

The rugged mountain farm life Peck experienced as a boy, the gruff love and guidance of his father, the adventures with his friend Soup (who later became the Reverend Luther Wesley Vinson to whom Peck dedicated *Soup*), Miss Kelly's books, his love for animals, and his celebration of things natural all became a part of his books. In his books we celebrate boys becoming men. We cheer those people who nudge them, often unwillingly, toward maturity. We laugh at their foibles and cry at their sorrows. His characters become real because they are real—they are the people of Peck's world who have helped make him the man and the writer he is. ◆

Preadolescent Girls

Stories about preadolescent girls, such as *Little Women* and *The Secret Garden*, have been popular for many generations. However, in recent years these books have focused more and more on seeking independence from the family so that the protagonists can deal with the problems of emerging adolescence.

Physical Change   The problems girls face in dealing with physical maturation are far more common in young adult literature than problems boys face. Judy Blume has provided two frank, cutting-edge books in *Are You There, God? It's Me, Margaret* and *Deenie*. The importance of beauty has always been emphasized to Deenie. Both she and her mother panic when they discover Deenie has a curvature of the spine and must wear a back brace. The book talks frankly about the fitting of the brace, the difficulty Deenie has adjusting to it, and her concern that she is no longer beautiful. Margaret's problems, on the other hand, are not unusual for an eleven-year-old girl. She has just moved to a new neighborhood and is forced to deal with the onset of puberty while she is adjusting to new friends and a new school. Margaret's mixed-faith parents do not attend church as her friends' parents do, and she wonders whether she is Christian or Jewish. Her parents want her to decide for herself, but Margaret finds she is torn between her two grandmothers. She, like all young adults, seeks independence and at the same time demands answers from the adults in her life. Throughout the book she talks to God about religion, menstruation, wearing a bra, and anything else troubling her.

Other books about girls facing the problems of their emerging maturity are *The Trouble with Thirteen* (Miles), *Don't Look and It Won't Hurt* (Peck), *The Long Secret* (Fitzhugh), *All We Know* (French), *Halsey's Pride* (Hall), *Is It Them or Is It Me?* (Haven), *B, My Name Is Bunny* (Mazer), *Someday I'll Laugh about This* (Crew), *First Wedding, Once Removed* (Deaver), *Silver* (Mazer), and *Leap Before You Look* (Stolz).

Emotional Turmoil   Many young adult books do not deal simply with the physical problems of emerging adolescence but with emotional problems as well. In *Someday I'll Laugh about This*, for example, twelve-year-old Shelby can't understand why spending time at her grandparents' cabin is not the same now that her thirteen-year-old cousin Kristen has "gone and grown up!" Pokie in *First Wedding, Once Removed* finds that her world is no longer ideal now that her brother Gib has graduated. In *All We Know*, an Australian Book of the Year, Arkie begins to better understand her family members, her former best friend Kylie, and Ian Koh, a quiet, neglected neighbor boy. Sarabeth in Norma Fox Mazer's *Silver* must deal with being different. All the students in her school are snobby and rich and ask her questions like "Do you have a regular bathroom in your trailer?"

The Girl by Robbie Branscum is semiautobiographical. It takes place in the Arkansas hills of Branscum's own childhood. The girl, as the protagonist is called throughout the book, and her two brothers live in the midst of poverty. The children are threatened by the abuse of their grandparents with whom they are living. The girl's great-grandmother is the only adult in the book who appears to provide love and guidance. This book is more adult than many coming-of-age novels for younger adolescents in that it deals not only with physical abuse but sexual abuse. When it appears that the girl's uncle will finally have his way with her, her brother Gene intervenes.

Vera Cleaver's books *Sugar Blue* and *Sweetly Sings the Donkey* deal with emotional problems in a less intense manner. Amy in *Sugar Blue* no longer experiences the happy carefree days of childhood after her parents take on a new business and her four-year-old niece Ella comes for the summer. At first Amy resents Ella, but she soon learns how caring for someone else can be a rewarding experience. Lily in *Sweetly Sings the Donkey* is a remarkably mature fourteen year old. Because of the hardships and failures of her family she has been forced to grow up more quickly than most adolescents. She understands her family's frailties and dreams, and supports their strengths.

Horse Books   A subgroup of coming-of-age books for preteenage females is the popular horse books. Many of these are simply formula books that are precursors to teenage formula romances. However, one exception worth mentioning is *Summer's Chance* (Easton), about fourteen-year-old Elizabeth who is spending the summer on Grandmother Bates' horse farm. She hopes to find out more about her mother who died when she was young, but Grandmother refuses to tell her about Lizzie, even though everyone expects her to behave exactly like her and some call her by that dreaded nickname. Unlike Lizzie, Elizabeth is not good with the horses until she meets Maggie's Last Chance, the filly her mother prized. When Chance is hurt before the big race, Elizabeth attempts to nurse him back to health and, in the process, learns a great deal about her mother. Although in many ways a traditional horse book, this book is more about Elizabeth's search for herself than her love of a horse. Another good book for girls who enjoy horse books is Phyllis Reynolds Naylor's *Night Cry*.

The Transitional Phase

Once young adults have been separated from childhood, a lonely, frustrating transitional phase often begins. Now teenagers learn about themselves and how to fit into adult society. This phase of coming of age often involves an initiation of some kind. Sometimes these initiations are planned rituals or ceremonies; however, most important ones simply happen. During the transitional phase the adolescent must remove him- or herself from the protective environment created by parents and school and seek a place in which to grow. Frequently the transition from the cocoon of childhood to independence involves relationships with peer groups, but because self-assessment and struggle are necessary for growth, the adolescent must leave the peer group as well to finally achieve maturity.

This transitional period is a time of continual testing as the teenager evaluates and questions long-held values and beliefs. The value system of the family must be meshed with that of the peer group, and, ultimately, with the adolescent's own system of beliefs and values. As the stage of transition progresses, the adolescent acquires more and more the freedom and responsibility of adulthood. Adolescents have new experiences at this time and with these comes a loss of innocence.

Symbolism in Transitional Novels for Boys

Males have been much more common as protagonists in transitional literature than females, as seen in these classic coming-of-age books: *The Adventures of Huckleberry Finn* (Twain), *Catcher in the Rye* (Salinger), and *A Separate Peace* (Knowles).

The Journey   Literature about the teenage male in transition often involves an actual journey from one physical setting to another. This journey is symbolic of the passage from childhood to adulthood. Authors of young adult books recognize that if their characters are to grow it is essential that they separate them from the place and time of their childhoods. Huck in Mark Twain's *Adventures of Huckleberry Finn* does his growing up on a raft traveling down the Mississippi River. In *Up Country* by Alden R. Carter, Carl must leave the home of his alcoholic mother in Milwaukee and move to rural Blind River to live with a distant aunt and uncle. In *Growing Season*, also by Carter, Rich and his five siblings move during his senior year from the city to the country to start a dairy farm. In Kathryn Borland's and Helen Speicher's *Good-bye to Stony Crick*, Jeremy moves from Appalachia to Chicago. Josh in Richard Bradford's *Red Sky at Morning* moves from the South to a little town in New Mexico where he passes from childhood to adulthood as he and his mother wait out World War II. In *I'll Get There. It Better Be Worth the Trip* by John Donovan, Davy moves to New York City after the death of a beloved grandmother. In *Center Line* by Joyce Sweeney, five brothers leave their abusive, alcoholic father, steal a car, and head out to search for a better life. Evan in *Split Time* by Charles P. Crawford moves out of his suburban home with his father to a shabby apartment in a Victorian mansion after his mother announces she is leaving them because she has fallen in love with another man. Norma Fox Mazer's *Downtown* chronicles the life of Pete whose parents leave him with his uncle after their attempt to make the world a better place goes wrong and they blow up a laboratory, killing two people, in a protest against war. The uncle agreed to take Pete for a short time, but the two end up living together for eight years.

Transitional coming-of-age stories appear in many different genres. In Paula Fox's historical novel *The Slave Dancer*, Jessie is kidnapped and taken aboard a slave ship where he is forced to play his fife so that the slaves will dance and not lose their physical condition. Jessie struggles with the conflicting emotions of compassion and hate.

Summer   Because summer is a time of relative freedom and independence for many adolescents, it becomes a part of the setting for many transitional stories. Frequently in these summer coming-of-age stories the adolescent is removed from his home. *Summer of '42* by Herman Raucher takes place at the beach. During summer vacation three adolescent boys play the games of children while learning the lessons of adulthood. In *A Solitary Blue* by Cynthia Voigt, Jeff makes two trips to visit his mother, who abandoned the family. The solitary blue heron he sees near his mother's home becomes Jeff's symbol for himself. In another book that takes place in a similar sea island setting Simons in Padgett Powell's *Edisto* spends more of his time in the African American world in which he feels comfortable than in the prosperous white environment of his lawyer father and professor mother.

Isolation   Isolation or aloneness is an element in many young adult novels. This isolation allows characters like Jeff and Simons to learn more about themselves as they grope toward adulthood. Gary Paulsen's *The Island* is about a boy who moves from Madison, Wisconsin, to northern, rural Wisconsin with his family. During explorations on his bicycle, he spies an island. As the book progresses he spends more and more time on the island, exploring, observing, writing, and painting. When he decides to move to the island, his parents do not understand and send a counselor out to see him. As he explores the island, he receives food from Susan, a neighbor, and begins to learn that he cannot survive alone. The archetypal transitional novel for young males is probably *Catcher in the Rye* by J. D. Salinger. Holden Caulfield's relative freedom comes over the Christmas holidays after he flunks out of an exclusive boys school. Holden leaves the school after he has been humiliated by a history teacher and has several encounters with his "stupid" dorm mates. Although Holden is not physically isolated from others, he is psychologically alone throughout the novel. He meets people, goes to dances and plays and nearly has sex, but he is always alone within himself, absorbed in his own problems, coming closer and closer to a breakdown.

In *Summer Lion* by Liza Fosburgh, Leo moves to the private mountain estate of an eighty-year-old man to become his companion. In Paul Zindel's *The Amazing and Death-Defying Diary of Eugene Dingman*, Eugene goes to an Adirondack resort to work to help his sister pay her college tuition. While there he builds his own self-esteem as he takes to heart the message of the Indian mystic Mahatma: love yourself deeply and you can control the harshness around you. Richard Peck removes Andrew Wingate from his comfortable suburban home, his friends, and his driver's exam when he is forced to cruise the North Sea with his grandmother, whom he's never met, and his bratty younger sister in *Those Summer Girls I Never Met*.

Sports   Athletics is often a vehicle for growth in young adult novels aimed at adolescent males. Participating in sports and competition can be character building. More importantly, the field of play, whatever that field might be, removes the adolescent from his childhood environment and usually forces him to work in a peer group and, eventually, alone. Coming-of-age sports novels frequently include an adult mentor or antagonist, often the coach. This person usually differs from the adults who have been a part of the adolescent's life.

Bruce Brooks's *The Moves Make the Man* is an excellent coming-of-age sports novel. The setting is Wilmington, North Carolina, in the 1950s. Jerome Foxworthy, called Jayfox, is an outstanding student and an excellent basketball player who has been selected as the token African American to integrate the schools. Although the novel examines racial bigotry and injustice, the story is really about how Jayfox grows into a sensitive and mature adult after he meets Braxton Rivers the Third. Bix, as he is called, is also isolated. Although an excellent baseball player, he is exceedingly shy and troubled. The two young men become friends and through the metaphor of basketball, as Jayfox teaches Bix how to handle himself on the court, their friendship matures along with their attitude toward life. *Bridges to Cross* by Paul B. Janeczko, a well-known young adult poet, is another excellent coming-of-age story that employs sport, in this case baseball, as a metaphor for life. James Marchuk's mother forces him to leave public school, and give up his opportunity to play baseball, to attend Our Lady Queen of Angels. At the new school, a group of overzealous Christian Brothers become the target of James's frustration. James wants to think for himself, to attend the school he wants, and to not be told what to believe and how to behave. Finally, Mrs. Marchuk accepts James's need to be independent and find his own values, and she gives him the opportunity to do so. James discovers the root of his frustration and learns that only he can create the person he wants to become. *Hoops* by Walter Dean Myers deals with growing up in the streets of Harlem. Lonnie Jackson is seventeen and sees basketball as his way out of the ghetto. His coach, a frustrated basketball player, helps Lonnie see his dreams for what they are—just dreams. Marc Talbert's *Dead Bird*

Singing involves swimming. Matt is euphoric over his win in the swim meet until on the way home his mother and sister are killed by a drunk driver. Matt moves in with his best friend Jamie. Together they are able to survive the tragedy. Other good coming-of-age sports books include *The Shadow Brothers* (Cannon), *Rusty Fertlanger, Lady's Man* (Killien), and *The Whole Nine Yards* (Malmgren).

The Contender   Written in the late 1960s, *The Contender* by Robert Lipsyte is not only an important piece of realistic sports fiction, as discussed in Chapter 3, but a classic coming-of-age book with an exciting plot and a well-rounded protagonist. Alfred, although seventeen, still seeks comfort by escaping with his best friend to their childhood hideout, a cave in the park. But now his friend is more interested in escaping through drugs and tries to convince Alfred to come along on the trip. Alfred does not want to disappoint his aunt who has supported him. A good boxer, he dares himself to go to Donatelli's Gym to see if he can be somebody special, a champion. He's afraid, though; failure by not trying is always easier than failure by trying. He must force himself to head up the steps to the gym. When he meets Donatelli and tells him he wants to be a champion, the coach says,

> "Let me tell you what it's like." Donatelli walked toward Alfred until they were standing face to face. His square head settled down into the crisp collar of his open-throated, short-sleeved white shirt. He had almost no neck.
>
> "You get up at five-thirty in the morning, before the gas fumes foul the air, and you run in the park. That's to build up your legs and wind. You run smooth and easy, a little faster and a little longer each day. You run every day, rain or snow, unless you're sick. Then you go home and eat breakfast. Juice, two boiled eggs, toast, and tea. You go to school?"
>
> "I work."
>
> "You don't eat too much lunch, it just makes you slow and tired. No fried foods, no beans, no cabbage, no pies and cakes, no soda. After work you come to the gym. Jump rope, stretching exercises, sit-ups, push-ups, deep-knee bends. You do them until you can't do any more, then start all over again. You go home, have a good dinner. Meat, green vegetable, fresh salad, milk, fruit. You're asleep by nine o'clock. . . . You'll do it for a week, maybe two. You'll feel a little better physically, but all your friends, your family, will say you're a fool. You'll say to yourself, 'All this sacrifice, and I'll probably never even get to be a good fighter.' And you'll be right, nine times out of ten. . . . People will try to drag you down. Some will laugh at you for wanting to be a fighter. And others will tell you you're so good you don't need to train, to go to bed early. How far did you go in school?"
>
> "Eleventh grade."
>
> "What happened?"
>
> "I quit."
>
> "Why?"
>
> "Didn't seem like any reason to stay."
>
> "What makes you think you won't quit here too? . . ."
>
> "I want to be somebody."
>
> "Everybody is somebody."
>
> "Somebody special. A champion."
>
> Donatelli's thin lips tightened. "Everybody wants to be a champion. That's not enough. You have to start by wanting to be a contender, the man coming up, the man who knows there's a good chance he'll never get to the top, the man who's willing to sweat and bleed

to get up as high as his legs and his brains and his heart will take him. That must sound corny to you."

"No."

"It's the climbing that makes the man. Getting to the top is an extra reward." (Lipsyte, 1967, pp. 25–27)

School Settings   Some transition books have school settings. The most common setting in the transition book is the private school since it is essential that the adolescents be removed from their childhood environment. Private schools, particularly boarding schools, provide the adolescent with more independence. In such a setting, the young adult can deal with the problem of growing up in relative isolation from family and home. The best known of the boarding school transition novels is John Knowles's *A Separate Peace*. Written in the 1960s, the story takes place during World War II. A more recent transition novel reminiscent of Knowles's book is *At the Shores* by Thomas Rogers. It tells the story of Jerry Engles, a student in the Chicago Laboratory School of the 1940s (a progressive school of the University of Chicago that utilized the research of educator John Dewey). Jerry, like many boys who are approaching adulthood, finds women baffling and is not quite sure how to react to them or to his feelings. The book helps readers understand that the experiences of the young adult are universal, regardless of time or setting. In the 1981 *Books for Young Adults Poll* one young female respondent commented about this book, "Guys are still just like that." In the classic coming-of-age novel by Robert Cormier, *The Chocolate War*, Jerry Renault wants to be accepted by the Vigils, a group of students at the Catholic boys school he attends. He follows their evil plan to refuse to sell chocolates in the school's annual sale, and in so doing becomes the target of the school's cruel Brother Leon. Brother Leon intimidates the Vigils' leader Archie, who gets the Vigils to help rather than hinder the sale. Now Jerry is alone in his stand against selling the chocolates, opposed by the Vigils, the teachers, and the school administration. Eventually forced to leave the school, Jerry loses his faith in other people and his innocence. Although the novel does not end happily, readers know that Jerry, when he recovers, as he does in the sequel *Beyond the Chocolate War*, will grow into a person who can survive no matter what cruelty surrounds him.

Caring for Animals   Caring for an animal places the adolescent in a more independent and responsible position, and some authors have used this situation in a way that allows the main character to grow. Two good examples are horse stories. In *Moon in the Water* by Lucy Diggs, JoBob Draper lives in two worlds: the world of his impoverished family where he is the victim of his bigoted, abusive father and the world of the stable where JoBob is a welcomed, trusted member of the team of horse trainers. He takes on the care of Blue, a new Pinto regarded as a misfit by the other trainers. The bond between the young man and the horse grows as his relationship with his family worsens. When Blue is secretly sold by JoBob's father, JoBob must find a way to face the pain of this loss and move beyond it. In Patricia Harrison Easton's *Rebel's Choice*, Rob leaves his grandparents' financially secure home to work as a groom. He develops a relationship with the unmanageable Red Rat which becomes a metaphor for his relationship with his undependable father.

Tragedy and Conflict   Because growth often stems from tragedy and conflict, many young adult authors begin their coming-of-age novels with significant events that force the lives of the protagonist to change. As Margaret A. Edwards, a long-time young adult librarian and author of a useful book for librarians *The Fair Garden and the Swarm of Beasts*, says, "Whatever adversity life may bring, the young person must cast off the bonds of fear and have courage. He must reach down in himself to find strength" (1974). In *Page Four* by Sheila Solomon Klass, David drops out of life the day he finds out his father is leaving them to go to Alaska with a younger woman. He abandons his life—school, friends, sports—just as his father has abandoned him. A large portion of the book chronicles David's unhappy year, but in the end he begins to see through his self-pity and dreams of revenge to his mother's plight. He realizes she is grieving not only for her lost husband but for her lost son. As he helps her to recover, he begins the healing and growing-up process himself.

In Katie Letcher Lyle's *Dark but Full of Diamonds*, Scott Dabney also deals with the pain of loss. In this novel Scott experiences a double loss, or so it seems to him. First his mother dies. Then the woman he has loved since his mother's death, Hilah Brown, who is nine years his senior, returns to teaching drama and English. Scott throws himself into acting and football, but his love for Hilah continues. Eventually, Scott's father and Hilah fall in love and plan to marry. Scott is devastated and drops out of life. Concluding that Scott can't handle their relationship, Hilah and Scott's father call off the engagement. When Scott sees their sorrow, he feels no triumph and begins to grow into a caring and supportive individual.

Accidents are often the events that cause growth in young adult coming-of-age novels. In Frances A. Miller's *Cutting Loose*, Matt McKendrick realizes that his negligence contributed to the death of Katie, his deaf sister. Shunned by his friends and the people in his hometown, he struggles to make a new life in Los Angeles with new friends and adopted parents. There he comes to understand that he cannot begin life anew until he returns home and deals with his problems. In *Facing Up* by Robin Brancato, Dave is the driver of a car in a tragic accident. He is left with feelings of guilt and anger, and the ending of the novel is not a happy one. In Chris Crutcher's *Crazy Horse Electric Game*, sixteen-year-old Willie, a high school athlete, has an accident which handicaps him for life and makes glories like the "crazy horse electric game" a thing of the past. He runs away to escape his life at home and at school which he finds intolerable. He, too, learns that the only way he can deal with his life is by returning home. And when he does, he finds that those at home have changed too.

Many coming-of-age books could easily fit into the genre of the problem novel. The focus of these novels, however, is on the development and growth of the character as he or she moves beyond the problem. In Frank Bonham's *Durango Street*, Rufus thinks that he needs the gang for safety. When he is picked up by the police the night of his induction into the gang, he is not arrested. Alex Robbins, a special officer, has been assigned to Rufus's gang to channel its energies into constructive activities. Rufus decides ultimately to cooperate with Alex, and in the process he begins to learn how to live as an adult.

Far from Shore by Kevin Major takes place in a small town in Newfoundland. Chris's experiences and the reactions of Jennifer, Mother, Dad, and Reverend Wheaton to Chris's behavior prove that growing up can be painful in all cultures. Chris blames his typical adolescent problems on everyone and everything other than himself. Through the support of his friends and family, who never make excuses for his behavior, he learns to face the consequences of his actions and accept responsibility for his problems. Other excellent novels with young male characters in transition include *The Owl's Song* (Hale), *I'm Really Dragged But Nothing Gets Me Down* (Hentoff), *That Was Then, This Is Now* and *Tex* (Hinton), *If I Love You, Am I Trapped Forever?* and *The Son of Someone Famous* (Kerr), *Fog* (Lee), *The Chosen* (Potok), *Good Night, Prof. Dear* (Townsend), and *Confessions of a Teenage Baboon* (Zindel).

Symbolism in Transitional Novels for Girls

Most older coming-of-age novels have male protagonists; girls are rarely protagonists in such novels prior to the 1970s with the exception of a few books for early adolescents such as *Little Women* and *The Secret Garden*. "The traditional assumption [was] that girls experience menses as their rite of passage into womanhood and find males who have passed the test of manhood to take care of them. This choice will make their lives complete and give them meaning" (Endicott, 1992, p. 42). Although the girl-gets-boy theme is still common in many of the popular formula romances read by young adolescents (see Chapter 3), girls in transition are increasingly found as protagonists in young adult novels. In fact, young adult literature has given rise to some of the strongest female characters in all of literature. We will discuss many of these three-dimensional characters in this section.

The Journey   As with male protagonists, females often take a journey that is both physical and symbolic. As teenage girls travel through this difficult time, they often lose their innocence. Author Katie Letcher Lyle says of adolescents in transition, "They have left the Garden of Eden and seen their own nakedness, just as Adam and Eve in that parable of growing up" (1975). In Jean Craighead George's *Julie of the Wolves* thirteen-year-old Julie travels from the home of her Eskimo husband to the home of her father in search of herself. In *Shabanu: Daughter of the Wind* by Suzanne Fisher Staples, Shabanu's family are Pakistani desert people. Although Shabanu's age makes her still a child in our culture, she is one year removed from an arranged marriage. She does not want to become the traditional Muslim wife and lose her freedom. The wealthy brother of an unscrupulous landowner pays the bride price for Shabanu, and although she protests, no one but her aunt Sharma takes her side. Although she recognizes her duty to her family, she decides to run away in the middle of the night. When her father finds her in the desert, he beats her with a stick. She knows she has no other choice but to marry, but she vows to keep her secrets within her heart. In *Mr. and Mrs. Bo Jo Jones* by Ann Head, two young adults move from their parents' homes to their own apartment and struggle to maintain a marriage as they continue to grow apart from each other. In Isabelle Holland's *Of Love and Death and Other Journeys*, Peg must leave the home of the mother she has loved and move in with the father she has never known. Julie's journey in *Up a Road Slowly* by Irene Hunt begins when she is seven years old and ends when she is seventeen. After her mother dies, her father sends her to live with her strict Aunt Cordelia. Unhappy, she pays a visit to her married sister, only to discover that their once close relationship has changed. Returning on a train, she meets a friendly conductor who helps her understand that she must think of making others happy before she can be truly happy herself. When Julie's father remarries, she contemplates moving in with her father and stepmother but realizes she would be out of place. Discovering that she loves Aunt Cordelia, she makes her home with her while she works on her dream of becoming a writer.

Another book that uses a trip as a symbol of a girl's transition to adulthood is *The Green of Me* by Patricia Lee Gauch. As Jenny travels to meet her sweetheart, she recalls the joys and pains of her growing-up years. In Bette Greene's *Morning Is a Long Time Coming*, Patty travels to Europe to find the parents of her German soldier boyfriend. The search for the parents becomes a search for herself. Sibilance, a musical prodigy, and her father travel across the country in search of her mother in *Midnight Hour Encores* by Bruce Brooks. In *The Runaway's Diary* by Marilyn Harris, sixteen-year-old Cat runs away from her parents, ends up in an accident on a Canadian highway, and in the process learns many things about herself. In Katie Lyle's *I Will Go Barefoot All Summer for You*, Jessie, who lives with her cousin, is lonely and dreams of becoming famous as a way to find happiness. When Toby comes to visit, however, she discovers that love is the answer to her loneliness. In *The April Age* by Lavinia Russ, Peakie is almost eighteen in 1925. She is full of dreams and fantasies about life and men and love. On a trip to Europe she meets a handsome British lord, and through him she discovers herself. The heroine of *Homecoming* and *Dicey's Song*, by Cynthia Voigt, travels with her younger siblings in search of a new home. She finds that home with Gram in a rundown farm on Chesapeake Bay. In *Yesterday's Daughter* by Patricia Calvert, Leenie flees to a hideout in the swamp to escape from her mother, whom she resents for abandoning her as a baby. (Her mother became pregnant unexpectedly when she was only seventeen.) In the swamp she meets Axel Erickson, a photographer, and introduces him to the swamp's beauty. Following a moment of near passion with Axel, she begins to understand her mother. Throughout this novel Calvert uses the environment of the swamp—its fog, sunlight, flora, and fauna—to symbolize the murky transition between childhood innocence and adult understanding.

An actual journey is not always necessary in female transitional novels. In Sue Ellen Bridgers's *Home Before Dark*, the act of putting down roots, of finding a home after many years of migrant farming, leads Stella to grow up. Through her relationship with an aunt, an attraction to an egocentric young man, a growing friendship with another boy, the death of her mother, Mae, and the remarriage of her father, Stella learns much about herself.

Isolation   Making the transition to adulthood frequently involves a period of isolation. In the Newbery Medal winner *Jacob Have I Loved* by Katherine Paterson, Wheeze has a twin sister, Caroline, to whom she has always felt second place. Although most of the book takes place on an island in the Chesapeake Bay, a symbol of both childhood freedom and adolescent isolation, Wheeze travels to the mainland to continue her education. There she learns it will be impossible for her to become a doctor as she has dreamed. Instead, she moves to remote western Virginia and works as a midwife. As she helps deliver twins during a very difficult birth, in which one baby nearly dies, Wheeze realizes that there is sometimes a reason to treat one child differently from another. Suddenly she knows why she has always felt second. In each setting of the narrative Wheeze discovers something new about herself, and her isolation in an Appalachian valley away from home helps her better understand the relationship between her mother, her sister, and herself.

Zibby Oneal's *In Summer Light* is also set on an island. In this novel, seventeen-year-old Kate Brewer lives on an island off the coast of Massachusetts with her famous painter father and mother. Returning from boarding school, Kate finds herself trapped on the island that she once loved. She is ill, bored, restless, and resentful of her father's overwhelming presence. As she writes a paper on Shakespeare's *Tempest*, which is set on an island dominated by its aging ruler, as she befriends the graduate student doing a retrospective study of her father's work, and as she creates her own art on the rocks and the sand, she makes the transition from childhood to adulthood. She begins to understand her father as an aging man who is attempting to express himself through his art, begins to understand the complex relationship between the artist of one generation and the artist of the next, and begins to understand herself as an artist seeking her own voice.

◆ Between the Covers: *Authors at Work* ◆

ZIBBY ONEAL

Zibby Oneal is the author of coming-of-age literature featuring three-dimensional female protagonists. Her novels are carefully crafted, emotional, and complex. Each is full of the symbolic intensity of a young woman's rite of passage. In *The Language of Goldfish* thirteen-year-old Carrie actively resists growing up. Told in the third person, the novel begins after Carrie's breakdown and attempted suicide. As the novel unfolds, Carrie reveals her problems to her therapist, Dr. Ross. We learn that Carrie thinks of childhood as an unburdened time. She remembers her mother cooking as she and her sister Moira sit on stools and watch. She remembers their childhood games on the island and the language of goldfish she and Moira created. Carrie cherishes the memories of the island and refuses to move beyond them.

Another coming-of-age novel by Oneal profiles an older adolescent. *A Formal Feeling*, whose title is borrowed from the first line of an Emily Dickinson poem which appears as the frontispiece of the novel, is about sixteen-year-old Anne Cameron who comes home from boarding school for Christmas fourteen months after her mother's sudden death. She must not only deal with the death of her mother but with her father's recent marriage to Dory, a woman Anne thinks of as the opposite of her mother. Anne is trying hard to figure out who she is and who her mother was. People tell her how much she is like her mother and she wonders if the resemblance is more than physical. Anne has only cried twice since her mother's death and attempts to protect herself from pain. When she reads the first line of Dickinson's poem, "After great pain, a formal feeling comes," the reader begins to realize that everything Anne does is pervaded by a formal feeling. The only physical feeling Anne allows herself is the sensation of running which she uses to escape her emotional feeling that her father and brother have forgotten and betrayed her mother and, perhaps by extension, Anne as well. Throughout the story Anne turns to the Dickinson poem to find meaning. When she tries to write a paper about the poem, however, she loses the meaning of the words. Only then do her real feelings about her mother and herself begin to surface.

Zibby Oneal, born Elizabeth Bisgard in 1934, is married and the mother of two adult children. Today Zibby and her husband Bob live in Ann Arbor, Michigan. Zibby studied at Stanford University and completed her bachelor's degree at the University of Michigan. She has taught English, written for children and adolescents, and won numerous awards for her writing including the Christopher Award for *A Formal Feeling* and the Boston Globe–Horn Book Award for *In Summer Light*. Her father was a medical researcher, a keeper of goats, and a portrait artist. Zibby began her education in a convent school which she remembers lovingly, but was transferred because her sister hated the school and her parents wanted both of them in the same school.

Zibby remembers being read to as a child. She says that her family had something like a public library right in their home, and her mother was constantly quoting from their books. Zibby read a great deal as a child: "I can remember having a desire to read racy novels—and to do this privately and secretly the way my friends did (my mother wouldn't have objected so I had no real need for secrecy). *Forever Amber* was considered hot stuff in those days, and I bought a copy. One afternoon I had just settled in under my bed with the book on my stomach and a flashlight in hand. I was just approaching one of the 'good' parts when the dust ruffle lifted, and there was my mother, looking at me upside down. 'If you want to read something really racy,' she said, 'why don't you try *Ulysses*?' This was my introduction to James Joyce" (Bloom and Mercier, 1991, pp. 7–8).

Zibby also began writing at a very young age. She reports that she made up stories in her head before she could write. She loved to sit under a tree in her back yard and make up stories for herself.

Zibby has studied and taught the "great books," and from the writers of these books she has learned a great deal about writing. She has spent a good bit of time, she reports, studying how they write. She says of books like *My Antonia*, "It is almost as though the characters have grown out of the land in the way the coarse prairie grass has" (p. 8). She has attempted a similar kind of organic characterization in some of her young adult novels.

She says that she writes from the perspective of teenage girls because "I think I would have a hard time writing from a boy's point of view. For me that would be like writing from the perspective of a Martian. The tiny nuances of feeling that interest me in my female characters would simply not be available to me were I to write about boys" (p. 21).

Like many writers of young adult fiction, Zibby says that she was ignorant of the field until she had written *The Language of Goldfish*. Up to that point she had been writing children's books, but then, according to Zibby, "Carrie simply appeared to me. . . . To be afraid of growing up is a serious issue" (p. 27).

One of the things that make Zibby Oneal's books unusual in the young adult field is that, in spite of their strong young adult protagonists, each book is written in the third person. She says of first-person narratives, "I have spent the last year and a half trying to write in the first person, and I simply can't do it. It's too loose a form for me. I miss the control of a third-person narrator guiding the action, commenting obliquely" (p. 28).

She says of writing that it is "99 percent hard work—revising and rethinking and trying to get as close as you can to what it is you want to say, and failing. I think there is some general belief that writers sit down and whip off a chapter because they're inspired. Well, maybe some do. Not me. I'm more like a carpenter, sawing and planing and sanding a piece of raw wood, and being many times disappointed in the result before I get a little bit right" (p. 32). ✦

Overcoming Obstacles   In the struggle to grow up, the young adult must often overcome an obstacle that is placed in her way. In Kathryn Lasky's *Pageant* the obstacle is being a nice, middle-class Jewish girl from a liberal family in an ultraconservative Wasp private school where she has played a shepherd in the Christmas pageant for three years in a row. In Hadley Irwin's *Kim/Kimi* the obstacle is being half-Japanese and half-American in a small town Iowa high school.

In *Mel* by Liz Berry the obstacle is having to live with a violent, deranged mother in a filthy house in the slums of London. For Brieanna McQuade in *But in the Fall I'm Leaving*, by Ann Rinaldi, it is having to live up to the expectations of her newspaper editor father. In *Anywhere Else But Here* by Bruce Clements, the obstacles that Molly must overcome are the death of her mother, her father's failed business, and her desire to leave her home in upstate New York.

Being Different   Being different physically can present problems for adolescent girls. Grace Schmitt, in *Monday I Love You* by Constance Greene, is the target of cruel pranks because of the large size of her breasts. Heidi Rosenbloom, in *Wonderful Me* by Barbara Wersba, sees herself as anything but wonderful. She is short, unpretty, uninterested in clothes, and klutzy. *Life without Friends* by Ellen Emerson White is the story of Beverly Johnson. She is shunned by her friends because of her friendship with Tim Conners, who is found guilty in the death of two teenagers. In addition, she feels guilty because she had not revealed her suspicions about Tim or told anyone of his abusing her.

Personal Tragedies   Tragedy can move young adult females toward adulthood sooner than anticipated. In *Suddenly* by Hila Colman, Emily's life changes when a car she is in hits and kills the little boy she babysits and loves dearly. Kate Baker's parents were killed when she was eight years old in *Over the Moon* by Elissa Haden Guest, but at sixteen she has not yet come to terms with their death. When overachiever Wray Jean Child's father dies of cancer in *A Small Pleasure* by Patricia Hermes, she overextends herself and eventually suffers from exhaustion. During her physical recovery she must begin to address her father's death.

Romance   Developing relationships with males is often a part of coming of age for young female readers, but only part of it. Maureen Daly's *Seventeenth Summer*, written in 1942, may be the first honest account of an adolescent female's coming of age. By today's standards the novel may seem trite as it deals with whether Angie Morrow and Jack Duluth will stay together after Angie's seventeenth summer. However, in 1942 the book was revolutionary. Angie sees Jack and is immediately attracted to him. Within a few days he repays her interest. He asks her for a date and their seemingly idyllic relationship begins. How does this novel differ from teenage formula romances? First and foremost, Daly's characters are not one-dimensional; Angie does not focus solely on her romance. The characters are real people with real concerns and problems. They do things that real teenagers did and do, such as drink beer and smoke cigarettes. Angie tells her story in the first person, another breakthrough in the genre. This creates a closeness between Angie and the reader. We care about Angie and about what happens to her.

Although Angie is an innocent, (noticing but not understanding the red nail polish on the male piano player's fingers at the Rathskeller she and Jack visit), she is also far more independent than most female protagonists in traditional romances before or since. Not surprisingly, since the book was written in 1942 and Daly then was only eighteen, the book honors some of the taboos of the formula romance. Daly never deals with the role of sex in the romantic relationship, for example. Angie says of her first kiss, "I know you will think it's terrible after I had only been out with him three times but in a way I couldn't help it" (p. 53). Angie, like many other female characters in romances of the period, is unsophisticated and, like most female readers of the time, she values chastity. But, at the end of the novel, when Jack tells Angie he loves her and asks her to marry him, she chooses college over romance and marriage. She knows, as Katherine knows in Judy Blume's contemporary romance *Forever*, that first love is a part of the initiation into adulthood; there is a lot of life yet to be lived, and it must first be lived independently before a long-term relationship can grow.

Since Maureen Daly created the coming-of-age romance in 1942, many interesting books have followed. Katherine of Judy Blume's *Forever* begins to grow up as she experiences her first love affair. Critics of the narrative have pointed out that at the end of the book Katherine is not yet a responsible adult. When asked what she wants to do with her life, she replies that she has learned the meaning of the word *forever*. She leaves her "forever" love for a new boy on the college campus. Katherine, like many college freshmen, is still in the process of growing up.

Today, there are many contemporary romances worth reading. Teachers can direct young women who are hooked on formula romances to these books. *The Giver* by Lynn Hall is the story of Mary McNeal who is a good but not outstanding student, attractive but not beautiful. James Flicket, Mary's homeroom teacher, recognizes her potential, and through his guidance and attention she begins to bloom. Mary develops a crush on Mr. Flicket, and he, a lonely man with an overbearing mother, begins to fall in love with Mary. He stops short, however, recognizing what is happening and why and understanding the future consequences. *Seventeen and In-Between* by Barthe DeClements features the strong female protagonist she has written about in several other books. Elsie Edwards appears to be the typical heroine of the teen romance. However, she is far more independent and deals with more difficult problems than characters in formula romances. First, Craddoc, her boyfriend, is pushing her into an intimate relationship which she resists. Second, she becomes aware of an athlete's plot to change his grades while working in her school computer center. In spite of the personal risk, she makes the decision to expose him. Finally, Elsie's mother is attempting to reestablish a relationship with her daughter. At first, Elsie resists, but eventually she begins to forgive her. Many other romances are in part coming-of-age narratives and will be discussed in Chapter 6.

Fantasy   Some of the strongest female characters who come of age on the pages of the novel can be found in the genre of fantasy (fantasy is discussed at length in Chapter 7). Robin McKinley's *Hero and the Crown* and *Blue Sword* both contain a female heroine who expresses doubts about her self-worth. Aerin, in *The Hero and the Crown*, is the daughter of the King of Damar and his second wife. Because of her genetic and physical heritage she is distrusted by the people. After her eighteenth birthday, however, she takes action to win their trust and her own self-respect. In *The Blue Sword*, Harry (Angharad) Crewe's parents have died. Harry, who is not only penniless but "of no particular beauty," feels she is of little worth. However, Sir Charles and Lady Amelia offer her a new home among the Hillfolk. There she meets the Hill-King Corlath, who asks for help to fight the people of the North. Shortly after their meeting, Corlath kidnaps Harry and takes her to his kingdom Damar in the hope that she will inspire the Damarians to take up the defense of their land. She grows into this position and discovers her own physical and emotional strength.

Incorporation into the Adult Community

The culminating phase of the initiation ritual is the incorporation of the young person into the adult community. The rites of passage are endured in seclusion or in an unfamiliar environment, but in primitive societies incorporation rites are generally witnessed by the entire community, signifying to all that the novice is now "a new one," a member (Agee, 1973, p. 134). By this phase in the coming-of-age period, the adolescent has left the things of childhood behind and has accepted the new responsibilities of adulthood which include not only responsibility for self but also responsibility for the welfare of others. In addition, the emerging adult has begun to develop a mature value system by which she or he makes judgments based on a personal code of beliefs and values rather than simply the rules of family, the beliefs of a group of affiliated adults, or the law of the land. This, of course, does not mean that the young person's earlier beliefs are necessarily abandoned, but now they are considered in light of the new values and beliefs. Thus, incorporation into the community of adults involves an understanding and acceptance of the self. Not all adolescents reach this phase during the adolescent years. In fact, as many psychologists, sociologists, and anthropologists have pointed out some individuals are never fully incorporated into the adult community.

Elements of Emerging Adulthood in Novels for Girls

Many of the books dealing with a girl's transition from childhood to adulthood also depict the protagonist's new role in adult society. This is only natural since the growth that occurs during the transition often leaves the young person on the threshold of adulthood.

Separation and Reconciliation   In *Julie of the Wolves* (George), Julie understands that she cannot return to her primitive ways. This understanding, symbolized by the death of the bird with whom she has traveled, leads to her reunion with her father and her entry into his adult world. In *Morning Is a Long Time Coming* (Greene), Patty's lonely search for her German soldier's parents has ended and she rejoins the world she has abandoned, but this time as an adult who has come to terms with herself. In *Jacob Have I Loved* (Paterson), Wheeze is able to live with herself by forgiving her sister and mother. July in *Mr. and Mrs. Bo Jo Jones* (Head), reaches a new level of maturation when her premature baby dies. Even though there is no reason to keep the marriage together, July and Bo Jo decide to rebuild their relationship from their mutual respect and enter the adult world with a new courage that allows them to accept the lasting quality of marriage. In *Island of the Blue Dolphins* (O'Dell), Karana moves into adult society as the entire community watches. After her lonely existence on the island for eighteen years, she is rescued by a ship and is ready to enter a new world and a new life. In *In Summer Light* Kate reconciles with her father and again takes up her painting. At the end of the novel, the reader senses that Kate will assume responsibility for her artistic talent in the next generation.

Many novels about the incorporation period talk about careers or education as preparation for a career. In Paul Zindel and Bonnie Zindel's novel *A Star for the Latecomer*, Brooke's mother is dying of cancer and her boyfriend, Brandon, is moving from the gentle romanticism of young love to the superficial narcissism of Hollywood stardom. Brooke's mother has always wanted to be a star, and she pushes her dreams onto her daughter. The mother's cancer parallels the "cancer" that is growing in Brandon as his life becomes more and more consumed with his star status. Coping with the problems of her mother and Brandon helps Brooke grow into adulthood while gaining an increased understanding of herself. After her mother's death, Brooke is able to let go of the dreams of stardom and her love for Brandon, who has responded to Brooke's desperate love letter in a cold, impersonal way.

The End of the Journey   Although not as common in novels about incorporation, the journey is still a literary devise employed by some authors who want to show the movement between the transitional phase and achieving adulthood. In *A House Like a Lotus* by Madeleine L'Engle, for example, Polly O'Keefe, of the O'Keefe family of L'Engle's fantasy trilogy for younger readers, travels to Greece on her way to Cyprus for a conference for writers from developing countries. The trip gives Polly, now seventeen, time to reconsider her last year in school which she is beginning to recognize as a milestone. During the year, Polly learned about many kinds of love— some of them wonderful, like her first affair with a medical student, but others frightening. In flashbacks, Polly remembers how Maximilian Horne, the wealthy artistic neighbor for whom she felt great affection, attacked her. She is shocked by the attack but refuses to tell her parents about it. During her journey she struggles to understand love and forgiveness. Another interesting journey occurs in Amy Erlich's *Where It Stops, Nobody Knows*. This unusual novel takes us all over the country with Joyce and her daughter Nina, although it is not always easy to recognize which one is playing mother and which one child. Nina is used to being shuffled around the country, but in her need to leave childhood behind she is beginning to question these apparently illogical transplantings. Nina attempts to justify Joyce's actions by enumerating her many good qualities. She glosses over the difficulties of each move. However, in New York, when Nina finally learns the truth about these moves, she is forced to grow up. Nina learns from the two FBI men she finds in their apartment with her mother gone, that Joyce is not her real mother but is a nurse who kidnapped her soon after she was born. Suddenly, Nina is plunged into a new life with her birth parents and sister. Over the two years Nina learns to forgive Joyce, and when she visits Joyce in prison she tells her, "There's nothing to forgive. You brought me up. You were my mother."

New Responsibility   Some adolescents begin to accept responsibility as the adults of the next generation in novels of incorporation, as Kate does in *In Summer Light*. In Caroline Conney's *When the Party's Over*, high school senior Hallie is distressed to find that graduation seems to signal the end of the party. Everyone expects the seniors to be thinking about careers. Soon Hallie's friends are gone, and she is no longer a part of an in-group. Hallie is frustrated that she cannot find a job to suit her. She has no experience but regards all the low-paying jobs as beneath her. Then her parents leave town on vacation without leaving her any money. Cynthia Voigt's Dicey Tillerman, now twenty-one, is still searching for what to do with her life in *Seventeen against the Dealer*. She refuses Jeff's marriage proposal, drops out of college, and continues to live with Gram and her younger siblings. Dicey decides she wants to start a business building boats. Initially she is helped by Cisco, an older man who continually spouts quotations and biographical data. He betrays her, however, and at the same time her own arrogance and need for independence cause her to make some foolish mistakes. By the end of the book she is moving toward responsible adulthood. Just as Dicey appears in a series of coming-of-age books (beginning with *Homecoming*), so does Heidi Rosenbloom, at an earlier age, in books by Barbara Wersba. In *The Farewell Kid* Heidi is eighteen. She sets out on her own, moves into her own apartment, and, like Dicey, opens an ill-fated business. As Heidi struggles to maintain her Dog Rescue Business and her independence, she meets Harvey Beaumont who, like Heidi, is attempting to find himself.

Callie, in *Up Hill All the Way* by Lynn Hall, knows exactly what she wants to do with her life—she wants to be the best farrier (horseshoer) in Oklahoma. She is well on the way to her goal working for the summer for a veterinarian in order to save for the pickup truck she needs for her business. But then, Truman, the vet's new stepson arrives, just released from a state correctional ranch. Truman has been in all kinds of trouble, including committing robberies. Callie decides to reform him over the objections of her father, but her efforts fail and their friendship ends when Truman steals her father's pickup truck to carry out yet another robbery.

Other incorporation books explore the theme of premature adulthood. In *The Dark Card* by Amy Ehrich seventeen-year-old Laura's mother dies suddenly. Laura is devastated; she becomes increasingly withdrawn and is unable to eat. Her father and older sister are no help. Both are coping with the death in their own ways, and they leave Laura alone for the summer in the house on the Jersey shore near the glittering casinos of Atlantic City. Laura is drawn to the casinos which offer her a means of escape from her life. Using a stolen driver's license, her mother's clothes, and new makeup and hairstyle, Laura takes on a new adult identity. Her illusionary world, a sinister world for which she is not ready, begins to replace her real world. At the end of the novel Laura's boyfriend is able to convince her family that to help Laura they must admit that she has serious problems. In George Ella Lyon's *Borrowed Children*, sixteen-year-old Mandy Perritt takes on the responsibility for her four younger brothers and sisters and a newborn brother when her mother is bedridden after childbirth. In Nadine Roberts's *With Love, from Sam and Me*, fifteen-year-old Marylou Britten assumes the adult responsibility of caring for a two-and-a-half-year-old foster child who is brought into the home of her Uncle Ed and Aunt Bonnie, who are only interested in the money the foster child brings in.

Some adolescents, in spite of problems, are ready to grow up. Catriona (Cat) McPhie, in Mollie Hunter's *Cat, Herself*, lives in the Scottish countryside in a community of tinkers or travelers living by their wits and cherishing their freedom. Within the community gender roles are stereotypical and men are expected to own their wives. Cat, determined to be herself and maintain her independence, tells her fiancé who has promised not to beat her, "I can't be me as long as you have that sort of right over me. Because that way, you see, I'd belong to you." He asks Cat what she wants for herself. She replies simply, "Just to be Cat, herself. Always, Charlie. And for you to know that." A similar theme is dealt with in Phyllis Naylor's *Send No Blessings* in which Beth is caught in the poverty of her West Virginia family with many children and more "blessings" on the way. She wants to escape, but when a young man asks her to marry him, she realizes that the escape would be to a life like her parents'. Lyddie in Katherine Paterson's *Lyddie* is working in a textile mill in an attempt to regain her debt-ridden farm. When her goal is within grasp, however, she is inspired to seek more education and work for social change rather than take back the farm and her old life.

Elements of Emerging Adulthood in Novels for Boys

Traditionally, young men have been incorporated into the adult community when they begin a career or enter college. Young adult fiction today examines the problems young men face in the process of becoming adults. Not all young men find the path toward adulthood smooth; some are frustrated by problems and parents.

Death and Desertion   As in coming-of-age novels about young women, many novels about male protagonists entering the adult community actually span several phases of the coming-of-age period. Nathaniel Benchley's *Only Earth and Sky Last Forever* involves ancient primitive initiation rites. Dark Elk is an experienced brave at the beginning of the novel. He leaves childhood and enters the lonely transitional phase by trying desperately to prove himself in battle against white soldiers, and thereby gain the hand of the beautiful maiden Lashuka. At the end of the novel he is welcomed into adult society by Crazy Horse at Little Big Horn. In *Red Sky at Morning* by Richard Bradford, Josh is a young boy forced to move to a little town in New Mexico after his father leaves to fight in World War II. By the end of the story his father has died and Josh has assumed responsibility for his mentally disturbed mother. In Paula Fox's *Blowfish Live in the Sea*, eighteen-year-old Ben is a rebel. Deserted by his father when he was very young, he rejects the values of his mother and stepfather by dropping out of school and refusing to look for work. When he receives an unexpected message from his father, he agrees to meet him but is shocked by the alcoholic person he finds. This shock and the lies his father tells about successful business deals force him out of his rebellious stage and into adulthood. In making the decision to stay with his father and help him Ben finds a new purpose to his life.

In *Undertow* by Finn Havrevold, Jorn passes through the three classic stages of the initiation rite. At age fifteen he leaves home, against the wishes of his parents, with seventeen-year-old Ulf. Jorn expects to spend the summer at Ulf's family's cabin but soon discovers that Ulf has another idea—to go sailing in Norway's fjords. Unaware that the vessel is stolen, Jorn agrees to go along on Ulf's journey. During the days aboard the boat Jorn discovers that Ulf does not know the difference between right and wrong. Although Jorn knows he can leave at any time, he decides to stay because he believes Ulf needs him. During a land layover Ulf steals money, and when they believe they are being chased, the boys head out to sea. In a violent storm Ulf is drowned and the boat sinks. Jorn is rescued and reunited with his family. During the time between the rescue and the funeral Jorn reevaluates the meaning of his friendship with Ulf and his relationship with his parents. Through finding the good and bad in others, Jorn discovers the good and bad in himself. He rejoins society at Ulf's funeral, this time as an adult.

Sixteen-year-old Rob Dickson, in Sue Ellen Bridgers's *Permanent Connections,* is an immature sixteen-year-old who journeys from his suburban home to his father's boyhood home in the mountains of North Carolina. In this isolated environment where he is forced to stay while his parents travel in Europe Rob grows up. He moves from being an irresponsible youth who only cares about himself to a man who is willing to care for his elderly, eccentric relatives. The isolation of the mountains allows this transition to occur, and by the end of the novel Rob is ready to be welcomed by his family as an adult.

In *Travelers* by Larry Bograd, Jack is resentful of his father A.J. who was killed in Vietnam when Jack was four. He believes his father deserted him to fight in a pointless war. On the other hand, Jack's image of his father as a superman does not allow Jack his own identity. When Jack has the opportunity to travel to California to meet some of A.J.'s buddies, he learns a great deal about his father's identity but even more about himself.

Searching for Selfhood   Many young men do not know what to do with their lives after high school; they are still in the process of learning who they are so they find it impossible to think about what they should do for the rest of their lives. In *From Rockaway* by Jill Eisenstadt, Timmy and his buddies spend the summer as lifeguards on a Queens, New York, beach. During the winter, the lifeguards work odd jobs, drink, smoke dope, and date around, waiting for the glory days of summer to return. Timmy's life changes, however, when a riptide sweeps thirty people under and he loses a person he was trying to save. Afterward he is subjected to a horrifying ritual by the other lifeguards. Like Holden Caulfield in J. D. Salinger's *Catcher in the Rye,* Timmy uses language that is realistically raw and hard-hitting. Unlike Holden, Timmy is nudged toward adulthood by a tragedy. *Losing Joe's Place* by Gordon Korman is the story of three teens who move to the big city for the summer to work in a soap-bubble wand factory. They stay in the apartment of Jason's brother's Joe who gives them only one rule: "Don't lose my lease." On the first day at work computer wiz Don loses all of them their jobs by coming up with a more cost-effective way of making wands. Later, the stingy landlord of the apartment, who owns a deli, is hospitalized and the boys take over the deli. From this experience, they begin to grow in their sense of responsibility toward others.

Lorne in Kevin Major's *Thirty-Six Exposures* searches for himself in the fishing village of Marten in his native Newfoundland. Lorne and three of his classmates are putting together a class project based on his poetry and photographs. Without his intention, the project allows him to explore his past and the history of the people in his village. Each of the thirty-six chapters, like the thirty-six photographs, exposes some bit of knowledge about the past and provides a path toward the future. Lorne learns that photographs, like human perceptions, are two-dimensional and often frozen in time and space. The final photograph and chapter provide a tragic conclusion to Lorne's search. However, in his search he finds the truth that life is only revealed through life itself.

Careers   Manolo Olivar in *Shadow of a Bull* (Wojciechowska) is the son of Spain's greatest bullfighter. Although afraid of the bull, Manolo is expected to follow in his father's footsteps. He goes into training on his twelfth birthday. Manolo experiences great conflict between his fear of failure and his desire to fulfill his father's wishes. When he must fight his first bull, he is terrified, but, once he enters the ring he realizes he can be successful. He proves his courage to himself, his father, and the community, and this demonstration frees him to pursue his own dreams.

Not all young adult males want to follow in their father's footsteps. In Sandy Asher's *Everything Is Not Enough*, Michael is seventeen and seems to have everything including a guaranteed career in his parents' business. Against his father's wishes he takes a summer job working in a restaurant where he meets Linda, a determined waitress working two jobs so that she can pursue her goal to go into fashion design. Michael quickly learns that Linda wants to stay free of any emotional ties that might get in the way of her goal. At the same time Linda's friend Traci is being battered by her boyfriend Pete, and Michael is drawn into a conflict with brutal consequences. Through this experience Michael, Linda, and Michael's father learn a great deal about themselves and their relationships.

Like Michael, seventeen-year-old George Richards in *The Year of the Gopher*, by Phyllis Naylor, does not want to follow the Ivy League career path chosen by his attorney father. Rather than defy his father, he sabotages his college applications and interviews and is turned down by all except his hometown university. When George announces he will not attend college at all, a split occurs between father and son. After graduation George becomes a gofer in a garden shop and later works as a bicycle messenger. During this year George builds his self-confidence as he succeeds on the job and experiences fear when his best friend almost drowns. After a year of getting to know himself George decides to attend the local college and pursue a career as a guidance counselor. His father becomes reconciled to his son's choice.

In *Ask Me Tomorrow* by Betty Bates, fifteen-year-old Paige is not happy about the idea of being the third generation to manage the family apple orchard in Maine. He sees it as a life sentence to hard labor and little excitement compared to his dream of being a TV news correspondent. He agrees to work one more summer on the family farm when thirteen-year-old Abbey Winch, a talkative nuisance, arrives from Texas. Her unusually mature insights cause him to reexamine his relationships with his popular friends, his girlfriend, and his family. His dream of becoming a TV newsman fades as his life on the apple orchard comes into clearer focus.

Epilogue: Young Adult Books End at a Beginning

In a talk to the Assembly on Literature for Adolescents of the National Council of Teachers of English, author Joan Aiken said, "Helplessness is a basic ingredient of every child's life." Good literature written for and read by young adults can help readers overcome, or at least understand, the feeling of helplessness as they progress through the often difficult years between childhood and adulthood. Teachers, librarians, and parents should help young readers locate books that deal with the conflicts and difficulties that arise in the process of coming of age. According to Joan Aiken, one of the legitimate aims of literature for young people is to show the "tragic tension of life." In encountering this part of life through literature, the reader can better deal with the feeling of helplessness and better understand the tragedy that is part of the human condition. Author Richard Peck has noted that a characteristic of the young adult coming-of-age book is that it must "end at a beginning," so the young adult understands there is much of life to still be lived. The young adult book that ends at a beginning gives adolescent readers hope that they can survive life's tragic tension and move into adult life with confidence.

SUGGESTED READINGS

Agee, H. "Adolescent Initiation: A Thematic Study in the Secondary Schools." In *Literature for Adolescents*, ed. R. Mead and R. Small. Merrill, 1973.

Bloom, S., and Mercier, C. *Presenting Zibby Oneal.* Twayne Publishers, 1991.

Edwards, M. A. *The Fair Garden and the Swarm of Beasts: The Library and the Young Adult.* Hawthorn, 1974.

Endicott, A. Q. "Females Also Come of Age." *English Journal*, April 1992, pp. 42–47.

Aiken J. In *Something about the Author: Autobiography Series*, vol. 1, ed. A. Sarkissian. Gale Research, 1986, pp. 17–37.

Lyle, K. L. *News from ALAN*, March–April, 1975.

Mines, J. "Young Adult Literature: Female Heroes Do Not Exist." *ALAN Review.* Fall 1989, pp. 12–14.

Monseau, V. "Seventeenth Summer: A Modern Old-Fashioned Romance." *ALAN Review.* Spring 1988, pp. 5–6.

Moody, Anne. *Coming of Age in Mississippi.* Dial, 1968; Dell, 1980.

Peck, D. *Novels of Initiation: A Guidebook for Teaching Literature to Adolescents.* Teachers College Press, 1989.

Peck, R. "Some Thoughts on Adolescent Literature." *News from ALAN*, September–October, 1975, pp. 4–7.

Peck, R. N. "Robert Newton Peck: Soup's Best Pal. "In *Something About the Author: Autobiography Series*, vol. 1, ed. A Sarkissian. Gale Research, 1986, pp. 235–47.

VanderStaay, S. "Young Adult Literature: A Writer Strikes the Genre." *English Journal*, April 1992, pp. 48–52.

5 Across Time and Culture

Focus Questions

1. How does reading fiction about the past help make adolescents less egocentric?
2. How do historic and historical fiction differ, and how are they similar?
3. What are the characteristics of good historical and historic fiction for young adults?
4. Why is cultural diversity important in young adult fiction?
5. What are the characteristics of good multicultural books for adolescents?
6. Why is it important that young adult books provide readers with windows into other worlds and parallel cultures?

Prologue

> Clemente is not a quitter. He overcomes a lot of difficulties. He plays better than the other players on his baseball team. . . . Not a quitter . . . that's right. . . . I don't want to be a quitter either . . . no giving up during hard times.

Michael, fifteen, held up the biography of the baseball star Roberto Clemente as he talked in my literature-discussion group. The assertive nod, the determined tone, and the slight pounding of the fist gave me glimpses of Michael's affective response to the book. Shifting from Clemente's life to his own, Michael had been living through an empowering experience while reading the biography.

The evidence suggests that Michael has become empowered through his literary experience. What does this mean? He has increased his belief in his ability to act, often resulting in capable action. Or, as Leslie Ashcroft has defined it, he has received "nourishing belief in capacity and competence" (1987). How has literature helped Michael achieve this empowerment? Well, in the case of *Pride of Puerto Rico: The Life of Roberto Clemente* (Walker, 1988), the book has enabled him to inspect situations and to relate the [subject's] experiences and responses to his own.   ❖

From Belinda Y. Louie and Douglas H. Louie, "Empowerment through Young-Adult Literature," *English Journal,* April 1992, p. 53.

After middle school students from rural Carroll County, Maryland, read a Russian young adult novel *Shadows across the Sun* [by Albert Likhanov] in Rita Karr's English class, they examined their earlier journal entries where they had brainstormed about what they would anticipate daily life would be like in the U.S.S.R. Reflecting on what they would change in those entries, made before they read the novel, they made comments such as, "It doesn't seem as strict as I thought it was," or "I'd write now how they're similar to us." Sam's reflection captures what many students felt:

> I'd change the part about "I'd probably die" because reading the book, I see that it's not that hard to adjust to the Russian way of life, especially with friends like Fedya and Lena.

In fact, it probably would be hard for American young adults to adjust to such a different way of life; however, what their responses say is that they have a willingness to focus on the commonalities of the adolescent experience while examining, and perhaps even celebrating, the differences resulting from growing up in different environments.   ❖

From Lois Stover, "Exploring and Celebrating Cultural Diversity and Similarity through Young Adult Novels," *ALAN Review,* Spring 1991, p. 12.

Young Adult Books as Windows

In Chapter 3 we examined the young adult book as a mirror that reflects back to the egocentric adolescent reader his or her own life. Thus Sam, the middle school student in Ms. Karr's class from the anecdote above, saw the similarities in his life and the life of an adolescent in Russia. As Stover points out, his perceptions are only partially correct. However, it is because adolescents are so preoccupied with self that they are uniquely receptive to literature (Probst, 1988). They are drawn into the literature, sharing the plight of the protagonist, helping to make decisions along the way, and waiting, often impatiently, to learn the consequences. Through their empathy with the protagonist, they become a part of the story. Michael, in describing Roberto Clemente, exhibits his involvement in the story. He, like Clemente, refuses to be a quitter. As Louie and Louie point out, Michael is empowered by Clemente's story because he can see himself in it.

The personal involvement of students in a young adult book gives the teacher an important opportunity to help them see beyond themselves, to see not only the similarities between the lives of the characters in the book and their own lives, but the differences. As author Richard Peck suggests, students need to see books not only as mirrors of their images, but as windows into the world (1975, p. 5). Young adult books written about earlier times and about different cultures provide adolescents with this opportunity. I vividly remember Lee Hall, an undergraduate student in my adolescent literature class, announcing to the class after he had read Mildred Taylor's *Roll of Thunder, Hear My Cry,* "After reading it I felt less white." When I asked him what he meant, he replied that he could empathize with the characters. Although he was not African American and had never been in the characters' situations, he had had enough problems in his life to be able to put himself in their shoes. Lee, a more mature reader than Sam or Michael, recognized that by empathizing with the characters he could understand their actions. Additionally, he could learn more about life by viewing the book as a window into another world.

Historical and Historic Fiction

Even those of us who love the study of history can understand egocentric adolescents' frustration with reading about people and events that seem far removed from their lives. At the same time, we have read the results of tests such as the National Assessment of Educational Progress and shuddered at adolescents' lack of historical knowledge. According to a 1988 NAEP test (Educational Testing Service, 1990) only 0.1 percent of eighth graders and 4.6 percent of twelfth graders can interpret historical information and ideas. Even more horrifying, only 12.7 percent of eighth graders and 45.9 percent of twelfth graders can understand basic historical terms and relationships. Why do adolescents have so much difficulty learning history? It is certainly not because it is not emphasized in the curriculum; in fact, certain periods of history are taught at several grade levels. Christopher Collier, a historian who with his brother writes historical fiction for young adults, suggests that engaging historical narratives can hook kids on history:

There is no better way to teach history than to embrace potential learners and fling them into a living past. An historian must perform an act of creation that vivifies on paper scenes no longer replicable in concrete fact. An historian writing for young readers must become an active participant in the youngster's life, carry the youngster along as a participant in the historical narrative. Writer and reader must both feel part of the special history being told. (1987, p. 5)

One of the exciting aspects of young adult fiction is its ability to make history come to life for today's young readers. The heroes of young adult historical fiction have needs and interests that are similar to the readers'. Thus today's readers can identify with the young characters of bygone eras and begin to understand the world in which they lived. At the same time, historical fiction must be accurate and allow young readers to see how life differed from the present. Again, historian Christopher Collier:

To vivify the past in detail and ambiance requires first-hand familiarity with the records and artifacts of time and place; and the professional training to interpret these materials in ways that make sense to living people. When working with youngsters, a teacher of history must also be able to create a narrative floodtide that sweeps over the learners' ground and carries them along as a willing swimmer. The teacher must understand the universals of psychology, and must be able to use them as the human context for the attitudes and actions of the pasts to be created, and must use these understandings as a door to the learner's mind. . . . This is a very big order. Perhaps such a bundle of talents and skills is beyond the ability of one human to carry. (p. 5)

Collier suggests that teachers of history and writers of historical fiction for young adults can work together to engage students in learning about history. Writers can provide the well-documented, fun-to-read narratives, while teachers can put these stories into historical context. If students read historical fiction as well as history textbooks, their knowledge of history will be richer. Certainly, what we know about the psychological development of adolescents (see Chapters 1 and 2) should convince us that the use of historical fiction to teach history is likely to succeed.

There is a wide range of fiction with historical settings and characters. The more accurate a work's representation of people and events—the closer it is to nonfiction, or actual history. This type of fiction could be considered *historic* fiction. *Historical* fiction, on the other hand, has more fictional elements, an extreme case being a television minidrama about an actual event that is only minimally accurate. See Figure 5.1 for the characteristics of good historical fiction for young adults, and Figure 5.2 for the characteristics of good historic fiction. This chapter will primarily discuss historical fiction for young adults.

The period piece is a type of historical fiction that is not represented in Figure 5.1. The period piece brings to life a historical time period rather than a specific event or series of events. This type of literature presents an accurate picure of a certain time and place, but real historical figures are unlikely to appear in the period piece, except in the far background (they may be mentioned by a character to set the scene for the narrative). The main characters are not based on historic figures, although their behaviors are appropriate for the historical setting.

Figure 5.1
Characteristics of Good Historical
Fiction for Young Adults

Purpose
• bring history to life
• change reader's opinions

Character
Protagonist
• fictional
• realistic adolescent who could have lived during the period
• heroic; bigger than life
• has typical concerns and problems of adolescent
• accessible to the reader
Other Characters
• major characters are usually fictional
• minor characters may be real persons from history

Plot
• fictional character is placed in a real historic situation (war, political conflict, social unrest, etc.)
• sequence of events in which character is involved is historically possible
• sequence of events occurring in the novel is plausible
• actions of any real persons are accurate or plausible
• events may be romanticized to some extent

Point of View
• usually protagonist's
• sometimes multiple points of view are presented
• third-person point of view may be needed to relate historical events

Voice
• often protagonist's second self viewing the event in a reflective manner
• sometimes the author or narrator

Setting
• in the past
• historically accurate (e.g., could the character really get from point A to point B in one day?)

Theme
• patriotism, regionalism, heroism
• "War is evil"
• "You can!"

Many young adult novels fall in between historic and historical fiction. For example, Christopher Collier and James Lincoln Collier create characters that are fictional but based in historic fact. As Christopher Collier writes about their Newbery Award–winning novel *My Brother Sam Is Dead,* "The historical narrative is a fairly hard recreation of fact; the human relationships, though universally authentic, are fictitious." Teachers of history and English can help adolescents read these books critically by teaching them to recognize the differences between historic and historical fiction. Students who can place the narratives they read on the historic-historical continuum will be better able to judge the television minidramas they watch to

**Figure 5.2
Characteristics of Good Historic
Fiction for Young Adults**

Purpose
- reveal history
- reveal true character of historic figures

Characters

Protagonist
- adolescent
- often a real individual in history (e.g., young Abraham Lincoln)
- if not real, based on a real individual (documented in diaries, public documents, letters, etc.)
- heroic

Other Characters
- real individuals in history
- based on real individuals

Plot
- incorporates real events
- accurate in historical details
- allows the protagonist to develop
- reveals the history and personalities of the period

Point of View
- protagonist's
- third person

Voice
- usually the author's
- sometimes the protagonist's

Theme
- patriotism, regionalism, heroism
- "War is evil"
- "You can!"

determine whether the story is accurate or merely the scriptwriter's and producer's loose interpretation of the facts.

U.S. History in Fiction

Life in the Colonies

The story of an adolescent boy who survives the destruction of the Roanoke settlement is recounted in *Roanoke: A Novel of the Lost Colony* (Levitin). Jamestown during the time of Pocahontas is the setting for Scott O'Dell's *The Serpent Never Sleeps*. Readers enter the world of servants and masters in 1681 Boston in *Saturnalia* by Paul Fleischman. *Sarah Bishop* (O'Dell) is set in the pre–Revolutionary War period. *The Witch of Blackbird Pond* (Speare) is the story of Kit, a young islander from the Bahamas who is accused of witchcraft in Connecticut. A young settler is the heroine of *Constance: A Story of Early Plymouth* (Clapp). Esther Forbes' *A Mirror for Witches* tells of the New England witch hunts.

The Revolutionary Period

A classic young adult novel, *Johnny Tremain* by Esther Forbes, is about a young pre–Revolutionary War hero in Boston. *My Brother Sam Is Dead* (Collier and Collier) is the story of 12-year-old Timmy who is torn between the patriotism of his brother Sam who has run off to serve in the army and his father who is a loyalist. This book is one of a trilogy that attempts to "elucidate a set of ideas that underlay events of the Revolutionary Era" (Collier, 1987, p. 5) for young readers. All the books in this trilogy (which includes *The Bloody Country* and *The Winter Hero*) deal with the question of "war as a solution to human problems." *Bloody Country* follows pioneers from Connecticut to the Wyoming Valley of Pennsylvania in a dispute that the two states eventually go to war over, and *Winter Hero* is set in Massachusetts in 1787 during Shays's Rebellion. A second trilogy by the Collier brothers about the Arabus family relates the story of African Americans during the Revolution. In *Jump Ship to Freedom, War Comes to Willie Freeman,* and *Who Is Carrie?* the Colliers examine how the new Constitution affects African Americans. The period immediately following George Washington's crossing of the Delaware on Christmas Eve, 1776, is described from the perspective of fifteen-year-old Jemima Emerson in Ann Rinaldi's *Time Enough for Drums.*

Thirteen-year-old Jonathan in Avi's *The Fighting Ground* joins a small group of American militia in April 1778 against his father's wishes. He learns that good and evil are found on both sides, and even the hated Hessians are capable of compassion. This theme is explored from the Hessian perspective in *The Hessian* by Howard Fast, which tells of a drummer boy who is hidden by a Quaker family until he is discovered by the authorities. Another story about a young Hessian is Deborah H. DeFord's and Harry S. Stout's *An Enemy among Them.* Fast depicts a young hero of the Revolutionary War in *April Morning.*

The title character of Patricia Clapp's *I'm Deborah Sampson: A Soldier in the War of the Revolution* is a heroine who appeals to female readers. Rinaldi's *Ride into Morning: The Story of Tempe Wick* is another Revolutionary War story told from a female perspective. This story is based in the legend of Tempe Wick who hides her horse in the house overnight so the soldiers won't steal him.

After the Revolution

The period following the Revolutionary War is documented in Joan Anderson's *1787,* in which she tells the story of the Constitution through the eyes of the young nephew of Thomas Mifflin, an influential Philadelphian, who has apprenticed his nephew to James Madison. Rinaldi's *Wolf by the Ears* tells the story of teenager Harriet Hemings, daughter of the slave Sally and allegedly of Thomas Jefferson. In *The True Confessions of Charlotte Doyle* Avi tells the exciting story of a ship journey taken by thirteen-year-old Charlotte in 1832. *The Dunderhead War* (Baker) is a novel about a young man and his German immigrant uncle who travel on a wagon train from Missouri into Mexican territory and become involved in the early stages of the war with Mexico.

Robert Newton Peck's *Fawn,* set during the French and Indian Wars, is the story of Fawn, whose father is a French Jesuit and whose mother is an outcast Mohawk. A fourteen-year-old Shoshone girl, Sacagawea, along with the other members of her tribe, is captured by the Minnetarees in Scott O'Dell's *Streams to the River; River to the Sea*. The wars between white settlers and Native Americans have been the subject of several adolescent novels. *The Life and Death of Yellow Bird* (Forman) chronicles the life of a Native American seer from the battles of Little Bighorn to Wounded Knee. In *Save Queen of Sheba* (Moeri), two children are the only survivors of a Native American attack on a wagon train.

The Emerging Nation

Many young adult books incorporate important historical events of the nineteenth century. Life in the textile factories where many teens of the early 1840s worked is presented in Katherine Paterson's *Lyddie*. An unusual segment of U.S. history is presented in Joan Lowery Nixon's Orphan Train quartet. These four books (*A Family Apart, Caught in the Act, In the Face of Danger,* and *A Place to Belong*) tell the story of orphans from New York City who were sent out West to be adopted, not always for the best reasons.

Kathryn Lasky's *Beyond the Divide* is about fourteen-year-old Meribah who decides to accompany her father on the 1849 Gold Rush, leaving the Pennsylvania Amish community where she has been shunned for attending a non-Amish funeral. It is 1851 in the frontier town of Kanesville, Iowa, in Theodore Taylor's *Walking Up a Rainbow.* Orphaned Susan Carlisle, fourteen, has just inherited a house and 2,000 sheep. She sells the sheep to settle her father's debt and heads off to California. In Lloyd Alexander's *The El Dorado Adventure,* sixteen-year-old Vesper Holly travels with her guardian, Professor Brinton Garrett, to explore her property in El Dorado on the Central American isthmus.

The Bone Wars by Kathryn Lasky is an unusual novel set in the American West of the 1870s. The conflict is between paleontologists who want to dig up dinosaur bones and Native Americans and whites who want control of the land. Pam Conrad's *Prairie Songs* and *My Daniel* are set in Nebraska in the 1880s. The plots of both of these novels involve the finding of dinosaur bones. The westward movement of settlers is also described in *The Snowbird* (Calvert) and *Stout-Hearted Seven* (Frazier). The "Little House" books by Laura Ingalls Wilder depict the life of a family on the unsettled plains. *The People Therein* (Lee) is a love story that takes place in late-nineteenth-century Appalachia. The tale unites two unlikely lovers: Janthy, who is crippled and resigned to a life without marriage, and Drew, a botanist who comes from Boston to overcome his alcoholism.

Borderlands by Peter Carter and *Behave Yourself, Bethany Brant* by Patricia Beatty are two books set in turn-of-the-century Texas. *Borderlands* possesses many of the elements of the classic Western novel, such as buffalo hunts, outlaws, and cattle drives. However, Carter incorporates humor and a respect for the Native Americans' stewardship of the land. *Bethany Brant,* told from a female's perspective, is about ordinary settlers in Texas rather than the typical heroes of the old West. *Her Own Song* (Howard) is about Mellie who finds her heritage in Chinatown in turn-of-the-century Portland, Oregon. Another Howard book set in Oregon is *Edith, Herself.* Edith goes to live with her older sister Alena on a small farm. Wilson Rawls's *Summer of the Monkeys* is set in turn-of-the-century Oklahoma. This book for early adolescents is about a young boy who tries to catch a group of monkeys who have escaped from a circus. Also set in rural Oklahoma is Ouida Sebastyen's *Words by Heart*. In this book an African American family must deal with prejudice in rural Oklahoma during the 1890s. A little-known part of American history is examined in Hadley Irwin's *I Be Somebody*. This book is the story of Rap, a young African American boy, who along with the rest of his town of African Americans is transplanted from Clearview, Iowa, to Athabasca, Canada.

A book that is difficult to categorize is Paul Fleischman's *The Borning Room,* an unusual novel that interweaves issues of the Civil War, slavery, resistance to the draft, World War I, women's suffrage, emerging science and medicine, religion, and the rituals of birth and death. The plot is tied together by the setting of the borning room, which is set aside for births, serious illness, major family events, and deaths. Georgina Caroline Lott, a strong young woman who is greatly influenced by her beloved grandfather, is the protagonist of this novel which spans her youth and marriage. Another interesting historical novel by Fleischman is *Coming-and-Going Men: Four Tales*. Each story is about a traveling man whose interactions with the town of New Canaan, Vermont, in 1900 changes both the town and the visitor.

New York City in 1871 is the setting for Peter Burchard's *Digger: A Novel*. This book is about a newspaper boy who becomes a part of gang warfare while investigating arson. Kathleen Karr's *It Ain't Always Easy* is another book that takes place in New York City. In 1882 an eleven-year-old street urchin befriends a runaway girl fleeing from her home in New Hope, Pennsylvania.

The Civil War

The life of pre–Civil War Americans is examined by Julius Lester in three fascinating short stories in *This Strange New Feeling*. *Across Five Aprils* by Irene Hunt is about a family torn apart by the Civil War. In *Rifles for Watie* (Keith), a Union soldier is befriended by the rebel soldiers on whom he has been spying and sees the horrors of the war from the other side. *Eben Tyne, Powdermonkey,* by Patricia Beatty and Phillip Robbins, is the story of a young Southern boy whose difficult life as a teenager during the Civil War is well documented. The historic fiction novel *Gentle Annie: The True Story of a Civil War Nurse* by Mary Frances Shura is the story of Anna B. Etheridge, a nurse and sergeant. The period immediately following the Civil War is dealt with in Patricia Beatty's *Be Ever Hopeful, Hannalee*.

Slavery

In addition to the Collier brothers' Arabus family trilogy, a number of young adult books deal with the disturbing topic of slavery in the United States. In Joan Blos's Newbery Medal book, *A Gathering of Days: A New England Girl's Journal,* a girl helps a slave escape. Gabriel, a slave, leads a revolt on an 1800 Richmond plantation in *Black Thunder* (Bontemps).

In Joyce Hansen's *Which Way Freedom?,* Obie serves in a black Union regiment and fights at Fort Pillon, Tennessee, after escaping from slavery. Virginia Hamilton's *The House of Dies Drear* is a mystery about the Underground Railroad. *Amos Fortune, Free Man* (Yates), *Long Journey Home: Stories from Black History* (Lester) also deal with slavery.

The Early Twentieth Century

Several excellent young adult books deal with the period during World War I and the Depression. Books about young adults in World War I include *How Many Miles to Babylon?* (Johnson), *Johnny Got His Gun* (Trumbo), and *Company K* (March). Cynthia Voigt's *Tree by Leaf* is set in Maine in 1920. Twelve-year-old Clothilde's father returns from the war with a horribly disfigured face. He had gone to war thinking it a great adventure and now hides himself in the boathouse away from his family. Chester Aaron's *Lackawanna* is a mystery set during the Depression. The story is about abandoned children who form their own family and name it after the railway line on which they do their train-hopping. *Cave under the City* by Harry Mazer is set in New York City during the Depression. Tolley has to assume responsibility for his five-year-old brother while their father goes to Baltimore to seek work and their mother is hospitalized.

Three books by Mildred Taylor chronicle the life of an African American family, the Logans, in rural Mississippi from the 1930s through World War II. In *Roll of Thunder, Hear My Cry* Cassie Logan learns about bigotry and hatred as her family attempts to maintain their dignity and self-respect in the face of racial prejudice. In the sequel, *Let the Circle Be Unbroken,* the Logans are suffering economic hardship during the Depression. The family members, in spite of the frightening night riders and daytime harassment, find strength in each other. *The Road to Memphis* takes place during the first days of World War II. Stacey and Cassie are now teenagers with many teenage interests and problems. However, they are still battling with the prejudice of their time and region. Unexpectedly, a white boy helps their friend Moe escape a tense situation. This leads to a show of intolerance by the boy's father. Each of these books accurately depicts the lives of African Americans in the first half of the twentieth century in the South.

Immigration

Many young adult books deal with the problems of young people who have immigrated to the United States during different periods of its history. In the books discussed here immigrant teenagers are striving to become part of mainstream U.S. culture despite hardships and prejudice. (The concept of multiculturalism will be addressed later in this chapter.) Many immigrants' stories are told in biographies or autobiographies which will be discussed in Chapter 8.

Sonia Levitin's *Journey to America* is an excellent introduction to the subject of immigration because it chronicles a family's journey from Europe to the United States. The Platts, a Jewish family fleeing Nazi Germany, are separated during their escape and finally reunited in New York.

Most stories about immigrants to the United States chronicle the prejudice they experience. The heroes of Chaim Potok's *The Chosen* and *My Name Is Asher Lev* are boys who were born and raised as Hasidic Jews. A book depicting the internment of Japanese-Americans in the United States during World War II is *Farewell to Manzanar* (Houston and Houston). In this true story Jeanne Wakatuski Houston recalls the fears and frustrations she experienced living at the internment camp in California. *The Moved-Outers* (Means) is the tale of a Japanese family prior to and during their relocation.

Fifth Chinese Daughter (Wong) is a story about an American-born Chinese girl in San Francisco that describes her family, her education, and her budding career as an artist. *Dragonwings* by Laurence Yep tells of eleven-year-old Moon Shadow's experiences in San Francisco's Chinatown in the early twentieth century. Yep's *Star Fisher* is a fictionalization of the life of his own grandmother whose family was the first Chinese family to settle in Clarksburg, West Virginia, in the 1920s. *Year Walk* (Clark) is the story of a Basque sheepherder in Idaho in the early 1900s. In Linda Crew's *Children of the River,* Sundara is a refugee from the Khmer Rouge Army. Now seventeen, she struggles to adjust to life in Oregon. Growing up as an Irish Catholic boy in Pittsburgh in the 1930s is the theme of *Duffy's Rocks* (Fenton). Ganesh in *Ganesh* by Malcolm J. Bosse is uprooted from his home in India to live in rural midwestern America. The book shows the struggles between Western and Eastern cultures and philosophies. In *Viva Chicano* (Bonham), Joaquin "Keeny" Duran struggles to rise above the problems of the Mexican-American ghetto in which he lives. Life as a Mexican-American girl is dealt with in *Go Up the Road* (Lampman). The human side of illegal Mexican immigration is shown in Ted Conover's *Coyotes.* The novel is episodic, telling the story of several undocumented workers who are struggling for a better life.

The Morning of the Gods by Edward Fenton is a different sort of immigration novel, set in the 1970s. Carla Lewis at age thirteen is sent to Greece from New York after her mother's death. She lives with her Great-Aunt Tiggie and Uncle Theo and adopts her Greek name Ersi. She quickly becomes involved with her new culture and country and even protests against the dictatorship of the junta of colonels who rule Greece.

World War II

Because the war was not fought on the U.S. continent, many young adult books about this time are period pieces about life in the states during the war. *Summer of My German Soldier* (Greene) is about a German prisoner of war and a young Jewish girl. *The War at Home* by Connie Jordan Green is about twelve-year-old Maggie McDowell whose father has taken a job at Oak Ridge, Tennessee, where much of the reserach on the nuclear bomb was conducted. *Bethie* by Ann Rabinowitz is about being a Jewish girl in New York City during the war. *Other Bells for Us to Ring* by Robert Cormier shows the anxiety of Darcy and her mother when they receive word that Darcy's father is missing in action. Some young adult books deal with Americans fighting in battles. Harry Mazer's *The Last Mission* is about a young boy who lies about his age so he can enlist in the air force. When all his buddies die during a mission, he learns that war is not so glorious.

Recent Wars

Walter Dean Myers' *Fallen Angels* is an excellent book about the Vietnam War. Richie Perry is seventeen in 1967 and is on his way to Vietnam. He is sure the war is over and that his bad knee will keep him out of combat. He sees the army as his ticket to college to fulfill his dream of becoming a writer like James Baldwin. On the flight over he meets Peewee Gates. The two remain side by side in combat and stand up to racists they encounter within the army. Other good books for adolescents that deal with the

Vietnam War include *#1 Echo Company Welcome to Vietnam* by Zack Emerson, about Michael Jennings's first two weeks in Vietnam in Echo Company at Chu Lai, the area closest to the DMZ. Emerson continues the story of Michael Jennings and Echo Company in *Echo Company #2 Hill* and *Echo Company #3 'Tis the Season*. Another excellent, mature book about Vietnam is *If I Die in a Combat Zone, Box Me Up and Ship Me Home* by Tim O'Brien. O'Brien's book chronicles an entire tour of duty in Vietnam from boot camp in the summer of 1968 until he returns to Minnesota.

Other books do not deal directly with the Vietnam War but with its effects on the survivors. Written in 1988, *December Stillness* by Mary Downing Hahn is about Kelly, a teenage girl trying to make sense out of the effect the Vietnam War had on the men of her father's generation. In *Pocket Change* by Kathryn Jenson, published in 1989, Josie, who has a close relationship with her father, is suddenly faced with his having flashbacks about his time in Vietnam. Despite Josie's attempt to help him and get help for him, he barricades himself in the house with his son, Josie's half brother, and shoots at the neighborhood. Another book about the effects of war deals with the Persian Gulf War. *The War Began at Supper: Letters to Miss Loria* by Patricia Reilly Giff is a book for younger adolescents. Miss Loria is a student teacher to whom the youngsters write. They talk of many of the events of early adolescence, but most poignantly discuss their concerns about one student's father who is serving in the Persian Gulf.

Standing Tall, Looking Good by Gloria Miklowitz is not about war, but it is about being in the army. Two young men and a young woman have enlisted in the army. The book is about their basic training and the relationships they form during it.

European History in Fiction

Prehistory and Early History

Jean Auel has written a series of books about a Cro-Magnon girl and woman. The first, *The Clan of the Cave Bear,* and the only one that is suited to young adults, is the story of the girl's childhood after being adopted by a Neanderthal tribe. Although this book is only loosely historical fiction, since there is no written history on which to base it, it is an interesting anthropological account of a strong female character who grows up in a male-dominated society. In Elizabeth Speare's *The Bronze Bow,* the hero, who lives in the time of Jesus, is obsessed with hatred for the Romans and a desire for revenge until he meets the rabbi Jesus.

European History Through the Nineteenth Century

Rosemary Sutcliff is one of the most highly regarded British authors of historical fiction for young adults. *The Eagle of the Ninth* takes place in A.D. 125 in Roman Britain as Marcus sets out to trace the lost Ninth Hispana Legion. *The Shining Company* is narrated by Prosper, a young shield bearer in King Mynyddog's company. This book, about Roman Britain in A.D. 600, is based on an obscure poem, "The Gododdin." The King gathers together 300 men, each with two shield bearers, to train into a fighting brotherhood to protect Scotland against the invading Saxons. Prosper tells how he came to join the company, forming friendships that transcend class, and how the company showed honor and bravery in the face of almost sure defeat. The book reveals the horror of battles which seem so noble at the start but end in death and destruction.

> The last charge of the Companions had become an ugly swirling soup of fire and mist and moonlight and snarling faces, the cries of men and the screams of stricken horses, the smell of blood and filth.

Sutcliff sets another novel in England in A.D 700. A young Englishman in *Blood Feud* is sold into slavery to the Vikings. He travels through the Baltic Sea, down Russian rivers, and finally to Constantinople. Two other novels set in Roman Britain by Sutcliff are *The Silver Branch* and *The Lantern Bearers*. Sutcliff's other books—*The Capricorn Bracelet, The Mark of the Horse Lord, Warrior Scarlet, Song for a Dark Queen, Knight's Fee, Simon,* and *Rider on a White Horse*—are historical novels set in England from the days of Roman occupation to the English Civil War and Cromwell. Fans of the romantic heroes of Arthurian legend will particularly enjoy Sutcliff's *Sword at Sunset*. Also set in the sixth century is a novel about ancient Greece: In *The Dancing Bear* (Dickinson), a young Greek slave and his dancing bear journey with an old holy man to rescue Lady Ariadne.

Many other young adult books are set in Great Britain. Gunnar, the young hero of Nathaniel Benchley's *Beyond the Mists,* is the sole survivor of a Viking raid on Britain. Gunnar meets Leif Ericson, who takes him on his next journey. *The Maude Reed Tale* (Lofts) is set in fifteenth-century Britain. Maude's problem is that she doesn't want to learn to be a lady; instead, she wants to manage the family's wool business.

Leon Garfield's books are set in eighteenth-century England. The young hero of *Jack Holborn* searches for his home. A second novel, *The Sound of Coaches,* is in the tradition of Henry Fielding's *History of Tom Jones.* It tells the story of Sam, who is taken home and cared for by passengers on a coach who witness the death of his mother in childbirth. Part of the book talks of his early years and his desire to become a coachman. The next two parts of the narrative describe his journey to London, his apprenticeship, and his search for his father.

1066 is one of the most famous dates in history. In Norha Loft's *Madselin,* Madselin is left a widow at age seventeen following the Norman invasion of Anglo-Saxon England. She marries one of the conquering Normans.

During the eleventh century in Meghan Collins's *Maiden Crown,* sixteen-year-old Sophie leaves Russia to marry King Valdemar of Denmark. Sophie is a strong female protagonist who struggles to keep intact her independence and sense of values.

Captives by Malcolm Bosse presents a picture of medieval Europe as seen through the eyes of sixteen-year-old Anne Valens. The book begins with the brutal murder of Anne's parents by marauding soldiers, an event which she and her younger brother Niklas witness. Forced to flee, they travel in search of their uncle, whom they have never met, and a new home. Another, less gruesome story of medieval Europe is Geraldine McCaughrean's *A Little Lower Than the Angels.* Young Gabriel, fleeing from the unscrupulous stonemason to whom he is apprenticed, is rescued by Garvey, a playmaster, after being forced to hide in the "Mouth of Hell," a prop from the mystery play he has just witnessed. He begins to travel with the players from one medieval village to another and innocently associates key members of the group with the characters in the pageant; Garvey becomes God, and Lucier, a French actor, is Lucifer. Gabriel begins to perform miracles during the plays and reaps the profit from his sham.

E. L. Konigsburg sets *A Proud Taste for Scarlet and Miniver* in twelfth-century England and France. The novel is based on the interesting life of Eleanor of Aquitaine. Wife of two kings and mother of two others, she set the tone of court life by sponsoring poets and promoting the legend of King Arthur.

Italy in the thirteenth century is the setting for Scott O'Dell's *The Road to Damietta*. Ricci di Montanaro and Francis Bernardone are both children of prosperous merchants. Ricci falls in love with Francis, known for his outrageous antics. One day Francis becomes pious and begins to dress in robes and sandals. At first Ricci thinks she can change him back to the Francis he was. Her parents forbid her to see him and send her away. However, she escapes and eventually she and Francis go on the Fifth Crusade to Damietta on the Nile River. Also set in the thirteenth century, *Quest for a Maid* by Frances Mary Hendry is about Meg, the daughter of a Scottish shipbuilder, who is sent to accompany the Maid of Norway on her journey to marry Edward, King of England. Robert de Brus, claimant to the Scottish throne, enlists powerful allies to stop the marriage which will unite Britain and cost him his power. In the spring of 1349, Anne, in Ann Turner's *The Way Home,* is accused of being a witch, causing Lord Thomas' death, and bringing on the great plague. The young hero in *The Trumpeter of Krakow* (Kelly) lives in Poland in the 1400s. Barbara Dana's *Young Joan* examines the life of Joan of Arc before she goes to save the dauphin. In this book Joan is an adolescent who dreams of marriage and plays and gossips with her friends. She lives in a sheltered family but sees angels and saints who guide her activities.

Fifteenth-century Italy is the setting for E. L. Konigsburg's *The Second Mrs. Giaconda*. This book, based on true events, attempts to answer questions behind Leonardo da Vinci's painting the Mona Lisa. The late fifteenth and early sixteenth centuries provide the setting for Scott O'Dell's fascinating novel *The Hawk That Dare Not Hunt by Day,* which is based on the story of William Tyndale, the translator of the Bible into English. The young narrator of the story and his uncle attempt to smuggle Tyndale's Bible out of England.

Robert Westall, also an excellent author of British historical fiction for young adults, sets *The Cats of Seroster* in sixteenth-century France. This historical fantasy is about Cam, a young Englishman who is bored at the university and travels the continent as a jack-of-all-trades. Through a series of unlikely events, involving a knife with a will of its own and cats who try to establish their rightful ruler on his throne, Cam is forced into the role of hero, the Seroster.

Erik Christian Haugaard is another critically acclaimed author of young adult historical fiction. In *A Messenger for Parliament,* Oliver Cutter, born in 1630 and named for Oliver Cromwell, reminisces as an old man about the uprising of protestants and Parliament, the new rights of common people, and the beheading of King Charles. In *Cromwell's Boy* King Charles has turned England into a battlefield and thirteen-year-old Cutter acts as Cromwell's trusted messenger and spy.

The year is 1666 in Jill Paton Walsh's *A Parcel of Patterns*. The village of Eyam in Derbyshire is struck by the Plague. Mall Percival, the narrator, says she hopes that by recording the events of the Plague she will rid her life of its terrors. We learn of the effects of the disease on her, her family, and the town. *The Ship for Simnel Street* by Jenny Overton is set in England in the early 1800s. The story focuses on the Olivers, the master baker's family. Polly, the baker's daughter, falls in love and runs away to war in Portugal with her beloved. Mr. Oliver goes to find Polly, but Mrs. Oliver concocts a scheme involving twelve hundred bride-cakes to be shipped to the Regiment to get Polly home.

An interesting picture of seventeenth-century Vienna can be found in Claudia Von Canon's *The Moonclock*. This book is based on the true story of Barbara Schretter who lived only one year after marrying Jacob. A fictional set of letters provides the narrative for the novel.

Two books about Ross Poldark by Winston Graham, *Ross Poldark: A Novel of Cornwall, 1783–1787* and *Demelza: A Novel of Cornwall, 1788–1790,* provide an interesting perspective on the American Revolution. Ross has just returned home to Cornwall in 1783 after having fought against the American rebels. He finds many changes at home, including the engagement of his fiancee to his cousin. These novels were made into a PBS television series.

Victorian Great Britain is the setting for several good historical novels for young adults. *The Tiger in the Well* by Philip Pullman is one of a series of historical mysteries set in Victorian London. The heroine of this book, *The Ruby in the Smoke,* and *The Shadow in the North* is Sally Lockhart who must protect herself and her daughter from Ah Ling and the opium trade. Gillian Avery's *The Elephant War* is a humorous look at Victorian England. This story, first published in 1960, is based on the 1800s sale of Jumbo, a London Zoo elephant, to the American P. T. Barnum for his circus. *The Throttlepenny Murder* by Roger J. Green is the story of thirteen-year-old Jessie Smith who is in prison awaiting trial for the murder of her miserly employer. The Chartist labor movement in the Yorkshire pottery factories is the context for Constance Heaven's romance novel *The Wildcliffe Bird*. In Scott O'Dell's *The 290,* the year is 1862 in Liverpool, England, where the 290, a new sloop of war, is being built for the Confederate navy.

East Prussia and the post–Civil War American South of the 1860s provide the settings for Willi Fahrmann's *The Long Journey of Lukas B.* This first young adult novel of a prominent German author received the German Children's Book Prize. Unlike most young adult novels, the book has almost fifty characters, of whom a dozen play major roles. The novel follows the two-year journey of Lukas Bienmann, who is fourteen at the start of the book, in search of his father who left the family, defaulting on a loan. The story takes Lukas from Liebenberg, a village in turbulent East Prussia, to America via a sea voyage in the Neptune of Danzig. Although Lukas and his father never meet, Lukas comes to understand his father's need to develop his talent in painting.

The World Wars in Europe

World War I England is the time period of *Then the Zeppelins Came* by Dorothy Horgan. Prewar Edwardian life is depicted in a realistic manner. Emily and Lizzie are best friends, even though Emily's mother disapproves of Lizzie's lower class. Emily, like most children, is oblivious to the dangers of the imminent war with Germany until German families in their neighborhood are vandalized by German-baiting thugs. The early stages of the war are even more threatening when the munitions factory in which her mother works is attacked by zeppelins. In *Khaki Wings* by Milton Dank, Edward is not quite seventeen when Britain declares war on Germany in 1914. He becomes part of the Royal Flying Corps and is sent to France as a mechanic and observer. After he becomes a fighter pilot, each flight is a nightmare.

Rudolf Frank's novel *No Hero for the Kaiser,* first published in 1931, poignantly portrays the effects of World War I on Jan Kabitzky, a fourteen-year-old Polish villager. Jan and his dog Flox become part of the invading German battery after their village is devastated.

The years prior to World War II in Europe are chronicled in several good young adult books. Edith Baer's *A Frost in the Night* is set in 1932 in Germany when Hitler is gaining power. Eva Bentheim is a Jewish girl moving from an idyllic childhood into adolescence as Germany is changing. The turbulent days ahead are foreshadowed throughout the book. *The Other Way Round* by Judith Kerr is the story of Anna and her family who are early refugees from Nazi Germany in 1932.

In *Shadow of the Wall* by Christa Laird, thirteen-year-old Misha, a Polish Jew, and his two younger sisters live in the Orphans' Home in the Warsaw ghetto because their widowed mother is too ill and poor to care for them. They smuggle food to their mother and are inspired by Mr. Doctor, a physician who devotes his life to Jewish children. Misha joins the Nazi resistance and literally goes underground, traveling through the sewage canals, as an anti-Nazi liaison worker.

The horrifying story of Ruth Minsky Sender's *The Cage* follows a sixteen-year-old Jewish girl from Lodz ghetto to Auschwitz and finally to a work camp. *I Am Rosemarie* by Marietta D. Moskin also details the horrors of the concentration camps. A Russian Jewish teenage boy is the protagonist in Ephraim Sevela's *We Were Not Like Other People.*

In *Lisa's War* by Carol Matas, Lisa finds her life drastically changed when the German army invades Denmark in 1940. Lisa and her family work hard in the anti-Nazi resistance, and by the end of the novel Lisa must commit a dangerous and painful act to help warn her people.

Young people in Europe fight for their survival and the survival of others in *Chase Me, Catch Nobody!* (Haugaard), *The Upstairs Room* (Reiss), *Bright Candles: A Novel of the Danish Resistance* (Benchley), *A Ceremony of Innocence* (Forman), *A Bag of Marbles* (Joffo), and *Forever Nineteen* (Baklanov). Among the numerous good books about young people in the Holocaust are Uri Orlev's *The Man from the Other Side* and Renée Roth-Hano's *Touch Wood: A Girlhood in Occupied France.* In Orlev's book, Marek is a teenager in Nazi-occupied Warsaw who crawls through the sewers to help his stepfather smuggle food to Jews trapped in the ghetto and to help people escape from the ghetto to save them from "resettlement" in the Nazi death camp at Treblinka. In her historic fiction novel, Roth-Hano tells the story of Renée and her family who flee from their home in Alsace to Paris only to watch their Jewish neighbors taken away by German soldiers.

The fifteen-year-old hero of Brian Garfield's exciting tale *The Paladin* is a personal secret agent of Winston Churchill. He is involved in murder, assassination, and sabotage on both sides of World War II front lines. *Fathom Five* by Robert Westall is about sixteen-year-old Chas who flushes out a German spy in 1943 England. Chas is also the protagonist-narrator of Westall's Carnegie Medal winner *The Machine Gunners,* set in Garmouth, England, in 1940 and 1941. Another Westall novel *Blitzcat* uses a cat narrator to tell about World War II England.

Historical Fiction from Other Countries

Central or South America is the setting for a number of good young adult historical novels. Louise Moeri's *The Forty-Third War* is about a civil war in a Central American country where boys between the ages of twelve and fifteen are abducted by revolutionaries to serve in the army. *The Honorable Prison* by Lyll Becerra de Jenkins is set in South America. Marta's father is a journalist who is arrested with his wife and children. The family is held hostage in a house near an army barracks in the mountains. *My Name Is Not Angelica* by Scott O'Dell is about the West Indian Slave Rebellion of 1733. Raisha, a daughter of a subchief, is promised in marriage to Konje, the Barato king's son. Deceived by a rival king, they are captured by slave traders, and sent on a horrifying journey to the Danish Caribbean island of St. John where they are sold as slaves. Raisha's work on the van Prok plantation is demeaning, and her owners change her name to Angelica.

Canada in 1945 is the setting of Brian Doyle's *Angel Square.* This award-winning book takes place in the multiethnic, multireligious, working-class neighborhood of Ottawa's Lowertown. Tommy, the protagonist and narrator, enlists the help of his friend to discover who injured the father of a Jewish schoolmate. *A Nugget of Gold* by Maureen Pople is set in the Australian gold rush of the 1870s. Sally Matthews, a modern teen, and Ann Bird Shipton, a teen of the gold rush era, tell their love stories in alternating chapters.

Asian historical heroes are found in several young adult books. *Young Fu of the Upper Yangtze* (Lewis) is a young hero of early-twentieth-century China. Heroes from Japan appear in two young adult books by Katherine Paterson. Twelfth-century Japan is the setting for *Of Nightingales That Weep.* During the Keike-Genji civil wars, Takiko, the daughter of a famous samurai killed in the wars, becomes the personal servant of a musician. In *The Master Puppeteer,* Jiro is the son of a starving puppetmaker in eighteenth-century Japan. He runs away from home and becomes an apprentice to the master of the Nanza puppet theater. Sixteenth-century Japan is the setting for Erik Haugaard's *The Samurai's Tale,* the story of Marakamu, son of a Samurai knight, who is orphaned and captured by enemies of his father.

Cultural Diversity

Adolescents tend to select books with characters who are much like themselves. They also want the characters and the situations in these books to mirror their lives not as they are but as they would like them to be. The egocentrism of adolescence makes introducing young adults to cultures and ideas different from their own very difficult. Education, however, is the process of learning about new things. If adolescents do not learn about cultural differences, they are likely to have difficulty living in an increasingly diverse society. Mop, one of the characters in Walter Dean Myers's *Mop,*

Moondance, and the Nagasaki Knights, sums up what recognizing cultural diversity means. Talking to one of the baseball players on her team about playing teams from France, Japan, and Mexico, she says, "Intercultural means that you figure out how somebody's different and let them know that you know it and don't mind too much" (p. 89).

The task of the teacher is to introduce students to various cultures so they can come to understand that differences between cultures do not matter nearly as much as our shared humanity. Doing this is not an easy task. Young adult novels that deal with a variety of cultures can help adolescent readers relate to different characters and situations. (Fiction books that deal with a variety of cultures may be called multicultural, cross-cultural, or parallel-culture. The three terms are used interchangeably in this chapter.) Through such books adolescent readers can develop relationships with fictional young adults from parallel cultures which may then be transferable to real life.

Another reason it is essential to introduce adolescents to books depicting young people in a variety of cultures is so that all readers have a chance to read about people from their own culture. For generations, students in Amerian schools have read books populated by white, Eurocentric protagonists. Patricia Ann Romero and Dan Zancanella in an article "Expanding the Circle: Hispanic Voices in American Literature" suggest that the school bias toward majority literature still exists:

> The new Prentice-Hall American literature textbook, *The American Experience* (1989), is imposing. . . . Weighing in at what must be almost fifteen pounds, its sheer size holds the promise that its covers enclose the whole of literary America. The advertisements for the series tell us that "3,000 teachers nationwide acclaim what is at the heart of the program—our remarkable collection of literature." Yet only twelve of the 1,399 pages in the text (less than 1%) are devoted to works by writers with Hispanic surnames (the nature writer Barry Holstun Lopez and the Filipino poet Jose Garcia Villa), and not a single page is devoted to literature about Hispanic experience in the United States. The contents of American-literature anthologies offered by Scribner's, Scott-Foresman, and other well-known publishers include little more. (1990, p. 24)

Young readers need to be able to identify with the characters and situations in the books they read. Perhaps part of the reason African American, Native American, and Hispanic students have scored lower on standardized reading tests than white students is that they have encountered primarily books with white protagonists and have read much Eurocentric history. (NAEP reading tests results from 1971 through 1990 indicate that African Americans and Hispanics score significantly lower on reading tests than whites.) Studies on reading development, such as those done by Margaret Early in 1960 (see Chapter 1), imply that if young readers do not read books with which they can identify they are unlikely to progress beyond the egocentric stage of reading development and become mature readers.

We cannot expect minority students to be successful readers if we do not provide them with reading experiences that speak to their lives. Bear in mind that in nearly half of the largest cities in the United States minority students are now in the majority, and that most projections indicate that by the year 2000 minority enrollments will be anywhere from 35 percent to 50 percent of the total school enrollment nationwide. Nor can we expect all students to understand cultures different from their own unless we provide them with accessible books about characters who differ from them and at the same time share common fears and goals. See Figure 5.3 for a list of the characteristics of good multicultural books for young adults.

Figure 5.3
Characteristics of Good
Multicultural Books for Young
Adults

Purpose
• developing cultural awareness
• developing self-esteem
• coming to terms with differences between cultures

Character
Protagonist
• adolescent
• realistic
• a part of the culture in which he or she lives
• often more mature than age of character indicates
• develops self-esteem as a member of his or her culture
• may struggle with his or her differences but learns to rejoice in them
• growth within own culture
Antagonist
• usually from the majority culture
• sometimes the system or the government
Other Characters
• peers within the culture; frequently undeveloped
• an adult mentor within the culture; usually not a parent

Plot
• often more complex than typical young adult novel
• frequently deals with confrontation between cultures (protagonist vs. antagonist; protagonist vs. reader)
• the character learns about him- or herself within the culture
• increased awareness of the culture

Point of View
• protagonist's
• often written in first person

Voice
• protagonist's
• sometimes second self; more mature protagonist
• sometimes the mentor's voice is evident
• never preachy or dogmatic

Setting
• accurately portrays culture
• often presents clashing cultures (minority vs. majority; parents' vs. adolescent's)

Theme
• heroism
• combatting prejudice and discrimination
• individual against society
• ''You can!''

African Americans

Virginia Hamilton, a successful author of young adult books with African American protagonists, speaks of the difficulty involved in having complex parallel-culture books published:

> Our young adult literature tends to remove from the young adults, themselves. The slim presence of parallel culture literature would give the impression that such large parallel cultures have no presence and do not exist in America. I wrote *A Little Love, Sweet Whispers* [*Sweet Whispers, Brother Rush*] and *A White Romance* with the concept of voiceless, somewhat hopeless young adults, who never have enough words, money, love. Before they are out of their teens they seem beaten, dispirited, characterized by unease.
>
> Will the young people about whom my triptych books are written ever read them? Are these young adults capable of reading books; do they have the mental ease to concentrate long enough; do they care to read?
>
> Most of the time, I avoid such questions. What I must remember is that if there is a young adult somewhere who wishes to extend his/her comprehension of life and lifestyles, who wants to find something between the covers of a book that reflects his or her personal struggles, dreams, or even to find a new sort of entertainment, than these three books will be there for the reading. (1987, p. 3)

Authors of young adult books with African American protagonists have had difficulty finding publishers for their books because publishers like to publish books that can be sold in large numbers. Also, many people in publishing, like Virginia Hamilton, fear that young African Americans do not choose to read, and others maintain that schools and libraries rarely buy books with African American protagonists. This, of course, creates a problem for teachers wishing to introduce their students, both African American and non-African American, to such books. Despite such obstacles, the number of outstanding African American authors of young adult books is growing, and many titles can be recommended.

A wealth of books explore the world of the young African American male. In *The Second Stone* (Brown), fifteen-year-old Henry Wilson is struggling between loyalty to his family and acceptance by his friends. In *Cornbread, Earl, and Me* (Fair), Earl and Wilford witness the murder of their hero, Cornbread, by a policeman. The two boys eventually come to understand the circumstances that allow the African American community to accept the political corruption that resulted in Cornbread's death.

The masterfully written books of Virginia Hamilton are about young African Americans in a variety of environments. Examples include *M. C. Higgins, the Great; The Planet of Junior Brown; The House of Dies Drear; The Mystery of Drear House; Zeely; Justice and Her Brothers; A Little Love; Sweet Whispers, Brother Rush; A White Romance; Junius Over Far; The Magical Adventure of Pretty Pearl;* and *Arilla Sun Down.* The plots, themes, and genres are varied, but the literary style is always of highest quality. Virginia Hamilton writes of adolescents who experience the universal problems of all adolescents and, in addition, must deal with the difficulties of living in a parallel culture.

Four books by Rosa Guy—*The Friends, Ruby, The Disappearance,* and *Edith Jackson*—and many of Walter Dean Myers's books—*Crystal; Mojo and the Russians; Motown and Didi: A Love Story; Scorpions; Hoops; The Young Landlords; The Mouse Rap; Fast Sam, Cool Clyde, and Stuff; Me, Mop, and the Moondance Kid;* and *Mop,*

Moondance, and the Nagasaki Knights—examine city life. Others focus on rural life. *Roll of Thunder, Hear My Cry; Let the Circle Be Unbroken; The Road to Memphis,* and *Song of the Trees,* all by Mildred Taylor, take place in rural Mississippi. Ouida Sebestyen writes about a rural African American family in the Southwest in *Words by Heart* and *On Fire.* Other excellent young adult novels about African American protagonists in rural settings include *Marked by Fire* by Joyce Carol Thomas, *M. C. Higgins, the Great* by Virginia Hamilton, and *Sounder* by William Armstrong.

—————————— ❖ **Between the Covers:** *Authors at Work* ❖ ——————————

ROSA GUY: THE INFLUENCE OF HER EARLY YEARS

Rosa Guy, author of multicultural books for young adults, was born in Trinidad, Jamaica, the third child of Henry and Audrey Cuthbert. Her early years on the island were idyllic; she enjoyed the security and warmth of her family as well as the land's natural beauty. Exposure to her culture's oral tradition made Rosa Guy a storyteller before she was even seven.

Rosa's parents had emigrated from Trinidad to New York City to find work just after World War I. The immigrants were initially welcomed and work was plentiful. Leaving their children behind with relatives seemed a small price to pay for the promise of work and prosperity. As the immigrant ranks swelled, they became a political force in the industrialized cities. In the 1920s, when the Cuthberts arrived in Harlem, they found a large, self-contained community of African Americans in which African American institutions and cultures flourished. West Indian immigrants in Harlem, often found themselves doubly isolated, from the larger white community and, because of their language and culture, from African Americans as well. However, according to Jerrie Norris, a biographer of Rosa Guy, "the pressure-cooker effect of this crowded mixture of African American life-styles also produced the magic of the Harlem Renaissance and a spirit of African American nationalism that has had an enduring effect upon African Americans. Those of West Indian heritage were especially active in African American cultural, political, and entrepreneurial activities" (1988, pp. 4–5). Marcus Garvey, a Jamaican leader who is sometimes called the "black Moses", became a leader in this African American urban community, and later had an important influence on young Rosa Guy.

In 1932 Rosa and her sister Ameze joined their parents in New York City. By the time the girls arrived in New York, the Renaissance that had made Harlem internationally famous had been replaced by the hard economic times and deteriorating social conditions of the depression. Harlem for the girls was the opposite of Trinidad—cold, large, and unfriendly.

In 1933 the girls lived with a Garveyite cousin while their mother was ill. Here Rosa was first exposed to Garvey's nationalistic philosophy. From this short period with her cousin, according to biographer Norris, Rosa gained a knowledge of Africa, an awareness of languages, and a firm educational background. After her mother's death in 1934, the sisters returned to the Harlem home of their capitalist father whose dreams of African American enterprise were dashed by the depression. When he died in 1937 the orphan girls were forced to grow up quickly. In 1939 Rosa left school to work in the garment district, in 1941 she married Warner Guy, and in 1942 she bore a son, Warner. By the age of sixteen, Rosa was both a wife and a mother. These beginnings made an impact on Rosa Guy, the writer. Her cross-cultural experiences, her knowledge and love of language, her desire to learn and grow, her political beliefs, and her involvement with some of the greatest African American artists of the era are all evident in her novels for young adults.

For example, in *The Friends,* one of her most critically acclaimed works, Guy brings together two cultures in two characters. Fourteen-year-old Phylissia represents Guy's early years in the West Indies; she is loved, well cared for, intelligent, and proud. Edith, who eventually becomes her friend, is from Harlem; she is poor, outspoken, shabby, and nearly parentless. Phylissia is shunned in Harlem by poor African Americans like Edith who resent her prim and proper upbringing, her education, and her West Indian accent. The well-to-do children of Harlem's professionals also dislike her; they think she talks funny. Through Phylissia we become aware of some of the cultural prejudice Guy experienced when she moved to Harlem as a child.

The world of Jamaica and the world of Harlem begin to come together for Phylissia when Edith, Harlem's scruffiest girl, befriends her. At first Phylissia rejects Edith's overtures of friendship, but she realizes she needs Edith to protect her from their hooligan classmates. Edith shows Phylissia *her* New York—including how to shoplift and take "free" subway rides; while Phylissia, embarrassed to take Edith home and include her in her life, shares only her stories. The bond between the friends, however, grows stronger over the summer as Phylissia begins to take on Edith's ways. In addition to their antics, the girls share their many problems, fears, and hardships; Phylissia tells of her mother's illness and Edith tells of her father's departure from town. Edith becomes Phylissia's wonderful secret.

When she shares the secret with her family, the friendship falls apart. Phylissia finally takes Edith home and humiliates her in front of her parents. This incident, the loss of the friendship and the loss of her connection to Harlem, marks the beginning of a long period of unhappiness for Phylissia. She loses Edith's friendship, her mother dies, and her relationship with her father becomes more distant. She is again a part of neither culture.

Phylissia grows through these losses. She eventually recognizes the false image she portrayed, her insecurities, and her cruelty. Defying her father, she goes in search of Edith and finds her grieving over the death of her baby sister and facing life in an orphanage. Now Phylissia truly commits herself to her friend. At the end of the novel, she acknowledges the importance of her new friendship as she confronts her father. She makes an impassioned plea to be allowed to stay in Harlem rather than be sent back to Jamaica. Phylissia has become a West Indian American forging, along with her friendship, a life in the African American culture of Harlem. ❖

Biographical information from Jerrie Norris, *Presenting Rosa Guy* (Twayne Publishers, 1988).

Many books about African American adolescents deal with developing relationships. In Joyce Carol Thomas's *The Golden Pasture,* Carlton has an African American father and a Cherokee mother. He spends the summer on his grandfather's ranch, and the book is about the relationship between the boy and his grandfather. Walter Dean Myers's *Fallen Angels* is about the relationship between soldiers during the Vietnam War, and *Somewhere in the Darkness* (Myers) is about a father-son relationship. Romantic relationships are dealt with in *My Love, My Love; or, The Peasant Girl* by Rosa Guy, *A White Romance* by Virginia Hamilton, and *Motown and Didi: A Love Story* by Walter Dean Myers.

There are also many fine mysteries with African American protagonists, such as Virginia Hamilton's *The House of Dies Drear* and *The Mystery of Drear House.* Joyce Carol Thomas's *Journey* is an excellent murder mystery about a girl named Nutmeg (Meggie) who uses her ability to communicate with tarantula spiders to scare some young people to death. Walter Dean Myers has written several humorous mysteries including *Mojo and the Russians, The Young Landlords,* and *The Mouse Rap.* Some African American protagonists solve personal mysteries, as they search for their family origins. Two examples are Eleanora Tate's *The Secret of Gumbo Grove* and *Water Girl* by Joyce Carol Thomas.

The history of African Americans in this country is chronicled in many books for young adults. Mildred Taylor's books follow the difficult life of one African American family in the Southwest. Hadley Irwin's *I Be Somebody* explains how a town of African American people came to be relocated to Athabasca, Canada. Harper Lee's *To Kill a Mockingbird* tells what happens in a small Alabama town when a African American man is tried for allegedly raping a white woman. Ernest J. Gaines presents the long hard life of one African American woman from immediately after the Civil War to the 1960s in *The Autobiography of Miss Jane Pittman*. In *A Gathering of Old Men* Gaines describes the history of African Americans in the South through the events of a single day. In two books of stories *Long Journey Home* and *This Strange New Feeling* Julius Lester illustrates the life of African Americans during the antebellum period.

Most of the books mentioned thus far show young adult African Americans dealing with prejudice to different degrees. Several other books that explicitly address prejudice are worth mentioning. In *Freedom Songs* by Yvette Moore the year is 1963 when fourteen-year-old Sheryl experiences segregation firsthand. Sheryl decides to support Uncle Pete and the Freedom Riders through a fund-raising church concert. Mildred Pitts Walker's *Because We Are* is about how a young girl's dreams are dashed after a confrontation with a white teacher. In *Blue Tights* by Rita Williams-Garcia, Joyce is rejected from her high school ballet group and finds acceptance in an African dance group. In *Iggie's House* by Judy Blume, Iggie is from the only African American family on the block. The vehicle for the plot of *The War between the Classes* by Gloria D. Miklowitz is the "Color Game," a four-week experiment to demonstrate the damage done by stereotyping in a California high school with Asian, African American, Hispanic, and Anglo students. *Choice of Straws* (Braithwaite) is about a white boy who has hated African Americans all his life and falls in love with an African American girl, and *In a Bluebird's Eye* (Kornfeld), set in the 1930s South, examines the secret friendship between a white girl and an African American woman. *Jazz Country* by Nat Hentoff also deals with African American teens facing prejudice.

Other notable authors of young adult books with African American protagonists include:

- *A Hero Ain't Nothin' but a Sandwich; Rainbow Jordan* (Alice Childress)
- *The Soul Brothers and Sister Lou* (Kristin Hunter)
- *His Own Where* (June Jordan)
- *Listen for the Fig Tree; Teacup Full of Roses* (Sharon Bell Mathis)
- *Ludell; Ludell and Willie; Ludell's New York Time* (Brenda Wilkinson)

Hispanics

Books about Hispanic protagonists are not numerous, but among those books are many good books for young adults. In Gary Paulsen's *The Crossing,* Manuel Bustos is a fourteen-year-old orphan in a Mexican border town. Manny imagines calling himself Pancho, after the Mexican hero Pancho Villa, but he chooses the name of a boxer instead. Manny would rather be a fighter than a revolutionary. Like other orphans, Manny sleeps on the street and eats what little food he can buy with the coins tossed to him by American tourists as they cross the bridge from El Paso, Texas, to Juarez, Mexico.

One night Manny attempts to cross the border and is able to flee the searchlights of the U.S. border patrol. In an alley he meets Sergeant Robert S. Locke, who regularly visits a bar in Juarez. Robert decides not to turn Manny over to the border patrol even though Manny has attempted to steal the sergeant's wallet. Manny does not understand why anyone would do this and decides to seek out the sergeant. Through their first and other chance meetings Manny and the sargeant's lives become bound together. The novel has an exciting climax. In Paulsen's novel *Sentries* Manny becomes David Garcia after fleeing north across the border with the help of Sergeant Locke. At fourteen David goes to work in the beet fields of Nebraska. He believes that now that he is in the United States things will go right. At first he is puffed with pride as he hitchhikes across the vast Southwest and quickly finds work in the beet fields, but when one of his fellow workers gives birth to a baby in the fields, he begins to feel anger about the unfairness of life.

. . . *And Now Miguel* by Joseph Krumgold and *Bless Me, Ultima* by Rudolfo Anaya are about a young character's relationship with an adult. Miguel wants to travel into the mountains with his older brothers and father on the annual sheep migration. Ultima, who is a *curadera,* or healer, is seven-year-old Antonio's grandmother. *Bless Me, Ultima,* a novel for mature young adults, depicts a powerful relationship that transcends even death. A picture of the Los Angeles barrio is painted in Frank Bonham's *Viva, Chicano.* Joaquin (Keeny) Duran wants to continue the *la raza* (pride in his Mexican heritage) that his father gave him as a child. He searches for a better life in spite of his difficult homelife, the pressures of gang membership, and unfair juvenile authorities. Inspired by the Mexican revolutionary figure Emiliano Zapata, Keeny learns to face up to his problems. Gary Soto's *Taking Sides* is about fouteen-year-old Lincoln Mendoza, an aspiring basketball player in a suburban California high school. Lincoln's problems come from a misunderstanding with his best friend, a bad knee, and a coach who is prejudiced against Mexicans.

Several books with Hispanic characters and settings have Anglo protagonists. In Richard Bradford's *Red Sky at Morning,* Josh meets many memorable Hispanics when he moves to northern New Mexico during World War II. The book is about clashing cultures and beliefs. On his first day of school in New Mexico, Josh is told by one of his classmates, "We only recognize three kinds of people in Sagrado: Anglos, Indians, and Natives." Josh asks, What about the Negro? "I already explained that to you. He's an Anglo. That is, he's an Anglo unless you're differentiating between him and an Indian. Then he's white. I admit he's awfully dark to be white but that's the way it goes around here. . . . If there's a minority group at all around here, it's the Anglos." P. J. Petersen has written two books with Hispanic characters. In *Corky and the Brothers Cool,* Alfredo shows Tim, the protagonist, the truth about his new friend Corky; he is a bigot. In *Would You Settle for Improbable?* Michael Parker writes in his journal that he admires Salvadore Sanchez who is the eldest of eight children and can speak both English and Spanish. In contrast he calls himself a typical, normal "blah."

In *The Spanish Smile* by Scott O'Dell, the father of Lucinda de Cabrillo y Benivides tries to hide her from twentieth century life on an island off the coast of California. Her father has great contempt for Anglos, telling Lucinda, "Five million Hispanics know little of their heritage. But they grow angry at being people of the second class—*de clase sequnda*—looked down upon by the Anglos, underpaid, preyed upon by the unscrupulous, galled that their children attend schools where they are taught in gringo words the children do not understand." In the sequel *The Castle in the Sea,* Lucinda unravels the mystery of the plans her father had for her life and lives on the island as an heiress and its ruler.

O'Dell's major contribution to literature about Hispanics is historical fiction that depicts the rich heritage of Spanish Americans. The Mayan civilization figures in three books—*The Captive, The Feathered Serpent,* and *The Amethyst Ring*—that feature the hero Julian Escobar, a young, idealistic, Jesuit seminarian in sixteenth-century Mexico. In *The King's Fifth,* we journey with Coronado and a Captain Mendoza through the uncharted territory of Cibola in New Spain. This tale is told by fifteen-year-old mapmaker Esteban Sandoval. *The Black Pearl* is another O'Dell novel set in Mexico. In this novel Ramon Salazar grows up in a small Mexican village in Baja, California, and finds the "Pearl of Heaven." O'Dell's *Carlota* takes place during the Mexican-American War in California in 1846. Carlota's father is not concerned whether Spain or the United States wins the war. He only wants his family's land to be left undisturbed, and over this Carlota and her father go to battle. By the end of the novel, however, Carlota learns that neither she nor her values are necessarily an extension of her father and his beliefs.

Two other young adult books present more recent views of Hispanic culture. In Lyll Becerra de Jenkins's *The Honorable Prison,* Marta Maldonada becomes a political prisoner in a South American country in the 1950s. In *Among the Volcanoes* by Omar S. Castaneda, Isabel, the oldest daughter in the family, has responsibility for her three siblings in a poverty-ridden household in Guatemala. The people of her country lack education, are poor, and have been forced into "acceptable molds." However, Isabel wants to be a teacher. The clash between her dreams and her real life and between two cultures becomes clear as Alan, a young American, attempts to help Isabel's mother with her medical problems.

Native Americans

In recent years an excellent body of young adult literature with Native American protagonists has been published. These books celebrate the history, culture, and language of Native Americans. They also portray the struggle between the native cultures and white culture and the hardships faced by those living on reservations today.

The history of Native Americans is dramatized in a number of books. Soaring Hawk is a seventeen-year-old pre-Columbian Cherokee hero in *Long Man's Song* by Joyce Rockwood. *Creek Mary's Blood* (Brown) is the epic story of a Native American and her descendants. *To Spoil the Sun* (Rockwood) describes a girl growing up in a Native American tribe when the first white settlers arrive. In *Waterless Mountain* (Armer) a young Navaho boy who wants to become a medicine man must learn about his culture to achieve his goal. Hidden Poe in *We Are Mesquakie; We Are One* (Irwin) grows to maturity among the Mesquakie. *Sing Down the Moon* (O'Dell) describes the Navajos' forced march from Canyon de Chelly to Fort Sumner in 1864. In Hal Borland's *When the Legends Die*, Thomas Black Bull is embittered by the white man's deceit. He punishes the rodeo horse he rides until a crushing accident sends him back to his boyhood mountain home. Jamake Highwater tells the story of Sitko, a young first

American who searches for his identity as a descendent of Blood, Cherokee, and French Canadians in the book *I Wear the Morning Star.* The book is volume three of a trilogy known as "The ghost horse cycle," which also includes *Legend Days* and *The Ceremony of Innocence.* The series follows the life of Amana and her family from 1800 to the present, providing a realistic glimpse into Native American culture and revealing sharp images of the white culture from the perspective of a Native American author. Another book by Highwater, *Eyes of Darkness*, depicts the life of Charles Alexander Eastman, a Santee Native American physician practicing on the South Dakota reservation during the Wounded Knee massacre.

Several books are about white children who learn the ways of Native Americans by living with them. In *Ghost Fox* (Houston) sixteen-year-old Sarah is kidnapped by the Abnakis. She gradually adopts their ways and must choose between being a Native American or returning to her original culture. In Conrad Richter's classic *Light in the Forest,* True Son, a white boy, is captured and raised by the Delawares but is later forced to return to his white family, who no longer loves or understands him. In *A Country of Strangers* (Richter) Mary Stanton is kidnapped as a very young child and raised as a "Stone Girl." She is young enough that she forgets her white heritage and in her mind becomes a Native American. She marries, has a son, and is happy until she is forcibly returned to her natural parents and the white culture.

Many novels about Native American characters, including Borland's *When the Legends Die* and the two Richter novels just mentioned, show the conflicting cultural values of Native Americans and whites. *A Girl Named Wendy* by Beverly Butler is about fifteen-year-old Wendy who is taken from her reservation to Milwaukee to live with her aunt and uncle. Here she is caught between her relatives, some of whom attempt to deny their heritage and others who are openly militant Native Americans. In Virginia Hamilton's *Arilla Sun Down*, twelve-year-old Arilla perceives herself as a throwback; she doesn't look like her African American mother or her part-African American, part-Native American father. In *Jemmy* (Massler) a half-Native American boy grows up in Minnesota. In N. Scott Momaday's *House Made of Dawn,* Abel returns to his reservation after World War II and doesn't fit in any more. He kills a white man in a drunken brawl, is sentenced to prison in a public court, and relocates to Los Angeles after his release. In Will Hobbs's *Bearstone,* Cloyd becomes rebellious when he is forced to abandon his family and his Ute traditions to attend high school and must live with a lonely old rancher in Colorado. Annette, a mixed-blood Nootka in Victoria, British Columbia, is forced to choose between two separate and conflicting cultures in *A Woman of Her Tribe* by Margaret A. Robinson.

In *The Night the White Deer Died* Gary Paulsen tells the love story of Janet Carson, a white teenager, and Bill Honcho, an old, alcoholic Pueblo Native American. Janet first sees Billy in a dream, as a young man poised on the edge of a pool, taking aim at a white deer drinking in the moonlight. Through Janet's caring for the older, drunken Billy, readers can see the man he might have become.

Blood Red Ochre by Kevin Major is the story of fifteen-year-old David and Nancy, a new girl in David's class, who work on a high school research project about the Beothuk, an extinct Newfoundland tribe. Each chapter about David alternates with a chapter about Davoodaset, one of the last of the Beothuk tribe. Using a similar approach, Gary Paulsen in *Canyons* brings together two fourteen-year-old boys separated by more than one hundred years and two distinct cultures. In alternating chapters Paulsen tells their coming-of-age stories until only one of the boys, who knows he must act for both of them, is left.

A. E. Connon's *The Shadow Brothers* is about modern Native Americans and their need to recognize and learn about their cultural identity before they can be assimilated in white society. In the novel Henry Yazzie, a Navaho, is sent by his father to live with a white middle-class family. The story is told by his adoptive brother. When another Native American enters Henry's high school and refuses to accept its Anglo cultural values, Henry realizes that he feels estranged from both the white and Native American cultures. *The Owl's Song* by Coeur'd Alene tribe member Janet Campbell Hale is about Billy White Hawk who in the early 1970s must deal with the shockingly violent suicide of his cousin just returned from Vietnam. The novel focuses on death, not only the death of his cousin but of his father, and, perhaps, the whole Indian way of life. Another contemporary novel deals with Eskimo culture and the exciting Iditarod, the 1,179-mile dogsled race from Anchorage to Nome. In *Black Star, Bright Dawn* by Scott O'Dell, when Bright Dawn's father nearly dies on an ice floe that drifts away from shore, the family moves inland to Ikuma, a checkpoint on the Iditarod. Bright Dawn enters the race with her wolf-dog Black Star.

Young Eskimos are protagonists in several other young adult novels. In *The White Dawn: An Eskimo Saga* (Houston) a band of Eskimos discovers three survivors of a boat wreck and restores them to health. An Eskimo family in *Back to the Top of the World* (Ruesch) finds the ways of the white man strange but amusing. *A Hunter Comes Home* (Turner) is the story of an Eskimo boy. The heroine of *Julie of the Wolves* (George) is an Eskimo teenager torn between two cultures. She runs away from her young, mentally retarded husband and goes to her father's home. Her father has accepted white culture, which she rejects, but she soon learns that she cannot return to the culture of the Tundra.

Asian Americans

Numerous young adult books examine the lives of Asian American young people. Laurence Yep is well known for his historical and contemporary fiction about Asian Americans in California. All of Yep's book explore the Chinese American culture from the nineteenth century to the present. *Child of the Owl*, *The Serpent's Children*, and *Mountain Light* all examine the lives of children growing up among Chinese immigrants in America. Casey in *Child of the Owl* lives most of her life nomadically with her gambling father. When her father is badly injured in a fight, she is passed from one relative to another and finally stays with Paw Paw, her grandmother, in Chinatown. Cassia in *The Serpent's Children* tells of life in nineteenth-century China and later in the United States. *Mountain Light* is set in China and California in 1855. In China Squeaky, who thinks he is a coward and plays the comic, uses his cowardice as a weapon against the ruling Manchus. He falls in love with Cassia, helps her cope with the death of her father and the persecution of their companion Tiny, and travels with Tiny to America. In America, land of the "Golden Mountain," Squeaky finds that the feuds continue in the California goldfields. Migration from China to America is also explored by Yep in *Dragonwings*.

Contemporary stories about young Asian Americans include *More Than Meets the Eye* by Jeanne Betancourt, the story of Liz Gaynor and Ben Lee who are competing for the top standing in their Vermont high school class. *Kim/Kimi* by Hadley Irwin is about Kimi Yogushi who looks back at Kim Andrews when she looks in the mirror. Kim feels American but looks Japanese. Jean Davies Okimoto's *Molly by Any Other Name* is a similar story about a young Asian American who knows nothing about her birth mother or about her ethnic origins. In *China Boy* by Gus Lee, Kai Ting must survive the bullies on the streets of San Francisco. Two other books about growing up as an Asian American are *No-No Boy* (Okada), about growing up Japanese in America, and *It's Crazy to Stay Chinese in Minnesota* (Telemaque).

Regionalism

Recently in young adult fiction, as in adult fiction, books dealing with specific regions of the country have become popular. The region most commonly written about in young adult fiction is the South. Although many of the well-known authors of such books, including Sue Ellen Bridgers, claim that they do not write "southern fiction," their books provide different views of a region of the country that has frequently been stereotyped in literature. According to Robert Small, in the past young adult fiction set in the South tended to portray the region in one of three ways: readers encountered the romantic South in such novels as *Gone with the Wind;* the poverty-ridden South of the redneck sheriff, moonshine, and wrecked cars; or the literary South of such authors as William Faulkner. Although, according to Small, some young adult novels did deal with a South beyond these stereotypes, these tended to deal with the racial prejudice of southern towns. "More recently, however, a number of young adult novels have been set in the South and Southern Appalachia. In fact, there seems to be a renewed interest by young adult authors in the people and customs of the American South. Unlike the superficial, sentimental novels of the '40s and '50s, many recent young adult novels set in the South deal in profound ways with the Southern people, their culture and problems" (Small, 1986, pp. 62–63).

Probably the best-known and most highly regarded author of young adult books about the South is Sue Ellen Bridgers. Born and raised, and having lived most of her life, in rural North Carolina from the Piedmont to the Appalachian Mountains, Bridgers sets all of her novels in this region. Like the characters in the works of Carson McCullers, Flannery O'Connor, and William Faulkner, her books are populated with people who seem to come from the soil of the rural South. Her first novel, *Home before Dark,* is about Stella, the daughter of migrant workers, who seeks to find herself by settling down on the family's homeplace. Sue Ellen Bridgers speaks of the importance of the land and the homeplace in her life and in her writing:

> A house, especially an old house, a homeplace, owns us as much as we own it, maybe more so. Bleached boards hold memories. Crackled china catches light and holds it. Photographs on the mantel reflect our own faces. The timber of the house also provides the timbre — it creaks and squawks under foot, swells its window sashes and door jambs in summer, relaxes its hold in winter to let the cold in. The rafters make music, too, holding the roof steady in the wind. A summer storm blows up. Rain pellets the tin roof, a clattering music, and in the hallway downstairs, the bowl of crepe myrtle branches trembles as thunder

spreads the sky open and a streak of lightening, like the one that killed Mae Willis [in *Home Before Dark*], makes a hot, jagged path to ground.

Everything comes back to the earth. And so near every homeplace there must be a cemetery, set in a cornfield so that in summer it is invisible—the earth is breaking open to give out life, not to receive it—but in the winter, the narrow crosses and shallow etched stones stand above the frozen plowed-up fields, a reminder of pneumonia, killing colds, long nights of waiting through chills and fevers, the helpless biding of time.

And so Mae Willis, a migrant mother unable to accept a stationary life—a woman who had never had a homeplace or a sense of self—a powerless, disconnected woman—was laid to rest in the place from which she most wanted to flee. Her daughter Stella understood that because she knew the difference between them. Everything her mother rejected, Stella wanted and so she stayed in the tenant house, her own little homeplace set beside the real one, refusing to give up what belonged to her. The experience of ownership was new, a symbol of all the possibilities of her life. (Bridgers, 1985, p. 47)

Sue Ellen Bridgers understands the importance of land, homeplace, and ownership to the people of the rural South, the people whose ancestors fought and died in the War between the States. Brought up on the land and in the small towns of the South, she says of herself, "The blood tie to place and family is still intact. . . . Because I feel this attachment keenly I write about life in families" (Bridgers, 1986, p. 54). In some of her books it is hard to know whether the land is a character or is a part of the setting. Perhaps it is both, because to Sue Ellen Bridgers land and people cannot be separated. All of Bridgers's protagonists are seeking home, family, and ownership. Casey in *All Together Now* is seeking family; Kevin and Wren in *Notes for Another Life* are searching for home and love; Sara Will in *Sara Will* attempts to find her roots in a graveyard in the middle of the lake; and Rob in *Permanent Connections* at first rebels against his ancestral home and finally embraces it.

Other writers have written notable books about the rural South for young adults. Robbie Branscum writes of the land and the people of the Ozark Mountains of Arkansas in books such as *Johnny May, Cheater and Flitter Dick* and *The Girl.* Wilson Rawls's *Where the Red Fern Grows* is also about the Ozarks. Southern poet Jim Wayne Miller tells a coming-of-age story about a boy in the mountains of Tennessee in *Newfound.* Another story set in these mountains is Mildred Lee's *The People Therein.* Vera and Bill Cleaver examine the hardships of mountain life in *Where the Lilies Bloom* and *Trial Valley.*

Global Multiculturalism

Students need to extend their understanding of other cultures to countries around the world. Lack of intercultural understanding has been an underlying cause of wars and ecnomic conflicts between nations as well as diplomatic and personal errors. The following books can help young adults become more aware of other kinds of people who share their planet.

The Blanket Word (Arundel) is the story of a young woman who comes home from the University of Edinburgh to Wales to be at her dying mother's side. Another timeless story about life in Wales is Richard Llewellyn's *How Green Was My Valley,* a family chronicle that highlights the effects of coal mining on the people and the land.

Australia is the setting for the novel *The Min-Min* (Clark) in which young Sylvia finds life in the outback devastating. The family problems depicted in this modern adolescent novel make it an interesting companion to the popular adult novel *The Thorn Birds* (McCullough). *Eleanor, Elizabeth* by Libby Gleeson and Noreen Shelley's *Family at the Lookout* are two interesting stories about family life in contemporary Australia. Probably the two best-known Australian writers of young adult fiction in the United States are Ivan Southall and Patricia Wrigthson. Southall's books, such as the award-winning *Josh,* are about growing up in Australia between the two world wars. Wrightson's books deal with Aborigine culture. Her books, like many books about Native Americans in the United States, show the conflict between native and mainstream cultures. *The Ice Is Coming* and *A Little Fear* are both about the Aborigine culture in Australia today.

Canada is the setting for *Mrs. Mike* (Freedman and Freedman). Mrs. Mike is a sixteen-year-old Bostonian who marries a member of the Royal Canadian Mounted Police. The rugged life of the Canadian North causes many hardships and heartbreaks for the young heroine. Kevin Major's books depict life in contemporary Newfoundland. In all of his books *(Hold Fast, Far From Shore,* and *Thirty-Six Exposures)* adolescents struggle toward adulthood in the remote villages of this rugged island.

Fourteen-year-old Lesley in *One More River* (Banks) leaves her comfortable life in Canada to live in Israel. Her experiences there can be contrasted to life on a kibbutz as described in *Elsewhere, Perhaps* (Oz). *My Enemy, My Brother* (Forman) chronicles the early days of the Israeli state from the viewpoint of a Jewish boy who has just been released from a Nazi concentration camp. The power of this novel comes from the protagonist's relationship with a young Arab. Sonia Levitin's *The Return* is about a black Ethiopian Jewish girl who leaves her mountain homeland with her brother and younger sister to fulfill her dream of going to the promised land called Israel.

Rafik Schami's *A Hand Full of Stars* is about a fourteen-year-old boy growing up in Damascus under a repressive, authoritarian regime. Written in diary form, this translated book gives a vivid picture of life in an Arab country. Although not set in the Middle East, Suzanne Staples's *Shabanu: Daughter of the Wind* helps young readers understand life in a Muslim country through the eyes of a Pakistani girl.

Two excellent books about modern China, focusing on the Thammasart University idealistic movement and the Tiananmen uprising, respectively, are *Rice without Rain* by Minfong Ho and *Forbidden City: A Novel of Modern China* by William Bell. Modern-day Belfast is the setting for *Across the Barricades* (Lingard), in which a protestant girl and Catholic boy fall in love despite family opposition. *Don't Cry for Me* (Jarunkova) is a problem novel in which a Czech teenager attempts to find a place among her peers and revolts against adult values. *A Matter of Feeling* (Boissard) is a family-oriented love story set in France. The book centers on Pauline's first real romance, with an artist nearly twice her age.

Religion

Most young adults have little if any knowledge of religions different from their own. One way to introduce young adults to differences in religious beliefs, customs, and traditions and help them develop insight and tolerance is by reading young adult books with characters from a variety of religious cultures.

Christianity is an influence in many well-written books for young adult readers. Madeleine L'Engle, for example, ties Christian theology into many of her stories. Although only a few of her books deal directly with Christian themes, most of them include the symbols of her faith. In *A Wind in the Door,* for example, the Christian concept of naming is a central aspect of the book. The title of *A Ring of Endless Light* alludes to the concept of immortality. C. S. Lewis, a well-known theologian as well as author of books for young readers, uses Christian symbolism throughout his Narnia books, including *The Lion, the Witch and the Wardrobe; Prince Caspian;* and *The Magician's Nephew.* Walter Wangerin, author of *The Book of the Dun Cow,* is a Lutheran minister who incorporates theology into this book about talking animals. Entering the Christian religion is the subject of Robert Benard's *A Catholic Education.* Nick Manion is a student in a male-dominated parochial school. He also has an assertive father. Although accepted at Harvard, Nick decides to become a Jesuit priest and attend seminary. During his first year in seminary his world collapses as he questions his religion and has a homosexual encounter. This story recounts Nick's enlightenment and spiritual quest.

In recent years evangelical Christian religions and cults have been explored in young adult fiction. Robin Brancato's *Blinded by the Light* explores a teenager's search for self within a religious cult. *What I Really Think of You* by M. E. Kerr is about Opal Ringer, the daughter of a minister, and Bud Pegler, son of a successful television evangelist. Stephanie S. Tolan's *A Good Courage* is about fifteen-year-old Ty Rainey who has followed his mother from one commune to the next. They become a part of the Kingdom of Yahweh, a religious organization under the charismatic influence of Brother Daniel. The cult requires them to do hard manual labor seven days a week, eat meager meals, take cold showers, and be punished for infractions of rules. Ty commits the unpardonable; he teaches young children to read and tells them fantasy stories. In *No Way Home* by Marilyn Levy, Billy Goldman's mother, in a fit of despair, joins a religious cult after she and her husband separate. When Billy goes to see his mother, he becomes trapped within the cult. The book is about his attempt to escape from both the mother he loves and the cult.

Judaism plays a part in a number of young adult books. Yuri Suhl's *The Merrymaker* is based on the customs and folklore of Eastern European Jews, for example. Much of the literature of the Holocaust contains significant references to Jewish tradition. Books such as *The Upstairs Room* (Reiss), *A Bag of Marbles* (Joffo), and *The Devil in Vienna* (Orgel) tell of Jewish young people who strengthen their religious conviction as they attempt to survive the Holocaust. Orthodox Jewish traditions are dealt with in two books by Chaim Potok, *The Chosen* and *My Name Is Asher Lev,* about young American Jewish boys attempting to mesh their cultural heritage with life in the United States. A female perspective on Judaism is provided in Potok's *Davita's Harp.* How modern girls deal with their roles as Jewish women is dealt with in Susan Beth Pfeffer's *Turning Thirteen* and Merrill Joan Gerber's *Handsome As Anything.*

Judao-Christian history is brought to life in *The Eyes of the Blind* by Alison Morgan. Benjamin, the twelve-year-old grandson of the prophet Isaiah, escapes from the doomed city of Lachish just before it falls to the Assyrian army of Sennacherib.

Pamela F. Service's *Reluctant God* has as its theme the universality of religious thought. The daughter of an Egyptologist finds the repository for the "essence of life," a substance intended to guarantee the immortality of Egyptian souls.

Hermann Hesse's *Siddhartha* is the story of a soul-searcher who meets the Buddha. In an attempt to find the ultimate good, he abandons his friends and family, rejecting their values, and travels to the city to learn the true life he should lead.

Prejudice against religious groups is the topic of several young adult books. In *Chernowitz!* by Fran Arrick, Bobby Cherno tries to ignore the anti-Semitic remarks and personal attacks of the class bully, but when anti-Semitism spreads he and his parents must fight back. A protestant in a camp for Jewish children experiences prejudice in *The Summer Ends Too Soon* (Grossman).

Social Issues

Large numbers of young adult books address social issues. Many have been discussed on previous pages, and some additional titles are worth mentioning here. Fran Arrick frequently places her protagonists in situations in which they must confront difficult issues. In *God's Radar* Roxie has just moved from New York to a southern town dominated by the Baptist church. Roxie's new friends are the outcasts of the school; one is accused of destroying the radio tower that transmits the sermons of a television evangelist, while another spouts Bible verses at every chance. Roxie complains to her older sister, "Everybody pushes me in a different direction all the time!" *Nice Girl from Good Home* is about Dory Hewitt whose father is fired from an advertising agency and can't find another job because he is overqualified. *Where'd You Get the Gun, Billy?* is about a high school senior who intentionally shoots his girlfriend with a handgun. *Steffie Can't Come Out to Play* is about a fourteen year old who runs away and eventually becomes a prostitute.

Avi has also written numerous novels about social issues. In *Nothing But the Truth: A Documentary Novel* Philip wants to run on the high school track team but is unwilling to accept the coaches' advice, "Sometimes you have to go along to get along." In this novel apparently unimportant incidents mount into major problems. Philip thinks his English teacher Miss Narwin has no sense of humor. He sees his opinion confirmed by the C− he gets on a wisecracking analysis of Jack London's *Call of the Wild* which he thinks is boring. In Miss Narwin's homeroom he hums "The Star-Spangled Banner," disregarding a school rule requiring students to stand in respectful, silent attention during the playing of the national anthem. For this he is sent to the principal's office and eventually suspended. His father is appalled that his son has been suspended for "patriotism" and mentions this to Ted Griffin, a neighbor running for the schoolboard who is in search of a platform. Mr. Griffin repeats the story to a newspaper reporter, and it is picked up by the national news. Avi sides neither with Philip nor Miss Narwin, who is a disgruntled and easily annoyed person but also well-liked and respected by many students. In the end Philip transfers to another school and Miss Narwin is suspended. Avi makes it clear that no one wins when a conflict is allowed to escalate.

Larry Bograd writes interesting political novels for young adults. *The Kolokol Papers,* a love story that takes place in 1984, is about sixteen-year-old Lev Kolokol, son of a human rights activist in the Soviet Union, and Tanya Yakir, whose parents are involved with the Kolokols. *Los Alamos Light* is about sixteen-year-old Maggie Chilton who leaves Boston in 1943 with her physicist father who has been invited to work with Robert Oppenheimer at the atomic lab in Los Alamos. *Travelers* is about Jack Karlstad who was four years old when his father died in Vietnam. As a teenager Jack must come to terms with his superhuman image of his father. Sexual politics is the subject of *The Better Angel.* Each of the three main characters "must find their way around personal, peer, parental, and community pressures and expectations" (Bograd, 1984, p. 2).

Recently historical fiction author James Lincoln Collier has written novels focusing on social issues. *When the Stars Begin to Fall* is about how fourteen-year-old Harry White attempts to change himself and his community. Discovering that the local carpet factory is polluting the river, he sets out to expose it and meets resistance at every turn. In *The Winchesters,* a strike forces Chris Winchester to choose between his rich family and the people who work in the Winchester Mills.

Nat Hentoff has written several powerful novels on social issues. *The Day They Came to Arrest the Book* is about censorship and what happens in a school and community when a book is called into question. *Does This School Have Capital Punishment?* is about a teenage boy who faces false drug charges and makes friends with a famous African American jazz trumpeter. His nonfiction book *American Heroes: In and out of School* is a series of short biographies of young people who act to defend their constitutional rights despite personal risks. The censorship issue is also dealt with in Susan Beth Pfeffer's *A Matter of Principle* and Dallin Malmgren's *The Ninth Issue.*

Gloria D. Miklowitz is a writer who frequently uses social issues to advance her plots. In *The Love Bombers* Jenna's brother drops out of college to join a charismatic group, the Church of the World. *The War between the Classes* is about what happens at an ethnically mixed high school when students participate in a simulation called the "Color Game." A class simulation dealing with how the Nazis could gain power in Germany gets out of hand in Morton Rhue's *The Wave.*

Stephanie S. Tolan is another author of fiction for young adults dealing with important social issues. *A Good Courage* deals with communes and cults. *The Plague Year* is the year in which Bran finds out that his father is a mass murderer. *The Pride of the Peacock* is about a potential nuclear war. The threat of nuclear war is also dealt with in *Matt's Crusade* by Margot Marek.

Some young adult novels highlight international social issues. Two books whose plots revolve around apartheid in South Africa are *Chain of Fire* by Beverly Naidoo and *Waiting for the Rain* by Sheila Gordon. An adult novel appropriate for young adult readers that provides historical perspective on apartheid is the excellent coming-of-age saga *The Power of One* by Bruce Courtenay. *Wolf* by British writer Gillian Cross deals with the IRA and terrorism. *Talking in Whispers* by James Watson is about the suppression of basic human rights in Chile.

Many other social issues are the basis for young adult novels. Caroline B. Cooney's *The Face on the Milk Carton* is about a girl who recognizes her own face on a milk carton as a child who is missing. *Sex Education* by Jenny Davis has an unusual plot revolving around a biology project in which the students are required to care for someone else for the semester. Livvie and David choose a pregnant neighbor who is terrorized by her husband. Young people dealing with their father's involvement in Vietnam is the topic of several recent books such as *Effie's House* by Morse Hamilton, *Pocket Change* by Kathryn Jensen, and *And One for All* by Theresa Nelson. Homophobia is the issue of Bette Greene's *The Drowning of Stephan Jones*. Homelessness is the topic of these books:

- Felice Holman's *Slake's Limbo* and *Secret City USA*
- Adrienne Jones's *Street Family*
- Gary Paulsen's *The Crossing*
- Jerry Spinelli's *Maniac Magee*
- Barbara Corcoran's *Stay Tuned*
- Paula Fox's *Monkey Island*
- Vicki Grove's *The Fastest Friend in the West*
- Mary Downing Hahn's *December Stillness*

Each of these books give a face to the faceless homeless in America.

Epilogue: Books to Empower and Enlighten

Young readers need to recognize themselves in the characters in the books they read. Reading about situations in which they find themselves in their own lives helps affirm adolescents who lack a positive self-concept. Young adult novels with characters who suffer the same problems as readers and rise above them can empower readers to do the same.

At the same time, adolescents need to read books with adolescent characters from different times and cultures with whom they can empathize. This experience is enlightening for young people. Egocentric adolescents are frequently intolerant of differences in people. It is essential that young adults learn to accept these differences not as problems but as strengths in a culturally diverse society. As teachers, we can direct adolescents to books with multicultural and historic characters who are different from the adolescent readers but at the same time share many similarities with them. Such characters can move adolescents toward enlightened and empowered maturity.

Suggested readings

Ashcroft, L. "Defusing 'Empowering': The What and the Why." *Language Arts,* February 1987, pp. 142–56.

Bograd, L. "Political Animal." *ALAN Review,* Fall 1984, pp. 1–4.

Bridgers, S. E. "Stories My Grandmother Told Me. Part One." *ALAN Review,* Fall 1985, pp. 44–48.

———. "Stories My Grandmother Told Me: Part Two." *ALAN Review,* Winter 1986, pp. 53–56, 61.

Carroll, P. S. "Southern Literature for Young Adults: The Novels of Sue Ellen Bridgers." *ALAN Review,* Fall 1990, pp. 10–13.

Charles, J. "Celebrating the Diversity of American Indian Literature." *ALAN Review,* Spring 1991, pp. 4–8.

Chatton, B. "Our Emerging Nation—The Late 1800s." *Book Links,* January 1992, pp. 48–53.

Chatton, B. and S. Tastad. "The American Revolution: 1754–1783." *Book Links,* May 1993, pp. 7–12.

Colarusso, K. D. "World War II and Its Relevance to Today's Adolescents." *ALAN Review,* Winter 1986, pp. 12–15.

Collier, C. "Fact, Fiction and History: The Role of Historian, Writer, Teacher and Reader." *ALAN Review,* Winter 1987, pp. 5–8.

Donelson, K. "Conscience and the Battle with Fear: Two Novels of Robert Westall." *ALAN Review,* Spring 1986, pp. 25–29.

Educational Testing Service. *The U.S. History Report Card: The Achievement of Fourth-, Eighth-, and Twelfth-Grade Students in 1988 and Trends from 1986 to 1988 in Factual Knowledge of High-School Juniors.* 1990.

Hamilton, V. "The Spirit Spins: A Writer's Resolution." *ALAN Review,* Fall 1987, pp. 1–4.

Kemp, R. D., Jr. "The Search for Identity: A Theme Common to Adolescent and Native American Literature." *ALAN Review,* Winter 1989, pp. 10, 13.

Kettel, R. "Children and the Homeless." *Book Links,* May 1992, pp. 51–55.

Lindgren, M. V., ed. *The Multicolored Mirror: Cultural Substance in Literature for Children and Young Adults.* Highsmith Press, 1991.

Louie, B. Y., and D. H. Louie. "Empowerment through Young-Adult Literature." *English Journal,* April 1992, pp. 53–56.

Major, K. "The Truth about My Fictitious Friends." *ALAN Review,* Winter 1986, pp. 1–4.

Miller-Lachmann, L. *Our Family, Our Friends, Our World: An Annotated Guide to Significant Multicul-tural Books for Children and Teenagers.* Bowker, 1992.

Murphy, S. "Native Americans: Listening for a Voice." *Journal of Reading,* September 1991, pp. 66–69.

Myers, W. D. "Author's View." *Scholastic BookTalk,* Spring 1992, p. 6.

Nist, J. "Ten on Top from Down Under." *ALAN Review,* Spring 1988, pp. 54–55, 58.

Nixon, J. L. "A Link between Young People of the Past and Present: Providing the Common Ground." *ALAN Review,* Winter 1989, pp. 1–4.

Norris, J. *Presenting Rosa Guy.* Twayne Publishers, 1988.

Osa, O. "Touchstones in Nigerian Youth Literature." *ALAN Review,* Spring 1988, pp. 56–58.

Peck, R. "Some Thoughts on Adolescent Literature." *News from ALAN,* September–October 1975, pp. 4–7.

Perry, J. "Cultural Diversity through Literature." *ALAN Review,* Spring 1991, pp. 45–47.

Probst, R. E. *Response and Analysis: Teaching Literature in Junior and Senior High School.* Boynton, 1988.

Romero, P. A., and D. Zancanella. "Expanding the Circle: Hispanic Voices in American Literature." *English Journal,* January 1990, pp. 24–29.

Small, R. C., Jr. "The South in Recent Young Adult Novels." *ALAN Review,* Winter 1986, pp. 62–66.

Smith, H. M., and G. M. Kruse. "The African-American Struggle for Freedom." *Book Links,* January 1992, pp. 12–19.

Stover, L. "Exploring and Celebrating Cultural Diversity and Similarity through Young Adult Novels." *ALAN Review,* Spring 1991, pp. 12–15.

Tarry-Stevens, P. "The Hispanic in Young Adult Literature." *ALAN Review,* Winter 1990, pp. 31–32.

6 Adventure and Romance

Focus Questions

1. Why is escape literature important for adolescents?
2. What are the characteristics of good mystery novels for adolescents?
3. What makes suspense stories popular with adolescents?
4. How do survival stories differ from suspense stories?
5. Why is the romance genre controversial?
6. What are the characteristics of good adolescent romances?

PROLOGUE

If I had to sum up in one word [what I was interested in reading as an adolescent], I'd have to say that what interested me was the "Extraordinary." After all, I knew what ordinary life was like—I was living it. What I wanted to read about was other lands, other cultures, other times, past and future. Crises, mysteries. Situations in which I was extremely unlikely to find myself—especially if I stayed in the backwater town where I grew up.

It didn't matter if the protagonist was ordinary—in fact, so much the better. The more ordinary he was, the better I could identify with him.

I think kids still like to read about situations outside their own usually limited experience, and probably always will. But they also like to read books that reflect their own day-to-day concerns: school, dating, drugs, acceptance by their peers. There are some real drawbacks, however, inherent in writing books that mirror our contemporary culture too faithfully.

One is that, in writing books that speak to adolescents about themselves, we are crafting not literature so much as adolescent literature, in essence creating a separate genre, like murder mysteries or romance, which has conventions of its own, and concerns of its own, often even a morality of its own. We've already seen movies go down that declining path, becoming more and more "youth-oriented." Teenagers tend to live in a world of their own, at best. We need to offer them a wider universe to look at and not just more of the same.

Another danger is that, in writing about contemporary problems, we are turning out *temporary* literature. Too much of our society is temporary already. Our cars, our appliances, or kids' toys, our popular entertainment—they aren't designed for posterity, but for obsolescence. They're not meant to be preserved or treasured, but to be disposed of when we tire of them—which is, predictably, early on. I don't think it's too much to ask for something more from our literature.

Now, obviously, not every book can be expected to live forever, to be read by our children and their children, and so on. But we could do worse than to write with that goal in mind. What could it hurt to include, in even the most topical of books, something universal?

That's what I find so appealing about books which place an ordinary person in an extraordinary situation. They tend to deal with problems and emotions that are not transitory but timeless and elemental—matters of life and death, of good and evil. Almost, without exception, the classics of adolescent literature . . . are some species of adventure story. *Huckleberry Finn, Treasure Island, Two Little Savages, Swiss Family Robinson, Tarzan of the Apes, The Time Machine*—you can make your own list—all deal not with the life kids really lived in the time in which they were written, but with the sort of life they wished they could live. ❖

From Gary L. Blackwood, "Ordinary People, Extraordinary Situations," *ALAN Review*, (Fall 1989), p. 49.

Books as Dreams and Nightmares

Escape literature, literature of the extraordinary, is as popular with adolescents today as it was yesterday. In this chapter we will discuss some of the most popular forms of escape literature: mystery, suspense, adventure, and romance. These books take adolescents away from their day-to-day lives and place them in extraordinary situations, but as in all young adult books the protagonists are ordinary adolescents.

M. E. Kerr says that escape literature not only provides escape for readers but for authors as well. According to Kerr, in "Getting All Kids to Read My Books," she had been working on *Night Kites*, the story of a young, popular man, an unannounced homosexual, coming home to his family with AIDS. The year was 1985 and few people were talking about AIDS, which was still being called "gay cancer," making the writing of a book on the subject for adolescents even more difficult. She says, "Writing *Night Kites* ultimately resulted in the creation of the series *Fell*. I wanted a recess yard when I brake between more serious books: someplace familiar with the same people there." She turned to a character she knew well, based on a policeman who with his family lived in East Hampton, Long Island, and who had already appeared in her book *Gentlehands*. She learned a great deal about police work from her policeman neighbor:

> For example: that when a suicide with eyeglasses jumps from a high building, he invariably removes his glasses, puts them in his pocket, or leaves them behind on the dresser . . . so, if the police find a body of a person with the eyeglasses smashed beside it, he was probably pushed.
>
> And for example: that often on a dope surveillance, when a policeman is watching a particular house, two cops go to the neighborhood in an unmarked car. One of them hidden under a large box in the front seat, with eyeholes cut in it and with a hot water bottle for a bathroom. The other cop leaves the car. Then it just looks like a car with a box in it, and the cop inside the box stays there watching.
>
> Travel on a train, Bill used to tell me, if you want to be less noticed. The scenery distracts people, but on a plane people look at each other. (Meaker, 1989, p. 46)

Thus the *Fell* mystery series began as "an escape hatch" for an author who was tired of dealing with serious topics. The series, now numbering three books (*Fell*, *Fell Down*, and *Fell Back*), also provides a wonderful escape for kids.

Mysteries

Most readers of mysteries, whether young adult or adult, read the books for escape. We read them to find out how ordinary characters placed in unusual situations come up with extraordinary solutions to problems. The genre has always been popular with young adult readers. Mysteries are exciting and at the same time predictable. Many mystery writers create series involving the same detective, and use predictable plot lines. Publishing syndicates began to take advantage of this no-fail formula with series mysteries such as Nancy Drew and the Hardy Boys as early as the beginning of the twentieth century. Because these books follow a predictable pattern, they became known as formula fiction. Many young readers, attracted to these young adult mysteries, also found themselves reading adult mysteries by authors such as Agatha Christie.

Adult mysteries are often accessible to young readers because all mysteries use certain literary conventions. For example, the murder usually occurs in the early pages of the book, and the rest of the book is devoted to determining who the murderer is. Furthermore, all clues presented by the author are significant, even if they do not seem so at the time. If the writer has one of the characters lose her car keys prior to the murder, the loss of the keys is not included in the novel by accident. However, readers of mysteries soon figure out that some clues, called red herrings, are planted to befuddle and confuse them. Once a reader becomes familiar with the conventions of the mystery, reading a mystery is an easy task. And if readers read several novels by an author, they also get to know the author's protagonist, the individual who solves the crime, who is sometimes a professional detective. It is immaterial to the enjoyment of the mystery whether or not the reader can figure out the puzzle prior to the end of the novel. What is essential is that the reader becomes caught in the web the mystery writer is weaving. Because most adult mysteries tend to have few characters, limited character development, simple plot lines, and describe only what is necessary to solve or confound, they are accessible to adolescent readers. In fact, the main difference between adult and young adult mysteries is the age of the protagonist.

In the past few decades, authors of young adult literature have increasingly supplied the teenage reader with well-written mysteries. These mysteries are more appropriate to young readers than adult mysteries because the characters are young and deal with problems related to the young. They are also more interesting than the formula mysteries because their plots are more complex and challenging, and their characters are frequently multidimensional. Figure 6.1 lists the characteristics of good young adult mysteries.

Well-Known Writers of Young Adult Mysteries

Today there are many outstanding mystery writers who write for young adults and many excellent books. We will discuss a limited number of them here.

In 1978 the prestigious Newbery Medal was given to Ellen Raskin for her intriguing puzzle mystery *The Westing Game*. This award for literary quality in children's literature had never before been given to a mystery writer. The entire book takes place in a single apartment building. All of the residents are cast into the mystery which few readers are able to solve.

Jay Bennett has probably written more mystery books for young adults than any other writer. The author of such books as *The Birthday Murderer*; *Deathman, Do Not Follow Me*; *The Killing Tree*; *Slowly, Slowly I Raise the Gun*; and *The Pigeon*, Bennett has twice been awarded the Edgar Award (named after Edgar Allan Poe) for best juvenile mystery of the year.

Joan Aiken, author of *Nightfall*, has become a popular author of mystery-adventure stories for young adults. Most of Lois Duncan's books written during the past decade are macabre mysteries that combine suspense and the occult. *I Know What You Did Last Summer* is about four teenagers attempting to conceal their hit-and-run accident while being pursued by a mysterious person seeking revenge.

Robbie Branscum, the author of southern regional narratives including *Me and Jim Luke*; *Toby, Granny and George*; and *The Murder of Hound Dog Bates*, often uses mystery in her plots to help develop her characters.

Other popular authors of young adult literature have tried their hand at mystery writing. Paul Zindel's *The Undertaker's Gone Bananas* is a humorous whodunit. In *Dreamland Lake* Richard Peck's two young protagonists find a body in the woods near an amusement park.

Rosemary Wells is a well-known writer of mysteries for young adults. In *The Man in the Woods* Helen Curragh transfers from a parochial to a public high school and joins the newspaper staff. She accidently witnesses a crime and finds her own life threatened because she knows too much. *Through the Hidden Door* is about Barney Pennimen who tries to prevent a gang attack on the headmaster's dog at his New England boarding school. This incident leads to his being labeled as a traitor, a

Figure 6.1
Characteristics of Good Mysteries for Young Adults

Character
Protagonist
• detective; usually falls into the role by chance
• adolescent
Victim(s)
• usually undeveloped
• may not even be known to the reader
Antagonist
• murderer or perpetrator
• present throughout the book
• may be one of the better developed characters in the book
• not recognized as murderer or perpetrator until late in the book
Plot
• murder or mysterious event occurs early in the novel
• most characters, with the exception of the detective, could be the potential murderer or perpetrator
• every piece of information could be important in solving the mystery
• pieces of puzzle presented throughout the novel
• red herrings (misleading clues)
• verisimilitude; all events could be possible
• suspension of disbelief required
Point of View
• protagonist/detective; usually withholds information from the reader
Voice
• protagonist/detective
Setting
• contributes to the plot; may be an isolated island or a mysterious house
• weather is often important
• various; detective usually moves about
Theme
• usually unimportant

friendship with a strange boy named Snowy, and the discovery of a treasure hidden in a cave.

Other popular young adult authors have written mysteries that are likely to appeal to adolescent readers. Lynn Hall's *Ride a Dark Horse* will appeal to both mystery and horse story lovers. Gusty McCaw is seventeen and a thoroughbred exercise rider. Her father is killed in a freak accident. She senses something is strange when she is told he was drunk at the time but knows he had not taken a drink for thirty years. *The Freshman Detective Blues* by P. J. Petersen is an excellent transitional mystery for boys who have enjoyed the Hardy Boys books. Eddie Carter and Jack Mason accidentally discover a skeleton which they believe is Jack's long-missing father. Sandra Scoppettone's *Playing Murder* revolves around a family's move to Blue Haven Island to run a family restaurant. Anna resents the family's move which was precipitated by an unpleasant school episode involving her twin brother. She becomes involved with Kirk, the handsome son of the restaurant's previous owner, who is mysteriously murdered. In *The Christmas Killer* by Patricia Windsor, Nancy Emerson is kidnapped and dies and then appears in Rose Potter's dreams to give her clues about her body's whereabouts and murder.

Gothic Mysteries

The Gothic romance mystery is a subgenre of mystery. Most Gothic romances take place in a large, mysterious house in a remote setting, often on the misty moors of England. *Down a Dark Hall* (Duncan) is a Gothic mystery that deals with the supernatural phenomenon of ESP. Four adolescents find out they are more than students at an exclusive girls school, they are prisoners. Isabelle Holland writes Gothic mysteries marketed to adults but very popular with young readers. Cynthia Voigt's *The Callender Papers* is a Gothic mystery winner of the Edgar Award set in nineteenth-century New England. Jean Wainwright, an orphan raised by the headmistress of a girls' school spends her thirteenth summer with strangers in the old Callender family home cataloguing the family papers. Initially she is unaware of the danger lurking in the papers. A romance mystery by Barbara Michaels, *Wait for What Will Come*, is very popular with female readers. The book is about a young American who inherits an ancient, crumbling mansion in Cornwall, England, and learns of the mysterious legend surrounding it.

Historical Mysteries

Leon Garfield is the master of the young adult history-mystery genre. In *Footsteps*, set in eighteenth-century England, young William sets out to quiet his father's ghost by finding the old partner his father had swindled. The reader is introduced to colorful characters such as Shot-in-the-Head, a gangster who makes his living by "snick-and-lurk" and even contemplates stealing the gold on the dome of St. Paul's Cathedral. The story, which begins and ends in William's father's bedroom, is full of humor, suspense, historically accurate figures of speech, and amusing characters who will delight and intrigue the young reader. In *Devil-in-the-Fog* fourteen-year-old George Treet's life with traveling actors is disrupted after he learns his father is really a rich, powerful man. The book's suspense is heightened by the mystery of George's birth, his true identity, and the devil-like strangers he meets in the woods.

The Man Who Wanted Seven Wives by Katie Letcher Lyle is a fictionalized account of a famous historical murder mystery of 1897 supposedly solved by the testimony of a ghost. In Gary Paulsen's *Dancing Carl* twelve-year-old Marsh and his best friend Willy learn that Carl Wenstrom, a veteran of World War II, has experienced some terrible events.

Virginia Hamilton's critically acclaimed *The House of Dies Drear* and *Mystery of Drear House* spin out mysteries against the historical backdrop of the Civil War and the Underground Railroad. The author of the *Fell* mystery series, M. E. Kerr, writes about a young boy who discovers that his grandfather is an infamous Nazi war criminal in *Gentlehands*.

Humorous Mysteries

Walter Dean Myers, an author of parallel-culture fiction for adolescents, has written several humorous mysteries for young adolescents: *Mojo and the Russians*, *The Young Landlords*, and *The Mouse Rap*. The success of Myers's books shows the popularity of the humorous mystery among young adults. Elaine Konigsburg's *From the Mixed-Up Files of Mrs. Basil E. Frankweiler* is another popular humorous mystery. Readers who enjoy these funny mysteries will also want to read Dorothy Francis's *Mystery of the Forgotten Map*, about two young sleuths who attempt to prove their grandfather is not a thief by using an old map, and *Golden Girl*, about a girl who may be forced out of a pageant by being murdered. Georgess McHargue's *Funny Bananas: The Mystery in the Museum* is another funny mystery for young adolescent readers.

Multicultural Mysteries

Rosa Guy, like Myers and Hamilton, writes mysteries involving minority characters. In *And I Heard a Bird Sing*, the third in her series of mysteries, Imamu Jones is a likeable eighteen-year-old amateur detective who is attracted to Charlotte D'Arcy. The mystery is unusual in that much of it takes place in Imamu's thoughts and daydreams.

Supernatural Mysteries

Richard Peck writes about the supernatural in his humorous Blossom Culp books. Favorites of young adolescents include *The Ghost Belonged to Me*, *Ghosts I Have Been*, *The Dreadful Future of Blossom Culp*, and *Blossom Culp and the Sleep of Death*. These books feature a likable female protagonist who faces the typical problems of many adolescents—she is unattractive and unpopular—but she also has a supernatural ability that allows her to solve mysteries and travel through time.

Jane-Emily by Patricia Clapp is a suspenseful tale of mystery and the occult featuring a very unusual girl. Madeleine L'Engle's mysteries, including *The Arm of the Starfish*, *Dragons in the Water*, and *The Young Unicorns*, combine fantasy, suspense, science fiction, music, and theology.

Joan Lowery Nixon is another master of the young adult mystery genre. In *The Seance* Nixon introduces a touch of the supernatural. Lauren must welcome Sara Martin, a ward of the court, into her Aunt Melvamay's household. From the beginning there is something strange about Sara, and when she invites Lauren to a seance, Lauren agrees to go because she fears Sara's taunts more than the seance. During the seance Sara disappears and later her body is discovered in a swamp. Another teenager is murdered before the tragic and frightening mystery concludes. Other excellent mysteries by Nixon include *A Candidate for Murder*, *Caught in the Act*, *High Trail of Danger*, and *The Weekend Was Murder*.

Suspense

Suspense novels for young adults have gained popularity in recent years. Many such stories written for adults are also popular with adolescents, but the length and complexity of their plot lines often make them difficult for the immature reader.

Although suspense stories and mysteries have many similarities, they also have significant differences. Suspense, like mystery, catches the reader unaware. Readers of suspense must suspend disbelief in order to be caught up in the spine-tingling effect of the plot. Characterization in the two genres differs, however. Unlike in the mystery, where the victim is usually undeveloped, the protagonist of the suspense story is typically the victim or the intended victim. The protagonist may or may not suspect the villain. At times the victim will not know who the antagonist is, but the reader will. Unlike in the mystery, the various characters in the suspense story are often well developed. In fact, suspense differs from most other fiction in that the antagonist may be more completely developed than the protagonist. The antagonist is usually evil and intelligent.

Typically in the suspense story we await the enactment of the evil act rather than attempt to determine who committed the crime. The plot of the suspense story is often more complex than the plot of the mystery. Literary techniques such as foreshadowing and flashback are often employed.

The major difference between adult suspense, such as the stories of Stephen King, and young adult suspense is the age of the protagonist and the complexity of the plot. See Figure 6.2 for the characteristics of good suspense stories for young adults.

Killing Mr. Griffin

Lois Duncan's *Killing Mr. Griffin* provides an excellent example of the suspense genre. The protagonist and victim of the story (although readers do not recognize her as the victim until late in the book) is Susan, an unpopular girl whose only distinction is that she is a good student. Susan feels isolated from her family and peers.

The book begins on a wild and windy day with the dust blowing off the New Mexico mountains. Susan has the wonderful luck of saving the class president David's paper from being blown away in the wind. They walk together into school, but she loses him in the hallways. Readers empathize with this lonely girl. Susan's loneliness, which is central to the plot, also provides the novel with its most important subplot. Next we meet Mr. Griffin, the demanding English teacher, who makes it clear he will not accept late papers even on windy days. In the first chapter, which sets the scene and introduces the major characters, we also meet Betsy, the popular cheerleader, and Mark, an attractive, mysterious boy. The chapter is also full of foreshadowing that lets readers know the events to come will be horrifying. In the short segment that appears below, Susan has completed an assignment to write a song for Ophelia in Shakespeare's *Hamlet*. Many of the other students have been unable to do so and Mr.

Figure 6.2
Characteristics of Good Suspense Stories for Young Adults

Character

Protagonist

- victim (readers may not know he or she is a victim until late in the novel)
- adolescent
- vulnerable, isolated
- evokes reader empathy

Antagonist

- bold
- insensitive
- exceptionally cunning, insightful, manipulative
- believable
- well developed
- peer of protagonist and reader
- often someone the protagonist and reader care about

Plot

- several subplots common
- foreshadowing and flashbacks used
- tension and uncertainty builds
- clues given (may be misleading)
- character development important to plot
- chapters begin with hooks and end with cliff-hangers
- setting is important
- title of books is often a clue

Point of View

- protagonist/victim
- sometimes omniscient narrator is also used (reader knows what victim does not)

Voice

- protagonist/victim

Setting

- important to the plot
- creates sense of foreboding

Theme

- often unimportant
- sometimes subplot provides the theme
- "Things and people are not always what they seem"

Griffin has just finished chastising them. As she hands her song in, Susan worries that he might ask the students to read them aloud.

> Only this morning as she was leaving the house had the horrible thought occurred to her—what if he makes us read the songs in class? There was no way that she could have done that. Too much of Susan lay exposed in the neatly printed verses, intermixed with the person of Ophelia.

Now she scanned her words again—

Where the daises laugh and blow,
Where the willow leaves hang down,
Nonny, nonny, I will go
There to weave my lord a crown.

Willow, willow by the brook
Trailing fingers green and long,
I will read my lord a book,
I will sing my love a song.

Though he turn his face away,
Nonny, nonny, still I sing,
Ditties of a heart gone gray
And a hand that bears no ring.

Water, water, cold and deep—

Then Susan's attention turns to an event outside the classroom window:

The wind continued to blow. Gazing through the window toward the parking lot, Susan could barely make out the rows of cars, veiled as they were by swirling dust. Out of this wild, pink world a bird came flying, half blinded, carried by the wind, and crashed headlong into the windowpane. Its beak crumpled against the glass, and it seemed to hang there an instant, stunned by the impact, before it dropped like a feather-covered stone to the ground below.

Poor thing, Susan thought. Poor little thing.

Poor bird. Poor Ophelia. Poor Susan. She had a sudden, irrational urge to put her head down on the desk and weep for all of them, for the whole world, for the awful day that was starting so badly and would certainly get no better.

The chapter ends with a cliff-hanger: "From his seat behind her she heard Jeff Garrett mumble under his breath, 'That Griffin's the sort of guy you'd like to kill.' "

Throughout the first half of the book readers think of Mr. Griffin as the victim. Indeed, Duncan allows us to get to know him by devoting a chapter to him and to his pregnant wife. We see Mr. Griffin through his wife's eyes. Susan is manipulated by Mark and willingly joins in the plot to kidnap Mr. Griffin. For the first time in her life she feels a part of the group. Although she does not actually participate in the kidnapping, she acts as the bait by luring Mr. Griffin to stay after school to discuss a paper. The students take Mr. Griffin to a remote area of the mountains and leave him there.

By evening Susan feels remorse and convinces David to go with her to the mountains to find Mr. Griffin, apologize, and bring him back. They do find him, but when they do he is already dead, having died of a heart attack. They panic and Mark persuades Susan that they should bury him. The plot moves along with Susan caught under Mark's spell and falling deeper and deeper into the pit of her own lies. Once the students' act is discovered, the suspense does not diminish. Now, it is clear to the reader that Susan, even more than Mr. Griffin, is the vulnerable victim.

In addition to *Killing Mr. Griffin*, Duncan has written many other fine suspense stories for adolescents. *Five Were Missing* features a female protagonist; and deals with kidnapping. Other excellent suspense stories by Duncan include *Locked in Time*, *Stranger with My Face*, *Ransom* and *The Third Eye*.

British writer Joan Aiken is one of the best-known suspense writers for adolescents. *Died on a Rainy Sunday* is about a four-year-old child who is instinctively terrified, with just cause, by a new baby-sitter. In *The Wolves of Willoughby Chase*, winner of the Lewis Carroll Shelf Award, two cousins are left in the care of an evil governess in a creepy nineteenth-century house. Its sequel *Black Hearts in Battersea* involves wolves, a kidnapping, a long-lost heir, a bomb plot, the London criminal underworld, and a tragic death.

In addition to numerous mysteries, Jay Bennett has written many suspenseful young adult books. *Say Hello to the Hit Man* and *The Long Black Coat* are about Phil who discovers why two of his dead brother's army buddies are after him. Other excellent suspense stories by Bennett include *The Haunted One*, *The Dark Corridor*, *To Be a Killer*, and *The Executioner*.

Robert Cormier's Suspense Books

Probably the most acclaimed writer of suspense books for young adults is Robert Cormier. What makes his books so intriguing is not only their suspenseful plots and terrifyingly realistic antagonists but also the interweaving of numerous subplots. Unlike many suspense books, Cormier's works always have an underlying theme, making them excellent for classroom reading. His terrifying *After the First Death* involves a hijacked bus, terrorism, and family relationships. What makes this book so horrifying is how we and the victims come to know and empathize not only with the victims but the perpetrators. *The Bumblebee Flies Anyway* is about sixteen-year-old Barney Snow who is confined to an experimental hospital for dying teenagers. Adam Farmer in *I Am the Cheese* is not sure of his identity and neither are we. The plot develops through a series of flashbacks as Adam pedals his bike from Massachusetts to Vermont because he thinks his father is in a hospital there.

His first, and still best-known, young adult book, *The Chocolate War*, is the horrifying story of what can happen in a school when the school is more concerned about its reputation than its students. Who are the villains in this book: the vigilante gang at the Catholic school known as the Vigils or the brothers led by the malevolent Brother Leon? Like all good suspense books, the book begins with a hook that grabs the readers' attention: "They murdered him." The underlying themes of the book concern the struggle between individuals and institutions and the struggle to discover good in evil. The sequel, *Beyond the Chocolate War*, is also about the struggle of good and evil. Jerry comes back to school after nearly being destroyed by Archie and Brother Leon. He comes back to fight the system and the evils the system allows to exist.

We All Fall Down is the story of three characters who meet in violent confrontation. Buddy is an alcoholic adolescent who trashes a house and attacks a fourteen-year-old girl; Jane is the girl's older sister and moral touchstone of the novel, and "The Avenger" witnesses the attack and seeks revenge.

─────── ❖ **Between the Covers:** *Authors at Work* ❖ ───────

ROBERT CORMIER: EVIL AND THE INSTITUTION

Many people who have met Robert Cormier wonder how it is possible for such a nice man to create such evil characters. Some of the most evil villains in young adult fiction live within the pages of Cormier's books: Archie the leader of the Vigils and Brother Leon, the headmaster of Trinity, who is more concerned about his power than the welfare of his students; Artkin and Miro, hijackers of a bus filled with children; the powerful devil-like Handyman, the leader of the Complex, an institution where experiments on dying adolescents are conducted; and the Avenger, who has witnessed evil and seeks revenge but personifies evil himself.

Cormier was born in 1925 in Leominster, Massachusetts, where he still lives. He is the father of four children, has worked as a newspaper reporter and editor for much of his career, and has written both young adult and adult novels. His greatest critical and commercial success is as a writer of young adult books. Cormier has a strong attachment to his readers, even allowing his own phone number to appear on the pages of his novel *I Am the Cheese*.

Why do so many of the books by this man who obviously cares about and enjoys his readers portray the dark view of life? Cormier replied to such a question in a 1985 interview:

> *After the First Death* was occasioned by the violence and hijacking and by my influence as a newspaperman. [My novels] don't reflect any particular personal philosophy of mine. I try to write contemporary novels about what's going on. . . . Everything is to affect the reader. And, at any particular moment in the book, I want the reader to be angry or upset or even happy or laughing. . . . I said it all in *The Bumblebee Flies Anyway* when I had Barney say, ''The bad thing is to do nothing.'' I thought *Bumblebee* had moments of triumph. Even the downbeat pattern in *The Chocolate War* [provides some hope]. There's a time when Jerry was defeated yet nobody came to his rescue. What kind of book is it when people have to come to the rescue of others to survive? [Jerry is learning that he can survive on his own, that the bad thing is to do nothing.] (Bugniazet, pp. 14–15)

Although Cormier's suspense books may seem pessimistic, side by side with the pessimism is hope. Readers come to understand that they cannot rely on others to rescue them. They, like Jerry in *Beyond the Chocolate War*, must pick themselves up again and not only live life but attempt to right its wrongs. Cormier's heroes also help readers understand that evil is not always obvious; sometimes it lurks within innocence, sometimes within benevolence. Cormier, for example, calls Miro, the terrorist in *After the First Death*, ''the epitome of the innocent monster'' (Bugniazet, p. 17). This extremism within individuals can also be seen in his other villains such as Brother Leon, the Handyman, Brint, and the Avenger. A part of each protagonist's life is spent discovering that evil wherever it lurks.

Guy Ellis in an article ''Cormier and the Pessimistic View'' (1985) suggests that often the evil is in institutions rather than the characters, institutions that allow and even encourage the evil to exist and continue. We see examples of this in Trinity, the private boys school in *The Chocolate War* and *Beyond the Chocolate War*, in the military-police establishment in *After the First Death*, in the government and the psycho-medical institution in *I Am the Cheese*, and in the Complex in *The Bumblebee Flies Anyway*. Ellis suggests that Cormier is implying that we must fight the evil that hides in institutions that may be established for benevolent purposes, such as schools, hospitals, and the government. Evil does exist, but we have the power to fight it. Like Alan in *I Am the Cheese*, we will not always defeat the evil we find but we can keep pedaling. And like Jerry in *Beyond the Chocolate War* we may even get a second chance.   ❖

Other Authors of Young Adult Suspense Novels

Gillian Cross is a British writer of suspense for young adults. In *On the Edge* Tug Shakespeare, son of a prominent London journalist, is kidnapped by a terrorist group attempting to destroy the nuclear family. In *Born of the Sun* Paula is mysteriously withdrawn from boarding school to go with her family on an exploratory expedition into South America. *The Dark behind the Curtain* is a tale of good versus evil that unfurls during a secondary school play production of *Sweeney Todd*.

James Forman's *So Ends This Day* is a story about sea voyagers in search of whales, a ship, and a murderer. In *Cry Havoc* Forman recalls the line from *Julius Caesar*, "Cry havoc, and let slip the dogs of war." The story focuses on Jim Cooper who must deal with enormous killer animals who are terrorizing a quiet Long Island community.

Michael French's suspense story *Circle of Revenge* involves the family of an exiled South American dictator, two California teenagers, and a psychology professor who is an authority on mind-control. His book *Pursuit* takes place in an isolated area of the Sierra Nevada and describes a suspenseful week-long hiking trip.

Anthony Horowitz's *The Devil's Door-Bell* is about thirteen-year-old Martin Hopkins who is suddenly an orphan. He moves from London to a foster home in the country and the care of a strange and evil woman. Martin is again the protagonist of *The Night of the Scorpion* which takes place in England and Peru.

Norma Johnston has written several suspense tales for young adults. In *The Delphic Choice* Meredith, seventeen, meets Brandon Hurd while they are both in Delphi on their way to Turkey. While in Greece they learn that a close friend of Meredith's family is missing. The plot involves communication between terrorists, Meredith, and American agents. In *Whisper of the Cat* Tracy lives with her divorced mother. When her mother is offered a job in South America, she decides to stay with her father and his new wife on a Georgia sea island. The island, the ancestral mansion, and the people hold many secrets. Then Tracy discovers a body in a dark swamp.

Frances Miller's *The Truth Trap* is the tale of fifteen-year-old Matt and his little deaf sister Katie who flee from their home when well-meaning relatives suggest institutionalizing Katie. While on their way to Los Angeles Matt leaves Katie in an abandoned building while he seeks work to support them. When he returns, she has been brutally murdered and he is the suspect. Miller continues this suspense story in two sequels: *Aren't You the One Who——?* and *Losers and Winners*.

John Rowe Townsend's *The Intruder* is the eerie tale of a sinister stranger who claims to be a close blood relative of the young protagonist's friend, who is a shopkeeper. In Patricia Windsor's *Something's Waiting for You, Baker D.*, Mary the Hulk wants to protect Baker D. from something but she is not sure what. Barbara Corcoran's *The Clown* is a narrative about a young girl attempting to smuggle a Jewish circus clown out of Moscow. In Todd Strasser's *The Accident* Matt backs out of a dangerous dare and doubts his own courage. He drowns his sorrows in beer, becomes ill, and misses a trip, thereby saving his own life. To Matt, however, there is something about the accident that does not seem right. In Lawrence Yep's *Liar, Liar* Marsh is killed in an accident, but his friend and sister think someone tampered with the brakes.

Kidnapping Stories

Several young adult books deal with the relationship between a kidnapper and a young adult victim. These include *After the First Death* (Cormier), *Catch a Killer* (Wood), *Five Were Missing* (Duncan), *Taking Gary Feldman* (Cohen), *A Child Is Missing* (Paul), *Hitchhike* (Holland), and *Soul Catcher* (Herbert). In *The Kidnapping of Christina Lattimore* (Nixon) the victim is accused, after her rescue, of having conspired with her abductors.

Supernatural Elements

Perhaps influenced by Stephen King's remarkably successful adult suspense formula, a large number of today's suspense books for adolescents have an element of the occult, or supernatural psychological phenomena that seem to be beyond human understanding. In Charles Crawford's *Bad Fall*, for example, everyone is charmed by the new boy in school, but, what they do not know about him is terrifying. Almost all of Lois Duncan's suspense stories include an aspect of the supernatural. Mark in *Killing Mr. Griffin* possesses a strange, unexplainable power over his young friends; the headmistress in *Down a Dark Hall* has unusual, terrifying talents. In Dora Polk's *The Linnet Estate* an English girl visits a California widow who is interested in the occult. The girl becomes the object of what appears to be a supernatural campaign to drive her away. In Chester Aaron's *Out of Sight, Out of Mind* teenage twins can communicate mentally. They can even move heavy objects, such as guided missiles, using their combined mental powers.

A few young adult suspense novels actually deal with witchcraft or Satanism. In Barbara Michaels's *Witch*, Ellen purchases a house that formerly belonged to a witch. When Ellen moves into the house, she is labeled a witch and bizarre things begin to happen. In Thomas Cullinan's *The Bedeviled* a family moves to a quiet farmhouse in Ohio, but Dugg, the adolescent son, appears to become possessed by the spirit of his evil great-great-grandfather. *Haunted* by Judith St. George is a tale of murder, suicide, and unexplainable incidents. In Otfried Preussler's *The Satanic Mill*, set in seventeenth-century Germany, a boy attempts to escape from a master of necromancy who conjures the spirits of the dead.

Other suspense books include strange, unexplainable creatures or events not unlike those found in horror movies. For example, Edward Levy's *Came a Spider* is about a giant mutated spider that lays eggs in Lee's bloodstream as he hunts in the California hills. In *The Mirror* by Marlys Millhiser, Shay looks at an image of her grandmother in a strange mirror and sees their bodies switched. She continually attempts to return to the twentieth century through the mirror. *The Totem* by David Morrell is about a mysterious disease that plagues the small quiet town of Potter's Field, Wyoming. As the strange disease spreads death through the community, terror overcomes the population and the reader.

Books about Survival

Survival books are a popular subgenre of the suspense novel. In survival books, suspense is created as the characters confront the difficulties posed by the natural environments. There is usually no villain in these books, but often the protagonist must overcome some weakness or fear that lurks within. Many teenagers like to imagine what it would be like if they were caught in a situation in which they had to use their ingenuity or strength to survive. It's no wonder that survival books are very popular with adolescents because they show how ordinary adolescents overcome extraordinary situations.

Surviving Isolation

In Scott O'Dell's *Island of the Blue Dolphins*, a girl survives eighteen years alone on an island. Theodore Taylor's *The Cay* is the tale of a shipwrecked blind boy who at first lives with a black islander and a cat but later manages by himself on his deserted island home. Seventeen-year-old Cleo isolates herself on an island in Canada following her sister's death in Harry Mazer's *The Island Keeper*. *A Rumor of Otters* by Deborah Savage is the story of a young girl who runs away from the isolated sheep station on the South Island of New Zealand ostensibly to see the otters a Maori man told her exist, in spite of the common belief that there are no otters in New Zealand.

Overcoming the Environment

In J. Allan Bosworth's *White Water, Still Water*, Chris survives the Canadian wilderness on his homemade raft as he tries to find his way back to civilization before winter. In Mavis Clark's *Wildfire*, five young characters are united in a desperate struggle to escape a raging forest fire in Australia. *Incident at Hawk's Hill* by Allan Eckert is a strange tale of endurance about a young child who lives for weeks in the hole of a fierce badger. In John Ives's *Fear in a Handful of Dust*, four kidnapped psychiatrists struggle to survive in the desert after being abandoned to die by a psychotic killer. In *Canyon Winter* by Walt Morey, a fifteen-year-old boy lives through a plane crash but must then find a way to survive in the northwest wilderness. Harry Mazer's *Snow Bound* is about Tony, a runaway, and Cindy, the hitchhiker he picks up, who become stranded near the Canadian border in a raging blizzard. In *Yukon Journey* by Frank McLaughlin, insecure Andy Ferguson goes in search of his father whose plane has crashed in a remote area of the Yukon. Other good survival stories of young adults facing a harsh environment include *Cold River* (Judson), *Deborah: A Wilderness Narrative* (Roberts), *The Hall of the Mountain King* (Snyder), and *The Mountain of My Fear* (Roberts).

In some books about wilderness survival the protagonist also faces a human enemy. In *Wilderness Peril* by Thomas J. Dygard two boys on a canoe trip confront a hijacker of a plane who has parachuted into the area where they are camping. Barnaby Conrad and Niels Mortensen's *Endangered* is about a photographer who inadvertently photographs a murder and then must flee the murderers. In Oliver McNab's *Horror Story* a young couple and their five-year-old daughter are lost in the New Hampshire woods and become captives of a community led by a man seeking revenge against society. *Downriver* by Will Hobbs is the story of rebellious young people who are members of a wilderness survival group called Discovery Unlimited. This story is not only about challenging the wilderness of the Colorado River. It is about conflicts within a group, how leaders emerge, and how individuals struggle to find their own identities. Another book with the theme of young people in trouble working together to survive is Ivy Ruckman's *No Way Out*.

All of Gary Paulsen's survival books are exciting and realistic and have human interest as well. Brian's survival in the Canadian wilderness after a plane crash is chronicled in *Hatchet* and *The River*. Brian must not only overcome the hardships of the environment but must conquer his inner fears. *Tracker* is about deer hunting during the Minnesota winter. For John and his family deer hunting is not a sport, it is necessary for survival. When his grandfather is diagnosed with cancer, John must go out alone. Learning how to hunt on his own, John must also deal with the death of his beloved grandfather. *Canyons*, a historical novel, is about Coyote Runs, an Apache youth who goes on his first rustling raid, is caught, and is brutally executed by white soldiers.

In Otto Salassi's books the protagonists deal with all life has to offer with humor. *And Nobody Knew They Were There* is about a young teenage boy who solves a mystery the grown-ups cannot, stalks an elusive prey, and survives alone by his own native wit. *Jimmy D., Sidewinder, and Me* is a story of the Southwest in the 1940s; young Dumas Monk writes letters to a judge explaining his past actions. The letters, which make up the book, include stories about gambling and murder.

Survival Throughout History

In the historical novel by Sonia Levitin, *Roanoke: A Novel of the Lost Colony*, sixteen-year-old William tells of the hardships and struggles in the ill-fated colony. Robert Newton Peck's adventure *Eagle Fur* is a story of the Canadian frontier in 1754 in which sixteen-year-old Abbot Coe survives as a fur trader. In Joan Blos's *Brothers of the Heart* Shem, the fourteen-year-old handicapped son in a nineteenth-century pioneer family, runs away from home and becomes part of a trading expedition. However, as winter approaches he finds himself alone in the wilderness.

The Search

Another type of suspense novel that is particularly intriguing to young adult readers is the search story. Two books by Ian Cameron are two good examples. In *The Lost Ones* a father seeks his son who was lost while hunting whales in the Arctic. A dead man's diary leads to a search for a tribe of primitive men and an active volcano in remote Chile in *The Mountains at the Bottom of the World*. Danny of Walter Edmond's *Wolf Hunt* attempts to track down the "stump-toed wolf." In Hal Evarts's *Bigfoot* the abominable snowman is the object of the search. In *The Ides of April* (Ray), a historical novel, a seventeen-year-old boy looks for the killer of the Roman senator Caius Pomponius. *The Snake* by John Godey is about the hunt for a dangerous reptile that has escaped from the Central Park Zoo. Charlotte Paul's *A Child Is Missing* is about the kidnapping of a couple's eldest son. The surprise ending of the book, which suggests a solution to the Lindbergh case, is fast-paced and suspenseful.

Romance

Teenage romances are vastly popular with female readers. Take for example the following statistics. In 1979 Scholastic publishers noticed that paperback romances were selling exceptionally well in their Teenage Book Club which sells books directly to students at school via catalogues. Subsequently they established the first teenage series romance Wildfire Romances to extend to their bookstore market. According to Parrish and Atwood, "In just two years the new line of 24 titles grossed over two million dollars. The instant financial success of the young adult romance line has since lured 16 companies, with 25 series, into active competition for the reading interest and dollars of girls between the ages of eight and 18" (1986, p. 53). Apple in the introduction to *Becoming a Woman through Romance* reported that "adolescent romances . . . constitute the third most widely read books by teenagers and represent 35 percent of the total non-adult book sales at major national bookstore chains" (1990, p. x). According to Harvey in a 1981 article in *Interracial Books for Children Bulletin*, in only one year, the Scholastic Wildfire series sold approximately two million copies of teenage romances. Crossen in a 1988 article in the *Wall Street Journal* reported that Bantam's Sweet Valley High series averaged more than 350,000 books for each first print run with a total of over twenty-six million books printed (p. 25).

Why are romances so popular with adolescent girls? Parrish and Atwood report that publishers and educators see the success of the romances differently. Publishers and writers of romance tend to view their popularity as an example of young adults seeking escapism. Just as young male readers select adventures for escape reading, young female readers select romance to escape the unpleasant realities of their day-to-day lives. According to Wendy Smith in an article in *Publisher's Weekly* (1981), the boom in romance books was partly a reaction to the problem novels of the 1960s and 1970s which focused on such problems as divorce, suicide, and troubled sexual relationships. In addition, publishers point to the general conservatism of the adult population as a reason for the popularity of romance. Romance series novels show life with few problems, depict middle-class families with conservative values, and promote love without sex. Other publishers have pointed to the success of adult romances as a reason for the success of young adult romances. In fact, several publishers market adult romances and young adult romances together in bookstores, believing that mothers who read adult romances tend to recommend teen romances to their daughters.

Educators tend to have a negative reaction to the popularity of teenage romances, according to Parrish and Atwood. Some suggest that the books represent more than just escapism; they appeal to young women because they depict desirable relationships without the complication of sexual involvement (Nilsen and Donelson, 1980). Others claim that the books provide simple reading for adolescents. Linda K. Christian-Smith in *Becoming a Woman through Romance* (1990) suggests that the books are predictable and contain a "code" of romance, sexuality, and beautification. She points out that romances of the 1980s presented a version of femininity that prevailed in the romances of the 1940s and 1950s: women get their men if they are interesting, but do not challenge them, and they are "dutiful, weak, shy, and naive about boys" (p. 4). Susan G. Bennett and Alice Kuhn (1987) reviewed romance series books using literary criteria established by critics of young adult books and found them ranking "very low in overall literary quality," but they note that if the literary criteria used are based exclusively on adolescent literature, the books rank relatively high and "appear to be books that teenagers would find interesting and easy reading" (p. 44).

The Controversy

Virtually no one contends that the popular series romances are good literature. When evaluated against most literary criteria, they fall woefully short. Romances also tend to present a traditional view of women and girls. In a comparison of contemporary romances and those of the 1940s and 1950s, Litton concludes, "The new novels, with some notable exceptions, are as stereotyped in their own way as those of the earlier period. . . . For the most part, the newer novels do not present more positive women role models. The mother-daughter relationships in the newer books are more contentious than those of the older period. Authors still rely on stereotypes like the dumb blond flirt. Young girls still want to think of themselves as a certain boy's girlfriend. Friendships among girls have not changed much" (1987, p. 46). Litton, however, like many educators who review teenage series romances, points to some positive trends in certain books within series. "Some girls in a few of the more recent books are brighter, stronger and career-oriented" (p. 46).

Critics of modern teenage romances do not refute their popularity with teenage readers. Given this popularity, several of the more recent books and articles by these critics suggest that it is the educator's responsibility to help students read these novels critically. Christian-Smith claims that modern romances present two views of adolescent females: the shy, naive protagonist and her stronger, more assertive best friend. Kelly in a 1991 article "Transitional Novels for Readers of Teen Romance" suggests that teachers who begin with "respectful consideration of the books the girls are reading" (p. 19) can discuss the books with them, "helping them question, compare, and connect, and trying to determine which novels might tap into some of the romance characteristics but also provide opportunities for rich discussions" (p. 19).

Selecting Romances

If teachers are to help students find novels that have some of the characteristics of romances but are more literary and have more mature themes, it is essential that we know the characteristics of good teenage romances (see Figure 6.3). Some good romances will be found within the romance series, but most will be published outside of these series. The series novels follow a specific formula. Good young adult romances do not follow a formula, although they do contain many of the elements young readers seek in romance novels (a female protagonist, a developing relationship, realistic settings and situations to which the reader can relate). Good young adult romances provide an escape from day-to-day life, as suggested by author Gary Blackwood, by showing ordinary characters in extraordinary situations, formula romances fall short in this respect; the escapism they provide does not really allow the reader to get away from everyday life.

Authors of Good Young Adult Romances

The books described here meet many of the criteria for good romances. Some books may be flawed, but all provide readers with the elements of many of the series romances as well as a chance to develop mature relationships and cope with realistic problems.

It is ironic that the first teenage romance, published in 1942, was written by teenage author Maureen Daly. In *Seventeenth Summer* she developed the pattern for decades of romances to follow. It was not until 1986 that Daly published her second romance *Acts of Love*. This romance, unlike *Seventeenth Summer*, breaks many romantic stereotypes. For example. Retta's family is poor but genteel, and her

Figure 6.3
Characteristics of Good
Romances for Young Adults

Characters

Protagonist
- female adolescent
- realistic; flawed
- appearance is inconsequential
- intelligent; interested in education and career
- faces important problems in and outside of the romance
- sometimes reason and emotion conflict
- multidimensional; not stereotyped

Romantic interest
- teenage male
- realistic; flawed
- appearance is inconsequential
- may or may not provide a positive relationship for the young woman (if positive, values her strength; if negative, may be physically and psychologically damaging)
- multidimensional; not stereotyped

Family
- varied social and economic backgrounds
- realistic
- relationships between family members is often strained
- family relationships may provide a subplot
- multidimensional; not stereotyped

Plot
- more than one plot line
- main plot often centers on a moral dilemma
- love relationship is often difficult
- love relationship is realistic; sexual relationship is not avoided and not exploited

Point of View
- protagonist's
- third person

Voice
- protagonist's
- sometimes older, wiser self

Literary Elements
- figurative language
- motifs (hazy light, seasons, darkness, etc.)

Theme
- varied
- "There is more to life than romantic love"
- "Individuals must develop outside of relationships"

boyfriend Dallas is virtually the head of his family. Dallas faces a moral dilemma. He has evidence against the construction company for which his father works. If he provides it in a negligence suit that has been brought, his father is likely to lose his job. His dilemma is central to the plot rather than peripheral, as it would be in many series romances.

Daly followed this novel with *First a Dream*. In this novel both Retta and Dallas are growing toward maturity. Seventeen-year-old Retta and her family move to California from their Pennsylvania home when a six-lane highway is built near it. Nineteen-year-old Dallas, who needs just a few more credits to graduate from high school, comes to California for a summer job at Rancho Arabian. The owners of the champion horses set restrictions on how often Dallas can see Retta. Both are disappointed, but Retta uses her time to pursue new interests as a journalist.

Isabelle Holland has written numerous fine romances with Gothic motifs. *Summer of My First Love*, according to Holland, is based on *Romeo and Juliet*, the best teenage love story of all time. Sarah is the daughter of upper-crust academic parents; Steve's family is Polish Catholic. Sarah is one of the summer people at the beach; Steve is a townie. She is embarrassed by her appearance because of a limp she developed from an accident. Rather than sit on the beach and meet people, she wants to find a job to earn money for art school. When she meets Steve, their relationship is rocky at first because the townspeople favor developing a small strip of land and the summer people want to preserve it. Eventually, however, they overcome their differences and fall in love. Sarah becomes pregnant but loses the baby.

After the First Love is the sequel. Sarah has been attending art school. While her parents are in Europe, she is spending the summer babysitting the Brewster twins. She meets an interesting European man and another man who is fighting deafness. When Steve shows up and wants to marry Sarah, Charles Brewster, her friend and confidant, accuses her of "getting around" with all these men. Sarah is able to sort out her feelings by the end of the novel and make some mature decisions.

Together and separately, Harry and Norma Fox Mazer have written several excellent romance novels for young adults. Norma and Harry's *Heartbeat* has three main characters. Tod lives with his father whose engineering career was halted after his wife's death. Hillary is the daughter of a Ph.D., but to her family's distress she wants to become an auto mechanic. Amos, Tod's best friend, is in love with Hillary. However, when Hillary and Tod meet, they fall in love and neither knows how to tell Amos. When Amos dies, Hillary and Tod's relationship is stressed and comes to an end.

Harry Mazer's *City Light* is unusual in that it has a male protagonist who is dumped by his girlfriend and then meets an artistic, mysterious girl through a computer network. *Hey Kid! Does She Love Me?* is a book about an unconventional love triangle involving an eighteen-year-old boy, a twenty-year-old girl, and a baby. In *The Girl of His Dreams* eighteen-year-old Willis has two ambitions: to compete against the best middle-distance runners in the world and to meet the girl of his dreams. He meets a girl who is nothing like the one in his dreams and eventually wins a track scholarship.

Norma Fox Mazer's *Someone to Love* is about an insecure college sophomore Nina Bloom who believes she has found in Mitch, a college dropout, someone to love. After moving in with Mitch she discovers that he becomes aggressive when angry, each time apologizing and making her feel it was her fault. Eventually Nina realizes that she must get out of the relationship. *Up in Seth's Room* is about a nineteen-year-old boy who is pushing a sexual relationship on a fifteen-year-old girl before she is ready. Finn loves Seth, or thinks she does, but the book ends without a resolution of the conflict. In *When We First Met* Jenny, a high school senior who has never experienced romance, falls in love at first sight. When she finally meets Rob, the object of her affection, she is appalled to learn that his mother was the drunk driver who killed her sister two years earlier.

Other accomplished authors of young adult literature have written romances. A novel with the theme that strong relationships are based on mutual respect is Bruce Clements's *Tom Loves Anna Loves Tom*. Terry Farish's *Shelter for a Seabird* is a romance involving a family in crisis. Andrea's father is selling their ancestral, island home. Swede, a nineteen-year-old AWOL soldier, enters Andrea's life just after she has returned home from giving up her baby girl for adoption and is experiencing a great sense of loss. Slowly Swede and Andrea learn to trust each other and trust turns into love. Lynn Hall's *Fair Maiden* is about a high school senior's first love. Jennifer plays Guinevere at a Renaissance fair where she meets "John the Lutanist," and the two form a tableau of a maiden serenaded by an admiring troubadour. Each day the fantasy world becomes more real and attractive compared to her life with a divorced mother and violent older brother. Jenny's perceptions of John change, however, when the fantasy world extends to actually spending the night together. William Jaspersohn's *Grounded* is about a teenage boy, Joe, who runs away from home after being grounded by his parents. After a newspaper interview with his parents, he becomes famous and must hide. He meets Nan, and finds himself on an island off the coast of Cape Cod where Nan's wealthy grandfather lives. Eventually Joe and Nan fall in love. In Margaret Willey's *Finding David Dolores* Arly, a thirteen-year-old girl, has a secret obsession for the talented David Dolores, a high school student.

Multicultural Romances

Rosa Guy's romance *My Love, My Love; or, The Peasant Girl*, set in the Antilles, is about a poor girl who nurses to health a wealthy creole man who has been injured in an auto accident. The theme of this love story, based on Hans Christian Anderson's *The Little Mermaid*, is that color and class divisions are difficult to bridge. *A White Romance* by Virginia Hamilton has a similar theme. Walter Dean Myers has also written a romance, *Motown and Didi: A Love Story*. Didi is able to rise above the vices and temptations of her inner-city neighborhood from which she attempts to rescue her brother Tony. In her attempt to save Tony, she informs on Touchy, a drug dealer. When he sends three of his henchmen to teach her a lesson, Motown, a homeless orphan, interferes with Touchy's plans. In gratitude Didi finds Motown an apartment which she helps furnish. Friendship turns to love, although both characters attempt to deny their emotions.

Janine Boissard, a French writer, is the author of *Cecile*, the love story of a girl from a closely knit, middle-class French family who loses her innocence and comes to terms with love. An earlier novel by Boissard, *A Matter of Feeling*, is a sensitively written romance about Pauline's first love with an artist nearly twice her age. Eve Bunting's *The Haunting of Safekeep* is a well-written Gothic romance that could be a springboard to Charlotte Brontë's *Jane Eyre* and Emily Brontë's *Wuthering Heights*.

British historical fiction writer Mollie Hunter has written a sensitive account of love in World War II Scotland in *Hold On to Love*. A romance that begins during World War II is the three-generation love story by M. E. Kerr *I Stay Near You*.

Jean Ure's *What If They Saw Me Now?* also takes place in Great Britain. This book is unusual in that it was published as a romance series book but has the characteristics of a good teenage romance. Jamie dreams of coming to the United States to play baseball but inadvertently becomes the male star of his school's charity ballet. He enjoys dancing as long as his friends don't see him in tights, and he takes a romantic interest in the school's prima ballerina Anita. Jamie, however, has trouble juggling ballet rehearsals and baseball practice. Cynthia Voigt has written an exciting, romantic adventure story *On Fortune's Wheel*. Birle runs away at night to guide a handsome highborn stranger from her parents' inn rather than marry a lusting hunter from her village. Of course, Birle loses her heart to the lord who knows little about surviving in the wilds. Their perilous journey out of the kingdom involves a shipwreck, pirates, and slavery.

EPILOGUE: THE EXTRAORDINARY OFFERS ESCAPE

One reason for reading is to escape the routine and problems of everyday living. The best escape literature not only permits readers to lose themselves in a book but gives readers something to think about. Mysteries provide an intriguing, complicated puzzle to solve. Readers who read a lot of mysteries know what to look for as they solve the puzzles, but are often fooled by the ingenuity of the best mystery writers. Suspense stories allow ordinary people to confront situations and people that are not only beyond the ordinary but often terrifying. Readers of suspense can see themselves on the pages of the book because they are not unlike the ordinary characters in the book. However, the situations in which these characters find themselves provide page-turning excitement. In adventure stories ordinary characters manage to survive in extraordinary environments. They climb mountains, ford rivers, fight wars. Some adventures are historical, allowing readers to learn something about life in the past. Others take place in faraway places and in diverse cultures.

Romances, too, can provide escape and, at the same time, allow the reader to contemplate the difficulties of relationships. From the best romances readers learn that love does not conquer all, that individuals must first know themselves before they can give a part of themselves to a relationship.

Teachers can help young, egocentric readers become mature readers by recognizing the importance and validity of good escape reading. As Gary Blackwood suggests, we can encourage students to read books "about situations outside their own usually limited experience" (p. 49). And as educator Patricia Kelly suggests, by accepting the books immature readers select and read on their own, teachers can help young readers bridge beyond these books by helping them find "books that provide a broader reading perspective" (p. 19).

Suggested readings

Apple, M. W., ed. Series Editor's Introduction. In *Becoming a Woman through Romance*. Routledge, 1990.

Bennett, S. G., and A. Kuhn. "Love and Lust in the Secondary Schools: Do Formula Romances Have a Place in the Schools?" *ALAN Review*, Spring 1987, pp. 42–44.

Blackwood, G. L. "Ordinary People, Extraordinary Situations." *ALAN Review*, Fall 1989, p. 49.

Bugniazet, J. "A Telephone Interview with Robert Cormier." *ALAN Review*, Winter 1985, pp. 14–18.

Campbell, P. J. *Presenting Robert Cormier*. G. K. Hall, 1989, pp. 64–79.

Christian-Smith, L. K. *Becoming a Woman through Romance*. Routledge, 1990.

Crossen, C. "Book Publisher Finds Lucrative Niche in Soap-Opera Series for Teen-Age Girls." *Wall Street Journal*, 11 February 1988.

Daly, M. "Maureen Daly: One on One." *ALAN Review*, Spring 1988, pp. 1–4, 6.

Ellis, W. G. "Cormier and the Pessimistic View." *ALAN Review*, Winter 1985, pp. 10–12, 52.

Hartvigsen, M. K., and C. B. Hartvigsen. "The Divine Miss Blossom Culp." *ALAN Review*, Winter 1989, pp. 33–35.

Harvey, B. "Wildfire, Tame but Deadly." *Interracial Books for Children Bulletin*, 1981, pp. 8–10.

Kelly, P. P. "Transitional Novels for Readers of Teen Romances." *ALAN Review*, Fall 1991, pp. 19–21.

Litton, J. "Double Date to Double Love: Female Sex Roles in Teen Romances, 1942–1985." *ALAN Review*, pp. 45–46, 55.

Malmgren, D. "Knowing Your Audience." *ALAN Review*, Fall 1989, pp. 50–51.

Meaker, M. "Getting All Kids to Read My Books." *ALAN Review*, Fall 1989, pp. 46, 48.

Nilsen, A. P., and K. L. Donelson. *Literature for Today's Young Adults*. Scott Foresman, 1980, p. 221.

Parrish, B., and K. Atwood. "Romantic Fiction Revisited." *ALAN Review*, Spring 1986, pp. 53–56, 74.

Pilgrim, G. H., and M. K. McAllister. *Books, Young People, and Reading Guidance*. 2d ed. Harper & Row, 1968.

Rollin, L. "Isabelle Holland: A Nineteenth-Century Romantic for Twentieth-Century Realists (an interview)." *ALAN Review*, Fall 1985, pp. 9–12, 54.

Smith, W. "An Earlier Start on Romance." *Publisher's Weekly*, 13 November 1981, pp. 58–61.

7 Imaginative Literature

Focus Questions

1. Why is reading imaginative literature important for adolescents?
2. What is the definition of science fiction? How do "hard" and "soft" science fiction differ?
3. What is fantasy? What is the difference between high and low fantasy?
4. Why is the fantasy theme of the quest so important to adolescents?
5. What legends, myths, and folktales are explored in young adult literature?

PROLOGUE

The great biophysicist, J. B. S. Haldane said that "The universe is not only stranger than we imagine, it is stranger than we can imagine." More recently, Douglas Adams, in introducing Chapter 1 of *The Restaurant at the End of the Universe* writes:

> There is a theory which states that if ever anyone discovers exactly what the universe is for, and why it is here, it will instantly disappear and be replaced by something even more bizarre and inexplicable. There is another theory which states that this has already happened.

Well, it has happened. We are living in a new and extraordinary universe and we have, by and large, failed to notice it. We have failed to meet the demands that this new universe makes of us, because psychologically we are still living in the old universe, a universe that has vanished and is not likely to appear again.

Even with all the innovations and experiments in our educational system, we are still failing to understand that our students, having been born into the new universe, are more comfortable in it than we are. Often, what we teach them is confusing, rather than enlightening.

When did the old universe disappear, to be replaced by the present one? . . . For me the moment of radical universal shift came in New Mexico when the nuclear physicists exploded that first atomic device which opened the atom with a light brighter than a million suns.

. . . What had happened?

Several contradictory and paradoxical things.

Ordinary people in the United States of America now knew that we had a weapon with such capacity for destruction it was beyond the reach of our imaginations.

On the other hand, the opening of the atom revealed a universe of beauty and of interrelatedness also largely beyond the reach of our imaginations. We learned—or should have learned—that nothing in the universe happens in isolation. We did indeed start a chain reaction—a reaction of continuing technological change: everything that happens affects everything else. Indeed, if we kill a butterfly, that could cause an earthquake on a planet in a galaxy thousands of light years from ours. And how does volcanic explosion on a distant planet affect us?

It is in many ways a terrifying place, this new universe which . . . suddenly appeared . . . [with] that first atomic explosion. It would be even more terrifying if there were not assurances that there are basic things which do not change.

The first is that there *is* a universe. Even through the smog and our polluted skies we can see the stars. They are there, galaxies and galaxies of them, and we, on our little planet, are part of the glory of creation.

The love of human being for human being does not change. In the days when people lived in trees or caves just as now when many of us live in the great caves of apartment buildings, people meet, fall in love, and make babies. Those we love must die, and we grieve; we weep; we mourn. We are helped by the loving concern of our families, our friends. These are the basic elements of life, as basic as the atom with its nucleus and surrounding electrons.

Truth is eternal in all our universe. Knowledge is changeable. The trouble comes when we confuse the two, and that is one of the worst problems in our changed universe. Truth, love, courage, joy, creativity.

These do not change. These are basic. They are our foundation, and we, and the children, can survive and live in this universe as long as the foundation is firm. Because we are that amazing creature, the human being who has free will; we can by our thoughts and actions, change this changing universe. Don't let us be afraid to do so! This is how we become human. ✦

From Madeleine L'Engle, "Understanding the New Universe," *ALAN Review* (Winter 1988), p. 1.

Literature to Change the Universe

Madeleine L'Engle is one of the most highly regarded authors of young adult fantasy and science fiction, or imaginative literature. She told us why above; she also provided the teachers to whom she spoke these words at a conference in Los Angeles, California, a challenge. Ironically, the morning after her presentation there was an earthquake in Los Angeles, not a major one and not an unusual occurrence for that city. However, those of us who heard her speak could not help but wonder about connections; nothing, as she told us, happens in isolation.

Imaginative literature refers to books that allow readers to imagine worlds beyond the day-to-day world they know. Such books provide more than escape; they give readers the opportunity to think, to reason, to make connections. Teachers, through conversations with their students, can help young readers see these connections. Some kinds of imaginative literature can help young people understand the extraordinary changes that have occurred and continue to occur in our universe. At the same time, through such books students can begin to understand those elements that are unchanging.

The short excerpt from Madeleine L'Engle's essay above suggests a number of the questions teachers can ask students about imaginative literature: How does the world presented in the book differ from our world? How is it similar? What connections can you make between the two worlds? Is the other world created by the author one that could exist based on what we know today about our universe? What parts of it are possible? What parts are impossible? On what evidence do you base your opinion? What knowledge, scientific or otherwise, is the basis for the connections the author makes between the real world and the other world of the book? Are these connections based on current knowledge? Is this knowledge changing? What parts of the imaginative world in the book are based on basic human truths? What do the characters in the book do to change their world? Are their actions based on knowledge or truth?

Because imaginative literature is allegorical, providing an extended metaphor for our own world, we can ask students questions to help them make connections between characters and plots in the books and people and experiences in their own world. Teachers can examine current news stories about almost any aspect of our universe and attempt to understand these stories in terms of how various elements in them connect, how they might affect the future, and how our knowledge and values influence our interpretation of them. For example, students can examine the issue of the spotted owl and the lumber industry in the Northwest. They might be asked questions as follows: What do you know about this issue? What do you know about the issue of clear-cutting? What is your stand on the issue? On what knowledge and values do you base your stand? On what knowledge and values do the environmentalists base their opposition to clear-cutting? On what knowledge and values does the lumber industry base its defense? Is the knowledge base changing? In what ways? What parts of each side of the argument are based on universal truths? What connections between events and possible subsequent events does each side use to strengthen their arguments? What other connections might be made?

Science Fiction

Writers of science fiction make connections between the world as we know it and the world they create. According to young adult science fiction writer William Sleator, "Science fiction is literature about something that hasn't happened yet, but might be possible some day. That it might be possible is the important part" (1988, p. 4). Science fiction is based on scientific knowledge, or what we know about our universe; that is, it shows us something that *could* happen.

According to Sleator, the author of imaginative fiction must do everything the author of realistic fiction must do. In addition, the author of imaginative fiction must "convince the reader to believe in something that has never happened" (p. 5). The story must be plausible and the author must establish credibility by basing the story on hard scientific evidence. H. M. Hoover, author of young adult science fiction, agrees, "Good science fiction must make you see what is not known. Good science fiction teaches as well as entertains. . . . By wondering, the reader is led to the image of space. From the image the reader enters into real science" (speech to the International Reading Association convention, Atlanta, Georgia, April 1979). Sleator contends that young adult science fiction must be just as accurate, just as scientific, as adult science fiction. However, he suggests that young adult science fiction should begin in the real world and be peopled by realistic characters. (See Figure 7.1 for the characteristics of good science fiction for young adults.)

The Science Fiction Continuum

The wide variety of science fiction novels can be arranged along a continuum. At one end of the continuum is what many critics call "hard" science fiction, fiction based in the hard sciences of biology, chemistry, physics, and mathematics. The harder the science fiction, in terms of scientific content, the more difficult it is to read without substantial scientific knowledge.

"Soft" science fiction is based in the social sciences of psychology, sociology, anthropology, and political science. The term *soft* is not pejorative but simply indicates a difference in the academic orientation of the novel. In the mid-range of the continuum are novels based in such fields as ecology, computer science, and robotics.

Knowing the difference between the variety of novels within this genre can help teachers determine in which subject areas to teach the novels. Hard science fiction novels are more likely to be appropriate in science classrooms. Soft science fiction novels offer good, challenging reading in social studies classrooms. The novels in the middle of the continuum are often appropriate in both science and social studies classrooms.

Figure 7.1
Characteristics of Good Science Fiction for Young Adults

Characters

Protagonist
- adolescent
- believable; similar to the reader
- has superhuman qualities that are humanly possible (e.g., extreme intelligence, bravery, psychic abilities, insight)
- may be a victim
- has real human problems

Antagonist
- not always a person, sometimes a situation or the setting
- evil
- alien
- may be other self of the protagonist

Plot
- based on the laws of science
- events are plausible
- requires suspension of disbelief
- begins in the real world as the reader knows it
- follows rules set by the author which must have a foundation in the laws of science
- fast-moving, exciting

Point of View
- protagonist
- third person
- omniscient

Voice
- protagonist
- sometimes second, older or wiser self

Setting
- based on the laws of science
- moves from reader's real world to imaginary world
- often set in past or future

Theme
- "Science has important effects on our lives"
- "We can better understand the world by examining other imaginary but possible worlds"
- "The world of the future is an outgrowth of our world today"

Authors of Young Adult Science Fiction

While fantasy is as old as humankind, science fiction is a relatively new genre. Two of the earliest science fiction works are Mary Shelley's *Frankenstein,* written in 1818, and Jules Verne's *Journey to the Center of the Earth,* written in 1864. The genre did not gain popularity with either writers or readers until the twentieth century. Science fiction written specifically for young adults perhaps dates from Madeleine L'Engle's *A Wrinkle in Time,* first published in 1962.

Because the number of science fiction works written and published specifically for young adults is so small, we will first discuss the few major authors in the genre. (Madeleine L'Engle will be discussed in the fantasy section of the chapter.) In later sections of the chapter we will examine science fiction by topic.

H. M. Hoover   H. M. Hoover, one of the few female writers of hard science fiction for young adults, tends to set her novels in other worlds. *Another Heaven, Another Earth* is set on the planet Xilan which was colonized by Earth and then forgotten. The colonists adapt to their environment and develop their own skills, tools, and values. When an expedition from Earth arrives, these values are challenged. *The Bell Tree* takes place on the planet Tanin which is unpopulated except for the workers at a high-level research station and the miners who mine gemstones and rare wood. Jenny and her father unravel the mystery of a lost city after her father is given an ancient artifact. *Return to Earth* is about Galen Innes, a wise, old governor-general of an outlying colony, who returns to Earth to help fifteen-year-old Samara, who has become Corporate Director of one of the giant corporations that rule the Earth in the year 3307. Following the assassination of her mother, she has gained unlimited power.

William Sleator   Probably the most prolific and popular writer of science fiction for young adults, William Sleator writes books based in the hard sciences. Unlike Hoover's books, each of Sleator's begins on Earth. Sixteen-year-old David in *The Duplicate* is able to duplicate himself by using a machine he has found washed up on the beach. *House of Stairs* is about a psychological experiment on conditioned human response in which five kids are taken from a state institution and find themselves in a place without walls, ceiling, or floor, but with endless stairs. Sixteen-year-old Barney in *Interstellar Pig* is invited by three exotic neighbors to play a very unusual board game. In *The Boy Who Reversed Himself* Laura finds a mirror-image message written in her locker and later discovers that her biology report has been written likewise. The next thing she knows her neighbor Omar mirror-reverses himself. In *Singularity* twin boys discover a time contraction field in a small, isolated playhouse. *Strange Attractors* also deals with time travel and the altering of historic events.

Robert Westall   Robert Westall is a British author who incorporates soft science fiction and fantasy in many of his works. In *Urn Burial* a shepherd sees a piece of metal protruding from a heap of stones in the Lake District. He finds a coffin beneath it containing a six-foot, humanlike cat creature, two helmets, a blaster gun, and a red capsule. Whenever he wears one of the helmets he goes back in time and becomes the helmet's owner. *Futuretrack 5* is reminiscent of Orwell's *1984;* the plot involves hidden microphones, concealed cameras, and psychocopters that can detect danger.

Margaret Mahy   Mahy sets her soft science fiction novels in her native New Zealand. *Aliens in the Family* is about an alien who returns from the future to be tested while visiting Earth. *Memory* emphasized the psychological. Jonny is attempting to learn more about his sister's death. In the process he moves in with Sophie, a strange old woman with Alzheimer's disease, who confuses him with someone in her past. However, through her snatches of memory he begins to piece together the truth about Janine's death. *The Tricksters* is the tale of a very strange trio of tricksters who claim to be descendants of the builder of the house in which Ariadne, called Harry, and her family are spending their summer holiday. Mahy's most terrifying novel is *The Changeover: A Supernatural Romance,* the story of fourteen-year-old clairvoyant Laura and the older vision of herself she sees in her mirror. In her mirror into the future she sees dangers, some of which she cannot prevent. One such danger is the destruction of her brother Jacko by Carmody Braque, a demon who preys on human vitality. She convinces a witch named Sorensen Carlisle to conduct a changeover. Laura herself becomes a witch and uses her powers to destroy the evil Braque and release Jacko from the grip of death.

Ursula K. LeGuin   Ursula LeGuin in *The Dispossessed: An Ambiguous Utopia* explores the difference between anarchy in Anarres and capitalism in Urras. Neither of the systems, taken to extremes, provides an atmosphere in which people can work creatively in freedom. In *The Left Hand of Darkness* she explores the relationship of Genry, an envoy from the most technologically advanced world in the galaxy, and Estraven, who comes from the underdeveloped winter kingdom of Karhide. LeGuin explores another side of humankind in the far-off world of the planet Athshe in *The Word for World Is Forest*. The human invaders of the planet enslave the natives and despoil the forest of Athshe. The Athsheans, who have learned how to kill from the humans, turn the tables on their captors.

Monica Hughes   Monica Hughes writes both soft and hard science fiction for young adults. *Beyond the Dark River* is about Benjamin, a fifteen-year-old Amish boy of the twenty-first century, who has survived the nuclear holocaust. In *Devil on My Back* Hughes explores the question: What would happen if our personal computers were attached directly to our brains? *The Keeper of the Isis Light* is about Olwen whose parents have been sent to the planet Isis to prepare for future colonizers from Earth.

Richard Peck   Although it is difficult to classify Richard Peck as a writer of science fiction, he utilizes many aspects of the genre in his Blossom Culp books and *Voices after Midnight*. For example, Blossom in all her novels, is able to deal with current problems because of her ability to travel back and forth in time. The Blossom Culp books, including *The Ghost Belonged to Me* and *Ghosts I Have Been,* are accessible to young readers just beginning to explore the science fiction genre. *Voices after Midnight* also uses the device of time travel to take a brother and sister back to New York City during the blizzard of March 12, 1888.

Robert Cormier   Although only one of Robert Cormier's novels ventures into the genre of science fiction, his other realistic suspense novels (see Chapter 6) are so focused on the field of psychology that they could almost be classified as soft science fiction. A good example is *Fade,* in which thirteen-year-old Paul Moreaux possesses a haunting secret with terrifying responsibilities—he can fade from the visible to the invisible world. At first Paul finds this genetic ability very appealing, but as he learns the secrets of others' lives, he realizes that he must control the fade or it will control him. Like the best science fiction, this novel makes clear that everything we do has consequences and that each action is connected to a subsequent action and each individual is connected to others. Therefore, like Paul Moreaux in Cormier's novel, each of us has responsibility for assessing our actions and determining how they connect with other actions and other people.

The Past

Projection into the past is explored in Lester del Rey's *Tunnel through Time,* in which Pete and Bob are the only ones who can save Pete's father from a perilous fate after his jammed time machine strands him in the Mesozoic era. When time traveling in Jack Finney's *Time and Again* takes Simon Morley back to New York of the 1880s, he experiences difficulty because he is out of step with the times. In Eleanor Cameron's *Beyond Silence,* Andy travels back nearly one hundred years ago to the world of Deirdre which he indirectly affects by his presence. *Vision Quest* by Pamela F. Service involves two layers of time, the present, in which Kate finds an old Native American healing stone, and the past, in which she has an encounter with the stone's owner. In Paul Samuel Jacobs's *Born into Light,* streaks of lightning appear in the sky and wild children emerge from egglike structures scattered across Earth in the year 1913. Two of these children are taken in by a poor New England family. They mature from their wild state to brilliance in a relatively short period of time, and they begin to age rapidly.

In Joan Aiken's *The Shadow Guests,* Cosmo Curtoys discovers from his cousin Eunice, an Oxford mathematics professor, that his family line carries a deadly curse that has afflicted every generation since the Roman occupation of Britain. Cosmo sets out to discover and break the curse. Traveling through time he encounters three of his ancestors just before they become victims of the curse. Aiken combines Einstein's theory of relativity, parapsychology, and mysticism to create a believable tale.

The Present or Near Future

In some science fiction books the effects of new technological advancements are examined and often taken to the farthest extremes of possibility. In Phyllis Gotlieb's *O Master Caliban!* human genetic mutation leads to disaster. In the mature novel *The Boys from Brazil* (Levin) and *The Paper Dolls* (Davies), scientists face serious ethical issues as they conduct research into genetics. The possible dangers of computers are considered in *The God Machine* (Caidin) and *The Tale of the Big Computer* (Johannesson). What would happen if a child had a twin robot he could send to school in his place? Mildred Ames's *Is There Life on a Plastic Planet?* examines this scenario. Will technology take us too far? Will machines become our masters? Ten science fiction writers explore these questions in *Men and Machines,* edited by Robert Silverberg. These topics are also explored in *Traitors from Within* by R. A. Montgomery.

Ecological disaster is a common theme of science fiction set in the present or the near future. In John Brunner's *The Sheep Look Up,* an ecologist battles to alert the world to impending doom. In Thomas Baird's *Smart Rats,* the world is polluted and overpopulated, and the ozone layer has been destroyed.

What are some of the likely results of a nuclear attack? The possibilities are investigated in books such as D. C. Halacy's *Return from Luna,* Ruth Hooker's *Kennaquhair,* H. M. Hoover's *Treasures of Morrow,* Walter M. Miller's *A Canticle for Leibowitz,* Denis Johnson's *Fiskadoro,* Gloria Miklowitz's *After the Bomb,* Robert Swindells's *Brother in the Land,* and Robert O'Brien's *Z for Zachariah.*

John Rowe Townsend's *Noah's Castle* is set ten years from now in a world suffering from a shortage of food. Some families have stockpiled large quantities of food and attempt to hide it from neighbors. Ray Kytle in *Fire and Ice* explores what happens when a new ice age threatens. Another more recent book on this topic is Gary L. Blackwood's *The Dying Sun.* Daniel Keyes's narrative *Flowers for Algernon* examines the consequences of unchecked scientific experimentation. Charlie, a young retarded man, lives for a short time with superior intelligence. The loss of his intelligence is heartbreaking to him and the people around him. In *House of Stairs* by William Sleator, five teenagers find themselves in an experiment in which they are conditioned to become robots.

The Far Distant Future

Isaac Asimov is the editor of *Tomorrow's Children,* a collection of stories about children of a hundred, a thousand, and a million years from now. *Children of Infinity,* edited by Roger Elwood, is a collection of original science fiction stories for young readers. Although not written for young adults, Asimov's Foundation trilogy, including *Foundation, Foundation and Empire,* and *The Second Foundation,* is a favorite with teenage science fiction fans. Protagonist Hari Seldon creates the Foundation to preserve human culture during the dark ages after the collapse of the first galactic empire.

In Gregory Benford's *Jupiter Project,* a living laboratory is orbiting Jupiter, and Matt must prove himself or be returned to a hostile Earth. *Cities in Flight* by James Blish is another set of novels not written specifically for teens but enjoyed by those who are already science fiction fans. The tale centers on the "spindizzy" drive that people in the cities use to escape the repressive environment on Earth for an existence in space. Earth is no longer inhabitable two thousand years from now in Louise Lawrence's *Andra. Star Trek 1–12* and *Star Trek Reader 1–10,* also by Blish, are pure entertainment for teenage devotees of the "Star Trek" reruns on television and the "Star Trek" films. The books enjoy almost the same cultlike following as the television series.

The Earth of the future looks rather bleak in Ben Bova's *City of Darkness,* in which Ron Morgan explores life in the isolated dome that once was New York City. World War IV has brought an end to the technological age in Leigh Brackett's *The Long Tomorrow.* Len Colter must decide whether to join a group of dissident scientists who want to restore science. An Earth that is controlled by superior beings is explored in John Christopher's *The City of Gold and Lead, The Pool of Fire,* and *The White Mountains,* as well as Arthur C. Clarke's *Childhood's End.* Six teenagers in John

Neufeld's *Sleep Two, Three, Four!* are running away from the totalitarian police state of the future. Kurt Vonnegut's book *Cat's Cradle* is a satire about the end of the world. Although this book is too difficult for many young readers, mature adolescent readers who enjoy science fiction usually find it interesting and humorous.

Alien Beings

In Alexander Key's *The Forgotten Door,* Little Jon can read people's minds, communicate with animals, and run like the wind. Sirius, the Dog Star, is falsely accused of losing the Zoi in *Dogsbody* by Diane Jones. As a punishment he must roam Earth in search for it. Lucinda, in Jean Karl's *Beloved Benjamin Is Waiting,* meets an alien mentor in a deserted house on the grounds of a cemetery after she is abandoned by her parents. In *Alien Child* by Pamela Sargent, Nita, who was born when her alien protector accidentally released an embryo in a research lab, believes that she is the only human left on Earth. Martin comes to Earth as a spaceman in *Down to Earth* by Patricia Wrightson. In John Rowe Townsend's *The Visitors,* sixteen-year-old John is baffled by the unconventional behavior of three visitors from the future. An excellent novelization of the movie script *Close Encounters of the Third Kind* by Steven Spielberg tells of Earth's first encounter with aliens from outer space. In Robert Heinlein's *Stranger in a Strange Land,* an Earthling raised by Martians returns to Earth and upsets society. Although not written only for young readers, this book is often a favorite, even with teenagers who have not yet discovered science fiction.

Robots, Machines, and Cyborgs

In Martin Caidin's *Cyborg,* an air force test pilot becomes the first cyborg, a human being modified for life in a non-Earth environment through the substitution of artificial organs and other body parts. This book became the basis for television's "Six Million Dollar Man" series. Ron Goulart's *What's Become of Screwloose?* is a series of stories about mechanical devices gone wild and humans' problems in dealing with the cyborgs they have created. In Arthur Clarke's *2001: A Space Odyssey* we meet a computer that goes crazy. David Gerrold's *When Harlie Was One* is about a computer that thinks it's human. The robots in *The Unsleeping Eye* by David Guy Compton and the humanoids in *The Humanoids* by Jack Williamson can see. In Walter Tevis's *Mockingbird* robots and clones have replaced most of the human population, reading and writing are no longer useful, and human lives are without purpose. The book ends on a hopeful note, however, as two of the remaining humans discover the lost emotion of love.

The Sea

The future and the sea are part of the science fiction genre. In Carl Biemiller's *The Hydronauts,* 80 percent of Earth is covered by water, and its inhabitants live in hive cities, communicate with dolphins, and listen to songs with titles like "Amoeba Though I Am, Nothing Can Divide Me." The underwater world in Karel Capek's *The War with the Newts* supports a giant race of intelligent newts that are enlisted to do people's work under the sea. They dig harbors and canals, and learn human ways. Eventually, they turn against their masters.

Faraway Worlds

The Martian Chronicles by Ray Bradbury, a classic science fiction work not written specifically for young adults, is about the colonization of Mars by Earth in the late twentieth century. Possibly because of its near-time proximity, even students who are not fans of science fiction usually enjoy this book. Another book about Mars is Gordon R. Dickson's *The Far Call.*

Some science fiction narratives take place on spaceships or space stations somewhere in space. Jeffrey Carver's *Star Rigger's Way* is about an apprentice starship pilot who drifts into the Flux, a strange area of space that carries vehicles at speeds faster than sound. Interstellar warfare is the backdrop for Gordon Dickson's *Dorsai!* Robert Heinlein's *Rocketship Galileo,* a narrative about an early flight to the moon, is a good selection for less mature readers. The story of the flight is particularly interesting in comparison with the actual moon voyages. In Leonard Wibberley's *Encounter near Venus,* four young people take a cruise on their uncle's custom-built flying saucer. *Splinter of the Mind's Eye* by Alan Dean Foster is a sequel to the film *Star Wars* in which the spaceship on a diplomatic mission crashes on Mimban.

Imaginary societies in other galaxies are often described by science fiction writers. H. M. Hoover creates a new world in *The Delikon* and *The Rains of Eridan.* In Lester del Rey's *Prisoners of Space,* the maze of tunnels beneath the lunar surface holds secrets to life in space. In *Enchantress from the Stars* and *The Far Side of Evil,* Sylvia Engdahl tells of the adventures of Elana, whose mission is to aid developing civilizations without interfering with their natural evolution. In *This Star Shall Abide* and *Beyond the Tomorrow Mountains,* Engdahl depicts the coming-of-age of young Noren, a rebel against the establishment in his faraway world.

Combining Science Fiction and Reality

Not all young adult readers are attracted to the world of science fiction. The joining of science fiction and reality in many novels, however, helps bridge the gap between the real world as the adolescent knows it and the hypothetical world created by the science fiction writer. In *Stardance* by Spider Robinson and Jeanne Robinson, Shara Drummond wants to become a professional dancer but is unable to. However, the zero-gravity environment of the orbiting Skyfac gives her the chance. Shara is an Earth child with humanlike dreams, but she achieves her dreams in space. In Jean Karl's *Beloved Benjamin Is Waiting,* a realistically portrayed girl who has been abandoned by her parents meets a fantastic mentor who is an alien from another galaxy. The narrative takes place in a deserted house in a cemetery. In T. W. Hard's *Sum VII,* a well-preserved Egyptian mummy at a state university is resuscitated by a team of medical students. He turns out to be a visitor from outer space.

In *Mastodonia* by Clifford Simak, a dog returns home with an ancient spear in his side and meat and bones from a 10,000-year-old dinosaur. The dog's owner soon learns the secret of traveling to the Pleistocene era. The people of Earth exploit the secret as big-game hunters plan safaris into Mastodonia and the government finds a solution to the world's overpopulation problem. *The Hunters* by Burt Wetanson and Thomas Hoobler takes place in the normal everyday town of Bear Paw, Montana, but when a strange couple walk down Main Street and promise the residents a journey into a better world, peculiar things begin to happen.

Outer Space and All That Junk by Mel Glidden joins together several genres: humor, mystery, realistic fiction, and science fiction. Fourteen-year-old Myron Duberville is sent off to spend the summer with his uncle who runs Astronetics Corporation and collects junk in case there is an alien among it. This joining of real people and real places to unreal events and places makes the science fiction narrative believable and allows young readers to see themselves in the story.

The writer of good science fiction, as well as the writer of good fantasy, must make the unreal seem real. The characters must possess believable human traits, even if they are aliens. The problems of the protagonists must seem real, even if they are experienced on a flying saucer. While good science fiction is plausible and believable, it also removes readers from the real world and allows them to feel invincible.

Fantasy

Fantasy, like science fiction, is far more than escape literature. It is literature that instructs through the use of allegory, or extended metaphor. The world constructed by the author of a fantasy is a world unlike the real world but one in which the problems of the hero are similar to the problems of the reader.

The Magical Moment

According to highly acclaimed author of young adult fantasy Meredith Ann Pierce, every fantasy has a "magical moment." This is the instant in the fantasy in which "the 'real' world intersects the 'other' world," the construct of the author. Pierce contends that in most fantasies the real world is "recognizably Earth," and the magical moment comes when the hero of the fantasy transcends this world and enters the other world: "Lucy enters Narnia from World War II England in C. S. Lewis's *The Lion, the Witch, and the Wardrobe.* Will encounters the magical world of Gramarye from Buckinghamshire of the 1970s in Susan Cooper's *The Dark Is Rising.* Lewis Carroll's Victorian Alice falls down the rabbit hole" (1988, p. 39).

In some fantasies, including Pierce's own *The Darkangel,* the real world is not Earth but a world of the writer's imagination. "The culture, customs, politics and so on found there are likely to be very different from what we, the readers, are used to. . . . [For example,] before she meets one upon the Steeps of Terrain, the moongirl Aeriel doesn't believe in darkangels." When Aeriel meets the darkangel, she moves from her real world to the other world; this is the magical moment when real meets the fantastic. According to Pierce what distinguishes the other world from the real world is "the *kind* of place it is. The 'other' world is *magical.* . . . Miracles occur here. Birds speak. Magic operates. Here be dragons. Time itself may be distorted . . . compressed, as when Lessingham and Antiope enter Dr. Vandermast's 'house of heart's desire' in E. R. Eddison's *Mistress of Mistresses* . . . or [dilated] as in the well-known folk tale *Sleeping Beauty,* where the princess Briar Rose awakes from what must have seemed to her but an hour's dreaming only to discover her swoon has lasted a hundred years" (Pierce, 1988, pp. 39–40).

According to Pierce, the other world of the fantasy is like a dream world, "strange, haunted, changeable," and private. The people and situations the hero encounters in the dream world are "metaphors for private concerns. By slaying the dragon, as Hugh does in Ursula K. LeGuin's *The Beginning Place,* our hero is actually slaying some dragonish part of his own soul, cowardice, in this case. Sometimes it's something else: greed or pride." When the hero leaves this dreamlike other world and returns to the orderly waking world, he or she has changed and will never again be the same.

The Importance of Fantasy

The fantasy, like the fairy tales of childhood, allows for self-transformation. Dorothy in *The Wizard of Oz* will be able to handle Miss Gulch after she has faced down the witch and unmasked the wizard. Like the Cowardly Lion she has gained backbone, like the Scarecrow she has used her intelligence, and like the Tin Woodsman she has learned the importance of caring about others. Readers of fantasy, like children who have been introduced to fairy tales, as scholar Bruno Bettelheim points out in his classic *The Uses of Enchantment,* will be better able to face the difficulties of life because they have learned

> that a struggle against severe difficulties in life is unavoidable, is an intrinsic part of human existence—but that if one does not shy away, but steadfastly meets unexpected and often unjust hardships, one masters all obstacles and at the end emerges victorious. . . . The child needs most particularly to be given suggestions in symbolic form about how he may deal with these issues and grow safely into maturity. "Safe" stories mention neither death nor aging, the limits of our existence, nor the wish for eternal life. The fairy tale, by contrast, confronts the child squarely with the basic human predicaments. (Bettelheim 1976, p. 8)

The Hero's Quest

The hero of the fantasy may or may not be a real human being, although in young adult fantasy the protagonist almost always is a real adolescent. However, as young adult fantasy writer Walter Wangerin, Jr., pointed out in a speech to the National Council of Teachers of English in November 1980, even if the hero is not a real person, as in his *The Book of the Dun Cow,* "heroes are the gathering of all characteristics of people. The hero in the epic is the people—to have a hero you must have a community of people."

The theme of the fantasy is the quest. The hero's quest may be for self-transformation or self-awareness, or it may be a quest against evil. Whatever the quest, in the world of fantasy, the hero must strive to overcome evil through a quest in which a multitude of problems must be solved. While in the other world the protagonist need not conform to the natural laws as we know them but can use fantastic means to reach his or her goal. Within the world the fantasy writer has created, however, those laws must be consistent. At the end of the fantasy the hero has achieved something. What has been achieved is not necessarily what the hero expected to accomplish. Evil is not destroyed, but it is temporarily defeated; it will return to be conquered again.

The fantasy world is often totally different from the real world. Animals may speak or humans may use a new language. People may be unnaturally small or large. Mythological beasts may roam the landscape. The world may look nothing like the world in which the reader lives. It may be under the sea or upside down. It may be a realm of total darkness or total light. Regardless of how unusual the world of the story is, the main characters must struggle and accept the consequences of their actions. By being steadfast in the quest the hero conquers the odds. Temporarily victorious, the hero knows that the struggle will not end. Figure 7.2 summarizes the characteristics of good young adult fantasy.

The Fantasy Continuum

Fantasy, like science fiction, can be viewed on a continuum. High fantasy contains all of the elements listed in Figure 7.2. It presents a complex other world that follows value-laden rules. The higher the fantasy, the more complex the allegory. Readers of high fantasy look for the multiple meanings of the story. Low fantasy may take place primarily in the real world. The book will involve a quest, but the fantasy world may be only in the mind of the protagonist.

Authors of Young Adult Fantasy

Lloyd Alexander   Although Lloyd Alexander is probably best known for his historical fiction for young adults, his Westmark trilogy is an enjoyable fantasy series set in a mythical kingdom. The first book in the trilogy, *Westmark,* won the 1981 American Book Award. In this book Theo is forced to leave town because of a murder he thinks he committed. He becomes involved with a showman, a dwarf, a beautiful girl, and with Cabbarus, who is influencing the king against him. In *The Kestrel,* the second book in the trilogy, Theo is prince consort-to-be, and his friend Mickle has ascended the throne as Queen Augusta. Theo sets out incognito to assess the condition of the realm. While on his quest, powerful elements of the nobility conspire with neighboring Regia to overthrow the queen. Theo and his friends battle these forces of evil to save the queen and the kingdom. *The Beggar Queen,* the final book, pits Theo and his friends Florian and Justin against their old enemy Cabbarus. Theo, the protagonist, continues to grow throughout the trilogy, from an unwilling hero to a hero who recognizes his weaknesses and knows his many strengths. As in all good fantasies, as Madeleine L'Engle has told us, the essential qualities of humankind are present in the characters: love, loyalty, deceit, hatred, suffering, and compassion.

Ursula K. LeGuin   LeGuin's Earthsea trilogy is popular with young adults. In *The Wizard of Earthsea* Ged must master the monster within himself by facing and defeating the gebbeth from the other world. *The Farthest Shore,* the third book in the trilogy (and the sequel to *The Tombs of Atuan*), is the most complex. It introduces the new character Arren, a young prince who travels with Archmage Ged on his last and most perilous mission. The book includes ornate language and discussions of life and death, and love and courage. Ged and Arren travel to the far reaches of Earthsea to seek the evil spirit who is choking the land and taking the mystic powers from the mages and dragonlords. In a final heroic effort, Ged uses all his magic powers to seal the breach through which the potency of the land is being drained and gives up his life in the process. The continuation of a trilogy after many years have elapsed is an unusual phenomenon in fantasy writing. In 1990, however, LeGuin extended the trilogy of *Earthsea,* begun in 1968. *Tehanu: The Last Book of Earthsea* reintroduces Ged. In this book LeGuin not only explores the powers of good and evil but the

**Figure 7.2
Characteristics of Good Fantasy
for Young Adults**

Characters

Protagonist
- represents every adolescent ("everyman")
- usually a reluctant hero with self-doubt
- possess characteristics of good and evil
- transforms self by encountering and defeating problems
- although humanlike, may possess superhuman characteristics (some of which are discovered during the course of the adventure)
- very well developed

Antagonist
- may or may not be human
- may not be recognized by the protagonist until late in the novel

Others
- usually part of either the real or other world, but rarely both

Plot
- begins in the waking world
- a magical moment occurs when the protagonist transcends the real world and enters the other world
- most suspense develops in other world
- involves quest to solve problems and conquer evil
- life-and-death situations are encountered
- events have many levels of meaning
- protagonist's growth is central to the plot
- protagonist may not conquer evil by the end of novel
- conclusion may be a resting place for the beginning of new quests in subsequent novels

Point of View
- protagonist's

Voice
- author's

Setting
- both real and other worlds are believable
- moment of transcending real world to other world must appear to be possible
- wide-ranging
- magical world must follow rules set by the author
- there may be talking animals, magical or mythological beasts

Literary Elements
- allegory (imaginary world makes the real world more visible)
- invented words or a new language may be used
- language is often central to the plot and theme

Theme
- relates to hero's quest
- involves self-transformation and self-awareness
- "Problems in the real world can be conquered"
- "Good can triumph over evil"

relationship of men and women. Teran, the Priestess of the Tombs, is now a widow. Ged has been stripped of the magical powers he had as Archmage, and Lebannen is the young king of Havnor. As always in LeGuin's work the language not only sets the scene but is an important aspect of her characters. LeGuin has written numerous other fantasies for young adults including *The Beginning Place, The Left Hand of Darkness,* and *Very Far Away from Anywhere Else.*

Madeleine L'Engle   When *A Wrinkle in Time* was published in 1962, it was an immediate, surprise success, but its full impact on the young adult publishing would not be known for many years. Today, after its thirtieth anniversary, it is viewed by many as the breakthrough book in fantasies for young adults. Although published as a children's book (young adult books were not yet a publishing category), it is today read primarily by young adolescents. For many young readers, the book is their introduction to the world of fantasy.

The book is also unusual in that it combines elements of both science fiction and fantasy, and is therefore difficult to categorize. Although many of the elements of the book are fantastic, they are based on principles of science, as in much science fiction. For example, to write *A Wind in the Door,* the second book of the Time trilogy, L'Engle studied cellular biology, particularly mitochondria. L'Engle says she was introduced to the subject by her oldest friend who is a physician and first read about cellular biology in an article by Lewis Thomas in the *New England Journal of Medicine.* Throughout *A Wrinkle in Time* and its sequels, mystical characters do appear, and language and the quest are central to the plots and the themes. L'Engle, however, classifies her books as science fiction: "Well, it is science fiction. I'm basing the stories on the new way of looking at the world since we opened the heart of the atom" (Schmidt, 1991, p. 11).

Each book in the Time trilogy is about the O'Keefe and Murry families, particularly the children, who grow older in each book. The Murry family is a loving family, unusual for its time in that both parents are professionals. Meg Murry is the unwilling hero, the sister of two handsome twin brothers, and a brilliant younger brother. She feels awkward and is unsure of her place in the world until she must rescue four-year-old Charles Wallace by tesseracting through time in *A Wrinkle in Time* and traveling through his mitochondria in *A Wind in the Door.* In the third book in the series, *A Swiftly Tilting Planet,* Meg's twin brothers, who communicate mentally, are central to the plot, in which the young people must rescue their father.

Many other books by L'Engle deal with the Murrys and O'Keefes of the next generation. In *An Acceptable Time* Polly O'Keefe, the daughter of Calvin O'Keefe and Meg Murry, travels through the time gate to a civilization three thousand years old to learn the truth about love and hate, good and evil. Other L'Engle books involving the Murry and O'Keefe families include *Dragons in the Water, Many Waters,* and *The Arm of the Starfish.*

Madeleine L'Engle's fantasies are remarkable for many reasons. Not only do they provide an allegory for the real world, but also for the stories of Christianity. Readers do not need to recognize Christian allegory to enjoy the books. In fact, L'Engle maintains that this element should be subtle in a novel. In her nonfiction work

Walking on Water: Reflections on Faith and Art, L'Engle explains that she employs Christian allegory because without it in the technocratic world, which she distinguishes from the positive aspects of science and technology, we have "lost abilities that are innate in the human being. . . . Whatever Jesus did while he was alive we should be able to do too, but we've forgotten" (Schmidt, 1991, p. 13). She remembers as a child being able to float downstairs and reports that many adults who have similar experiences as children are told they have vivid imaginations or not to lie. According to L'Engle, this world of marvel is drummed out of children at home and at school. L'Engle is also concerned about fear: "I'm just so convinced that, if our own true faith is thoroughly grounded in God's love, we needn't fear." She maintains that this is the message of the Time trilogy, "but I didn't write the message; the story did" (Schmidt, p. 14). And that, of course, is the nature of an allegory.

❖ Between the Covers: *Authors at Work* ❖

MADELEINE L'ENGLE: TO CROSSWICKS

In the concluding lines of L'Engle's *Two-Part Invention: The Story of a Marriage,* the moving adult, autobiographical book about her forty-year marriage to the actor Hugh Franklin, she talks of the music of their home Crosswicks, the Connecticut farmhouse they purchased in the first year of their marriage.

> It is good to be part of the laughter as we sit around the table by candlelight. A wood fire both lightens and warms the room. None of the fullness of life in this old house is lost. The forty years of Hugh's and my marriage is part of the rhythm.
> *Music I heard with you was more than music, and bread I broke with you was more than bread* [Conrad Aiken].
> Yes. And always will be. (1988, p. 232)

With these words she concludes her tribute to her husband, who had recently died after a long, agonizing, but life-affirming battle with cancer. Although *Two-Part Invention* is primarily about Hugh and Madeleine's love and marriage, it is also a celebration of intellect, love, life, home, and family. Crosswicks, which appears on the book's dustjacket, is symbolic of all of these things. A home much like Crosswicks is the setting for many of L'Engle's best-loved young adult books.

L'Engle spent much of her adult life and much of her childhood in New York City. She recalls being a much-loved but lonely child who supped alone in her room while her parents entertained guests or attended the theater. While these years were difficult for young Madeleine, they provided the opportunity to read, to become acquainted with artistic and intellectual adults, and to learn about the culture surrounding her parents' lives. Madeleine's love of language, knowledge, and art were well established during her childhood.

Madeleine's parents sent her to Anglican boarding schools where she says the virtues she was taught were all self-protective: "do not show emotion; do not grieve; do not ask for help; do it yourself" (L'Engle, 1988, p. 39). When her father died she was seventeen, and these virtues nearly did her in. It was not until much later that L'Engle learned that Anglican virtues and Anglican theology are "barely compatible." She rediscovered the church when she first entered Ascension Episcopal Church, a New York City church open twenty-four hours a day, after being propositioned by a man she had respected. She went to that church each midnight, "not so much to pray as to take time to *be*" (p. 39). Throughout her adult life she has steadily studied theology; eventually she came to the church for prayer as well.

L'Engle once told students in a class she was teaching at Wesleyan University not long after Hugh's cancer was diagnosed, "I do not believe true optimism can come about except through tragedy" (p. 147). She reports that this comment surprised her, but understands that it was a personal revelation—one, of course, that is revealed to her readers in all of her books. She writes in *Two-Part Invention*, "If we are not willing to fail we will never accomplish anything. All creative acts involve the risk of failure" (p. 173). She has lived her life understanding this; the characters in her books are willing to risk failure, and she hopes that her readers will learn to do the same. Her science fiction–fantasy writing is a combination of those things she has learned and experienced. She does not write only about mythical beasts but about the science and theology she has studied. Her books embody her underlying belief in the beauty of the simple things of creation, in the complexity of the galaxies, in humankind's ability to change the universe, and in the existence of a creator who hears when we cry "Help!" and who "can be glimpsed only in metaphor, that chief tool of imagery of the poet" (p. 168). ❖

Anne McCaffrey   The Harper Hall trilogy by Anne McCaffrey introduces the reader to a real girl with real problems who lives in an unreal world on a fantastic planet. In the first book, *Dragonsong,* Menolly, ordered by her father to stop "tunemaking," runs away from home and develops a friendship with the fire lizard, whom she teaches to sing. In *Dragonsinger,* Menolly arrives at Harper Hall to continue her music studies. During her stay she learns about the extraordinary role she must play in the future of her planet. The final book of the trilogy, *Dragondrums,* tells the story of Piemur, a mischievous boy introduced in *Dragonsinger.* Piemur grows from a restless troublemaker to a self-sufficient young man while endeavoring to quell the political unrest in Pern during the perilous Threadfall. The realistic characters in McCaffrey's stories meet the unrealistic trials of the quest to conquer evil in both real and unreal ways.

The Dragonriders of Pern series is six overlapping books about the planet Pern where dragons and telepathic riders protect the world from deadly silver threads that fall from the sky and destroy everything they touch. Other good fantasies by McCaffrey, which possess all the elements of a good young adult fantasy without the metaphorical language and complexity of LeGuin's books, include *Killashandra* and *Crystal Singer.*

Robin McKinley   *The Blue Sword,* a Newbery Honor book, and *The Hero and the Crown,* a Newbery Medal winner, are set in Damar, a land not unlike early outback Australia. Each of the books has a strong female protagonist. In *The Blue Sword* Harry is kidnapped and then thrown into situations that test her strength and courage. *The Hero and the Crown,* which precedes the other novel in time, is about Aerin, the motherless misfit princess of Damar. Aerin takes up dragon killing with the help of the old lame war-horse Talet when her father refuses to let her ride into battle with the warriors of the kingdom. McKinley has also edited a good anthology of short fantasy stories by authors such as Robert Westall and Jane Yolen entitled *Imaginary Lands.*

Meredith Anne Pierce   Pierce's Darkangel trilogy is about Aerial, a servant girl whose mistress Eoduin is kidnapped by the Darkangel, a vampire. Aerial lacks faith in herself, but this does not keep her from seeking revenge for the kidnapping. She too is abducted to serve as one of the Darkangel's wives. In *A Gathering of Gargoyles* Aeriel searches for an answer to the riddle that holds the secret of how to dispel the wicked White Witch's power over the kingdoms on the moon of Oceanus. Six gargoyles, each of a different shape, serve as allies during her travels through the Sea-of-Dust. Although the riddle is solved at the end of the book, it is not clear whether good will finally conquer evil. In *The Woman Who Loved Reindeer* the young female hero is in love with a golden demon deer-man she has reared. With his help she leads her people on a long and dangerous trek to safety away from a geothermal cataclysm.

Laurence Yep   Although best known for his multicultural, historical fiction, Yep is also the writer of some fine fantasies for young adults. A three-book series beginning with *Dragon of the Lost Sea* is about Shimmer, a shape-changing dragon, who tries to restore her clan's traditional home and regain her former status in the clan. Like many of Yep's books, this series is loosely based on a Chinese myth. This book and its sequels, *Dragon Steel* and *Dragon Cauldron,* are particularly good for young adolescents because of their fast-moving, exciting plots as well as well-drawn characters in interesting relationships. In *Dragon Steel* Shimmer returns home with Thorr, her trusted human friend. She expects to be greeted with honor because she has captured the evil witch Civet. Instead, she is imprisoned in an underwater home of her uncle, King Sambar. She escapes with the help of a human enslaved by Sambar and the magic of a colorful group of allies and continues her long struggle to restore the Inland Sea Home of her clan. In *Dragon Cauldron* a group of shape-changing dragons attempt to find the Smith and the Snail Woman to mend the dragon's magic cauldron. The Boneless/Nameless One, whom they accidentally released from prison, and the ruthless Butcher are their adversaries. At the end of the book the newly mended magic cauldron is stolen by the Butcher whose body has been appropriated by the Nameless One.

One of the reasons young fantasy readers enjoy Yep's books is that they are very humorous. *Dragon Cauldron* is told from the perspective of a funny, sometimes sarcastic, flying monkey. In another Yep book *Monster Makers, Inc.,* the evil Xylk Empire invades the world of Carefree. The Xylks come in the form of urya, household pets, and bring the Rell, their fighting slaves. Piper Kincaid, son of the gene-splicer known as the Monster Maker, foils the plot with the help of Godzilla, a miniature version of his namesake. The plot of the book is fast-paced and silly.

Jane Yolen   Most of Yolen's works are for children. However, her Pit Dragon trilogy is excellent for young adolescents. In *Dragon's Blood,* the first book, Jakkin, the young hero, steals a hatchling dragon from a nursery and raises it secretly in the desert in order to enter it as a fighter in the Krakkow gambling pit. Akki, a young girl who is a bond servant in the dragon barns, aids him in the theft and training. At the end of the book Jakkin's freedom is ensured when his dragon, Heart's Blood, wins his first fight. Heart's Blood is a full-grown dragon and Jakkin is the Dragon Master in the second book of the trilogy, *Heart's Blood.* Jakkin is looking forward to training Heart's Blood's hatchlings to be fighters like their mother when Akki disappears and is rumored to be involved with rebels and in danger. Jakkin infiltrates the gang in order to save her. In book three, *A Sending of Dragons,* Jakkin has taken Akki into hiding in the desert caves of Austar IV. Jakkin and Akki communicate with each other and with the dragons through telepathy. Although their lives are difficult in the desert, they are happy until a helicopter starts flying over the cave with regularity. They search for another hiding place and come across a world of tunnels under the desert. The "men not-men" who live there also communicate by telepathy. However, this world, in which the "men not-men" see in gray rather than bright colors, is even more hostile than the one they have fled. Jakkin and Akki must eventually face their responsibility not only to themselves but to their world.

Quest Fantasies

A good fantasy communicates basic truths about human existence. The quest in a fantasy is often improbable, and the actions of the hero are unlikely, but through the author's skill the quest and the hero become believable. Many quest fantasies are appropriate for young readers.

If the quest takes the form of a series, each book can stand alone; however, the quest, usually against evil, is never complete. The Prydain Chronicles by Lloyd Alexander is an excellent series that can be read by readers as young as nine or ten years of age or enjoyed, on a higher level, by older readers. The cycle, based on Welsh legend and myth, is about Taran's search for his true identity. The cycle includes *The Black Cauldron, The Book of Three, The Castle of Llyr, The High King,* and *Taran Wanderer.* Although easy to read, the books create such a complex world that an encyclopedialike reference guide, *The Prydain Companion* (Tunnell), has been published. This reference catalogs each character, object, place, and major theme in the novels. A pronunciation guide for Welsh words is included as well as information about the sources of many of the ancient words and names used throughout the novels.

Susan Cooper's *The Dark Is Rising* series is about Will Stanton, last of the Old Ones, or immortals, and his dedicated fight against evil. The series also includes *Over Sea, Under Stone; Greenwitch; The Grey King;* and *Silver on the Tree.* Sparrowhawk in Ursula LeGuin's Earthsea trilogy, which includes *The Wizard of Earthsea, The Tombs of Atuan,* and *The Farthest Shore,* grows from boyhood to old age. Throughout his life he attempts to overcome the evil force he released when he misused his gift of magic. In old age he must use his hard-won wisdom to fight the forces that wish to destroy his gift. Patricia McKillip's *The Riddle-Master of Hed* and *Heir of Sea and Fire* are the stories of Morgan, prince of Hed, and his betrothed, Raederle. The two are linked in the fate that awaits Morgan as they search for his true identity. Roger Zelazny's Amber series, including *Nine Princes in Amber, The Guns of Avalon, Sign of the Unicorn,* and *The Hand of Oberon,* takes place in a strange world of purple clouds and Kentucky fried chicken. This saga of the royal family of Amber tells of their attempt to control the evil powers that threaten their world and all the worlds of Shadow. The stories contain a quest as well as sword-and-sorcery elements, mystery, suspense, and humor.

Although not written specifically for young adults, J. R. R. Tolkien's Ring trilogy has many young adult fans. The trilogy—*The Fellowship of the Ring, The Two Towers,* and *The Return of the King*— is an epic account of the defeat of the Dark Lord through the destruction of the One Ring of power.

L. Frank Baum's *Ozma of Oz* is a tale of good versus evil that is easy reading for many young adolescents. Jay Williams's *The Hero from Otherwhere,* another good fantasy for younger readers, tells about two boys who are called in to save a world that mirrors our own. In Poul Anderson's and Gordon Dickson's *Star Prince Charlie,* a boy accompanied by his tutor, Charlie Stewart, travels to Talyina, where he discovers and fulfills an ancient prophecy. In *A Spell for Chameleon* by Anthony Piers, Bink must search to find his magic talent or be exiled and lose Sabrina. In Joyce Ballou Gregorian's *The Broken Citadel* and *Castledown,* Prince Leron goes on a quest to free Princess Dastra from her glass prison. Valentine of *Lord Valentine's Castle* by Robert Silverberg joins a troupe of jugglers and gathers a motley party of supporters as he journeys across Majipoor to regain his rightful throne.

Numerous quest fantasy novels begin in the real world and then a magical moment comes when the hero enters another, fantastic world to learn more about the real world. Some good examples of this type of fantasy include Charles de Lint's *The Dreaming Place.* Ashley's mother has died and her father has rejected her, so she lives with her cousin Nina's family. Although Ashley and Nina are not fond of each other, Ashley enters the Otherworld to save Nina's soul from a manitou winter spirit. In *Colors in the Dreamweaver's Loom* by Beth Hilgartner, Zan is upset by her father's sudden death. She drives away to escape reporters and the lingering resentment she feels toward her father. When she stops the car and wanders into the woods, she falls and ends up in another world. Two children find her and take her to the dreamweaver Eikoheh who has woven Zan into this strange world. Julia, in *Gates of Glass* by Eric Houghton, is drawn through a mirror into a cavern world of glass. She is summoned by the magician Quorgrun who wants her help to recover the pieces of the Crystal of Darkness which supplies his evil power.

Walter Dean Myers's *The Legend of Tarik* is an excellent fantasy with a parallel-culture hero. Tarik is uprooted from his home west of the Niger River. He seeks revenge for the slaughter of his family by the evil El Muerte. Tarik is nursed to health and taught the skill of a knight by a one-handed priest and a blind philosopher. He acquires a magnificent horse, a magic sword, and the powerful Crystal of Truth. Stria, a girl seeking a similar revenge, and the practical baker Capa join Tarik on his quest across North Africa. Other good quest books include *Juniper* by Monica Furlong, *The Warriors of Taan* by Louise Lawrence, *Moon-flash* by Patricia A. McKillip, *The Dragonbards* by Shirley Rousseau Murphy, *Flute Song Magic* by Andrea Shettle, and *The Boy Who Was Thrown Away* by Stephanie Smith.

Magical Elements

Some fantasies for young adult readers catapult the main character from one world to another by magical means. In Norton Juster's *The Phantom Tollbooth,* Milo passes through a magical tollbooth into a land where the mathemagician rules the world of numbers and King Dictionopolis rules the kingdom of words. This humorous book contains many plays on words, idioms, and unusual phrases. In Marvin Kaye's *The Incredible Umbrella,* the umbrella transports the hero to another universe. An ancient Scottish tower becomes a door to the fifteenth century for children of the twenty-second century in Margaret Anderson's *In the Keep of Time.* In *The Butterfly Kid* by Chester Anderson, blue pills make fantasies become real. In *The Dragon and the George* by Gordon R. Dickson, Jim goes into a time machine a man and comes out a dragon.

Wizards are common in fantasies. In Lloyd Alexander's *Wizard in the Tree,* a kitchen maid learns the secret of magic from a rusty, humorous, and heartwarming wizard. Another wizard is found in Grace Chetwin's *The Crystal Stair.* In this novel Gom Gobblechuck of Windy Mountain is the child of a human and a wizard.

In Suzy McKee Charnas's *Golden Thread,* the final book in the Sorcery Hall trilogy, fourteen-year-old Val Marsh is pitted against Bosanka Lonat, an evil sorceress from another dimension. Val, however, has inherited magical powers from her Scottish grandmother. These along with a chemistry created by the Comet Committee, a group of six friends, create a mysterious force. The other two books in the series, which also have witches and wizards, are *The Bronze King* and *The Silver Glove.*

Dragons and Other Mythological Beasts

Valgard is a changeling, half elf, half troll, in *The Broken Sword* by Poul Anderson. In Peter Beagle's *The Last Unicorn,* the beautiful unicorn, knowing she is the last of her species, is told to be brave and she will find others. *Unicorns in the Rain* by Barbara Cohen is a tale of violence, pollution, and overcrowding. One family builds a large ship and, when it begins to rain, fills it with animals. In the seven books of the Narnia series by C. S. Lewis (including *The Lion, the Witch, and the Wardrobe*), the mythological animals are ruled by a wise lion, Aslan. Mermen, mermaids, and menehunes are characters in *My Sister Sif* by Ruth Park, a book with the theme of the importance of cleaning up the environment of the seas.

Dragons are also common in fantasy. In *The Forgotten Beast of Eld,* Patricia McKillip introduces readers to a wonderful world of strange, magical animals. A dragon and a feisty robot are both characters in *Norby and the Oldest Dragon* by Janet and Isaac Asimov.

A nonfiction book by Peter Dickinson, *The Flight of Dragons* (illustrated by Wayne Anderson), is an interesting companion work to the study of mythological creatures in fantasy. In the book Dickinson contends that dragons did exist, and he presents his theory of why no physical evidence of them is left except in artwork and mythology.

The lost world of Atlantis is the setting of Robert Silverberg's *Letters from Atlantis.* The protagonist discovers that the people of Atlantis are humanoid aliens. This book could either be studied as a work of science fiction or paired with myths in a unit on mythology.

Animal Worlds

A fantasy world may be inhabited by talking animals. Some examples are the engaging rabbits in Richard Adams's *Watership Down,* the talking barnyard animals in Walter Wangerin's *The Book of the Dun Cow,* certain sentient cats in Clare Bell's *Ratha and Thistle Chaser,* and the peace-loving mice of Redwall Abbey in Brian Jacques's *Redwall* and *Mattimeo.* Arthur is turned into a stray dog by an African schoolmate he has ridiculed in *The Dog Days of Arthur Cane* by T. Ernesto Bethancourt. However, he learns a great deal about life and love, good and evil, and human and canine nature. In Russell Hoban's book for young adolescents, *The Mouse and His Child,* a toy wind-up mouse searches for his first home and family. Kenneth Grahame's classic children's book *The Wind in the Willows,* a favorite of readers of all ages, follows the adventures of Mole, Badger, Rat, and Toad. The lizards in Daniel Pinkwater's *Lizard Music* not only talk but sing.

The fantastic world of Tolkien is explored in *The Atlas of Middle-Earth* by Karen Wynn Fonstad, a geographer whose knowledge of her subject makes this intriguing book seem very realistic. The maps include topography, trails, highways, territories, cities, forts, castles, cave works, battles, and even troop positions. This book will fascinate the sophisticated young reader with a taste for Tolkien.

Invented Languages

Many fantasies make use of invented words or languages. The vocabulary of the rabbits in *Watership Down* is so complex that a lexicon is provided at the end of the book. "Tolkienese" has practically been merged into the English language. Many of his readers use the language in his books to name stores or restaurants or children. Because language is an aspect of the power of humans, language is essential in all fantasies to separate the real world from the other world. Alexander's Prydain chronicles provide an excellent example of how an author uses language to help define a world. In the forward to Tunnell's *The Prydain Companion,* Alexander tells how he insisted that the Welsh words and names were essential to the story when his editor Ann Durrell initially feared they would make the books too difficult for young readers. Alexander writes, "Ann agreed they should be kept, but warned me that I would be haunted ever after by readers trying to puzzle them out. My attitude was, and is, simply have fun with them" (1989, p. x).

Combining Realism and Fantasy

Books that join realism and fantasy in a single narrative may assist young readers in developing a taste for fantasy. Bruno Bettelheim points out in *The Uses of Enchantment* that the fairy tale is an important aspect of the young child's life because it teaches children, through simplification, that they can master fears and overcome obstacles. Most young children are enthusiastic about fairy tales. Many young adult readers, however, find the related genre of fantasy confusing, unrealistic, and hard to follow. Perhaps young adults, in putting away childish things, have also put away their imaginations, the desire to fantasize, the need to leave the real world and enter a world in which they can be victorious. This is unfortunate. The lessons to be learned in fantasy and fairy tales are important, and teachers and parents should encourage young adults to read in these genre.

Teachers and parents who discover that adolescents are reluctant to read fantasy can use books that join realistic characters and situations with fantastic situations and characters to bridge the gap. When the realistic world is joined with the fantastic, the young realistic hero, who is like the reader in almost every way, is involved in a fantastic situation among fantastic people. In *Hangin' Out with Cici* (Pascal) young Victoria is plagued by problems in her relationship with her mother that are typical of difficulties experienced by many young adults. Their arguments are continual. One day the young heroine is taken back in time to an unfamiliar era. In her search for the familiar in this new world, she meets Cici. After many unusual experiences she realizes that Cici is her mother as a teenager. She and Cici become great friends. When she returns to her real world, she has a new understanding of her relationship with her mother. *Saturday, the Twelfth of October* (Mazer) uses a similar technique to transport an unhappy girl into a fantastic situation and return her, a changed person, to the real world. In Richard Parker's *A Time to Choose,* Stephen and Mary move back and forth between their own world and a parallel world in which they live in a utopian commune. They must finally choose in which world they will remain.

John LeVert's *The Flight of the Cassowary* is a particularly good book for adolescent boys. John, a believable high school junior, must work through typical problems—first love, making the football team, getting along with his father and teachers. However, John is unusual in that he has an extraordinary empathy for animals. Readers know the story will take on a fantastic twist when he begins talking to Ken, a neighborhood dog. His family, friends, counselors, and therapists think he's crazy until, at the end of the novel, he learns to fly. As Jim Brewbaker (1986) said in a review of the book for the *ALAN Review,* "The line between illusion and fantasy is muddy. I discussed the whole business with Mitzie, my cocker spaniel, who noted that LeVert just hints of John's gift (or curse) early on and then, once his reader is hooked on the boy's everyday problems, springs his fantasy trap. 'By then,' Mitzie concluded, 'it's too late.' "

Another humorous, realistic fantasy is Julian F. Thompson's *Herb Seasoning.* In this book Herb is sent by his high school guidance counselor to Castles in the Air, a place where he transcends time and space by traveling in the Upwardmobile to test various careers. Herb is able to do this because he was born during a leap second, a period of time added every few years to keep clocks in sync with the earth's rotation.

Cynthia Voigt's *Building Blocks* is about Brann, a twelve-year-old boy who retreats to the basement when he hears his parents arguing yet again. He awakens thirty-seven years earlier during the Great Depression in his father's boyhood bedroom. After spending a day dealing with Kevin's problems he is better able to understand why his father is so argumentative and unsuccessful. Kevin has an abusive father, a pregnant bickering mother, and five younger, difficult siblings for whom he must care. His knowledge of his father's childhood allows him to help his parents find a solution to their latest argument: whether to sell the farmhouse in which his father grew up and just inherited so that his mother can attend law school.

Katherine Paterson in *Bridge to Terabithia* never allows Jesse and Leslie to exit their real world totally, but the imaginary world they create in Terabithia helps Jesse transcend his limitations and learn to accept himself and the life he is living with increased maturity and understanding. In *The Beginning Place* by Ursula LeGuin, Irena and Hugh enter the fantasy world of Tembreabrezi where they struggle to save their friends and find a place for themselves in the real world.

Folklore, Legend, and Myth

Young readers can find an ever-growing number of books based on folklore, legend, and myth. These books can spark the storytelling and creative writing talents of young adults. Comparing the actual myth to a story based on it may provide young writers with the creative seed they need to begin their own story. Examining folklore and legends of the region or area in which the students live may encourage them to begin gathering legends and lore from living persons, in the tradition of the students in Rabun Gap, Georgia, who compiled and wrote the remarkable *Foxfire* books under the tutelage of Eliot Wigginton.

For many years, folklore, legend, and myth have been fertile sources for children's books. Unfortunately, the same cannot be said for most young adult literature. In recent years, however, we are seeing more works that use these sources enter the marketplace. Perhaps this is a sign that young adult literature is indeed coming of age.

Legend

Welsh legend is the source of several interesting young adult books. Alan Garner's *The Owl Service* is based on the legend of the Mabinogion. In this interesting tale three children find an old set of dishes in an attic. They discover that an ancient Welsh myth involving love, hatred, and jealousy is expressed in a symbolic way in the pattern on the dishes. The story describes the children's attempt to determine the hold the old myth has on their dreams and actions and those of their parents. The third book in Madeleine L'Engle's Time trilogy, *A Swiftly Tilting Planet,* is based on the legend of Madoc of Wales. The seven Narnia tales by C. S. Lewis are also based on an ancient Welsh legend. The Prydain Chronicles of Lloyd Alexander are drawn from Welsh legend and many other mythologies.

Virginia Hamilton's *The Magical Adventures of Pretty Pearl* is based on an African legend of Pretty Pearl, a god child from Mount Kenya who convinces her brother and best god, John de Conquer, to take her among the humans.

Several young adult books begin with the Arthurian legend. Constance Hieatt's *The Minstrel Knight* is the story of Sir Orfeo, a traveling knight who comes to King Arthur's court. This tale is interesting in that it is also based on the Orpheus tale of Greek legend. The two legends combine to provide romance and excitement. *Here Abide Monsters* by Andre Norton is about a boy, a girl, and a dog who are transported through time to Avalon of Arthurian legend. T. H. White's *The Sword in the Stone* retells the tale of the boy Wart who becomes King Arthur. Rosemary Sutcliff's three-book Arthurian cycle is an excellent bridge to Sir Thomas Malory's *Le Mort D'Arthur* and can be used as an introduction to Arthurian legend and values. *The Light beyond the Forest* is a retelling of the quest for the Holy Grail. The second book in the cycle, *The Sword and the Circle,* is a tale of King Arthur's knights and the round table. The final book, *The Road to Camlann,* is the story of the death of King Arthur.

The French legend of Charlemagne is the basis for Norton's *Huon of the Horn.* Huon, betrayed in Charlemagne's court, must complete an almost impossible task to return to France.

Mythology

Other young adult books use Greek or Roman mythology. Leon Garfield and Edward Blishen's *The God beneath the Sea,* which is divided into three parts, is the story of Hephaestus, first son of Zeus. Patrick Skene Catling's *The Chocolate Touch* is a retelling of the Midas myth. A collection of twenty-four myths from different cultures can be found in Juliet Heslewood's *Earth, Air, Fire and Water.* The myth of Orpheus, who plays his lyre in an attempt to rescue his wife from Hades, is retold by Patricia A. McKillip in *Fool's Run*. Native American myths are collected and retold in Jean Guard Monroe and Ray A. Williamson's *They Dance in the Sky: Native American Star Myths*.

Folktales

Epic folktales are a source for some young adult books. *A Song for Gilgamesh* (Hodges) is an interesting retelling of the ancient epic. *Beowulf* by Rosemary Sutcliff retells the old English epic. *Beowulf: A New Telling* by Robert Nye is a different interpretation of the tale. The story of Oedipus is retold in *The Days of the Dragon's Seed* by Norma Johnston.

The medieval Child Waters ballad provides the foundation for Katie Letcher Lyle's beautiful, believable *Fair Day, and Another Step Begun*. The story is about sixteen-year-old Ellen Burd who loves John Waters and is pregnant with his child. She is convinced that someday she and John will be united even though he seems indifferent to her.

Arabic folktales are the source for two notable young adult books. Barbara Cohen and Bahija Lovejoy's *Seven Daughters and Seven Sons* is the retelling of an Arabic tale of a poor merchant's daughter who, disguised as a boy, makes a fortune and takes revenge on seven male cousins who have insulted her. Inea Bushnaq's *Arab Folk Tales* is a compilation of 128 tales gathered from a variety of Arab traditions. Vietnamese folktales, which provide information about the culture ranging from belief in reincarnation to moral admonitions, can be found in Alice M. Terada's *Under the Starfruit Tree: Folktales from Vietnam*. Native American tales from forty tribes dealing with the legend of Coyote the trickster are presented in Barry Holstun Lopez's *Giving Birth to Thunder, Sleeping with his Daughter*. Legends known to Chinese Americans are collected by Laurence Yep in *The Rainbow People*.

Another interesting trend in young adult literature is the retelling of the fairy tale. Three excellent books retell the Beauty and the Beast story. *Roses* by Barbara Cohen has a modern setting in which Isabelle, called Izzie, works in a florist shop and is drawn to its owner Leo out of compassion for and curiosity about his grotesque appearance, the result of burns from an automobile accident. *Beauty* by Robin McKinley is a beautiful retelling of the story from the female perspective. Jonathan Fast's *The Beast* also sets the tale in a modern setting. The beauty of the story is a beautiful movie actress unable to find roles consistently. The beast is a former director of a napalm chemical company. They are brought together by Beauty's homosexual manager.

Adèle Geras, a popular young adult author in Great Britain, has written a trilogy about Alice, Bella, and Megan. The novels, each with a different protagonist, are modern versions of classic fairy tales. *The Tower Room,* the first book of the trilogy, which is based loosely on the story of Rapunzel, takes place in the tower room of a cloistered girls boarding school from which the three friends spy on Simon Findlay, a laboratory assistant who is the only man allowed on campus. Megan soon finds herself secretly seeing Simon and their love blossoms during clandestine meetings. However, Dorothy, the school's science teacher, has also fallen in love with Simon. When the teacher discovers Megan with Simon, Megan's world begins to fall apart. The second novel, *Watching the Roses,* is the Sleeping Beauty story with an ironic twist.

Alice's friends eagerly await her eighteenth birthday party. By the time the party is over, however, Alice lies in her childhood bedroom in a comalike state. She is silent to everyone other than her diary. At Alice's birth her evil aunt Violette had presented her with the frightening prophecy of death at the age of eighteen. It appears that the prophecy will come true until Alice realizes that she ultimately must save herself. In the third novel, *Pictures of the Night,* which is based on *Snow White,* Bella is living a Bohemian lifestyle in Paris. She finds her life threatened by two mysterious women, both of whom remind her of her stepmother.

The fairy tale motif is not uncommon in realistic young adult fiction. Zibby Oneal suggests that her novel, *In Summer Light,* could be considered a retelling of Sleeping Beauty in that it is a story about the reawakening of Kate. Oneal writes in an article "Fairy Tales: The Ambivalent Awakening of Maturity:" "It was not from a jealous fairy's spell that Kate suffered. Here was a thoroughly modern disease called mononucleosis, but the symptoms were much the same. Drowsy, dozing, full of lassitude, Kate rested, deep among the thorns of the family thicket" (1988, p. 11). Sharon Chinn suggests that the archetypal structures of fairy tales are present in many young adult novels; these include quests, "heroic figures who must hurdle nearly impossible obstacles" in spite of their own inadequacies, and cyclical and dialectical structures such as seasonal motifs and literary images. She notes that many young adult authors, such as Marc Talbert, "employ these very motifs as their protagonists confront growing up in a hostile world" (1990, pp. 35–37). For example, in Talbert's *Dead Birds Singing,* Matt is orphaned after his mother and sister are killed in a tragic automobile accident. His quest is to make sense of his life without a family. At the end of the novel, Matt runs naked through a meadow, "symbolically [releasing] his ties to his now-dead family while at the same time embracing the warmth and love of his new one" (p. 35). Matt overcomes many obstacles, but he is also a powerless victim who doubts himself. The action in the novel symbolically begins in the fall of the year, "that time of the year that traditionally is associated with failure and death, and ends in the spring, that season that typically is associated with triumph" (p. 37).

Epilogue: Literature that Illuminates the Real World

Imaginative literature not only ignites the imagination and allows the reader to escape the real world, it helps the reader better understand the real world. Adolescents who read these books picture other worlds in their mind's eye. The opportunity to imagine is, in itself, an important aspect of reading imaginative literature for a generation of young people brought up on the images of television, motion pictures, and computers.

Adolescents who read imaginative literature can stand back from their own problems when they enter a new imaginary world. As they step back, they do not leave their problems behind but instead look at them from a new vantage point. For many readers, seeing their problems in a new way can lead to innovative solutions.

At the same time, adolescents who read imaginative literature think beyond their problems to the problems of humankind, the earth, and the universe. Many social and ethical problems are dealt with in imaginary settings. As young realistic heroes overcome these problems, adolescent readers see that they too can make a difference in the future of the world. If they persevere, like the protagonists of these books, they can succeed and meet the challenges of their lives.

Imaginative literature that is allegorical can be read on many levels. This makes the books accessible to both poor and capable readers. Students can read the best imaginative literature several times and each time see something new in the plot and theme. In a first reading of the book students may see simply a good, exciting story. Reading it at a later date, or by discussing it with peers and teachers, they may come to understand the book's deeper meaning. Once students grasp that books often have a meaning beyond the superficial plot, they read with deeper understanding and increased interest. Seeing beyond their initial reaction to the book is an important step to becoming a mature reader. Discussing imaginative literature is an excellent means for helping adolescents move beyond surface knowledge to deeper understanding.

SUGGESTED READINGS

Bettelheim, B. *"The Uses of Enchantment: The Meaning and Importance of Fairy Tales"*. Knopf, 1976.

Brewbaker, J. Review of *The Flight of the Cassowary,* by John LeVert. *ALAN Review,* Fall 1986, p. 35.

Chinn, S. "Modern Fairy Tales: Archetypal Structure in the Novels of Marc Talbert." *ALAN Review,* Spring 1990, pp. 35–37.

Gunn, J., ed. *The Road to Science Fiction.* 3 vols. New American Library, 1978–1979.

Lehman, R. L. "Margaret Mahy: Mixing the Family with the Unfamiliar." *ALAN Review,* Winter 1990, pp. 33–34, 40.

L'Engle, M. *Two-Part Invention: The Story of a Marriage.* Crosswicks, 1988.

———. "Understanding the New Universe." *ALAN Review,* Winter 1988, pp. 1–3.

Lind, D. "The Importance of Fantasy in Young Adult Literature." *ALAN Review,* Winter 1988, pp. 13–14.

McIntosh, M. E., and M. J. Greenlaw. "Ladies First: Teaching Characterization through Strong Female Protagonists in High Fantasy Literature." *ALAN Review,* Winter 1988, pp. 47–50.

Nugent, S. M. "Quests for Self-Awareness." *ALAN Review,* Winter 1988, pp. 43–44.

Oneal, Z. "Fairy Tales: The Ambivalent Awakening of Maturity." *ALAN Review,* Winter 1988, pp. 11–12, 10.

Pierce, M. A. "The Magical Moment in Fantasy." *ALAN Review,* Winter 1988, pp. 39–42.

Schmidt, G. D. "The Story as Teller: An Interview with Madeleine L'Engle." *ALAN Review,* Winter 1991, pp. 10–14.

Shadow, L. "The Challenge of Alan Garner's Fiction." *Connecticut English Journal,* Fall 1980, pp. 151–54.

Sidorsky. P. G. "Voicing a Concern." *Book Links,* January 1992, pp. 56–58.

Sleator, W. "What Is It about Science Fiction?" *ALAN Review,* Winter 1988, pp. 4–6.

Tunnell, M. O. *The Prydain Companion: A Reference Guide to Lloyd Alexander's Prydain Chronicles.* Greenwood Press, 1989.

8 Nonfiction, Poetry, Short Stories, and Drama

Focus Questions

1. Why is it important to teach nonfiction to adolescents?
2. What are the categories of biography and autobiography, and why is it important to be aware of them?
3. What should you look for when selecting nonfiction?
4. What are some of the important subjects covered by young adult nonfiction?
5. How can you help adolescents appreciate poetry, and why is it important to do so?
6. Why are short stories written for young adults useful in the classroom?

PROLOGUE

My childhood had two homes simultaneously, my own, that is to say, belonging to my parents, and my grandmother's house by the sea. Both were filled with books and each in a different style. . . . Remembering my grandmother is to remember her among her books. It is to sit again in a corner of her cavernous and usually deserted living room when Sunday dinner was over, the blue haze of cigarette smoke had cleared and the decanters were still. She would be doing the *New York Times* crossword, with a dictionary [and] a red ballpoint pen, in what she called "the card room."

On one of the lower bookshelves were several collections of cartoons, mostly from the *New Yorker*. I pored over these for years, drinking in each Helen Hokinson and Peter Arno, trying to understand the sophisticated wit but not being put off when I couldn't. I was soaking in, without knowing it at all, just how artists got a whole world of character and feeling into a four by five square with a few strokes of a pen.

Another book that fascinated me Sundays over a period of years was a collection of David Low, the British political cartoonist who documented the Second World War in such a fashion that it came to life and made sense to me. To this day I can picture his evil Von Ribbentrop, his clueless Colonel Blimp and his wissy Neville Chamberlain. These wicked caricatures in brilliantly clear poses explained history to me in a time when that war loomed large and in a way I have never forgotten. It taught me more than a course at Harvard. I have the book still. . . .

In my own house, which was dustier and much smaller than my grandmother's, where chaos reigned and one could relax in any position in any piece of furniture there was no end of books, dogs and different patterns of floral upholstery. If I go upstairs in my mind's eye I find about two hundred books in my own room, all well thumbed and read many times. . . . In the upstairs hall was another bookcase with a collection of Matthew Brady on Lincoln. . . . Down in the living room are at least three bookcases. In them is my father's unending love of history. There is Carl Sandburg, Winston Churchill and an immense chronicle of the First World War. My father is sitting in a wing chair reading a book called *Capricornia* for the dozenth time. It is about his beloved native Australia. . . . Around the fireplace and on the porch were books which reflected my mother's love of England, oddities of any kind, and anything related to her life in the theater.

There were also large full-color books with great paintings from the world's most splendid museums.   ❖

From Rosemary Wells, "Books Remembered," *CBC Features* (January–June 1991).

Lately I've been reading the books of my childhood and finding them as wonderful as ever. I am also finding to my amazement how deeply these books affected me. I am what I've read.

"The city of Calcutta," I hear my mother begin as she reads *Gay-Neck* to my brothers and me, "which boasts a million people, must have at least two million pigeons. Every third Hindu boy has perhaps a dozen pet carriers, tumblers, fantails, and pouters." John, Frank and I glance at each other. Here at last is our kind of story. Real children are learning about nature as they raise pigeons, just as we were learning about nature by raising falcons.

The story of *Gay-Neck: The Story of a Pigeon* by Dhan Gopal Mukerji (Dutton) was the winner of the seventh Newbery Medal, I also would learn many years later that *Gay-Neck* seeped into my subconscious and became part of my brothers and me. We all grew up to become nature writers, and we all grew up, like Gopal Mukerji, to write about wild animals we had raised, trained and studied in their natural environments.   ❖

From Jean Craighead George, "Books Remembered," *CBC Features* (January–June, 1992).

Nonfiction: Rarely Taught, Often Read

It is impossible to read the reading memoirs of Rosemary Wells and Jean Craighead George and not notice that these two writers, one of historical fiction and one of fiction about nature, were inspired most as children by nonfiction books. This phenomenon is not unusual. Many avid readers include nonfiction among the books that influenced them most. In fact, a large percentage of adult aesthetic readers read mostly nonfiction. Why is it then that nonfiction is rarely taught in the schools?

Of course, students' lockers and desks, classrooms, and school libraries are filled with works of nonfiction. These works, however, are generally meant to be used as textbooks or for reference; rarely are they considered for study of the genre or for independent reading. According to W. Geiger Ellis, in an article "To Tell the Truth or at Least a Little Nonfiction": "A large portion of the reading material chosen by students is nonfiction. It is not uncommon to find in a check of library circulation records that from half to two-thirds of the books checked out by high school students are nonfiction. Further inquiry reveals that this circulation pattern occurs independently from classroom assignments" (1987, p. 39). He suggests that the nonfiction books read by adolescents, not those selected by anthologists and certainly not textbooks, should be read and taught as literature in the English classroom.

Nonfiction Publishing and the Curriculum

In recent years the reliance on textbooks to teach such subjects as history and science and the lack of nonfiction in the English classroom may be changing. Frank Sloan, the editorial director of three nonfiction imprints of Macmillan Children's Book Group, comments:

> Nonfiction is enjoying an unprecedented boom in the nineties. Everyone who has published nonfiction all along is now publishing more of it. And even publishers that have traditionally given nonfiction wide berth are looking at the category more and more seriously. They too are testing the new waters. (1991)

Sloan explains why more and more publishers are publishing more and more nonfiction. According to Sloan, publishers have always looked to the school curriculum to help them determine nonfiction topics on which to publish.

> For example, there is no point in doing a major series on dinosaurs for junior high students. Unless the books take a detailed, scientific approach to the topic, the chance of their success is marginal. They *may* get read, and they may even enjoy good sales, but they do not tie into the curriculum being taught at that level. (1991)

Changes in the school curriculum, according to Sloan, are encouraging publishers to publish more and better nonfiction for children and young adults. The most important change is the focus on "whole language," an approach that synthesizes the teaching of language with all elements of the curriculum (see chapter 9).

Finding the Books

A large number of nonfiction books for young adults are now available for use in the classroom. Unfortunately, learning about and evaluating this vast number of books is impossible for the busy teacher. Sloan (1991) claims that publishers recognize the need to assist teachers in getting to know the books and learning "how to use them effectively in enriching their courses of study." He contends that publishers, such as Macmillan, are "finding ways to link the books thematically across genres and imprints." (Imprint refers to a subdivision of a publisher's booklist, used for marketing purposes, that usually denotes a type of book or the age level or type of intended reader.) For example, publishers are presenting sets of books around topics such as the Civil War, Native Americans, or self-esteem. These sets may include "poetry, picture books, middle grade and young adult novels, and, of course, nonfiction." In addition, according to Sloan, publishers are providing teachers with teaching techniques for using these books in the classroom.

Because the genre of nonfiction is so broad, it is useful for the teacher to have criteria for selecting nonfiction for the classroom. The criteria listed in Figure 8.1 are based on the work of W. Geiger Ellis (1987, pp. 40–41) and can be taught to students to help them recognize good nonfiction.

This chapter will describe a variety of nonfiction books suitable for young adults related to many different topics, themes, and disciplines. Although how to use these books will be the focus of Part 3, ideas on how to incorporate them in the curriculum are touched on in this chapter when appropriate.

Biography and Autobiography

One of the best-known scholars of young adult literature G. Robert Carlsen writes: "Teens want the same qualities in biography as in fiction. They seek real-life stories about heroes and heroines who resemble the characters in their fiction. Boys prefer to read about men; girls about women. Both sexes want a fictionalized biography rather than a factual account. They enjoy undocumented dialogue, thoughts and feelings of the subject" (1980).

Biographical and autobiographical works written for or enjoyed most by young adults are short in length (150 to 250 pages). In addition, as in the fiction enjoyed most by teenagers, the subject of a biography must seem real, so that by the end of the book the reader has a sense of knowing the person. The person should not be portrayed as so good or so bad as to seem unbelievable. The situations must also seem true to life.

The writer of the young adult biography should not preach to the reader, sensationalize the account of events, or invent situations that are impossible in light of the facts of the subject's life or the historical period in which the subject lived. Good biography for young adults is like good fiction; it is readable and relates to the needs and interests of the reader. Sloan reports that biographies "are now proliferating throughout the [publishing] industry. Everyone is doing them, making them lively and interesting" (1991). Because there are so many biographies on the market, it is important that teachers help students learn to distinguish between those that are particularly good and those that are merely readable. The characteristics of good biography and autobiography for young adults are listed in Figure 8.2.

G. Robert Carlsen (1980) identifies seven categories of biography: fictionalized, definitive, interpretive, objective, monumental, critical, and collected. Although it is often hard to place a biography or autobiography in a specific category (for example, an account that attempts to be objective or critical may also be fictionalized to some degree), these categories are useful for talking about biography and autobiography appropriate for young adults. Teaching students to identify books by these categories will help them understand whether a book will give a historically accurate picture of the hero or merely a sense of the hero's life.

Fictionalized Biography

An account of a historical figure can seem real even when it is part of a fictionalized biography as long as the fictionalization is consistent with the person's character and

**Figure 8.1
Characteristics of Good
Nonfiction for Young Adults**

Readability
- appropriate for reading level of adolescents
- appropriate for developmental level of adolescents
- jargon and technical language is minimal or carefully defined
- should be of interest to individual student (does not necessarily have to interest the teacher)

High-Quality Writing
- use of language adroit or distinctive
- appropriate and acceptable use of dialects of English

Material Logically Organized
- format allows easy access to information
- index, table of contents, and other devices help locate information
- book covers what it purports to cover

Visuals Aid Understanding
- visuals appear with appropriate textual material
- photographs are of high reproduction quality
- visuals are clear and generally attractive
- content of visual is easily understood

Accurate Information
- author's credentials are appropriate
- information is up to date for field covered
- information does not contain errors
- supporting evidence given for all assertions

the historical period of the narrative. Fictionalized biography includes events and dialogue that might have happened but cannot be verified with historical documentation. Many works about historical figures are fictionalized because there is little or no primary source documentation of their lives. Even when primary sources are available, the author may choose to fictionalize to make a point about the person, describe the person's thoughts, or show the person's relationship to other historical figures. Rhoda Lerman's *Eleanor* is a good example of a fictionalized biography. It covers the life of Eleanor Roosevelt during the four years following her discovery that Franklin was having an affair with another woman. Although based on documented evidence, Gene Smith's *The Horns of the Moon: A Short Biography of Adolf Hitler* is also fictionalized. The book deals with Hilter's first love, his boyhood friends, and his fascination with astrology, and relates these experiences to what he later became.

Young adults enjoy fictionalized biographies and many such books are available. *Beyond Myth: The Story of Joan of Arc* by Polly Schoyer Brooks is a good example of a fictionalized biography for young adults. The author presents Joan, who was burned at the stake at nineteen, as a normal, healthy peasant girl who possesses both shrewdness and idealism. Jean Fritz is well known for her excellent and accurate,

Figure 8.2
Characteristics of Good Biography and Autobiography for Young Adults

Hero
- real and realistic
- portrayal is based on fact; the subject is neither denigrated nor romanticized
- focuses on life of hero as young adult
- well-developed; reader should feel as if she or he knows the subject by the end of the book

Other Historical Figures
- real and realistic
- based on fact, but may be fictionalized to some extent
- less well-developed; serve as foils for the hero

Storyline
- based on real events
- if fictionalized, story must be consistent with hero's development, historic events, time period, and setting
- readable; follows a storyline not unlike that in fiction
- relates to the needs and interests of the readers

Point of View
- young hero's

Voice
- author's
- knowledgeable about hero and historic period

Setting
- accurate
- helps develop the storyline

Theme
- proves that history is interesting
- "You, too, can accomplish great things if you believe in yourself"

fun-to-read biographies for younger adolescents. Two more recent works are *The Great Little Madison* and *Bully for You, Teddy Roosevelt!*.

Definitive Biography

Definitive biographies are usually long works based on all the known facts about the person. Such works are scholarly and well documented. Consequently, definitive biographies are enjoyed most by mature young adult readers. The four-volume *Henry James* by Leon Edel is too long and too involved for most young readers, but may be enjoyed by the mature young adult. The same is true of Carl Sandburg's six-volume *Abraham Lincoln* and Carlos Baker's *Ernest Hemingway*. Fawn Brodie's *Thomas Jefferson: An Intimate History* is an interesting scholarly portrait of the Jefferson's attitudes and relationships. Because of its length, over 800 pages, it is likely to be overlooked by immature readers.

The young reader who is fascinated by a particular historic figure may be able to read a definitive biography. Many young adults enjoy Virginia Hamilton's *Paul Robeson: The Life and Times of a Free Black Man*. Fewer than 250 pages, it is a well-researched account of the singer's life, including the disruption of his career in the United States owing to his political sympathy for the Soviet Union. Another definitive biography young adults enjoy, not for its reading ease but for its subject, is *Buried Alive: The Biography of Janis Joplin* (Friedman). This book portrays the rock idol of the 1960s as a troubled young woman who thought herself ugly and attempted to dull her pain with drugs and alcohol. *Sorrow's Kitchen* by Mary E. Lyons is about the recently rediscovered, African American Southern writer Zora Neale Hurston. *Uncommon Eloquence: A Biography of Angna Enters* by Dorothy Mandel is a well-researched and readable work about a gifted woman who was a writer, dancer, mime, painter, and costume and set designer from the 1920s to the 1970s.

Interpretive Biography and Autobiography

Interpretive biographies attempt to find patterns in a person's life and explain why the person behaved in a particular way. The interpretive biographer may purposely omit evidence that does not support the portrait being drawn. Many autobiographies enjoyed by young adults can be placed in this category. One good example is Eldridge Cleaver's *Soul on Ice*. Cleaver's prison recollections are short, spiritual, and intellectual. The book may be difficult for some young adults, but many teenagers find it illuminating.

Many other interpretive biographies or autobiographies are easier to read, such as Maya Angelou's *I Know Why the Caged Bird Sings*. This autobiography and its three sequels—*Gather Together in My Name, Singin' and Swingin' and Gettin' Merry Like Christmas,* and *The Heart of a Woman*—tell the life story of this gifted African American writer, poet, and actress who grew up in the South. Another interpretive autobiography set in the deep South is Anne Moody's *Coming of Age in Mississippi*. Jimmy Carter in *Why Not the Best?* interprets his own life from his depression-era childhood to his nomination as president.

Some memoirs attempt to capture a particular period in an individual's life. *Farewell to Manzanar* by Jeanne Wakatuski Houston and James D. Houston is told through the eyes of five-year-old Jeanne when she was a child in an internment camp for Japanese Americans during World War II. Gale Sayers in *I Am Third* interprets his own life from his youth in an African American ghetto through his professional football career and the death of his close friend and teammate Brian Piccolo. In *Breakout: From Prison to the Big Leagues,* Ron LeFlore reflects on the events that led him from drug addiction and crime to the Detroit Tigers and the All-Star game. Tim O'Brien recounts his experience in the Vietnam War in *If I Die in a Combat Zone.* Robert Maiorano's *Worlds Apart: The Autobiography of a Dancer from Brooklyn* is about a soloist with the New York City Ballet and the contrast between the world of his youth and that of the dance studio. Another good interpretive account of the world of dance is Tony Bentley's *Winter Season.* In *Birthmark* Lorraine Dusky writes of her experience of having a child out of wedlock, putting her up for adoption, and later searching unsuccessfully to find her. *Iron and Silk* by Mark Salzman is about his teaching English at the Hunan Medical College in Changsha, China, from 1982 to 1984.

Rod Ansell and Rachel Percy have written *To Fight the Wild* about surviving in Australia's northern territory. Colin Fletcher's *The Thousand Mile Summer* is about his summer-long trek on foot from Mexico to Oregon. *Adrift* by Steve Callahan is about surviving seventy-six days adrift on a rubber raft after his boat sinks in the Atlantic.

Robyn's Book, a True Diary by Robyn Miller is taken from her journal and tells about her struggle to survive cystic fibrosis. Another similar book about a girl suffering from cystic fibrosis, *Give Me One Wish,* is taken in part from the diary of Chris Gordon but was written by her mother, Jacquie Gordon, after her death.

Starring Sally J. Freeman As Herself is an autobiographical sketch of Judy Blume's younger years. This humorous book is appropriate for younger adolescent readers. Many interpretive autobiographies by popular authors of young adult fiction describe becoming an author and growing into a writer. Some examples are Lois Duncan's *Chapters: My Growth As a Writer,* M. E. Kerr's *Me Me Me Me Me, A Girl from Yamhill: A Memoir* by Beverly Cleary, Rosemary Sutcliff's *Blue Remembered Hills, Boston Boy* by Nat Hentoff, Laurence Yep's *The Lost Garden, I Have Words to Spend: Reflections of a Small-Town Editor* by Robert Cormier, and *The Cookcamp* and *Woodsong* by Gary Paulsen. These memoirs are particularly appropriate for adolescents who have enjoyed the books of these authors. For many adolescents reading these autobiographies may provide them with their first glimpse into the lives of authors. Both teachers and writers are often surprised at how many young adults do not have a concept of a real, live person who wrote the book they read.

Among the many interpretive biographies of interest to young adult readers is *Anyone's Daughter* by Shana Alexander. This sensitive account of the Patty Hearst case traces the events from her kidnapping to the trial. Robert Conot's *A Streak of Luck: The Life and Legend of Thomas Alva Edison* tells of the inventor's career and personal life. Conot paints Edison as a complex and contradictory man. William Bradford Huie's *A New Life to Live: Jimmy Putman's Story* tells of the illegitimate son of Alabama's governor "Big Jim" Folsom. The book follows Jimmy through his troubled adolescence to his decision to devote his life to Christ. In *The Right Stuff* Tom Wolfe portrays the ascent of astronauts from test pilots to the beginning of the space program to space flights. *Free to Be Muhammad Ali* by Robert Lipsyte is a look into the life of the great boxing champion. The book examines the controversies that have surrounded Ali's career.

Objective Biography

The objective, or factual, biography records documented facts about the subject's life, usually in chronological order. The author does not attempt to judge, criticize, or interpret. There is no attempt to show how incidents in the person's life developed his or her character. An objective biography may or may not be definitive.

Being objective in an autobiography is more difficult than being objective in a biography. However, James Herriot's books about his life as a Yorkshire veterinary surgeon can generally be called objective autobiography. The four books record the events of his life in the Yorkshire Downs from Herriot's first years as a vet to his life after World War II. The very humorous accounts never judge or criticize, only report. Herriot does not attempt to show how one event leads to another. Each chapter can stand alone as a piece of writing in its own right. These books, although not written specifically for young adults, have been enjoyed by teenage readers. The warm, simple, funny tales have won the books many accolades, including the Best of the Best Books for Young Adults Award from the American Library Association for *All Creatures Great and Small* and *All Things Bright and Beautiful.*

Another author who writes funny books about the adventures and misadventures of his own life is Farley Mowat. *The Dog Who Wouldn't Be* is the tale of his boyhood adventures with Mutt. The story of his leaky old schooner, Happy Adventure, is told in *The Boat Who Wouldn't Float.* Mowat's books not only relate incidents in his own life but paint an interesting picture of Canada.

Periodically authors of young adult fiction attempt to write an objective biography for young adults. Many of these books are not very readable and can be boring. There are some exceptions, however. Although *Martin Luther King, Jr.* by Jean Darby is unlikely to help adolescents understand why King is a hero, this readable account covers the major events of his life. Neil Baldwin's *To All Gentleness: William Carlos Williams, the Doctor Poet* is interesting in that it presents the conflict in Williams's life between his poetry and his practice of medicine.

Kindling Flame: The Story of Hannah Senesh, 1921–1944 by Linda Atkinson is the story of a Hungarian Jew who was a member of a Nazi resistance group. The story is told through letters, photographs, interviews with family and colleagues, diary excerpts, and poems. Other objective biographies and autobiographies about life during the Holocaust include

- Corrie ten Boom's *The Hiding Place*
- Moshe Flinker's *Young Moshe's Diary: The Spiritual Torment of a Jewish Boy in Nazi Europe*
- *Anne Frank: The Diary of a Young Girl*
- Alfred Kantor's *The Book of Alfred Kantor*
- Ilse Koehn's *Mischling, Second Degree*
- Janusz Korczak's *Ghetto Diary*
- Primo Levi's *Survival in Auschwitz: The Nazi Assault on Humanity*
- Jakov Lind's *Counting My Steps*
- Johanna Reiss's *The Upstairs Room*
- Elie Wiesel's *Night; Dawn; and the Accident: Three Tales*
- Maia Wojciechowska's *Till the Break of Day*
- Joseph Ziemian's *The Cigarette Sellers of Three Crosses Square*

Monumental Biography

Many biographers make their book a monument to the person about whom they are writing. These biographies minimize the faults of the subject. In the past, young adult biographies leaned in this direction. Today, however, we are seeing more and more biographies using the opposite approach. Young adults today are increasingly interested in antimonumental biographies. The widely read *Mommie Dearest,* a book about actress Joan Crawford by Christina Crawford, is an example of this phenomenon. Many such books have been written about entertainers and politicians but most of these cannot be recommended as literature.

The teenage reader also likes to read touching tales about real-life heroes who seem too good to be true. Many books that deal with the handicapped or recently deceased celebrities may tend to deify the person. *The Story of Stevie Wonder* (Haskins) and *Brian Piccolo: A Short Season* (Morris) fit this category. *Elvis, We Love You Tender,* by members of Presley's family, reviews his final, difficult years and his strict code of conduct. Like the Presley book, many titles of monumental biographies give away the author's intent, as in *Cudjoe of Jamaica: Pioneer for Black Freedom in the New World* by Milton McFarlane, *Paul Robeson: Hero before his Time* by Rebecca Larsen, and *Pride of Puerto Rico: The Life of Roberto Clemente* by Paul Robert Walker. Although none of these biographies, by omitting or downplaying faults, can claim to be an objective work, each can be useful for certain readers. Each can show young readers that they can overcome and be successful.

Critical Biography

Critical biography looks at the subject in relationship to the times and assesses the value of the person's contribution to society. This type of biography neither deifies nor denigrates the person, but rather presents both strengths and weaknesses. The critical biography seems to be more predominant today than it was several years ago, when most biographies, particularly those written for the young, seemed to idealize their subjects. *Scoundrel Time* by Lillian Hellman is not just an autobiography but also a portrait of a historic period, the witch-hunting, blacklisting years of the Joseph McCarthy era. Because this book is short, it can be an excellent companion to the textbook presentation of the 1950s in a U.S. history class. Another short biography that is appealing to many young adults, particularly those interested in a career in art, is Donald Walton's *A Rockwell Portrait. Isaac Bashevis Singer: The Story of a Storyteller* by Paul Kresh is a part of Dutton's Jewish Biography Series for young adults. The book shows the influences on the life of this Nobel Prize–winning author who began his life in a Warsaw ghetto. A book that became an Academy Award–winning film is Ladislas Farago's *Patton: Ordeal and Triumph,* which portrays George S. Patton as a real person, not as a hero. Although the book is over 400 pages, students who have seen the movie or are interested in the military will enjoy it. Phyllis Bentley's *The Brontës and Their World* examines the Brontë sisters against the backdrop of the world in which they lived. Students who have enjoyed reading Pam Conrad's *Prairie Songs* are also likely to enjoy *Prairie Visions: The Life and Times of Soloman Butcher,* the real-life photographer who took the picture of the Downing family in Conrad's novel. *Malcolm X: By Any Means Necessary,* an excellent biography by Walter Dean Myers, makes the life of this controversial African American Muslim leader accessible to younger adolescents.

Biographical Collections

A collection of biographies contains short accounts of a number of people's lives or descriptions of particular events in their lives that tie the people in the collection together. John F. Kennedy's *Profiles in Courage,* an excellent example of this type of biography, describes several congressmen who risked their careers by taking unpopular stands. Although this is a valuable book for helping teenagers see another side of the political arena, many teenagers find it difficult and consequently boring. Assigning a few chapters of the book, reading several aloud to the class, or allowing students to elect to read the entire book or parts of it would be preferable to requiring all students to read the entire book.

Hettie Jones's *Big Star Fallin Mama: Five Women in Black Music* is an easy-to-read biography collection for young blues fans, as is Donald Bogle's *Brown Sugar: Eighty Years of America's Black Female Superstars.* In *GirlSports!* Karen Folger Jacobs has collected stories about fifteen young women athletes age nine to seventeen, some famous, others not. Steven Clark's *Fight against Time: Five Athletes—A Legacy of Courage* is the story of athletes faced with personal tragedy. *Glorious Triumphs: Athletes Who Conquered Adversity* by Vernon Pizer includes thirteen stories of athletes who combat cancer, drug abuse, severe burns, and paralysis. Some of the athletes included in this book, first released in 1966 and revised in 1980, will be familiar to today's young adults; others will be new to them. Two good collections about women are *Mothers: Memories, Dreams and Reflections by Literary Daughters* edited by Susan Cahill and *American Women: Their Lives in Their Words* by Doreen Rappaport.

Recollections of people experiencing the same historical event or living the same lifestyle make interesting biographical collections. John Hersey's *Hiroshima,* about six survivors of the atomic bomb, is an important example. In *Hillbilly Women,* compiled by Kathy Kahn, nineteen women tell in their own words about living in Appalachian coal mining and mill towns. This collection paints a vivid picture of the region and its people.

Collections of biographies are useful as reference sources and for reluctant readers who prefer not to read an entire book. Two general biography collections that are particularly appropriate for young adults are *Great Modern American Short Biographies,* edited by Joseph Mersand, and *American Dreams: Lost and Found,* compiled and edited by Studs Terkel.

Historical Nonfiction

For years enjoyable, entertaining, and illuminating historical accounts were solely the possession of the adult audience. The works of historians such as T. S. Morison or Dee Brown were too long and too difficult for most young adults. Fortunately, many authors are now writing enjoyable historical accounts for young adult readers. These books are valuable resources for many subject areas and can be used to supplement or replace textbooks. Students are much more likely to learn to appreciate history when the books they are reading are more than catalogues of facts. Good works of nonfiction enliven history because they present history through anecdotes and stories, photographs and paintings, and the words of those who lived it. The best books about history have a heart, a soul, and a voice.

Historians Who Write Young Adult Nonfiction

The historian and fiction writer James Forman has written some excellent histories for young adults. His *Anarchism: Political Innocence or Social Violence?* is a historical analysis that introduces young readers to the philosophies of Rosseau, Sorel, Spencer, Tolstoy, Thoreau, and others. His *Capitalism: Economic Individualism to Today's Welfare State* follows capitalism from its origins through industrialization and the depression to the big businesses of today. Two other excellent ideological histories are *Communism: From Marx's Manifesto to Twentieth-Century Reality* and *Fascism: The Meaning and Experience of Reactionary Revolution,* an examination of fascism's roots and its future. *Nazism* is an informative history of the Nazi party, covering the writings of Hitler and the social and political climate in which Nazism developed. *Socialism: Its Theoretical Roots and Present-day Development* examines the history of socialism and the differences between it and communism.

Forman's *The Mad Game* examines the question of why we have war. The author traces the history of war from the beginnings of human history to the Russian invasion of Afghanistan. This unique historical account would be an excellent book to use in a history class studying war. As a counterpoint Forman also examines the history of pacifism from its roots in Eastern religions and Christianity. He discusses the successes of pacifists in this century, such as the Quakers, Gandhi, and Martin Luther King, Jr., pointing out that peacemaking efforts require as much courage, patriotism, and heroism as fighting a war. The book is readable, but many historical references are cited to support the author's views. The book includes a bibliography for further reading and an index. All of Forman's books are interesting, well documented, and present a variety of viewpoints.

The historian Milton Meltzer has also written several appealing histories for the young adult reader. One of his best is *Never to Forget: The Jews of the Holocaust.* This book is divided into three sections: "History of Hatred," "Destruction of the Jews," and "Spirit of Resistance." Meltzer says of his book: "When I went to work on *Never to Forget,* it was with the idea of trying to provide young people, particularly of junior and senior high school age, with a deeper understanding of the origins of the Holocaust. There had been a number of very good novels about the experience of the Holocaust written for young people, some based on personal experience and others purely imagined experience. But there has been almost nothing nonfictional trying to deal with the Holocaust" (in Weiss, 1979).

Some other young adult histories written or edited by Meltzer include *Taking Root: Jewish Immigrants in America, World of Our Fathers: The Jews of Eastern Europe, In Their Own Words: A History of the American Negro, 1619–1965* (three volumes), *Bound for Rio Grande: The Mexican Struggle, 1845–1848,* and *Violins and Shovels: The WPA Arts Projects.* In a recent book *The Bill of Rights: How We Got It and What It Means,* Meltzer examines not only a history of the Bill of Rights, but provides a commentary on its application today. *The American Promise: Voices of a Changing Nation, 1945–Present* deals with U.S. history since World War II: the atomic bomb, the cold war, the Korean War, the Vietnam War, the civil rights movement, the generation gap, the women's movement, immigration, poverty, and chemical pollution.

Adaptations of Adult Works

An interesting recent trend is the adaptation of adult histories for young readers. The best current examples are the rewritings of Dee Brown's outstanding adult works. His *Hear the Lonesome Whistle Blow,* which describes the building of the transcontinental railroad, became a book for adolescents titled *Lonesome Whistle: The Story of the First Transcontinental Railroad.* His *Bury My Heart at Wounded Knee* was adapted for young readers and retitled *Wounded Knee.* If this trend continues, many adult histories that are too difficult for most young readers will become available to them.

Histories by Period

Books about specific historic periods can often be used to teach important concepts and themes in both social studies and English. For example, *Columbus and the World around Him,* by Milton Meltzer, brings to life not only a historical figure but the time period in which he lived.

Other important books about various periods in American history have been written for young adults. Meltzer's *The American Revolutionaries: A History in Their Own Words* and *Brother, Can You Spare a Dime? The Great Depression, 1929–1933* tell the story of two very important periods in American history through the eyes of those individuals who experienced them. An award-winning series by Daniel J. Boorstin provides an accurate and fun-to-read account of politics in American hisory: *The Americans: The Colonial Experience, The Americans: The National Experience,* and *The Americans: The Democratic Experience.* An unusual book told partially in stories and songs, *Scalded To Death by Steam* by Katie Letcher Lyle, provides vivid accounts of American railroad disasters. Juan Williams's excellent account *Eyes on the Prize: American Civil Rights Years, 1954–1965,* which was made into a public televison series, will help adolescents better understand this difficult time in U.S. history. A terrible day during the Vietnam War crisis is told in James A. Michener's *Kent State: What Happened and Why.*

The Rights of Man, the Reign of Terror: The Story of the French Revolution by Susan Banfield presents the social changes in France from 1789 through 1799. The book makes clear the impact of the French Revolution on human rights today. This book would be excellent in a thematic unit coupled with Dickens's *A Tale of Two Cities.*

The Civil War

Many good histories deal with the Civil War and the decades surrounding it. *Anthony Burns: The Defeat and Triumph of a Fugitive Slave* by Virginia Hamilton is an excellent narrative of ten days in the life of Anthony Burns who attempted to escape slavery in Virginia and whose plight galvanized antislavery groups in Boston in 1854. In *To Be a Slave,* a Newbery Honor book by Julius Lester, slaves themselves eloquently relate their stories. *The Brothers' War: Civil War Letters to Their Loved Ones from the Blue and Gray,* edited by Annette Tapert, shows the human aspects of war from both sides of the battlefield. Other excellent books about the Civil War period include

Escape from Slavery: Five Journeys to Freedom by Doreen Rappaport, *Gentle Annie: The True Story of a Civil War Nurse* by Mary Frances Shura, *The Boys' War* by Jim Murphy, *A Nation Torn: The Story of How the Civil War Began* and *Behind Blue and Gray: The Soldier's Life in the Civil War* by Delia Ray, and *All for the Union: The Civil War Diary and Letters of Elisha Hunt Rhodes,* edited by Robert Hunt Rhodes. Russell Freedman's *Lincoln: A Photobiography* is an excellent supplement in any unit on the Civil War.

World War II

Of the many excellent nonfiction books for young adults on World War II, only a few can be mentioned here. Although not specifically about World War II, an excellent book to use in any unit about war is Sue Mansfield and Mary Bowen Hall's *Reasons for War,* which can be paired with Forman's *The Mad Game.* The book surveys all the possible reasons for war. The authors begin with a definition of war and make clear their premise that war is neither instinctive nor inevitable. Then they present five beliefs about and approaches to war and the part they played in wars throughout history. In the conclusion the authors make a plea for an international peace movement.

The Holocaust has been the focus of numerous books on World War II in the past several decades. An excellent overview of the events of the Holocaust can be found in Meltzer's *Never to Forget: The Jews of the Holocaust,* discussed above. Other excellent accounts of the Holocaust present it from the perspective of a particular individual who lived at the time. *Anne Frank: The Diary of a Young Girl* was published in 1952, after her death, by her father. *The Last Seven Months of Anne Frank* by Willy Lindwer is a sort of sequel to the events in Anne's diary. Other personal accounts include *Alicia: My Story,* by Alicia Appleman-Jurman, about a Jewish girl who was able to escape imprisonment in a Nazi concentration camp; *As the Waltz Was Ending,* by Emma Macalik Butterworth, about her life in Vienna from 1935 to 1945; and Lena Küchler-Silberman's *My Hundred Children* about a Polish girl who survived the Nazi extermination of the Jews and her campaign to help survivors. *Grace in the Wilderness,* by Aranka Siegal, is about Piri Davidowitz's life following her liberation from Auschwitz. Siegal's *Upon the Head of the Goat* describes Davidowitz's childhood under Hitler's dictatorship. Knobel Fluek's *Memories of My Life in a Polish Village, 1930–1949* covers the years prior to and during the Holocaust.

The stories of the children and grandchildren of many Holocaust victims are presented in Yale Strom's *A Tree Still Stands: Jewish Youth in Eastern Europe Today.* A book that will help students understand that the Nazi persecution was not just of Jews is Ina R. Friedman's *The Other Victims: First Person Stories of Non-Jews Persecuted by the Nazis.* Milton Meltzer's *Rescue: The Story of How Gentiles Saved Jews in the Holocaust* is an excellent work for helping students understand how brave men and women risked their lives to save others.

After having read books on how the Holocaust affected millions of Europeans, students may wonder how someone like Hitler could have possibly come to power. They can better understand this phenomenon by reading William L. Shirer's *The Rise and Fall of Adolf Hitler.* Another book that attempts to explain how and why the Holocaust could happen is Barbara Rogasky's *Smoke and Ashes: The Story of the*

Holocaust. Life on the home front at the start of World War II is chronicled in Margaret Poynter's memoir *A Time Too Swift.* Letters home from American GIs during World War II help bring the lives of the young men who fought the war to life in *Lines of Battle* by Annette Tapert.

The Vietnam War

Numerous good books have been written on the war in Vietnam, particularly from the perspective of the young men who fought. A book that chronicles a young marine officer's year in Vietnam is Charles Coe's *Young Man in Vietnam.* Another personal account of the war is *Don't Cry, It's Only Thunder.* In this book Paul G. Hensler tells of his two tours of duty in Vietnam and his attempts to provide for 125 war orphans. *Dear America: Letters Home from Vietnam,* edited by Bernard Edelman, tells the stories of many of the young soldiers in their own words. A book that can bring the Vietnam years to life for many students is Dorothy and Thomas Hoobler's *Vietnam: Why We Fought: An Illustrated History.*

Other Good Books on U.S. History

Many good young adult books focus on the western movement. These books can be combined with fiction books about this period (see Chapter 5) and books about Native Americans for an interesting unit on the American West. The following are good nonfiction sources for this period: *The United States in the Indian Wars* by Don Lawson, *Native American Testimony: An Anthology of Indian and White Relations, First Encounter and Dispossession* edited by Peter Nabokov, *The Oregon Trail* by Leonard Everett Fisher, *The Great American Gold Rush* by Rhoda Blumberg, *Faster Than a Horse: Moving West with Engine Power* by Suzanne Hilton, and *Cowboys* by Robert H. Miller. An interesting book to read while examining the industrialization of the United States is *A Long Hard Journey: The Story of the Pullman Porter* by Patricia and Frederick McKissack. This book spans the period from the Age of Steam in 1852 to the death of A. Philip Randolph, the man who unionized the porters, in 1979. *The Eagle and the Dragon* by Don Lawson tells of the two hundred year history of America's relationship with China. There are many good books about John F. Kennedy. One that may particularly appeal to adolescents is *John F. Kennedy: Young People's President* by Catherine Corley Anderson.

Contemporary Social Issues

Social issues can be taught in many subject areas. Of course, social issues are an important part of social studies, but they also figure in science courses, in which students may deal with issues such as the environmental damage, using animals for experimentation, and the right to die. Social issues may also be a part of English courses under themes such as "Women in literature" and "The changing family." An English teacher and a social studies teacher might team-teach a unit on a particular social issue with the social studies teacher examining the issue's history and implications and the English teacher helping students analyze the issue through critical reading and writing. This section of the chapter offers many books on contemporary social issues that are appropriate for classroom use or independent student reading.

Individual Rights

Many nonfiction books on issues of social importance are being written for the young adult audience. Alan Sussman's *The Rights of Young People: An American Civil Liberties Union Handbook* catalogues the legal rights of young adults in all fifty states. It includes such topics as driving, drugs, and alcohol, employment, search and seizure, rape, pornography, child abuse and child neglect, adoption, and more. *The First Freedom: The Tumultuous History of Free Speech in America* by Nat Hentoff also addresses the rights of teenagers. The struggle for international human rights including the role of the United States is chronicled by young adult writer Marvin E. Frankel in *Out of the Shadows of Night: The Struggle for International Human Rights*. Another book that deals with the rights of individuals is Milton Meltzer's *Poverty in America*. Told from the perspective of an individual, *Socrates, Plato, and Guys Like Me: Confessions of a Gay Schoolteacher* by Eric E. Rofes, argues for homosexuals' rights. The issue of AIDS is addressed from the perspective of one of its young victims in the powerful book *Ryan White: My Own Story*, by Ann Marie Cunningham and Ryan White.

Women's Issues

Heart Songs: The Intimate Diaries of Young Girls, edited by Laurel Holliday, is a collection of writings by ten young girls across several centuries. The diaries reflect the same joys and fears of approaching womanhood that young women experience today. Carol Hymowitz and Michaele Weissman's *A History of Women in America* spans the years from the colonial times to the present. This easy-to-read book presents many first-person accounts. *Growing Up Female in America*, edited by Eve Merriam, another easy-to-read book, is about ten American women from different times and places. Dell's Women of America paperback series, under the general editorship of Milton Meltzer, includes *Ida Tarbell: First of the Muckrakers* and *The Senator from Maine: Margaret Chase Smith* (Fleming), *The World of Mary Cassatt* (McKown), *Probing the Unknown: The Story of Dr. Florence Sabin* (Phelan), *Fanny Kemble's America* (Scott), and *Sea and Earth: The Life of Rachel Carson* (Sterling). Richard Deming's *Women: The New Criminals* describes the increase in the number of women criminals in the 1970s and 1980s and discusses some reasons for it.

Teenage Sex and Pregnancy

Changing Bodies, Changing Lives: Revised and Updated, by Ruth Bell and others, can help teenagers understand the changes they are experiencing both physically and emotionally. An account of one young man's changes in adolescence can be found in the humorous and fun-to-read book *Will the Nurse Make Me Take My Underwear Off?* (Schwartz, MacFarlane, McPherson). *Learning about Sex: The Contemporary Guide for Young Adults* by Gary F. Kelly is a straightforward, nonjudgmental guide for young adults. Eric W. Johnson's *Love and Sex in Plain Language* is far more than a book on sex education. Johnson addresses the values of caring, responsibility, self-control, honesty, and respect for self and others and at the same time provides an accurate explanation of human sexuality and reproduction. Sol Gordon's *You Would If You Loved Me* examines the lines used by boys to entice girls into sex. Gordon gives scientific, historical, psychological, and sociological information in this nonjudgmental guide.

Janet Bode's *Kids Having Kids: The Unwed Teenage Parent* discusses the sexual conduct of teenagers and the health risks associated with pregnancy and birth control. Options such as adoption, abortion, and keeping the child are frankly discussed. Other good books dealing with the topic of teen pregnancy include *Teen Pregnancy* by Sonia Bowe-Gutman and *What Do I Do Now? Talking about Teenage Pregnancy* by Susan Kuklin. One of the great values of Bowe-Gutman's book is its controlled reading level which makes it accessible to the middle school students and poor readers of all ages. *The Ambivalence of Abortion* by Linda Bird Francke is a compilation of the feelings of adults and teenagers, both male and female, about abortion.

Drugs and Alcohol

Drugs and alcohol are discussed in Robert deRopp's *Drugs and the Mind,* Greg Felsen's *Can You Do It until you Need Glasses? The Different Drug Book,* and *Worlds Apart: Young People and Drug Programs,* edited by Dennis T. Jaffe and Ted Clark, *Drug Wars* by Margaret O. Hyde, and *Should Drugs Be Legalized?* by Susan Neilburg Terkel. *Alcohol: The Delightful Poison* by Alice Fleming traces the history of the discovery and use of alcohol. Wayne Coffey's *Straight Talk about Drinking: Teenagers Speak Out about Alcohol* dispels myths about alcohol from a scientific perspective and from the perspective of recovering teenage alcoholics.

Environmental Issues

Ecological issues are discussed in Jonathan Schell's *The Fate of the Earth,* Laurence Pringle's *Lives at Stake* and *What Shall We Do with the Land? Choices for America,* and Betty Sue Cummings's *Let a River Be.* The issue of toxic chemicals is examined in Michael Brown's *Laying Waste: The Poisoning of America by Toxic Chemicals.* Gail Kay Haines's *The Great Nuclear Power Debate* defines both sides of the issue. Animal rights are explored in *The Forest* by Roger Caras. Patricia Curtis's *Animal Rights: Stories of People Who Defend the Rights of Animals* offers seven imaginary case studies in animal rights. *Ourselves and Other Animals,* by Peter Evans, based on the television series of the same name, deals with the connections between animals and humans. A case for the scientific and spiritual need to save our environment is made by Terry and Renny Russell in the Sierra Club's *On the Loose.*

Family Concerns

Family problems are considered in Richard Gardner's *The Boys and Girls Book about Divorce* and Arlene Richards and Irene Willis's *How to Get It Together When Your Parents Are Coming Apart,* and *Putting It Together: Teenagers Talk about Family Breakup* by Paula McGuire.

Death and illness are dealt with in *Afraid to Ask: A Book for Families to Share about Cancer* by Judylaine Fine, *Losing Someone You Love: When a Brother or Sister Dies* by Elizabeth Richter, and *Meeting Death* by Margaret O. Hyde and Lawrence E. Hyde.

South Africa

Jonathan Paton, son of the South African author Alan Paton *(Cry, the Beloved Country)*, points out that if the story of South Africa is told from the white's perspective it is the history of "courageous" whites fighting off "hordes of fierce, heathen black warriors." Paton's own *Land and People of South Africa* exposes the myths of South Africa that have been taught to South African school children for generations. *Voices of South Africa* by Carolyn Meyer presents a view of the oppressed indigenous people of the country dramatized through anecdotes of Meyer's travels through villages, towns, and cities. *Winnie Mandela: Life of Struggle* by Jim Haskins describes Winnie Mandela's life from her birth in 1936 through the mid-1980s.

American Schooling

The quality of public education in the United States has been a major issue during the past two decades. Therefore, it is not surprising that schooling is being addressed in many books that are appropriate for adolescent readers. Eleanor Craig's *If We Could Hear the Grass Grow* is about a school for twelve severely disturbed children. *I Am a Teacher: A Tribute to American Teachers,* by David Marshall Marquis and Robin Sachs, makes it clear that in spite of the criticism of American schools many marvelous teachers are succeeding. Although this book is written primarily for adults, young adults thinking about a career in education are likely to find it inspirational. Other inspirational accounts by teachers of their experiences in the schools include *Lives on the Boundary* by Mike Rose, *Small Victories: The Real World of a Teacher, Her Students, and Their High School* by Samuel G. Freedman, who spent a year shadowing Jessica Sigel at Seward Park High School in Manhattan, and *Sometimes a Shining Moment: The Foxfire Experience* by Eliot Wigginton, the teacher in the Georgia mountains who taught students language by allowing them to share their stories with the nation.

Other Social Issues

A wide range of other social concerns is presented in nonfiction written for young adult readers. Involvement in religious cults is addressed in Christopher Edward's firsthand account *Crazy for God: The Nightmare of Cult Life.* The contemporary phenomenon of the game Dungeons and Dragons and its power over one individual is the subject of William Dear's *The Dungeon Master: The Disappearance of James Dallas Egbert, III.* The issue of police brutality is addressed in *Best Intentions* by Robert Sam Anson, a book about the killing of a seventeen year old by a plainclothes policeman. A plea for nonviolence in books, media, and in life is made by Jane and Paul Annixter in *The Last Monster.*

Two good books about money by economist John Kenneth Galbraith are useful to young adults. *Money: Whence It Came and Where It Went* is a history of money from ancient times to the present. *Almost Everyone's Guide to Economics* (Galbraith and

Salinger) is a short, simple introduction to the world of supply-and-demand curves. Another good money book for older teens is Jane Bryant Quinn's *Everyone's Money Book*. It is filled with useful personal financial advice of particular interest to young adults, including handling college expenses, buying a car, and renting an apartment.

Cross-Cultural Studies

Few textbooks can give an in-depth picture of another culture. For that students need to turn to nonfiction books, especially those by people who have lived in specific cultures. Through such books students can learn how all humans are similar and how all cultures differ. The books described in this section are appropriate for social studies and English classrooms and for student independent reading.

African Americans

An interesting historical account of African Americans in the West is given in William Katz's *Black People Who Made the Old West*. In *Young and Black in America,* edited by Rae Pace Alexander and Julius Lester, eight men and eight women tell of their experiences. *Growing Up Black,* edited by Jay David, is a compilation of the views of nineteen young people. *A Pictorial History of Black Americans* is edited by Langston Hughes, Milton Meltzer, and C. Eric Lincoln. June Jordan's *Dry Victories* contrasts Reconstruction and the civil rights era using photographs and dialogue between two young African American boys. *Selma, Lord, Selma: Girlhood Memories of the Civil Rights Days,* by Sheyann Webb and Rachel West Nelson, is a recollection of events from the 1965 Selma civil rights campaign. Walter Dean Myers's *Now Is Your Time! The African-American Struggle for Freedom* is an excellent, readable history of African Americans by a gifted writer of young adult books. An excellent companion to Myers's book is Milton Meltzer's *The Black Americans: A History in Their Own Words, 1619–1983. Black Ice* by Lorene Cary is a memoir about growing up African American in the United States. Unlike many African Americans, Lorene had the benefit of a private education, having been recruited to attend an exclusive school in New Hampshire. In this book Lorene must affirm her blackness in a white environment and deal with racism.

Increasingly in the field of young adult literature the achievements of African Americans are being cataloged. Two excellent sources for learning about the accomplishments of African Americans are *Black Music in America: A History through Its People* and *Black Dance in America: A History through Its People,* by James Haskins. Haskins has also written other excellent books about African Americans for young adults. *Witchcraft, Mysticism and Magic in the Black World* traces the development of beliefs from their sources in West Africa. *One More River to Cross* tells about twelve African Americans who achieved greatness in spite of racial prejudice.

Native Americans

Alvin M. Josephy's *The Indian Heritage of America* is an archaeological, ethnological, and historical account of the tribes and cultures of the Indians of the Americas. Russell Freedman's *An Indian Winter* is about the Mandan Indians of North Dakota. *Ishi, Last of His Tribe* by Theodora Kroeber is an account of the Yahi Indians of California that is especially suited to young adolescents. Mari Sandoz's *These Were the Sioux* is an interesting history of the tribe. Vine Deloria's *Behind the Trail of Broken Treaties: An Indian Declaration of Independence* makes a strong case for a federal policy defining the Native Americans' sovereign states. T. C. McLuhan's *Touch the Earth: A Self Portrait of Indian Existence* helps explain Native Americans' attachment to the environment.

Other Ethnic Groups

Other nonfiction books with ethnic themes include *Rising Voices,* edited by Al Martinez, containing brief biographies of fifty-two outstanding Chicanos. *Strangers in Their Own Land* by Albert Prago is a history of Mexican Americans. How immigrant Jews have made their lives in America is the subject of books such as *Growing Up Jewish,* edited by Jay David, *The Jewish Family Album,* edited by Franz Hubmann, and Meltzer's *Taking Root.* The Chinese Americans' immigrant experience is discussed in *The Chinese Americans: A History in Their Own Words* by Milton Meltzer and *Tales from Gold Mountain: Stories of the Chinese in the New World* by Paul Yee. J. Joseph Huthmacher's *A Nation of Newcomers: Ethnic Minority Groups in American History* is a short, easy-to-read survey. In Janet Bode's *New Kids on the Block: Oral Histories of Immigrant Teens* young immigrants of the 1980s talk about their experiences. *Pride and Protest: Ethnic Roots in America* edited by Jay Schulman, Aubrey Shatter, and Rosalie Ehrlich, is a selection of essays, fiction, drama, and poetry that reflect the views of the diverse cultures that make up the modern United States.

Careers

The selection of an appropriate career is very important to the young adult. A unit on careers in English or social studies may help students begin to think about appropriate careers. Many books have been published to guide teenagers in considering their options.

Studs Terkel's *Working: People Talk about What They Do All Day and How They Feel about What They Do,* although not written specifically for young adults, is an excellent resource guide to jobs — from gravedigger to piano tuner, from copyboy or copygirl to editor, and hundreds of other jobs. Another book containing interviews with workers is Sheila Cole's *Working Kids on Working.* The book shows the positive side of young adults in the work force. The young people interviewed are enthusiastic about the jobs they do, from washing dishes and busing tables to delivering newspapers. The book emphasizes the responsibility needed for and developed through a job. The interviews help young readers understand what can be obtained from a job besides the money earned.

To learn more about specific careers, young adults can turn to any of the hundreds of books written about individual fields. The best of these books describe a typical work schedule, the benefits and problems of the job, the training needed for the job, the possibility for advancement, and other information helpful to those pursuing a lifelong career or a summer job. Most school and public libraries have these books listed in the subject card catalogue. Several good examples include these books by young adult author William Jaspersohn: *A Day in the Life of a Marine Biologist, A Day in the Life of a Veterinarian,* and *The Ballpark.* Students can also read memoirs by individuals who have pursued particular career paths such as James Herriot's books about being a veterinarian in England and the books about teaching noted under "American Schooling."

Other books that give an overview of career choices and tell how to gain access to different professions are *The American Almanac of Jobs and Salaries* (Wright), *I Can Be Anything: Careers and Colleges for Young Women, The Men's Career Book: Work and Life Planning for a New Age* and *The Work Book: A Guide to Skilled Jobs* (Mitchell), and *Modern Sports Science* (Kettelkamp). *A Not Entirely Benign Procedure* by Perri Klass is about getting a medical education. *Conversations: Working Women Talk about Doing a "Man's Job,"* edited by Terry Wetherby, presents interviews with twenty-two women who work in traditionally male-dominated fields as welders, carpenters, butchers, and board chairpersons. A book that is designed to help the reader identify skills and aspirations and set a realistic career target is Tom Jackson's *Guerrilla Tactics in the Job Market.* All of these books are interesting to young adults and can help them in pursuing, obtaining, and keeping a job.

How-To Books

How-to books tell readers how to do everything from losing weight to making a million dollars in the stock market. For many students these kinds of books are their only pleasure reading. Therefore, it is important to help them learn to select good how-to books. Furthermore, it is important that students learn how to read these books. They need to understand that a how-to book is not read like most other works of nonfiction. Because it is rarely essential to read the entire book, knowing how to use the indexes to find information is important. Students also need to learn how to read directions using a step-by-step process and how to utilize photographs, charts, diagrams, and tables. Often these features are critical to understanding the information presented. Assessing the value of these books is difficult because one misleading sentence can render a book useless.

An intriguing series of how-to books is the *Foxfire* books. Edited by Eliot Wigginton, these books were written by high school students in Georgia as part of an English program in which the students interview local people to report on the everyday life of Rabun Gap. The books include information on how to slaughter hogs, make moonshine, read weather signs, build furniture, hook rugs, and many other skills mastered by the self-sufficient mountain people.

Every bookstore and library has hundreds of how-to books for young and adult readers. Before purchasing a book for classroom use, it is a good idea to check it out of the library to be sure it can be easily understood by teenagers, has easy-to-follow directions, and does not present misleading or dangerous information. The readability can easily be determined by having a young adult read a section and try to follow the author's directions. If the directions are hard to follow, the book is not for teenagers.

The novice or the person who knows nothing about a topic cannot easily detect misinformation in a book. However, the following guidelines are useful in selecting an accurate, helpful how-to book. The book is likely to be accurate and helpful to the teenage reader if (1) the reviewers' comments printed on the book jacket are from reputable persons who know something about the topic; (2) the publisher is well known for other how-to books in the field; (3) the author's biographical sketch indicates that he or she has the appropriate background; (4) the points the author makes in the first few pages seem logical and well thought out; (5) there are no physical, emotional, or financial reasons why teenagers should not do what this book suggests.

Here are a few good how-to books written primarily for adolescents: *Too Fat? Too Thin? Do You Have a Choice?* by Caroline Arnold; *Safe, Strong, and Streetwise,* by Helen Benedict, about sexual assault and how to protect yourself from it; *I Hate School: How to Hang In and When to Drop Out* by Claudine G. Wirths and Mary Bowman-Kruhm; *Speak to Me,* by Patricia Sternberg, to help adolescents become better conversationalists; *The Young Writer's Handbook* by Susan and Stephen Tchudi; and *Literature Unbound,* by Sam Tanenhaus, to help young adults understand how to read books. One of the most enjoyable and fun-to-read nonfiction books of recent years is author and artist David Macaulay's *The Way Things Work.* This humorous presentation of technology uses marvelous drawings to show how devices such as computers and CD players work.

Science Books

Since many teachers are using science trade books, written for the popular market, to supplement or even teach science, it is important to recognize quality science trade books for young readers. In "Science Trade Books and Teachers," Lazer Goldberg (1991) suggests the following criteria:

Intellectual and Aesthetic
1. Facts, generalizations and theories must be accurate.
2. Scientific evidence should be provided to support assertions whenever possible.
3. Illustrations in the book should be correct, eye-catching, and significant.

Developmental Level
1. Content and style should be appropriate for the ability and interests of the students.
2. The books should stretch the reader's capacity to comprehend.

The Science Program
1. Books should address not only *what* scientists have discovered but also *how* they have done so.
2. The book should allow readers to ask productive questions.

Connections
1. The book should make connections between science and the rest of the curriculum.
2. Biographies of scientists are useful for this purpose.
3. The book should help students make connections between science and graphic and musical arts, physical education and sports and health.
4. Science and human values must be connected in the book.

Special Interests or Needs
1. The book should address the particular needs and interests of the students.
2. The book should reduce the mystery surrounding a scientific topic.

Among the many sources that recommend good science trade books to teachers are *Outstanding Science Trade Books for Children* and *Appraisal.* These will be specifically discussed in Chapter 14.

An increasing number of accurately detailed science books are available for young readers. Issac Asimov was a prolific writer whose books are appropriate for many older teenage readers and span the entire world of scientific study. Appropriate books in astronomy include *Asimov on Astronomy, The Nearest Star, Of Time and Space and Other Things, The Collapsing Universe* (about black holes in space), *The Solar System and Back, The Universe: From Flat Earth to Quasar,* and *From Earth to Heaven. Life and Energy* is about the physical and chemical bases of biology. *The Tragedy of the Moon* is a collection dealing with cosmology and the physics of light and sound, microbiology, astronomy, and sociology. *The Left Hand of the Electron* discusses problems of left and right, numbers and lines, and history and population. *The Planet That Wasn't* involves astronomy, biology, chemistry, sociology, religion, and economics. All of Asimov's books are readable, many of them being written at eighth-grade level or below, and all make connections between science and other disciplines.

Most other science writers emphasize one branch of science in their writings. Older adolescents are often interested in the works of Lewis Thomas on biology. His *Lives of a Cell: Notes of a Biology Watcher* won the National Book Award. The second biology-watcher diary, *The Medusa and the Snail,* won the Christopher Award. Teenagers interested in biology will also enjoy the following: David Carroll's *Wonders of the World,* a beautiful book of photographs of tundras, tidal waves, blue whales, polar lights, and more; Jacques-Yves Cousteau and Phillippe Diole's *Life and Death in a Coral Sea;* Ronald Glasser's *The Body Is the Hero,* an account of how the body protects itself from disease; the books of the Diagram Group entitled *Child's Body, Man's Body: An Owner's Manual* and *Woman's Body: An Owner's Manual;* Margaret Hyde's *Your Brain: Master Computer;* Paul Lewis and David Rubenstein's *The Human Body;* and Dorothy Hinshaw Patent's *Evolution Goes on Every Day.*

Students interested in ecology are likely to find these books on the rain forest interesting: *The Last Rain Forest: A World Conservation Atlas* edited by Mark Collins, *Wildlife in a Rainforest* by Andrew Mitchell, *Rainforests* by Lois Warburton, and Jean Craighead George's *One Day in the Tropical Rain Forest.* The last book can be used in conjunction with George's many fictional books that are also based in the biological sciences and ecology. (See pages 316–317 for using the books of Jean Craighead George to teach science.) These books on extinction and endangered animals are also of interest to adolescents; *Extinction A–Z* by Erich Hoyt, Dorothy Hinshaw Patent's *The Challenge of Extinction,* and *Saving Endangered Animals* by Virginia Alvin and Robert Silverstein.

Young students of physics and astronomy are often interested in Lincoln Barnett's *The Universe and Dr. Einstein,* which makes Einstein's theories understandable to a lay audience. *Cosmos* by Carl Sagan is based on the PBS series. This beautifully illustrated catalogue of life includes history, physics, biology, astronomy, and philosophy. *A House in Space* by Henry Cooper is about the daily working regimen in a skylab. The student astronomer is also likely to enjoy Sune Engelbrekston's *Stars, Planets, and Galaxies.*

Books for young experimenters include Magnus Pyke's *Butter Side Up! The Delights of Science,* which teaches many basic concepts and dispels many myths. John Gunter and his students put together the delightful book *The Gunter Papers,* a do-it-yourself guide to experiments in biology, earth science, chemistry, and physics. It even contains a play, "A Visit with the Cold Germ Rancher." *The Formula Book* by Norman Stark is for teenagers who enjoy creating their own products. This simple guide to "consumer chemistry" shows the reader how to make personal, pet-care, and household products from easily acquired materials. *The Quest for Artificial Intelligence* by Dorothy Hinshaw Patent is likely to interest young adults who are fairly sophisticated users of computers.

Science biographies and autobiographies are also interesting to students and make important connections between science and other aspects of an individual's life. *A Passion to Know: 20 Profiles in Science,* edited by Allen L. Hammond, is a good anthology of the lives of important scientists. *Dr. Wildlife: The Crusade of a Northwoods Veterinarian* by Rory C. Foster is an autobiographical memoir that describes a career in science and the practical side of life as a northwoods veterinarian.

Mathematics and Puzzle Books

The poor mathematics knowledge of American students has been well documented in the national media. Teachers who introduce students to motivational books on mathematics may help solve the problem. Many of the mathematics books written for young adults can turn on students to math. Those who have already discovered the delights of numbers will also enjoy many of these books.

Asimov on Numbers covers the uses of numbers, the meanings of symbols, and more. *Fantasia Mathematica,* edited by Clifton Fadiman, presents the strange and unusual facts from the world of mathematics. *Figuring: The Joy of Numbers* by Shakuntala Devi demonstrates puzzles, shortcuts, and mathematical tricks that make figuring fun.

Playing with numbers through games and puzzles can make mathematics enjoyable even for the reluctant student. Some interesting game books in mathematics include

- *Coin Games and Puzzles* by Maxey Brooke
- *More Posers* by Phillip Kaplan
- *The Moscow Puzzles: 359 Mathematical Recreations* by Boris A. Kordemsky
- *Perplexing Puzzles and Tantalizing Teasers* (including "droodles for nimble noodles") by Martin Gardner
- *The Tokyo Puzzles* by Kobon Fujimura
- *Timid Virgins Make Dull Company and Other Puzzles, Pitfalls, and Paradoxes* by Dr. Crypton
- *Fun with Figures* by J. A. Hunter

- *We Dare You to Solve This!* by John Adams
- *Your Move* (100 decision problems) by David L. Silverman
- *Mathematical Magic* (tricks using numbers) by William Simon
- *100 Geometric Games* by Pierre Berloquin
- *Pocket Calculator Game Book* by Edwin Schlossberg and John Brockman
- *The Mathematical Magpie* (stories, rhymes, music, anecdotes, and epigrams) by Clifton Fadiman
- *Mathematical Carnival* and *Mathematical Circus* by Martin Gardner

Books about the history of mathematics and mathematicians can be appealing to adolescents, particularly those interested in mathematics. *The Ages of Mathematics: The Modern Ages* by Peter D. Cook presents the latest mathematical theories and the people behind them. This book is part of a four-volume set edited by Charles F. Linn which explores the complete history of mathematics in both East and West. A briefer history of mathematics can be found in Lancelot Hogben's *Mathematics in the Making*. Hogben's *Wonderful World of Mathematics* shows that the growth and development of civilization is also the growth and development of mathematics as a science. Julia Diggin's *String, Straightedge and Shadow* is the story of geometry. *Men of Mathematics* by Eric Bell is a series of short biographies from Zeno to Poincare. *Women in Mathematics* by Lynn Osen tells of mathematicians from A.D. 370 to 1935. *Math and Aftermath* by Robert Hooke and others shows how practicing mathematicians contribute to the community. Nathan Court's *Mathematics in Fun and in Earnest* explains how mathematicians think.

Mathematics, a Human Endeavor: A Textbook for Those Who Think They Don't Like the Subject, by Harold Jacobs, shows the beauty and symmetry of mathematics. *Impromptu Magic* by Bill Severn is not a mathematics book but is an excellent book for adolescents who like puzzles and illusions.

Poetry

The Child as Poet

Poetry is a part of our oral language. We listen to it on records, tapes, radios, and jukeboxes. We sing it in the shower, in cars, at parties, at church. We recite it in playground jump-rope chants, in rhymes sung to babies in their cribs, and in advertising jingles from television. Poetry is living language. It is the language of the street, the home, and the playground.

Poetry comes naturally to us when we are young children. As preschoolers we are chased away by other children with rhyme: "Fat and skinny had a race around the pillow case; fat fell down and broke his face, and skinny won the race." We reply in rhyme: "Sticks and stones can break my bones, but names can never hurt me." We learn nursery rhymes and Bible verses as we sit on our parents' laps. As poet, anthologist, and educator Nancy Larrick suggests, "Poetry, beyond any other literary form, solicits participation from the listener or reader. Indeed, some people insist that a poem is not complete until there is a partner adding his own experiences and feelings to those of the poet" (1971).

Poetry and the Adolescent

Hooking young readers on poetry at a very early age is quite easy when they are introduced to the humorous verse of a Shel Silverstein or a Judith Viorst. Keeping that interest alive as readers progress through their teens should be possible given contemporary poets like Nancy Willard and Mel Glenn, who write for young readers, and anthologists like Lee Bennett Hopkins and Paul Janeczko, who write and compile poetry collections attuned to the different ages of young readers. However, when you ask most typical adolescents what they think about poetry, a common response is "Yuk." Why?

For many young people, their natural love of rhythm and rhyme is lost between the playground and the classroom. Though they may warm to poetry on the radio and television, they often tune out poetry on the printed page. Perhaps the turnoff comes about because of the way poetry is often taught.

Myths about Teaching Poetry

Paul B. Janeczko, a poet, collector of poems for adolescents, and teacher of adolescents, claims that before teachers can successfully teach poetry to adolescents, seven myths must be dispelled:

Myth 1: Only Certain Teachers Can Teach Poetry Well.

This myth is correct, but, as they say, it ain't right. Only certain teachers *CAN* teach poetry well, but it's not hard to be one of those teachers. To begin with the teacher who expects to teach poetry well must read poetry. And not just the stuff that's in the classroom anthology, the stuff we're expected to "cover." I happen to agree with James Dickey who said that poetry is "just naturally the greatest goddamn thing that ever was in the whole universe. If you love it, there's no substitute for it.". . .

Myth 2: Modern Poetry Is Impossible To Understand.

While some modern poetry *IS* impossible to understand, much of it is delightfully accessible. . . .

Myth 3: Poetry Units Must Be Three or Four Weeks Long for Students to Get the Most Out of Poetry. (Myth 3a: Poetry Units Should Be Taught/Work Best in the Spring, Usually May.)

Poetry units *MAY* be long, but there's no law demanding it. In fact, one of the wonderful things about poetry is that so many poems are short; students can read a complete literary work (a couple of times, in fact) in a class period and still have time to discuss it.

Poems can fit into a lesson almost any time. . . . We can read a couple of relevant poems in connection with a short story or a novel. . . . We don't need to "cover" every poem we share with our students. We should spend more time reading poems aloud. . . . Read sports poems when your school is caught up in the frenzy of the basketball tournament. Read apple poems in the fall, early morning poems to your first period class and spring poems when winter won't let go. . . .

Myth 4: Poetry Works Best with Older/Younger Students. (Myth 4a: Poetry Works Best with Smarter Students.)

. . . The key with poetry, as with any classroom activity, is to find material that is appropriate for our students. . . .

Myth 5: There Is No Connection between Reading Poetry and Writing Poetry.

You're right. I can't disprove this myth. However, I think students who play with language, who try to write poetry might have insight when they read poetry that nonwriters won't have. . . .

Myth 6: There Aren't Very Many Places to Find Good Ideas about Teaching Poetry to Young Readers. . . .

Myth 7: All Students Should Enjoy Poetry.

For a poetry lover/teacher, this is a toughie. But, let's face it; not everyone is going to enjoy one thing. . . . Poetry is no exception. However, the poetry lover/teacher will do everything s/he can to lead young people to good poetry. By exploring poetry, the students will have the opportunity to taste the richness of a good poem. The rest is up to them. . . . (1987, pp. 13–16)

The Poem as Experience

To the child a poem has been an experience, a part of life; the child has lived the poem. When children are asked to divorce the poem from the experience and read it, they resist. Rhyme and rhythm, chant and song are to be lived, committed to memory because they are loved and used. Often the poetry in the textbook is to be read, analyzed, memorized, and reproduced on a test. It is no longer alive; it is no longer loved; it is no longer experienced. Charles R. Duke and Sally Jacobsen suggest in the introduction to their book *Reading and Writing Poetry:*

> For too long, far too many students have considered poetry as some mysterious artifact, meant to be observed at a distance always, under the eye of a critical curator. But this distancing is contrary to all we now know about how readers develop a liking for various types of literature. Growth comes from direct engagement, not from distancing of reading and text. We believe, therefore, that the teaching of poetry needs an expanded view which emphasizes student interaction with the text, as well as creation of new texts. (1983, p. vii)

Nancy Larrick, in a book that grew out of a poetry festival at Lehigh University, reports that no textbooks are used in the poetry workshop she teaches. Instead, the workshop participants are encouraged to discover poetry in readings of their own selections, and by listening to the students they teach. The teachers who take the workshop learn to allow their students to experience poetry "as naturally as they talk." The teachers help their students "to see and dream and feel as a poet does" (1971, p. 49).

In order to feel and dream like a poet, the student must become the poet. Fortunately, the student already is a poet. The child has been a poet since the discovery of two words that rhyme, since the singing of the first song. To help students understand their natural poetic talents, the teacher begins with the poetry of the students themselves. According to Lee Bennett Hopkins, "Children have no need to have poetry explained to them, they don't need to know what it is; they need to be part of it. Poetry comes in to the students's life as naturally as breathing" (from a speech to the National Council of Teachers of English, November 1980).

Found Poems

No textbooks or poetry anthologies may be needed then. The class can create its own. The teacher encourages the students to remember rhymes they chanted while playing as youngsters. The students begin an anthology of collected chants. The anthology might be posted on an empty classroom bulletin board.

Television and radio are another source of found poems. Teachers could alert the students to listen for new jingles or search their minds for ones from the past. Students could also consult parents and other adults for older advertising jingles they remember.

Billboards, newspaper and magazine advertisements, signs on store windows, even the names of businesses produce a variety of different rhymes and rhythms. Students can keep their eyes open for these bits of commercial poetry.

Greeting cards include bits of poetry that are familiar to all young adults. Students could begin recording their favorites, or even the ones they think are trite or corny. To illustrate the poetry of greeting cards, three anthologies are useful: *Postcard Poems: A Collection of Poetry for Sharing* and *Pocket Poems,* edited by Paul Janeczko, and *Best Wishes, Amen,* edited by Lillian Morrison.

Most teenagers listen to music continually. The words of the songs they listen to and sing could be written down from memory or from their album covers and added to the class anthology of poetry. Rap music is a newer, often controversial, form of poetry that appeals to many teens. Because of their interest in music, teenagers are likely to enjoy a poetry anthology entitled *Grandfather Rock,* edited by David Morse. This book compares rock lyrics with classic poetry. It is a lively resource for helping teenagers understand that poetry is a part of their lives.

Poetry by Adolescents

One of the ways to keep poetry alive for young readers is to share with them poems that are written by their peers. Some good collections of teenage poetry include *It Is the Poem Singing into Your Eyes* (ed. Adoff), *Almost Grown: A Book of Photographs and Poems* (eds. Szabo and Ziegler), *I Heard a Scream in the Street: Poetry by Young People in the City* (ed. Larrick), *I Really Want to Feel Good about Myself: Poems by Former Drug Addicts* (eds. Hopkins and Rasch), and *Who I Am* (eds. Lester and Gahr).

Poems Written for Young Adults

Shel Silverstein has written numerous volumes of poems for older children and young adults, and most adolescents have already been introduced to his books *A Light in the Attic* and *Where the Sidewalk Ends.* However, many adolescents may have yet to meet the warm, humorous poems written by poet and teacher Mel Glenn. Glenn's poetry volumes include *Class Dismissed! High School Poems, Back to Class,* and *My Friend's Got This Problem, Mr. Chandler.* Mel Glenn teaches adolescents and writes poetry about and for them to prove to them someone is listening.

—————— ❖ **Between the Covers:** *Authors at Work* ❖ ——————

MEL GLENN:
GABE KOTTER LIVES

Most people, when they find out I teach in a New York City public high school, ask to see my licensed hand gun and bullet-proof vest. They marvel at the fact that I have survived the public school wars for over 20 years. They are even amazed to learn that I actually like kids and don't regard them as human land mines that will blow me out of the field.

I teach in the same high school I went to as a kid. Gabe Kotter lives, and, if I wasn't a sweathog like in the old TV show, I nevertheless teach in some of the same rooms I sat in while I went to Lincoln High School in Brooklyn. Lincoln graduated Arthur Miller, Neil Diamond, Neil Sedaka, Lou Gosset, Jr., three Nobel laureates, and ME! If high school is the universal experience Vonnegut says it is, I am still part of that universe. I'm first and foremost a teacher. My teaching gives me the material to *be* a writer. With a balding head and myopic eyes, I even look like the quintessential English teacher, as Robert Winograd says in my book *Back to Class:*

> *I met a person at my health club who said,*
> *"You look like an English teacher."*
> *How does an English teacher look?*
> *Let me count the ways:*
> *A noun for a nose,*
> *A verb for a vein,*
> *A fragment for a forehead.*
> *Does he conjugate in public*
> *Or only among his friends?*
> *Does he speak in full sentences?*
> *Is his jacket pretty, his face bold?*
> *Wouldn't it be a novel experience*
> *If, just once, I met someone who said,*
> *"Hey, you look like a big-league ballplayer"?*

Big-league ballplayer or no, I find joy in small moments in the classroom, the naive and humorous questions I get like: Who wrote the Diary of Anne Frank? Or when you double space for a term paper, does that mean between words? Or why does Shakespeare write in a foreign language? Or is the opposite of dilate, dying early?

I teach English, not the most popular of subjects where "yo, man" is considered a compound sentence, and, if you have the temerity to assign a book of over 100 pages to adolescents who often have the attention span of advanced fleas, students will look at you as if you just landed from Mars. A book as long as *Grapes of Wrath* can make a student grow pale with terror and go running to the Cliff or Monarch notes. If they read at all, you wonder if it's during the commercial breaks of their favorite soaps.

The challenge is enormous.

Teenagers are the most ego-centric beings alive. The world revolves around them. Industry caters to their wants. Entertainment caters to their tastes. Parents cater to their whims. They believe with full conviction that the sun rises and sets with their permission. They go through life majoring in theater where every small problem is a catastrophe and every medium problem is Armageddon. Students are increasingly materialistic. They are all going to make a million dollars—quickly.

But beneath the bravado, the fundamental things still apply. Between the silences and the outbursts, the haunting questions of self-worth and future direction loom large. We don't listen to these questions, we teach instead the properties of a parallelogram and the reasons for the War of 1812. As Ellen Winters says in *Class Dismissed:*

> *Feeling closed in and cut off from life, I told my*
> *Parents,*
> *Who told me to tell my*
> *Teacher,*
> *Who referred me to my*
> *Guidance counselor,*
> *Who sent me to the*
> *Assistant Principal,*
> *Who informed the*
> *Principal,*
> *Who said I should go back to my*
> *Teacher,*
> *Who told me to speak to my*
> *Parents.* ❖

From Mel Glenn, "Back to Class Again," *ALAN Review* (Spring 1990, pp. 2–3)

Collections on a Single Theme or Topic

Some anthologists select poems written for adults that are appropriate for young adult readers and, therefore, particularly useful in the classroom. Some useful anthologies are listed below by topic:

Love
- *A Book of Love Poems* (ed. Cole)
- *If Only I Could Tell You: Poems for Young Lovers and Dreamers* (ed. Merriam)
- *Love Is Like the Lion's Tooth: An Anthology of Love Poems* (ed. McCullough)

Friends and Family
- *Going Over to Your Place: Poems for Each Other* (ed. Janeczko)
- *Who Do You Think You Are? Poems about People* (ed. Woolger)
- *Strings: A Gathering of Family Poems* (ed. Janeczko)

Being Young
- *Sounds and Silences* (ed. Peck)
- *Mindscapes* (ed. Peck)
- *Pictures That Storm inside My Head* (ed. Peck)
- *Bring Me All Your Dreams* (ed. Larrick)

Sports
- *Hosannah the Home Run! Poems about Sports* (ed. Fleming)
- *Sprints and Distances* (ed. Morrison)
- *The Breakdance Kids: Poems of Sports, Motion and Locomotion* (ed. Morrison)
- *The Sidewalk Racer and Other Poems of Sports and Motion* (ed. Morrison)

Science and Nature
- *Earth, Air, Fire and Water* (ed. McCullough)
- *Overhead in a Bubble Chamber, and Other Science Poems* (ed. Morrison)

- *Why Am I Grown So Cold? Poems of the Unknowable* (ed. Livingston)
- *My Mane Catches the Wind: Poems about Horses* (ed. Hopkins)

African Americans
- *I am the Darker Brother: An Anthology of Modern Poems by Negro Americans* (ed. Adoff)
- *My Black Me: A Beginning Book of Black Poetry* (ed. Adoff)
- *The Poetry of Black America: An Anthology of the Twentieth Century* (ed. Adoff)

Holidays and Pleasure
- *Poems for Pleasure* (ed. Ward)
- *Eye's Delight: Poems of Art and Arhitecture* (ed. Plotz)
- *Straight On till Morning: Poems of the Imaginary World* (eds. Hill, Perkins, and Helbig)
- *O Frabjous Day: Poetry for Holidays and Special Occasions* (ed. Livingston)

Work and School
- *Gladly Learn and Gladly Teach: Poems of the School Experience* (ed. Plotz)
- *Saturday's Children: Poems of Work* (ed. Plotz)

General Collections

Some anthologists compile a wide variety of poems in a single volume. Some good anthologies for young adults include

- *Reflections on a Gift of a Watermelon Pickle* and *Some Haystacks Don't Even Have Any Needles* (ed. Dunning)
- *Don't Forget to Fly: A Cycle of Modern Poets* and *The Crystal Image* (ed. Janeczko)
- *A Poison Tree and Other Poems* (ed. Mayer)
- *Talking to the Sun: An Illustrated Anthology of Poems for Young People* (eds. Koch and Farrell)
- *Monkey Puzzle and Other Poems* (ed. Livingston)
- *Waltzing on Water: Poetry by Women* (eds. Mazer and Lewis)

Paul Janeczko has two excellent poetry anthologies that help make teaching poetry easier: *Poetspeak: In Their Work, about Their Work* and *The Place My Words Are Looking For: What Poets Say about and through Their Work*. A third anthology edited by Janeczko, *The Music of What Happens: Poems That Tell Stories,* tells young readers about the lives and craft of poets.

Other Collections Appropriate for Young Adults

Many poetry anthologies are appropriate for readers other than those for whom they were specifically written or selected. Some good examples of poetry anthologies for children that are enjoyed by many young adults are *Rainbows Are Made: Poems by Carl Sandburg, Moments: Poems about Seasons, I Am the Cat* and *Munching: Poems for Eating* (ed. Hopkins).

Adult poetry can also be accessible to young adults if carefully chosen to meet their needs and interests. The following are anthologies containing many poems that will appeal to adolescents:

- *A Green Place: Modern Poems* (ed. Smith)
- *Peace and War: A Collection of Poems* (eds. Harrison and Stuart-Clark)
- *Under All Silences: Shades of Love* (ed. Gordon)
- *When I Dance* by James Berry
- *Those Who Ride the Night Winds* by Nikki Giovanni
- *I Am Phoenix: Poems for Two Voices* by Paul Fleischman
- *A Latch against the Wind* by Victoria Forrester

Paul Janeczko (1990) recommends the following anthologies, compiled for adults, that he has tried with his students:

- *The American Poetry Anthology* (ed. Halpern)
- *American Sports Poems* (eds. Knudson and Swenson)
- *Geography of Poets* (ed. Field)
- *The New American Poetry, 1945–1968* (ed. Allen)
- *Carrying the Darkness: The Poetry of the Vietnam War* (ed. Ehrhart)
- *The Voice That Is Great within Us* (ed. Carruth)
- *Harper's Anthology of Twentieth Century Native American Poetry* (ed. Niatum)

Janeczko maintains that anthologies of poems by single poets are more difficult to locate for young adults. However, he has successfully used the following:

- *Yarrow* by Robert Currie, a Saskatchewan poet writing about Canadian life
- *Blue Like the Heavens: New and Selected Poems* by Gary Gildner, poems that have emotional depth
- *Daily Horoscope* by Dana Gioia, a young but traditional poet
- *Naming Our Destiny: New and Selected Poems* by June Jordan, "the definitive collection of work by a major black poet"
- *Cross Ties: Selected Poems* by X. J. Kennedy, poems in meter and rhyme
- *At the Edge of the Orchard Country* by Robert Morgan, poems about rural life
- *Hugging the Jukebox* by Naomi Shihab Nye
- *Black Hair* by Gary Soto, family poems by a well-known Chicano poet
- *Family Reunion: Selected and New Poems* by Paul Zimmer, "witty, sensitive, and fierce poems"

Books to Make Teaching Poetry Easier

Many English teachers report that they dislike teaching poetry. Perhaps this is because their own experiences of learning poetry were not very positive. They may have been required to interpret poetry in the same way as their teachers and professors interpreted it. I remember a time in my own college experience in which I was to do an oral report on my interpretation of Milton's *Paradise Lost.* I spent a great deal of time preparing the report and based my own interpretation on a Biblical exegesis. My professor had a different interpretation. I got a C. Several weeks later I had to do a second oral report on Milton's *Paradise Regained.* Instead of doing my own research I used only my class notes, echoing the interpretation of the professor. On that report, I got an A. My college students today tell me my experience was not unusual.

Because my experiences learning poetry had not been positive, I was reluctant to teach it. I did not want to teach as I had been taught, but I didn't know how else to proceed. When I began teaching, few poetry anthologies were available for young adults. However, I had not been teaching long when I discovered Kenneth Koch's *Wishes, Lies, and Dreams: Teaching Children to Write Poetry* which encourages teachers to begin teaching poetry with the students' own poems. Not long after, I read Koch's *Rose, Where Did You Get That Red? Teaching Great Poetry to Children* which discusses poetry across the curriculum. Although these books were written primarily for teachers of younger children, they struck a chord in my high school classroom. Today there are many more wonderful books available on teaching poetry (see "Suggested Readings" at the end of this chapter).

Incorporating Poetry into the Curriculum

In the classroom, poetry should be incorporated into the regular curriculum. The students should continually share and discover poems. For example, poetry can be a part of examining the great themes of literature. Richard Peck's *Sounds and Silences* groups poems under a variety of themes. Other thematic poetry anthologies for the classroom bookshelves are described in the following sections.

Women and Minority Poets

Teaching a unit on African American literature would not be complete without reading selections of powerful African American poetry. Some useful anthologies are:

- Arnold Adoff's *Celebrations, the Poetry of Black America: Anthology of the Twentieth Century* and *Black Out Loud: An Anthology of Modern Poems by Black Americans*
- Maya Angelou's *Just Give Me a Cool Drink of Water 'fore I Diiie, Oh Pray My Wings Are Gonna Fit Me Well,* and *And Still I Rise*
- *On Our Way: Poems of Pride and Love,* edited by Lee Bennett Hopkins
- *The Black Poets,* edited by Dudley Randall

Ntozake Shange's powerful collection *Nappy Edges* is autobiographical. *Don't Explain: A Song of Billie Holiday* is an unusual book by Alexis De Vaux about the singer's life which is written in a free-verse song that reflects her music. Two exceptionally valuable anthologies are *American Negro Poetry* (ed. Bontemps) and *Black Voices* (ed. Chapman). Some of the writers included in these two anthologies are Claude McKay, Jean Toomer, Countee Cullen, Paul Laurence Dunbar, June Jordan, Phillis Wheatley, and Jupiter Hammon.

In a unit on women and literature, students can read poems by women collected in anthologies such as *Alone Amid All This Noise* (ed. Reit), *The Other Voice* (eds. Bankier et al.), *The World of Gwendolyn Brooks* and *No More Masks!* (eds. Howe and Bass), Sylvia Plath's *Colossus and Other Poems, I Became Alone* (ed. Thurman), and *Emily Dickinson.*

In a unit on Native Americans, anthologies such as William Brandon's *The Magic World* and Terry Allen's *The Whispering Wind* and *Arrows Four: Prose and Poetry by Young American Indians* can be used.

Humor

Most young readers enjoy humorous poetry. The following collections contain not only poems but also fables, folktales, short stories, jokes, and other types of humor:

- *Fireside Book of Humorous Poetry* (ed. Cole)
- e.e. cummings's *95 poems*
- *Pocketbook of Ogden Nash*
- May Swenson's *Poems to Solve*
- Herman M. Ward's *Poems for Pleasure*
- *Speak Roughly to Your Little Boy: A Collection of Parodies and Burlesques* (ed. Livingston)
- *The American Way of Laughing* (ed. Weiss and Weiss)

The works of Lewis Carroll should be included in a unit emphasizing humor. Myra Cohn Livingston has selected some of the best of Carroll's poetry in *Poems of Lewis Carroll,* a collection of poems from *Alice's Adventures in Wonderland* and *Through the Looking-Glass.* When read aloud, "Jabberwocky" will delight young readers with its humorous, imaginative language. An interesting visual interpretation of the poem appears in *Jabberwocky,* with watercolors by Jane Breskin Zalben.

In mentioning "Jabberwocky," which is sometimes used by teachers as a model of poor grammar rather than good poetry, I feel compelled to repeat a warning voiced by Myra Cohn Livingston in protesting the "assaults" by publishers of basal reading texts on her poem "Whispers." She criticizes publishers for using her poem to teach skills and warns teachers against asking students inane questions about poetry, as in some of the exercises suggested by publishers. Livingston cautions: "Do not use [the poem] to teach about rhyming words or punctuation, do not ask . . . inane and unanswerable questions. . . . Is it any wonder we lose children to poetry after the early grades? Is it any wonder we have lost many adults to poetry because they have long memories for the poetry and even the prose selections that were ripped apart and made whole again?" (1983, pp. 143–144). To enjoy and understand poetry, students must have the opportunity to develop their own images, to recreate the poem, not as the poet wrote it or the teacher taught it, but as the reader-listener imagined it.

The poetry of Edward Lear is also a must in a unit on humor. Two favorite collections are *The Complete Nonsense Book* and *The Nonsense Book of Edward Lear.* Lear's poetry, influenced by his friendship with Alfred Lord Tennyson, includes limericks, nonsense verse, narrative poems, tongue twisters, and songs. Lear's poetry could be used as a bridge to the poetry of Tennyson.

Other poets have written collections of humorous verse appropriate for young readers. N. M. Bodecker's poems are most often used with beginning readers, but *Hurry, Hurry, Mary Dear* is appropriate for older students. The poems in this volume often tell a story. The title poem, for example, tells about poor Mary who is continually verbally harassed by a man who does nothing but sit in his rocking chair. Students enjoy the way the poet plays with words; in the poem "Bickering," Bodecker asserts, "I find it downright sickering!"

Nancy Willard's *A Visit to William Blake's Inn: Poems for Innocent and Experienced Travelers* made history when it won the Newbery Award in 1982, the first book of poetry to do so. This book is appropriate in a unit on humor because of its cast of characters: two dragons who bake the bread and a rabbit who makes the bed. It is also useful as a bridge to the work of such classic poets as William Blake.

John Ciardi's poetry appeals to readers of all ages. His first volume *Fast and Slow,* which contains many satirical observations, is particularly appropriate for young adult readers.

Nature

Poetry about nature is important in helping students develop the ability to see the world in new and creative ways. Many excellent poets as well as compilers of poetry explore the natural world in words. Ann Atwood's collection *Fly with the Wind, Flow with the Water* contains haiku verses that celebrate movement. Byrd Baylor's *The Other Way to Listen* gives young readers the opportunity to hear, through words, cactus booming or hills singing. *To Look at Any Thing,* compiled by Lee Bennett Hopkins, combines the unusual nature photographs of John Earl with poetry that depicts haunting scenes in nature.

Another unusual way of looking at nature is found in Arnold Adoff's *Under the Early Morning Trees.* In this work Adoff writes from the perspective of a young girl who goes out to explore a line of one hundred trees that protect her farmhouse from the weather. The girl finds ants working near a rock, beetles in deadwood, and a redbird in the branches. She hears the sounds of animals moving in the dry leaves and sees the farm animals beyond the line of trees. She feels secure in the newly discovered fact that the trees will still be there to protect her tomorrow.

Moments, compiled by Lee Bennett Hopkins, is a collection of poems about the seasons that includes the work of David McCord, Langston Hughes, and Karla Kuskin. Another seasonal collection is *Sun through Small Leaves: Poems of Spring,* which includes poems by Emily Dickinson, Gerard Manley Hopkins, Rudyard Kipling, and William Blake.

Science and Mathematics

The value of poetry in language arts, English, and even social studies classes is clear. Less obvious is that poetry can be of great value in science and mathematics classes. The anthology *Of Quarks, Quasars, and Other Quirks: Quizzical Poems for the Supersonic Age,* compiled by John E. Brewton and Sara Brewton, introduces students to scientific concepts from the perspective of the poet. *Imagination's Other Place: Poems of Science and Mathematics,* compiled by Helen Plotz, introduces the poetry of many of the best-known poets to young science and math students. At the same time, poetry students are introduced to new ways of examining the world of science and mathematics. The poems can be used to introduce new concepts or reinforce previously learned skills. The scientist and the poet have in common their ability to observe the world in detail. Students could develop their observational skills by viewing slides of animals, by determining common characteristics of the various animals, by creating their own classification system, by reading poems about specific animals, by thinking of a new animal that fits into the classification system, and, finally, by writing their own poems about the animals they have invented.

Short Stories

An encouraging new trend in adolescent literature is the introduction of short stories written for the teenage audience by well-known young adult novelists. These "short-read" books are attractive to readers reluctant to tackle longer fiction as well as to busy teenagers who enjoy reading but find their schedules too busy for full-length books. Short stories are also excellent classroom tools for introducing students to the literary craft of specific writers, such as Robert Cormier or Norma Fox Mazer. Often short fiction can whet the student's appetite for longer works on a similar theme or by the same author.

Collections by a Single Author

Some short story collections by a single author are written specifically for young readers. Norma Fox Mazer's *Dear Bill, Remember Me?* contains eight stories that deal with the maturation of a teenage girl. This Christopher Award–winning book is particularly enjoyed by young women. Mazer's *Summer Girls, Love Boys* is also an appealing collection for the classroom library. The maturation of a young African American woman is explored in Kristin Hunter's short story collection *Guests in the Promised Land.* Nicholasa Mohr's *In Nueva York* is a series of interrelated stories about growing up Puerto Rican in New York City's Lower East Side.

Robert Cormier has compiled his short stories in *Eight Plus One.* All of these stories had been previously published in magazines. The book is particularly useful for students who wish to try their hand at writing their own short stories because Cormier introduces each selection with information about the sources of the characters and plots, the difficulties he experienced writing the story, and other information about the story's creation. (M. E. Kerr's autobiographical *Me Me Me Me Me* uses a similar technique.) All of Cormier's stories, except the "plus one," deal with the growing up of young people. The stories take place either in the 1930s, the time of Cormier's youth, or today. Though the times are different, the young reader can see the similarities in adolescents' problems and their solutions.

The popular author Roald Dahl has compiled seven of his short stories for preteen and early teenage readers in *The Wonderful Story of Henry Sugar and Six More.* The book is filled with exciting and suspenseful stories that are injected with Dahl's special sense of humor. Kurt Vonnegut's *Welcome to the Monkey House* is a controversial collection of stories and essays that often appeals to mature young adult readers.

Anthologies

Anthologies of short stories are a good way to introduce young readers to the work of a number of different authors. One of the best of these anthologies is *Authors' Choice 2* (ed. Aiken). Eighteen writers selected their favorite short story for inclusion in this book. The authors include Joan Aiken, Vera Cleaver and Bill Cleaver, and Damon Runyon. Donald Gallo has compiled several short story anthologies featuring the best young adult writers: *Sixteen Short Stories, Visions: Nineteen Short Stories by Outstanding Writers for Young Adults,* and *Connections.* These books include writers such as M. E. Kerr, Sue Ellen Bridgers, Todd Strasser, Richard Peck, Robert Lipsyte, Robert Cormier, Norma Fox Mazer, Chris Crutcher, and many more.

Some collections of well-known short story writers are of particular interest to young adult readers. *The Complete Short Stories of Mark Twain* are appealing for their humor. Edgar Allan Poe has been a favorite with teenagers for generations. Some of his best and strangest short stories have been compiled for young readers in *Eighteen Best Stories by Edgar Allan Poe* (ed. Wilbur). An adaptation of the works of Arthur Conan Doyle for immature readers is available in four books entitled *The Adventures of Sherlock Holmes* (ed. Sadler).

Mystery and Suspense

A Touch of Chill and *A Whisper in the Night: Tales of Terror and Suspense,* edited by Joan Aiken, are two collections of suspenseful tales. The stories are fantastic but never unreal. Everyday events become strange and terrifying, and the feeling of horror builds throughout the book. The macabre character of these stories attracts young readers, and their literary quality is very high.

Other good collections of mystery and suspense include *Fifty Great Ghost Stories* and *Fifty Great Horror Stories* (ed. Canning), *Great Tales of Action and Adventure* (ed. Bennett), *Handle with Care: Frightening Stories* (ed. Kahn), and *Dark Imaginings* (ed. Boyer and Zahorski). These five books include selections by some of the great authors of horror and suspense fiction: Frank Usher, Arthur Conan Doyle, Agatha Christie, Ellery Queen, Edgar Allan Poe, Arthur C. Clarke, Ursula K. LeGuin, Ray Bradbury, and others. More young adult authors, such as William Sleator and Jane Yolen, are featured in *Things That Go Bump in the Night* (eds. Yolen and Greenberg).

Imaginative Literature

Dream's Edge (ed. Carr) is a science fiction anthology for young adult readers that includes stories by Larry Niven, Ursula K. LeGuin, Frank Herbert, Poul Anderson, and others. Two excellent books offer science fiction shorts by well-known young adult novelists: Margaret Mahy's *The Door in the Air and Other Stories,* peopled with seemingly normal human beings with strange powers, and *Break of Dark* by Robert Westall. Jane Yolen's *2041* is a twelve-story collection about a bizarre future in which many of today's social issues are taken to extremes. Other good imaginative short stories can be found in *Hidden Turnings: A Collection of Stories through Time and Space* (ed. Jones), *Catfantastic* (ed. Norton and Greenberg), *Imaginary Lands* (ed. McKinley), and *Survival* (ed. Lord).

Being an Adolescent

Arriving at a Place You've Never Left by Lois Ruby is a short story collection that was selected by the American Library Association as a Best Book for Young Adults. Its unifying theme is that each of the young protagonists is placed in a stressful situation, such as leaving a loved one to enlist in the army, being caught stealing, and watching a parent go mad. Two anthologies edited by Robert Gold—*Point of Departure* and *Stepping Stones*—contain stories about growing up. These two collections include stories by John Updike, Elizabeth Enright, William Saroyan, D. H. Lawrence, Grace Paley, and other well-known writers. Other anthologies that deal with the adolescent experience are *Do You Like It Here?* (ed. Benard), *A Gathering of Flowers: Stories about Being Young in America* (ed. Thomas), and *Early Sorrow* (ed. Zolotow). Barbara Girion has written her own group of short stories on growing up in *A Very Brief Season.* Martha Brooks's *Paradise Cafe and Other Stories* is a collection featuring bizarre adolescent characters; each story examines love from a different adolescent's perspective.

Sport Shorts

Many adolescent males who do not like to read can be wooed by sport stories. Chris Crutcher, a well-known and highly regarded young adult author, has written *Athletic Shorts,* a collection of short stories about many of the characters in his novels. If students get attached to these stories, they may be willing to learn more about the characters by reading the novels. *Baseball in April and Other Stories* by Gary Soto is another good collection of simple-to-read sport short stories. *The Random House Book of Sport Stories* (ed. Schulman) is an illustrated anthology of many well-known authors' sport shorts, including Thurber, Hemingway, London, Faulkner, and Updike. The anthology also includes stories by young adult writers such as Bruce Brooks.

Multicultural Short Stories

Some anthologies compile the works of authors of another generation or a different culture. *Giving Birth to Thunder, Sleeping with His Daughter* (ed. Lopez) is a collection of sixty-eight stories from the oral tradition of more than forty tribes of Native Americans. *Great Jewish Short Stories* (ed. Bellow) assembles twenty-nine short stories by authors such as Heinrich Heine, Sholom Aleichem, Philip Roth, and Grace Paley. *Long Journey Home: Stories from Black History and Black Folktales* (ed. Lester) intertwines history, oral storytelling, and literature. *Modern Black Stories* (ed. Mirer) is designed specifically for classroom use, with study aids that include "Questions for Discussion," "Building Vocabulary," and ideas for "Thinking and Writing." The collection includes stories by two African authors as well as well-known American writers such as Arna Bontemps, Frank Yerby, Rudolph Fisher, Ralph Ellison, James Baldwin, and Richard Wright. Julius Lester's *This Strange New Feeling* is his own collection of three short stories about slaves in pre–Civil War America. Kevin Major offers tales of Newfoundland in *Doryloads.*

Students can compare the stories across two cultures in two interesting anthologies. In *Face to Face: A Collection of Stories by Celebrated Soviet and American Writers* (eds. Pettepiece and Aleksin) students can read stories about shared human problems. Many of the stories in *Face to Face* are excerpts from young adult novels by American authors such as Robert Cormier, Virginia Hamilton, and Cynthia Voigt. Well-known Russian contemporary writers are also featured. Another comparative book of modern short stories, this time British and American, is *To Break the Silence* (ed. Barrett).

War

British young adult author Robert Westall often sets his novels during World War II in Great Britain. *Echoes of War* contains five provocative short stories about the continuing effects of war. An anthology of short stories that examine the futility of war is

Georgess McHargue's *Little Victories, Big Defeats: War as the Ultimate Pollution*. This collection includes stories by T. H. White, Kurt Vonnegut, Frank O'Connor, William Dean Howells, John Dos Passos, and others.

Drama

Finding good, short drama appropriate for adolescent reading and production is not always easy. Fortunately, several recent works, some published specifically for adolescents, fill the bill. All of these works contain plays appropriate for adolescent actors and audiences. The plays can be performed informally in the classroom, using such techniques as readers' theater in which students rehearse and read their lines but do not act them, or they can be performed as a stage production.

Donald Gallo is not only collecting short stories by young adult writers, he is now collecting plays. *Center Stage: One-Act Plays for Teenage Readers and Actors* features short plays by such young adult novelists as Alden Carter, Ouida Sebestyen, Cin Forshay-Lunsford, and Walter Dean Myers. Other collections include plays not specifically written for young adults but appropriate for them. Recommended collections include *All the World's a Stage* (ed. Swortzell), *Hey Little Walker and Other Prize-Winning Plays from 1989 and 1990 Young Playwright's Festivals* (ed. Lamp), and *Plays by American Women, 1900–1930* (ed. Barlow). Not every play in each of these anthologies is appropriate for all adolescents. It will be necessary to read them carefully before selecting them for classroom or stage performance. Another prize-winning play by a young adult author that could be used in the classroom is Paul Zindel's *The Effect of Gamma Rays on Man-in-the-Moon Marigolds*.

Epilogue: Literature is More Than Novels

The world of nonfiction for adolescents is rich indeed. As skilled writers write more books for adolescents and publishers publish these books, the possibility of hooking readers on nonfiction increases. Educational trends, such as whole language, mean that more and more teachers will use nonfiction trade books either to supplement textbooks or as primary materials for teaching the content of the curriculum. This, of course, will require that teachers not only become familiar with the nonfiction that is available, but also develop ways to incorporate it in their classes.

Poetry, like nonfiction, can be introduced across the curriculum. Today more than ever, accessible poetry collections for adolescents are available. Although many young adults have been turned off by poetry as it is sometimes taught in the schools, poetry is an increasing presence in their lives.

Another recent trend in young adult literature is the short story written for young adults and the short story anthology compiled with the interests and needs of adolescents in mind. Both of these trends can help teachers turn students on to reading books.

Finally, collections of plays for adolescents are very useful in the classroom. No longer must teachers use plays with all adult characters and themes. Today, plays are being written specifically for adolescent actors and audiences, and other plays are being collected to be read and acted by adolescents.

Today's adolescents have the opportunity to grow through the literature they read. The wealth of young adult literature available in nonfiction, poetry, short stories, and drama can help adolescents become avid readers and develop a lifelong appreciation for good books.

SUGGESTED READINGS

Abrahamson, R. F. "A Retrospective Look at Young Adult Literature of the 1980's." *ALAN Review,* Winter 1992, pp. 12–15.

Agee, H. "Experiencing Poetry: An Expanded View." *ALAN Review,* Spring 1987, pp. 17–20.

Alexander, A. *The Poet's Eye: An Introduction to Poetry for Young People.* Prentice-Hall, 1967.

Baldwin, N. *The Poetry Writing Handbook.* Scholastic, 1981.

Carlsen, G. R. *Books and the Teen-Age Reader.* 2d rev. ed. Harper & Row, 1980.

Chatton, B. "Settling the West." *Book Links,* July 1992, pp. 20–29.

Duke, C. R., and S. Jacobsen, eds. *Reading and Writing Poetry: Successful Approaches for the Students and Teacher.* Oryx Press, 1983.

Eames, A., and D. Grabeck. EarthBeat: Tropical Rain Forest. *Book Links,* July 1992, pp. 37–41.

Ebensen, B. *A Celebration of Bees: Helping Children Write Poetry.* Winston Press, 1975.

Ellis, W. G. "To Tell the Truth or at Least a Little Nonfiction." *ALAN Review,* Winter, 1987, pp. 39–41.

George, J. C. "Books Remembered." *CBC Features,* January–June, 1992.

Glenn, M. "Back to Class Again." *ALAN Review,* Spring 1990, pp. 2–4.

Goldberg, L. "Science Trade Books and Teachers." *CBC Features,* July–December, 1991.

Grossman, F. *Getting from Here to Here.* Boynton, 1982.

Healy, M. P. *Teaching History through Literature: A Teacher's Manual.* New American Library, 1983.

Hopkins, L. B. *The Best of Book Bonanza.* Holt, Rinehart & Winston, 1980.

———. "The Gift of Poetry." *ALAN Review,* Spring 1987, pp. 1–2.

———. *Pass the Poetry, Please: The Revised Edition.* Harper & Row, 1987.

Janeczko, P. "Seven Myths about Teaching Poetry; or, How I Stopped Chasing Foul Balls." *ALAN Review,* Spring 1987, pp. 13–16.

———. "What If . . . Poetry for Young Adults." *Booklist,* 15 June 1990, pp. 1968–69.

Kennedy, X. J., and D. M. Kennedy. *Knock at a Star.* Little, Brown, 1982.

Koch, K. *Rose, Where Did You Get That Red? Teaching Great Poetry to Children.* Random House, 1973.

———. *Wishes, Lies, and Dreams: Teaching Children to Write Poetry.* Harper & Row, 1970.

Koch, K., and K. Farell, eds. *Sleeping on the Wing: An Anthology of Modern Poetry with Essays on Reading and Writing.* Random House, 1981.

Koch, K., with K. Farrell. *I Never Told Anybody: Teaching Poetry Writing in a Nursing Home.* Random House, 1977.

Larrick, N., ed. *Somebody Turned on a Tap in These Kids: Poetry and Young People Today.* Delacorte, 1971.

Livingston, M. C. "An Unreasonable Excitement." *The Advocate,* Spring 1983, pp. 141–45.

McKim, E. *Beyond Words: Writing Poems with Children.* Wampeter Press, 1983.

Myers, W. D. "Walter Dean Myers' *Now Is Your Time!*" *Book Links,* January 1992, pp. 22–23.

Powell, B. *English through Poetry Writing.* Peacock, 1968.

Simons, S. J. "History Seen through People's Lives: A Look at the American Civil War and World War II in Books for Young Adolescents." *Journal of Reading,* February 1992, pp. 420–22.

Sloan, F. "Publishing Nonfiction for the Classroom." *CBC Features,* July–December, 1991.

Turner, A. *To Make a Poem.* Longman, 1983.

Wallace, R. *Writing Poems.* 3d ed. Harper College, 1990.

Weiss, M. J., ed. *From Writers to Students: The Pleasures and Pains of Writing.* International Reading Association, 1979.

Wells, R. "Books Remembered." *CBC Features,* January–June 1991.

Wiseman, C. "Endangered Animals." *Book Links,* May 1993, pp. 58–62.

PART THREE

CURRICULUM AND METHODOLOGY

9 Young Adult Literature in English and Language Arts

Focus Questions

1. Why do so many of today's secondary school students not read?
2. What is the nonreading curriculum? How can teachers change it into a reading curriculum?
3. Why is it difficult to achieve the goals of contemporary English and language arts study?
4. How does a thematic unit help achieve the goals of the English classroom?
5. What is whole language? Why is the young adult book essential in the whole language curriuclum?
6. How can the secondary reading classroom help encourage reading?

PROLOGUE

At the National Council of Teachers of English conference in Los Angeles last November, a friend from Harper and Row kept pointing out people in receptions, luncheons, and workshops, and giving them an enthusiastic designation: "There's a good teacher," my friend would say, mentioning a name and a city; "she (or he) uses *books.*"

"Imagine that," I said, or something else feigning understanding of why this made those teachers so terrific. I was feigning because I couldn't see what was so extraordinary about using books, not because I don't like books, but rather because I had never imagined there was any alternative to them in English teaching. But from the way my friend spoke I sensed there was some Other Path to the classroom, some well-lighted corridor, with florescents and fire sprinklers in the ceiling, that did not pass in twists through the shadowy forest of literature.

I learned at NCTE . . . that . . . the florescent alternative to the dark woods of books . . . was something I came to regard as the *nonbook.* The nonbook—which reflected a noncurriculum and was purveyed, necessarily, through nonteaching, to produce children who were passable at the skill of nonreading—took a few forms, including anthologies of selections from literature, collections of texts selected for their value on an arcane scale of reading-comprehension evaluation, workbooks, sourcebooks, and all kinds of compendia. Their common features seemed to be two: (1) they were committed to the fact that *reading* is recognizing letters and assembling them into words and associating meanings with those words; (2) they were determined to demonstrate that reading is absolutely nonfun.

Since that conference I have been a speaker at half a dozen others held for English teachers. . . . I have learned at these conferences that nonreading is the order of the day, and that because of it a lot of ambitious teachers are being turned into nonteachers. And, of course, a lot of ambitious readers are being turned into nonreaders.

These conferences have been full of teachers committed to the growth of their students and frustrated by imposed curricula that pinch every bud of growth. These teachers are all English teachers . . . because they recognize that there is nothing in the world of education that can touch reading and writing in producing a holistic response of the intelligence. These teachers know that reading a work of literature takes everything that a human being has at his/her command; it stretches every muscle, fires every neuron, tests reaction time and mind-eye coordination, demands coherence of left-brain and right. And—just to distinguish it from some kind of mental aerobics—it reaches and expands all levels of feeling, too. ❖

From Bruce Brooks, "The Difference between Reading and Reading," *ALAN Review* (Fall 1988), p. 1.

Selecting Books for Different Kinds of Reading

Bruce Brooks is an author of highly regarded books for young adults. Books like *Moves Make the Man* are not only critically acclaimed by reviewers and scholars but widely read and enjoyed by adolescents. Like all good teachers of English, he knows that reading is not simply a skill. He also knows that readers read not only to illuminate their worlds (although this is certainly an important reason to read) but for fun, entertainment, pure joy. Reading uses not only the head but the heart.

As Brooks suggests, the problem with the "nonreading" curriculum—the curriculum of workbooks, blue dittos, anthologies, and standardized tests—is that it may teach students the skills of reading, but it is not likely to encourage them to read. It tends to make reading drudgery; it takes the fun and the heart out of the process. Standardized reading tests such as the National Assessment of Education Progress (NAEP) and the Scholastic Aptitude Test (SAT) show the negative results of this nonreading curriculum. Today's students can read; they can recognize letters and assemble them into words and associate meaning with those words. What they can't do is interpret what they have read. They cannot find deeper meaning in the passages they read. American students do quite well on the basic levels of these tests, but when it comes to higher-level skills that require more than simple recall and comprehension, they fall apart. Why?

Bruce Brooks gives us a large part of the answer. Students today do not read. In fact, as Brooks points out, the nonreading curriculum may encourage them not to read. In "Between the Covers" in Chapter 8, poet and teacher Mel Glenn commented that if you ask today's student to read a book over a hundred pages long, they panic and run to the closest store to buy the Monarch or Cliff Notes. As standardized tests scores indicate, students' lack of interest in reading has little to do with not being able to read; rather, they read so rarely that they are unable to sustain the attention needed to read longer works. And the less they read, the less they are inclined to read. Many educators and scholars call this the "nonreading cycle."

How can we break this cycle? As Paul Janeczko has suggested in his remarks on teaching poetry, breaking the cycle is not nearly as difficult as it might seem. First, we know that all students *can* be good readers (Atwell, 1987). As teachers, we recognize that when students come into our classrooms, they do not all read on the same level, nor do they all enjoy reading. But by giving them the time to read, helping them learn that they too can "own" books, and by allowing them to respond in their own way to books they can meet as equals, we can begin to break the nonreading cycle.

Second, we must do everything in our power to ignore the nonreading curriculum of the schools. We must bring books and more books into our classrooms. (I tell my university teacher certification students, and I'm only half joking, that if I enter their classrooms after they begin teaching and don't find shelves of real books, I'll personally go to the state certification office and rip up their certification papers.) Teachers, particularly English teachers, who teach without real books should not be in the classroom, for they are perpetuating the nonreading curriculum in the schools and the nonreading cycle in their students.

Finally, we need to recognize that there are many important reasons to read. Louise M. Rosenblatt (1989) suggests that every text requires a reading stance. Either we read the work for what we can learn from it (efferent) or for personal enrichment (aesthetic). Her studies indicate that the reading students do in school or for school primarily requires an efferent stance, and this stance is unlikely to produce the greatest understanding of a work or a personal appreciation of the work. Indeed, it may conflict with the adolescent's egocentric reading development.

Margaret Early's study of reading development (discussed in Chapter 1) clearly shows that our reasons for reading change as we mature as readers. It is not until we become mature, aesthetic readers that our reasons for reading include enlightenment and knowledge. She suggests that younger, less mature readers read primarily for self-enhancement and fun. This is normal; there is nothing wrong with an adolescent who is an immature reader. Of course, as teachers of adolescents we want them to grow into mature, aesthetic readers. Therefore, we must help them distinguish the reasons why reading is important (see Figure 9.1).

As teachers, we can use the reasons to read (see Figure 9.1) as a guide in selecting a variety of books for our classroom libraries. We can also use these reasons to read as a guide in suggesting books to students. And, finally, we can use them in making selections for our English or language arts curriculum. The careful selection of a variety of books for all readers, for a variety of types of reading, will help our students become lifelong readers. If they read for all of these reasons, there can be no doubt that the reading they do will help prepare them for their future education and careers.

History of Literature Study in the Schools

In colonial schools the only literature that was taught was the Bible. The first initiative to provide students with broader literature occurred in England during the late nineteenth century when Her Majesty's School Inspector, Matthew Arnold, championed English literature's educational value. In the United States, until the twentieth century literature was taught only to the select few who could attend private academies. The curriculum in these schools included literature designed to teach "morals," and the classics were justified in the belief that reading them would lead to improved character (Beach and Marshall, 1991, p. 16). By the 1920s a greater variety of students were attending school. Reading interest studies done during this period, according to Beach and Marshall, show a wider range of literature offered in the school curriculum. Instruction using these works was largely didactic, however, with

Figure 9.1
Reasons for Reading

1. Reading is fun.
2. Reading builds reading skills.
3. Reading gives us new knowledge.
4. Reading is therapeutic.
5. Reading provides new insights.
6. Reading makes us more empathetic.
7. Reading provides the opportunity to create images.

the teacher telling the students what the author intended the reader to learn. The books taught were largely American and British books written by white males.

The 1940s, 1950s and early 1960s represented the beginning of the study of literature as a discipline. The New Criticism, a method of analyzing a work apart from its historical or biographical context, influenced what literature was taught and how it was taught. During this period, particularly in the 1950s, the concept of Great Books predominated. The belief prevailed that all students, particularly college-bound students, needed a common literary and cultural foundation. In this era education was geared to the interests of the "best" students, those who were college material, and the college curriculum, organized primarily around historical periods, largely dictated what was taught in high schools.

The integration of public education in the early 1960s began the era of equalization of educational opportunities for all students. As in the 1920s when a new population of immigrants and middle-class students affected the curriculum, the new multicultural population of the schools influenced the curriculum of the 1960s and 1970s. Beach and Marshall suggest that since the 1960s the teaching of literature in the schools has shifted widely between two poles.

> On the one hand, broad social changes associated with the civil rights movement, the Vietnam War, and the highly politicized atmosphere on many college campuses led to a strong liberal trend in the high school literature curriculum—a trend that saw the advent of phase-elective programs [students selecting between a variety of theme-, topic-, or period-based English courses], the wider use of adolescent literature, and an increasing interest in literature by minorities and women. The study of literature could be justified, in this view, by emphasizing the ability to help students understand themselves, their community, and their world more thoroughly. (1991, pp. 16–17)

On the other hand, reactions to this liberal trend, the decline in student test scores, and, I would suggest, the more conservative political climate, influenced by the writings of President Reagan's Secretary of Education William Bennett, have lead to a more conservative view of the English curriculum, a view not unlike that of the 1950s, in which literature suited to the most able students was emphasized. Ironically, at the same time that the curriculum moved, in the late 1970s and 1980s, to an increasing use of classical literature, the instructional emphasis was on basic skills teaching. Beach and Marshall suggest that these two different curricular and pedagogical approaches have led to a justification of literature based on (1) the *usefulness* or practical value of reading (the basic skills approach) and (2) *cultural literacy* (the approach advocated by such scholars as E. D. Hirsch) whereby students are exposed to a common cultural background to help them succeed in college and in society.

Despite these strong currents, the teaching of literature was changing. In the 1970s the student became far more central to the process. What students thought about what they read was at least as important as what the teacher thought. Educators and scholars such as James Britton *(Language and Learning)* and Louise Rosenblatt *(The Reader, the Text, the Poem)* were revolutionizing how literature was taught. For the first time, the study of literature was providing students with the opportunity to think about how their own experiences related to a work of literature; they could examine a work using their own background of knowledge and values. Britton suggests that the study of literature requires the student to be not only a spectator but also a participant. English teachers were being trained to begin instruction with the student's response to the literary work as a way of encouraging students to strive for a deeper understanding. We'll discuss what has become known as response strategies in Chapter 11. In this chapter we will focus on choosing books for the contemporary curriculum and how to use them to meet the diversity of goals in today's English classroom.

Goals of the English Curriculum

Before we proceed, let's summarize the goals of today's English curriculum:

1. Teaching the basic skills of reading and writing.
2. Developing cultural literacy.
3. Preparing students for future education and careers..
4. Developing critical thinking skills by encouraging students to respond to literature.
5. Helping students understand the variety of reasons for reading so that they become lifelong readers.

Some educators maintain that meeting these diverse goals is not possible, particularly in situations where some groups of adults want to dictate what students should not read. However, the purpose of this book is to show how it is possible to meet these goals and to demonstrate how the incorporation of young adult literature is essential for meeting these goals.

Curricular Structures

The most effective curriculum begins with the individual students. The best way to help students understand why they read, is to design a curriculum and select books based on the students' needs, interests, and abilities. Motivating young adults to read and encouraging them to respond to what they read means letting them make their own choices from a wide range of books available in the classroom or library. At the same time the teacher must organize a curriculum that will help students learn necessary skills, concepts, and ideas, that teaches them both their common and uncommon cultural heritage, and that prepares them for further education and the world of work.

Clearly, in a secondary school classroom in which students select their own reading materials, not every student is reading the same book at the same time. Possibly no two students are reading the same book at the same time. Traditional teaching methods that require students to read a chapter in the text, answer the questions at the end of the chapter, discuss the material in class, and take a test on the skills, ideas, or concepts presented in the chapter will not work in the classroom in which students are reading self-selected materials. Similarly, the traditional method of having all students read the same literary work, analyze the work, complete the same activities, and finally take a test on the reading is inadequate in a classroom in which John is reading *Death Be Not Proud* (Gunther), Jane is reading *Questions and Answers on Death and Dying* (Kübler-Ross), and Sam is reading *Death of a Salesman* (Miller). Of course, there are times when it is appropriate for every student to read the same book. However, the goal of having students become capable, lifelong readers who have the ability to respond critically to what they read requires a variety of books and a diversity of teaching techniques.

If every student is reading a different book, or if five or six small groups of students are each reading a different book, the teacher must find a common thread that becomes "the cohesive strand running through all learning and teaching activities" (Kniep, 1979, p. 388). This strand is often a common theme. In the example above, the common theme of all the books being read might be "Facing Death." The common theme becomes the building block of the curriculum during planning and instruction. The common thread in another classroom might be a historical period, such as "The Civil War in History and in Literature," or a common literary genre, such as "Mystery and Suspense." Alternatively, students could be asked to find commonalities among different books or fields of knowledge using a technique called webbing (see p. 269).

A variety of activities should be used to help students explore the books they read. In the whole language classroom these activities might include talking about a book with peers, writing about the book in a response journal, presenting parts of the book through dramatic activities, creating a mural that represents the book, searching for and reading other books similar to the book or by the same author, or doing vocabulary exercises based on the book. If a book is used across the curriculum, activities might involve researching the historical period in which the book takes place, examining the scientific principles behind the author's imaginary world, discussing the political orientation of the author, illustrating the book, or selecting and performing musical works related to the book.

Students should be involved not only in selecting reading material but in choosing reading response activities. Curricular approaches based on a common thread allow for variety and diversity. They will be discussed in this chapter and Chapter 10.

Teaching Thematically

Thematic units join together a number of concepts, ideas, and skills related to a single or several disciplines. (A curricular unit is a group of related activities designed to help students meet specified goals during a specified period of time.) This fusion of elements allows students to practice their skills as they discover important concepts and ideas of the discipline(s). Thematic units also enable teachers and students to use a wide variety of reading materials at various reading levels. Activities, discussions, projects, reports, tests, and the like relate to the common theme, rather than to a single shared piece of reading, such as a chapter in a textbook. Through large-group, small-group, and individual activities, students are able to work simultaneously on a common concept or problem while using a wide range of materials and participating in a variety of activities in different interest areas and at different ability levels.

The thematic unit serves three functions: (1) it integrates the various areas of the discipline(s) by relating them all to one theme, (2) it allows the teacher to incorporate into the curriculum a wide variety of materials at different reading levels, including young adult literature, and (3) it lets the teacher incorporate a variety of grouping and individual instructional patterns that accommodate individual needs, interests, and abilities.

Elements of a Thematic Unit

The students in Mrs. Smith's ninth-grade English class, in a small North Carolina city, are examining the theme "Youth's Alienation from Adult Society." One group of six students is busily reading Paul Zindel's *The Pigman*. This novel presents the story of two teenagers and their relationship to an elderly man. At the end of the book the old man dies. His death may, or may not, be the result of John and Lorraine's actions. After the students finish reading the book, they will begin to work on a problem. The assignment asks them to suppose that John and Lorraine have been arrested for the murder of Mr. Pignati. One student in the group will play the role of Lorraine, another will be John. Two other students will act as their defense attorneys. The remaining two students will act as the prosecution. The trial will take place in the classroom, with Mrs. Smith as the judge and six students, selected by the defense and the prosecution, as jurors.

The students' assignment is to prepare the defense and the prosecution based on evidence extrapolated from the book. They must also investigate the legal procedures they will need to perform in the courtroom. During their group work, Mrs. Smith will help them by suggesting resources, asking them questions about the story that will lead them to better understanding, quizzing them on the legal vocabulary they will need during the trial, helping them write a legal brief, and introducing them to a real attorney they can interview as a resource person. These students will use a variety of skills needed in the English classroom. They will be reading, writing, interviewing, learning vocabulary, role-playing, doing research, and analyzing the book they have read.

Variety of Reading Materials

Not all students in the class are reading *The Pigman*. There are five other groups working. These groups are reading *That Was Then, This Is Now* (Hinton), *The Catcher in the Rye* (Salinger), *The Chocolate War* (Cormier), *Dinky Hocker Shoots Smack!* (Kerr), and *Hamlet*. One student, who elected not to participate in the groups, is reading *Where the Lilies Bloom* (Cleaver and Cleaver). Through their assignments the various elements of English language teaching have been integrated, serving the first function of the thematic unit. Second, the students have been allowed to select from books at a variety of different reading levels that are tied together by a common theme, "Youth's Alienation from Adult Society."

Variety of Instructional Patterns

Mrs. Smith is able to incorporate a variety of grouping and individual instructional patterns during the unit. Most of the students are working in groups of five or six students. One student is working alone. The group work requires students to divide into subgroups of two or three. For example, the groups preparing for the trial work in three pairs: Lorraine and her attorney, John and his attorney, and the two prosecutors.

Introducing the Unit: The Turn-on Event

Before reading, the entire class meets as a group for an introductory activity, or turn-on event, which presents the theme and provides a common experience. The turn-on event in this unit is a viewing of the video *Breaking Away*. While watching this film about a teenager's attempt to gain independence, symbolized by winning a bicycle race, the students are instructed to particularly notice the teenager's interactions with the adults in the film. After the film the class explores questions such as the following: Why was Dave breaking away? What was he breaking away from? Was he really breaking away? At the end of the film, was he more independent than at the beginning? In what other ways do teenagers attempt to break away? Is breaking away a necessary part of growing up? Several interesting points are raised during the discussion. Mrs. Smith lists the major areas of disagreement on the board.

The following day the students divide into self-selected discussion groups based on the disagreements of the previous day. Mrs. Smith has prepared a list of possible discussion questions after reviewing a tape recording of the class discussion. The class period of fifty minutes is divided so that the first ten minutes are used for group selection and organization. Each student selects a first- and second-choice problem to discuss. Mrs. Smith quickly organizes the groups based on each student's selection and her knowledge of the student's ability to work in a group. Once the groups are formed, the students randomly draw marked index cards indicating group leadership positions. One student acts as chairperson and fields responses to the questions; another student acts as recorder and reports the results of the group discussion. The groups are told to try to come to an agreement on the issue being discussed. The questions Mrs. Smith prepared are used for guidance, but are not used if the discussion is proceeding without them. The discussion lasts fifteen minutes. The group problems ranged from "Is the support of a peer group necessary for all teenagers?" to "Must teenagers rebel against their parents to become independent?" At the conclusion of the discussion, each of the six small groups is given a maximum of three minutes to summarize the results of their discussion for the class.

The Tie-Together

During the remaining several minutes of the period, Mrs. Smith synthesizes, with the help of the students, the result of the discussions and gives the tie-together assignment. Tie-together projects can be group or individual and allow students to synthesize the content and activities of the unit. Students are instructed to select one of the problems they have been discussing, to solve the problem on their own, and to seek support for their solutions in their reading. Several class periods are devoted to research, and the project is due at the end of the unit.

Teaching Basic Skills

During the eight-week unit Mrs. Smith uses other instructional approaches. In each of Mrs. Smith's classes the students are required to keep a journal. They are asked to jot down any unfamiliar words they discover during their reading. They need not find dictionary definitions for these words. Every Friday, half the class period is devoted to a discussion of the words. Each student presents one or two unfamiliar words. All the words are listed on a piece of newsprint. The students select no more than five unfamiliar words each week. These words become the basis of the next week's intensive vocabulary study. On Monday, the class is given a sentence based on the theme they are studying. For example, on one Monday the sentence is "Larry despised everything his father stood for." Small groups of three or four students write a brief composition based on the sentence using as many of the vocabulary words from the previous week as possible. Fifteen minutes are given for this exercise. The words during one particular week are *indeterminate, exonerate, iconoclast, metamorphism,* and *ethos.*

The success of Mrs. Smith's vocabulary lessons becomes obvious one Monday morning in homeroom. The students in her classes are busily discussing the words they will be using that day. Even though no weekend assignment has been given, they already know the definition of each word. An announcement of an assembly comes over the public address system. A groan goes up from the dictionary perusers: "Not during third period, that's English class!"

During the week, Mrs. Smith's students complete individual activities based on the five vocabulary words. They do crossword puzzles, often designed by volunteers from Mrs. Smith's study hall. They try to use the words correctly in the writing they do during their small-group work. They search magazines and newspapers for the words, and an extra point of credit goes to the first person to find the word in a particular type of source (this encourages students to read on their own time). Finally, when they feel they know the words sufficiently, they complete a mastery test on these words and on words randomly selected from lessons of weeks past. They may take the test as many times as they like, but must place the completed test in their folders by the end of their English class period each Friday.

Organizing the Thematic Unit

The various activities in Mrs. Smith's unit are tied together by the theme "Youth's Alienation from Adult Society." Essential language skills are incorporated into the unit work rather than taught in isolation. During the unit the students read, analyze literary works, learn vocabulary, do research, practice composition skills, role-play, discuss, prepare oral and written reports, and work together in groups. Mrs. Smith also incorporates a wide variety of literature at many different reading levels. The students not only read the book they use for their small-group projects, but also are required to read three to five other books, depending on the grade they hope to receive for the unit's work. The activities Mrs. Smith selects allow for a variety of grouping and individual instructional patterns. The patterns may include individual conferences with Mrs. Smith on independent reading materials, small group work, discussions by the entire class, individual research, and so on. The basic organizational pattern for Mrs. Smith's thematic unit is shown in Figure 9.2.

Involving Students in the Planning Process

In planning of the thematic unit, Mrs. Smith, often with the help of her students, selects the theme and decides on the objectives for the unit. The turn-on event is selected by Mrs. Smith to give all of the students a common introduction to the unit, to set the tone for the unit, and to help fix the unit's objectives in the students' minds. The alternative activities are based on the objectives and stem from the turn-on event.

For example, the student's individual project is selected following a discussion of the introductory film. The student also selects a book to use during small-group book discussions based on information gained from the film and an annotated bibliography prepared by Mrs. Smith. Other reading materials are selected by the student in the course of working on the project. Usually these independent selections are related to needs and interests discovered during the project. The small-group skill work is developed following the discussion of the turn-on event, and language-related strengths and weaknesses of each student are discovered through the reading, group work, and reporting. The individual skill and reporting activities are established as a result of needs uncovered during group work and individual work.

The culminating activity, which is designed to help the students and Mrs. Smith assess the extent to which they have reached the unit's objectives, is developed during the unit's alternative activities. In the case of the youth alienation unit, the culminating activity is the small-group project, such as *The Pigman* trial. In other units, Mrs. Smith and her students have developed culminating activities such as field trips to the opera, to a play, or to a funeral home. At times the culminating event has been a film, a panel discussion, a guest speaker, or a telephone hookup with an author. After each culminating activity, the class discusses how well the unit's objectives have been achieved.

Figure 9.2
Organization of a Thematic Unit

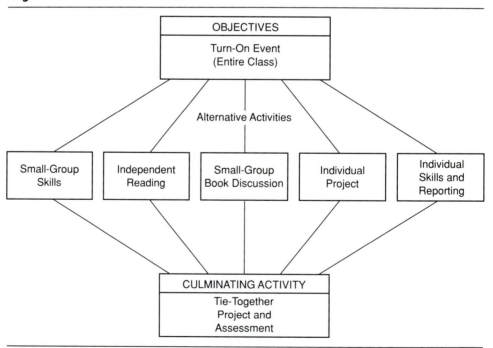

Based on Willard M. Kniep, "Thematic Units: Revitalizing a Trusted Tool," *Clearing House* 52, no. 8 (April 1979):380–94, a publication of the Helen Dwight Reid Foundation. Used by permission.

Evaluation

The completion of the tie-together project on which the students have been working throughout the unit also helps Mrs. Smith and the students assess the progress that has been made in understanding the unit's theme and reaching the unit's objectives. (The tie-together project in the youth alienation unit involved the definition of a problem, research to help select a solution to the problem, and a short individual paper or project presenting the problem and solution.) Various assessment techniques are used to evaluate student progress toward different objectives. Vocabulary tests are completed each week. Students report on their individual reading in a variety of ways. Essay tests are given to help determine the student's ability to analyze and synthesize the readings and activities completed during the unit. Group and individual compositions or positions papers (e.g., the legal brief) are written throughout the unit. Group oral reports or projects are completed at the end of the unit.

The Thematic Unit in the English Classroom

The goal of the thematic unit is not only to teach the theme but also to use it as a vehicle for teaching English. (A sample thematic unit is shown on pages 263–267.) The theme is the means by which the English teacher can encourage secondary school students to write, read, and speak. When writing, reading, and speaking revolve around a meaningful theme, students are more likely to complete the tasks with enthusiasm.

Selecting a theme that incorporates each of the skill areas of English, motivates students to read, helps them reach the aims and goals of the high school English program, and is of interest to a large variety of students in the classroom can be a monumental task. Dwight Burton (1974) gives some helpful guidelines for selecting a theme. His guidelines are based only on the literature portion of the English classroom. The creative teacher, however, will incorporate the other skill areas into the unit. According to Burton, a secondary school literature program is made up of concepts and activities. Burton proposes themes based on the literary concepts of substance, mode, and form.

Substance

Burton claims that all literature is about human beings in four relationships: with their gods, with the natural world, with other humans, and with themselves. The archetypal themes or central myths of all human experience, and therefore all literature, grow from these relationships. In recent years most high school English programs have been built around the historic survey of literature, particularly in the junior and senior year. Burton (p. 30) suggests that thematic units for American literature could address the following myths:

1. The Puritan myth
2. The frontier myth
3. The myth of the significance of the individual's everyday life
4. The myth of the importance of material success
5. The myth of youth's alienation from adult society

The substantive approach could be taken when designing units for a British literature course. Basing thematic units on substance would be appropriate for the teacher who must teach American literature to all juniors and British literature to all seniors. Dividing the year into themes can provide the flexibility necessary for reading a wide array of materials, for teaching all of the language arts skills, and for incorporating a variety of instructional and grouping strategies.

Mode

Mode, the second literary concept on which thematic units could be based, refers to the general point of view of the author or the kind of life experience that the literary work represents. Burton adapts the four literary modes identified by Northrop Frye—romantic, comic, tragic, and ironic—to thematic teaching.

> Frye, in his book *Fables of Identity,* differentiates these modes in terms of the human condition which they frame: the nature and predicament of the hero or protagonist. If the hero is superior in degree to other men and to his environment, we have the typical romance and its literary affiliates, the legend and folktale. If the protagonist is superior in degree to other men and is a leader but is not superior to his natural environment, we have the hero of most tragedies and epics. If the hero is superior to neither other men nor to his environment, we have the comic mode. If he is inferior in power or intelligence to ourselves so that we have a sense of looking down on a scene of frustration and absurdity, the protagonist belongs to the ironic mode. (Burton, 1974, p. 30)

The English teacher can develop units based on the modal approach to help the students understand how literature can be a study of the human condition.

A unit based on the tragic mode, for example, could highlight such young adult novels as *The Contender* and *One Fat Summer* (Lipsyte), *Bridge to Terabithia* (Paterson), *Heads You Win, Tails I Lose* (Holland), *Across Five Aprils* (Hunt), *April Morning* (Fast), *His Enemy, His Friend* (Tunis), *Very Far Away from Anywhere Else* (LeGuin), *Tunes for a Small Harmonica* (Wersba), *Pardon Me, You're Stepping on My Eyeball* and *The Pigman* (Zindel), and many others. Once the students understand the tragic mode in these books, they can be directed to the more adult classics written in this mode. Reading Howard Fast's *April Morning,* in which Adam Cooper runs from the Continental Army at Lexington after his father is shot by British redcoats, will help students understand and appreciate Stephen Crane's *The Red Badge of Courage,* for example.

Form

Form is the third literary concept that can be used in developing thematic units. "Form refers to the various genres of literature—fiction, drama, and poetry—and their subgenres, as well as to certain elements of structure—point of view, setting, dialogue, and the like—and to certain devices—metaphor and symbols" (p. 30). Burton says it is form that separates the teaching and study of literature from the study of other disciplines.

Once having selected the genre or element of structure to emphasize, the teacher can develop a unit based on this literary form. For example, in a unit entitled "Location, Location, Location," the teacher might choose to emphasize young adult novels and classics in which the setting is of particular importance. In Robert Newton Peck's *A Day No Pigs Would Die* the plot would lose its meaning without the rural Vermont Shaker setting of the 1920s. The same, of course, is true in regional stories such as *Hawaii* and *Chesapeake* (Michener), *When the Legends Die* (Borland), and *Dust of the Earth* (Cleaver and Cleaver). Often, historic events become settings that are essential to the plot. For example, the Nazi invasion of the Netherlands was the setting in which Anne Frank and her family fled to their attic hiding place. Similarly, the plight of poor African Americans creates the setting and forms the plot of books like William Armstrong's *Sounder*. Teachers emphasizing the setting as an essential element of structure in the novel can also examine books like Lois Duncan's *Down a Dark Hall,* in which the remote Victorian house in which the private girls' school is located adds to the suspense created by the headmistress and her son. In Katherine Paterson's *Jacob Have I Loved,* the isolated island setting allows the characters and the plot to develop.

─────────── ❖ Between the Covers: *Authors at Work* ❖ ───────────

SANDY ASHER: TEN YEARS AND A MILLION LOUSY WORDS

At an NCTE workshop on adolescent literature, author and English teacher Sandy Asher was asked what it took to make her a writer and where her teaching fits in.

It took a kind of neediness, ten years, a million lousy words, and some cheerleaders.

First, the need: Writing does have a lot to do with keeping my body and soul together. There is the income, of course, but that's not what I mean. Without the writing itself, on those days when real life interferes—weeds and laundry and dentists—I'm not, as my daughter would say, a happy camper.

Writing soothes my soul. It's reason to wake up in the morning, it helps me sleep better at night, and it occupies my mind, if not always my typewriter, much of the time in between. When the writing goes well, I go well. When the writing goes badly, I go badly. I have GOT to organize, analyze, create, and recreate my world on paper—or whatever it is that binds me up and holds me together begins to unravel.

Like most writers, I have another job, one that pays, if not generously, at least regularly. During my semester of student teaching fifteen years ago, I discovered why I liked both teaching and writing enormously and why I couldn't do both full time. They are terrifically creative activities that draw on every resource available: intellectual, emotional, spiritual, and physical—and I simply do not have enough of all that to go around twice. Even one and a half is a stretch, but putting two kids through college can be wonderfully inspiring.

So I teach part time. The negative effects of my teaching on my writing are minimal, but they are annoying. I can no longer spell. Commas placed just about anywhere on a page are beginning to look right to me.

But my students have done me far more good than harm. When Drury College hired me to teach creative writing, I'd sold a few stories and poems and one article to *Parents Magazine.* I was still receiving approximately forty-nine rejection slips for every fifty submissions to publishers, and I had no idea why. I had no objective understanding of my work at all.

As a teacher, for the first time, I had to read, not just for enjoyment, not just to appreciate great writers at their finest moments, but critically, taking apart works-in-progress and analyzing where they went wrong and why, where they succeeded and why. Instead of admiring buildings from the outside, I got in under the floors, behind the wallpaper, and learned what held it all together, learned it thoroughly enough to be able to explain it to my students—and finally, to myself.

[Do] I analyze the work of other published writers? I *should*. I know that. All the writing books say to do it. I tell my students to do it. In fact, I require them to do it, and I force myself to do it with them. . . .

. . . My teachers made all the difference in the world. But before I start—and conclude with—my love letter to teachers, let me touch ever so gently on the negative side of their influence.

I am thinking of the day I learned to hate poetry. A high school English teacher spent an entire hour of our class time urging us to decide what the word "snow" meant in A. E. Housman's phrase "to see the cherry hung with snow." Was it really snow? Or was it the whiteness of the blossoms? Were the blossoms really blossoms? Were the cherries really cherries? Could anyone ever really know? *Did anyone ever really care?* . . .

I'm thinking also of the principal who came to the dress rehearsal of our sixth-grade play, one I'd written myself, based on an African folk tale. We'd made a huge relief map of Africa for it and this principal watched the rehearsal, glanced at the map, and made only one comment: "You left the 'y' out of Tanganyika." I'll never forget that man. I wish I could.

And I am thinking of those college professors who informed me that writers worthy of the trees that died for their immortal words did not lead ordinary, middle-class lives—the only kind of life I've ever known.

True artists, I was taught, constantly teeter on the brink of insanity, with regular excursions across the border. They drink to excess and make spectacles of themselves in public, leaping into fountains or collapsing into gutters, preferably in full evening dress. Attempts at suicide are an absolute requirement—unless one develops terminal tuberculosis before the age of thirty. Mad, passionate, and inevitably tragic love affairs are to occur at regular intervals, and all mortal laws are to be brushed aside. An artist answers only to the muse. . . .

Hard work. Discipline. Frustration. Tenacity. Maybe they make for a less colorful lecture, but that's where literature comes from, years of hard work, often done under very difficult circumstances. . . .

So how did I get past all that: the insensitivity of principals, the drudgery of "taught" poetry, the nagging feeling that I wasn't nearly bizarre enough to write anything worth reading? Who gave me the gift of self-confidence that saw me through? Mrs. Lomozoff, my second grade teacher.

Mrs. Lomozoff loved stories and theater with passion, and she shared that passion with us. . . . Sometimes she acted out whole scenes of *Arsenic and Old Lace* for us, gallumphing around the room as the crazed brother who thinks he's Teddy Roosevelt, blowing blasts on an imaginary bugle and charging up San Juan Hill. We adored every minute of it. Second grade. To this day, I wonder what her lesson plans looked like.

Mrs. Lomozoff was the first to take my little plays and poems and stories seriously, and to find ways for me to show them off. She knew that everybody, not just athletes, needs cheerleaders. She was my first. Then came Mr. Leggieri and Mrs. Spector and Miss Hirschfield and Mr. Santner and Mr. Krimmins and Miss Glassberg. . . . When the going gets rough, I still think of them all, and I see their smiles. Not their grammar lessons, of which there were many, and I'm grateful for those, too. Not their exams. Not the grades. Just the smiles: encouragement, approval, affirmation. ❖

From Sandy Asher, "Ten Years and a Million Lousy Words," *ALAN Review* (Spring 1989), pp. 58–59.

✦

SAMPLE THEMATIC ENGLISH UNIT

The Individual Versus Society
by Nadine Shimer

OVERVIEW

This unit is designed to enable students to experience vicariously some situations in which the demands of society conflict with other individual values: artistic, intellectual, religious, or humanitarian. Having these vicarious experiences and responding to them may help students to have more empathy with individuals encountering similar situations, may help them to clarify some of their own attitudes and values, and perhaps will enable them to deal with comparable real-life situations.

GENERAL OBJECTIVES

As a result of this unit, the student:

1. Will recognize that social pressures exist in different forms in different situations;
2. Will recognize that different cultures favor different values with different priorities;
3. Will recognize that individuals may internalize conflicts between different ideal courses of action;
4. Is better able to empathize with an individual in conflict with social pressures;
5. Becomes more comfortable with discussion of values;
6. Examines and clarifies some of his/her own values;
7. Becomes more aware of the impact of slang and colloquial language on fiction;
8. Improves reading and viewing skills, especially sensitivity to expression of intangibles, of attitudes;
9. Improves oral and written communication skills.

EVALUATION

The students's progress toward these objectives may be evaluated by his/her:

1. Participation in a number of small- and large-group discussions;
2. Short essay based on the conscription issue;
3. Short essay based on the short story;
4. Participation in oral presentation of a novel (or play);
5. Written response to a language research assignment;
6. Performance on a test, partly objective, largely essay.

MATERIALS

- Films
  "The Dehumanizing City . . . and Hymie Schultz"
  "The Man Who Had to Sing"
  "My Country Right or Wrong"
  "The Violinist"

- Novels
  Robert Cormier's *The Chocolate War*
  Ken Kesey's *One Flew Over the Cuckoo's Nest*
  Harper Lee's *To Kill a Mockingbird*
  Sinclair Lewis' *Main Street*
  Robert McKay's *The Troublemaker*
  Sandra Scoppettone's *Trying Hard to Hear You*
  Mary Stoltz's *Pray Love, Remember*
- Plays
  Henrik Ibsen's *An Enemy of the People*
  William Saroyan's *The Man with His Heart in the Highlands*
- Poetry
  W. H. Auden's "The Unknown Citizen"
  e. e. cummings' "i sing of olaf"
  Patricia Goedicke's "Jack and the Beanstalk"
  Phyllis McGinley's "The Angry Man"
- Recording
  Arlo Guthrie's "Alice's Restaurant"
- Short Stories
  Frank O'Connor's "The Idealist"
  John Updike's "The A & P"

LESSON PLANS AND ACTIVITIES

1. Have class see the film "The Dehumanizing City . . . and Hymie Schultz" and discuss Schultz's frustrations and his responses to them. Even though students recognize Schultz's efforts to break the red tape are often irrational, most of them will tend to identify and empathize with him.

2. Have class read aloud the short play *The Man with His Heart in the Highlands* and discuss the way the artist's relationship to society is presented. Many students are apt to identify with the storekeeper, Mr. Kosak, and feel that, as a representative of society, he is victimized.

3. Have students, working in groups of 5 or 6, undertake the following values exercise:

   Assume that you are the city council of a small city badly hit by economic problems. Your staff has determined that by instituting a rigid austerity program, you can continue to provide "essential services" (fire and police protection, hospitals, etc.) *if* you abolish one of these institutions or services: asylum for the mentally ill, institution for the citizen's center, or park and golf course. Decide which institution or service you would vote to do away with (underline it). After each member of the council has decided, try to reach a consensus as to which one the council will determine to abolish.

   After all the groups complete their work, collect their reports, compare results, and ask them to describe any interesting features of their group deliberations. Try to elicit from group members who defended minority positions and descriptions of how they felt as they did so.

4. Assign (or ask students to choose from among) the 7 novels and the play *An Enemy of the People*. Arrange to have at least 3 students reading each major work. Give them some time to begin reading in class; estimate a date they should be finished reading them.
5. Read aloud in class the poem, "The Unknown Citizen," and discuss the implications of it. Follow with readings of "Jack and the Beanstalk" and "The Angry Man." In discussion try to resolve the contrasting attitudes revealed in these two poems.
6. Have class see the film "My Country Right or Wrong?" and discuss it only to establish the plot—what they are to assume has actually happened. Then sketch in the historical context and basic situation of "Alice's Restaurant" and play Arlo Guthrie's recording of it. Finish by reading aloud "i sing of olaf."
7. Elicit in a brief discussion an identification of the issue of conscription and then ask each student to discuss the issue more fully in a short essay written in class.
8. Have students see the films "The Violinist" and "The Man Who Had to Sing" and discuss the attitudes revealed in them.
9. Distribute language assignment sheets which define the status labels used by many dictionaries, "slang" and "colloquial," and give several examples of each. The assignment is to find and list several examples of "colloquial" language in the works in which it appears. These assignments should not be turned in until after all the novels have been completed, and then can be used as a basis for discussing the use of these kinds of language in works of fiction and its impact on them.
10. Have each group reading the same novel (or play) meet and construct a Johari window [see Figure 9.3] for a central character—Jerry Renault, Dr. Stockman, McMurphy, Atticus Finch, Carol Kennicott, Jesse Wade, Jeff Grathwohl, or Dody Jenks. (The Johari window is a technique I learned from Linda Shadow of Bozeman, Montana.)

Figure 9.3
The Johari Window

The Johari window, developed by Joseph Luft and Harry Ingham, is a diagram used to show the many ways people see and don't see themselves, and the ways they are seen and not seen by others. There is often a wide gap between what a person seems to be and what he is. A Johari window is arranged like this:

	Self-Aware	**Self-Blind**
Other-Aware	Things in a personality that both the person and others are aware of—traits, habitual actions, etc.	Things in a personality which others can observe but the person is not conscious of
Other-Blind	Traits, facts, or intentions which the person deliberately withholds from others	Facts or traits not known either to the person or to others (the sort of things discovered by a psychologist)

11. Have students read either "The Idealist" or "The A & P" and write a short essay in response to this question: "Where did (the central character) get the values he determined to defend at such expense to himself?"

12. Lead students in discussions of the various responses to the question about the characters in the short stories.

13. Have students who have read the same novel (or play) meet and prepare to share that experience with the rest of the class. Each group should be given a work sheet designed for that book with a number of questions that elicit the ways in which the character(s) was in conflict with his/her society, how pressures were manifested, and how the conflict was resolved. (I would suggest that each member of each group be required to participate in the oral presentation for full credit in this activity.) As much as 15 to 25 minutes could be allowed for each book, to permit the rest of the class to ask questions the presentation raises.

14. Each group shares its reading experiences with the rest of the class. (This should be a student-directed activity as much as possible, but if members of a given group don't see parallels between their book and other works studied in the unit, the teacher may want to lead them to discover these similarities.)

15. Lead the entire class in a discussion of the theme "individuals vs. societies" in order to help them perceive the entire scope of the unit and formulate some generalizations about issues. For example, students may not have observed that Carol Kennicott's dissatisfaction with her adopted home, Zenith, is paralleled by Dody Jenks' feelings about the town she was born and reared in. They may need guidance to realize that individuals' conflicts range from these subtle disaffections with cultural narrowness to the direct confrontations with powerful authorities in *An Enemy of the People* and *The Troublemaker*. Students can discover that multiple assaults on an individual's integrity can be provided by such massive issues as white supremacy, as in *To Kill a Mockingbird,* or by utter foolishness, as in *The Chocolate War*. They can recognize that Camilla's distress with sexual mores is, in some measure, comparable with McMurphy's struggles with society's assessment of sickness and sanity. It is best to help students identify parallels and let them articulate generalizations rather than telling them anything.

16. Have students take a unit test. I would urge that the test consist of about 1/3 objective items—simple identification tasks to help fix titles, authors, well-known characters, and basic situations in the memory—and 2/3 essay items. The essay items might ask students to defend a choice of a character they know of who had to resolve the most pressing internal conflict and another character who had to display the greatest courage in defending his/her personal choice of a course of action.

Let me reiterate emphatically that any of these materials and activities are optional—there may be many others better suited to a given group of students. Teachers can select and devise the best strategies for their own classes. The same is true of the thematic unit and book titles that follow. I've simply identified some topics and books that have been useful for me with students I've known.

HISTORICAL SURVEY UNITS

- "Puritan New England," Miller's *The Crucible,* Speare's *The Witch of Blackbird Pond*
- "What will the future bring?" Frank's *Alas, Babylon,* Levin's *This Perfect Day,* Neufeld's *Sleep Two, Three, Four,* Orwell's *1984,* Vonnegut's *Player Piano*
- "The Civil War," Crane's *The Red Badge of Courage,* Gaines' *The Autobiography of Miss Jane Pittman,* Hunt's *Across Five Aprils,* Mitchell's *Gone With the Wind,* West's *Except for Thee and Me*

THEMATIC UNITS

- "Search for identity through commitment to others," Byars' *Summer of the Swans,* Cleavers' *I Would Rather Be a Turnip,* Donovan's *Remove Protective Coating a Little at a Time,* Malamud's *The Assistant,* McCullers' *The Heart Is a Lonely Hunter,* Saroyan's *The Human Comedy*
- "Difficult decisions," Bradbury's *Farenheit 451,* Kerr's *Son of Someone Famous,* Richard's *Pistol,* Steinbeck's *The Pearl,* Stewart's *Fire,* Tunis' *His Enemy, His Friend,* Wouk's *The Caine Mutiny*
- "The impulse to escape," Brautigan's *A Confederate General at Big Sur,* Hamilton's *The Planet of Junior Brown,* Harris' *The Runaway's Diary,* Hemingway's *A Farewell to Arms,* Hinton's *The Outsiders,* McCarthy's *Birds of America*
- "Learning through commitment," Fitzgerald's *The Great Gatsby,* Holland's *The Man without a Face,* Kerr's *If I Love You, Am I Trapped Forever?* Knowles' *A Separate Peace,* Mather's *One Summer In Between,* Steinbeck's *Of Mice and Men,* Zindel's *The Pigman*
- "Loving and losing," Agee's *A Death in the Family,* Brontë's *Wuthering Heights,* Hemingway's *A Farewell to Arms,* Horgan's *Whitewater,* Kirkwood's *Good Times, Bad Times,* Peck's *A Day No Pigs Would Die,* Stolz's *The Edge of Next Year*
- "On self-reliance." Cleavers' *Where the Lilies Bloom,* Crane's *Red Badge of Courage,* Defoe's *Robinson Crusoe,* Donovan's *Wild in the World,* Hemingway's *For Whom the Bell Tolls,* O'Dell's *Island of the Blue Dolphins*

From Nadine Shiner, "Adolescent Novels in Thematic Units: Bridging the Gap," *Arizona English Bulletin* (April 1976), pp. 209–15.

The Whole Language Classroom

One of the trends of recent decades in the teaching of English and, more particularly, middle school language arts is the whole language approach. Whole language has been defined in many ways. James Moffett and Betty Jane Wagner in *Student-Centered Language Arts and Reading, K–13: A Handbook for Teachers* (1991) define it in terms of the communication concept of complete discourse. According to Moffett and Wagner a complete discourse is the only unit of language worthy of instruction and requires a sender, a receiver, and an understood message. Hence, whole language involves two active events of the sender, speaking and writing, two passive events of the receiver, reading and listening, and the message which must be understood by both the sender and the receiver. Moffett and Wagner conclude, as do most other educators who affirm the concept of whole language, that all elements of language must be included in each unit of teaching: reading, writing, speaking, listening, and critical or creative thinking.

Moffett and Wagner further contend that whole language must be understood in terms of the processes required to teach it. If language is to be taught as a complete discourse, students must be active participants in the process. One cannot develop language unless it is both read and written, listened to and spoken, and, finally, clearly understood. The teaching of whole language requires that teachers individualize instructional methods based on the needs and abilities of the students, create situations for interaction between teacher and students, and students and students, and integrate all language arts elements with the other content areas. It is essential, according to Moffett and Wagner, that students can communicate about and in a variety of different disciplines.

Although educators and scholars supporting whole language basically agree on its definition, some suggest slightly different ways of describing it. Ken Goodman says of whole language, "If language is learned best and easiest when it is whole and in natural context, then integration is a key principle for language development and learning through language. In fact, language development and content become a dual curriculum" (1986, p. 30). In its most integrated and natural form, whole language is the synthesis of all teaching. Without language the learning of any content is impossible. Likewise, the learning of content requires the continual development of new language skills to communicate completely within that discipline. Some terms that are often used as synonyms for whole language are integrated curriculum, interdisciplinary study, and holistic approach.

In the development of whole language curricula teachers in different content areas often work together, selecting a central topic, theme, or concept that allows connections to be made between various elements in each subject area. Elinor Parry Ross, in "Moving toward a Whole Language Classroom," suggests a webbing approach to curricular development. Figure 9.4 shows a literature web based on Katherine Paterson's young adult book *Park's Quest.*

The Interdisciplinary Thematic Unit

The interdisciplinary thematic unit reflects the whole langue approach to curriculum development. (A sample interdisciplinary unit is shown on pages 271–277.) Like all the examples in this chapter, it not only meets the goals of language in the language arts or English classroom but uses language to achieve the goals of other content areas. In addition, reading selections in an interdisciplinary unit reflect all the reasons why we read.

A common concern, interest, or activity must provide the impetus for developing an interdisciplinary thematic study. Several years ago I visited a high school in a suburban area that bordered a large city. Many of the children in the area had contracted the same serious disease. The community was concerned that the illness was the result of air or water pollution possibly aggravated by industries in a neighboring city. One of the biology teachers in the school brought up the problem at a departmental meeting. He suggested the development of a departmental unit

Figure 9.4
A Literature Web

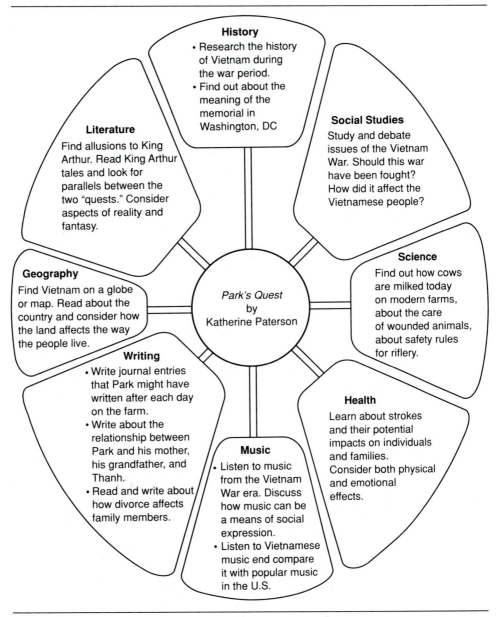

History
- Research the history of Vietnam during the war period.
- Find out about the meaning of the memorial in Washington, DC

Literature
Find allusions to King Arthur. Read King Arthur tales and look for parallels between the two "quests." Consider aspects of reality and fantasy.

Social Studies
Study and debate issues of the Vietnam War. Should this war have been fought? How did it affect the Vietnamese people?

Science
Find out how cows are milked today on modern farms, about the care of wounded animals, about safety rules for riflery.

Geography
Find Vietnam on a globe or map. Read about the country and consider how the land affects the way the people live.

Park's Quest
by
Katherine Paterson

Writing
- Write journal entries that Park might have written after each day on the farm.
- Write about the relationship between Park and his mother, his grandfather, and Thanh.
- Read and write about how divorce affects family members.

Health
Learn about strokes and their potential impacts on individuals and families. Consider both physical and emotional effects.

Music
- Listen to music from the Vietnam War era. Discuss how music can be a means of social expression.
- Listen to Vietnamese music end compare it with popular music in the U.S.

From Elinor Parry Ross, "Moving toward a Whole Language Classroom," *Journal of Reading* (December 1991–January 1992), p. 277.

investigating pollution, its causes and its effects. One of the members of the department commented that the problem was as political as it was scientific. She suggested that the social studies department be brought into their discussions of the unit. In the teachers' lounge the chairperson of the English department heard two social studies teachers discussing the unit and suggested that the English department might be interested in developing bibliographies of literature dealing with ecological issues. The interdisciplinary unit was born.

With the help of the school administration, members of the community were contacted and asked to join a curriculum committee to develop the unit. The student council was also involved in the curriculum development discussions. Each department developed activities, based on the theme, that were appropriate to its own discipline. All of the teachers agreed that in addition to content-specific goals, the unit would have the overriding goal of enlightenment. They quoted young adult author Maia Wojciechowska on their unit plan:

> I want to give you a glimpse of the choices you have before you, of the price that will be asked of you. . . . When you know what life has to sell, for how much, and what it can give away free, you will not live in darkness. I hope that in books you'll find your light, and that by this light you may cross from one shore of love to another, from your childhood into your adulthood. I hope that some of the light will come from my books and that, because of this light, life will lose its power to frighten you. (1976)

In English classes the students read books such as *Swift Water* (Annixter), the story of a young man's attempt to develop a game preserve in Maine; *M. C. Higgins, the Great* (Hamilton), about a boy who grows up as he attempts to rescue his family from an encroaching strip mine; *The Lion's Paw* (Sherman), about a young African who is caught in a conflict between efforts to protect the lion and the opposing views of white hunters; *Deathwatch* (White), an exciting novel about hunting, murder, survival, and escape; *The Martian Chronicles* (Bradbury), a science fiction commentary on humankind's self-destructiveness; *Born Free* (Adamson), a true story about the relationship of humans and animals; and *Cities in Flight* (Blish), a science fiction work, actually four books, about people who are evacuating into space to escape an overpopulated Earth.

In science classes the students examined the ecosystem of a local stream, analyzed the water contents, and investigated the materials being dumped into the stream by industries and municipalities. Wildlife in and around the stream was also studied. Other classes studied techniques for measuring the pollutants in the air, tested the air for specific chemicals, and analyzed industries' air pollution protection equipment and emissions. Other classes examined the emissions from cars, buses, and trucks, and sought to establish a pattern of high and low pollution periods.

Social studies classes examined federal, state, and local pollution guidelines and enforcement. Students visited city council meetings at which the pollution problem was discussed. They completed a case study on pollution guidelines enforcement in one highly polluting industry. Similarly, they examined the regulations in smaller municipalities upstream from their community.

Mathematics classes became involved in quantifying the results of some of the scientific studies. They calculated the probability of the passage of stricter pollution regulations by city council and surveyed the community on an anti-pollution referendum.

Journalism classes reported the results of the different class studies in the school newspaper. They interviewed officials of industry and government. They wrote feature articles on the families of sick children.

The interdisciplinary unit produced no solid conclusions, but the students became aware that there were no easy, or even right, answers. They learned that there were many sides to the issue. They developed their own opinions and supported them with evidence. They thought, they reasoned, they argued, they became involved citizens. And all the while, they were learning skills, concepts, and ideas central to the disciplines they were studying.

❖

SAMPLE INTERDISCIPLINARY UNIT
by Mark Finley

Unit—Dealing with the Fear of Death
Duration—Four weeks
Subject(s)—Art, Math, English, Social Studies, and Music

OBJECTIVES
Concepts   The student will

(Engl./S.S.)	1.	identify the different kinds of fears that people have toward death
(Engl./S.S.)	2.	explore how some fears stem from a lack of knowledge
(S.S.)	3.	explain how death can stimulate more than one reaction/feeling at the same time

Skills   The student will

(Art)	1.	do tombstone rubbings and create the images
(Engl.)	2.	read books dealing with the theme
(Engl.)	3.	compose a piece of writing that has a central theme
(Math)	4.	learn how to collect statistical data
(Math)	5.	learn how to chart statistical data once it is compiled
(Music)	6.	examine a variety of music used at funerals, both modern and classic
(Engl.)	7.	identify new vocabulary words related to the theme
(S.S.)	8.	learn about the occupations that deal directly with death
(Engl.)	9.	compose a piece of writing that deals with a hypothetical situation (e.g., obituary)
(Engl./S.S.)	10.	use the newspaper to compile facts and examine current events

Values   The student will

(S.S.)	1.	express an understanding of the importance of dealing directly with a problem rather than consequences

(Music)   2. express an appreciation of music and its purpose
(S.S.)   3. express an appreciation of those professional people who make dealing with death less of a burden for others
(Engl.)   4. read from a wide variety of literature
(Math)   5. derive answers mathematically to help to explain a trend

CONTENT OUTLINE

I. Identification of the most feared deaths (other than death of self)
   A. death of a family member
   B. death of a close friend
   C. death of a classmate
   D. death of a teacher
   E. death of a neighbor
   F. death of an adult friend

II. Establishing a basis for the collection from the newspaper of statistical information concerning death
   A. Using a data sheet to record the following information from obituaries for one week
      1. name
      2. age
      3. sex
   B. Charting the findings on graphs
      1. *Line graph:* to show the relationship between the male and the female death rate
      2. *Bar graph:* to show the average age of people who have died each day during one week

III. Identification of people and methods that aid in dealing with the fear of death
   A. Examining the ways that music can help in dealing with death
   B. Examining professional people who deal directly with death and help to ease our fears
      1. coroner
      2. clergy
      3. funeral director
      4. physician
      5. social worker

INSTRUCTIONAL STRATEGIES

I. Completion of an interest inventory (see Chart A)
II. Turn-on event: visiting a graveyard
   A. Examine the tombstones for different types of epitaphs. Do rubbings of the stones.
   B. Conduct a group search for the newest and the oldest graves and compute the difference in years. Attempt to determine how old the graveyard is.
   C. Examine the various types of grave markers.

Chart A

Student's Name_____

Interest Inventory

1. What is your greatest fear? _____
2. Do you feel that others share this same fear? _____
3. Is there any way that you know to help overcome this fear? _____
4. To whom would you like to speak about this fear? _____
5. Does this fear involve only you or other people? _____
6. Does this fear create problems for you at home? _____ in school? _____ with friends? _____

III. Examination of different types of fears we have about death
   A. Brainstorm various feelings aroused after the visit to the graveyard.
      1. What were your personal feelings before, during, and after the visit?
      2. What emotions did you experience?
   B. Discuss the messages that the various epitaphs contained. How were they different or similar?
   C. *Assignment:* Create a tombstone that tells something special about you and write an epitaph on it as if it were your own grave.

IV. Examination of how we deal with death
   A. List various situations in which death is most feared.
      1. death of a family member
      2. death of a close friend or classmate
      3. death of a teacher, a neighbor, or some other adult friend
   B. Conduct an informal survey to determine which is most feared by individual students.
   C. Place the students into small groups based on their fears.
   D. *Assignment:* Select one of the following books to read:
      1. *A Day No Pigs Would Die* (Peck)
      2. *A Ring of Endless Light* (L'Engle)
      3. *After the Rain* (Mazer)
      As you read the book, notice how the main characters deal with their feelings toward death. Are these feelings similar to the ones you have? Are there any differences?

V. Examination of various words that are commonly used in connection with death
   A. In your group discuss death-related terms with which you are familiar.
      1. One member should list words or phrases on newsprint.
      2. Share list with the class.
      3. Which words or phrases increase the fear of death? Why?
      4. *Assignment:* As you read your book, list all other words that create a feeling of fear toward death.
   B. In your group discuss how the actions or words of the characters in the book help to overcome the fear of death.

1. One member should list actions and words.
2. Share this list with the class.
3. How do the actions or words deal directly or indirectly with death?
4. How do the characters' situations or life-styles alter their reactions or fears?

VI. Collection of data from current newspapers concerning death.
   A. Give each student the data sheet (Chart B).
   B. Each day for one week keep the information required on the sheet.
   C. Supply daily newspapers to the class.

VII. Chart of compiled statistical data.
   A. Using Charts C and D, draw conclusions from the data compiled.
   B. Chart the findings.

VIII. Examination and discussion of the various means by which people deal with death.
   A. In your groups discuss the music used by different denominations at funerals. (Supply each group with a number of different hymnals and song books.)
      1. What do the lyrics indicate about fear or acceptance of death?

Chart B

Record name, sex, and age of each person listed in the obituary column.

MONDAY	1. 2. 3. 4.	5. 6. 7. 8.
TUESDAY	1. 2. 3. 4.	5. 6. 7. 8.
WEDNESDAY	1. 2. 3. 4.	5. 6. 7. 8.
THURSDAY	1. 2. 3. 4.	5. 6. 7. 8.
FRIDAY	1. 2. 3. 4.	5. 6. 7. 8.
SATURDAY	1. 2. 3. 4.	5. 6. 7. 8.
SUNDAY	1. 2. 3. 4.	5. 6. 7. 8.

Student's Name: _____   Source of Information: _____

2. Are there any major differences or similarities that you find in the lyrics?
3. What mood do you feel while you read them?
4. Which do you prefer? Why?
5. Sing selected hymns as a class.
6. As a class discuss
   (a) most familiar or frequent titles and themes.
   (b) hymns that make you feel sad.
   (c) hymns that give reassurance.
B. Identify classical music that deals with death.
   1. As a class, listen to either Verdi's or Brahms's *Requiem*.
      (a) What feelings do you experience while listening?
      (b) How do these compare to those you experience when hearing and singing hymns that are used today?
      (c) List these feelings on the board.
   2. *In-class assignment:* Write a brief creative explanation as to why or why not you feel music helps to overcome the fear of death. Support your view with examples from the music that we have discussed.
C. In groups discuss the professional people who deal directly with death.
   1. One member should make a list.
   2. Decide which professionals aid in overcoming fear and which ones make death more fearful.
   3. As a class discuss people in these professions from the books read.
   4. Assign each group one of the following professions to research; eventually the groups will invite representatives of the professions to the classroom for a panel discussion.

Chart C

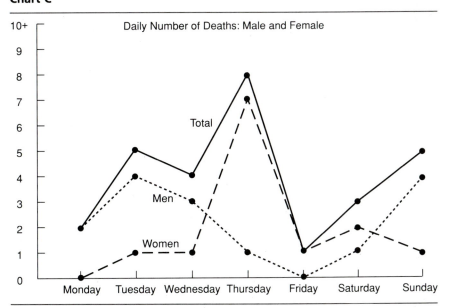

Chart D

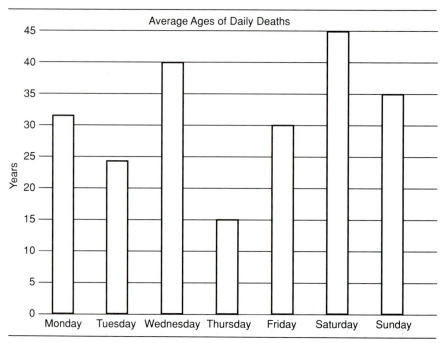

Average Ages of Daily Deaths

(a) coroner
(b) clergy
(c) funeral director
(d) doctor
(e) psychologist
(f) social worker

D. Set up the panel discussion with four professionals who deal directly with death.
　　1. Prior to discussion each group presents introductory material gathered from its research.
　　2. Class discusses each of the roles these people play in dealing with death.
　　3. Class lists questions to be asked during the panel discussion.

IX. Tie-together event
　　A. Four professionals meet in class with the students.
　　　　1. After the discussion, students examine reaction to each professional.
　　　　2. What similarities or differences existed among how they deal with death?
　　　　3. Do you think they helped you to deal with your fear of death?
　　　　4. Do they help others deal with the fear of death?
　　B. *Assignment:* Complete any one of the following:
　　　　1. Write a letter of sympathy to a character of your choosing from the book you read. Include methods that you have learned from this unit that may help that character deal with death.

2. Write a eulogy for any of the characters who died in the book you read. How could you comfort the family of the character by what you have to say about him or her?
3. Write a creative paper on what you have gained from this unit. Include any changes that have occurred in your personal attitude toward death. Is the fear that you expressed at the beginning still as great as it was?

The Reading Classroom

The only way to improve reading skill is by reading. Reading, like any other skill, takes practice. Unfortunately, many young people do not have the opportunity to improve their reading skill. Once reading instruction ends in about the fifth grade, they often quit reading. These students never learn to read for pleasure, and they do not think of reading as a skill that needs practice. Consequently, their reading skill does not improve.

The Parents' Role in Adolescent Reading

In the spring of 1980 I made this same point to a small group of junior and senior high school parents whose children were in a special reading program. It was a warm evening, the flowers were in bloom, and a Little League game was in progress outside the classroom window. Very few parents attended.

I began my presentation by telling the parents, "There is no great mystery in learning how to read, even though many of us who teach reading would like you to believe that what we do is somehow miraculous. The key to learning to read is in reading. The more a child reads, the greater the likelihood that he or she will be a good reader." I was encouraging the parents to help their sons and daughters get started on a reading habit. I gave them many suggestions for accomplishing this: reading out loud as a family, discussing articles from the newspaper, going to the library together, visiting free museums and exhibits around the community and reading about them afterward, reading about television shows the family watches together, reading magazines, perusing cookbooks to find interesting recipes, and, probably most important, letting their children see them reading.

Right in front of me sat a teenager who seemed to scowl at every word I said. The next day I received this note from her reading teacher:

> The one student in the whole [high school reading] program who has been most reluctant to read anything was seated directly in front of you. She said after the meeting that she felt like you were talking directly to her throughout the speech. She has since selected a book on her own and begun reading (a very positive step for her). She is also considering enrolling for the reading program next year. This may have been one of those times when who attended was more important than how many.

In the Reading Classroom

In the reading classroom, too, the most effective way to improve a student's reading ability is by allowing and encouraging the student to read. Of course, in every secondary school reading classroom there are students who need remedial help to learn reading-related skills, but all students need practice reading. Most of the students in secondary school reading classes have the basic skills needed to read; what they lack is reading practice. They are nonreaders, not because they cannot read, but because they do not read.

Many of these students do not see themselves as readers and are convinced they cannot read. Like all reasoning people, they find every way possible to avoid doing what they think they cannot do well. If we are convinced we are all thumbs, we are unlikely to take up needlepoint. If we believe we cannot hit a ball, we will not play softball. If we do not swim well, we will not enter the pool when a dozen of our friends are sitting around watching. Students who are convinced they do not read well will do anything in order not to read. The task of the reading teacher is to break down those inhibitions, to get the students into books, without throwing them in head first, and persuade them that they *can* read if they *do* read. Reading teachers who succeed in this task can undo years of frustration, fear, misbehavior, and bad grades.

To get students involved in reading materials, the students must be given time to read, and during their in-school reading time they should be encouraged to select books for any reason, including fun. As Nancie Atwell (1987) found in her eighth-grade classroom, reading during the school day may be one of the most important activities in which students participate. Her students' significantly improved reading test scores suggest that nothing improves reading skill more than actively reading.

In addition, teachers can learn a lesson from the successful bookstores. Being a book lover, I go to bookstores whenever possible. Some stores always seem to be full of people; others have few customers. Why? Surely, there are many variables—location, price, friendliness of sales personnel—but I suspect the major difference is the outward appearance of the store. My favorite bookstore is a feast for the eyes. Colorful, easy-to-find books, magazines, and records cover the walls, the tables, the counter, and, in the children's section, even the floor. The books are displayed in an eye-catching way.

The young adult section of that bookstore is always crowded with teenagers reading the book covers and the books themselves. The other day when I was in the store, I noticed that one young man was reading Lipsyte's *The Contender;* he was on page 102. He didn't hear me approach, but as he saw me out of the corner of his eye, he quickly closed the book. I said, "Please don't stop. I'm glad to see you enjoying that book. It's one of my favorites, too." I continued by asking him if he'd gotten to Alfred's first fight yet. When he sheepishly replied that he had, we began discussing the story. After several minutes I asked him where he had begun reading the book. "Here," he said. "I come every day after school and read." I suggested that he might see if the school or community library had a copy that he could take home with him. He looked at me with a smile and replied, "I'd rather read here. I like it better."

This young man is as captivated with the bookstore as I am. Apparently, according to the bookstore manager, he is not alone. "We've got dozens of kids who come in here to read. Some of our books get so dog-eared that we can't sell them. But we don't stop the kids; someday they'll be our best customers." In addition to the colorful displays, each section of the bookstore has its own comfortable chairs: rocking chairs, leather wingback chairs, and small chairs for young children. All of these chairs are in private nooks between the shelves. This bookstore encourages reading in a way few classrooms do.

Brand-new books seem to have a special appeal to readers. Daniel Fader in *Hooked on Books* tells about the first day the paperback books arrived in the school. The students were so excited that they did not want to give the teacher time to check the shipment. Many of us have experienced similar excitement. I remember the day our book distributor gave me a bookstore-type rolling book rack. There were so many students gathered around the rack that they could barely see the books. Every student left with a paperback. The paperbacks were not new to the classroom—they had been on the regular shelf for a month or more—but the new display made the difference. The students could see the front covers of the books and, like children in a toy store, they were captivated. Merchandising is an important part of reading instruction.

I visit many reading classrooms that invite quiet reading and group work. My favorite reading classroom is in a local high school. Like the bookstore, the room is sectioned off by shelves displaying books. Between many of the bookcases are comfortable, private chairs. None of the chairs are new; all have been recycled from the homes of teachers, school staff, and students. On each chair is a colorful pillow that the students made out of materials donated by a local fabric store. The walls are covered with posters of book jackets drawn, painted, and put together in collages by the students. Small, library-style tables with four chairs around each are the instructional center of the room. There is no lectern, but the teacher's desk is placed against the back wall to allow for more private discussions. In the front of the room is a stool and a small table; on the table are books the teacher plans to introduce to the students today. Small study carrels, some with computers, are placed along two walls of the classroom. Wherever possible there is a lamp, again recycled from local homes. Lamp lighting provides much better reading light than the flourescents on the classroom ceiling. Although the room is an interior room and has no windows, it is bright and colorful and full of books. It is the kind of environment that makes nonreaders want to read.

Activities That Encourage Reading

Teachers can encourage reading through a number of specific activities:

1. Have students keep a list of books they look at and write down the number of pages they read (completing the book is not important).
2. Have students "sell" the book to other students in an informal small- or large-group situation.
3. Set aside time for in-class free reading.
4. Read aloud from one of the books to the class or to small groups. Young adult author Paula Danziger notes, "What turns kids off to reading are teachers who don't read and kill the story by asking a thousand picky questions."
5. Develop motivational activities based on one of the books, such as seeing the film *Summer of My German Soldier* or *The Outsiders*.
6. Relax the rules; allow students to be accountable only to themselves for book titles and number of pages listed.

7. Go to the public library. Ask the young adult librarian to give a booktalk, get library cards for all of the students, and check out books.
8. Visit your favorite bookstore. Arrange for a discount on student purchases during the visit.
9. Hold an author discussion over the phone or in person.
10. Have parents or other members of the community come to class and talk about their favorite books.
11. Develop creative ways for students to share their books, such as storytelling, giving book reviews, or taking part in an interdisciplinary schoolwide book-sharing program.
12. Set up a school bookstore or a school book fair.

Teachers must keep in mind, as Beers's study of aliterate seventh-grade readers points out, that not all students will be motivated by the same activities. Therefore, students should be able to choose from a variety of activities in the reading classroom.

Getting secondary school students into high-interest reading materials is the best way to increase reading ability. Through practice, reading skills will improve, motivation to read will increase, and confidence in ability to read will grow. As a result, students will be more likely to read in their other classes. The reading teacher must create a classroom environment that displays books in an appealing way and encourages reading. Books, particularly young adult books, magazines, and newspapers on many different reading levels must be available and a variety of motivational activities should be offered. Teachers themselves should show their enthusiasm for reading. They should also help students feel good about their ability as readers and discover that reading need not be punishing but can be enjoyable. The reading teacher who gets students into books will be far more successful than the reading teacher who teaches reading skills but never motivates the students to practice them.

Individualized Reading

Individualized reading programs have many different names, such as free reading, uninterrupted silent sustained reading (USSR), free-choice program, reading work-shops, silent reading program, direct individualized reading, read-it-and-like-it, and paperback book program. All of these programs have three things in common: (1) students select the books they will read, at times from a teacher-prepared bibliography or a classroom library, (2) students read during class time, and (3) students are encouraged to respond personally to books both orally and in writing.

Making Time for Reading

In many schools the individualized reading program is schoolwide. For example, in one Florida middle school I visited, I was sitting in the principal's office when a bell rang. The principal looked at me and asked, "Do you have something to read?" After examining my briefcase I found nothing that was particularly appealing, so he thrust a magazine in my hand, demanding that I read it. I sat there examining the magazine for fifteen minutes as the principal busily turned the pages of a popular novel. When another bell rang, he put down his book and explained that the schoolwide reading program required *everyone* to read. "Everyone" meant not just students and teachers but the principal, the janitors, the cooks, and anyone else within the school. Several students wandered the hall each day to enforce the reading rule. He explained that one day, to his great embarrassment, he was meeting with the superintendent of schools and had ignored the reading bell. One of the student enforcers visited his office, discovered that they were not reading, and sentenced them both to reading detention hall for a half hour that afternoon. Both he and the superintendent enjoyed a half hour of enforced reading at 3:30 that very day.

In other schools the individualized reading program is a single course sometimes elected in place of a study hall or an English, language arts, or reading class. In still others fifteen minutes of every English, language arts, or reading class session, or thirty minutes twice a week, or some other specific, set time is allotted for free, independent reading.

Successful Programs

Many individualized reading programs have been extremely successful. As early as 1936, Lou L. LaBrant in an evaluation of the free reading program at the Ohio State University High School found that students who participated in the program acquired reading habits that they carried into their adult lives. Margaret Willis (1961), in a research report published by the Ohio State University, followed up on the group of students who had participated in the free reading program and found that they still read a variety of materials, read more than their peers, and read more to their children; also their children read more than their peers.

In 1976 Harrison J. Means completed a similar, nine-year study on individualized reading. He analyzed eighteen semesters of reading records of students enrolled at the University of Iowa Laboratory School. He found that the individualized reading program encouraged extensive reading, particularly of popular fiction. Students read an average of twelve books per semester. That represented a significant increase in the number of books read in typical English, language arts, and reading programs. Likewise, Bruce Appleby (1971) found that students who took elective, individualized reading courses were more aware than their peers of how literature contributed to their lives. They also liked a wider variety of literature than students who did not elect the course. Nancie Atwell (1987) discovered that her eighth graders who participated in a reading workshop not only read an average of thirty-five books in a single school year and purchased more books for their own libraries, but improved their standardized reading achievement test scores from the fifty-fourth percentile to the seventy-second percentile in a single year (p. 158).

Barbara Blow (1976) has delineated the most common elements of successful free reading programs:

1. The teachers read what the kids were reading—not every book, necessarily, but always the most popular.
2. A classroom paperback library offered students many different titles and several copies of the most popular titles.
3. Librarians were involved in the program and often gave short book talks to stimulate interest.

4. A record of titles read were kept so that additional copies of the most popular books could be purchased as needed. The records also assisted the teachers in recommending popular titles to other students. Students, according to Blow, are more likely to take recommendations from other students than from the teacher.

5. Regular conferences were held between teachers and students to discuss the books. During the conference the teacher suggested additional titles that might interest the student.

6. Students prepared for the book conferences. They were instructed to focus on a single aspect of the book, such as characterization, setting, or theme. They were also encouraged to examine the social theme of the book, such as friendship, growing up, or family relationships. If they wished, they could discuss books from specific genres, such as autobiography, sports, and science fiction. Before the conference the student selected the appropriate discussion topic for the book and answered teacher-prepared questions on the topic chosen.

7. Each student conference was scheduled for ten to fifteen minutes every two weeks. The students signed up for the conference at least a week in advance.

8. Students were provided with a reading record in which they entered each day the number of pages read during the class period. Students were able to use this record to check progress in their reading speed.

9. An evaluation and grading system was set up prior to the course, and the students understood the system. The grading system could be individualized; for example, it could be based on improvement of reading speed or the difficulty and the number of books read and discussed.

Bruce C. Appleby and John W. Conner (1965) suggest an evaluation and grading system based on three criteria: number of books read, quality of conferences and bookcards (summary reviews on index cards), and the difficulty of books read. They provide this explanation of the system:

(1) Number of books read. This measure alone is unreliable in that books vary so greatly in length and difficulty. Nevertheless, the students have always felt that quantity of reading is important.

(2) Number of books is multiplied by an estimate of the student's perceptiveness into what he has read. The student is graded on the conference and card on a cumulative 1 to 4 scale: 1—no understanding beyond the plot; 2—some application to his own life; 3—some implications for larger human ideas; 4—understanding of levels of meaning; aesthetic values, and relationships with other reading.

(3) The product of criteria one and two is multiplied by an estimate of the level of the book. Each book is given a numerical rating on the following scale:

Other successful individualized reading programs take a somewhat different approach. One of the most interesting programs I have observed uses group as well as individual conference techniques. The titles of especially popular books are printed on sheets of newsprint posted near the classroom paperback library. When students check out one of these books, they enter their name and the date on the list. The teacher arranges a meeting of all the students on a list after each has had time to complete the book. During this meeting the students select one or several topics to discuss with the teacher. After the initial meeting, a group conference of twenty to thirty minutes is scheduled with the teacher. Students may also select from a variety of reporting techniques that do not involve a conference with the teacher. For example, they may design a poster or write a skit on the book they have completed. (See Chapter 11 for a list of book-reporting techniques.) Since not all students elect the teacher-student conferencing, the teacher has time for scheduling more time-consuming reporting activities, such as videotaping a student dramatization of parts of a novel.

In another successful individualized reading program I observed, bibliography charts based on specific themes are posted around the room. When a student reads a book that fits into a specific theme, he or she writes the title and author of the book on the chart. The student then dates and signs an index card, writes on it a brief paragraph about the book, and files the card in a catalogue under the appropriate theme. Since students receive 5 points of credit in a 100-point credit system for each new book placed in the annotated card catalogue, they are challenged to read books not being read by other students. A student may complete only one card on each book read, even if it fits under several themes. The card catalogue serves a variety of purposes. It assists students in selecting books similar to ones they have just read. It helps students seek out other readers of the book. Finally, it is extremely useful to the teacher in developing thematic unit bibliographies for the regular classroom.

An individualized reading class activity that also encourages student writing is keeping a journal. Teacher Robert Garcia asked students to write about the books they are reading in their journals each day. The entry can be as simple as copying a passage from the book or as complex as the rewriting of a section of the book. The student can also use the journal to express feelings about the book, the author, the characters, or the setting. Mr. Garcia does not check the journal for specific content or for grammar and punctuation. Rather, he skims through the journal with the student prior to the biweekly conference. He reads only the entries the student suggests, and he asks that he be allowed to read a minimum of two entries for each two-week period. Students may choose to use their journal entries as the basis for their book discussion with Mr. Garcia.

The journal technique serves several functions:

1. It encourages the student to write something every day.
2. It reinforces in the student's mind the content of the book and the student's evaluation of it, making the individual conference with the teacher easier.
3. It helps convince the student that what he or she has to say about the book is valid.
4. It allows the student to relate personally to the book without the constant supervision of the teacher.
5. It encourages the student to share his or her best work with the teacher.
6. It gives the teacher the opportunity to suggest additional writing activities.

Individualized reading can increase motivation to read, ability to read books critically, reading enjoyment, the habit of reading, reading rates, and even reading achievement scores on standardized tests. However, independent reading courses in one way are no different from any other course in the school curriculum. To be successful they must have specific objectives and be well planned, carefully organized, and easily evaluated.

EPILOGUE: TURNING KIDS ON TO BOOKS

The key to a successful English, language arts, or reading classroom is turning kids on to books. Getting kids to read so that they can learn to read more successfully, read with increased understanding, and become mature aesthetic readers is the number one goal of the language-oriented classroom. No one will argue with the concept that the only way to improve a skill is through practice. Reading more, however, does more than improve students' basic reading skills. Reading helps students improve all language-related skills and opens up a world not available to them except through books. How to turn kids on to books is no great secret. The key is getting them immersed in books. This chapter has suggested many ways to get students hooked on books and keep them reading once they leave the classroom. In addition to breaking the nonreading cycle, these techniques will make reading more fun for students— and, as a bonus, they will make teaching more fun for teachers.

SUGGESTED READINGS

Abrahamson, D., and E. Tyson. "What Every English Teacher Should Know about Free Reading." *ALAN Review,* Fall 1986, pp. 54–58.

Appleby, B. "Individualized Reading as Environment for the Literary Experience." In *The Creative Teacher,* ed. W. Evans. Bantam, 1971, pp. 1–10.

Appleby, B. C., and J. W. Conner. "Well What Did You Think about It?" *English Journal,* October 1965, pp. 606–12.

Asher, S. "Ten Years and a Million Lousy Words." *ALAN Review,* Spring 1989, pp. 58–59.

Atwell, N. *In the Middle: Writing, Reading and Learning with Adolescents.* Boynton/Cook/Heinemann, 1987.

Beach, R., and M. Marshall. *Teaching Literature in the Secondary School.* Harcourt Brace Jovanovich, 1991.

Beers, G. K. "Choosing Not to Read: An Ethnographic Study of Seventh Grade Aliterate Readers." Unpublished doctoral dissertation. University of Houston, 1990.

Blow, B. "Individualized Reading." *Arizona English Bulletin,* April 1976, pp. 151–53.

Britton, J. *Language and Learning.* Penguin, 1970.

Brooks, B. "The Difference between Reading and Reading." *ALAN Review.* Fall 1988, pp. 1–2.

Burton, D. L. "Well, Where Are We in Teaching Literature?" *English Journal,* February 1974, pp. 28–33.

Early, M. "Stages of Growth in Literary Appreciation." *English Journal,* March 1960, pp. 161–167.

Fader, D., and E. B. McNeil. *Hooked on Books: Program and Proof.* Berkeley, 1966.

Frye, N. *Fables of Identity: Studies in Poetic Mythology.* Harcourt, Brace & World, 1963.

Goodman, K. *What's Whole in Whole Language?* Heinemann, 1986.

Hirsch, E. D. *Cultural Literacy.* Houghton Mifflin, 1987.

Janeczko, P. "Seven Myths about Teaching Poetry; or, How I Stopped Chasing Foul Balls." *ALAN Review,* Spring 1987, pp. 13–16.

Kniep, W. M. "Thematic Units: Revitalizing a Trusted Tool." *Clearing House,* April 1979, pp. 388–94.

LaBrant, L. L. *An Evaluation of the Free Reading in Grades Ten, Eleven, and Twelve.* Ohio State University Studies, Contributions in Education, no. 2. Ohio State University Press, 1936.

Means, H. J. "Nine Years of Individualized Reading." *Journal of Reading.* November 1976, pp. 144–149.

Moffett, J., and B. J. Wagner. *Student-Centered Language Arts and Reading, K–13. A Handbook for Teachers.* 4th ed. Boynton/Cook/Heinemann, 1991.

Reed, A. J. S. *Comics to Classics: A Parents' Guide to Books for Teens and Preteens.* International Reading Association, 1989.

Rosenblatt, L. M. *The Reader, the Text, the Poem: The Transactional Theory of the Literary Work.* Southern Illinois University Press, 1978.

———. "Writing and Reading: The Transactional Theory." In *Reading and Writing Connections,* ed. J. M. Mason. Allyn & Bacon, 1989, pp. 153–76.

Ross, E. P. "Moving toward a Whole Language Classroom." *Journal of Reading,* December 1991–January 1992, pp. 276–81.

Shimer, N. "Adolescent Novels in Thematic Units: Bridging the Gap." *Arizona English Bulletin,* April 1976, pp. 209–15.

Tuccillo, D. P. "Getting Kids Hooked on Reading: What Public Librarians Can Do for Teachers." *ALAN Review,* Fall 1987, pp. 15–16.

Willis, M, *The Guinea Pigs after Twenty Years: A Follow-Up Study of the Class of 1938 of the University School Ohio State.* Ohio State University, 1961.

Wojciechowska, M. Newbery Award acceptance speech. In *Current Biography Yearbook,* September 1976.

10 Young Adult Books across the Curriculum

Focus Questions

1. Why are young adult books important across the curriculum?
2. How can young adult books be used in the social studies classroom?
3. How can multicultural literature be incorporated into the curriculum, and why is this essential?
4. How can literature be included in the science curriculum without overcrowding it?
5. Why are young adult books useful in nonreading classrooms such as physical education, the arts, and mathematics?

PROLOGUE

In October, 1987, the Ku Klux Klan staged a march in Marietta, Ohio, our home town. As we met with other concerned people to plan a response, we became aware of how little most people know about the history and activity of hate groups. Common responses to the Klan's announcement were: "Why here?" (the county is 98% white); and "If we just ignore them, they'll go away." Knowing instinctively that the latter was untrue, our group (an *ad hoc* committee calling itself the Celebration of Unity Coalition) staged a successful anti-Klan rally, and afterwards continued to explore ways to counteract hate group activity.

As educators, we were interested in how young students, who may never have known a black person, can be made aware of the motivation of hate group members and of the impact such groups' activities have on people who are targets. We were interested in how adolescents respond to fiction that introduces black characters in diverse settings. We also wanted to explore fiction that presents themes related to the work of hate groups.

The Autobiography of Miss Jane Pittman and *A Gathering of Old Men,* both by Ernest J. Gaines, stand out as works of literary quality which, while not written specifically for young adults, are accessible to adolescents. Both novels portray adolescent characters in crisis situations, even though adolescence is not the focus of either novel. Since most students expressed surprise at the Klan's choosing our town for recruitment, we selected these novels to elicit responses, in the hope that students would come to understand the historical roots of hate groups.   ❖

From Rebecca Phillips and Meg Philbin, "Fiction about Hate Groups: A Case Study Approach," *ALAN Review,* Fall 1988, p. 16.

> If I chose painting, it is because it seemed to me the most natural occupation for me. It was as indispensable to me as food. It was a kind of window through which I escaped from all that surrounded me.
>
> —Marc Chagall

To be a teenager is to be on a quest for one's identity. What a teenager wears and says and does reflects his/her need to communicate who s/he is to others and him/herself. Feelings and ideas about life and identity evolve, explode and harden, only to melt. In this quest to realize a fluid identity, the adolescent may seek an equally fluid form of expression in the fine arts.

"Art interest is something natural and robust, not a precarious hot house flower reserved for the very cultured initiate" (Susanne K. Langer, *Feeling and Form,* 1953). Teenagers in young adult novels who are interested in the arts are hardly the "cultured initiate." These adolescents make a claim on the accessibility of the arts for all. Readers and characters alike may find their suspicions about peers who sing or make pots or act or write replaced with respect for the artist, the creative process and the art.   ❖

From LuAn Keller, "Portrait of the Young Adult As an Artist," *ALAN Review,* Fall 1987, p. 10.

Books Should Be Central to the Curriculum

Young adult literature can be incorporated into almost any subject area in the secondary school. Rebecca Phillips and Meg Philbin use literature to teach about hate groups using the case study approach to history. LuAn Keller uses young adult fiction to encourage students to both feel good about their own artistic endeavors and respect others who are artists. One of the most effective teachers I've ever visited uses science fiction to teach scientific fact.

Carol M. Butzow and John W. Butzow in *Science through Children's Literature: An Integrated Approach* suggest that "fictional literature can be used as the foundation of science instruction" (1989, p. 3) and reading can be taught through the use of literature in the science classroom. According to the Butzows:

> Reading is the interaction of the reader's experiential background and knowledge (schema) with the author's background and purpose, and with the text itself. Comprehension is actively constructed by the reading as these three elements interact. Skills are interdependent and cannot exist alone. No single process can be performed without overlapping others. (p. xvii)

These overlapping reading processes, according to the Butzows, are needed to understand science. Quoting Patricia Blosser (1986), they note: "The major purpose for studying science should be to comprehend the conceptual basis of the everyday things that constitute our world. The strategies and process skills needed to understand and interpret the scientific world are more significant than specific facts" (Butzow and Butzow, 1989, p. 3).

Research studies of the 1980s, according to the Butzows, suggest that using the traditional textbook and worksheet approach to teaching science and breaking it into "isolated bits bearing little meaning and relevance to the child's life" is not effective. Nor is it effective to teach using the hands-on approach if "misconceptions are not addressed and new concepts explained and made relevant." They cite numerous studies that show that students are turning away from the world of science. In some studies middle school students called studying science "uninteresting." It was considered by these students to be "too abstract and discipline-oriented."

The solution to this problem, the Butzows conclude, is an integrated approach to the study of science that includes both fiction and nonfiction written for the age level of the students. Such an approach presents "facts and concepts in a form that is motivating and understandable" and allows teachers to reinforce essential reading processes that are central to understanding science. Because of the importance of experience in the development of reading skills, there is no better discipline to encourage reading than science. Likewise, because the overlapping of reading processes is essential to the understanding of scientific concepts, the use of literature in the science classroom can improve the students' comprehension of the subject and motivation to study it.

The Social Studies Classroom

Good young adult historical fiction and nonfiction have the potential to bring the study of history to life. The need for revitalizing the teaching of history is evident in the results of standardized history tests such as the National Assessment of Educational Progress (NAEP). Although the tests show that most eighth and twelfth graders know "simple historical facts," the tests also show that fewer than half of twelfth graders can understand basic historical terms and relationships and fewer than five percent of twelfth graders can interpret "historical information and ideas" (National Center for Educational Statistics, 1990, p. 16).

The dismal results of the NAEP history test reflect how history is typically taught in the schools. Factual knowledge is often stressed at the expense of higher-level skills. Less commonly is history taught in a way that helps students make connections between various historical events and between history and other disciplines or helps them interpret historical information and ideas. An overreliance on textbooks can discourage higher levels of understanding. Not infrequently the single textbook adopted for and used in the social studies classroom is inappropriate for many of the students. It may be too difficult for some students and boring to others. The coverage of events may lack depth or balance. For a variety of reasons the teaching of history is not succeeding with the majority of our students.

One solution to this problem is to incorporate a myriad of interesting reading materials both nonfiction and fiction, at a variety of reading levels.

For example, after Alex Haley's *Roots* was first shown on television, one teacher divided his tenth-grade class into six small work groups, based on each student's selection of a segment of the *Roots* story. Each group's task was to read a specific section of the novel, take notes on the personalities, locations, and events; investigate the actual locations, events, and personalities using material available in the classroom and in the school, public, and nearby university library; and then defend or refute Haley's interpretation of history in the book. This challenging assignment led to many serious discussions about the difference between fact and fiction, a fiction writer's right to color an event to fit the plot or theme of the story, and the facts surrounding slavery in this country.

Types of Books to Use

Historical Fiction   Good historical fiction should be realistic. Yet, even in very accurate novels, authors often take certain creative liberties to make a point. The main characters, for example, are often not real people. They may meet real people, but the situations created are fictional. The famous figure may never have visited the location of the contrived meeting, but usually, in good historical fiction, the encounter could have taken place at the time and place the author suggests. These fictional encounters give the teenage history student the opportunity to play the role of detective. Could the meeting have taken place? Is it likely to have taken place when and where the author suggests? The contrast between fact and fiction, and the often convincing nature of the fiction, provide students with a chance to practice many of the skills required of the historian: observing, questioning, predicting, hypothesizing, gathering data, comparing, interpreting data, and making inferences.

There are many excellent authors of historical fiction for young adults. Rosemary Sutcliff deals with the period of Roman occupation in England. Her books, such as *The Capricorn Bracelet,* allow the teenager to view the period from the perspective of the people living at the time. Like most authors of good historical fiction, Sutcliff is a historian who cares about bringing history alive for young readers.

Leon Garfield's historical novels for young adults, including *Jack Holborn* and *The Sound of Coaches,* portray life in eighteenth-century England. The novels, which depict orphans searching for a home, show much of the unpleasant side of British life during this period.

The creative history teacher can develop units based on specific historical periods and season them with a wide array of good historical fiction for young adults. *Johnny Tremain,* written in 1945 by historian and Pulitzer Prize winner Esther Forbes, has become a classic tale of the pre–Revolutionary War period in America. Told by fourteen-year-old Johnny, the novel introduces students to Samuel Adams, John Hancock, and Paul Revere. Another excellent young adult historical novel about the Revolutionary War is *April Morning* by Howard Fast. This story of a young boy fleeing from battle rivals Stephen Crane's *The Red Badge of Courage* in its account of the hardships of war. Another Revolutionary War tale is *I'm Deborah Sampson* by Patricia Clapp, based on the true story of a girl who, disguised as a boy, fights bravely in battle.

Other Revolutionary War books particularly appropriate in middle and junior high school classrooms include the humorous biographical stories by Jean Fritz: *And Then What Happened, Paul Revere?, What's the Big Idea, Ben Franklin?, Where Was Patrick Henry on the Twenty-Ninth of May?, Why Don't You Get a Horse, Sam Adams?,* and *Will You Sign Here, John Hancock?* Each of these books is short and easy to read, and reveals interesting, little-known facts about these famous men. An excellent book to use in conjunction with Fritz's biographical works for preteen readers is *Mr. Revere and I* by Robert Lawson. This is the story of Paul Revere's famous ride told from the perspective of his horse Scheherazade. The book is beautifully illustrated with engravings by the author. (Because of the quality of this work I would recommend it to history students of all ages. It is a wonderful work to share with the entire family.) Poetry can be incorporated into the study of history with Henry Wadsworth Longfellow's well-known poem, which has been beautifully illustrated in the book *Paul Revere's Ride* by Paul Galdone.

Wars have provided much material for great literature. This is as true in the field of young adult literature as it is of adult literature. James Forman stands out as one of the best authors of young adult literature about World War II. In *Ceremony of Innocence,* based on an actual incident, a brother and sister produce anti-Nazi literature in spite of the certainty of their capture and execution. Several of Forman's other books revolve around the theme of young people fighting or questioning Nazism. In addition, he has written many well-researched nonfiction works (see Chapter 8).

An interesting and frightening book that could be a useful addition to a bibliography of readings on the Holocaust is Morton Rhue's *The Wave.* (Morton Rhue is a pseudonym of Todd Strasser.) It is a factually based novel that first appeared as an ABC television movie about a 1969 high school history class studying Nazism. The students ask, "If all the Germans weren't Nazis, why did they let the horrors happen?" The teacher answers with "the wave," a system of discipline in which students must sit straight in their seats and spring to attention when answering a question. The system has a membership card and special salute. The wave moves beyond the classroom;

other students want to become involved. As the momentum for the wave grows, an anti-wave movement begins to form. Anti-wave students are threatened and beaten. The experiment gets out of hand, and the teacher is told to put a stop to it. At an assembly of wave members the teacher stops a movie on a frame of Hitler and his followers and says to the students, "Yes, you all would have made good Nazis. Fascism isn't something those other people did, it is right here in all of us."

James Forman writes about the civil war in Greece during the 1940s in *Ring the Judas Bell,* about Israel in *My Enemy, My Brother,* and about Northern Ireland in *A Fine, Soft Day.* Theodore Taylor's *Battle in the Arctic Seas* is based on naval records and a personal diary. *Across Five Aprils* by Irene Hunt is a fictional tale about growing up during the Civil War period.

The Vietnam War is the subject of a number of young adult books. Two of the best accounts, which combine fiction and nonfiction, are *If I Die in a Combat Zone, Box Me Up and Ship Me Home* (O'Brien), a memoir, and *First Blood* (Morrell), the story of a veteran's return home and his conflict with a small-town sheriff. (See Chapter 5 for historical fiction works and Chapter 8 for nonfiction works dealing with war and other historical topics and time periods.)

Problems Novels   Social studies teachers teach far more than history. In the contemporary curriculum, social studies includes the disciplines of anthropology, sociology, psychology, political science, economics, geography, as well as history. Three of these fields—sociology, political science, and psychology—can be taught effectively using young adult problem novels. In psychology classes students can read some of the many problem novels cited in Chapter 3 to better understand the psychological concepts they are studying. Problem novels provide case studies for them to explore. For example, if students are studying adolescent suicide, they might read novels such as *Notes for Another Life* by Sue Ellen Bridgers and *Chinese Handcuffs* by Chris Crutcher. Young adult fiction deals with societal concerns in addition to individual problems. Many of these novels, appropriate for sociology classes, can help young adults better understand parallel cultures or how prejudice affects individuals and harms groups.

The treatment of Native Americans by Americans of European heritage may be studied in political science as well as sociology classes. Some appropriate titles on this subject are *The Massacre at Fall Creek* (West), *Only Earth and Sky Last Forever* (Benchley), *Yellow Leaf* (Capps), *The Life and Death of Yellow Bird* and *People of the Dream* (Forman), *The Valley of the Shadow* (Hickman), *White Crow* (Quimby), and *Betrayed* (Sneve).

Teachers developing units on African Americans will find a wealth of relevant young adult literature, both fiction and nonfiction. Reading about African American characters in young adult novels from 1950 to 1990 can help students learn about how African Americans have coped with a Eurocentric white culture. In many cases novels from the earlier periods do not paint a realistic picture of society. For example, in the 1950s Hope Newell wrote two career books, *A Cap for Mary Ellis* and *Mary Ellis, Student Nurse*, in which an African American heroine is presented in integrated situations. Mary Ellis is the only African American in an all-white nursing school, but her color in no way affects the plot, and the problems she faces are the same as those of white student nurses. She lives in Harlem in a rather atypical tree-shaded apartment. Nicknamed "Tater" by her classmates, she is snubbed by only one girl, who is from the South. Mary Ellis is capped as a student nurse, and the Southern belle flunks out. In another book of the period with an equally rosy outlook, *Hold Fast to Your Dreams* by Catherine Blanton, an African American teenager works to become a ballet dancer. In *South Town* (Graham), a white racist is reformed and a white doctor states that "progress is being made all the time. . . . In spite of what happened last week, things are better now than they were; in some places, I understand, you might be very comfortable, and the children could grow up to forget this." The message for African Americans in these novels tends to be "Pull yourself up by your bootstraps and whites will grant acceptance." For whites the moral is "Treat black people as individuals and you will learn that they're as good as you are" (Kraus 1976, p. 156). Students can benefit by comparing the situations in these novels to actual historical events of the period in which they are set. These books will also give them a sense of how cultural attitudes about race relations have changed.

Among books published prior to 1960 very few openly deal with racial integration. A rare exception is *Call Me Charley* (1945) by Jesse Jackson. This story about an African American boy whose family moves to an all-white neighborhood and encounters racial discrimination is one of the few in which an African American protagonist faces the real world, rather than the "wouldn't it be nice if we could all live together in peace and harmony" world of Mary Ellis. Another fairly realistic early book is *Hard to Tackle* (1956) by Gilbert Douglas. Clint, an African American football player, moves to an all-white neighborhood, meets Jeff Washington, who persuades him to join the team, is helped by his team members when his house is damaged by hostile whites, and is accepted into the community after his house is burned. In this book Clint talks of the prejudice he faces; however, his acceptance by the white community is not totally realistic.

The civil rights movement of the 1960s increased the number of realistic novels with African American protagonists: Some recommended titles are *The Soul Brothers and Sister Lou* (Hunter), *Daddy Was a Numbers Runner* (Meriwether), *A Hero Ain't Nothin' but a Sandwich* (Childress), *The Friends* (Guy), *Sounder* (Armstrong), *Ludell* and *Ludell and Willie* (Wilkinson), *The Contender* (Lipsyte), *Cool Cat* (Bonham), *Manchild in a Promised Land* (Brown), *Five Smooth Stones* (Fairbairn), *The Autobiography of Miss Jane Pittman* (Gaines), *Fallen Angels* and *Somewhere in the Darkness* (Myers), *A White Romance* (Hamilton), and *The Learning Tree* (Parks). A study of these novels, published from 1950 to the 1990s would reveal some interesting parallels with the civil rights struggle.

The place of women in our society is reflected in many good young adult novels. A study of the women characters in young adult literature from 1950 to the present in conjunction with an examination of the factual history of the period would yield interesting parallels. Some girls in sociology classes might be interested in studying how the roles of women and girls in romance novels have changed, as suggested in Chapter 6.

Other social issues are appropriate for exploration in sociology classes. Drugs, alcohol, aging, institutionalization of the mentally ill, discrimination against handicapped persons, abortion, environmental damage, homosexual rights, AIDS, rape, religious cults, and changing roles and values are all topics dealt with in young adult literature. A unit dealing with the problem of abducted and missing children might include such books as *The Third Eye* by Lois Duncan and *One Child* by Torey L. Hayden. (See Chapter 5 for fiction appropriate for units on these topics and Chapter 8 for nonfiction.)

Science Fiction   Science fiction can be useful for examining a number of social problems. Science fiction often deals with the theme of society gone crazy. Many soft science fiction novels (based primarily in the social sciences) ask the question, What if society continues on the same course it is on today? Often the answer presented in the "other" world of the novel calls into question existing societal practices and values. Soft science fiction can be effectively used in the secondary school social studies classroom when examining subjects such as ecology, other cultures, overpopulation, technology and its abuses, revolt against conformity, and theology and religion.

In an American history thematic unit entitled "Technology: From the Industrial Revolution to the Third Wave," Stephen Sapp incorporates many science fiction books. He uses the books to help students deal with the question, What if industrialization continues at the same pace for the next generation? The unit begins with the reading aloud of several short sections from the book *Future Shock* (Toffler) and a viewing of the film based on it. The bibliography includes books such as *The God Machine* (Caidin) and *The Tale of the Big Computer* (Johannesson), about computer technology gone wild; *The Fourth "R"* (Smith), about the terrifying possibilities of technological advancement in the classroom; *I Sing the Body Electric* (Bradbury), nine short stories of mechanical grandmothers, four-dimensional babies, and humanoid heroes; *Is There Life on a Plastic Planet?* (Ames), about a child robot; *Noah's Castle* (Townsend), about the stockpiling of food; *Fire and Ice* (Kytle), which presents the possibility that technological advancements are hastening the advent of a new ice age; and *Flowers for Algernon* (Keyes), the sad story about what happens to humans when scientific experimentation proceeds without caution. The unit ends with the oral reading of several sections from Alvin Toffler's *The Third Wave,* and with the question, What can we do to ensure that technological advancements will help rather than hinder society? (See Chapter 7 for other science fiction books appropriate for use in the social studies classroom.)

Biography and Autobiography   For many students the study of history is a very impersonal experience. The pages of many secondary school history textbooks do not reveal the feelings, concerns, abilities, and weaknesses of the real people behind the events. Teenagers often cannot see themselves as a part of the history of their country, nor can they imagine parents, grandparents, or friends on the pages of the textbook. Learning theorists have carefully researched and documented the learner's need to relate all new learning to past experiences and already acquired knowledge; learning must be personalized.

Studies of American students show that high school graduates are often ignorant of basic history. A *New York Times* education questionnaire on history given to 1,856 college freshmen indicated that the respondents had limited knowledge of the colonial period, that two-thirds had no idea what Jacksonian democracy means, and that less than half knew that Woodrow Wilson was president during World War I (Wellington, 1977, p. 528).

This ignorance may be the result of a widespread distaste for the study of history, as exemplified by an intelligent woman named Janie, who holds a major administrative position in state government. Janie lacked one course for completion of her undergraduate degree. Although she had been able to obtain major professional advancements without the degree, she was constantly worried that she would be denied a promotion in the future. However, she continued to procrastinate and failed to complete the single course she needed. The course was a sophomore-level history course. When I asked her why she didn't just take the course, she replied, "I hate to study history." To Janie, and to many other students, history is the study of a series of wars with endless lists of dates and names to memorize. On the other hand, Janie loves historical fiction. She has read the entire John Jakes bicentennial series; her favorite book is *The Thorn Birds* (McCullough), a historical novel about a family in the Australian back country.

Finally, after a bit of persuasion, Janie decided to see what it would take to complete this single degree requirement. She called a history professor at her undergraduate school and arranged an individualized reading program. The program required her to read a series of six books. The first book, *From These Beginnings* (Nash), was a biographical presentation of many historic figures, designed to synthesize her other reading. Janie loved the course, and she continually discussed historical trends, personalities, and events. The difference between this study of history and her previous experience in the history classroom was the personalized nature of the material; the character of each historical figure was revealed. She became part of the history she was studying.

Middle school and high school history teachers can bring their subject to life by including the reading of biography and autobiography in the curriculum. The accounts need not be about famous people; they can be about everyday people with whom the students can identify. Biography and autobiography can provide the jumping-off point, the organizational "coatrack," the introductory turn-on event, or the synthesizing tie-together for secondary school history study. "It is often stated that history is biography and biography is history" (Adejunmobi, 1979, p. 349). Biography, after all, is a history, or a written account, of a person's life.

> Good biography is sensitive reportage. Biography is writing that captures the heart and spirit of a man, his zest for life, his passion to know, to explore and discover, to reveal. . . . Over two centuries ago Samuel Johnson said that the first purpose of literature is to teach the art of living. Herein lies the relevance of biography. Good biography does teach living. (Osterlind, 1976, p. 176)

Through the study of good biography and autobiography, students are better able to understand the personality of the subject, increase their knowledge of historic events surrounding the subject's life, develop a sense of people as individuals, begin thinking of groups as being made up of many individuals, and acquire self-knowledge through an increased understanding of others. Such books allow teenagers to see how the study of history relates to their own lives. This is particularly true with biographies and autobiographies that present a person's life from childhood, through the teenage years, into adulthood. As teenage students read about the person as a young adult, they can often see themselves in that person. The need for teenagers to personalize reading is essential for developing adult reading skills as well as for understanding the book. In addition to personalizing the study of history, biographies and autobiographies develop student interest in history and provide an organizational framework for thinking about new concepts, phenomena, and problems.

Many good biographies and autobiographies are available at different reading levels. The history teacher can begin with those written for young adults. Criteria for judging good biography and autobiography for young adults, along with suggested titles, can be found in Chapter 8.

Instructional Approaches

The Case Study Approach to Higher Level Thinking Skills   As Phillips and Philbin (1988) suggest, a case study approach in which the students first complete a case study of events from a historical fiction work and then apply these skills to conducting a community study of historical events can lead to increased understanding. According to Phillips and Philbin, "The case study approach . . . encourages high order thinking skill and the ability to organize and categorize material drawn from primary sources. Writing case studies requires gathering evidence (either fictional or factual) drawing conclusions based upon it, leading to a cause and effect analysis of the event described" (p. 16). Using fiction in the history classroom in this way allows the students to move beyond a grasp of the facts to an understanding of the interrelationship of events and human motivation. The case study approach to history allows students to practice the high-level skills on which they have tested poorly to date.

Writing from History   Studies of writing across the curriculum have shown that students more fully comprehend what they have read when they write about it. Similarly, scholars who have examined how students become involved with poetry have found that beginning with poems the student finds or ones the student has written is more motivating than beginning with poems by adult writers. Mike Angelotti suggests combining these two educational theories in an interdisciplinary approach to the study of history and poetry. In "Writing from Local History: Try Historical Poetry," he maintains that students can learn more about local history and how to study it and at the same time improve their ability to write poetry by beginning with local history.

> The historical society proved to be the prime source. The average age of their members must have been 85, so they could authenticate much of the material we uncovered and could provide the interesting nuance, the human quality often missing from straight historical pieces. They were also the oldest families, knew the cemeteries best and had access to the oldest buildings. They provided us a history of the county published in 1935, a tour of the museum, personal commentary on each artifact contained therein and volunteered as guides for automobile tours of the historical markers and landmarks. As they (or their immediate ancestors) were there when the history behind the markers was happening, their talk significantly enriched the experience.

On all of this we took copious notes and began writing fragments of pieces we hoped to finish, or at least rough out. . . . We discovered during review sessions that personal responses were shaping themselves into fiction and nonfiction narratives, descriptive and narrative sketches, essays (written and photographic), drama and poetry. (1987, p. 21)

Angelotti began his unit with a talk by a member of the local historical society and a class interview following it. Trips to the museum, cemeteries, historic homes and other buildings, and historical markers followed. Many of these trips were made on foot, others with the help of historical society members. After students wrote their own pieces based on the notes they had taken, they began to read historical works of fiction and nonfiction. These works could be introduced earlier to help the students with their writing. One interesting book that could provide a good introduction to a unit like the one described is Eleanora Tate's *The Secret of Gumbo Grove* in which the young African American protagonist researches the history of her small Southern town and the African American citizens who helped make it thrive.

Studying the Region   Linda G. Gober and Mike Angelotti suggest that a good way to teach students how to study history is by studying the region of the country in which they live. Adolescents are egocentric, both psychologically and intellectually. Therefore, any study that begins with them is likely to be more successful than a study that begins with people, locations, and time periods that are foreign to them.

In the regional approach to the study of history, the teacher can select from a series of novels with strong regional flavor or ones that deal with the region's history and people. Gober and Angelotti suggest some of the following as examples: Kevin Major's *Hold Fast,* with a strong flavor of Newfoundland; James Lincoln Collier's and Christopher Collier's *The Bloody Country,* about the Revolutionary War in the middle Atlantic colonies; *Prairie Songs* by Pam Conrad, which deals with a young girl's life on the Nebraska prairie; *Leroy and the Old Man* by W. E. Butterworth, which focuses on the Mississippi delta; and Larry McMurty's *The Last Picture Show,* which paints a picture of Texas.

In developing a regional unit Gober and Angelotti suggest centering the unit around the students' backgrounds and interests. The teacher should create a beginning bibliography of short stories, poems, novels, works of nonfiction, and other resources to match the reading level of the students. Then the teacher should preview the unit with the students by helping them see history as an integral part of their everyday lives. For example, the teacher might point out where examples of writing containing historical information can be found: business reports relating the history of a company, advertisements comparing yesterday's and today's styles, newspaper articles describing past events, diaries and letters, genealogies, patient histories aiding a physician's diagnosis, minutes of clubs and committees about past activities, lawyers' briefs citing precedents in past cases, and novels using historical facts to make a narrative more vivid and meaningful. Students should also have a chance to study maps to become familiar with the geographical aspects of the setting of a book. Teachers should also make use of local and state resources to expand their collection of historical fiction, and make use of this information in oral history assignments (Gober and Angelotti, 1987, pp. 37–38).

Multicultural Approaches   According to scholar and educator James Banks, who writes widely about multiculturalism, multicultural education is "at least three things: an idea or concept, an educational reform movement, and a process" (1989, p. 201). We will examine it as an idea and as a process in relation to the social studies curriculum.

In the 1970s, according to Puglisi and Hoffman, the dominant approach to multicultural education was "the culturally disadvantaged model in which the person from the parallel culture was considered to be disadvantaged by not being a part of the Eurocentric culture." The authors argue instead for a "culturally different model" of multiculturalism (1978, p. 495). This concept of multiculturalism maintains that there is richness in cultural diversity, that differences do not disadvantage an individual but enrich the individual and the entire society.

According to James Banks, multiculturalism is translated into the curriculum in four different ways. The first curricular approach he calls the "contributions" approach. In this approach the contributions of a group are discussed in isolation of the rest of the curriculum. For example, contributions of African Americans are studied during Black History Month in February.

The "additive" approach is more integrated that the first approach. This approach consists of "the addition of content, concepts, themes, and perspectives to the curriculum without changing its structure" (p. 201). For example, this approach might add a unit on Japanese Americans' internment during World War II to a U.S. history course, but not deal with the contributions of Japanese Americans in any other unit. Or the approach might examine ethnic foods without studying the cultures from which they come.

A third and more integrated curricular approach to multiculturalism is what Banks calls "transformation." This approach changes the basic goals and structure of the curriculum to enable students "to view concepts, events, issues, problems, and themes from the perspectives of diverse cultural, ethnic, and racial groups" (p. 201). For example, a unit on the American Revolution might examine the period from the perspective of such groups as Anglo revolutionaries, Anglo loyalists, African Americans, Native Americans, and the British. Or a unit on twentieth-century literature might incorporate the works of parallel-culture American authors (this is the primary approach to curriculum suggested in this text).

The most integrated approach deals not only with curriculum, but with the students' role in learning. Banks calls this fourth approach "decision making and social action." In addition to doing what the "transformation" approach does, it helps students identify important social problems and issues and encourages them to work at solving these problems. For example, students study prejudice and discrimination in society, discuss how the problems affects their school, and take action to improve race relations. (See the thematic unit "Aging in America" as an example, pp. 302–305.)

The value of young adult literature in the two most integrative multicultural approaches is crucial. Reading young adult literature allows students to become acquainted with adolescent characters from parallel cultures. Chapter 5 discusses how young adult multicultural books act as both a mirror for the adolescent reader and a window into cultures she or he does not know. Incorporating these books into appropriate units can allow students to see how various individuals dealt with life during a particular period of time. It is difficult to imagine how any history course based primarily on a textbook could convey the richness of cultural diversity in the way that historical fiction and nonfiction told from the perspective of protagonists from different cultures can. Take for example a unit on the Civil War. Students could read works such as *Across Five Aprils* (Hunt) to examine how families were divided in their loyalties to the South and North. They could learn about slaves in pre–Civil War America by reading Julius Lester's *This Strange New Feeling*. Nonfiction books also provide a variety of perspectives, as in *Anthony Burns: The Defeat and Triumph of a Fugitive Slave* (Hamilton), *The Brothers' War: Civil War Letters to Their Loved Ones from the Blue and Gray* (Tapert), and *Behind Blue and Gray: The Soldier's Life in the Civil War* (Ray).

The Thematic Unit in the Social Studies Classroom

An integrative curriculum that teaches the content required of the social studies classroom, meets the needs of the students, and encourages an understanding of the rich cultural diversity of the United States is not as difficult to develop as it may seem. This type of curriculum can be developed by using the thematic approach to teaching social studies.

In social studies, as in English, the goal of the thematic unit is not merely understanding the theme; the theme is also a vehicle for teaching history, sociology, geography, political science, and economics. The theme is a means through which the secondary school social studies teacher can help students grasp the discipline's major organizing tools and use them to gain a better understanding of the world.

According to Willard M. Kniep (1979), the four major organizing themes in social studies are (1) processes of inquiry, (2) concepts as building blocks, (3) certain phenomena that delimit the field, and (4) persistent problems (see Table 10.1). Kniep suggests that these four organizers can become the sources for selecting thematic units for the social studies classroom. If the four organizers are balanced in designing units of study, students will gain the skills and concepts necessary for understanding social studies.

Units Based on Processes   A thematic unit based on a process theme might focus instruction on the discovery process often employed by the social scientist. This process can assist the student in developing an ability to make decisions, solve problems, and generate knowledge. Process units can also be thought of as skill-development units. Another example of a process unit is the case study approach suggested on page 295. It is essential that students develop skills such as those listed in Table 10.1 to effectively explore concepts, phenomena, and problems.

Units Based on Concepts   A unit based on concepts emphasizes fundamental ideas students need to understand and describe the world in which they live. For instance, a unit developed around the concept of conflict would give students the chance to study various types of conflict and examine the components of each so that they would be able to identify conflict-causing events in new situations and determine whether they are likely to develop into open confrontation.

Table 10.1
Organizing Themes for Developing Thematic Social Studies Units

Processes (skills)	Concepts	Phenomena (human and natural)	Persistent Problems
Observing	Cause/Effect	Art	Communication
Questioning	Change	Banks	Conflict
Predicting	Cooperation	Cities	Crime
Hypothesizing	Community	Communities	Cultural change
Gathering data	Conflict	Consumers	Energy needs
Quantifying	Culture	Cultural groups	Inflation
Comparing	Evolution	Dress	Overcrowding
Classifying	Family	Economic systems	Pollution
Measuring	Group	Elections	Poverty
Interpreting data	Human being	Exploration	Powerlessness
Making inferences	Interaction	Families	Racism
Communicating	Interdependence	Feelings	Sexism
Making models	Land use	Governments	Technological
	Motivation	Groups	displacement
	Nation	Land forms	Unemployment
	Opportunity cost	Literature	Urban decline
	Population	Markets	War
	Power	Media	
	Resources	Mythologies	
	Producer and	Oceans	
	consumer	People	
	Roles	Political	
	Rules	organizations	
	Scarcity	Producers	
	Self	Religions	
	Specialization	Rural areas	
	Supply and demand	Schools	
	System	Small towns	
	Technology	Technology	
	Time/Space	Wars	
	Tools		
	Values		

From Willard M. Kniep, "Thematic Units: Revitalizing a Trusted Tool," *Clearing House,* 52, no. 8, pp. 380–94, April 1979. Reprinted with permission of the Helen Dwight Reid Educational Foundation. Published by Hedret Publications, 1319 Eighteenth St., N.W., Washington, D.C. 20036-1802. Copyright © 1979.

George Hemmingson developed an interesting eighth-grade social studies unit on conflict. The unit began with a study of conflicts between parents and teenagers. Various young adult books, fiction and nonfiction, on different reading levels were employed. His bibliography included the following titles:

- *Mom, the Wolfman, and Me* (Klein)
- *Mama* (Hopkins)
- *Of Love and Death and Other Journeys* (Holland)
- *Summer of My German Soldier* (Greene)
- *Dinky Hocker Shoots Smack!* and *Is That You, Miss Blue?* (Kerr)
- *The Boy Who Could Make Himself Disappear* (Platt)
- *Richie* (Thompson)
- *It's Not the End of the World* and *Deenie* (Blume)
- *Run Softly, Go Fast* (Wersba)
- *Anne Frank: The Diary of a Young Girl* (Frank)
- *The Cat Ate My Gymsuit* and *Can You Sue Your Parents for Malpractice?* (Danziger)
- *Ronnie and Rosey* (Angell)
- *I Know Why the Caged Bird Sings* (Angelou)
- *Mommie Dearest* (Crawford)

Each student, after reading one book, was asked to identify the major conflict between the parent and the young adult. Then the student was instructed to search the book for the events that led to the conflict. The conflict-producing events were assigned to one or more of three categories: situations attributable to the teenager, situations that stem from the actions or lack of actions of the parent, and situations that arise from neither the teenager nor the parent. Next the student was asked to examine each situation and determine the particular cause of the conflict, for example, lack of communication between the teenager and the parent. After the causes were identified, the students met in small groups to develop a list of the apparent causes of conflict between teenagers and parents. A final class list was developed and much discussion ensued.

During the next class session the students saw a film of the events leading up to the Watts riots of 1965 in Los Angeles. Afterward, they formed small discussion groups and examined the events of the film, identifying the probable causes of each event. These causes were then compared with the list the class had developed after reading about and discussing teenage-parent conflict. Similarities and differences were discussed by the class.

Then Mr. Hemmingson suggested that it might be interesting to look at the current city council discussions about the annexation of a new subdivision to determine whether open conflict was likely to develop around this local issue. The students examined the newspaper for information about the annexation, interviewed local residents, invited city council members to attend their class, and interviewed members of the local broadcast media. They concluded that open conflict was likely to develop, basing that conclusion on the fact that all the major causes they had identified in the parent-teenager conflict and in the Watts film were present in the annexation issue. The students were right; open confrontation arose at the next meeting of the city council.

Units Based on Human and Natural Phenomena   Thematic units based on human and natural phenomena allow students to study events, places, structures, and organizations, often through actual experience. In late 1991 the history department of a high school decided that the best way to teach the democratic election process was to involve students in the process from the start. Therefore, about three months before the primaries, students developed files of information about the announced candidates. Small groups of students developed files of information on each candidate. From these files oral reports were prepared and delivered to each of the history classes. Next, the students obtained information about the presidential primary in their state. After collecting data about how to register and vote in the primary election, they made a videotape of a mock television interview show on registration and voting, which was shown to an assembly of the school. Afterward, the students conducted a register-to-vote campaign among the student body and school community.

During this time the students were continuing to seek information about each candidate and review the data in each candidate's file. Several weeks prior to the primary election, the students wrote editorials supporting particular candidates, defending their choices by citing the candidates' qualifications. The editorials, without identification of the candidate, were copied and distributed. Small groups of students were assigned to examine the editorials for incorrect or biased information. Each group reported the results of its study to the class.

Finally, the students were asked to select a candidate to support. Based on their decisions, groups of students developed a campaign for each candidate. The campaign included posters, articles in the school paper, announcements over the intercom, and speeches to other classes. On primary day a mock schoolwide election was held and the votes were counted. Also on primary day the students assisted in getting the local population out to the polls.

A similar thematic unit on the presidential election was developed at another high school. The bibliography for this unit included many titles for young adults:

- *Politics from Precinct to Presidency* (Liston)
- *Facts about the Presidents* (Kane)
- *We Elect a President* (Weingast)
- *The Nature of Politics* (Curtis)
- *Lies, Damn Lies, and Statistics* (Wheeler)
- *Defender of the Constitution: Andrew Johnson* (Green)
- *Young Man in the White House: John Fitzgerald Kennedy* (Levine)
- *John F. Kennedy: Young People's President* (Anderson)
- *President from Missouri: Harry S. Truman* (Martin)
- *Those Who Love* (a historical novel about John and Abigail Adams by Irving Stone)
- *Breach of Faith: The Fall of Richard Nixon* (White)
- *They Also Ran* (Stone)

The reading and maturity level of this bibliography was widely varied so that all the students in the class could participate in the study of the politics of the American presidency.

Units Based on Persistent Problems   Focusing on persistent problems in thematic units will help students understand and explain the causes of these problems. A unit based on problems allows students to use the critical thinking skills developed in units based on processes and concepts, thereby increasing their skills in analyzing and problem solving. As young adult author Alice Childress says, "The art of living cannot be taught or learned by rote, so I believe we should encourage our children to make inquiry and seek answers, directly, with honesty, through reading and open discussion in the home as well as at school."

For example, in a unit on aging, the students in one high school examined the problems of growing old in our society, developed solutions, and examined the consequences of their solutions. This unit allowed the students to practice skills such as observing, questioning, and predicting. It also required them to examine concepts such as cause and effect, change, cooperation, community, family, and culture.

In developing units on phenomena and persistent problems, the teacher can incorporate the processes (skills) and concepts essential for learning in social studies. For example, the unit on elections calls for skills such as observing, questioning, gathering data, comparing, interpreting data, and communicating. The unit also teaches the concepts of cooperation, community, interaction, interdependence, nation, and rules. The social studies teacher who is aware of the processes and concepts to be taught at each grade level will be able to incorporate many different skills and concepts in thematic units on phenomena or problems. A sample thematic unit for social studies follows.

SAMPLE THEMATIC SOCIAL STUDIES UNIT

Aging in America

Grade: 10–12
Course/Subject: Problems in Democracy/Social Studies
Unit: Aging in America
Duration: Two weeks

I. Brief Introduction
   A. The main concept to be covered by the unit is that aging is part of the natural life cycle, and we must learn to deal with old age as part of our life and the lives of others. The problems involved in doing this, however, are complex.
   B. The unit utilizes the process of inquiry. Since inquiry is a social process, the students interact with other students to solve a puzzling problem. By comparing their actions with others' the students will be better able to understand themselves.
   C. The students will be working at the highest levels of the cognitive domain: analysis, synthesis, and evaluation. Similarly, the students will develop high-level affective skills through defending a hypothetical solution to the problem. Defending the solution will require the organization of new values.

II. Objectives
   A. The student will formulate a problem statement given limited information.

B. The student will use the library to investigate the problem statement(s).

C. The student will help organize a group to investigate problems and to lo-cate and formulate solutions.

D. The student will locate, read, and comprehend articles in journals and books related to the problem statement.

E. Given information gathered, the student will formulate, with other group members, a solution hypothesis.

F. With the group the student will identify problem solutions, defend them, and discuss possible consequences of them.

G. The student will listen to and show respect for the problem solutions of other groups.

H. The student will express in writing his/her contributions to the group's investigation of the problem.

III. Content Outline
  A. Day 1
    1. Puzzling situation is presented (film: *Peege,* in which family members visit their grandmother, whose vital life is described in flashbacks).
    2. Student writes his/her reactions to the film on a small piece of paper.
    3. Student selects one book from attached bibliography.
  B. Day 2
    1. Reactions to the film are presented orally and key words are listed on the board.
    2. Key words are analyzed and synthesized into categories. These might include:
      a. differing reactions to old age
      b. care systems for the elderly
      c. family support systems
      d. societal attitudes
      e. historical aspects of aging
      f. medical aspects of aging
    3. Each student selects three categories he or she finds interesting and lists them in order of preference.
  C. Day 3
    1. Groups are assigned based on student choices.
    2. As a class, the students develop a problem statement to serve as a model.
    3. Each group develops a problem statement for its category.
  D. Day 4
    1. The students visit the library and discover the resources available to them in the areas of concern. The class develops a local resource list.
    2. The assignment is given: Your task is to solve the problem and present to the class a hypothetical solution. The solution must be defensible from the research you do.
  E. Days 5–8
    1. Class time is used for research and for designing hypothetical solution. Teacher acts as resource person.

2. A final evaluation instrument for the oral reports is designed by the class. The discussion will include the function of the report, what the other students need to know, and how best to present the information.

F. Days 9–10

    1. Hypothetical solutions are presented and defended.

IV. Instructional Strategies

A. Turn-on event (film: *Peege*)

B. Technique

    1. The primary technique is group inquiry. The first element is the identification of problem statements. Since successful group interaction is the key to completing this lesson, the groups will be expected to keep a daily (or more frequent) log of assignments, objectives, and progress. Similarly, they will be required to designate each person's responsibility on a group plan handout provided during the first small-group session. Five minutes before the end of each session, the groups will be given an assessment form to complete. At the end of each week, the students will be given a progress report to complete.

C. Closing the lesson

    1. Each group will orally present a hypothetical solution. The day before the presentation they will hand in a one-page summary of their solution. These summaries will be duplicated and silently read by the other students in the class. Students will then write questions to ask after the presentation. Each presentation will last ten to fifteen minutes, and a fifteen-minute question period will follow.

V. Instructional Aids and Resources

A. Film: *Peege*

B. Library facilities handout

C. Community resource list, to be developed by the teacher in consultation with the students during the visit to the library

VI. Evaluation

A. Each group will develop a problem statement and a group plan for defending their solution. The solution and its defense will be presented during class time. The presentation will be evaluated by the other students in the class, using an instrument developed by the class. The instructor will evaluate the presentation, using a similar instrument.

B. Each student will read one book from the accompanying bibliography. A brief report on the problems faced by the elderly character will be required.

C. Each student will keep an individual journal, recording contributions to the group's work. Five minutes before the end of each session, an individual evaluation will be completed by all students and collected by the instructor. These will be returned to the students for recording in the journal. The journal will be handed in after the oral presentation.

D. Each day a group meeting assessment form will be completed by all group members. At the end of each week, a group progress report will be completed.

VII. A Bibliography of Young Adult Books
Aaron, C. *Better Than Laughter*.
Branscum, R. *Toby, Granny, and George*.
Bridgers, S. E. *Notes for Another Life*.
Glass, F. *Marvin and Tige*.
Holland, I. *Man without a Face*.
Irwin, H. *Lilith Summer*.
Kerr, M. E. *Gentlehands*.
L'Engle, M. *A Ring of Endless Light*.
———. *The Summer of the Great Grandmother*.
Mazer, N. F. *A Figure of Speech*.
———. *After the Rain*.
Paterson, K. *Jacob Have I Loved*.
Ruby, L. *This Old Man*.
Taylor, T. *The Cay*.
Zindel, P. *The Pigman*.
———. *The Pigman's Legacy*.
———. *A Begonia for Miss Applebaum*.

———————— ✦ ————————

Selecting a theme that incorporates key social studies skills and concepts can be challenging in disciplines that require the teaching of a specific body of knowledge, such as U.S. history, European history, civics, or economics. However, it is essential to develop interesting themes in social studies classrooms to prove to students that different periods of history do interrelate, that the study of history usually does not end in 1920, and that history is more than a body of facts.

Key Constructs for Social Studies

Before selecting a theme that incorporates the concepts and skills of the social scientist, teachers should establish in their own minds a cluster of key themes (phenomena or problems) that bring out the essence of the discipline or culture being studied. In 1957 the National Council for the Social Studies established a list of key constructs for designing thematic units in U.S. history which synthesize national ideals. Robert Waller (1978) further outlined these constructs for the history teacher. According to Waller, "by identifying select themes recurring throughout the nation's history, the instructor can provide an interpretive framework within which to develop a meaningful exposure to this nation's heritage of ideas and ideals" (p. 202). The ten key constructs elaborated by Waller provide a useful reference point for social studies teachers developing themes for their courses.

Economic Opportunity   This theme is "readily apparent in American history from colonization efforts through contemporary society." The theme is concerned with the high value placed on utilizing scarce resources to attain the best for all citizens. According to Waller, the theme can be approached by examining one's home state as a "frontier environment," the labor movement as a collective drive toward prosperity, the Puritan work ethic, and the country's contrasting identification with equal opportunity and crass materialism.

Political Participation   An understanding of government of, by, and for the people can be gained by studying the twin concepts of "consent of the governed and the importance of public opinion in decision-making." To appreciate the wide participation of American citizens in government, students could study the two-party system as well as the Progressive movement, referendum, and constitutional amendments that have expanded the electorate.

A Belief in Reform   The belief in social change through evolution rather than revolution is the third key theme. Teachers should help students understand the delicate "balance between social stability and social change." An understanding of this theme is essential if students are to appreciate the "revolutionary heritage from which the United States originated and to perceive the dichotomies inherent in the Jeffersonian tradition of civil disobedience." Students should become familiar with the reforms of the Progressive era, the system of checks and balances that has been devised to encourage cooperation and yet allow for dissension, and the missionary zeal with which our nation has attempted to export its ideals to the rest of the world.

Population Mobility   This theme helps students develop a sense of historic continuity in the nation's development. The theme includes social mobility, economic mobility, and personal freedom. The movement westward is an example of geographic mobility. "The concept of the city and its place within society deserves special consideration in this category," says Waller. The study of the growth of the middle class is an excellent way to approach this theme.

Status of Women   This is another theme that ties together two centuries of the nation's development. A study of the history of the women's movement can shed light on this theme. Women's changing roles in the family, the job market, and politics parallels the country's economic development. "Study of this theme enables one to draw some definite distinctions between women's rights, women's emancipation, feminism, and women's liberation in order to illustrate the complexity of the issue in past as well as present time." Waller suggests that a study of changes in women's clothing styles reveals parallels with the suffrage movement. The relationship of women to the male culture might be an interesting area of study for some perceptive high school students.

Widespread Educational Opportunity   Strangely, this theme is rarely dis-cussed in educational institutions. Students should understand how the concept of democracy is inherent in the public school system. The goal of universal, free public education could be traced. A study of the school as a socializing agent within the society could be of interest. Is the school an institution devoted to maintaining or transforming the values of society? Do all students have access to equal educational opportunity?

Concern for the Welfare of Others   According to Waller, the United States is populated by people "hard-headed about making money but soft-headed about spending it." A study of U.S. philanthropic concerns can shed light on this theme. The twentieth-century phenomenon of social welfare is also a fascinating subject. Studies of foreign aid for humanitarian causes will interest students as well.

Toleration of Differences   Focusing on this theme allows high school history students to examine how various groups have been assimilated, or not assimilated, into American culture. An examination of immigration from the first days of the nation to the present as well as groups known for intolerance (Know-Nothings, the Klan, McCarthyites) can help students understand the complexities of the issue of tolerance.

Respect for the Rights and Abilities of Individuals   This theme is closely related to the previous one. An examination of individualism as the foundation of the nation is an interesting study to develop; it could include the Bill of Rights, the Four Freedoms, slavery and emancipation, Native Americans, the internment of Japanese Americans, the civil rights movement, and so on. An examination of school integration from the 1954 *Brown* decision of the Supreme Court to the present can show students how respect for individual rights has been interpreted by the courts and legislatures. The threat of violence to the rights of the individual cannot be ignored in the study of this theme.

Worldwide Responsibility   The interdependence of the world's nations, a twentieth-century phenomenon, should be studied, and the concepts of isolationism and internationalism should be compared. Students should be aware of how each president's personality affected the conduct of foreign policy. "The emergence of this nation as a world power is a theme with significant implication for comprehending domestic politics as well as understanding the character of Americans," says Waller.

Selecting Books for Social Studies Themes

Units based on subthemes of these ten key constructs of U.S. history can employ young adult literature in many different ways. For a unit on population mobility, entitled "Movement, Migration, and Mobility," the teacher might develop a bibliography of literature on the westward migration. Although much of this literature is not specifically written for young adults, its major characters are usually young, adventurous, and exciting. The following titles would add interest at a wide variety of reading levels to a unit on westward expansion.

- The *Little House* books (Wilder)
- *The Snowbird* (Calvert)
- *The Massacre at Fall Creek* (West)
- *The United States in the Indian Wars* (Lawson)
- *Native American Testimony: An Anthology of Indian and White Relations, First Encounter and Dispossession* (ed. Nabokov)

- *The Virginian* (Wister)
- *The Log of a Cowboy* (Adams)
- *Borderlands* (Carter)
- *Behave Yourself, Bethany Brant* (Beatty)
- *Laughing Boy and the Enemy Gods* (LaFarge)
- *The Way West* (Guthrie)
- *The Man Who Killed the Deer* (Waters)
- *The Bone Wars* (Lasky)
- *The Taste of Time* (Egan)
- *Down the Long Hills* and *The Quick and the Dead* (L'Amour)
- *The Brave Cowboy* (Abbey)
- *The Spirit Is Willing* (Baker)
- *A Woman of the People* (Capps)
- *My Antonia* (Cather)
- *Words by Heart* (Sebestyen)
- *I Be Somebody* (Irwin)
- *The West of the Texas Kid, 1881–1910* (Crawford)
- *To Be a Man* (Decker)
- *The Adventures of the Negro Cowboys* (Durham and Jones)
- *The Chisholm Trail* (Gard)
- *To the Last Man* (Grey)
- *You Bet Your Boots I Can* (Hosford)
- *Home Below Hell's Canyon* (Jordan)
- *Jim Bridger, Mountain Man* and *The Missouri* (Vestal)
- *Once in the Saddle: The Cowboy's Frontier, 1886–1896* (Seidman)
- *Faster Than a Horse: Moving West with Engine Power* (Hilton)

The history teacher can have each student select one title and then join a work group of students whose book choices are based on a similar historic event, geographic location, or character. Activities that integrate these novels into the theme of the unit can be completed by the groups and presented to the class. In this way students can share information presented in all of the books.

If multiple copies of several titles are available, the teacher can give book talks, presenting some of the book's highlights to help students decide if they want to read the book, allowing the students to select from among them. The students can be grouped according to the titles selected, and activities can be planned for each group. This arrangement allows the teacher to preselect the best titles for meeting the unit's objectives, while the students still have the opportunity to choose books and work in groups in an area of special interest.

Bibliographies of young adult titles can be developed for all of the subthemes suggested by Waller. John Ney's *Ox* books, about a boy growing up in wealthy Palm Beach society, are excellent choices for a unit on prosperity and materialism. Stories of poor families struggling to survive in the midst of a prosperous community, such as Sue Ellen Bridgers's *Home before Dark,* Mildred Taylor's *Roll of Thunder, Hear My Cry,* and Lee Bennett Hopkins's *Mama,* will add food for thought to units dealing with equality of economic opportunity. The importance of public opinion can be seen in a personal sense in books such as Isabelle Holland's

Heads You Win, Tails I Lose; Sticks and Stones (Hall); *Night Kites* (Kerr); and S.E. Hinton's tales of teenage peer relationships, *The Outsiders; That Was Then, This Is Now; Rumble Fish;* and *Tex.*

The need to find a balance between social stability and social change is a theme of many books dealing with multiculturalism in the United States. The following books can help students view life from the perspective of people seeking to claim their fair share of freedom and prosperity and from the perspective of those attempting to adjust to new social demands:

- *It's Crazy to Stay Chinese in Minnesota* (Telemaque)
- *Moves Make the Man* (Brooks)
- *The Crossing* (Paulsen)
- *The Education of Little Tree* (Carter)
- *Sing Down the Moon* (O'Dell)
- *The Brave* (Lipsyte)
- *The Autobiography of Miss Jane Pittman* (Gaines)
- *Roll of Thunder, Hear My Cry* and *Let the Circle Be Unbroken* (Taylor)
- *I Know Why the Caged Bird Sings* (Angelou)
- *Bury My Heart at Wounded Knee* (Brown)
- *Manchild in the Promised Land* (Brown)
- *The Friends* (Guy)
- *Ludell, Ludell and Willie,* and *Ludell's New York Time* (Wilkinson)

The status of women can be studied by examining women's roles as seen through the literature of the period. Anne Eliot Crompton's *A Woman's Place,* told in five sections (1750, 1800, 1850, 1900, 1950), is a good place for young adults to begin their study. Other useful sources include these titles:

- *I Speak for My Slave Sister: The Life of Abbey Kelley Foster* (Bacon)
- *Born Female* (Bird)
- *Never Jam Today* (Bolton)
- *First Woman Editor: Sarah J. Hale* (Burt)
- *Silent Voices: The Southern Negro Woman Today* (Carson)
- *A Minority of Members: Women in the U.S. Congress* (Chamberlin)
- *Bloomers and Ballots: Elizabeth Cady Stanton and Women's Rights* (Clarke)
- *Women of Crisis: Lives of Struggle and Hope* and *Women of Crisis II: Lives of Work and Dreams* (Coles and Coles)
- *An American Girl* (Dizenzo)
- *Women Out of History: A Herstory Anthology* (Forfreedom)
- *The Ladies of Seneca Falls* (Gurko)
- *The Lady Is a Jock* (Haney)
- *Claws of a Young Century* (Hunt)
- *Jeanette Rankin: First Lady in Congress* (Josephson)
- *Zanballer* (Knudson)
- *Margaret Sanger: Pioneer of Birth Control* (Lader and Meltzer)
- *Jane Addams: Pioneer for Social Justice* (Meigs)
- *Growing Up Female in America: Ten Lives* (Merriam)
- *That Crazy April* (Perl)
- *Dorothy Thompson* (Sanders)

- *Indian Women of the Western Morning: Their Life in Early America* (Terrell and Terrell)

A unit on immigrants' impact on and contribution to the culture of the United States could involve books such as *My Name Is Asher Lev* and *The Chosen* (Potok), about the life of young Hasidic Jews. An excellent nonfiction account of Jewish-American life is *How We Lived* (Howe and Libo). The immigrants' experience in getting to the United States and the first months in the new country are presented in Sonia Levitin's *Journey to America.* The experiences of non-white citizens in the United States can be better understood through young adult books such as *It's Crazy to Stay Chinese in Minnesota* (Telemaque), *Year Walk* (Clark), *Farewell to Manzanar* (Houston and Houston), and *Viva Chicano* (Bonham). Much of Laurence Yep's historical fiction addresses being Chinese in the West. Two more comprehensive, nonfiction books for young adults that are particularly useful in studying immigration are *Coming to America: Immigrants from the Far East* (Perrin) and *Coming to America: Immigrants from the British Isles* (Blumenthal and Ozer).

History textbooks sometimes lump people into faceless groups, speaking of the Japanese or African Americans or Native Americans. Supplementary books, including good young adult books, can introduce students to individuals. Thus literature is exceedingly important in a unit on the rights and abilities of the individual. Scott O'Dell's *Sing Down the Moon,* for example, examines the impact of the Navajo's forced march from Canyon de Chelly to Fort Summer, New Mexico, on several individuals. Through Ann Nolan Clark's *Year Walk,* young adults can step into the life of a single immigrant to the United States, in this case a Basque sheepherder. *Beyond the Divide* by Kathryn Lasky introduces Meribah and her father Will who travel from their Amish community to the West. After Meribah is shunned by her Amish community, she and her father face hardships in the new life they seek. An understanding of individuals from different ethnic groups is especially important in the 1990s, a decade in which the nation is experiencing greater immigration than at any time in its history.

Christy Hammer, a teacher in Lincoln, Nebraska, suggests that using young adult novels to teach about the struggle for independence makes great sense since most adolescent literature deals with this theme. Hammer lists the following group research topics for students in a unit on the struggle for independence in the American West: Jim Bridger, Mormons (Joseph Smith and Brigham Young), Jedidiah Smith, Donner Party, Cochise, Isabella Bird, fur traders, Jim Bowie, workers on the transcontinental railroad, forty-niners, John Colter, Marcus and Narcissa Whitman, Sacajawea, Davy Crockett, pioneers on the Oregon Trail, Father Junipero Serra, Daniel Boone, Kit Carson, Wyatt Earp, miners, John Charles Fremont, Zebulon Pike, and the cowboys (1987, p. 17). She suggests that, using these topics, teachers might incorporate some of the following activities in a unit on independence in the American West. (These work best in an integrated English and social studies curriculum.)

1. Write a journal or diary of the character.
2. Make a model (Alamo, a Spanish mission, a wagon, a fort, the Northern Mountains).
3. Compose poems written by the person you have studied.

4. Interview your character. (Assume he/she is visited by someone from our time, who conducts the interview.)
5. Write a report, pulling together the materials which you have found in all your sources.
6. Write a short story from the point of view of a character who may have known the person you researched.
7. Prepare part of a meal the pioneers may have served, and serve it to the class.
8. Visit an old graveyard with markers from the 1800s; write a play including the cause of death and the funeral of one of the people buried there.
9. Make a slide/tape, movie or videotape showing sections of the Oregon Trail, and make a map illustrating it.
10. Make a newspaper revolving around the key elements you research. Include several news articles, an editorial, a political cartoon and advertisements.
11. Make your own candles or soap using the techniques of the pioneers.
12. Write a time travel story in which you go back in time to change something that happened in that time period. Include details from your research in your story to make it seem more realistic.
13. Locate songs from that time period. Play or sing the songs to the class. (This project relates especially to topics on cowboys, Jenny Lind or the Oregon Trail.)
14. Dress in an outfit similar to one that your character would have worn. As that character, present an argument to the class on why you took the action you did. (pp. 17 and 35)

Thematic approaches in the social studies classroom allow the teacher to teach the skills and concepts needed by the social scientist, to encourage all students to learn by providing a rich array of materials to suit various interests and reading levels, to create a sense of historic continuity, and to give attention to cause–effect relationships. Studying a theme allows students to ask questions, and motivates them to learn the concepts of social studies and develop the skills of a social scientist.

Individualized Reading

An individualized reading program is as important in the social studies classroom as it is in the English classroom. In such a program, the student chooses from a variety of books at his or her reading level, regularly reads books of interest in addition to the textbook, individually or in small groups reports on the reading to the teacher, and writes about the reading at regular intervals. Individualized reading allows the student to become personally involved in the study of history, geography, sociology, economics, and other areas and enlivens the content.

> Reading can help make events in history or concepts on topics such as prejudice come alive and be unforgettable for the student. We are talking about incorporating literature, biographies, and other personal accounts of events into the curriculum, integrating all types of reading material into the content, and encouraging reading as a lifetime habit: one that gives pleasure, expands the experience of the individual and creates an atmosphere of a historical era in a memorable way. (Cline and Taylor 1978, p. 27)

With an individualized reading program in a social studies classroom, the student selects from an array of books suggested by the teacher. Usually the books relate to the subject being studied. The selections are likely to include many different kinds of books, as shown in Table 10.2.

Table 10.2
Books for Individualized Reading Programs in Social Studies

Topic/Genre	Example
Biography	*Josh Gibson: A Life in the Negro Leagues* (Brashler)
Autobiography	*The Autobiography of Malcolm X* (with Haley)
Historical fiction	*The Distant Summer* (Patterson)
Personal account	*First Blood* (Morrell)
Nonfiction adventure	*The "Ra" Expeditions* (Heyerdahl)
Dissent literature	*Soul on Ice* (Cleaver)
Nonfiction reporting	*Anyone's Daughter: The Times and Trials of Patty Hearst* (Alexander)
Social problem	*Sarah T.—Portrait of a Teenage Alcoholic* (Wagner)
Religion and culture/fiction	*Beyond the Mists* (Benchley)
Religion and culture/nonfiction	*Gypsies* (Greenfeld)
Changing mores/fiction	*Mom, the Wolfman, and Me* (Klein)
Changing mores/nonfiction	*A Woman's Place* (Crompton)
Human conflict	*Deathwatch* (White)
Struggle against nature	*Snow Bound* (Mazer)
Historic events	*Battle in the Arctic Seas* (Taylor)
Sports figures	*Life on the Run* (Bradley)

If the students are studying multiculturalism in the United States, all of the books may relate to that theme. Similarly, if the unit covers a historical period such as World War II, all of the individualized reading selections may relate to the various aspects of that period. Some may deal with battles, some with the Holocaust, some with Nazism, some with military figures, and some with life on the home front.

If a concept such as conflict is being studied, all of the books may deal with the various types of conflict: interpersonal, group, political, or international. If a phenomenon such as oceans is being examined, the books may deal with conquests on the high seas, explorations, sea journeys, or sea battles. For a study of a persistent problem such as the scarcity of natural resources or ecological destruction, the books selected could present fictional and nonfictional examples of the problem as well as solutions to the problem and problems created by the solutions.

An individualized reading program in the social studies classroom should be well organized and a regular part of the classroom activities. The essential elements of a successful program for social studies are the same as those for the English classroom. (See Chapter 9 for a description of the elements of a successful individualized reading program.)

An individualized reading program in the social studies classroom gives students the opportunity to view problems from many different vantage points and helps the student understand that there are often many right answers to any given question (and that there is often no right answer). It also motivates students to read books, increases the likelihood of their developing a lifelong reading habit, and helps students become more enthusiastic about specific subject areas.

The Science Classroom

Science Fiction

Good science fiction is based on scientific fact. Robert Heinlein, a major science fiction author, calls science fiction "speculative fiction in which the author takes as his first postulate the real world as we know it, including all established facts and natural laws" (1953, p. 1188). He further contends that science fiction must be based on a thorough understanding of the scientific method (1969, p. 22). Educator Paul Cook underscores this criterion, pointing out that in 1937, when John W. Campbell became editor of *Astounding Stories* (now *Analog Science Fiction*), he sought "technically minded stories of speculative fiction, wherein the science as well as the characterization was believable" (1975, p. 87). According to L. David Allen, editor of *The Ballantine Teachers Guide to Science Fiction,* science has four basic functions in science fiction:

1. Science fiction "explores a situation which is in some way different from conditions as we now know them. In many cases, the science involved provides the basic element of change."
2. Science provides "the basis for the exploration and interpretation of a new and different situation."
3. The use of the scientific method is another facet of the use of science in the science fiction story.
4. Science in science fiction provides a "sense of possibility and of plausibility to a situation which might otherwise be strange and unbelievable." (p. 12)

The science teacher who wants to use science fiction in the classroom can determine the scientific authenticity of a book by learning about the author. Many authors of hard science fiction are scientists (see Chapter 7). Heinlein, a scientist himself, points out that the world-famous astronomer who writes under the pen name of Philip Latham would be a good source for science fiction literature about space travel.

The teacher who uses science fiction to help students better understand scientific fact should be familiar with the categories of science fiction. Hard science fiction, which is most appropriate in the science classroom, is based on chemistry, physics, biology, astronomy, geology, and mathematics. A good example of the use of mathematics in hard science fiction is in Isaac Asimov's Foundation trilogy, which probes the question of whether science can and should pinpoint the future of the universe. The action of the trilogy begins when a character works out a series of equations that predict the empire's fall.

In soft science fiction the major framework for the action is one of the social sciences, such as sociology, psychology, anthropology, or political science, or a related area such as historiography, theology, linguistics, or myth. Novels in this category, such as the works of Margaret Mahy, are more appropriate in the social studies or English classroom.

The genre known as fantasy is sometimes classified as a subgenre of science fiction. It assumes "an orderly universe with regular and discoverable natural laws" and proposes that "the natural laws are different from those we derive from our current sciences" (Allen, 1975, p. 20). This category, including works by Madeleine L'Engle and Ursula LeGuin, can be used in the science classroom in a comparison of natural laws with the fictional "new natural laws" created by the author. Students reading this science fiction could be encouraged to invent their own fictional societies, each with its own "natural laws."

Science can inform a work of science fiction in several ways. The first, and most common, is through the setting. According to Sheila Schwartz, the setting is never unimportant in science fiction. The setting includes the initial situation as well as the time and space involved. Because the scientific nature of a novel's setting is less pure than the science in a textbook, it must be understood "in relation to how things really are on earth" (Schwartz, 1975, p. 121). Students in science classes can examine the setting of science fiction novels for scientific accuracy and try to discover the natural laws on which they are based. According to the late scientist and science fiction author Isaac Asimov, comparing the science fiction world and the natural world can be a motivator for the young science student:

A law of nature ignored or distorted can rouse more interest, sometimes, than a law of nature explained. Are the events of the story possible? If not, why not? And in tracking that down, the student may sometimes learn more about science than from any number of correct classroom demonstrations. (quoted in Pell, 1977, p. 259)

The plot in science fiction also involves the use of science, by extrapolation. The author extrapolates from what is known to create new situations. Thus technological possibility is one of the major characteristics of science fiction plots. For example, the short story "Caught in the Organ Draft" (Silverberg) starts with the present actuality of organ transplants and develops a society in which the young are drafted to give up their organs to the "splendid seniors." Currently the transplanting of organs from one living human being to another is a technological possibility. Through extrapolation Silverberg creates a new but scientifically plausible situation. However, readers will understand the extrapolation only if they are familiar with the ideas, events, and technology involved in the scientific reality. To help students make connections between the real and the fictional, the science teacher can pose questions like the following: On what scientific reality has the author based his extrapolation? Is the extrapolation a technological possibility? How far in the future is the author projecting? What things would have to occur before this extrapolation could become fact? Do we want science to continue moving in this direction? If not, how can we prevent science from moving in this direction?

Robert Heinlein relates science fiction plot to speculation. The student is able to relate current scientific knowledge to future possibilities by posing the question, What if . . .? The science fiction writer answers this question. Often the answer can lead to new human problems. "In the speculative science fiction story, accepted science and established facts are extrapolated to produce a new situation, a new framework for human action. As a result of this new situation, new human problems are created—and our story is about how human beings cope with these new problems

(Heinlein, 1964, p. 17). According to Heinlein, the science fiction plot follows these principles:

1. The conditions must be, in some respect, different from here-and-now, although the difference may lie only in an invention made in the course of the story.
2. The new conditions must be an essential part of the story.
3. The problem itself—the "plot"—must be a human problem.
4. The human problem must be one which is created by, or indispensably affected by, the new conditions.
5. And lastly, no established fact shall be violated, and furthermore, when the story requires that a theory contrary to present accepted theory be used, the new theory should be rendered reasonably plausible and it must include and explain established facts as satisfactorily as the one the author saw fit to junk. (1964, p. 17)

The science teacher can use these principles in developing science units based on science fiction. Students could examine the conditions presented in the novel and compare them with the here and now of science. They could be asked to explain why these conditions are essential to the story and determine whether the story could occur if no new conditions were created. Using the scientific method and knowledge of scientific fact, students could attempt to solve the problem presented in the story. Students could also determine which new conditions were essential for creating the problem and discuss what would have occurred had the new conditions not been present. Finally, students could examine each theory presented in the story to determine its scientific plausibility.

Of course, the works of Heinlein and Asimov are particularly notable in their use of scientific fact, but many immature readers will find these authors too sophisticated for their reading interest and skill. Fortunately, an increasing number of science fiction authors are writing for young readers and are knowledgeable about the hard sciences. Among the best authors in the field of science fiction for young adults are William Sleator and H. M. Hoover. Teachers should also consider the books of Madeleine L'Engle which incorporate elements of hard science fiction and fantasy.

L'Engle's books are difficult to categorize. Their common theme of good versus evil often places them in the fantasy genre, but their use of scientific concepts aligns them with science fiction. In L'Engle's Time trilogy—*A Wrinkle in Time, A Wind in the Door,* and *A Swiftly Tilting Planet*—the son of two scientists is a genius who has trouble relating to his elementary school peers—how many first graders are interested in mitochondria? *A Wrinkle in Time* deals with the physics principles of a tesseract (the four-dimensional equivalent of a cube), and *A Wind in the Door* examines cellular biology. Science plays a predominant role in several other books by L'Engle. *The Arm of the Starfish* examines the concept of regeneration, and *A Ring of Endless Light* looks at the life and death of stars, starfish, and dolphins. L'Engle's books not only present the concepts of the hard sciences but examine their relationship to theology, human values, and family life. (For a discussion of the works of H. M. Hoover and William Sleator see Chapter 7.)

Using science fiction in the science classroom can help students understand the difference between scientific fact and science fiction. Reading these books also allows students to gain a better understanding of cause–effect relationships and explore value judgments based on these relationships. Finally, the use of good science fiction gives students the opportunity to apply scientific knowledge vicariously, read materials written at the right reading level, reinforce new learning, analyze a myriad of possibilities, and gain new appreciation for the potential of science.

─────────────── ❖ Between the Covers: *Authors at Work* ❖ ───────────────

JEAN CRAIGHEAD GEORGE: NATURE WRITER

Jean Craighead George writes books with a style and clarity of purpose that reflects her solid scientific background and love of the subject matter. George is the daughter of an entomologist and has twin brothers who work as wildlife ecologists. Her brothers, she says, "took me with them on hunting and camping trips, to the tops of cliffs to look for falcons, down the white water rivers to fish and swim, and over the forest floors in search of mice, birds, wildflowers, trees, fish, salamanders, and mammals. So absorbing and carefree were these excursions that my childhood in retrospect seems like one leaping, laughing adventure into the mysteries and joys of the earth" (quoted in Hopkins, 1973, p. 1049). Perhaps it is because of these childhood experiences that she writes so graphically of life on this planet.

George's work is characterized by a concern with ecology and an uncommon respect for the delicate checks and balances of nature. The scientific accuracy demonstrated in both her fiction and nonfiction works is a result of research, study, and consultations with scientists in many fields. In order to sharpen her senses and develop her powers of observation, she literally lives with and draws every animal character about which she writes, with the exception of bears and mountain lions.

Jean Craighead George has written over forty books, and many have been award winners. *My Side of the Mountain* was a Newbery Honor book as well as being included in the Hans Christian Andersen International Honor list. *Hold Zero!* and *Spring Comes to the Ocean* were on the American Library Association's Notable Children's Books list. *Julie of the Wolves* was winner of the Newbery Award in 1973.

If the science teacher is to justify the use of George's fiction in the classroom, he or she must be prepared to show that it is scientifically accurate and fits other criteria for scientific materials suitable for classroom use. Science writer Millicent Selsam defines good science books as follows:

> By good science books . . . I mean those that show the methods of science at work, that elucidate basic principles of science and are not a mere assembly of facts, that convey something of the beauty and excitement of science, and that interest young people in thinking up good questions for new young scientists to test by experiment. (1967, p. 99)

Mary K. Eakin stresses the need for social consciousness in science, as well as social studies, books:

> When children's books of science are written with an awareness of the responsibility of science for its contribution not only to technological progress but also for the social problems that technology creates; when books of social studies are written with an awareness of mankind's responsibility for insuring the wisest use of science's discoveries, then we can truly say that children's books are meeting the challenge of a changing world. (1973, p. 322)

Another writer, Alice F. Randall, encourages teachers to "see science as a method of discovery, and to make judgments that can be translated into social, political, and personal action" (1979, p. 19). "Teachers must be committed to portraying science as a human endeavor, with a philosophy and history closely tied to societal issues. In order to do this, however, we must give our students the chance to read beyond the science text" (p. 18). Jean Craighead George takes her readers beyond the textbook and leads them directly to the scientist's greatest laboratory, the world of nature.

Probably no other book by George does a better job of showing the scientific method at work than *Who Really Killed Cock Robin?*, an ecological mystery that proves that scientists must use imagination, that their work is not error-free, and that some scientists are concerned about the effects of their work on society. Another of George's books, *Gull Number 737,* is an excellent example of how pure scientific research can be used to solve practical problems. Beautifully written and filled with interesting observations about the gulls, this book also includes the story of a father and son whose relationship is strengthened by their common interest.

In her award-winning novel *Julie of the Wolves,* George again shows her expertise in writing about animal behavior. Julie is Miyax, an Eskimo girl lost on the Alaskan tundra. She is able to survive only through the kindness of a pack of wolves and her ability to finely tune her senses to the ways of nature, as she carefully observes the animal life around her. George is able to write about animals in such a way that they come alive on the page, while she carefully avoids the pitfalls of anthropomorphism. *Julie of the Wolves* has practical application in both the sociology and science classroom.

My Side of the Mountain and *River Rats, Inc.* are both about the ability of humans to survive in the wild by paying careful attention to the environment. These novels are adventure stories filled with accurate and fascinating descriptions of wildlife and plants. Although basically stories of survival, *Julie of the Wolves, My Side of the Mountain,* and *River Rats, Inc.* involve self-discovery by the main characters. Thus, these three books in particular may aid adolescent science students in confronting and coping with challenging situations that will allow them to grow (Wright, 1979).

The works of Jean Craighead George to date span a period of over thirty years. During this time she has consistently written exciting fiction that shows characters involved in various phases of problem solving using the scientific method and presents accurate and scientific observations of nature and animal behavior. Readers of George's works not only feel intrigued by the unsolved mysteries of science but feel keenly aware of their obligations and responsibilities toward life on our planet.   ❖

From Carol Burnette, unpublished paper, 1981.

Books about Scientists and Careers in Science

Many librarians report that students ask for books about science. "Students want to know how scientific discoveries are made. They need to identify with men and women working in science to see that they, too, can become scientists, an idea they often do not believe. High school students are trying to discover where their interests lie and they are troubled about career choices" (Guerra and Payne 1981, p. 583).

Offering books about scientific discovery, scientists, and careers in science can help students see the practical side of the sciences and make decisions about their career options. Two useful books that deal with these topics are Farley Mowat's *Never Cry Wolf,* about a scientist's adventure in the Arctic as he attempts to discover how wolves live, and *Dr. Wildlife,* by Rory C. Foster, about being a veterinarian in the Northwoods. *The Making of a Surgeon* by William Nolen relates the day-to-day events in the life of a doctor in a hospital. *Kon Tiki* by Thor Heyerdahl is an adventure story about a group of scientists who cross the ocean on a raft; *Aku-Aku* by Heyerdahl is the tale of a scientific expedition that led to the discovery of a lost civilization. *Sea and Earth: The Life of Rachel Carson* (Sterling) is a biography of the famous biologist and writer. *Woodswoman* is an autobiography by Anne La Bastille, who lived by herself in the mountains. In *Doctors for the People: Profiles of Six Who Serve* (Levy and Miller) six doctors discuss their careers. *Marie Curie* (Reid) is the biography of one of the most remarkable scientists of all time. James Herriot's books *All Creatures Great and Small, All Things Bright and Beautiful,* and *All Things Wise and Wonderful* describe the humorous adventures of a country veterinarian. Lewis Thomas's *Lives of a Cell: Notes of a Biology Watcher* and *The Medusa and the Snail* are entertaining essays by a scientist who is fascinated by nature, science, life, and death. Jean Craighead George's books also shed light on scientists and careers in the sciences. All of these books and many more give the student a personal glimpse into the world of the scientist.

SAMPLE THEMATIC SCIENCE UNIT

The Exploitation of Wildlife

by Joanne Gentry Bartsch

INTRODUCTION

The purpose of this unit is to introduce students to the variety of ways in which people exploit the environment, in particular, wildlife. Literature is used throughout the unit. The motivating activity for the unit is the viewing of *A Whale for the Killing,* which is both a movie and a book. In addition, passages are read from Amory's *Mankind?* and a variety of other books. Students may choose, from an extensive reading list, a book based on their interests and abilities. The information gained from their reading is used in several ways throughout the unit. On the content outline, sections III.B, III.C, and IV relate to questions raised during the course of individual reading. Both fiction and nonfiction titles are on the reading list. Students are likely to select fiction at first and read the nonfiction as the unit progresses and more information is required.

The unit could be developed into an interdisciplinary study. This particular outline considers the biological aspects of wildlife exploitation, but there are several points in the outline at which other disciplines could be incorporated. Also, there are several places at which other biological facts could be studied.

The first deviation could occur at I.B on the outline. *Mankind?* is an interesting book that explores the humane side of the hunting issue, but the author is overemotional at times in his appeal to the public. The people who argue for the right to hunt are often guilty of the same emotionality. "Persuasion and Propaganda in Literature" is an appropriate English unit to be taught in conjunction with this science unit. Where does the objectivity stop in the arguments of both sides? What are the pros and cons of using persuasive writing? In what kinds of situations is it used? The issue of persuasion could be examined in a communications, speech, or psychology class.

Section II.B opens an avenue for the study of people's relationship to animals; adolescent novels could be used extensively here. *The Naked Ape* by Desmond Morris investigates this topic in some detail. What traits do we like to see in animals? What traits do we not like to see? What is anthropomorphism? What is our relationship to pets?

If a unit on ecology has not already been completed, then section III.B offers a good springboard. In particular, 1 and 3 would be points for discussing community dynamics. At III.B a discussion of dinosaurs could be initiated. What are some of the more up-to-date theories about dinosaurs? Were they cold-blooded? Why did they disappear? An excellent short story to introduce here would be "Our Lady of the Sauropods," found in the September 1980 issue of *Omni* magazine.

Natural history is mentioned in section III.C. If this subject has not already been discussed in class, it can be at this point. Teaching this topic effectively, however, requires examining it in great detail.

Section IV.F could be discussed in conjunction with a political science or history class studying governmental operations, in particular lobbying. What are some groups that lobby in favor of wildlife legislation? Which groups lobby against it? How do they work? A class studying Congress could follow the passage of the Marine Mammals Act. Who introduced it? Who supported it? What does it say? What doesn't it say?

This unit leaves many unanswered questions that could be used as a starting point for another unit. For example, what efforts are being made to protect wildlife? What are game refuges and reserves? What special problems occur when we try to protect wildlife? (This question could lead to a unit on animal migration.) Should we keep wild animals in zoos? What efforts are being made to breed rare species in zoos? Off we go with that question into a study of genetics and genetic engineering. Will extinct animals ever return? (This leads to the topic of evolution.) Is there such a thing as an endangered plant? (This gets into botany.) A class could probably go on for a whole year with this one unit.

UNIT OBJECTIVES

1. The student will describe several ways in which wildlife is exploited by people.
2. The student will know five extinct or endangered species of animals and be able to describe the natural events or human actions that caused these animals to become extinct or endangered.
3. The student will understand the ecological interrelationships of all animals within an ecosystem, or natural community, and will be able to predict the impact on the community if a species becomes extinct.
4. The student will become aware of the efforts being made on behalf of wildlife.
5. The student will be able to present accurately both sides of a modern wildlife issue and will be able to defend his or her position on that issue.

CONTENT OUTLINE

I.   Turn-on Event
    A. Show movie, *A Whale for the Killing.*
    B. Read passages from Cleveland Amory's *Mankind?*
    C. Discuss movie as a class.

1. What does *exploitation* mean?
2. Where have you heard the word used before?
3. In what ways was the whale in this movie exploited?
4. What are some other animals that you believe are being exploited, or have been exploited, in the same or different ways?

II. Group Reading
   A. Class reading list (attached)
      1. The teacher reads aloud bits and pieces from a few books.
      2. The student selects a book he or she would like to read.
   B. Individuals read books, answering the following questions.
      1. What animals are being exploited in this book?
      2. What are some ways in which they are being exploited?
      3. What are the reasons given for the actions being taken against wildlife?
      4. What actions are being taken to oppose this exploitation?
      5. What are the reasons given for opposing exploitation?
   C. Teacher groups students randomly to discuss findings from individual readings.
   D. Groups synthesize individual findings and report to class.
   E. Class synthesizes and discusses group findings.

III. Extinction
   A. Definition
      1. What is extinction?
      2. What animals are now extinct?
   B. Compare natural with unnatural extinction.
      1. Discuss reasons for extinction of prehistoric animals.
         a. Competition
         b. Climatic change
         c. Failure to adapt
      2. Discuss reasons for modern-day extinction (see II.B).
         a. Development and consumption
         b. Hunting and trapping
         c. Other
      3. Discuss consequences of unnatural extinction.
         a. Niche filling
         b. Aesthetic losses
         c. Examples
   C. Investigation of Endangered Species List
      1. Description and explanation of list
      2. Individual project concerning list
         a. Students choose one species from list to investigate.
         b. Students answer questions on species.
            (1) What is the natural history of the animal?
            (2) Why has this animal been placed on the list?
            (3) What are the statistics concerning the survival of this animal?
            (4) What is being done to protect this animal from extinction?
            (5) What are some possible consequences of the loss of this animal?

3. Students may refer to reading list, periodicals, and other sources for information.
4. Students write a report and share their findings with other members of the class.

IV. Culminating Activity
  A. Class chooses one "wildlife versus special interest" controversy.
  B. Class members choose a side of the controversy to defend.
  C. Opposing sides thoroughly investigate the issue, taking into account the questions raised and discussed in class.
  D. Resources available to the student include the reading list, information from other students, pamphlets from special-interest groups that represent each side of the issue, books, periodicals, interviews.
  E. Debate is held between opposing sides.
  F. Students discuss the results of the debate.
    1. Was the issue resolved?
    2. Was either side right?
    3. What particular problems are faced when we consider wildlife legislation?
    4. On which side of the fence do you sit? Has your position changed as a result of the discussion or debate?

SUGGESTED READING LIST

Adamson, Joy. *The Searching Spirit: Joy Adamson's Autobiography.*

Amory, Cleveland. *Mankind? Our Incredible War on Wildlife.*

Beddall, Barbara G. *Wallace and Bates in the Tropics: An Introduction to the Theory of Natural Selection.*

Brooks, Paul. *The Pursuit of Wilderness.*

Brown, Philip. *Uncle Whiskers.*

Caras, Roger. *The Forest.*

Carroll, David. *Wonders of the World.*

Clarke, James Mitchell. *The Life and Adventures of John Muir.*

Collins, Mark. *The Last Rain Forest: A World Conservation Atlas.*

Cummings, Betty Sue. *Let a River Be.*

Curtis, Patricia. *Animal Rights.*

Davis, J. A. *Samaki: The Story of an Otter in Africa.*

Diole, Philippe. *The Errant Ark.*

———. *Life and Death in a Coral Sea.*

Domalaim, Jean-Yves. *The Animal Connection.*

Donovan, John. *Family.*

East, Ben. *The Last Eagle.*

Ehrlich, Paul. *Extinction.*

George, Jean Craighead. *Gull Number 737.*

———. *Hold Zero!*

———. *Julie of the Wolves.*

———. *My Side of the Mountain.*

———. *One Day in the Tropical Rain Forest.*

———. *Spring Comes to the Ocean.*

———. *Who Really Killed Cock Robin?*

Hays, James. *Our Changing Climate.*

Herriot, James. *All Creatures Great and Small.*

———. *All Things Bright and Beautiful.*

———. *All Things Wise and Wonderful.*

Humphrey, William. *My Moby Dick.*

Jenkins, Alan. *Wildlife in Danger.* (1970).

Kevles, Bettyann. *Thinking Gorillas: Testing and Teaching the Greatest Ape.*

Kohl, Judith, and Herbert Kohl. *The View from the Oak.*

Lawrence, R. D. *Secret Go the Wolves.*

———. *The Zoo That Never Was.*

L'Engle, Madeleine. *A Ring of Endless Light.*

Linnaeus, Carl. *Travels.*

Lopez, Barry Holstun. *Of Wolves and Men.*

Maclean, Norman. *A River Runs through It.*

McClung, Robert M. *America's Endangered Birds: Programs and People Working to Save Them.*

McPhee, John. *Encounters with the Archdruid.*

Mitchell, Andrew. *Wildlife in a Rain Forest.*

Moser, Don. *A Heart to the Hawks.*
Mowat, Farley. *Never Cry Wolf.*
———. *A Whale for the Killing.*
O'Dell, Scott. *Island of the Blue Dolphins.*
Rawls, Wilson. *Summer of the Monkeys.*
———. *Where the Red Fern Grows.*
Ryden, Hope. *America's Last Wild Horses.*
———. *God's Dog.*
———. *Mustangs: A Return to the Wild.*
Samson, John G. *The Pond.*
Silverberg, Robert. *The Auk, the Dodo and the Oryz: Vanished and Vanishing Creatures.*

Stoutenburg, Adrien. *Out There.*
Swarthout, Glendon. *Bless the Beasts and the Children.*
Thomas, Lewis. *The Medusa and the Snail.*
Wallace, David Rains. *The Dark Range: A Naturalist's Night Notebook.*
———. *Idle Weeds: The Life of a Sandstone Ridge.*
Walton, Bryce. *Harpoon Gunner.*
Warburton, Lois. *Rainforests.*
Warner, William W. *Beautiful Swimmers.*

Incorporating Literature into the Science Classroom

Incorporating young adult literature into the science classroom may sound like a good idea to the teacher who watches the blank looks on the faces of students who cannot read the text or who find it boring and irrelevant. Dole and Johnson have commented on the usefulness of such literature in teaching science: "Many students (and adults) enjoy reading short paperback books, and many students both want and need to read material beyond the class curriculum. Even more importantly, these books can provide needed background for science concepts covered in class, and they can help relate these concepts to students' everyday lives" (1981, p. 579). But the curriculum in the typical junior and senior high school classroom is already overflowing with concepts and skills that must be taught if the student is to succeed in the next course in the sequence and in college. How can the teacher incorporate one more thing into the overcrowded curriculum?

Cathy L. Guerra, a biology teacher at Bolton High School in Alexandria, Louisiana, in collaboration with DeLores B. Payne, suggests that before the science teacher incorporates nontextbooks in the classroom the students must be encouraged to read course-related material outside of class. They propose that the teacher develop a regular, changing bulletin-board display that emphasizes appropriate books and authors. The display can lead students to general topics that they might enjoy learning about. According to Guerra and Payne, "Interests develop naturally out of discussions about the material on the bulletin board." In addition, they suggest that the teacher read passages aloud from books related to the content being studied or to the interests of the students. This oral reading should be done regularly to acquaint students with the variety of science books that are available to them. At the same time, a reading center stocked with relevant books should be organized in a corner of the classroom. The center should also include magazines such as *National Geographic, Science World, Science News, Science Digest, Science, Scientific American,* and others related to the subject of the course. As in the social studies and English classrooms, independent, free reading time should be set aside to allow the students to sample the reading material.

Once the students have developed an interest in the outside reading, according to Guerra and Payne, the teacher should begin to consider ways in which course-related young adult books can be assigned and class time set aside for activities dealing with the books. They suggest that students reading the same book work in small groups. The groups can report to the rest of the class on course-related concepts they discover in the book. Panel discussions about the books might prove valuable as well. These discussions can center on scientific issues and problems as well as moral and ethical dilemmas that are discussed in the books. If science fiction is being read, the panel might discuss how the fiction of the book relates to scientific fact.

Another way to involve the entire class in the reading of a nontext science book is to read one aloud to the class daily. After each reading, the class could note scientific facts and events, discuss the book's plausibility based on the concepts being learned in the class, and argue whether the information presented in the book is substantiated with scientific facts. These discussions could lead to a research project in which students attempt to prove or disprove theories presented in the book.

Incorporating literature that deals with scientific concepts and scientists need not take away from time used for demonstrations, lectures, films, or lab work. Rather, it can supplement these activities and help personalize the study of science for the student.

The Non-Reading-Oriented Classroom

When university physical education majors who plan to teach are told they must take a class in teaching reading in the content areas, they may wonder, Why do I need a course in reading? Many state departments of education are committed to the belief that every teacher, including those who traditionally do not incorporate reading into their classes, must become teachers of reading. The hope is that if all teachers encourage reading, students will be more likely to read and therefore more likely to improve their reading skills.

Physical education teachers, art teachers, and music teachers who have taken my class on teaching reading in the content areas affirm that reading is essential. They agree many students flock to their courses because they have difficulty in reading. They also know that many students look up to them, and realize that no teacher is more likely to motivate students to read than a teacher they respect.

Physical Education

Several years ago a young man entered my reading education classroom with a frown on his face. By the end of the first class session I knew why. He was a coach; he saw no reason to take this class which took time away from his major concern, his losing basketball team. I made a deal with the coach: "If you'll give this class a chance, I'll try to give you some ideas to help you motivate your team, as well as help them become better readers." He agreed. I gave him an individual assignment and freed him from some of the usual course requirements. His assignment was to search the young adult literature for motivational sports books to (1) read to his students for a few minutes before practice and (2) encourage them to read.

The coach began his task unenthusiastically. By the end of the second week of class, however, he had read John Tunis, James Summers, and Robert Lipsyte. One day he came to class with a big smile on his face. "Did you know that Robert Lipsyte is a sports reporter for *New York Times?*" he asked. "I was reading the paper this Sunday and I saw his name on several articles. I made a poster of some of the articles and read sections of some of them to the team. Next week I'm going to begin reading *The Contender* to them." After he had read *Zanballer* (Knudson), he sent the girls basketball coach to me to get some additional books. He began passing out copies of the books to members of the team. They came back and asked for more. Bill Bradley's *Life on the Run* provided some real inspiration, he reported. By the end of the university class, he was convinced that reading is important even in physical education. He wrote me a note, "You were right! If the brain is not being exercised properly, how can the rest of the body work? My team's record has not improved much, but we are a closer group, we are much more optimistic, we practice better together, we don't feel so down about our losses, and we're really excited about next year. Thanks."

Art

At the start of each university class on reading in the content areas, I read a chapter from a young adult novel. One semester two art teachers were in the class, so I decided to read *Bridge to Terabithia* (Paterson). In the book Jesse is a budding artist, but he is convinced he must hide his interest from the world. His father laughs at him, his teachers yell at him because he is drawing instead of paying attention, his mother gets annoyed because drawing keeps him from doing his chores. Leslie, the girl who becomes his friend, convinces him that his talent is important. Through his friendship with Leslie he acknowledges his ability and openly begins to practice his skill.

A young art major was taking the class in the evening after he had student taught all day. He was frustrated by the fact that many of his students had the potential to be quite good in art but were unwilling to acknowledge their creative abilities, particularly the boys. He decided to borrow the book I had been reading aloud and read it to his junior high school art students. The results were almost immediate. He reported that the students were totally attentive as he read, they began asking if he had other books they could read, and he noticed a marked improvement in their willingness to use their talents.

Many other titles are appropriate in the art classroom. Max in *Max's Wonderful Delicatessen* (Madison) dreams of being a sculptor of junk metal. However, the practical problem of making enough money to live on intrudes on his dream. The climax of the book comes when Max accidentally wrecks a $10,000 car and finds that creating something beautiful out of junk is indeed practical. In Zibby Oneal's *In Summer Light,* Kate Brewer is an artist who denies her talent because she believes she is unable to live up to her father's expectations. Her father Marcus Brewer is a famous painter who did not praise her work when she had won an art competition. Gary Paulsen's *The Monument* is about Rachael Ellen Turner whose life is changed when artist Mick Strum visits town to design a commisioned war memorial. Five of David Macaulay's intriguing books are particularly appropriate in the art classroom: *Cathedral: The Story of Its Construction, Castle, City: A Story of Roman Planning and Construction, Pyramid,* and *Great Moments in Architecture,* a tongue-in-cheek guide to what could have happened if archtects had gone wild.

Art Cop (Adams) is a good book for boys who want to become artists but are afraid that being an artist is not masculine. Since the protagonist of the book is both an artist and a crime detective, he is assigned to the Art Squad, a unit that attempts to solve thefts from museums and galleries and art frauds and forgeries. The stealing of art treasures is the subject of Milton Esterow's *The Art Stealers.* This nonfiction book describes various art thieves, from Vincenzo Perugia, who in 1911 stole the Mona Lisa, to modern art plunderers. Another book about the problem of protecting great works of art is John FitzMaurice Mill's *Treasure Keepers.*

Biographies and autobiographies of famous artists are good additions to the reading corner in the art classroom. The great art scholar Kenneth Clark frankly tells of his early life and his growing appreciation for art in *Another Part of the Wood;* this is another good book for reluctant students of art. Biographies of artists who were scorned, criticized, or ignored can be inspirational reading for young readers. Sylvia Horwitz's *Toulouse-Lautrec: His World* demonstrates the possibility of success despite handicaps. The life of Mary Cassatt, who was scorned by her father, is told in *American Painter in Paris* (Wilson). Other biographical accounts of artists show a variety of struggles. *Paintbox on the Frontier: The Life and Times of George Caleb Bingham* (Constant) and *Indian Gallery: The Story of George Catlin* (Haverstock) are stories of two artists who recorded the events of the early American western frontier. *The Double Adventure of John Singleton Copley* (Flexner) discusses the early life of Copley, a portrait painter who grew up in colonial Boston without the opportunity to see the world's great art. Nevertheless, he devised a style of his own and became a major artist.

A series of art history books by Christine Price is particularly useful for young readers. It includes *Made in Ancient Egypt, Made in Ancient Greece, Made in the Middle Ages, Made in the Renaissance: Arts and Crafts of the Age of Exploration, Made in West Africa,* and *The Story of Moslem Art.*

Music and Dance

Music is dealt with in many young adult books, as is dance. Several excellent books about adolescents and music were discussed in Chapter 3. *Midnight Hour Encores* by Bruce Brooks is among the best. In this book a sixteen-year-old internationally acclaimed cellist is attempting to find herself within her world of stardom. Many books deal with rock and roll; among the best of these are: Todd Strasser's *Rock 'n' Roll Nights, Turn It Up,* and *Wildlife,* and Bernie MacKinnon's *Song for a Shadow.* Other good books that have protagonists who are musicians include Katherine Paterson's *Come Sing, Jimmy Jo* and *I Will Call It Georgie's Blues* by Suzanne Newton. *Buried Alive: The Biography of Janis Joplin* (Friedman) is a good nonfiction book on a rock idol.

Thursday's Children by Rumer Godden is a fictional account of one adolescent's struggle to become a dancer. Two excellent interpretive autobiographies tell of the difficult life in the world of dance: *Worlds Apart: The Autobiography of a Dancer from Brooklyn* by Robert Maiorano and *Winter Season* by Tony Bentley.

Mathematics

Young adult books also have their place in the mathematics classroom. The world of literature can open up new possibilities for the student who is turned off by math.

Puzzle books are one kind of book that can help make mathematics fun and challenging. Consider this riddle-poem from *The Mathematical Magpie* (Fadiman):

Make three-fourths of a cross,
and a circle complete,
And let two semi-circles
on a perpendicular meet;
Next add a triangle
that stands on two feet;
Next two semi-circles and a circle complete.

Do you know the solution to this riddle? It's the word tobacco. (Other mathematical puzzle, game, and fun books are listed in Chapter 8.)

Books about mathematicians and careers in mathematics are useful additions to the reading shelf in the math classroom. Victor Boesen's *William P. Lear: From High School Dropout to Space Age Inventor* tells the life story of the mathematical, business, and scientific genius who developed the Lear jet, among other things. *Charles Babbage: Father of the Computer* (Halacy) is about a pioneer of the modern technological age.

Books and magazines that contain statistical data are useful in the mathematics classroom. Books about sports, major sports magazines, and sports pages of the daily newspaper may be the most valuable resources in this category. There are unmotivated math students who can compute the batting average of all the major league baseball players. Many books about individual sports stars such as *The Home Run Kings: Babe Ruth/Hank Aaron* (Gault and Gault) can be included on the math class bookshelf. Other books such as *Basketball's Fastest Hands* (Sahandi) and *The Great NFL Fun Book* (Gelman) offer a variety of statistical information. Other compilations of statistics are worthwhile additions to the math classroom. A current almanac gives information that can be included in many interesting math lessons. Any book that compiles statistical data, such as *Guinness Book of World Records* (McWhirter), whether on sports, weather, superhuman tasks, or politics, is a good beginning place for reluctant math students or mathematical geniuses who desire a broader understanding of the world of numbers.

Other recent additions to the literary marketplace, such as books about computer games, books about robotics, and puzzles for hand calculators can be incorporated into math instruction. Today's world is filled with technology that is familiar and fun to students. Many of these technological advancement are possible because of our knowledge of mathematics, and teachers of math should bring this world into the math classroom.

EPILOGUE: THE WORLD OF BOOKS

For too long the only book found in many classrooms was the textbook. Although textbooks provide basic information, they often must sacrifice depth for breadth, especially in the case of social studies. Abraham Lincoln was president during the most difficult time in American history, when the nation was divided. But who was Abe? Textbooks may tell students that Lincoln grew up in a log cabin and studied law by candlelight, but they do not help students understand why he made the decisions he made or why he wrote the famous speeches he gave. In describing Civil War battles, history textbooks may give the commanding officers for the Union and the Confederacy, the death count, the location, and even the battle plans of each side. They often cannot fully describe, however, the thoughts, feelings, and experiences of individual soldiers: the hard physical conditions in which they often lived, their family ties or conflicts, the moral questions they wrestled with, their fears, hates, and loves. Why did one brother support slavery and the other decry it? How did African Americans in the South and in the North view the war? How do the issues over which the war was fought affect various regions of the country today? Many of these questions can only be answered by exploring numerous fiction and nonfiction works about the Civil War.

Students often find science dull and boring or difficult to understand. The textbook may not capture the excitement of scientific discoveries; it may not help students understand how to use the scientific method to prove or disprove theories. In some cases the textbook is far too abstract. In others, as the Butzows suggest in *Science through Children's Literature,* the hands-on approach is fun for students, but leaves them with many unanswered questions. When good fiction and nonfiction are incorporated into the science classroom, students venture beyond the textbook to the real world of science and the scientist. Students who have found science too abstract may gain a new understanding of scientific theories by viewing them from a new vantage point.

If books are incorporated into such disciplines as art, music, dance, and physical education, students are more likely to understand the importance of these disciplines to themselves and to civilization. Books can also help adolescents to pursue their own talents even if they are not acknowledged or encouraged by peers or families.

Real books, books young people can sink their teeth into, can bring any discipline to life in a way no textbook can. And the life brought to the discipline is not simply presented by an author but imagined by the student.

SUGGESTED READINGS

Adejunmobi, S. A. "The Biographical Approach to the Teaching of History." *History Teacher,* May 1979, pp. 349–57.

Allen, L. D., ed. *The Ballantine Teachers' Guide to Science Fiction.* Ballantine, 1975.

Angelotti, M. "Writing from Local History: Try Historical Poetry." *ALAN Review,* Spring 1987, pp. 21, 40, 59.

Banks, A. "Integrating the Curriculum with Ethnic Content: Approaches and Guidelines." In *Multicultural Education: Issues and Perspectives,* eds. J. A. Banks and C. A. M. Banks. 1989, pp. 189–207.

Blosser, P. "What Research Says: Improving Science Education." *School Science and Mathematics,* November 1986, pp. 597–612.

Butzow, C. M., and J. W. Butzow. *Science through Children's Literature: The Integrated Approach.* Libraries Unlimited, 1989.

Chatton, B. "Using Young Adult Literature in the Content Areas." *ALAN Review,* Fall 1985, pp. 49–52.

Cline, R. K. J., and B. L. Taylor. "Integrating Literature and Free Reading into the Social Studies Program." *Social Education,* January 1978, pp. 27–31.

Collier, J. L. "Doing the Literacy Tango." *ALAN Review,* Winter 1987, pp. 1–2, 4.

Cook, P. H. "Teaching Proper Science Fiction." *Arizona English Bulletin,* April 1975, pp. 86–89.

Dole, J. A., and V. R. Johnson. "Beyond the Textbook: Science Literature for Young People." *Journal of Reading,* April 1981, pp. 569–82.

Eakin, M. K. "The Changing World of Science and the Social Studies." In *Children and Literature: Views and Reviews,* ed. V. Haviland. Scott, Foresman, 1973. Lothrop, Lee and Shepard, 1974.

Gober, L. G., and M. Angelotti. "Historical Fiction Starts with the Student." *ALAN Review,* Winter 1987, pp. 37–38.

Guerra, C. L., and D. B. Payne. "Using Popular Books and Magazines to Interest Students in General Science." *Journal of Reading,* April 1981, pp. 583–86.

Hammer, C. "Beyond the Divide: A Springboard for Discussion of Current Concerns of Young Adults." *ALAN Review,* Winter 1987, pp. 17, 35–36.

Heinlein, R. A. "On the Writing of Speculative Fiction." In *Of Worlds Beyond,* ed. L. A. Eschback. Advent, 1964.

———. "Ray Guns and Rocket Ships." *Library Journal,* July 1953, pp. 1188–91.

———. "Science Fiction: Its Nature, Faults and Virtues." *The Science Fiction Novel: Imagination and Social Criticism,* ed. B. Davenport. 3d ed. Advent, 1969.

Hopkins, L. B. "Jean Craighead George." *Horn Book,* August 1973, pp. 1048–51.

Keller, L. "Portrait of the Young Adult as an Artist." *ALAN Review,* Fall 1987, pp. 10–12, 14.

Kniep, W. M. "Thematic Units: Revitalizing Trusted Tool," *Clearing House,* April 1979, pp. 380–94.

Kraus, W. K. "From Steppin Stebbins to Soul Brothers: Racial Strife in Adolescent Fiction." *Arizona English Bulletin,* April 1976, pp. 154–60.

Kraus, W. K., Ed. *Murder, Mischief and Mayhem: A Process for Creative Research Papers.* National Council of Teachers of English, 1978.

National Center for Educational Statistics. *The U.S. History Report Card.* (NAEP 19-H-01). U.S. Department of Education, 1990.

Osterlind, S. J. "Autobiographies and Biographies for Young People." *Arizona English Bulletin,* April 1976, pp. 176–78.

Pell, S. J. "Asimov in the Classroom." *Journal of Reading,* December 1977, pp. 258–61.

Phillips, R., and M. Philbin. "Fiction about Hate Groups: A Case Study Approach." *ALAN Review,* Fall 1988, pp. 16, 35.

Puglisi, D. J., and A. J. Hoffman. "Cultural Identity and Academic Success in a Multicultural Society: A Culturally Different Approach." *Social Education.* June 1978, pp. 495–98

Randall, A. F. "Scientific Writing Beyond the Textbook." *Science Teacher,* May 1979, pp. 18–21.

Schwartz, S. "Choosing Science Fiction for the Secondary School." *Arizona English Bulletin,* April 1975, pp. 119–26.

Selsam, M. E. "Science Books: Reflections of a Science Writer." *Children's Literature in Education,* Summer 1980, pp. 82–84.

———. "Writing about Science for Children." In *A Critical Approach to Children's Literature,* ed S. Fenwick. University of Chicago Press, 1967, pp. 96–99.

Waller, R. A. "A Thematic Unit Approach to Teaching U.S. History." *History Teacher,* February 1978, pp. 201–10.

Wellington, J. K. "American Education: Its Failure and Its Future." *Phi Delta Kappan,* March 1977, pp. 527–30.

Wright, J. L. "The Novel as a Device for Motivating Junior High Science Students." *American Biology Teacher,* November 1979, pp. 502–4.

11 Responding to, Experiencing, and Sharing Books

FOCUS QUESTIONS

1. Why is it important for students to become engaged with texts?
2. How can students be encouraged to respond to books through discussion and writing?
3. How can teachers build a community of readers?
4. Why is it important for students to experience books?
5. What are some ways in which students can experience books?
6. What are some ways in which students can share books?

PROLOGUE

A writer cannot help but be pleased to hear that her work is the subject of a doctoral dissertation but imagine my added delight in learning of Sissi Carroll's plan to look at my books as Southern literature. Southern by birth, I am also a Southerner by intent, having strayed beyond the Mississippi only once, to live three years at Ellsworth Air Force Base in South Dakota. At least, I consoled myself, it's SOUTH Dakota.

Reading Carroll's dissertation, I was reminded of many of the tenets of our Southern tradition, especially our history which contributes so powerfully to our experience and subsequently to our literature as well. . . . The fact is we Southerners have a "thing" about history, and this abiding need to look backwards for lessons to live by has affected me profoundly, although only a few years ago I might have denied it. . . . I bring the past with me even if I don't journal and could never keep a diary for more than a week. When I was a girl I knew a secret place where I might stow a tiny book with its cheap lock and key but I also knew what I wrote there was hardly worth protecting. Occasionally I would try again, spend with hopefulness my meager allowance on yet another little diary only to find, several weeks later, that my entries had not magically sprung life, were not rich in insight, were not even entertaining.

As an adult, I again tried keeping a journal because it was expected of writers urged to encourage the flow every moment, an exhausting and, for me, unproductive way of working. . . .

But is fiction a way of journaling? To explore this possibility, I have looked back at my early published fiction, pieces done sporadically in the sixties and early seventies, to find that the majority of these pieces were set in the past and involved children. The plots—a neighbor-lady going to a nursing home, the death of a policeman-father, a daughter's internal battle with a domineering mother, a child's attempt to reconcile her parents—were all drawn from the Southern child's impression of experience. . . .   ❖

From Sue Ellen Bridgers, "My Life in Fiction," *ALAN Review*, Fall 1990, pp. 2–3. Reprinted with permission of Sue Ellen Bridgers.

Engagement with Literature

Sue Ellen Bridgers understands that stories are a part of the writer, not something separate. The stories she tells relate to what she knows, what she feels, the problems she faces, the life she lives. Although most authors believe they can write about things that have not happened to them directly or places they haven't been to, they also recognize that they cannot ignore their own experiences. At the same time, the stories are not necessarily autobiographical. Bridgers says of her stories, "These were impressions of experience because the events were not autobiographical" (1990, p. 2). Bridgers recognizes that her stories are not diary entries that exactly catalog experience, but, instead, are extrapolations of experience. Embellished by dreams, stories take on new dimensions. And, according to Bridgers, as each story takes on its own life, it becomes separate from the experience that may have inspired it.

The writer is engaged with her text while she is writing it. Sue Ellen Bridgers on several occasions has told students in my university adolescent literature class during her annual visit that the level of engagement an author has with a story can get in the way of real life. She recalls that when her children were in elementary school she would begin writing shortly after the school bus picked them up in the morning and not stop until she heard the school bus round the corner in the afternoon. When her children came in the door wanting to tell her of their days, she found herself resenting their intrusion on the story she was creating. When the text is published, however, it is no longer the author's task to transact with it; now the transaction is between the readers and text.

The Reader and the Text

Readers who are engaged with a text may also find themselves so caught up in the story that real life becomes an intrusion. You can probably remember times when you were so engrossed with a powerful story that you found it difficult to answer the phone or go to the supper table.

Although the author's interaction with the text is a fact of the creative process, once the text is published, it belongs to its readers. As readers recognize and identify with the experiences in the text, as they become part of the story and the story affects their lives, then the work comes alive as literature. Much of literature instruction in the schools, however, ignores the important transaction between the reader and the text.

In fact, in many English, language arts, and reading classrooms, the text is something the teacher tells the student about. Or, perhaps, the text is the key to the student's ability to answer the teacher's questions about it. Reading in such instances is a passive act. In lesson plans, the teacher may indicate that "the students will discuss the text." However, often the discussion takes the form of answering questions that lead the students to discuss the teacher's interpretation of the work.

Transactional Theory of Literature

The transactional theory of literature, also called reader-response theory, assumes that the reader is an active participant in the reading process. This theory, first introduced by Louise M. Rosenblatt in *Literature as Exploration* and further expounded in *The Reader, the Text, the Poem*, contends that the reader and the text act on each other, "affecting each other to evoke an experience, a meaning, for the particular reader of the text" (Karolides, 1992, p. 22). The word *text* is purposefully used here to indicate that until this transaction occurs, the text is merely words, or symbols, on the page. Only through the transaction between reader and text does the text become a literary work, or in Rosenblatt's terms a "poem."

The transaction between reader and text is a very personal experience in which "meaning evolves from the fusion of the author's text and the reader's personality and experience" (Karolides, 1992, p. 22). There can be as many responses to a single text as there are readers of the text because the reading process for each reader is unique.

This assumption would appear to make dealing with a single text or even several texts in the classroom difficult. This need not be the case, however. As Karolides points out, the reading process is evolutionary:

> The reading is not linear, but rather, recursive, a backward-and-forward exploration of what is being evoked in relation to the text. Clues of context are perceived and integrated. The reader constructs a constantly adjusted scaffold of understanding attempting to account for the text's many features. A second reading, if there is one, can reveal additional or revised nuance. (1992, p. 24)

The teacher who encourages each reader's response to the text aids in this recursive process in which the students explore the text looking for new clues. Discussions and activities that encourage individual response allow students to revise the meaning they derive from the text by adding new insights, often provided by other readers, to their reading.

Selecting Books for Student Response

One of the keys to successful transactional approaches is selection of reading materials. According to Karolides, there are several prerequisites to reader-response teaching: (1) marks on the page are decipherable as words—the printing is clear and easy to read and the reader understands the meaning of the bulk of the words; (2) the text is understandable—the situation, characters, and expressed issues can be comprehended by the reader, and (3) the reader is willing to engage in the text. All of these prerequisites point to the careful selection of appropriate works.

Robert C. Small, in a fascinating article (1977) on using the young adult novel to teach the art of literature, addresses the issue of understandable text:

> A study of most novels for adults, surely almost all the so-called "classics," puts students at a great disadvantage. The well-written junior novel, in contrast, invites, welcomes, students to meet as equals. . . . As you can be a successful literary critic in relation to a Peter Benchley or a John Hersey, so students can apply with reasonable success a critical approach to Virginia Hamilton or M. E. Kerr. (p. 57)

Small compares the English teacher's desire to plunge the students head first into the classics to attempting to teach a child how an automotive engine works by having him examine the engine of a 747 or an advanced modern racing car: "Their size, complexity, and refinement would make them poor starting places for the beginner" (p. 58). He suggests, instead, the use of working models. In the automotive engineering class the teacher would probably want to begin with a working model of a simple jet engine, a combustion engine with a single cylinder. In an English class the working model of a mature piece of literature, or classic, according to Small, is the young adult novel.

Most teenage students are developmentally prepared to actively read, enjoy, and respond to the young adult novel. Similarly, the vast majority of teenagers prefer young adult novels to the classics and are therefore more likely to be willing to discuss young adult books enthusiastically. The young adult book can act as a working model for studying the form of literature: plot, setting, characterization, dialogue, theme, and even metaphor and symbol. Once the student becomes an expert in the literary craft of the young adult novelist, the step to the classics is easier.

Encouraging Student Response

Students can respond to literature in many ways. Most response techniques revolve around discussion between teacher and student or small groups of students. Some encourage the student to respond through writing. Other techniques allow the student to experience the work in a variety of different ways from films to storytelling to creative dramatics. All of these techniques will be examined in this chapter.

Discussion Response Techniques

The most common way of implementing the transactional approach to literature is through discussion. The keys to encouraging successful oral response include teaching students how to respond, creating an atmosphere that encourages response, and carefully correcting incorrect response.

Teaching Students How to Respond   Concentrate initial discussion on the students' responses. Students should be encouraged to accept their own responses and those of others. Beach and Marshall (1991) have identified the following techniques as appropriate for first discussions:

1. *Engaging.* The reader's articulation of her or his level of engagement with the text may be the first step in responding to it. The engagement is reflected in the reader's emotional reaction, ranging from "This is BOR—ING" to "I couldn't put it down."
2. *Describing.* Restating or reproducing information that is provided in the text requires selecting out some important aspect of the text and is often the next level of response.

If students seem unable to make initial responses to a text, provide them with a context for the text. For example, in an eleventh-grade class with below-average reading skills, students were attempting to respond to John Hersey's *Hiroshima.* When at first the students' only response was that they could not understand the book, the teacher moved the discussion closer to home. She asked the students "to imagine they had just heard that Minneapolis–St. Paul, a metropolis some forty miles away, had been targeted for a nuclear attack, expected in about an hour. They, in their windowless classroom, were relatively safe. She paused and asked, 'How would you react? What would you do?'" (Karolides, 1992, p. 29) Their discussion, after some initial reluctance, becomes lively. Karolides points out that the teacher had "created involvement among her students, . . . had raised feelings and issues that could be applied to their primary text, *Hiroshima*" (p. 30).

A third key to encouraging good oral response is to help students understand the difference between what she or he has brought to the text and what is found within the text. The student needs to be able to distinguish "between having feelings and inferring those of writer or character" (Probst, 1984, p. 34). The following techniques are useful:

1. *Conceiving.* The student makes statements about meaning or draws inferences from important aspects of the text. For example, if a character stutters, we may infer that the character is nervous.
2. *Explaining.* The reader explains why the characters do what they do, or examines their motivation. What is causing the character to stutter beyond the immediate situation? Is it his difficult relationship with his father? Is it his inability to make friends? Is it his fear of girls? Or is the stuttering *the cause* of his other problems?
3. *Connecting.* The reader connects her or his own experiences with the text. As in all forms of responding to text, connecting is a recurrent movement between the text and one's experiences, knowledge, and attitudes. The reader may first recall a similar experience, next elaborate on that experience, next apply the experience to the text, later use the text to reflect on her or his own experience, and finally, interpret the text and the experience.
4. *Interpreting.* The reader uses all the reactions above to interpret an overall theme or point.
5. *Judging.* The reader makes judgments about the characters in the story or the literary quality of the story.

Creating an Atmosphere for Response   Encourage cooperation rather than competitiveness, using these guidelines:

1. Do not allow debating. Debate is not an appropriate model since one side wins and one loses.
2. Help the response discussion build, so ideas feed new ideas, "with participants gradually acquiring sharper insights, changing their minds, and adding the observations of others to their own, broadening their perspectives on the work" (Probst, 1989, p. 34).
3. Encourage students to make "tentative statements, aware that they are not bound to them, that they may later be withdrawn or revised" (Probst, 1984, p. 34).
4. Help students understand that their opinions are important and errors they make will not be held against them.

Correcting the Incorrect Response   Gently correct incorrect responses. Incorrect responses that can limit ability to respond include

1. Incorrect identification of a character
2. Misinterpretation of a word
3. Prejudicial judgment

An example is a student assuming that a character who is a physician is a male when in actuality the character, whose name is Leslie, is female.

Writing

The most common response technique next to discussion is writing. Students respond by writing about texts they have read. Jane Ann Zaharias (1984) recommends four types of written responses, which are described below, with sample activities.

Personal Statement   These statements include emotional reactions, expressions of identification or empathy with characters or places, conjecture about characters, and autobiographical associations.

- In many adolescent books music is important to the characters. In *The Keeper* by Phyllis Reynolds Naylor, for example, the song "Cat's in the Cradle" is particularly meaningful to Nick. List music that is particularly meaningful to you and explain why. Put together a tape of the music that is special to you. Write a script to go along with the tape (McKinney, 1991, p. 37).
- After reading Gary Paulsen's *Hatchet* or Harry Mazer's *The Island Keeper*, write an imaginary diary of what it would be like to live on an island or in a remote place waiting to be rescued (McKinney, 1989, p. 44).
- Read an essay on the plight of today's college graduates, and write about your own fears of the future (Warawa, 1989, p. 48).

Description   Descriptive statements attempt to classify or describe the form, language, structure, or content of a work. Such responses can range in complexity from the simple recall of explicitly stated information to analysis of the stylistic properties of a text.

- After reading Paula Fox's *The Moonlight Man* and Cynthia Voigt's *Solitary Blue*, write a letter that might have been written by Jeff or Catherine to each other, or to another character in the novels.
- Both Fox and Voigt are particularly good at writing descriptions; copy some that you particularly like or find interesting in your journal.
- Read *Prank* by Kathryn Lasky and *In Summer Light* by Zibby Oneal. The protagonist in each book likes to write and finds in their writing truths about their own lives. Write a description of a painting Kate might paint for her father, mother, or for Ian.
- After the students have read *In Summer Light*, read to them about Zibby Oneal on pp. 107–108 of this text. Tell the students, "Notice how often she uses the word *light* in various forms to describe characters. The amount of light in a character's life has to do with how much personal growth and identity that has been found. Kate has lived in the shadow of her father for many years. Her mother still lives in his shadow. To stand out in the right light seems to be too painful for some. Bright light reveals truth as well as pain. Contrast these descriptions to those in *Prank* in which 'the water appears leaden and still. Even on a sunny day the water looked gray.' " (McKinney, 1989, pp. 43–45).

Interpretation   Interpretive responses are aimed at identifying the symbolic or thematic meanings of a work. Interpretation requires of readers an ability to infer the intentions of authors.

- Write your own version of Robert Browning's poem "Porphyria's Lover." You may change the setting, the point of view, the sequence of events, and the ending (Warawa, 1989, p. 48).
- Read *One Fat Summer* by Robert Lipsyte and write a short story based on it from a female's perspective (McKinney, 1989, p. 44).

- After reading *Macbeth*, retell an important episode of the play from the perspective of either Macbeth, Lady Macbeth, Malcolm, or Macduff. Be faithful to the events of the play but interpret them according to the character's viewpoint (Warawa, 1989, p. 49).

Evaluation   Evaluation responses assess the construction, meaningfulness, or appropriateness of a work.

- Gary Paulsen's book *Hatchet* is a Newbery Honor book. Look at the criteria for this award; what makes this book worthy of receiving the award? (McKinney, 1989, p. 44).
- After reading any novel you think is particularly good, make a list of what made the novel good. Compare your list of criteria to other students' lists who have read the same novel. Revise your list. Now compare your list with a group of students who have each read different novels. Revise your list for criteria of good books across genres. Construct a class list of criteria. Now, use the class criteria on another novel you think is particularly good (Nugent, 1990, pp. 4–7).

Journals and Letter Writing

Probably the simplest and one of the best ways to respond to literature in writing is through the use of journals or logs. These are sometimes called literature logs or dialogue journals. Both of these techniques are based on the writing workshop model of Nancie Atwell. They allow students to respond independently while feeling a part of a community of readers.

Marie Dionisio (1991) uses the technique of dialogue journals in her middle school classroom. She does a series of book talks on adolescent novels throughout the school year, reading particularly motivating sections aloud to the students. The students are permitted to select books from the classroom library, including those on which book talks have been done. When the students read, the teacher also reads an adolescent novel. The students write letters to the teacher in their dialogue journals about the books they are reading. The teacher responds to some of the students' entries in writing. When the students select books mentioned in book talks, the teacher designs mini-lessons on literary elements found in the books such as setting, characterization, theme, conflict, use of language, and relationship of the author's ideas to the reader's world.

Students begin to discuss some of these elements in the letters in their dialogue journals, the teacher responds in writing. Here is an example:

> Dear Ms. D,
>   I'm reading *Snow Bound* by Harry Mazer. I remembered what we said in the mini-lessons a few weeks ago, the setting ones. I think Harry Mazer did some of those things too. In one part Tony is walking away from the car. He is just like a speck in the white snow walking and walking. The way Mazer wrote it I can see Tony in my mind. It makes me feel like he's so alone and will probably die. I think Tony feels like that too. And Cindy too because she sees him from the car window. Ken.
>
> Dear Ken,
>   Mazer sure does use setting in *Snow Bound* in many of the ways that we saw Jean George use setting in *Julie of the Wolves*. The example you used in your letter is great. It

illustrates an author using setting to make the reader feel a certain way. The picture of Tony getting smaller and smaller as he walked up the snow covered hill made me feel hopeless too. It made me think that the chances of their surviving were next to impossible. You made a good point. Thanks for sharing it with me. Ms. D. (Dionisio, 1991, pp. 40–44)

In Sandra L. Robertson's junior high school classroom students write to their teacher and their peers about the books they are reading in literature logs using a technique that Nancie Atwell calls writing and reading workshops. One of the goals of this approach is to encourage cooperation rather than competition. Although another goal of this approach is to encourage students to self-select reading material, Ms. Robertson sometimes reads to the class to model the techniques. Often she asks for a volunteer to read from a text that has been selected by the teacher or a student. After reading aloud she asks the students to say aloud any word or sentence that they especially liked or one that they found confusing (writing teacher Peter Elbow calls this "text rendering"). After about five minutes of oral responding, Ms. Robertson asks the students for questions or comments. She tells the students they can use the "text rendering" approach when they listen to each others' compositions during the writing workshop. She tells them that it often helps a writer if she or he can hear which phrases work and which ones are confusing.

Students then write letters in their literature logs about what has been read or what they are reading. In the logs there are no right or wrong answers. This guideline helps create the kind of atmosphere that is necessary for responding to literature successfully. After students have spent some time writing in their lit logs, Ms. Robertson asks them to copy a sentence or phrase from the book that they liked or found confusing. Then they speculate in writing about what it might mean. She defines *speculate* simply as "guess." They are to write to a friend or to Ms. Robertson, and they are assured that they will receive a response. In this classroom students are responding to literature individually, with peers, and with their teacher. Through Ms. Robertson's coaching they are learning new techniques to improve their responses to literature and to their own writing.

Quite by chance, high school teacher Patricia Stoddart and university instructor Joyce Kinkead found a similar approach that allowed both high school and university students to respond to the same text and learn from each others' responses. Students in Ms. Stoddart's high school class were reading Robert Cormier's *I Am the Cheese*. The college students in a "Literature for Teachers" class were to read the same book. Because the logistics of having high school and college students meet face to face to discuss the same book were so complicated, their instructors decided to use letter writing to allow students to write about a piece of literature and receive comments on their response.

Within two pages of the start of Cormier's novel, Adam, the protagonist, says, "I am afraid of a thousand things, a million." To get the students into the book, the instructors selected a prereading activity in which the high school students first brainstormed a list of fears. Each student then selected one fear from the list and wrote a letter about it to an unidentified college student:

Dear ?
I am afraid of deep water. I can go in water, but deep water I can't stand. The way I stand it is that I never go near deep water. I like to go on boats, but I don't like to swim. Sometimes I like to swim in a swimming pool. I really don't like to swim after seeing *Jaws*.

Each college student selected a letter about a fear with which they could empathize and responded in writing:

Dear Jason,
When I was eight or nine years old I almost drowned in a canal ditch. Luckily, I somehow grabbed the edge of the bridge that was touching the water since the ditch was full. If I'd have gone under the bridge I probably wouldn't be alive because the water was barely moving and the bridge was really wide so trucks could cross it. After that, any thought of being in the water, unless it was the bathtub, really scared the hell out of me. (Kinkead and Stoddart, 1987, p. 40)

The college student's letter continued by describing his first experience with the ocean ("see was the right word for me. Not feel"), focusing on four good things about water ("drinking, bathing, fishing, and duck hunting"), and offering reassurance about one fear ("I don't sweat it because I know lots of guys besides us that don't like to swim").

When the high school students received the responses they were very excited. They silently read them and then shared parts of them with their peers. The students were eager to meet their correspondents and write again. After finishing the book, the students did write again, this time to discuss the book. The high school students often began their letters with a reference to the first exchange. The college students often reinforced the high school student's interpretation of the novel and answered their questions.

Students can also be given specific topics to write about in journals. Figure 11.1 provides a list of topics for responding to books. Many of these writing topics also help students understand the literary characteristics of books.

Building a Community of Readers

For many adult readers there is no greater pleasure than discussing a good book with a peer. We can provide some of this same delight for students while, at the same time, helping them to respond in ever more sophisticated ways to literature. As an added benefit, a classroom community of readers develops. Carol Gilles reports that Chris, a seventh grader, had commented glumly about school, "You've gotta do it: the homework, the worksheets, the tests, you just gotta do it." After his teacher initiated literature study groups, Chris's response was more enthusiastic, "We're doing literature groups. We read real books, interesting ones, and talk about and write about them. I like what I'm reading, and it is just funner. I don't feel limited about what I have to do. . . . I'm even reading some at home" (1989, p. 38). In literature study groups, according to Gilles, "Students are given a choice of books to read; those reading the same book meet together with the teacher to discuss the book; students keep a literature log in which they respond to their reading; they are often involved in a culminating project using some other media; and both students and teachers take part in the evaluation process" (p. 38).

The careful preselection of motivating, well-written literature appropriate for adolescents for the classroom library is the most important step in building a community of readers. (The criteria for good young adult books in a variety of genres in Chapters 3 through 8 can be used in selecting these books.) Teachers then

Figure 11.1
Reacting Directly to a Book in Writing

General Ideas for Writing about a Book

1. Choose the book you would most like to have with you if you were stranded on a desert island and explain why.
2. Discuss in writing your reactions to the book. Did you enjoy reading it? Why?
3. Write a letter to the author explaining why you liked the book and ask specific questions about how it was written.
4. Put together a reader's support kit for a book.
5. Write a letter to a friend recommending the book.
6. Write the material for the front and back inside flaps of the book jacket.
7. Write a review of the book from some other person's viewpoint—an English teacher, a parent, a person of the opposite sex.

Writing about Plot

8. Retell the story of the book.
9. Discuss whether or not the book is believable.
10. Write a new ending for the book.
11. Write a different resolution for the major conflict in the book.

Writing about Character

12. Discuss the major character in the book in terms of whether or not you would like to know that person.
13. Discuss a minor character in terms of whether or not you would like to meet that person.
14. Write a letter to a character in the book in which you react to something that character said or did.
15. Describe how a character's life-style would change if he or she lived in your community today.
16. Pretend you are the major character in the book and write a letter to a friend telling about some of the things that have happened to you recently.

Writing about Setting

17. Discuss an important place where the book is set in terms of whether or not you would like to visit that place and how you would feel about being there.
18. Write about how the book would change if it was set in your community.

Writing about Theme

19. Discuss one thing you think the book tells about people and their lives.
20. Discuss one new idea about people and their lives that you got from the book.
21. Disagree with one of the author's ideas or opinions.

Defending the Book

22. Write a nomination for the book for the School Book Award.
23. Write a letter to the local public library asking the librarians to order the book and explain why it should be purchased.
24. If the book is controversial, defend it, in writing, to your parents, teacher, or another adult (or student) who might object to the book.
25. Explain why certain scientific or historic facts discussed in the book are correct or incorrect.

Some of these writing response ideas were generated by Robert Small and his students at Virginia Tech in 1979.

introduce the books to the students. Typically, students select their top two choices, and teachers organize the groups based on these choices.

After students have selected books and been placed in groups, they have the rest of the class period to begin reading the book. Often the teacher will meet with each group to establish how far the students will read. Teachers can decide how much in-class reading time is appropriate. In basic or remedial classes it may be necessary to do most of the reading during class time.

While reading the book students keep a literature log. They can also use these logs to write questions and comments they want to share with their groups. A double-entry, modified "dialectical" journal (Berthoff, 1978) is an approach suggested by Deb Allai, a seventh-grade reading teacher. On one side of the page, students take notes on the book, and on the other they respond to their notes or to the book. Students use these logs during their literature study group discussions.

During discussions students are encouraged to discuss the books seriously and tie the books into their experiences, other books, movies, and events in history. The teacher participates as a knowledgeable, mature member of the group. Teachers, according to Gilles, can provide labels for the ideas students bring up. For example, when a student offers an example of irony teachers can tell them what it is called. These discussion techniques help all students become members of a community of readers.

How to Experience Books

If today's students are to be exposed to the accumulated knowledge of humankind, it is essential that they become involved with the concepts and ideas expressed on the pages of a variety of books by a variety of authors of all times. Unfortunately, many things seem to get in the way of reading and talking about books. It is junior prom week and the students are so excited that they can't sit still. Snow just started to fall outside the classroom window. The secretary in the school office is making announcements over the new public address system. How can the teacher keep the attention of the class with so many interruptions?

To minimize the effect of interruptions that occur daily in the classroom and to keep the students' minds on the lesson, teachers must find ways to make students feel more involved in what is going on in the classroom than in what is happening outside the window, in the hallway, or in the office. Most adolescents are actively involved in life: they drive, they work, they bungee jump, they listen and dance to ear-splitting music, they take risks, some of which are healthy, others of which could threaten their futures. For many of these active adolescents, books seem unexciting. If we are to turn them into readers, it is essential that we find ways to help them experience books. One good way to do this is by inviting students to respond to literature, as discussed above. Other ways to become actively involved with books are discussed in this section of the chapter.

Edgar Dale's well-known "cone of experience" (see Figure 11.2) shows that experiences vary from the direct to the very abstract. As the cone illustrates, the best starting point for meaningful learning is a lesson based on direct, purposeful experiences. Since creating direct, purposeful experiences is very difficult in most classrooms, the next best alternative is a lesson using contrived experiences.

According to Dale, the most difficult way to learn is through visual and verbal symbols. For most students who have yet to experience active involvement in the world of ideas, symbols are abstract and learning through them is passive. Therefore, the teacher must find ways to convert the visual and verbal symbols that emerge in reading and discussion into active learning experiences that are direct, contrived, or

Figure 11.2
Cone of Experience

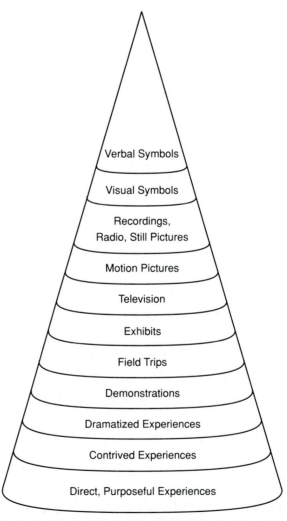

Verbal Symbols

Visual Symbols

Recordings,
Radio, Still Pictures

Motion Pictures

Television

Exhibits

Field Trips

Demonstrations

Dramatized Experiences

Contrived Experiences

Direct, Purposeful Experiences

Source: Figure from *Audiovisual Methods in Teaching,* Third Edition by Edgar Dale, copyright © 1969 by Holt, Rinehart and Winston, Inc., reprinted by permission of the publisher.

dramatized. Dale is not saying that symbolic learning is unimportant. On the contrary, symbolic learning is essential in our society. To be understood, however, symbolic abstractions must be based in the reality of the learner's life.

Abstract visual symbols in a book are more likely to come alive for students when the books that students experience relate to their needs and interests. For teenage readers, this type of book is often a young adult novel.

Direct, Purposeful Experiences

Creating a direct, purposeful experience in the classroom is difficult, and the results can never be guaranteed. The only way an experience can be direct and purposeful is if it touches the life of the student in a meaningful way. An experience can be meaningful for one student and not meaningful for another. However, there are several ways in which the teacher can create direct experiences for learners that relate to the books they are reading or being encouraged to read.

One possibility is a direct author hookup, either a classroom visit by an author or a phone conversation with the author. The first, of course, is more desirable, but it is also the most expensive and difficult to achieve. Students should be involved in the process of deciding which author they would personally like to meet. As Holden Caufield says in J. D. Salinger's *Catcher in the Rye*, "What really knocks me out is a book that when you're all done reading it, you wish the author that wrote it was a terrific friend of yours and you could call him up on the phone whenever you felt like it."

Most schools cannot pay much in the way of travel expenses and fees for authors to visit classrooms. However, there are several ways to arrange author visits even without extensive funding (see Appendix B).

In addition to careful planning of the visit, the most important element in the success of an author hookup is the preparation of the students. Many authors talk about visiting schools in which none of the students have read their books prior to the visit. Authors also complain that in some schools they have been told the students have read their books, but they learn while talking to the students that they have only seen a film or video based on the books. If students are ill-prepared for the author visit, the visit will have only limited educational value. Such lack of preparation also sends two wrong messages: that it is not necessary to prepare for meetings and that books are unimportant. (See Appendix B for ideas for preparing students for author interviews.)

After the author visit or phone hookup, follow up the event by encouraging students to continue reading the author's books. Suggest other books by authors who write on similar topics or in the same genre. Have students write original thank you notes to the author. Suggest that they try turning one of the author's books into a script. In small groups have students write new chapters for the author's book as they think the author would write them. Or they might develop a research project based on the topic, theme, period, or characters.

An author hookup provides an opportunity for the students to meet an author directly. Students can compare their ideas about the books with the author's ideas. A sense of kinship with the author develops. Students often learn something about the author that very few readers know. This direct, purposeful experience can spark a great deal of learning.

Contrived Experiences

When a direct experience is impossible for the teacher to arrange, contrived experiences can be developed to motivate the students to read or to encourage them to learn more about what they have been reading. A contrived experience is one in which the students participate but which is orchestrated by the teacher.

A good example of a contrived experience (see Figure 11.3) uses characters from six young adult books: *Gently Touch the Milkweed* (Hall), *The Pigman* (Zindel), *Swift Water* (Annixter), *Teacup Full of Roses* (Mathis), *After the First Death* (Cormier), and *Winning* (Brancato). The teacher presents an imaginary situation that challenges students to think critically about what they have read.

This particular contrived experience encourages students to read the novels carefully, understand the characters thoroughly, and reexamine the books for additional information about each character. Should we save Gary Madden, the quadriplegic with a good mind, or John Conlan, the healthy teenager who appears to be egocentric, or

Figure 11.3
A Contrived Experience for Stimulating Reader Response

WHO SHOULD SURVIVE?

Following a worldwide nuclear disaster, a few survivors gathered. The only available shelter from the effects of radiation has enough supplies to support only ten people. A slow death will be the likely fate of the others.

From a list of characters below, choose the ones that you believe should survive. Have one or more reasons for each of your decisions. Then compare your list of survivors with other members of your group, trying to agree on a single list of ten.

Think clearly and carefully. Your choices reflect much about you and may shape the world's future.

1. Janet Borofen	15. Ma Calloway
2. Vesta Borofen	16. Joe Brooks
3. Willard Borofen	17. Paul Brooks
4. Mel Makinick	18. Matti Brooks
5. Mary Pat Makinick	19. Ellie
6. Jay Zupin	20. Davey Brooks
7. Mr. Conlan	21. Miro
8. Mr. Pignati	22. Artkin
9. Lorrain Jensen	23. General Marchand
10. Mrs. Jensen	24. Ben Marchand
11. John Conlan	25. Kate Forrester
12. Bucky Calloway	26. Gary Madden
13. Bridie Mellott	27. Diane
14. Cam Calloway	28. Anne Treer

Key: 1–6, *Gently Touch the Milkweed;* 7–11, *The Pigman;* 12–15, *Swiftwater;* 16–20, *Teacup Full of Roses;* 21–25, *After the First Death;* 26–28, *Winning*

Source: W. Geiger Ellis, "Who Should Survive," unpublished classroom activity. Reprinted by permission of W. Geiger Ellis.

Cam Calloway, the kind-hearted dreamer? On what will we base our decision? Can we reach a consensus? A contrived experience can introduce a thematic unit, conclude a study of the works of a particular author, act as an introduction to a concept, illuminate a discussion topic, and encourage students to read books with new enthusiasm.

Dramatized Experiences

Viewing or participating in live dramatic performances is a good way to make learning more interesting for students. In most communities students have some access to amateur or professional theater productions. I have used local college presentations of *The Diary of Anne Frank, Romeo and Juliet, West Side Story,* and *Of Mice and Men* as turn-on events for thematic units. *The Diary of Anne Frank* was an excellent beginning for an interdisciplinary unit on the Holocaust. *Romeo and Juliet* and *West Side Story* were both used as jumping-off points for a unit on love. *Of Mice and Men* served as the introduction to a unit on violence. All of these productions helped students become involved in the theme before any reading assignments were made or any discussions conducted. The teacher who keeps abreast of upcoming theater productions has a wealth of dramatic experience on which to build units in many subject areas.

Students can also become involved in dramatic experiences in the classroom as teachers incorporate classroom drama into the teaching of reading, writing, and speaking. After students have read the young adult novel *The Night Swimmers* (Byars), Creighton Linder divides his eighth-grade English class into small groups to turn the chapters into a script that the class will produce. Mr. Linder uses the writing and producing activities to teach abstract language skills. The students carefully analyze the book's plot, theme, characters, and setting. Then they write and revise the play. During the revision they use many of the grammatical rules they have been studying and often consult grammar books, a thesaurus, and dictionaries. Each student participates in the oral reading during the initial readers' theater presentation of the script. In producing the play, the students consult texts and manuals on staging, costuming, lighting, and directing a stage production. Throughout the unit all of the students are reading, writing, and speaking.

The selection of an exceptionally well-written adolescent novel is particularly important in this unit. The students are able to relate to the story of Roy, Retta, and Johnny because the characters are young adults facing typical adolescent problems. On the other hand, the problems they deal with in their parentless home situation are far enough removed from their lives as students that they are able to act in the play without feeling they are revealing too much of themselves. The novel is also a good choice for teaching the literary techniques of plot, theme, character, and setting, which students will encounter in more mature literature later in the year. Similarly, the language of the characters in the book is easy for the eighth graders to turn into dialogue because it is similar to the English spoken in Mr. Linder's class.

Many of today's students are familiar with the world of television, video, and motion pictures. Producing videos and films based on young adult novels can provide students with reading, writing, speaking, and listening experiences and skills. Many young adult books have been made into films. Students can learn to script and produce their own videos by reading young adult books on which films have been based, watching these films in class, discussing how the narrative in the book differs from the script of the film, and examining the techniques script writers, producers, and directors use to make the books come to life.

Cheryl Christian of Conway, New Hampshire, suggests the following approach for preparing to dramatize part of a book:

> Frequently these days, when I bring a class a novel, such as Gloria Miklowitz's *After the Bomb*, I will direct the students in a number of acting exercises to get them personally, actively involved in the book. I introduce the book with exercises, add new ones for each chapter discussed as we get to it, and finally, have them develop their own reader's theatre production once we, as a class, have finished the book.
>
> Students first need to be introduced to the idea of improvisation. At this point, it's helpful to take students to a more theatrical setting. Our school does not have a theatre, but I have turned a lecture hall into a theatre. We've hung lights, and have developed a costume wardrobe, prop room, and scene dock. . . .
>
> To overcome their fears of "performing," I use a number of orientation exercises from Viola Spolin's *Improvisation for the Theatre*. . . . The idea behind improvisation is to have players work out a "problem," spontaneously and collectively. If everyone is working on a problem, then any self-consciousness can be easily removed. . . .
>
> Once the groundwork has been laid, I'm ready to begin with a specific book.
>
> I generally like to begin with the moods the book creates, and give the students a physical preview of what the book holds in store. [The technique of standing as] statues, a form of tableau, handles an introduction simply. It can be adapted easily to fit any piece of literature.
>
> Players are to organize themselves in groups of three, and cast themselves as A, B and C. . . . Players are to move into position and hold that position silently for a few moments. If we were to use *After the Bomb,* I would set up the following series of tableaux.
>
> 1. Player A is jealous of the relationship between Players B and C.
> 2. B refuses to help A and C.
> 3. C wants to run away from A and B.
> 4. A tries to help B and C, who are wounded.
> 5. B tries to protect A, while trying to scare away hostile C.
> 6. C regrets having to leave B and C.
> 7. A, B and C are all suspicious of each other.
>
> Once we have completed all of these scenes, we discuss how the students created each of them. . . .
>
> After the players have worked through a series of physical exercises, it is time for them to add voices. In [a decision-making exercise] players form in groups of three, again taking parts A, B and C. A is vomiting. B is emotionally weak. C is injured. They decide by playing the roles who gets the last of the water, and who goes out of the bomb shelter for help. All of the groups work simultaneously on this one. . . . We then discuss the exercise and the conclusions they have reached. . . . (Christian, 1989, pp. 6–7)

After doing these kinds of improvisational exercises, the next logical step is actually scripting part of a young adult book. Students doing their own scripting might be interested in hearing the experience of authors such as Gloria D. Miklowitz in the excerpt below.

--- ❖ **Between the Covers:** *Authors at Work* ❖ ---

GLORIA D. MIKLOWITZ: BOOKS INTO FILMS

About ten years ago I sat at a luncheon honoring children's book authors and illustrators and watched as Martin Tahse, the film producer, received the first award of its kind for his "Significant Contribution for the Interpretation of Literature Through Film." As I listened to the presenter explaining the kind of films Martin Tahse had made, my pulse raced. Could he be interested in any of *my* books for an after-school special?

. . . [Indeed he was, but the film of *Did You Hear What Happened to Andrea?* about a young girl who is raped, was almost not made.] Time went by and I assumed Martin Tahse had given up on filming my book. Then one day the phone rang. "Sorry, but ABC thinks the subject matter is too adult for its after-school audience."

"Oh," I said, surprised he had followed through. Not having really counted on it the disappointment was minimal.

"However—don't lose heart," he added. "I really want to do this book, and I'll keep trying."

. . . One day, perhaps 18 months after I met Mr. Tahse, I received another call from him. This time he said, "they have a new children's program director at ABC—Judy Price—a very gutsy lady. She's really excited about your book and has gone to bat with the administration to do it. They just gave her the go-ahead, so I'll draw up a contract."

. . . Months later, I received a copy of the script as a courtesy. I suggested a few changes—but don't believe they were incorporated.

. . . When filming started, Martin invited me to watch. . . . That day's experience . . . planted the seed for a new book. . . . I wondered what an actress's life was like, and the plot for *Love Story, Take Three* emerged.

[Sometime later another Miklowitz book *The Day the Senior Class Got Married* was being made into a film and she asked for the opportunity to write the screenplay. Although this was denied—as she explains, when an author sells the rights to her book for a film, she gives up all control—she was made a consultant on the film. She says of this experience:]

The scriptwriter invented two new characters, a "valley girl" type and her handsome, but dumb husband. On paper, the girl's dialogue struck me as dippy. "Tell me he's not seriously gorgeous. I'm gasping!" I objected, but was over-ruled. Also, the book's subplot was eliminated . . . because of time. The subplot added so much richness to the book that it broke my heart to see it left out. . . . I also had some problems with the script's ending because Garrick, the boyfriend, does an about face when he suggests he might go on to engineering school after all, making the viewer wonder if maybe Lori *should* have married him. . . .

I did not see the film until the day it was televised. I sat down before my TV set full of hope and fear. But it was wonderful! The settings were interesting; the characters well cast; the story involving. The dippy character Diane, who I didn't like on paper, became a nice contrast to the serious subject matter. . . .

[The screenwriter won the Humanitas Prize for his work, based on Miklowitz's book. Since the prize is awarded for the humanitarian values of the work Miklowitz was hurt that her book was not acknowledged as the basis for the script. When her next book, *The War between the Classes,* was contracted for film, she was signed to write the script. However, before her treatment, the first stage toward a final script, reached New York, another writer was working on the teleplay.]

Perhaps an author *is* inclined to stick closely to her own scenes and concepts. Why not? They work well in the book. . . . Authors tend to believe scriptwriters, adapting a book to film, need to show *their* originality and, so, change or add scenes that achieve the same as scenes written by the author. [The *War Between the Classes* won the Emmy for Best Children's Special in 1986.]

Looking back, and looking ahead to new books converted to film, I feel extremely fortunate. Without deliberate plans, my books and their themes have attracted the TV medium. It is gratifying to know that because of TV, my message can reach way beyond the several hundreds of thousands who might read a single title, to the millions of young people who watch TV, and, perhaps, turn the TV watchers on to books. ❖

From Gloria D. Miklowitz, "Books into Children's TV Specials," *ALAN Review,* Spring 1989, pp. 1–3. Reprinted with permission of Gloria D. Miklowitz.

Demonstrations

A demonstration, after the reading of a book or before reading, can make the book seem more real to the students. In Bill Cleaver and Vera Cleaver's book *Where the Lilies Bloom,* fourteen-year-old Mary Call Luther and her brother and sisters are able to support themselves after the death of their father by "wildcrafting." In spite of the Cleaver's description of this picking and digging of medicinal plants, the students in one tenth-grade sociology class studying Appalachian life were unable to understand wildcrafting. Their teacher, Christina Derrough, invited an Appalachian native who grew up with wildcrafting to her class. The guest, Ms. Chestnut, demonstrated the craft to the students. She brought with her many samples of plants, explained why roots were sometimes more valuable than flowers, showed some of the products made from the plants, and discussed the local uses for wildcrafted medicines. The students were fascinated and asked Ms. Derrough for more information. She contacted a local agriculture extension agent who provided the class with several booklets on the topic. Early in the spring it was agreed that Ms. Chestnut would return, and she and the students would go wildcrafting on the school nature trail.

The demonstration of the craft, initiated by reading a young adult novel, stimulated much learning in Ms. Derrough's class. The students developed a better understanding of Appalachian culture, gained an appreciation of the resourcefulness of the mountain people, and learned a valuable new skill.

Field Trips

Field trips are usually great fun and if well planned can be educational. The students in Henry Frame's history class were studying America during the period before colonization, and as part of the unit the students examined the life of Native Americans. As an introduction Mr. Frame read aloud from Joyce Rockwood's books *To Spoil the Sun* and *Long Man's Song.* (Rockwood's books are particularly appropriate in a history class because of their accurate presentation of Native Americans.) The first of these young adult historical novels is about a Cherokee girl and the impact European settlers had on her life and on the Cherokee nation; the second is about a Cherokee apprentice medicine man who attempts to save his sister's life.

Early in the unit Mr. Frame also planned a trip to Cherokee, North Carolina, to visit the Oconoluftee Indian Village and the Museum of the Cherokee. Before the trip he arranged for a Cherokee historian employed by the museum to meet with the students to discuss the Cherokee of the precolonization period and how the European settlers affected them. The day before the field trip the students wrote questions to ask the historian, primarily based on the books Mr. Frame had been reading. Since Mr. Frame had previously visited the field trip location, he was able to prepare a handout for the students with a series of questions about the Cherokee. He also allowed the students to choose from a list of assignments to be completed while in Cherokee. The assignments included these activities: sketch the Cherokee "houses" as they developed through the ages and are displayed in the village; briefly explain how the Cherokee hunted with the blowgun; sketch or make a typical ceremonial outfit worn by the Cherokee; explain why the Native Americans at most of the commercial establishments in the town of Cherokee are not wearing Cherokee clothing; assume that you experienced the Trail of Tears and write a letter to a friend who remains in North Carolina telling him or her about it; describe the Cherokee craft of basket weaving or try to make a basket using the technique; interview a Cherokee about life on the reservation today.

After the field trip, the visit to Cherokee was carefully discussed in the classroom, beginning with the answering of the questions assigned prior to the trip. During this discussion Mr. Frame and the students made a time line of the history of the Cherokee with plenty of space to add new information throughout the year. Other activities linked the field trip, the books, and information about different historic periods. One group of students made a time line of what was happening in Europe during the periods examined in the books. Another group created dioramas of a Cherokee town (houses, grounds, meeting place) during the historical periods discussed in *To Spoil the Sun* and *Long Man's Song*. A third group outlined a typical day in the life of a Cherokee girl in the sixteenth century, an American-European girl of the sixteenth century, and an aristocratic girl living in Europe during the same period. Another group of students outlined the life of fifteenth- and sixteenth-century Cherokee girls and compared them to a Cherokee girl during the time of the Trail of Tears and a Cherokee girl of today living on the Qualla Reservation.

The field trip was the basis for an effective unit of study in Mr. Frame's class, providing the impetus for a yearlong study of the Cherokee throughout U.S. history. By the end of the school year the time line begun the day after the field trip reached two-thirds of the way around the room and encompassed events from around the globe.

Exhibit

An exhibit based on a book or an exhibit of books is an an excellent way to get students interested in books or in a specific subject. If the students are involved in setting up the exhibit, they are more likely to become involved in the books or the topic. For example, students could be encouraged to select a visual way to tell about a book they have just completed. During a unit on alcoholism and drug addiction in Karen Lang's tenth-grade health class, one of the students elected to sketch two important scenes from Frank Bonham's *Cool Cat*. Another student shared a book by designing a jacket cover for Sandra Scoppetone's *The Late Great Me*. John Donovan's *I'll Get There. It Better Be Worth the Trip* was the source for a poster advertising the book. Costumes for the characters were sketched by one student for a dramatic presentation of Alice Childress's *A Hero Ain't Nothin' but a Sandwich*. Another student wrote a poem based on *That Was Then, This Is Now* by S. E. Hinton and mounted it for display. Using the anthology of poems compiled by Lee Bennett Hopkins and Sunna Rasch, *I Really Want to Feel Good about Myself: Poems by Former Drug Addicts,* a student elected to make a chart of facts learned from the poems in the book. Another student constructed a diorama of one of the scenes in Robert Lipsyte's *The Contender.*

After the projects were completed, Ms. Lang set aside a table and bulletin board in the room to display the projects as an exhibit about books on drug addiction and alcoholism. Next to the exhibit she placed a book rack with paperback books that relate to the exhibit. After examining the books and projects displayed, the students were encouraged to select a book of their choice to read as they continued the unit.

Exhibits take very little time to create and are an excellent way to get students into books. Display techniques such as carousel book racks, which allow books to be displayed with their jackets showing, or racks constructed from pegboard and small metal shelves that place books in easy reach, increase the number of circulations from the classroom library. Changing exhibits of sales posters or jacket covers, often available free from publishers, will also attract students to the new books on the classroom display rack.

In each of Janice William's eighth-grade English classes two students per month are in charge of the reading corner. As part of their responsibility they unpack and catalogue the new paperbacks that arrive, watch the mail for new posters, display information about books that have recently appeared on the shelves, distribute material that comes from the book club to which the class belongs, and select and display student projects related to the books. Ms. Williams's classroom is a constantly changing exhibit about books and authors. It is a rare student in Ms. Williams's class who walks the halls without carrying a paperback.

School Bookstores as Exhibits

In 1985 in Great Britain, approximately 7,000 schools had bookstores that stocked not only pencils and notebooks but books. According to John Mason, Marketing Manager for Trade Books at Scholastic Publishers, that means one in every six schools in the country had a bookstore. The phenomenon of school bookstores began in 1962 when high school English teacher Peter Kennerly conducted a survey of his students' reading habits and found that a frighteningly large proportion of his students had "given up reading" by the upper grades. To help counteract this, Kennerly, like many teachers, had a paperback library in his classroom and read to his students aloud. His enthusiasm for books began to rub off on his students. Because there was not a bookstore in their immediate neighborhood, Kennerly decided to start one in the school. The idea caught on and by the mid-1970s publishers, teacher associations, and booksellers were recognizing that school bookstores had become an important phenomenon in education. The School Bookshop Association was born to provide central support and guidance.

John Mason suggests that school bookstores are needed if we are to improve adult literacy in the United States (in 1985, 26 million were functionally illiterate, 46 million marginally literate). In 1985 a book industry study showed that readers under the age of 21 had declined from 75 percent in 1978 to 63 percent in 1983. According to Mason, we must give adolescents easy access to books and turn them into consumers of books if we are to improve the U.S. rank of 49th in literacy.

The organization of a school bookstore need not be complicated. A school can begin by sponsoring a bookfair, a one- or several-day event that can be set up by a local book distributor. Usually, the school benefits from some of the profits of the sale, and the students benefit from discounted prices on paperback books selected to meet their needs and interests. Book clubs, sponsored by some publishers, can also get books into the hands of students. Typically book clubs send catalogs and order forms to classes of students once every month. Students can order from the annotated book lists in these catalogs, and the books are sent to the classroom and distributed by the teacher. Usually the school benefits by receiving bonus books if a certain number of books are purchased by the students. Often teachers can arrange for students who receive free or reduced-cost lunches to purchase books using funds provided through special parent- or community-sponsored projects.

Bookstores have a larger impact than bookfairs and book clubs because they allow students to browse through books for a longer period of time, display books in ways that attract student attention, and stock books geared to the specific student needs and interests. Bookstores can also provide an ongoing fund-raising project for the school, be staffed by students, and increase parent and adult volunteer involvement in the school. A school bookstore, for example, could be run by a group of senior volunteers from a retirement center. (For ideas on how to organize a school bookstore, see Appendix C.)

Television

Many teachers complain that television is one of the causes of students' inability to get involved in the learning process. According to many researchers, television encourages passive viewing rather than active participation. The classroom teacher, however, can use television to make books and authors come to life for students.

There is no doubt that children watch a great deal of television. A. C. Neilsen, the television rating group, found that the average child of elementary school age watches approximately twenty-five hours of television per week or four to six hours per day. This means that upon entering high school, a student will have spent approximately 11,000 hours in the classroom and 15,000 in front of the television set.

A landmark study of television and reading found that when junior high school students were given a choice of reading books connected with television programs or books not connected with programs, over two-thirds selected television-related books (Hamilton, 1976). A similar study, conducted in 1978 in Virginia, found that 89 percent of the students surveyed were influenced to read a book by at least one television program. Other studies have found that television was more effective in increasing the reading of books related to television programs than teachers, parents, or peers.

The television and publishing industries have begun to capitalize on the information gained from these studies by producing tie-ins, books and television shows that are related. The tie-ins take several different forms: Television shows or movies based on books, books based on television scripts, books about celebrities or special programs, books about the development of a television series, books about the subjects treated in television programming, and actual scripts of television shows.

All the major broadcast networks, the Public Broadcasting System, and cable networks are involved in book–television tie-in programs. Most school libraries receive listings of educational and tie-in television programming from the major networks. These can be duplicated for distribution to teachers, displayed on a library bulletin board for teachers, or displayed in the section of the library devoted to educational materials. Most networks publish these on a monthly basis and issue them several weeks prior to airing. In addition, most publicity departments of publishers send out periodic newsletters giving information about books that have been made into television movies. Many libraries regularly receive these newsletters. Teachers can easily be placed on mailing lists by contacting the publishers (addresses are provided in Appendix F). Of course, teachers will need to check local listings for actual times of broadcast. Large numbers of young adult novels have been made into television movies both for the young adult and general audience. Many of these are now available on videotapes that can be rented or purchased for classroom use.

Teachers can encourage active television viewing by creating a bulletin board on which notices of future television shows of educational value are posted. Next to the bulletin board, reading material related to the show can be displayed. Books related to television or news media events such as major elections, the Olympics, or other major sports or news events can be placed on the table. In science and social studies classrooms, teachers can place books that relate to science and nature shows or historical documentaries. Books about television and television personalities (including sports figures) can be part of the display.

Films and Other Audiovisual Media

The videotape has made films more accessible in the classroom than ever before. Although the wide screen of motion pictures is the best way to view films crafted for theaters, they can be brought into the classroom on 16-mm film or on videotape. Students can experience film in much the same way as television. (Prior to copying films or television programs off the airwaves or using rental films in the classroom, teachers should familiarize themselves with copyright laws. These materials can be used in the classroom, but their use is restricted by law and teachers have been sued for abuse of those laws. Most schools have copies or summaries of these laws, which are often printed in teacher handbooks.) A film is particularly useful when the teacher arranges for students to participate actively in the viewing of the film through creative activities before and after the film showing. These activities must involve the student with the subject of the film.

Thousands of good films are available for classroom use in all subject areas. Most schools have access to free film-lending libraries. School librarians can help teachers locate these sources and obtain the films, but most films must be ordered several months in advance to ensure that the show date occurs at the right point in the instructional unit. Other difficulties in using films include failure of films to arrive on expected dates, arrival and return dates that do not permit teacher preview (a very dangerous situation), and equipment failure. Nevertheless, films or videotapes of films are an excellent way to assist students in understanding difficult concepts and ideas. They also help bring books to life for students who are often more comfortable with visual media than with print media.

While it is impossible to mention all of the films that are particularly useful in units that use adolescent literature, some films deserve particular attention. The following young adult books have been made into feature-length films:

- *Sounder* by William H. Armstrong. (Directed by Martin Ritt. Screenplay by John Alonzo.)
- *The Chocolate War* by Robert Cormier. (Directed by and screenplay by Keith Gordon.)
- *I Am the Cheese* by Robert Cormier. (Directed by Robert Jiras. Screenplay by Robert Jiras and David Lange.)
- *Ordinary People* by Judith Guest. (Directed by Robert Redford. Screenplay by Alvin Sargent.)
- *The Outsiders* by S. E. Hinton. (Screenplay by Kathleen Rowell. Directed by Francis Ford Coppola.)
- *That Was Then, This Is Now* by S. E. Hinton. (Directed by Christopher Cain. Screenplay by Emilio Estevez, who also stars.)
- *Tex* by S. E. Hinton. (Directed by Tim Hunter. Screenplay by Charlie Haas and Hunter.)
- *Are You in the House Alone?* by Richard Peck. (Two-hour television movie made by CBS-TV. Screenplay by Judith Parker.)
- *The Ghost Belonged to Me* by Richard Peck. (Ninety-four minute film retitled *Child of Glass* by Walt Disney Productions.)
- *Father Figure* by Richard Peck. (Screenplay by William Hanley. Ninety-five-minute CBS-TV television movie.)

Every year the Young Adults Committee of the Young Adult Services Division of the American Library Association selects films to recommend for use in "programs planned to be of interest to young adults." The committee's pamphlet offers annotations on the content of each film, information about the film's producer, and listings of the distributors and price. (See Chapter 14 for how to order films from the American Library Association.)

Other nonprint media can motivate students to read and introduce them to authors and books. Videocassettes of author interviews, for example, are available in Temple University's Profiles in Literature series. The series features many young adult authors, such as Katherine Paterson, Scott O'Dell, Madeleine L'Engle, Kristin Hunter, Beverly Cleary, Judy Blume, Jean Craighead George, and others, who discuss their books, their lives, and their writing.

Another series that helps students learn more about authors and their books is Miller-Brody's filmstrip and audiocassette series Meet the Newbery Author. The filmstrips show pictures of the authors as the authors speak about themselves, their books, and the art of writing on cassette. Also available in this series are audiocassettes and filmstrips depicting key action sequences from Newbery Award–winning books. Teacher guides and still pictures are included along with copies of the books. Teachers can use this series in many different ways and incorporate a variety of different reading, writing, and literature activities. The sound filmstrips would be viewed by the class or made available in learning centers and book nooks for individual use.

The Center for the Humanities produces sound slide shows. Many of the productions use young adult literature, poetry, and music. *I Couldn't Put It Down: Hooked on Reading*, based on six adolescent novels, is designed to encourage reluctant readers to get into books.

A number of media distribution companies have extensive offerings related to young adult literature. Weston Woods offers films, recordings, filmstrips, cassettes, and other multimedia items. Caedmon produces records of readings of young adult books, classic children's books, and modern and classic literature. Some of the young adult authors available on Caedmon records are Norma Klein, Roald Dahl, Jean Craighead George, C. S. Lewis, Isaac Asimov, Ursula LeGuin, and Anne McCaffrey. Many of the young adult television specials as well as feature-length films of young adult novels are available for rent or purchase from Learning Corporation of America. Films based on books by authors such as Betty Bates, M. E. Kerr, Francine Pascal, Marion Dane Bauer, Harry Mazer, Mildred Lee, Maia Wojciechowska, Louise Fitzhugh, and Thomas Thompson are available in thirty-minute segments. Feature-length films based on books by Robert Cormier, S. E. Hinton, Gale Sayers, Ernest Gaines, John Gunther, Thomas Thompson, Margaret Craven, Maya Angelou, Mildred Taylor, Bette Greene, and others are also available for classroom use.

An increasing number of books are available as interactive computer programs for adolescents. According to Jane Ann Zaharias:

> Text-based adventures or interactive fiction soft-ware programs require the user to assume a character's identity and interact with text in a very personal way. Like readers of what have come to be known as pick-a-path books, adventure game players create stories by determining what actions to take at various "decision" points within the program. Unlike readers of pick-a-path books, however, interactive fiction software enthusiasts are not limited to three or four options in developing a plot. In fact, they can do almost anything that occurs to them—providing, of course, that the writer and programmer have anticipated the action. For example, by typing commands on their computer's keyboard, players may pick up, examine and discard objects; move from room to room; and attack or befriend other characters. In addition, by issuing appropriate commands, players can generally question the people they meet in any given scene within a story. Based on its analysis of instructions received, the computer responds by bringing up the next scene in a story, altering the existing scene to fit the actions taken by the user or providing a response on the part of one of the story's characters. (1986, p. 58)

Zaharias suggests that interactive computer fiction fosters both critical reading and problem-solving skills in students who are already hooked on computers. Teachers can also use such software to encourage writing. Students who can create their own stories on computers can then transfer them to paper. For example, students could take plots they have created and flesh them out with dialogue and description. According to Zaharias, "Interactive fiction is normally written in second person, present tense. In this respect, it closely resembles drama" (p. 61). Thus, another possibility might be for students to create scripts from the software plots. Students who already have computer programming skills might also be able to create their own interactive fiction using a young adult novel as the model for their program.

Sharing Books

Many of the response techniques discussed earlier in the chapter encourage students to share books with each other. By sharing books students will not only become familiar with far more books and authors than they can read, but they may discover some new books or authors they want to read themselves. In addition, sharing techniques allow teachers to incorporate the books in class activities even if all students have not independently read them.

Reading Aloud

One excellent way to involve all students in reading, learning, and thinking is by reading aloud to them. Reading aloud is an art that has been all but lost with the predominance of television. For generations families used the evening hours as a time to gather together and read aloud. The shared experience was entertaining, educational, motivational, and therapeutic. Jim Trelease in his popular book *The Read-Aloud Handbook* encourages parents of adolescents to continue reading aloud as a family tradition.

Many people think that reading aloud is only for small children, that the elementary classroom is the last place in which books can legitimately be read aloud. But reading aloud continues to be wonderful entertainment. The age of the audience doesn't matter; all listeners can be captivated by the spoken word. Each listener pictures the story as he or she pleases. Each story fulfills a different need for each individual. A fantasy takes the listener to new and strange worlds. A mystery keeps students on the edge of their seats, groaning at the end of each day's chapter, begging the teacher to continue reading, and happily anticipating the reading time during the next class. Historical fiction illuminates the human side of history. As the teacher reads *The Witch of Blackbird Pond* by Elizabeth George Speare, the students question the motives of the New England Puritans. They wonder why the citizens of Wethersfield, Connecticut, are so unaccepting of Hannah, the "witch." They fear for the welfare of Kit, the niece from Barbados. And they begin to question their own motives and lack of acceptance of others different from themselves.

Reading humorous books aloud produces outbursts of laughter and eager anticipation of the next insane episode, as in *How to Eat Fried Worms* by Thomas Rockwell. Sad books bring students together as they empathize with the character's plight. The slow, agonizing death of Johnny Gunther in *Death Be Not Proud* often brings tears to the eyes of the toughest boy in the class. Reading aloud gives students and teacher the opportunity to share reactions even if they are never discussed. Reading aloud is superb, shared entertainment. Here are some other reasons to read aloud:

1. Reading aloud is educational.
2. Students' reading skills are improved through reading aloud.
3. Students' writing skills are improved as a result of the read-aloud sessions.
4. Reading aloud improves students' listening skills.
5. Students' thinking skills are improved by reading aloud.

6. Reading aloud is motivational.
7. Reading aloud is therapeutic for the class, the teacher, and the individual student.

Reading aloud can be a daily event at any grade level. It allows the teacher to share exceptional books with students and gives the students something to anticipate each day. It helps develop a sense of community and sets a comfortable atmosphere for learning. It also allows students to hear well-written English, encourages equal participation, and motivates the students to read more books by the same author or on the same theme. Reading aloud can be the basis for the day's lesson.

There is probably no easier and, at the same time, no more useful teaching method than reading aloud. Your students are likely to remember you for it and thank you for introducing them to books they might not have read. I had a poignant experience one day several years ago that I will always remember as one of those rewarding moments in my teaching career. I had been reading young adult novels to my university students for several years. I often read *Killing Mr. Griffin* (Duncan) in the English methods course I taught. I read many different books in my adolescent literature class. One day, after a particularly difficult advising session with a student, I opened my mail. I had received a letter from a faculty member I had never met at another university. The letter read in part:

> I just had to write to you to tell you this. I was one of the readers of student papers [on a national standardized exam]. The students were to write on a teaching method they had experienced that was meaningful to them. I read one by a student who talked about being read aloud to in a university class. I was moved by it. And, then, I read another one. A few papers later there was another. And, in this one the student named the professor, you, and the university. I'm sure they won't tell you how much your reading influenced them, so I just had to.

The teacher who plans to institute a reading-aloud program should look at the reading as a vital part of the daily lesson. The book selected could be one that fits the subject being studied. For example, students studying the early settlement of this country could begin each day with a reading selection from *Constance* by Patricia Clapp. Students studying humans' reliance on nature could begin each day with a chapter from a book by Jean Craighead George. Or the book could be one that introduces the wide world of literature. For instance, a book like Richard Peck's *Ghosts I Have Been* could be used to introduce the world of mystery and fantasy.

The book should also be one that will interest students and hold their attention. Most young people are attracted to books with action, suspense, and a lot of dialogue. Therefore, the teacher may want to begin reading aloud to the students from a suspenseful novel. Then, as the students develop their listening skills, a variety of moods and genres can be incorporated. Each book fills a different need for students. Fantasy and science fiction stretch their imagination. Humor gives the class an opportunity to laugh together. Sad books give them a chance to share emotions that are rarely revealed in public. Figure 11.4 lists some helpful hints for reading aloud to a class.

Storytelling

Storytelling has many of the same attributes as reading aloud and several additional benefits. Like reading aloud, storytelling is entertaining, educational, motivational, and therapeutic. Storytelling is an event enjoyed by people of all ages. In some parts of the country, such as the mountains of North Carolina and Tennessee, storytelling continues to be a means of entertainment and a way to communicate knowledge and folklore. A colorful, oral literary tradition has been passed down from generation to generation. In such sections of the country storytelling has never died. In recent years, however, the art of storytelling has experienced a rebirth nationally and is gaining a new, active following. (The National Association for the Preservation and Perpetuation of Storytelling is based in Jonesborough, Tennessee. The association presents a storytelling conference each June and sponsors a storytelling festival in October. The association also maintains a National Storytelling Resource Center, which contains a

Figure 11.4
Helpful Hints for Reading Aloud

1. Select a book that appeals to you, not a book selected by a friend or a colleague. Be sure the book can be divided into easily read daily sections. As Jim Trelease (1989) advises, "Don't read stories that you don't enjoy yourself. Your dislike will show in the reading, and that defeats your purpose."

2. Be thoroughly familiar with the book. Look up the pronunciation and definition of unfamiliar words.

3. Practice reading aloud. Be aware of phrasing. Practice ending each sentence without raising or dropping your voice. Practice looking up from time to time, and looking at a different person each time.

4. Never change words to simplify the text. However, dropping "he said" and "she said" in long segments of conversation may improve the movement of the dialogue. If you feel the book contains objectionable words, either select a different book or tell the students you have made substitutions for these words. Be sure any changes you make do not affect the mood of the story or the intent of the author.

5. Try to create a signal that indicates that the reading is about to begin. For example, pull an easy chair or stool to the front of the room and invite the students to gather their chairs around you.

6. Be sure the students are comfortable and can see and be seen by you, the reader. It is best to sit with a blank wall or curtain behind you; sitting in front of a window causes glare for the listeners.

7. Try to minimize classroom interruptions. Do not read at the end of class if announcements are always given at that time. Put a sign on the door that announces, "Reading aloud. Do not interrupt."

8. Set aside a time each day for reading aloud. Do not confine reading to this time, however. Read as often as is possible and practical.

9. When possible, duplicate sections of the book for take-home reading, or have available other books by the same author or on the same theme.

resource library and an archive of audio and video recordings. For more information about the association and the art of storytelling, write to NAPPS.)

The story selected by the storyteller might come from the oral literary tradition of the region in which the story is being told (in recent years many of these tales have been collected and made into anthologies that are usually available in local libraries), or it could take the form of a children's book, a poem, a song, or a section of a young adult book. One of the great benefits of storytelling is that any story can be told to any age group. A storyteller need not limit the audience to the age group for which the work was originally written. Recently, for example, I attended a storytelling session given for 120 adults by Barbara Freeman and Connie Regan-Blake (The Folktellers), two well-known storytellers who work in tandem. They told the story of Maurice Sendak's *Where the Wild Things Are.* Even though the book was written for very young readers, it had great appeal to the adult audience when related orally, with the storytellers' words providing the pictures. With storytelling listeners are able to experience a variety of different stories that they would be unlikely to discover or enjoy in other media.

Storytelling actively involves the listener in the story. The storyteller may involve the audience by asking listeners to repeat a refrain or make a sound that creates a special effect for the story, but in all cases the listener is actively involved through imagining what the storyteller is describing and dramatizing. The storyteller brings the listener into the story through hand gestures, voice, and eye contact. Being able to maintain eye contact is one of the advantages of storytelling over reading aloud. As the storyteller's eyes meet the eyes of the listener, the listener becomes a part of the story.

Learning to Tell a Story in the Classroom   Many people are afraid to attempt to tell a story without using the book as a crutch. It is true that telling a story is more difficult than reading orally from a book, but the benefits to both the listeners and the teller make it worthwhile. Telling a story well, like reading a book well, takes practice. Caroline Feller Bauer, in her *Handbook for Storytellers,* says that in her experience as a teacher of storytelling, "almost everyone who takes the time to learn [a story] can become a competent storyteller" (1977, p. 48).

The key to learning to tell a story competently is taking the time to learn the story. The time invested need not be great if the novice storyteller does not worry about creating a large repertoire. As Barbara Freeman and Connie Regan-Blake remarked in a storytelling workshop, "If you learn only one story a year, think how many you will know by the time you are eighty." Figure 11.5 gives some helpful hints for learning a story you will be telling out loud.

Caroline Feller Bauer has identified several common faults of beginning storytellers. She suggests that the storyteller have a friend listen to a rehearsal of the story for these faults: speaking too rapidly or too slowly, speaking too softly, speaking with too high a pitch, failing to make eye contact, and using distracting gestures. Once these faults have been noted, the storyteller's practice sessions can be directed toward correcting them.

Once you have learned the story, you can prepare to tell it to an audience. The first thing to do is be sure that the location in which the story will be told is comfortable for you and your listeners. As in oral reading, the storyteller should be able to see and be seen by the audience. Choose a location away from windows and doors. The best backdrop is a solid wall or curtain. If possible, the entrance should be behind the audience so they will not be disturbed if someone enters the room. As in reading aloud, placing a sign on the door ("Storytelling in Progress. Do Not Disturb.") is a good idea. Before the storytelling session the storyteller should sit where the audience will sit to test the room. Telling a story outdoors may seem romantic, but it can be disastrous, particularly for the beginning storyteller. All teachers know what the appearance of a bee can do to the attention of a class. Imagine what will happen if a neighborhood dog decides to join the group.

It is a good idea to establish a signal that shows that storytelling is about to begin. The signal could be the same one you use for oral reading. You may want to incorporate storytelling into your reading sessions, for the effect on students when

Figure 11.5
Helpful Hints for Learning a Story

1. Select a story you would like to learn. Read several stories, wait for several days to a week, and choose the story that keeps coming to mind. As Ruth Sawyer points out in *The Way of the Storyteller,* (1976), be sure you really love the story you plan to learn. It is probably a good idea to buy the book from which you plan to learn a story so you can truly make that story your own.

2. Identify separate sequences of action into which the plot can be divided. (When I am learning a new story, I actually list each bit of action on separate note cards that I use as I learn the story.) Learn these segments of action in order. You do not need to memorize the entire story. Practice saying what needs to be said in the first unit of action to move the listener on to the next action, and so on.

3. Identify sections of the story that must be memorized. These sections include segments in which the author's words contribute to the mood of the story or repeat a refrain, and passages that have special beauty, rhyme, rhythm, or other importance in the narrative. For the novice storyteller, choosing a story with only a few passages for memorization is probably best.

4. Practice telling the story. Incorporate the memorized sections into the action sequence you have already practiced. Rehearse the story aloud in a place where you feel comfortable so you become accustomed to the sound of your own voice. Try to tell the story at least twice a day until you can do it without error. If you confuse the action or forget the lines you have memorized, stop your practice and come back to it later. Connie Regan-Blake and Barbara Freeman say that "a gift you can give to your listeners is knowing the story so well that you are comfortable telling it." You can't be comfortable telling a story if you are not enjoying the process.

5. Record your progress. After you feel secure telling the story, put it on tape. Don't listen to it immediately because you have been too involved in the process to evaluate the performance objectively. John Warren Stewig (1978, pp. 341–42) suggests asking these questions as you listen to the tape: (1) What parts of the story need more practice to achieve greater fluency? (2) What parts of the story need to be changed to make them more effective? (3) Would different words better evoke the mood set by the author? (4) Should I change my pitch, stress, pauses or tempo for greater effectiveness?

you have been reading a section from a book and suddenly put it down and begin telling the story is dramatic. Some good signals include pulling forward a special chair, briefly playing a musical instrument, or even lighting a candle.

It is important for the storyteller to set the mood for the story. "The introduction to a single story or program as a whole often sets the mood of the entire period. A question such as "How many of you enjoy being scared out of your wits?" suggests a suspense or ghost story, and in effect you have set the mood that will elicit a humorous response to whatever you tell" (Bauer 1977, p. 35). An introduction to a story also gives listeners an opportunity to get accustomed to your voice. Thus, the introduction should serve three purposes: setting the mood, getting the audience involved, and helping the listeners get used to listening to you.

As you tell the story, you can draw the audience into the story by developing a one-to-one relationship through eye contact, by holding out your hand(s) toward the audience and slowly pulling them back in toward your body, and by using your voice to command the listeners' attention. The storyteller does not act out the story, but rather relates it. When you tell a story you are yourself, not an actor playing the role of a character in the story.

Props can enhance your story if they are used judiciously. A single prop to represent a single character or refrain that occurs throughout the story can be effective. Props can be good transitional tools to use with younger students. Many students are not used to listening without visual cues. A prop helps build a bridge between a story told with pictures and a story told without pictures. If props are used, they should be carefully worked into the practice sessions; they are as important to the story as presenting the correct action sequence.

After the story has been told, be sure to show the listeners the book from which it is taken and acknowledge the author. This is a good way to encourage students to read the complete book or find other books by the same author or on the same theme. Try to have such books available in the classroom at the time of the storytelling session.

Table 11.1 lists some young adult books that have worked well in storytelling sessions. Owing to their subject matter, not all of the books are appropriate for all ages. However, limiting certain books to a single age group defeats one of the major advantages of storytelling. The teacher is cautioned to know the maturity level of the students and the precise content of the book before selecting a book for storytelling.

The storytelling program, whether it is one or several stories long, should end with a signal linked to the one chosen at the beginning: the putting away of the chair, a final chord on the guitar, or the blowing out of the candle.

Teaching Students to Tell Stories   Students can become involved in the storytelling process by telling stories or giving book talks. Teaching students to tell stories is an excellent motivator for reading and writing. Author Sue Alexander points out that telling stories was important to her development as a writer:

> I'll tell you how I began writing stories. . . . I was the smallest person in my class and I was very clumsy. I couldn't walk down the hall without tripping over my own feet. Consequently, the kids in my class didn't want to play with me at recess time because I was so clumsy I ruined the games; so I sat by myself. Then one day I was very sick and tired of

Table 11.1
Young Adult Books That Work Well in Storytelling Sessions

Book	Author
Watership Down	Richard Adams
The Wolves of Willoughby Chase	Joan Aiken
Bugs in Your Ears	Betty Bates
Freckle Juice	Judy Blume
Superfudge	
Tales of a Fourth Grade Nothing	
Blinded by the Light	Robin Brancato
Toby, Granny and George	Robbie Branscum
Toby Alone	
Toby and Johnny Joe	
Beezus and Ramona	Beverly Cleary
Ramona the Pest	
Henry and the Clubhouse	
Henry and the Paper Route	
The Dark Is Rising	Susan Cooper
Charlie and the Chocolate Factory	Roald Dahl
The Cat Ate My Gymsuit	Paula Danziger
Down a Dark Hall	Lois Duncan
Killing Mr. Griffin	
Incident at Hawk's Hill	Allan Eckert
Julie of the Wolves	Jean Craighead George
The Planet of Junior Brown	Virginia Hamilton
Mama	Lee Bennett Hopkins
Moon and Me	Hadley Irwin
We Are Mesquakie; We Are One	
A Wrinkle in Time	Madeleine L'Engle
One Fat Summer	Robert Lipsyte
Ox: The Story of a Kid at the Top	John Ney
The Black Pearl	Scott O'Dell
Bridge to Terabithia	Katherine Paterson
The Great Gilly Hopkins	
The Ghost Belonged to Me	Richard Peck
Soup	Robert Newton Peck
Soup and Me	
The Resident Witch	Marian T. Place
How to Eat Fried Worms	Thomas Rockwell
Words by Heart	Ouida Sebestyen
Who Put That Hair in My Toothbrush	Jerry Spinelli
The Cay	Theodore Taylor
Timothy of the Cay	
The Weirdo	
The Loner	Ester Wier

Source: Compiled and tested by the adolescent literature classes of the University of North Carolina, Asheville.

sitting by myself. There was a boy who wasn't playing either, and I said, "Come on; I'll tell you a story." And I began to tell a story that I made up as I went along. Before I was finished with the story, all the rest of the class had come to listen. It made me feel good and I figured, this is the way I'm going to have company every recess. (in Weiss, 1979, p. 4)

Older students can find a purpose in their reading by preparing and telling stories to younger children. In the early stages of learning the storytelling technique, the student reads aloud a passage or an entire book to young children. This is a painless way of practicing oral reading and speaking skills. Once proficient in reading aloud to an audience, the student can then be encouraged to read part of the story and then put the book down and tell the next part of the story. The same techniques that teacher uses to learn a story can be taught to students. Eventually the student can try learning an entire story to tell the children. It is essential to give students the opportunity to practice their skills, so teachers should arrange for students to tell their stories in an elementary school or preschool classroom. Students should know the age group with which they will be working before they select a story. Figure 11.6 lists some other activities that will encourage students to tell stories.

Giving a Book Talk   An interesting storytelling technique that combines reading aloud and telling stories is the book talk. A book talk is a talk usually based on four or five books that have a common theme or author. This technique is particularly useful in the secondary classroom where the teacher wants to encourage students to read one or more books with the same theme or author.

In Barbara Soileau's English classroom, for example, the students were investigating the theme "Love and Infatuation: Discovering the Difference." Ms. Soileau's book talk presents five books: *Gentlehands* (Kerr), *Love Is Like Peanuts* (Bates), *The Great Gatsby* (Fitzgerald), *Summer of My German Soldier* (Greene), and *Toby and Johnny Joe* (Branscum). The book talk includes short readings from each book as well as storytelling. After the talk students are asked to select the book that is most interesting to them. They are given five minutes to begin reading the book. Then they have the opportunity to exchange the book they originally selected for another book. This process continues until each student has settled on a book he or she is interested in reading.

Students Sharing Books with Students

One drawback of the traditional book report is that the student shares the book only with the teacher. One of the most effective ways to motivate a student to read is to get a peer to do the motivating. Students motivate other students to read a book by sharing it with them in a way that makes the book seem interesting to students of similar interests.

The teacher motivates students to read by sharing books through reading aloud, storytelling, and book talks. How can the teacher encourage students to do the same sharing?

One way is to make sharing a common event in the classroom. Gloria Deaton, an English teacher, conducts a book-sharing discussion every Wednesday. On that day the students share what they have been reading. Since her class is designed thematically, most of the books discussed relate to a certain theme. Ms. Deaton believes that literature becomes exciting to students when they have a chance to respond to it and become involved in it. She thus deems it essential that the teacher help students choose books that relate to their interests and are on their reading level. If the book does not interest the student, or if it is too hard or too easy to read, the student will

Figure 11.6
Activities for Encouraging Students to Tell Stories

1. *Forming Groups*
   Divide the class into five groups. Have each group select a story to learn to tell, and work together to practice telling the story and to critique each other. Then rearrange the students into five new groups comprised of one member from each of the previous groups. Each student in the new group will then tell the story he or she learned. In that way, each student learns one story and hears four others.

2. *Pass It Along*
   Working in pairs, one person tells a story to a partner. The partner then retells the story varying the emotion, the language, the culture, the setting, and the time of the story.

3. *Story Grammar*
   As the students hear, learn, and practice storytelling they will develop an awareness of story grammar, for example, the use of "three's" in stories from Europe, such as three brothers, sisters, bears, pigs, attempts to solve the problem, etc. Students can discover that most folktales involve a hero or heroine with a problem and that he or she has to leave home to find a solution to the problem. Generally, the hero or heroine has three tries or three tasks to complete before the ending of the story.

4. *Video Tape*
   Video tape each student telling a story. These tapes can be used for self-evaluation or to share with other groups.

5. *Story Mapping*
   Have students practice story mapping or webbing. The name of the story is at the center and then the sequence of events are mapped around it.

6. *Compare/Contrast*
   Encourage the students to compare and contrast how the stories they hear and tell are alike and how they are different.

7. *Continue the Story*
   Have the students select a story to use. One student starts the story and then at some selected signal (a bell, a knot in a soft rope, a new color of yarn in a ball of knotted yarn, or the storyteller breaks off and points to the next person), the next person continues the story until the next signal is given.

8. *Story and Art*
   Have the students illustrate stories they have heard. These illustrations can be put together into class books or made into media productions.

9. *Folksongs*
   Have the students make up new verses to well-known folksongs. Have the students take some current event, tell it in story form, and then put it to the tune of some familiar folksong.

From Norma J. Livo, "Using Storytelling to Enhance the Literature Program," *ALAN Review*, Spring 1990, pp. 42–44. Reprinted with permission of Norma J. Livo.

have difficulty responding in a meaningful way. Therefore, Ms. Deaton incorporates many young adult books into her curriculum. It is not unusual in her class to find one student reading both a young adult novel and a classic at the same time. Ms. Deaton claims that reading begets reading, and that the adolescent who reads is likely to read a wide variety of books. If students are allowed to choose their own books, they are usually willing and able to share them with other students.

The students in Ms. Deaton's class work in small groups to discuss the book they have all read. Five to seven books are often being read in the class at any one time. The students are instructed to begin their small-group discussions with general impressions of the plot and the characters. One of the students in each group acts as a recorder and writes down a few key words in each student's response. After approximately ten minutes of these preliminary responses, the recorder summarizes briefly what each student has said. The group members are instructed to look for any disagreement in their responses and examine them for a cumulative change in attitude toward the book. For example, does one student's response seem to influence the response of the next student? Students are then asked to elaborate on the initial response they had to the book by defending their opinions based on the book itself. Students with divergent opinions are asked to examine their differing feelings closely. After about fifteen minutes of discussion, Ms. Deaton instructs the group members to restate their opinions about the book, this time in writing, citing examples from the book to support each opinion. After the students have completed the written exercise, the recorder reads each original opinion as the student examines the essay to determine how his or her opinion has changed. A class discussion about how and why initial reactions to the book changed completes the lesson.

Through this exercise students have the opportunity to share their varied reactions to the book. All reactions are valued. Through the course of the discussion, however, opinions begin to change, just as initial superficial reactions to a subject change in any conversation. This book-sharing exercise not only enables students to react to the book they are reading, but prepares them for looking at the literary attributes of the book by helping them get beyond first impressions. Likewise, it gives members of the class who have not yet read the book some understanding of it through the final class discussion. Often the comments made during this discussion motivate other students to read the book.

Students can share the books they are reading in many other ways. Some are very simple and require little or no student or teacher preparation. One such way makes use of three-by-five-inch file cards and the inside back pocket of the book which usually holds a checkout card. After finishing a book, the student fills out a blank file card with the date, a brief response to the book, and signature and then places the card in the book pocket. This technique encourages students to respond to the book in their own way, to value their responses, and to share them with other students.

Other book-sharing techniques are more formal and require student preparation. If the student is allowed to select the book-telling technique for sharing the book he or she has read, the student is more likely to enjoy reading and telling about the book and to motivate other students to read the book. Reports on books can range from the casual to the formal, but their primary use should not be to check up on students or to give them a grade. Instead, the goal is to get students talking about books as a natural part of their day-to-day conversation. (See Appendix D for sixty ways to tell about books.)

Teri S. Lesesne offers another interesting book-sharing technique. She suggests that students use Maurice Sagoff's book *Shrinklits: Seventy of the World's Towering Classics Cut Down to Size* as a model. In this book Sagoff takes the plot summaries of numerous literary works and turns them into humorous, rhymed couplets. According to Lesesne, *Shrinklits* are particularly appropriate for high school students because they appreciate the sophisticated satire and irony involved. The summaries Sagoff creates are nontraditional in form but relatively easy to mimic.

> For example, Sagoff's version of Lewis Carroll's *Alice in Wonderland* describes Alice as a prepubescent badly in need of psychiatric assistance because of her extraordinary hallucinations about tarts, queens, and bunnies. Sagoff manages to accomplish this tremendous feat in only 10 lines, a total of 17 words. (Lesesne, 1991, p. 17)

Below is an example of a shrinklit by one of Lesesne's students on *Killing Mr. Griffin* by Lois Duncan:

> *Mr. Griffin was a teacher, very tough.*
> *The students in his class had it rough.*
>
> *They soon decided to play a trick on him.*
> *A cruel trick it was, mean and grim.*
>
> *They kidnapped Mr. Griffin in a car*
> *And took him to a mountain far.*
>
> *Soon, though it was not intended.*
> *Mr. G's life was suddenly ended*
>
> *The students wouldn't take the blame,*
> *But it will catch up with them, just the same.*
>
>

Nina Ahluwalia
>

Sharing Books in a Schoolwide Program

At Shoreham-Wading River Middle School in Shoreham, New York, three teachers have developed a program that involves the entire school. "Booktalks: An Innovative Approach to Reading" is a regular part of the English curriculum for all eighth-grade students. A book talk, as defined by project directors Diane Burkhardt, Ross Burkhardt, and Esther Fusco, is "a discussion of a book read by a group of up to ten students under the direction of a Booktalk discussion leader." The objectives of the book talks are to "(a) encourage independent reading, (b) stimulate interest in reading, (c) provide a selection of book titles that will appeal to students of diverse interests and reading abilities, and (d) provide an opportunity for students to discuss books on several different levels."

During the school year each eighth grader participates in at least nine book talks, conducted on nine Booktalk Days scattered throughout the school year. Discussion leaders for the book talks include all eighth-grade teachers, the principal and assistant principal, the librarian, art teachers, teaching assistants, and teaching aides—"in short, all staff members are encouraged to lead a Booktalk."

On Booktalk Registration Day, approximately three and one-half weeks prior to each Booktalk Day, the students select a book (they may participate in two talks by selecting two titles) from a list of twenty-five or thirty titles. Each student indicates five selections on a registration form in order of preference. Every effort is made to give students their first choice but no more than ten students may participate in each booktalk group.

The book talks take place during two class periods on Booktalk Day. Approximately twelve book groups meet during each period. Students who do not have a book talk scheduled during that period attend a large-group program. Booktalk leaders evaluate the students using the Booktalk Evaluation Form. Leaders are also given a list of sample general questions to help them plan their talks. For example: Does the book answer any questions or solve any problems you have faced? Which ones? How? At what point in the book does a very slight incident alter an entire life? A suggested format also is given to the leaders. The format includes an objective quiz, word associations, interpretive questions, evaluative questions, and factual questions. Each booktalk leader gives a member of the English staff a copy of the format used in the book talk, including the questions asked and handouts provided to the students.

The success of this program is due to several factors. All of the students are involved, and all staff members are encouraged to participate. Students are allowed to select books from a limited list of titles that cover a wide range of interests and reading levels, and staff members, as much as possible, select the titles to be discussed. No more than ten students participate in a single book talk. The booktalk format and questions are left up to the leader, although significant guidance is given. The leaders evaluate the participants using a common evaluation form. Students who are not involved in a book talk can participate in a motivational large-group program.

Epilogue: Active Participation in Reading

Active adolescents need to be actively involved in what they read. The goal of the English classroom is not only to get students to read but to teach them how to read, to grasp the meaning behind the words. English teachers want students to understand texts as works of literature through their knowledge of the author's craft. Response techniques that encourage students to initially respond to books on a personal level and work up to understanding those books at a deeper level will foster mature reading skills and an interest in books as literature.

All teachers seek active ways for students to share books. We know that students learn better if they are able to share their learning in creative ways. Using Edgar Dale's cone of experience as a guide, we can create activities that allow students to share books with their teachers, parents, and peers. While they are sharing these books, they are learning more about the world of books and the wider world beyond.

If today's students are to become readers, they must actively experience what they read. This has been said in many different ways by different researchers. In reading, scholars talk about the need for a schema, a way to relate the book to oneself. In the study of literature, English teachers discuss the transaction between texts and students, the dynamic nature of responding to books. In mass communications, scholars cite the need to experience books. And librarians talk about sharing them with others. By creating situations for adolescents to experience books, we can turn them into avid readers who can see the world not just through their own eyes but through a broad range of perspectives.

SUGGESTED READINGS

Atwell, N. *In the Middle: Writing, Reading and Learning with Adolescents.* Boynton/Cook/Heinemann, 1987.

Bauer, C. F. *Handbook for Storytellers.* American Library Association, 1977.

Beach, R., and J. Marshall. *Teaching Literature in the Secondary School.* Holt, Rinehart and Winston, 1991.

Berthoff, A. *Forming, Thinking and Writing: The Composing Imagination.* Boynton/Cook, 1978.

Bridgers, S. E. "My Life in Fiction." *ALAN Review,* Fall 1990, pp. 2–5.

Christian, C. "The Full Picture: Living the Life of a Character." *ALAN Review,* Winter 1989, pp. 6–7.

Dionisio, M. "Responding to Literary Elements through Mini-Lessons and Dialogue Journals." *English Journal,* January 1991, pp. 40–44.

Fader, D., and E. B. McNeil. *Hooked on Books: Program and Proof.* Berkeley, 1966.

Fusco, E. "Authors' Week in a Middle School." *Journal of Reading,* November 1973, pp. 122–24.

———. *Everybody Reads: A Step-by-Step Guide to Establishing a Book Discussion Group Program in Your School.* Dell, 1983.

Gilles, C. "Reading, Writing, and Talking: Using Literature Study Groups. *English Journal,* January 1989, pp. 38–41.

Hamilton, H. "T.V. Tie-ins as a Bridge to Books." *Language Arts,* February 1976, pp. 129–30.

Hendee, R. "Young Adult Novels and Film." *ALAN Review,* Spring 1989, pp. 6–8.

Kane, S. "Turning Teenagers into Reader Response Researchers." *Journal of Reading,* February 1991, pp. 400–401.

Karolides, N. J. "The Transactional Theory of Literature." *Reader Response in the Classroom: Evoking and Interpreting Meaning in Literature,* ed. N. J. Karolides. Longman, 1992, pp. 21–32.

Kinkead, J., and P. Stoddart. "Pen-pals and I Am the Cheese." *ALAN Review,* Fall 1987, pp. 40, 42–43.

Lesesne, T. S. "An Alternative to Traditional Book Reporting: Shrinklits." *ALAN Review,* Winter 1991, pp. 17–19.

Livo, N. "Using Storytelling to Enhance the Literature Program." *ALAN Review,* Spring 1990, pp. 42–44.

McKinney, C. "Breaking Down the Walls." *ALAN Review,* Spring 1991, pp. 35–38.

———. "How I Really Spent My Summer Vacation." *ALAN Review,* Winter 1989, pp. 43–45.

Mason, J. "Promote Reading for Pleasure: Start a School Paperback Bookstore." *ALAN Review,* Spring 1985, pp. 43–46, 53–54.

Miklowitz, G. D. "Books into Children's TV Specials." *ALAN Review,* Spring 1989, pp. 1–3.

Nugent, S. M. "Young Adult Literature: Opportunities for Thinking Critically." *ALAN Review,* Winter 1990, pp. 4–7.

Parker, M., and J. Hickman. "Teacher Feature: An Author Is Coming to School?" *The WEB: Wonderfully Exciting Books,* Spring 1981, pp. 24–26.

Pinkster, J. "Surviving the First Novel: From Script Writer to Young Adult Novelist." *ALAN Review,* Spring 1989, p. 4.

Probst, R. E. *Adolescent Literature: Response and Analysis.* Charles E. Merrill, 1984.

Robertson, S. L. "Text Rendering: Beginning Literary Response." *English Journal,* January 1990, pp. 80–84.

Rockwood, J. "Can Novelists Portray Other Cultures Faithfully?" *The Advocate,* Fall 1982, pp. 1–5.

Rosenblatt, L. M. *Literature as Exploration.* 4th ed. Modern Language Association, 1983.

———. *The Reader, the Text, the Poem: The Transactional Theory of the Literary Work.* Southern Illinois University Press, 1978.

———. "The Lost Reader of Democracy." In *The Triumph of Literature: The Fate of Literacy: English in the Secondary School Curriculum.* Teachers College Press, 1991, pp. 114–44.

———. "Writing and Reading: The Transactional Theory." In *Reading and Writing Connections,* ed. J. M. Mason. Allyn & Bacon, 1989, pp. 153–76.

Sacco, M. T. "The Reading/Writing/Media Connection." *ALAN Review,* Fall 1988, pp. 18–19.

Sagoff, M. *Shrinklits: Seventy of the World's Towering Classics Cut Down to Size.* Workman, 1980.

Sawyer, R. *The Way of the Storyteller.* Penguin, 1976.

Scales, P. *Communicating through Young Adult Books: How Parents Can Understand More about Their Teenagers by Reading and Discussing Their Books.* Bantam, n.d.

———. "Parents and Students Communicate through Literature." *ALAN Review,* Spring 1984, pp. 10–12, 52.

Singer, D. G. "Television 'Tie-ins' in the School Library." *School Library Journal,* September 1979, pp. 51–52.

Small, R. C. "The Junior Novel and the Art of Literature." *English Journal,* October 1977, pp. 55–59.

———. "The YA Novel in the Composition Program: Part II." *English Journal,* October 1979, pp. 75–77.

Spolin, V. *Improvisation for the Theatre.* Northwestern, 1963.

Stewig, J. W. "Storyteller: Endangered Species." *Language Arts,* March 1978, pp. 338–45.

Trelease, J. *The Read-Aloud Handbook.* 3d ed. Penguin, 1989.

Warawa, B. "Write Me the Story: Responding to Literature through Storytelling." *English Journal,* February 1989, pp. 48–50.

Weiss, M. J., ed. *From Writers to Students: The Pleasures and Pains of Writing.* International Reading Association, 1979.

Zaharias, J. "Fiction on a Floppy Disk." *ALAN Review,* Spring 1986, pp. 58–63.

———. "Promoting Response Agility through Literature for Young Adults." *ALAN Review,* Fall 1984, pp. 36–41.

12 Teaching Skills with the Young Adult Book: An Inclusive Approach

Focus Questions

1. Why is young adult literature an important tool in teaching students how competent readers read?
2. How does teaching basic skills facilitate students' ability to respond to books?
3. What are some ways teachers can teach the elements of fiction while encouraging students to respond to texts?
4. How can young adult books be used to teach language?
5. How can young adult books be used to teach writing?
6. Why is it important to teach reading and writing simultaneously?

PROLOGUE

I used to gnash my teeth when children came home from school with their reading homework, which was always "read the next chapter and answer these questions." Like miners they would chip laboriously away at the story until it lay around them in little pieces, some of which they slotted into the blanks on their mimeos. The rest of it, as far as I could tell, was discarded.

The last thing I ever expected to find myself doing as a middle school English teacher was taking a book apart in class—asking my eighth graders to think about and answer questions as we read it aloud. But there was no other way to share my all-time favorite with them. *To Kill a Mockingbird* is filled with four and five syllable words, universal ideas and themes, subtle relationships that shift and grow, discoveries and events that demand response from readers. It is a feast for mind and soul, and I refused to have the class nibbling resentfully at crumbs.

We read the book together, dealing with the vocabulary as a homework exercise the night before, and the questions in discussion during class each day. I wanted these 13-year-olds alert and watching for clues, preparing to draw their own inferences because they knew there would be inferences to draw. I wanted them to stop now and then instead of racing to finish the chapter; to savor the language; to look back at what had happened and why; to speculate on what lay ahead; to explore their own relationships to the people and events in this extraordinary book. Like my children's teachers, I wanted them *reading* in every sense of the word.

Having been a reader for fifty of the last fifty-three years, I discovered long ago the truth about fiction—that at its best it is more than story. I did not realize how much more than story there can be, and how important it is that we share this truth with our children and teach them how to mine stories for their deeper treasure, until I began writing fiction myself. ❖

From Frances A. Miller, "More Than Story," *ALAN Review,* Winter 1992, pp. 6–7. Reprinted with permission of Frances A. Miller.

Reading in Every Sense of the Word

Frances Miller, author of the very popular Matt McKendrick series including *The Truth Trap* and *Cutting Loose,* is also a middle school English teacher. She points out that if students are to learn to read books for more than their stories, teachers must teach them how. Often, as Miller suggests, students are not ready to read books that will personally enrich their lives and broaden their horizons. Teachers—by reading the book orally with the students, making assignments that help them fathom the complexity of the book, and discussing the book with them—can open up the vast world of literature for adolescent readers. Miller's suggestions at first glance may appear to contradict the transactional and experiential literary techniques suggested in Chapter 11 but when explored more closely they can be seen to be compatible.

If we expect students to learn to read books for more than their stories, we must help them gain the skills that will allow them to do so. We must teach them how authors write. And, we must teach them to mine books so that they can get beyond the surface elements of the plot.

Middle school teacher Nancie Atwell describes reading skills as "the things good readers do" (1987, p. 216). Likewise, scholar Frank Smith, in his book *Reading without Nonsense* (1984), suggests that the skills teachers need to teach involve an understanding of how competent readers read. To help young readers learn how competent readers read, we must provide them with books they can and want to read. We must make available to them well-written books they can use as models. Many good young adult books can be used as working models of more complex, classical works. It is important to note that a working model need not be an inferior work. As Robert Small points out, "some of the most beautiful objects ever made by human hands have been working models—models of the solar system crafted of brass and walnut in the eighteenth century, models of ships built with perfect detail in the nineteenth century, models of steam engines and locomotives and automobiles constructed in our own time" (1977, p. 58). In fact, some young adult literature may be superior in its literary craft to the classical works we want our students to read and understand. Of a young adult novel by Howard Fast, literary critic J. Donald Adams wrote:

> Another kind of book of the same length might well have taken me longer, but this was one of compelling narrative power, of unflagging interest. It was Howard Fast's *April Morning,* a story of the battle of Lexington as seen through the eyes of a 15-year-old boy who took part in it. When I had finished it, I said to myself, "This is an even better book than Crane's *The Red Badge of Courage.*" I still think so. I readily wager that *April Morning* will someday reach the standing of an American classic. (1961, p. 2)

The teacher's task is to help students learn to make the same kind of judgments. To understand how authors write and to develop the techniques required to read literature, students should begin by reading and responding to young adult books. Young adult author Sue Ellen Bridgers tells us why these goals cannot be reached without young adult books: "Young adult literature is transitional literature. By its nature, it should move the reader closer to maturity not only by its subject matter and philosophy, but also by its inventiveness of style, its characterization, sensitivity and discovery, and most of all, by the commitment of its writers to do their best work." To help students understand the craft of gifted writers, teachers must also provide historical or cultural information relevant to the book, an explanation of the elements of fiction, and opportunities to develop vocabulary and specialized reading skills. Without these, students will be unable to experience books, respond to them, and share them with their peers and instructors. As students learn the craft of writers, they can practice their own fiction writing skills. And, as Frances Miller suggests, they may begin to realize how much more there is to fiction than a storyline.

Elements of Fiction

English and language arts teachers need not—in fact, should not—lecture on the literary art found in young adult novels. Rather, the teacher should develop activities that allow young adults to discover, experience, and respond to elements of a literary work, such as plot, characterization, setting, and theme. Frank Smith (1984) suggests that one of the most important skills competent readers have is reading in the largest possible units. This skill allows readers to place large chunks of information in long-term memory. Since items are placed in long-term memory in units or chunks, readers who attempt to memorize what they read, according to Smith, experience the bottleneck that comes when they try to move the six or seven items that short-term memory can absorb at one time into long-term memory, which can only store one of these items about every five seconds. Teachers, therefore, need to teach students the skill of reading for large chunks of information. Throughout this chapter, ways to teach basic skills that are compatible with techniques encouraging student response and reading for long-term memory will be examined.

Plot

There are many ways to help students understand how a work of fiction is plotted. Teachers might want to begin with a short story or a novel that has a single plot line. Mystery and suspense stories are excellent books for examining plot. (See Chapter 6 for characteristics of the genres and examples.) All of the books by Gary Paulsen and by Lois Duncan, for example, are well plotted. Students can discover, with a few leading questions from you, how the author captures the attention of readers and holds it throughout the books.

Once students have dealt with books with single plot lines, they might move to adolescent books with imbedded plots. Robert Lipsyte's *One Fat Summer* and *The Contender* and Robert Newton Peck's *A Day No Pigs Would Die* are easy-to-read books with primary and secondary plot lines. More complex books with multiple plot lines include most of Robert Cormier's books, particularly *The Chocolate War, I Am the Cheese,* and *We All Fall Down.* Sue Ellen Bridgers's *Notes for Another Life, Permanent Connections,* and her more adult *Sara Will* are also excellent for teaching students how authors develop multiple and interrelated plots.

In addition to discussing the techniques authors use to develop plots, such as chapter openings and closings, alternating chapters or sections, building suspense to a climax, and moving toward resolution of the problems presented in the book, teachers can utilize other methods to help students understand plot. Robert Small suggests this activity: Examine a sports event for evidence of a clear cause-and-effect plot as well as connections between the plot and elements such as setting and character; compare the results to the plot of a novel like Havrevold's *Undertow* (1977, p. 59). Teachers could develop a similar activity using a videotape of a tabloid-type news program such as "Inside Edition." These shows employ many of the plotting techniques used by fiction writers. Or students could watch a video or movie version of a young adult book (many are suggested in Chapter 11) and develop a plot outline from the script. Usually, movies leave out the subplots of novels. After seeing the movie, students can read the book to see what the movie left out, thereby discovering the novel's subplots.

Characterization

Young adult novels are wonderful tools for beginning to understand how authors develop characters. Because students can personally relate to the characters in these stories, they are better able to see the techniques the author uses to bring the characters to life. For many young adult authors, the development of the character is the most important element of the novel. Some of the best books for exploring character development can be found in the coming-of-age genre (see Chapter 4). In most of these works the author focuses on the growth of the hero or heroine. Teachers may want to begin with short stories or novels that focus on the development of one character. Reading aloud Sue Ellen Bridgers's short story "The Beginning of Something" (in Gallo) is a good activity for introducing characterization. Young adult books that fully develop two characters can also be used for this purpose. Novels by Katherine Paterson and Cynthia Voigt, read aloud, would be good choices. For example, in *Bridge to Terabithia* Katherine Paterson develops ten-year-old Jesse and his female best friend Leslie, and the plot which would not work without the characters' careful development. Even minor characters such as Jesse's little sister May Belle and Jesse's father, whose name we never know, are well developed and important to a complete understanding of the story.

Numerous teaching techniques can be employed to teach characterization. Students can view films or video versions of young adult novels, such as the made-for-television video of *Bridge to Terabithia*. After discussing in small groups how the characters are developed in the film, they can compare this development to the author's development of character through words. They can also reverse this technique by developing characters for plays or videos from the books they have read. After reading the book, they can write a careful description of each of the major characters and discuss in a small group how the character should be portrayed in a play or film, including what things they might change to represent the character more appropriately in a movie.

Characters from Young Adult Literature (1991) by Mary Ellen Snodgrass is a useful reference book for teachers and learning tool for students. Teachers could explore the book for suggestions of young adult and adult fiction to use to teach characterization. The character descriptions will help teachers outline some of the important traits of each major and minor character in a work. Students could use this book in several ways. They might read about one or more of the major characters in a novel they are about to read and then search the novel to see how the author reveals the character's traits. Or students could review Snodgrass's character descriptions after reading a novel and rewrite them adding traits they believe are important. The descriptions can also serve as models for students who are writing about characters in their reading response journals or developing a script for a play or film.

Robert Small (1977) suggests some other activities for teaching characterization. Students could select characters from a television program and describe the appearance and personality of several of them, including one or more incidents that demonstrates each person's character. They could also use scenes and characters from a novel such as *Mom, the Wolfman, and Me* (Klein) to create a television series.

Setting

Young readers often complain that fiction books include too much description. Most immature readers want to know what will happen next. However, if we direct adolescents to books in which the setting is central to the development of the plot, the characters, and the theme, and help them understand how these elements are interrelated, they will begin to appreciate the importance of setting. Setting is very important in several genres including suspense, science fiction, fantasy, and historical fiction. If the author cannot help the reader envision the setting in his or her mind's eye, the novel is not likely to work. In books such as Gary Paulsen's *The Winter Room* and *The Haymeadow,* the setting is so important that it appears in the title of the book. This is not unusual in young adult fiction. You and your students might identify other books in which the setting is crucial to the development of plot and character. If you read one of the two Paulsen books orally to the class, ask the students to identify aspects of the story that could not take place in any other setting. Also ask them to notice how the author helps readers "see" the setting through his words.

Showing a film, such as the one based on Harry Mazer's *Snow Bound,* is another way to introduce students to the element of setting. After watching the film, students could discuss the setting in small groups, or they might write about the setting using as many adjectives as possible to describe it. After this activity, you could read aloud parts of the book that develop the setting, especially as it contributes to suspense. Students can identify how the author helps readers visualize the setting through his words. Here are some other young adult books that are excellent for studying setting:

- *Fantasy:* Phyllis McKillip, *The Night Gift;* Anne McCaffrey, *Dragonsong*
- *Science Fiction:* Robert O'Brien, *Z for Zachariah*
- *Historical Fiction:* Mildred Taylor, *Roll of Thunder, Hear My Cry;* Richard Bradford, *Red Sky at Morning*
- *Coming of Age Fiction:* Katherine Paterson, *Jacob Have I Loved;* Richard Peck, *Unfinished Portrait of Jessica;* Graham Salisbury, *Blue Skin of the Sea.*

Robert Small suggests another interesting technique for studying setting. Have students examine the settings in a number of different comic strips, looking at the way each artist creates the setting, how the setting suits the story and characters, and how much detail the artist presents. Then have them compare the presentation of setting in a novel such as *Where the Red Fern Grows* (Rawls) to the visual settings in the comic strips in terms of detail, style, and so on. Finally, students could draw several scenes from the novel in a style suitable to the book.

Theme

One of the best ways to teach the concept of theme in fiction is to use thematic units as discussed in Chapter 9. This approach allows teachers to group together a variety of books on a single theme. Students could discuss how the theme is approached in each of the books or use their reading response logs to write about the theme of the individual books they are reading.

Films, videos, and television shows can all be used to teach the concept of theme. Using films or videos of young adult novels can be particularly effective since the titles often reflect the theme of the film. If this is the case, students can discuss why the title was selected. An interesting twist can be added by using a novel such as *Bugs in Your Ears* (Bates) and the made-for-television movie "Family of Strangers," which is based on the novel. Questions like the following could be asked: Is the change in the title a reflection of a change in the theme? Why was the title (and perhaps the theme) changed for television? What other changes were made in the plot, characters, or setting?

Next, students could refer to several books read in class. Ask the students why the author selected the title for the book. List the criteria they suggest on the chalkboard. This technique can be used with theme-related titles such as *The Outsiders* (Hinton), *I Never Promised You a Rose Garden* (Green), *Morning Is a Long Time Coming* (Greene), *Home before Dark* (Bridgers), *Man without a Face* (Holland), *The Bumblebee Flies Anyway* (Cormier), and *Pardon Me, You're Stepping on My Eyeball* (Zindel). Finally, a short story, poem, or chapter from a novel could be read to the class. The title of the selection should not be revealed. Ask the students to decide on a title using the criteria they suggested previously. Have the students reveal their titles and discuss the reasons for their selection.

Robert Small suggests an additional activity for teaching the literary element of theme: reading a passage that presents only facts about some topic and then reading one from a young adult novel about the same subject but containing opinions or emotions. Comparing the two is a good way to explore the concept of theme. *The Pigman* (Zindel), with its several themes and numerous passages expressing the feelings and opinions of the two major characters, is especially effective for this exercise (1977, p. 59). Other books that are particularly good for teaching the element of theme are: *Dinky Hocker Shoots Smack!* (Kerr), *Bless the Beasts and the Children* (Swarthout), *Don't Play Dead before You Have To* (Wojciechowska), and *It's Not the End of the World* (Blume).

Language and the Young Adult Book

The study of language, its structure and its usage, is an important part of all middle school language arts and high school English courses. Students need to explore "items related to standard English as well as other varieties of English. They should explore language heritage, geographical and social dialect, semantics, and the silent language" (Bushman and Jones, 1975, p. 56). Language can be studied through language-related units dealing with semantics, the media, communication, changes in language patterns, and advertising. It is also possible to study language in non-language-centered units. For example, in a thematic unit entitled "People against People" students can study differing dialects and social, geographic, and cultural language variations presented in a book such as *Sounder* (Armstrong), a story set in an impoverished area of the South, and *The Chocolate War* (Cormier), a cruel tale of life in a private New England boys school. Students could also examine the difference between standard and nonstandard English as spoken by the characters in three books by Maya Angelou—*I Know Why the Caged Bird Sings, Gather Together in My Name,* and *Singin' and Swingin' and Gettin' Merry Like Christmas.*

Vocabulary

Learning vocabulary is much more than memorizing lists of words to be regurgitated on a weekly test. Being able to recognize a vast array of words and use them correctly is a valuable skill. The lack of an adequate vocabulary can keep students from learning all they are intellectually capable of learning. Without a good vocabulary, students cannot analyze what they read or verbalize their responses. Poor vocabulary is a major cause of poor scores on such aptitude tests as the SAT.

The goal of education is to prepare students for the world beyond the classroom and lead them to become independent learners. By integrating the study of vocabulary with the study of the theme, the teacher encourages students to use their vocabulary skills independently in identifying and using new words. To this end, a number of strategies using young adult books can be employed in the classroom.

Learning new vocabulary not only fosters the ability to identify and use new words, but increased understanding of concepts and ideas. For example, in a thematic unit titled "The Teenager in the Urban Environment," students selected one of five young adult titles to read: *The Outsiders* (Hinton), *That Was Then, This Is Now* (Hinton), *Durango Street* (Bonham), *Journey of the Sparrows* (Buss), or *A Raisin in the Sun* (Hansberry). Before reading their choices, students predicted words they expected to encounter in the books. The teacher, Martha Wight, made five columns on the chalkboard and listed the words the students identified.

To ensure that the students were able to use the words they had identified, Ms. Wight created groups based on the students' book selections. Each group copied the words on the board that related to the book chosen and then wrote a paragraph using the words. The students were allowed to use a dictionary and change the form of the words in constructing their sentences. At the end of the group work, the paragraphs were read aloud and the class decided whether the words were used correctly. Ms. Wight assigned one point for each word attempted and three points for each word used correctly, and one group was declared the winner. The students understood the point system before they began. The competition encouraged them to use the words and to try to use them correctly.

Finally, the students recorded the words as a checklist to use during their reading. Each time one of the words appeared in the book, the student checked the word and noted the page number on the list. At the same time, students kept lists of unfamiliar words found in their reading and page numbers on which the words appeared. These words were used in future vocabulary study in the classroom.

It is important that students learn to identify the meaning of words from context if they are to become independent learners. Therefore, Ms. Wight encouraged students to predict the meaning of words from context. To do this the students used the lists of unfamiliar words they compiled from their reading. Each week Ms. Wight reviewed each student's list and identified generally unfamiliar words and the page numbers on which they were found. Using an unfamiliar word, she developed a title for a chapter and listed on a transparency several sentences that gave different clues to its meaning, usually from the students' reading. Beginning with the title, she asked the students to write down the meaning of the word based on the title. She next flashed each of the sentence clues on the screen, asking students to predict the word meaning. After showing all the clues, she gave the meaning and asked each student to identify the clue that finally revealed the meaning of the word. She asked each student to tell how the particular clue helped to show the meaning. Through this practice the students learned to identify words in context. They also developed additional information about the unit topic being studied from the words and sentences Ms. Wight selected.

Ms. Wight understands that words and skills learned and used in class need constant reinforcement. Therefore, she creates games, activities, and worksheets to let students practice their vocabulary skills. In a vocabulary learning center, students complete crossword puzzles, design games, play Password and Scrabble, and complete worksheets based on the words studied in class. Each center contains activities that pertain to each of the adolescent novels being read and deal with parts of speech, definitions, associations, synonyms or antonyms, and connotations.

Figurative Language

Imaginative and descriptive language is difficult for teenagers, who tend to be quite literal. Attempting to teach figurative language in classic literature often leaves students scratching their heads or giggling at the "weird" use of the words. Adolescent literature provides an excellent source for helping students understand the power of figurative language.

Metaphor and Simile   Even with adolescent books, however, teaching forms of figurative language, such as simile and metaphor, is often quite difficult. Jane Hyder has discovered a painless method using young adult literature. The students are given a picture of an easily described item, such as a fancy sports car. In small groups they are allowed five minutes to write down every word they can think of that relates to the picture. When the five minutes are up, time is called and the class's words are listed on the board. The students are then given a picture of something that is totally unlike the described object, such as the school basketball team. The small groups must then attempt to match the words on the board with various aspects of the school team. Each group is given one point for every correct matching and two points if, in addition, no other group has selected the pairing. Ms. Hyder gives a few examples before the groups begin the exercise. The students have discovered interesting similes and metaphors such as "Joe and Raymond are the headlights of the team," "The team works together like a well-oiled engine," and "Coach Anal's heavily padded leather seat protects him during his fights with the official."

After the points have been tabulated and the winning group announced, the students are asked to begin reading or continue reading a young adult book. As they read the book, they keep a list of descriptive words or phrases that are paired with unlike objects. During the first five minutes of each class session for the next week, Ms. Hyder asks the students to report on the unusual word pairings they have found. Two lists of the discoveries are kept, one of metaphors and one of similes. At the end of the week the differences between each list are discussed by the class and Ms. Hyder places the correct heading on the list. These lists are displayed in the room for future reference.

Allegory   Science fiction and fantasy are a source of many interesting modern allegories. An allegory is an extended metaphor, a metaphor that goes beyond a phrase to an entire work. The characters, settings, and plots of fantasy and science fiction usually have a meaning beyond the exciting story. Often the author uses them to teach a difficult concept or encourage a particular value or belief. (See Chapter 7 for examples of imaginative literature as allegory.) The best young adult science fiction and fantasy can be read on several levels, from a literal understanding of the storyline to a sophisticated sense of the symbolism implicit in the actions and characters of the story. Therefore, teachers can use fantasy and science fiction successfully with a wide range of students. They can use it to help students understand the literary technique of allegory, but those students who are not yet mature enough to go beyond a literal interpretation of a work can still enjoy a good story and interesting characters. For many writers the process of writing science fiction leads to the discovery of truths beyond their own vocabulary and knowledge. Young adult science fiction writer Monica Hughes writes:

> Reading voraciously and longing to write like Rosemary Sutcliff and Alan Garner does not, unfortunately, automatically produce a publishable book, and I was struggling with unconvincing adventure stories when I happened to see a TV program by Jacques Cousteau in which he talked about an undersea habitat, which he called Cornshelf One, that he had designed and was testing on the continental shelf of the Red Sea, to find out human reactions to living beneath the sea at pressures of three to four atmospheres for a week or so.
>
> As I watched, I thought that it was a waste that they would all go back to France at the end of the experiment, leaving the little house empty. What would it be like to live under the sea? What would it be like to be a *child* growing up under the sea? [This experience was the beginning of Hughes's young adult science fiction novel *Crisis on Cornshelf Ten.*] (1992, p. 4)

Before reading any allegorical novel, teachers might read Hughes's words to students and then invite them to discover what questions the author was trying to answer by writing the novel. If students can discover these questions, they are likely to discover the allegory contained in the story. As students progress in reading the novel, the teacher can ask, "How is the author answering his or her own questions?" and "What other questions are you discovering as you read?" Students who get hooked on the books of Monica Hughes, for example, will discover that in some of her later books she asks ecological questions about the earth: "Is Earth heating up due to the greenhouse effect, or cooling down as a result of particulate pollution actually reflecting the sun's energy? What are the rights of a technological society? Whose rights should prevail? Is there another solution other than the weakest going to the wall?" (1992, p. 5). In more recent books she has explored other societal problems by asking questions such as these: "What would become of a society . . . in which there was absolutely no employment for the eager, imaginative young people leaving school? How could society contain all that wasted energy? What solutions would they come up with?" (p. 5). She asks, and attempts to answer, these questions in her novel *Invitation to the Game.*

Once students have discovered the kinds of questions that authors of imaginative fiction explore, the next step is to encourage them to ask and begin to answer similar questions of their own. Students can try this first in the writing vehicle of the nonfiction essay. First, the class can brainstorm a list of environmental, technological, political, and social questions and select one to explore in their journal writing. They can then go to the library and develop or practice their research skills as they attempt to find some possible answers to their question. Later, either in small groups or individually, they can incorporate their questions and answers into pieces of imaginative fiction. At this point students will be writing their own allegories.

————————————— ❖ **Between the Covers:** *Authors at Work* ❖ —————————————

LAURENCE YEP

I once asked a friend how many hours of maintenance her English-style garden required. She simply laughed and said that I was no gardener if I had to ask that. I think, perhaps, that I understand now—except my garden has grown green-scaled dragons instead of green-petalled snapdragons. For the last twelve years I have had those beasts romping not only in the garden of my imagination but wearing out a manual Hermes, an electric Olivetti, an Osborne computer, and now a Macintosh.

When I sold my first science-fiction story at 18, I had always intended to use Chinese mythology in science-fiction as well as in fantasy. Almost five thousand years have created layer upon layer of myth and history just as deep. I thought it would be easy to use what I wanted.

However, at the same time, I wanted to respect the culture that had produced that rich, mythical heritage. I didn't want to plunder odd bits willy-nilly the way less scrupulous writers had. For me, it was the difference between archaeology and grave-robbing.

To my surprise, I found it difficult to understand a set of myths where there was no ultimate evil. Instead, the creations of light balance the creations of darkness; and a legendary villain can wind up in Heaven as a bureaucrat.

More importantly, it was hard to reset my mental gyroscopes to enter that Chinese universe. In our western cosmos, the supernatural and the natural are opposing and even antagonistic forces. The fantastical is synonymous with illusion and has no existence in the real world.

However, in a Chinese universe, the supernatural and the natural are simply the different ends of the same spectrum. In fact, Chinese fantasy stories developed not from fiction but from early historical writing. In order to explain historical events, such as rebellions and changes in dynasties, writers recorded strange omens. At first, these were short, prose narratives—as bland as a police report. When it came time for later generations of writers to write down the strange occurrences of their time, they began to embellish their own accounts with imagery and dialogue. In subsequent centuries, writers began to make up stories that imitated the earlier factual narrative.

So Laurence Yep has taken the centuries-old Chinese myths, which attempted to explain real historical events, and turned them into adventurous and imaginative novels for young adults. He has employed the Chinese continuum of natural and supernatural to explore questions that are as old as history and as current as today's news stories. His series of novels called The Green Darkness is based on the Monkey King myth in which the Monkey King pursues Civit (a catlike skunk) to the real world. During the battle between them, in *Dragon of the Lost Sea,* several real-world children are drawn back into the other, imaginary world in which the dragon Shimmer becomes a princess. Although the other world he creates helps explain life in the real world, Yep says of his imaginative world:

After four books, I know that there is a certain point in creating a world where you stop being the owner and become an observer instead. It's rather like having the title deed to a garden. That scrap of paper is significant only to the lawyers; the garden's occupants, the flora and fauna, could not care less what I call myself; and I feel lucky when they show themselves to me. As Mr. Collins in Jane Austen's *Pride and Prejudice* would gush, "Such condescension!"

When they have deigned to appear, the dragons have taught me that there is more than one way to reach the truth and more than one way to portray it. There is more than one way to discover a heritage and more than one way to explore it. Fantasy may be the longer path, but its rewards are far more satisfying. ❖

From Laurence Yep, "A Garden of Dragons," *ALAN Review,* Spring 1992, pp. 6–8. Reprinted with permission of Laurence Yep.

Rich Language

Young adult literature offers many examples of rich language. Trade books, books that are not part of a regular classroom textbook series, can be used to show students how elements of language are used to develop plot, character and setting. Teachers can help students locate such elements as alliteration, onomatopoeia, rhyme, and rhythm. Reflection on language should produce "richer, more concise and precise use of words" (Burke, 1978, p. 145).

Imagery   Laura Ingalls Wilder in her book *Little House in the Big Woods* uses beautiful imagery and precise, carefully chosen words to evoke the feeling of the forest. Her language is deceptively simple, using short sentences and easily understood words, but the result is a rhythmical passage that is a very effective beginning for the book.

Once upon a time, sixty years ago, a little girl lived in the Big Woods of Wisconsin, in a little gray house made of logs.

The great, dark trees of the Big Woods stood all around the house, and beyond them were other trees and beyond them were more trees. As far as a man could go to the north in a day, or a week, or a whole month, there was nothing but woods. There were no houses. There were no roads. There were no people. There were only trees and the wild animals who had their homes among them.

Many young adult writers use imagery as a means of developing plot and theme. Suzanne Reid suggests that Cynthia Voigt's books are wonderful sources for studying imagery. According to Reid, Voigt uses music, especially singing, as a metaphor for "reaching out of oneself." She provides this example of Voigt's use of music from *Dicey's Song*:

Was this how Momma felt? Was this why Momma ran away? Because she couldn't think of anything more to do and couldn't stand any more to try to take care of her children? . . . Sitting around, her head not thinking, not worrying, . . . a melody came into her head and she sang one of Momma's old, sad songs: "The water is wide, I cannot get o'er. Neither have I wings to fly. . . . Give me a boat that will carry two, and two shall row—my love and I." (p. 80)

Other young adult authors use the imagery of music to develop their themes. Examples can be found in Sue Ellen Bridgers's *Notes for Another Life,* Suzanne Newton's *I Will Call It Georgie's Blues,* and Katherine Paterson's *Come Sing, Jimmy Jo.* After students have been introduced to various kinds of images, they can search for examples of it in other young adult novels.

Many of the coming-of-age novels discussed in Chapter 4 provide interesting examples of imagery. For example, Zibby Oneal's novels *The Language of Goldfish* and *In Summer Light* use imagery related to visual art and light.

Students can generally understand the images used by young adult writers because they come from their own lives. To help students understand how writers select images, challenge them to identify images, literal or symbolic, that represent their own lives. Some will tend to select rather literal images such as an athletic uniform whereas others will move beyond these to more metaphorical images such as a lone wolf. I still have a piece of my own adolescent writing completed after a wonderful English teacher had encouraged us to seek images of our lives. We constructed personal heraldic shields in which we included four images: two that literally represented how we saw ourselves, one that represented how someone else of our choice (a parent or a friend) saw us, and one that symbolically represented us. I selected as my symbolic image one that I have used many times since, the apple tree that shaded my childhood backyard.

Folklore   Alvin Schwartz has collected humorous folklore from around the country and published it in a series of books that can be used in the classroom to integrate the teaching of language with a unit on American folklore:

- *A Twister of Twists, a Tangler of Tongues: Tongue Twisters*
- *Tomfoolery: Trickery and Foolery with Words*
- *Witcracks: Jokes and Jests from American Folklore*
- *Cross Your Fingers, Spit in Your Hat: Superstitions and other Beliefs*
- *Whoppers: Tall Tales and Other Lies*

Each contains notes and sources that provide additional information about the material in the book. The collections not only provide wonderful examples of how alliteration, rhyme, and rhythm can be used to create humor and communicate ideas, but also show that humor is a valuable part of the nation's history and culture. Students can use the tongue twisters, jokes, superstitions, and tall tales in these books as models for creating their own humorous twists, "witcracks," and whoppers. Students could also collect bits of local folklore and transcribe them to create their own books of local folklore. In recent years many collections of folklore have been published. Teachers can find examples of folklore from their geographic region and other regions of the country in school and public libraries. Many of these offer inspiration for playing with language.

Onomatopoeic language is fun to reflect on and to compose. Words that sound like what they denote are found throughout literature. Stories that evoke feelings of eeriness often use vocal imitations of sounds. The best ghost stories told around the campfire are terrifying because of the evocative language used. Books that are particularly appealing to young adults include *Some Things Strange and Sinister,* edited by Joan Kahn, and two books compiled by Seon Manley and Gogo Lewis, *Masters of the Macabre* and *Mistresses of Mystery*.

Fun Language   Sam McKane has his eighth-grade students keep a journal of fun sounds and images they discover in their reading. His students are constantly playing with, sharing, and composing language that creates interesting sounds and pictures. This exercise makes them conscious of the use of rhythm, tunes, rhyme, pattern, metaphor, simile, alliteration, onomatopoeia, interesting adjectives, and even unusual sentence structures. Mr. McKane uses the examples the students record as the basis for many writing lessons.

The mature reader consciously attempts to discover new words or new meanings of familiar words. Similarly, the mature reader is interested in the structure and use of language for its own sake.

Playing with words has always been a part of Alyce Cramer's classes. To encourage interest in words, their meanings and their use, Ms. Cramer creates a variety of language lessons based on the words in the books the students are reading.

Because in-depth understanding of words and their uses is essential in the study of literature, Ms. Cramer teaches a unit on language, propaganda, and persuasion. As part of the unit students read young adult novels that illustrate how words can be used to persuade. For example, in *Blinded by the Light* (Brancato) members of a religious cult twist the words of the new recruits to force them to join the group. After reading aloud a section of the book, Ms. Cramer discusses with the students the persuasive techniques used by the cultists. Other fictional works that deal with persuasion or propaganda can be found in Chapter 5 under "Social Issues."

Examples of fun language abound in young adult literature, even in book titles. *A Ring of Endless Light* (L'Engle), *Blinded by the Light* (Brancato), *Heads You Win, Tails I Lose* (Holland), *Bugs in Your Ears* (Bates), *The Pigman* (Zindel), and *The Outsiders* (Hinton) are good sources for many lessons on the imaginative use of language.

The Structure of Language

Understanding the basic structure of the English language is essential to understanding the meaning of the written word. Sentence structure, punctuation and capitalization, tense and mood, point of view, and the like can all alter the meaning or emphasis of a written passage. Subtleties of language are difficult to recognize, but students must understand them in order to become independent, critical readers.

Books written for the age level of the student are one means of encouraging the recognition and use of appropriate language patterns. A book that relates to the student's needs and interests and is well written can serve as a good model for standard English usage. By selecting a book dealing with the theme being studied, teachers can help students learn concepts as well as language skills.

Sentence Combining   Cyrus Smith (1979) has developed an excellent way to guide students in learning the structure of the English language as well as the structure and content of a book. The technique uses an exercise that Smith calls "read a book in an hour." The teacher selects a young adult book that is interesting to the students and easily understood by them. The teacher divides the book into chapters and distributes a section of the book to an individual or group of students for silent reading. The length of the sections assigned varies depending on the student's (or group's) reading ability and speed.

After completing the silent reading, each group or individual recounts the important events of the chapter to the class. The teacher structures the discussion of the important story events by writing several headings on the chalkboard. These headings should relate to the unit theme and might include setting, significant events, scientific discoveries, conflicts, characters, and important historic events. As students retell the chapters, the teacher directs the discussion by asking open-ended questions that lead the student to not-to-be-missed information relating to the headings on the board. After the retelling of each chapter, the teacher summarizes and records the summary on the board beneath the appropriate heading.

Once the entire book has been retold, the teacher can use the chapter summaries to teach a variety of language skills, such as sentence combining. Smith gives the following examples of summaries from the first three chapters of Theodore Taylor's *The Cay*.

> *Chapter 1.* In February of 1942, twelve-year-old Philip Enright is growing up on the island of Curacao. Curacao lies off the coast of Venezuela, and its principal industry is an oil refinery. Philip's father is an engineer at the refinery.
>
> *Chapter 2.* Because of the threat of an attack on the refinery by a German submarine, Philip and his mother leave Curacao for the mainland on a ship called the Hato.
>
> *Chapter 3.* The Hato is torpedoed on April 6th. In the confusion of the attack, Philip is separated from his mother and knocked unconscious by a piece of flying debris. Philip awakens on a raft with a West Indian named Timothy and a cat called Stew Cat. (1979, p. 27)

These summaries can be transformed into short, simple sentences by the teacher.

1. Philip Enright is twelve years old.
2. He lives on the island of Curacao.
3. Curacao lies off the coast of Venezuela.
4. An oil refinery is on Curacao.
5. The time is February 1942.
6. A German submarine threatens to attack the refinery.
7. Philip and his mother leave Curacao.
8. They embark on the S.S. Hato

Working alone or in small groups, the students then combine these sentences. For example, they might write: Twelve-year-old Philip Enright lives on the island of Curacao, off the coast of Venezuela.

The "read a book in an hour" technique allows for the rapid reading of a book that relates to students' interests and to the theme being studied. The teacher, through the selection of headings for the summaries, manipulates the information gained from the book. The teacher creates simple sentences from the summaries that are important to the story and to the subject being studied. Finally, the students combine these into compound or complex sentences that require them to see interrelationships between the sections of the book.

The sentence combining can be taken a step further by having students use the combined sentences to create paragraphs relating to the unit being studied. For example, in a unit on World War II, students could combine their sentences about *The Cay* into a newspaper account or radio news report of the torpedoing of the Hato. Others students might turn their sentences into a short play or combine the sentences with additional information from books about the experiences of other World War II children to create a documentary about the children of the war. Each activity uses the "read a book in an hour" technique as the beginning point for examining and using language in experiences that relate to the unit being studied. This technique helps students understand the structure of language by searching for the essential aspects of the author's writing.

Summarizing   In an interview by Jean Greenlaw, in M. Jerry Weiss's *From Writers to Students: The Pleasures and Pains of Writing,* Mollie Hunter, an author of many historical novels for young adults, responds to the question of how she developed an appreciation of and ability to use language so well:

> I had grasped the language simply as a result of the fact that every English lesson consisted partly, at least, of a passage which had to be analyzed. I had to analyze sentences so that I understood what the structure of language was. Then we had to do a passage which we called precis . . . it was simply a long passage that had to be condensed, keeping the essential meaning of it. Now this meant that we were taught to understand the structure of language; we were taught to search for the words which had the strongest and most extensive meaning and to replace that whole sentence with that one word. (Weiss, 1979, p. 47)

In writing a summary students must analyze language to reduce it to its most concise meaning. Students can learn to do this by selecting a paragraph and summarizing it in a sentence, coming up with a short title for a chapter of a book, or selecting a poem or a song and writing a phrase or a word that best reflects its message.

Teaching Writing with Young Adult Books

The teaching of composition must be a central aspect of the thematic unit. "In a good thematic unit, emphasis is placed on frequent writing. The premise is that students have something to say and should be given ample opportunity to express themselves in writing" (Bushman and Jones, 1975, p. 55). Within the thematic unit students should be able to write about what interests them. Gone are the single-topic writing assignments; gone are the lists of one hundred composition topics. Students write because they have something to say, to share, to defend, to criticize, not because they must complete an assignment. Students are taught writing skills as they write, say, legal briefs about the guilt of Lorraine in *The Pigman.* They learn how to persuade as they write letters to the editor about the abuse of pollution regulations in their city. They learn how to describe as they write descriptions of the defense system for a new galaxy in a unit on space exploration. They write letters, advertisements, television and radio scripts, newspaper articles, legal briefs, plays, short stories, poems, and more.

They write often, as often as every day, and they learn to write well because what they are writing is not just an English assignment but personally meaningful.

The Writing-Reading Connection

Because writing and reading go hand in hand, it is essential that each unit emphasize and teach both writing and reading skills. A review of eighty-nine studies conducted between 1950 and 1978, compiled by Donald D. Hammill and Gaye McNutt (1980), found that there is a strong relationship between measures of written expressive language and reading. "This relationship may lend support to those who advocate teaching reading (and writing) through a combined reading and writing approach" (p. 273). If recent studies are correct, and students learn to write more effectively when writing is taught in conjunction with reading, then teaching writing during any unit of study that requires reading is a useful approach.

Published authors consistently tell students that reading is the first step in learning how to write. This advice is confirmed in a collection of interviews with authors of young adult books (Weiss, 1979), in which the authors were asked, "What advice do you give young authors?" S. E. Hinton, who wrote *The Outsiders* when she was only sixteen, replied, "First of all, they've got to read. Just read everything" (p. 36). Milton Meltzer, author of numerous nonfiction books for young adults, agreed: "First do a good deal of reading, read a great variety of writers" (p. 71). Norma Klein, author of *Mom, the Wolfman, and Me,* said, "I . . . read all the time, and I think you can be influenced by a writer that you really admire tremendously" (p. 157).

Author Sandy Asher further suggests that students must read what they themselves and their peers have written. Asher, who also teaches writing to college students, says:

> Kids love to read what they've written and what their classmates have written, so I've always tried to finish up with something in print that they could keep and refer back to. I've seen lovely poems and short prose pieces done on poster board with illustration. When I was in school I made up plays and my teachers let me rehearse them with my friends and perform for the class. Any chance to show off is great. It feels good, knowing that someone cares enough about what you've written to shine a spotlight on it. (Cramer, 1987, p. 44)

Models for Writing

Possibly the best reason for incorporating the young adult novel into the classroom curriculum is its suitability as a model for writing. Teenagers may find it difficult to study a so-called classic and use that book as a model for their own writing because most mature works are too intricate for teenagers to read critically. Students, however, can meet the young adult novel as an equal. As a result, they can respond to it with some confidence (see Chapter 11 for various response techniques) and can use it as a model for their own writing.

Characters as Writing Role Models

Several young adult novels have protagonists who write. Carl Anderson suggests that such characters encourage students to do the same.

> Bobby Marks, whose teenage summer adventures readers can follow in *One Fat Summer, Summer Rules,* and *The Summerboy* [all by Lipsyte], is a walking writer's handbook. For

example, he always keeps a notebook with him because "a writer has to get his good lines down or he'll forget them" (*Summer Rules,* p. 9). Bobby chooses to sit in the back row of a camp counselor's meeting because "writers should sit in the back, or off to one side, so they can observe the entire scene" (*Summer Rules,* p. 12). But he goes far beyond knowing good writing strategies. Bobby sees the world through the eyes of a writer: every experience, his own and those of others, is potential writing material.

Bobby collects others' experiences as squirrels gather acorns. After relating a story to the reader about how a local girl conquered polio, he reflects that it would "make a good story for *Reader's Digest*" (*One Fat Summer,* p. 21). After musing about some stories his mother had told him about her teaching in Harlem, Bobby comments, "I filed them away for when I'd be a writer" (*One Fat Summer,* p. 99).

His own life, too, is a source to mine for the raw materials of writing. After being drunk for the first time, Bobby thinks, "At least now I'd be able to write about a hangover without faking it" (*Summer Rules,* p. 61). And while being shadowed by Willie Rumson, an infamous local hood, Bobby observes, "it's sort of interesting being scared all the time. Good experience for a writer" (*One Fat Summer,* p. 115).

Bobby even seeks out new experiences to write about. Before his father forces him to work in a daycamp during his sixteenth summer, Bobby has other plans:

> I was going to work on a landscape gardening crew with rough guys who drag raced and hunted and had girl friends who went all the way. I was going to get into great physical shape and have the kind of exciting adventures I needed to become a writer like Ernest Hemingway (*Summer Rules,* p. 1).

Anderson cites other young adult books in which the protagonist is involved in writing. *The Cage* by Ruth Sender is about Riva Minska who writes about her experiences during the Nazi Holocaust. Discussion of the diary as a form of writing occurs in the nonfiction work *Anne Frank: The Diary of a Young Girl.* Two books in which the adolescent protagonists learn that writing is an interactive process are Cynthia Voigt's *Dicey's Song* and Robin Brancato's *Winning.* (Other good fiction books to use when teaching writing are discussed in Chapter 3. Autobiographies by writers who write about how they became writers are discussed in Chapter 8.)

Writing a Novel in Class   A well-written young adult book may inspire students to try writing a fictional narrative of their own. Hadley Irwin and Jeannette Eyerly's *Writing Young Adult Novels: How to Write the Stories Today's Teens Want to Read* (1988) is filled with excellent, helpful hints for the budding fiction writer. Successful young adult authors give students who are interested in writing many concrete suggestions on how to write a good young adult novel. If you use the group novel writing technique discussed in this section, you can assign appropriate chapters of the Irwin/Eyerly book for students to read prior to tackling a particular element of the novel.

Before narrative writing begins, students must first study the elements of young adult books. Making the leap from understanding the elements to using them in writing can be difficult, but the process is easier if students are allowed to work in small groups to develop setting, characters, plot, dialogue, and point of view. Working in small groups enables young writers to share and test ideas. The process is fun as well as educational.

Developing Setting.   Studying the setting of a young adult novel will help students learn to develop setting in their own writing. *Forever Island* (Smith) provides a good example of setting. The novel describes a Seminole Native American family living in the Big Cypress Swamp, north of the Florida Everglades. The family clings to the ways of its ancestors, refusing to be assimilated by the white culture. When a large corporation purchases the land on which they live, the streams become silted and the marsh is poisoned, forcing the family to move. Charlie, the young hero in the novel, leads his family as they search for the lost island of the Seminole legend, Forever Island.

After examining the importance of setting in the novel, students could practice developing setting by completing one of these activities:

1. Rewrite one chapter of the novel. Pretend that the family is faced with the same problem, except that this time the story takes place in New York City. The building in which the family lives is bought by a large corporation and is being turned into condominiums. How would the story by different? How would it be the same? Would the family search for a Forever Island?
2. Rewrite a chapter of the book in play form, emphasizing the descriptive details of the swamp.
3. Assume that Charlie finds Forever Island. Describe in detail how the island appears to him. What readjustments will Charlie have to make? How will his new surroundings affect his life? Do you think he will survive? How?
4. Charlie's family moves to the community in which you live. Write a chapter describing how they deal with their new environment.

In these exercises the student is encouraged to examine the setting and determine how the setting affects the mood and the action of the story. The settings of many young adult novels provide excellent models for student writing. Books such as *The War on Villa Street* (Mazer), *Johnny May* (Branscum), *Where the Lilies Bloom* (Cleaver and Cleaver), *Where the Red Fern Grows* (Rawls), *The Friends* (Guy), and *Junius Over Far* and *M. C. Higgins, the Great* (Hamilton) would change dramatically in another setting. By placing the same characters and basic plot line in a new setting, the student can begin to understand how the setting is essential to the plot, the character development, the mood, and the theme of the novel. To help students make the transition from the study of setting in these young adult novels to developing setting in their own writing, the teacher should have students form small groups. Each group is asked to select a mood, such as foreboding, fear, happiness, freedom, and to design a setting that evokes that mood. In designing their setting they might draw a map or diagram, find pictures, or create a diorama before writing. Once the setting has been developed in pictures, each student describes it in writing. The group reviews each of the descriptions, and by combining them develops a written description that accurately depicts the setting and creates the mood.

Characterization.   Similar small-group writing experiences can be developed to help students learn the art of characterization. *The Great Gilly Hopkins* (Paterson), *Mama and Her Boys* (Hopkins), *Man without a Face* (Holland), *Killing Mr. Griffin* (Duncan), *Of Love and Death and Other Journeys* (Holland), *Tex* (Hinton), and *Is That*

You, Miss Blue? (Kerr) are all excellent resource books to use as students examine how to develop characters in their own writing. Characterization is difficult for many beginning writers of fiction. Lee Bennett Hopkins told a group of middle-school students about problems he had writing his first autobiographical young adult novel *Mama:* "I left my sister out of my first novel, *Mama,* because I didn't know how to write a book with four characters." Irwin and Eyerly provide this helpful hint to developing good characterization:

> When a teenage reader says, "That's *me* in that book!" or "Whoever wrote that book must know my dad," or "I know a kid just like that," you, as an author, have succeeded in establishing reader recognition, not just a plus for a book but a *must*. For this to be achieved, characters must be given personalities suitable to the part they are to play. Whether they are timid, outgoing, secretive, brazen, cowardly, courageous, tenacious, or conniving, they must have particular mannerisms, individual ways of talking, walking, or acting. Some will have irritating habits. Are they always interrupting? Twisting a lock of hair? Flirting? Doodling? Are they usually late for whatever is going on? (1988, p. 69)

Plotting.   The structuring of plot is essential in narrative writing. Because young adult books emphasize plot, they are excellent models for students to use in their own writing. Several years ago I heard young adult author Scott O'Dell ask a group of young readers if they would continue reading a book if the first page were not interesting. All of them shook their heads in unison. The point O'Dell was making to the adults in the audience was that the young adult book must hook readers early and keep them turning the pages.

A good plot, according to Robert Newton Peck in *Secrets of Successful Fiction* (1980), another good source to use with student fiction writers, involves "two dogs and one bone." In other words, a good plot requires conflict. Author Isabelle Holland says that she develops conflict by beginning with "an enmity, which becomes a relationship between two people " (Weiss, 1979). Students can see how she portrays the conflict between two people and the resolution of this conflict in books such as *Man without a Face* and *Of Love and Death and Other Journeys*. Many other young adult books are exceptional models for helping young writers develop plot. Some of the best are *Fawn* and the Soup books (Peck), *Killing Mr. Griffin* (Duncan), *Home before Dark* (Bridgers), *Blinded by the Light* (Brancato), *The Spirit House* (Sleator), and *After the First Death* (Cormier).

Writing Dialogue.   Novice writers can find strong examples of effective dialogue in young adult novels. As Irwin and Eyerly note, "Strong, active narrative demands *showing,* not *telling,* and one of the best means of achieving *showing* is through dialogue, between or among characters or within one character's mind—interior monologue. The purpose of dialogue is always to help create character, reveal relationships, and advance the plot. Conversation for its own sake is a terrible waste of quotation marks as well as dull reading" (1981, p. 91). Effective dialogue reveals character and strengthens the plot. In Robbie Branscum's books, *Johnny May; Toby, Granny and George; Toby and Johnny Joe;* and *Toby Alone,* dialogue reveals both the strengths and weaknesses of the characters. The dialogue in Branscum's books is colorful and consistent, as in this example from *Toby and Johnny Joe:*

"Toby, do ye take Johnny Joe Treat to be yore wedded husband?"

"Reckon so, Preacher, else I wouldn't be here." I didn't mean to snap the words so sharp, but truth to tell, I was a mite jumpy and all of a sudden it sorta seemed like I didn't know big ole Johnny Joe a'tall. . . .

"Toby, do ye promise to love and obey Johnny Joe?"

My Chin shot up and I said, "I promist to love him, Preacher, but I ain't gonna say I'll mind him, 'cause I ain't a-marryin' me a pa to obey."

Establishing Point of View.   One of the most difficult aspects of narrative writing is deciding upon and maintaining a consistent point of view. By the time the young writers have explored setting, character, plot, and dialogue, they should be developing a point of view. They may have become aware of how professional authors of young adult books establish a point of view, but moving from understanding point of view to actually using it in writing is difficult.

Understanding of point of view begins with examining novels that present various points of view—personal, limited narrator, and omniscient. *The Cat Ate My Gymsuit* (Danziger) is a good example of a novel told from the personal point of view of the major character, Marcy. Sometimes authors tell stories from more than one point of view. In Robin Brancato's *Winning,* most of the story is told by English teacher Ann Treer, but substantial parts of it are told by Gary Madden, a young athlete paralyzed in an accident, and other parts by his girlfriend Diane. Since Brancato is working with the theme of how individuals relate to paralysis and death, she must present a variety of viewpoints. To do this she changes the point of view each time the chapter changes.

Students can begin to grasp point of view by rewriting a section of the book, changing it from one point of view to another. For example, in one chapter of *Winning* Gary examines his fears and frustrations about being strapped to a bed that allows him to be flipped over several times a day. Students could work in small groups to rewrite the chapter from Ann's point of view as she sees Gary on the apparatus. Once the chapter has been rewritten, the class can discuss how the change in point of view alters the development of the characters, the plot, and the author's message. Four excellent books for teaching point of view are Judith Guest's *Ordinary People,* Sue Ellen Bridgers's *Permanent Connections,* and Lynn Hall's *Sticks and Stones* and *The Leaving.* All are told from the personal point of view of two or more characters. It is not unusual to find young adult novels that use, at least in part, the limited narrator, or third-person point of view. Irwin and Eyerly (1988) provide this example from the Hadley Irwin book *I Be Somebody.* The book is about ten-year-old Rap, an African American boy who leaves Oklahoma for Canada in 1910. In this passage the third-person point of view is used to describe Rap's first train ride.

Rap took the tin cup and started down the aisle. At first he didn't know what had happened. Maybe it was because he had been sitting at the window so long his legs had forgotten how to walk. He didn't think he'd ever sat still so long before, longer even than Mrs. Crumpton's study periods. He took one step and bumped into the seat across the aisle. He grabbed to steady himself, but was thrown against the opposite seat. It was like trying to swim upstream in Salt Creek. He zigzagged down the length of the car like one of the big Smolletts when he got too much home brew.

This example allows the reader to get inside of Rap's head without any "he thoughts" or "he saids." The author can describe not only what Rap is thinking but also what those around him are likely to see him doing. Many authors intersperse third-person, limited-narrator point of view in first-person narration after they have carefully established the character. This allows for more flexibility in writing; the character does not have to tell the reader everything. The story still clearly belongs to the character, however, and the author's voice is not heard.

Since most young adult books address the development of young adult characters, very few are told from the omniscient, or all-knowing, point of view. Exceptions are memoirs such as *Death Be Not Proud* (Gunther), biographies such as *The Silent Storm* (Brown and Crone), and nonfiction accounts such as *Never to Forget: The Jews of the Holocaust* (Meltzer). These books and others using the all-knowing point of view can be used to show that the writer has the freedom to stand outside the narrative and enter the minds of any of the characters.

To better understand the omniscient point of view, students could examine a section of a book that uses this technique and then rewrite it in the point of view of one of the characters. Following the writing, discussion could stress the differences between the two points of view and the advantages and disadvantages of each.

Revising and Rewriting.   All established writers know that writing is a process that usually involves a significant amount of revising and rewriting. Most authors accomplish this on paper or on computer. Sometimes authors rewrite the previous day's pages before beginning any new writing. Others rewrite periodically throughout the process. Still others wait until the entire story is told and then rewrite and revise.

Many students are not convinced of the importance of revising and rewriting. One chapter of the Irwin and Eyerly book is particularly helpful in this regard. In addition to talking about the importance of rewriting, they provide examples of revising from their own work and other writers' works. Some of the examples show as many as four revisions. Students can locate the final versions within the novels and compare the different drafts to explore why the changes were important. After students have analyzed the drafts, you might want to share Irwin and Eyerly's discussion of why the changes were made.

Writing about the Books

One of the biggest complaints of students in composition classes is "I don't know what to write about." Teachers spend hours helping reluctant writers identify topics. Out of frustration, teachers often assign topics. Books have been written for students listing hundreds of topics for essays. Consequently, teachers read and students write hundreds of boring essays that do nothing to inspire the student to get into the writing habit. Young adult novels can act as raw materials to get students writing. Robert Small writes:

> We teachers know that the basis for writing does not have to be exotic, but most students will not believe us. Efforts to appeal to students' own experiences are, therefore, not particularly successful, although many of us suspect that teenagers, in fact, lead more

interesting lives than most of their teachers. Young adult novels can, however, provide the focused and intensified experiences the teacher must supply, experiences that are within the teenager's world, but not their own and thus devalued by them. (1979, p. 75)

The intensified experience illuminated in the young adult novel is the beginning point for the student's writing. If the novel was selected based on the student's own interest, it is likely, with some help from the teacher, to provide many good ideas for writing. In a thematic unit titled "Heroes," in Elaine McCracken's class, one three-week subunit was based on realistic heroes placed in times of trial. Each student elected to read one of nine books: *Canyon Winter* (Morey), *A Hero Ain't Nothin' but a Sandwich* (Childress), *The Edge of Next Year* (Stolz), *Toby Lived Here* (Wolitzer), *The Girl Who Had No Name* (Rabe), *The Kidnapping of Christina Lattimore* (Nixon), *Hatchet* and *Tracker* (Paulsen), and *Blinded by the Light* (Brancato). Ms. McCracken decided to use these books to teach journalistic writing skills. The entire class was involved in putting out a newspaper and using the plots and characters in these books in the development of news and features. The procedure Ms. McCracken established was as follows:

1. Students examine copies of the local newspaper.
2. They compose a list of the sections (such as editorials, news, features) they plan to include in their class newspaper.
3. An editor and assistant editor are chosen by the class.
4. Section assignments are made.
5. The sections of the newspaper are written and typed on the word processor.
6. Each article is checked by the editor, assistant editor, and teacher and revised by the writer.
7. The material is printed for distribution. Copies are run off by the teacher and stapled by the students.
8. Copies are distributed to members of the class.

This procedure not only helps students develop journalistic writing skills but also helps them learn the various elements of the novel. To write about the characters students must understand their development. To relate the events of a story they must understand the plot.

Using adolescent novels as raw material for encouraging student writing need not entail an entire class project. Robert Small and his students at Virginia Polytechnic Institute suggest nine ways to use young adult books to promote writing:

1. Create a scene in which the main characters from two books meet—*Then Again, Maybe I Won't* and *It's Not the End of the World* (Blume).
2. Write a letter to Dear Abby as a person with the same problem as a character in the book. Write the answer for the column—*Are You There God? It's Me, Margaret* (Blume).
3. Write a newspaper editorial commenting on a problem dealt with in the book—*A Figure of Speech* (N. F. Mazer).
4. Write the diary of the main character covering several crucial days—*Are You in the House Alone?* (Peck).

5. Write a biography of a minor character using what is in the book and inventing the rest consistent with the book—*The Chocolate War* (Cormier).
6. Write a description of a place in the book, using what the book provides and inventing other suitable details—*The Pigman* (Zindel).
7. Create fully a scene mentioned but not shown in the book—*Mr. and Mrs. Bo Jo Jones* (Head).
8. Write a poem that the major character might have written in reaction to an incident or other character—*The Iceberg Hermit* (Roth).
9. Interview a character for a TV talk show creating both questions to be asked and answers consistent with the book—*Are You in the House Alone?* (Peck). (1979, p. 77)

Writing about Personal Experience

A book often contains inspiration for writing, even when the student is not writing directly about the book or the characters in it. Something in the book makes the student want to sit down with pencil in hand and begin composing. Young adult novels that appeal to students' own experiences can help them realize that their own lives are a source for writing. After reading a young adult novel, the student may be moved to write a poem, a song, or a narrative that is not a direct response to or a rewriting of the story but is inspired by it.

Most beginning and even some experienced writers write best about their own experiences. Writer Judy Blume acknowledges the importance of personal experience in her writing when she says, "I write a lot of the child I was" (in Weiss, 1979). Teachers can encourage students to see young adult literature as an inspirational source for writing about personal experience by leading discussions about how an event in a book relates to the life of the student. The heart attack of Jorey's father, for example, in *The Ups and Downs of Jorey Jenkins* (Bates) could stimulate discussion, and perhaps writing, about relationships that change as a result of illness. Or students might identify an adult who is as important to them as Donatelli is to Alfred in *The Contender* (Lipsyte). *Lilith Summer* (Irwin) could prompt students to describe experiences they expected to be terrible but turned out to be very valuable. *The Friends* (Guy) is likely to stimulate thought, discussion, and writing about friendship. The sibling relationships in *Can You Sue Your Parents for Malpractice?* (Danziger) provide motivation for students to begin thinking and writing about relationships with brothers and sisters.

Young writers can also be encouraged to examine places they have lived in and visited. The description of the home in *Home before Dark* (Bridgers) might prompt readers to write about feelings of home. Discussing places of great importance in the young adult's life would be appropriate after reading books like *Where the Red Fern Grows* (Rawls) and *The Witch of Blackbird Pond* (Speare).

Reading novels about the problems of adolescents should stimulate thought and writing. The student who feels like an outcast for refusing to become involved in the drug scene might be influenced by the novel *The Contender* (Lipsyte) to write about drug-related experiences. The teenager who is coming to terms with the death of a parent will relate to the difficulties described in *A Season in-Between* (Greenberg), *The Empty Chair* (Kaplan), *Big Doc's Girl* (Medearis), *Of Love and Death and Other*

Journeys (Holland), *Break a Leg, Betsy Maybe!* (Kingman), *Grover* (Cleaver and Cleaver), and *Ronnie and Rosey* (Angell). These books might lead to the composing of a poem, a song, or a narrative based on the student's own experience.

Advice from Authors

Students need to become aware of the authors behind the books if they are to become authors themselves. A number of resources offer interesting information about young adult writers. Several are cited in the autobiography section of Chapter 8. Some other inspirational sources in which writers talk about their own writing are the series of interviews in *English Journal* by Paul Janeczko titled "In Their Own Words," the Twayne Young Adult Author series edited by Patricia J. Campbell (each book is titled "Presenting . . ."), *Behind the Covers: Interviews with Authors and Illustrators of Books for Children and Young Adults* edited by J. Roginski, and *From Writers to Students: The Pleasures and Pains of Writing* edited by Jerry Weiss. (See Chapter 14 for more books about young adult authors.) The following excerpts from these and other sources, offer inspiration to students:

> Write every day, even if it's only your name. Get into the habit of writing. (Mollie Hunter)
>
> More than anything else . . . keep on writing. . . . I cannot stress this enough—the habit of writing is the most important thing a writer can develop. (Isabelle Holland)
>
> Writing is primarily daydreaming; good writing is day-dreaming with a technical basis. (Paul Zindel)
>
> When I write, I never think of segments as chapters; I think of them as scenes. I always visualize them in my mind. Then I try to get the scene down on paper as closely as I can. That's the one thing the readers don't see—what you have in your mind. The reader can only see what you get on the page. (Robert Cormier)
>
> To be a writer you have to see the world for the first time and pretend you know nothing about it. . . . Writing is a process of self-discovery. . . . I write to find out who I am. . . . Every book is yourself. (Barbara Wersba)

EPILOGUE: AN INCLUSIVE APPROACH TO TEACHING BASIC SKILLS

The approach to teaching basic skills suggested in this chapter differs significantly from the still common approach of breaking language down into easy-to-teach, easy-to-test bits of information. Instead, the approach mirrors the one suggested by Frank Smith. Students must learn to read as capable readers read. They must learn to read by reading for large chunks of information. This requires a curriculum that does not teach skills in isolation from each other, but instead teaches all communication skills in an integrated fashion.

Often when teachers think of teaching basic skills, we think of workbooks, textbooks, and worksheets. Few of us deny the importance of teaching students how to read, write, and effectively use language. We know that the ability to communicate is essential for students to succeed in education and work. The worksheet and workbook approaches, however, are not only boring to students and teachers, there is little evidence that they improve communication skills. There is only one way to learn to communicate more effectively and that is to communicate.

Teachers can teach the basic skills of reading literature by using the young adult book as a model. The young adult book is perfect for this purpose, for not only is it accessible to adolescents because of its characters and themes, but many of the novels are as well written and as highly regarded as adult novels. Studying plot, character, setting, and theme in novels that are distinguished, in part, by their relative simplicity will allow students to move on to more complex works once they have developed the reading skills used by competent readers.

Young adult novels can also be used as models and inspiration for student writing. Few students are likely to read the work of Hemingway and say, "If I try, I can write just like him." For most students, the plots, characters, and themes of his novels are too far removed from their own experiences. As most authors confess, they write best from what they know. So, too, do adolescents.

SUGGESTED READINGS

Adams, J. D. "Speaking of Books." *New York Times Book Review,* 23 April 1961, p. 2.

Anderson, C. A. "Young Writers in Adolescent Literature: Models for Student Writers." *ALAN Review,* Spring 1990, pp. 12–14.

Atwell, N. *In the Middle: Writing, Reading and Learning with Adolescents.* Boynton/Cook/Heinemann, 1987.

Beach, R. *Writing about Ourselves and Others.* National Institute of Education, 1977.

Bernstein, J. E. *Fiddle with a Riddle: Write Your Own Riddles.* Dutton, 1979.

Burke, E. M. "Using Trade Books to Intrigue Children with Words." *Reading Teacher,* November 1978, pp. 144–48.

Bushman, J. H., and S. K. Jones. "Getting It All together . . . Thematically." *English Journal,* May 1975, pp. 54–60.

Campbell, P. *Presenting Robert Cormier.* Twayne, 1985.

Carlson, R. K. *Sparkling Words: Three Hundred and Fifteen Practical and Creative Writing Ideas.* National Council of Teachers of English, 1979.

Cassedy, S. *In Your Own Words: A Beginner's Guide to Writing.* Doubleday, 1979.

Cramer, G. "Sandy Asher Discusses Writing, Reading and Teaching." *ALAN Review,* Fall 1987, pp. 44, 46, 54.

Hammill, D. D., and G. McNutt. "Language Abilities and Readings: A Review of Literature and Their Relationship." *Elementary School Journal,* May 1980, pp. 269–77.

Hughes, M. "Science Fiction as Myth and Metaphor." *ALAN Review,* Spring 1992, pp. 2–5.

Irwin, H., and J. Eyerly. *Writing Young Adult Novels: How to Write the Stories Today's Teens Want to Read.* Writer's Digest Books, 1988.

Janeczko, P. "In Their Own Words: An Interview with M. E. Kerr." *English Journal,* December 1975, pp. 75–77.

———. "In Their Own Words: An Interview with Richard Peck." *English Journal,* February 1976, pp. 97–99.

———. "In Their Own Words: An Interview with Barbara Wersba." *English Journal,* February 1976, pp. 20–21.

———. "In Their Own Words: An Interview with Isabelle Holland." *English Journal,* May 1977, pp. 14–16.

———. "In Their Own Words: An Interview with Robert Cormier." *English Journal,* September 1977, pp. 10–11.

———. "In Their Own Words: An Interview with Paul Zindel." *English Journal,* October 1977, pp. 20–21.

———. "In Their Own Words: An Interview with Judith Guest." *English Journal,* March 1978, pp. 18–19.

———. "In Their Own Words: An Interview with Stephen King." *English Journal,* February 1980, pp. 9–10.

———. "In Their Own Words: Confessions of an Ex-Kid—Robert Newton Peck." *English Journal,* May 1979, pp. 18–19.

Miller, F. A. "More Than Story." *ALAN Review,* Winter 1992, pp. 6–10.

Nugent, S. M. "Young Adult Literature: Suggested Reading for Bridging the Gap." *ALAN Review,* Winter 1986, pp. 27, 45.

Peck, R. N. *Secrets of Successful Fiction.* Writer's Digest Books, 1980.

Reid, S. "Reaching Out, Holding On, and Letting Go: Images of Music, Wood and Sailing in Cynthia Voigt's Tillerman Series." *ALAN Review,* Fall 1991, pp. 10–14.

Roginski, J. "An Interview with Jane Yolen: Author of Fantasy and Fairy Tale." *ALAN Review,* Spring 1985, pp. 37–42.

———. *Behind the Covers: Interviews with Authors and Illustrators of Books for Children and Young Adults.* Libraries Unlimited, 1985.

Silvey, A. "An Interview with Robert Cormier: Part I." *Horn Book Magazine,* March–April 1985, pp. 145–55.

———. "An Interview with Robert Cormier: Part II." *Horn Book Magazine,* May–June, 1985, pp. 289–96.

Small, R. C. "The Junior Novel and the Art of Literature." *English Journal,* October 1977, pp. 55–59.

———. "The YA Novel in the Composition Program: Part II." *English Journal,* October 1979, pp. 75–77.

Smith, C. F., Jr. "Read a Book in an Hour: Variations to Develop Composition and Comprehension Skills." *Journal of Reading,* October 1979, pp. 25–29.

Smith, F. *Reading without Nonsense.* Teachers College Press, 1984.

Snodgrass, E. *Characters from Young Adult Literature.* Libraries Unlimited, 1991.

Vardell, S. "YA Writers on Writing." *ALAN Review,* Fall 1986, p. 50.

Weiss, M. J., ed. *From Writers to Students: The Pleasures and Pains of Writing.* International Reading Association, 1979.

Yep, L. "A Garden of Dragons." *ALAN Review,* Spring 1992, pp. 6–8.

13   Bridging to the Classics

Focus Questions

1. Why is it important to recognize that a wide variety of excellent books can be shared with readers of all ages?
2. Why is it essential that all of the goals of the English or language arts curriculum be reached by all students?
3. How can we create an inclusive curriculum that teaches a variety of great books from classical works to contemporary works from a variety of cultures?
4. Why is young adult literature useful in the advanced placement curriculum?
5. How can young adult literature and classical literature be grouped together by theme or genre?
6. How can young adult literature be used in historical literature survey units?

PROLOGUE

Watching the March snowfall, my mood matched the patches of grayish ice that had lain for months under the azalea bushes. I began to read a book that the flap copy was recklessly trumpeting as a "side-splitting romp." Knowing the fragility of humor, I was quite aware that it was the wrong moment for such a book, but there was no help for it. Through clenched teeth, I dared the author to split my sides, and began.

Absolute Zero [by Helen Cresswell], as I was soon forced to admit, begins well. Uncle Parker, related only by marriage to the multitalented and poli-eccentric Bagthorpes, has won a slogan contest for "Sugar-Coated Puffballs," which entitles him and his wife Celia (who writes poetry and pots) to cruise the Caribbean. By the end of Chapter One, the fiercely jealous clan are feverishly entering every competition in the British Isles. Before long the prizes, some rather more welcome than others, begin pouring in.

The plot of this book, even more than that of the first volume in the saga, *Ordinary Jack,* defies description. I would sound like one of my children relating a Marx Brothers movie. But the plot is not by any means the only thing that makes this a very funny book. Yes, funny, even hilarious. For there I sat, laughing out loud in my cold, dark, empty house, while the giant snowflakes falling outside my window not only continued but clung glumly to the wet ground.

The characters are marvelous, from Granma Bag, who cannot bear to lose at anything, even if the result is a Bingo Hall riot, to four-year-old Daisy, a reformed pyromaniac. It is, however, a good thing that we met the family in *Ordinary Jack,* for in this volume no one stands around long enough to be introduced. Except perhaps Zero, Jack's pudding-footed, mutton-headed mongrel, who has only been known to move rapidly on those several occasions when the house has caught fire. In this book, incidentally, Zero becomes the most celebrated and photographed dog in all of England. . . .

If Helen Cresswell's considerable talent is unknown to many American readers, it is not because she herself is a new writer. She has published more than fifty books for children, three of which have been runners-up for Britain's prestigious Carnegie Medal. A fair number of these books, many of them fantasies, have been published in this country. But if her American audience has been relatively narrow until now, "The Bagthorpe Saga" should remedy that. Everyone loves really funny books, don't they?

But, you ask, how many American children will understand, much less appreciate, Cresswell's very British brand of humor? Isn't humor the most fragile of literary commodities, the one most likely to perish in transition? Anticipating this question, I asked my thirteen-year-old to read the books. I can report that at least one All-American Boy found himself laughing out loud at *Ordinary Jack*—which was a problem, actually, because he was sneak-reading after lights-out and didn't want to be discovered. His report on *Absolute Zero* confirms my own opinion that it is even funnier. When I asked him how old a person would have to be to enjoy the books, he said that he thought children younger than he might have trouble catching on.

My feeling is that the plot and characters are strong enough to delight younger children who might not, as John suggests, catch on to the batting about of literary allusions, but there is plenty of humor for all. It would be a great series of books to read aloud. And as for catching on to all the jokes—I found myself, magnifying glass in hand, pouring over the small print of my compact edition of *Oxford English Dictionary* to find the definition of "absolute zero." I suspect Cresswell's tucked another joke in there, and I hate to miss even one.   ❖

From Katherine Paterson, "Not for Children Only: *Absolute Zero.*" *Washington Post Book World,* 9 April 1978, p. E4.

Books for All Ages

As Katherine Paterson recognizes in this book review (which also appears in *Gates of Excellence*), great books are great books are great books. They can be read or shared with readers of many ages, no matter when they were written, no matter the age level for which they were published.

Several years ago I had an experience similar to Paterson's when I first read Barbara Robinson's wonderful, heart-warming and hilariously funny Christmas story, *The Best Christmas Pageant Ever.* It occurred to me that this was a book that begged to be read aloud to an audience of children, young adults, and adults. So when a local radio talk-show host asked me to talk about children's books for the holidays, I asked if he would mind if I read part of a book aloud to his audience. He agreed. The day after the show I ran into a literature professor colleague at my university. "I was listening to you as I was driving to work," she said, "and I laughed so hard I had to pull the car over and stop driving." For weeks afterward, people I had never met told me how much they enjoyed hearing that short section of Barbara Robinson's book. Many had gone out to purchase it and found themselves laughing and crying as they read it to themselves or to their children. We all agreed, *The Best Christmas Pageant Ever* is a *great* book!

Author Madeleine L'Engle talks about similar reading events. For years she has read Shakespeare aloud to her children and grandchildren. All of them are lovers of the bard. Even as young children who could not understand all of Shakespeare's words and often did not comprehend the complexity of his plots, they loved the sound of the language and found humor in his slapstick role-switching and excitement in his swashbuckling action.

Of course, not all books can be shared with all ages of readers. No one would expect a twelve-year-old to appreciate, even if read aloud, James Joyce's *Ulysses.* Large numbers of books, however, can be read by or shared with readers of greatly varying ages or educational levels. My literature professor friend would be more likely to pick up Barbara Robinson's book on her own than Madeleine L'Engle's preteen grandchildren would be to pick up Shakespeare. They found these great books because someone who loved the books was willing to share them with them.

This, then, is the goal of this chapter, to show how the English and language arts curriculum can introduce great books to all preteen and teenage readers. Our goal as teachers is to help all students become what Margaret Early calls "aesthetic readers,"

readers who read for the love of reading and for the knowledge it gives them. It is possible for a far greater number of adolescents to become aesthetic readers before they leave high school than is currently the case. This cannot be accomplished, however, if our curriculum does not acknowledge that great books come in all lengths and are written for many audiences. Nor can it occur if we continue to assume that only books that have stood the test of time and generations of critics are great books. Great books are written every year. As teachers of literature we must trust our own ability to find them for ourselves and for our students, and we must help our students learn to find them for themselves.

Selecting Books for an Inclusive Curriculum

Many individuals and groups have developed lists of books that should be read by all students. The underlying assumption of these lists is that there is a specific canon of books that must be taught to all students if we are to share a common literary heritage. It is further assumed that knowledge of this common heritage is essential in a large country in which we come from so many different cultures and traditions. Most of the books in these lists tend to be derived from our Western cultural heritage beginning with the myths, philosophy, and plays of the Greeks and Romans, continuing through the renaissance of British literature, and moving to the industrial revolution of the United States. The books, although in many genres, are largely written by male writers of European heritage, although there are some females among the group, including the Brontë sisters and George Eliot. The list of essential books is frequently broadened to include writers who trace their origins to non-Western cultures such as African American authors like Langston Hughes and Toni Morrison. Although most teachers are familiar with the titles that frequently show up on such lists, even if we have not read them, it is unlikely that we could all agree on a single list of important books.

Nevertheless, if we are to reach the diverse goals of the English or language arts curriculum (see page 253), groups of teachers must develop a sort of literary canon for the curriculum. This can actually be great fun. You can start by polling the teachers in your school, asking each to list approximately ten books that should be read by all adolescents in school. Ask the teachers to leave off the list any books that might be classified as children's books, young adult books, or popular fiction. Explain that the goal of this initial list is to develop a sense of our common literary heritage. After you have compiled the list, call the teachers together with the goal of (1) agreeing on those books that all students should read and (2) determining at what grade level they should be included in the curriculum. This will take a while. Teachers who love books will argue for their choices even if no one else has heard of the book or the author.

Once you have completed your tentative list, examine alternative means of organizing the curriculum so that all the books can be taught. Don't ignore other subject areas. For example, could John Steinbeck's *Grapes of Wrath* be taught in American history instead of in literature? Next, broaden your list to include excellent adult books, popular fiction and nonfiction, and books that represent the multicultural heritage of Americans. Your goal is to be inclusive, selecting a wide variety of books that, taught together, will help students develop basic skills, an appreciation for the variety of reasons we read, and a sense of our common literary heritage. By teaching a variety of works you will automatically be encouraging students to develop critical and creative thinking skills. The specific response activities you choose to teach the works will further sharpen their thinking skills. In addition, you will be able to reach another goal of the English or language arts curriculum (touched on in Chapter 9), helping students define their personal values and understand the values of others.

─────────────── ❖ Between the Covers: *Authors at Work* ❖ ───────────────

PAUL ZINDEL: YOUNG ADULT BOOKS IN THE SCHOOL

The comments by Paul Zindel below are a part of an interview conducted by Mike Angelotti.

Q: What place has young adult literature in the schools?

A: Young adult literature has a firm place in the schools. In a sense it is like a young person choosing a friend, a friend his own age, a friend who talks to him in a way he can understand, a friend who talks to him about living, loving and surviving in a world that he finds himself. It prepares the very foundation of loving books. It shows a student that reading can be exciting and can give information and help and provide a mythology that is usable at a time when he needs it. Leading the right student to the right book is the secret—the greatest secret of demonstrating how important a book can be. Reading is not a useless snobbery. Reading is not a premature drudgery. Reading the right book allows the student to cry out—come, beast, mystery, come. . . .

Q: The book [*The Pigman*] is considered a young adult classic by most YA professionals and by its continued readership. How do you account for its capacity to touch so many generations of readers? So much has changed for them since the sixties.

A: Well, I think there are two main reasons I can think of. Number one is I did commit a great portion of my own emotional truth to it. Emotional truth tends to pretty much age fairly well, and so there is something about the book that does bring many people to tears towards the end of it. I think it is probably rooted in the fact that when the pigman dies, in some way it touches people, children of all ages in their own "lack of innocence," not lack of it, but loss of it. So, I think that often all through life human beings come across certain moments of growth, and when we remember them from the point-of-view of nostalgia or experience the insight for the first time, there's a weeping. We tend to not like to move on. There is some sadness because we are saying goodbye to a part of ourselves, and that reminds me of some of the more emotional farewells—almost as when a ship is sailing. I've seen some farewells around the world in which the tears and the emotions of the event are not covered by inhibition.

Then the other reason why it hasn't dated, I think, is a conscious choice. I knew from teaching over a period of ten years that kids changed their slang every few years. It is like them changing the color and shape and textures of their hair. They have a slang that gets to be unique for them and is something that seems only to fit properly on them. I didn't imitate that aspect of their language. There were certain elements that they did use that I think were timeless, for example, the use of bathos, or the use of hyperbole by taking some very common word and then juxtaposing it with something very lofty or by taking some very lofty concept or word and then juxtaposing it with something very common. This tends to give the illusion of slang, but there was really very little in *The Pigman* that was intended to *copy* the way young people spoke in the sixties. And I think that has allowed it some longevity.

At the tail end of that question you say that so much has changed for the readership since the sixties. And yet, again, I never picked themes or qualities that *do* change. My books always, and certainly in the case of *The Pigman,* are linked to timeless elements about the human being, which is what I have always been interested in. I am never very interested in something that is terribly trendy or a disguise of any type. I think my purpose has always been to look into the heart and soul of the human being in order to discover what truth I might find there—ironically, for myself probably more than anyone else. ❖

From Mike Angelotti, "The Effect of Gamma Rays on Man-and-the Writer Zindel: *The Pigman* Plus Twenty and Counting," *ALAN Review,* Winter 1987, pp. 21–22.

Young Adult Books as a Bridge to the Classics

Although the two curricular goals of teaching basic skills and developing cultural literacy are often thought to be contradictory, this need not be the case. In fact, it is possible to use accessible young adult books to teach basic skills so that students can more successfully read and interpret the classics. As Barbara G. Samuels, Rosemary Oliphant Ingham, and Hollis Lowery-Moore suggest, "Experience with a number of young adult novels can provide the tools teens need to prepare them for more complex classics. Adolescent novels can be used to teach the literary conventions in preparation for reading the classics or as parallels to help young adult readers understand specific classics" (1987, p. 42). In this way young adult literature becomes a bridge to the classics.

Using some of the best young adult novels, the English and language arts teacher can illustrate the author's technique in handling many aspects of literary craft. For example, the plot and interrelated subplots in Robert Cormier's young adult novels *The Chocolate War, I Am the Cheese, After the First Death,* and the very mature *We All Fall Down* provide an excellent working model for the more involved and subtle plots of Conrad and Hardy. Characterization in Fielding, Faulkner, Thackeray, and Updike can be approached through the character development in young adult novels such as *The Great Gilly Hopkins* (Paterson), *A Wind in the Door* (L'Engle), and *Notes for Another Life* (Bridgers). The symbolism used in the works of Hawthorne can be approached through a young adult book such as *The Contender* (Lipsyte) and *A Wrinkle in Time* (L'Engle). The importance of the settings in the classic works of Austen and Hemingway can be better understood after examining the settings in young adult books such as *Soul Catcher* (Herbert), *Trial Valley* (Cleaver and Cleaver), and *Island of the Blue Dolphins* (O'Dell).

The observant English teacher can find examples of metaphor and simile in almost every young adult novel. In M. E. Kerr's *Gentlehands,* we find this simple illustration of the simile: "Once I got to Beauregard, I always seemed able to put my life out of my head, and just wallow in theirs, with Skye. Beauregard was like a drug; so was she." Metaphors are one of the most common forms of figurative language. Teenagers use them all the time (usually without recognizing them), and they are omnipresent in young adult literature. Often the epithets teenagers apply to peers and teachers are examples of metaphor. In Paul Zindel's *The Pigman,* John and Lorraine call the librarian "the Cricket." Similarly, John refers to his friends Dennis and Norton as "two amoebae." One of the most difficult literary concepts to teach teenagers is theme. Although the theme of Hawthorne's *Scarlet Letter* might escape them, most teenagers can grasp the concept of theme in books such as *The Outsiders* (Hinton), *The Contender* (Lipsyte), and *Dinky Hocker Shoots Smack!* (Kerr).

Creating an Inclusive Curriculum: The Thematic Unit

The thematic approach to teaching literature encourages an egalitarian approach to reading and at the same time can expose students to major works from the English literary tradition. In 1985, during the height of the educational excellence movement, in which politicians and educators were advocating that students learn about their common literary heritage and at the same time acquire basic skills, the state of California developed a new English and language arts curriculum. The philosophy behind the curriculum is expressed both in its title "Literature for all students" and in the quotation from Dylan Thomas that introduces the program's sourcebook for teachers:

> I could never have dreamt that there were such goings-on in the world between the covers of books, such sand-storms and ice-blasts of words, such slashing of humbug, and humbug too, such staggering peace, such enormous laughter, such and so many blinding bright lights breaking across the just-awaking wits and splashing all over the pages in a million bits and pieces all of which were words, words, words, and each of which was alive forever in its own delight and glory and oddity and light.

The California curriculum is designed to be inclusive, to address the various cultural identifications of the state's diverse student population. At the same time, however, the curriculum does not ignore the great works that are likely to appear on the list of books compiled by your English department colleagues. The teaching of basic skills is combined with responding to literature in a variety of modes in the California curriculum. The sourcebook for teachers shows how teachers can integrate the various educational goals of the curriculum.

The California sourcebook for teachers suggests that literature be studied by examining ways into literature, ways through literature, and ways beyond literature. The authors of the sourcebook suggest that this process approach can help students "become fluent and comfortable with writing, [and] can get similar results in approaching reading" (California Literature Institute, p. 83). "Ways into literature" are techniques and activities used before reading a work. "Ways through literature" are student-oriented activities employed as the class reads a work. And "ways beyond literature" are activities that encourage further learning and open up the vast world of literature to the student.

The sourcebook presents a thematic, inclusive curriculum using teaching methodologies that integrate all aspects of language development. Figure 13.1 shows some appropriate teaching strategies for a sample unit titled "The Search for Justice and Dignity." In this single unit a variety of cultures are presented; at the same time students are introduced to at least one work that appears on many lists of important literary works. *Farewell to Manzanar* (Jeanne Wakatsuki Houston and James Houston) is a young adult novel written from the viewpoint of a Japanese person who was interned during World War II. *I Know Why the Caged Bird Sings* (Maya Angelou) is the autobiographical story of growing up African American in the United States of the 1950s and 1960s. Arthur Miller's *Death of a Salesman* is a classic American drama, and Percy Bysshe Shelley's "Ozymandias" is a poem by one of the great British poets about a classical Greek subject.

If you look carefully at the example, you will notice some other types of integration. Each of these works represents a different genre, allowing teachers and students to examine how different genres deal with the same theme. You'll also see a variety of student-oriented activities that encourage reading, writing, speaking, listening, and thinking. Also note that each work was written for a different audience. *Death of Salesman* was clearly written for an adult theater audience; *I Know Why the Caged Bird Sings* was a contemporary adult best-seller; *Farewell to Manzanar* was written and published primarily for adolescents. In addition, each work fulfills a different reading purpose. Most adolescents will read *Farewell to Manzanar* both for pleasure and to gain new knowledge; *I Know Why the Caged Bird Sings* may provide therapy for some and broaden the horizons for others; *Death of a Salesman* is likely to provide new insights into human nature and also expand students' reading skills; "Ozymandias" can also allow students to improve reading skills and may help them create new images. The simple approach used in this example represents integration at its best.

Another way to organize the curriculum thematically is to connect a particular classic with a young adult title on the same theme. Helping students see connections between the works may make each work more meaningful to students, particularly those who are not yet able to synthesize sophisticated concepts on their own. Many educators have suggested ways to incorporate both classic and young adult works into thematic units (see Chapter 9).

Joan F. Kaywell, the editor of the book *Adolescent Literature as a Complement to the Classics* (1993), suggests that pairing young adult books with classic books is essential if reading is to be "relevant and meaningful" to students. Each of the fourteen chapters of Kaywell's book pairs young adult books with one or more classic titles. Many of the pairings are thematic:

- "Family Relationships as Found in Arthur Miller's *Death of a Salesman* and Cynthia Voigt's *The Runner*"
- "*The Adventures of Huckleberry Finn* (Twain), Prejudice, and Adolescent Literature"
- "Leaving Home to Come Home: The Hero's Quest in *Great Expectations* (Dickens) and Three Young Adult Novels"
- "Reading from a Female Perspective: Pairing *A Doll's House* (Ibsen) with *Permanent Connections* (Bridgers)"
- "Exploring the American Dream: *The Great Gatsby* (Fitzgerald) and Six Young Adult Novels"
- "*Their Eyes Were Watching God* (Hurston) and *Roll of Thunder, Hear My Cry* (Taylor): Voices of African-American Southern Women"
- "Alienation from Society in *The Scarlet Letter* (Hawthorne) and *The Chocolate War* (Cormier)"
- "The Beast Within: Using and Abusing Power in *Lord of the Flies* (Golding), *The Chocolate War,* and Other Readings"
- "Dealing with the Abuse and Power in *1984* (Orwell) and *The Chocolate War.*"

Figure 13.1
A Sample Thematic Unit from the California English Curriculum

The Search for Justice and Dignity

Drama	**Autobiography**
Death of a Salesman	*I Know Why the Caged Bird Sings*
FOCUS/GOALS	FOCUS/GOALS

1. To study the struggle of the individual to find personal dignity in a materialistic society.
2. To provide an experience demonstrating that the process of maturation never ends.

1. To see how the main character, through her struggle to mature as a black female, evolves into a person who has a strong feeling of self-worth.
2. To connect in writing students' own experience with the author's.

WAYS INTO LITERATURE

1. Literature Journals:
   A. Define what is meant by the "American Dream."
   B. Describe someone, real or imaginary, who is successful in our society.
2. Prepare a collage or poster representing the American Dream.

1. In small groups, make a list of problems that teenagers face when growing up. Discuss whether there are any problems that could be considered typically male or female. Each group presents to class.
2. Literature Journals: After reading Dunbar's "Sympathy," as a large group attempt to define *discrimination*. Then write in journals about a time you felt discriminated against.

WAYS THROUGH LITERATURE

1. Read at least the first scene aloud.
2. Literature Journals: Jot down brief summaries of each dream sequence and tell what the sequence shows about Willy and his friends.

1. In small groups, after reading Chapter 5 discuss what the "contest" was, whether/how "Momma had won," and what they think Maya learned from the incident.
2. In small groups, after reading Chapter 32 discuss why Maya didn't call her mother immediately and what the result of her decision was.

WAYS BEYOND LITERATURE

1. Teachers presents a list of conflicts in the play. In pairs the students look for examples and symbols that represent the conflict. Journal writing follows.
2. Interview someone who is a salesperson. Ask them the favorable and unfavorable aspects of the work. Check the play to see if their ideas coincide with Willy's.

1. Prepare an oral presentation/interpretation by giving a dramatic reading of the poem "Sympathy" interspersed with readings of incidents taken from our own lives.
2. Write a stylistic imitation of Dr. King's speech "I Have a Dream" using Maya's voice.

The Search for Justice and Dignity

History
Farewell to Manzanar

FOCUS/GOALS

1. To show how the members of the Wakatsuki family struggled to maintain dignity in an unjust society.
2. To investigate that time in American history, seemingly at odds with the spirit of democracy, when Americans were imprisoned by Americans— when, how, why, by whom.

Poetry
Ozymandias

FOCUS/GOALS

1. To explore the question: What *is* dignity?
2. To become aware of the fleeting nature of power and fame.

WAYS INTO LITERATURE

1. As a home assignment, interview parents or grandparents to determine their ancestry and report on any injustices perpetrated upon their ancestors.
2. In small groups, share information from interviews and present findings to class.

1. Literature Journal: How would you want people to remember you? Based on the artifacts you would leave behind, what would future generations think of you?
2. The teacher shows slides of Egyptian statues and pyramids.

WAYS THROUGH LITERATURE

1. Teacher could invite a guest speaker who lived in an internment camp for a first-hand perspective.
2. Read the book in three sections focusing on how each member of the family exemplifies dignity and courage in the face of injustice.

1. Literature Journals: Record your initial reaction to poem and to Ozymandias.
2. Visualization: Circle descriptive words in poem. As poem is read, several of you draw poem on chalkboard.

WAYS BEYOND LITERATURE

1. Conduct a mock trial of our government's policy of internment during WWII.
2. Write persuasive letters to the legislators regarding reparations for those who were interned.

1. Extended Writing: What statue, building, work of art, etc., do you think will survive and remain useful in later years? Why? Share in small groups.
2. Some of you may wish to do independent research of Shelley's brief, productive life.

Marian Sheidy suggests an interesting pairing of *The Odyssey* and Paul Zindel's *Harry and Hortense at Hormone High* in a ninth-grade English class. Students can compare the concept of the hero as represented by two different heroes, Odysseus and Jason, in two different settings and times. According to Sheidy, her freshman class assigned the following characteristics to Odysseus: "responsible, wise, curious, egotistic, strong, patient, willing to take advice from people he respects (Circe) but not his own men, commanding, sympathetic over men's deaths, contemptuous of his enemies, respectful of the gods and their wishes, sorry when he defies them, courageous, perceptive, determined" (1988, p. 43). They described Jason as "nice looking—blond, godlike, penetrating eyes, kind, loving, easy going but paradoxically intense, lonely, perceptive enough to know that his own problems came from man's cruelty to his fellow man, determined, analytic at times—making the glider and escaping from the asylum, deranged and schizophrenic as the result of parental murder, desirous of reforming the world beginning with Hormone High" (p. 44).

Adolescent Literature in Advanced Placement Classes

One of the best arguments for using adolescent literature in the advanced placement curriculum is that advanced students who learn to appreciate literary technique through young adult literature will better understand the classic books they read. English teacher Tim McGee makes another important point in his defense of the young adult novel in the advanced placement curriculum: when readers make connections between two works of literature, both works of literature are enhanced. These connections are more likely when well-written young adult novels are a part of a curriculum that regularly features classical works. As McGee suggests, in the AP curriculum it is not necessary to find ways to link good young adult books with classic works, we simply need to teach both and allow our students to make the connections for themselves. He relates this story about introducing a novel by Robert Cormier to a class accustomed to reading challenging literary works.

At an AP conference in Salt Lake City last year I sat in a room with one-hundred other English teachers, listing books we found to be useful teaching texts, from *The Wide Sargaso Sea* to *Crime and Punishment,* but no mention was made of a Gary Paulsen or Cynthia Voigt novel! Therefore, when I made a choice recently to give my AP English students a week to jump into Robert Cormier's *The Chocolate War* (1974), I considered that reading on the same level as movies and crossword puzzles for the week.

Although most AP English teachers don't say it out loud, in private they admit that the young adult novels they may teach in other classes really have no place in the AP English curriculum. I always saw it simply as a question of literary value. We teach only the "best" works of literature; works that have stood the test of time merit inclusion in our curriculum. These works deal with the eternal questions of life using language that often is lofty and always is thought-provoking in its images. Quite frankly, the adolescent novel is what we feed to normal students because that is all they can handle. I had put it another way in my mind: "Why give them Cormier when I can give them Plato?"

. . . Tillie Olsen, in her sentinel *Silences* (1978), argues that to ignore a work is to silence it. We AP English teachers have ignored the YA novel long enough, and many of our students leave the high-school English classroom capable of discussing the Victorian era as it relates to the Brontë sisters but have no knowledge of the similarly challenging heroines of Voigt. What we have done as AP English teachers in the guise of preserving the best literature has in fact silenced a strong and intellectually stimulating alternative to the common AP canon.

Once AP English teachers begin to read the young adult novels of Paulsen, Voigt, Walter Dean Myers, and [Bruce] Brooks and consider them as something more than filler, a whole new world of literary stimulation will open up for students as well as teachers. . . .

The week of reading *The Chocolate War* in my classes turned into a remarkable learning experience for my students and a teaching epiphany for me. One given about the students we work with at the AP level is that they are searching for the truly mind-challenging questions. The honest truth is that often the archaic diction and syntax of the established works in the AP canon keep students from the intellectual debate they are striving for. Cormier cuts through all that. From the first line my students struck out on a serious investigative journey.

. . . From the discussions on topics ranging from the messianic motif to Cormier's treatment of women in the novel, I found that they were responding the same way they did to Shakespeare or Milton, with the intellectual search that had marked them as worthy of the AP English classroom. As for me, I must admit that what happened in my class was not planned. From the discussion of the spurned artist and comparisons to Stephen Dedalus to an application of Thrasymachus' edict to Socrates, "might makes right," I found students willing to experience a work of literature and walk away stronger thinkers.

Two weeks later during our discussion of Books 1–4 of *The Republic,* I didn't have to work through the merits of Platonic thought for the 90s mind; Cormier and my students had done that already. All I had to do was step back and watch as Archie met Thrasymachus. Glaucon's challenge to Socrates was now very real for my students. The challenge of *The Chocolate War* reconciles what students want to believe about the world and what they know the world is really like. Glaucon's challenge to Socrates to validate that the just life is really worth living is the hidden scream of all my students. Cormier's novel vocalized that scream, and Plato's *Republic* had a new place in my curriculum in terms of appreciation. This year we looked at *The Republic* as one man's attempt to explain that the Archies of the world are not really happy, nor really satisfied.

. . . Cormier allowed my students to see in vivid images and hear in modern language the eternal dilemma of whether one should stand up and live the just life or rule through force and fear. If a novel can promote this kind of thought, how can we devalue it simply because it is not on the AP reading list? (1992, pp. 57–58)

High school teacher M. Lisa Shattuck suggests that a pairing of Paula Fox's *The Slave Dancer* and Herman Melville's *Moby Dick* can lead students to a better understanding of Melville's complex novel. Highly motivated students can compare these two novels using composition and research to explore characters, themes, and figurative language. Shattuck suggests that students read *The Slave Dancer* independently and then investigate one of the composition or research topics:

I. Composition
   A. Comparison/contrast of authors' techniques: the use of irony, symbolism and imagery in Fox's *The Slave Dancer* and *Moby Dick.*
   B. Parallel themes in Fox's *The Slave Dancer* and Melville's *Moby Dick.*
   C. Foil characters: Ahab vs. Ishmael in *Moby Dick,* Jessie vs. Cawthorne/Stout in *The Slave Dancer.*

D. Literal, anagogical, moral and analogical levels of *Moby Dick* and *The Slave Dancer*.

E. Poetic forms presented in the literature of Paula Fox and Herman Melville.

II. Research Topics

A. The slave trade.

B. The Underground Railroad.

C. Sailing—whaling/slaving vessels.

D. The whaling trade.

E. Impressment.

F. Melville's background—relationship to works.

G. Fox's background. (1987, p. 12)

Genres, Classic Works, and Young Adult Books

Another way to organize the English or language arts curriculum is by genre. Chapters 3 through 8 include lists of the characteristics of each genre. Teachers can use these lists as they prepare units that include classic and young adult works in a variety of genres. If you go back to the list of books you and your colleagues agreed all students must read, you are likely to find classic titles that can be taught successfully in units on specific genres. For example, it is hard to imagine any list of essential books that does not include Mark Twain's humorous classic *The Adventures of Huckleberry Finn*. It would not be difficult to find young adult books to use in this unit to help students understand different types of humor. Two good books to pair with Twain's classic are *Absolute Zero* and *The Best Christmas Pageant Ever*. You might also include humorous poetry, perhaps by e. e. cummings or Edward Lear, or a humorous drama, such as Shakespeare's *Comedy of Errors*.

M. Lisa Shattuck, in her discussion of the parallels between Paula Fox's young adult novel *The Slave Dancer* and Herman Melville's *Billy Budd,* suggests a unit on the genre of the sea adventure.

A Unit: The Sea Adventure Genre

I. Filmstrips, historical background, other tales *(Old Man and the Sea)* may serve as starting points.

II. A study of nautical terms and/or vocabulary terms from Fox's book can follow.

III. General discussion on New Orleans and the South; pre–Civil War America; the slave trade.

IV. Role-playing activities (before reading):

A. Black/white encounter in which white expresses prejudice against the black or vice versa.

B. Students representing different minority groups explain ways in which they feel suppressed.

C. Pretended argument between captain of a ship whose primary goal is to deliver a cargo, and a concerned shipmate who worries about the safety of the cargo and the crew.

D. Power play—one person selects and assumes a position of power; the other chooses an inferior position; situation should develop.

   V. Reading *The Slave Dancer.*
  VI. Short writing assignment: students use the first person point of view and explain the arguments and reasoning of one of the following characters from *The Slave Dancer:* Jessie, Purvis, Ned, Cawthorne, Daniel, Ras or Stout.
 VII. Introduction to Melville—author's own sea background.
VIII. Reading of *Billy Budd.*
  IX. Concluding Activities:
     A. Create a sociogram which shows characters' relationships and varying levels of relationships.
     B. Give an oral report which explains parallels between *Billy Budd* and *The Slave Dancer.*
     C. Write a short paper discussing Billy and the slaves as victims.
     D. Test. (1987, p. 12)

High school teacher Sheila L. Haselhuhn presents a similar approach for teaching the epic. Haselhuhn maintains that although the epic is one of the most difficult forms of literature to teach, it is one of the most important. She found that using young adult epics to bridge the gap between students' lack of experience with the genre and works like the *Iliad* made students less anxious about studying the epic and also helped them understand the genre. She suggests that a good bridge to Homer's work is Ursula K. LeGuin's Earthsea trilogy consisting of *The Wizard of Earthsea, The Tombs of Atuan* and *The Farthest Shore.* Before beginning the unit, she points out to students that although the Earthsea trilogy fits the mold of the epic, it differs in that it does not use verse or elevated language. She suggests that for reluctant students the best approach is to entice them through the storyline first and then introduce the technical conventions of the epic. According to Haselhuhn, characteristics of the epic that can be found in LeGuin's trilogy include heroes, universal themes, divine aid, and struggles. She begins by reading the first page of *The Wizard of Earthsea* to introduce these characteristics through Ged, the "loud, proud, and full of temper" lad (p. 2). Through years of adventure, education, and growth, he becomes a classical hero.

According to Haselhuhn the epic characteristic of universal themes is evident in all three novels. LeGuin's books deal with the "ideas of death and life, dark and light, good and evil and knowledge and ignorance" (1985, p. 14). Students easily recognize these themes in the trilogy and question, along with Ged, their own fears of death.

The third characteristic of the epic, divine aid, is expressed through Ged's power of magic. Magic is a form of the supernatural in LeGuin's novels; it is found only in some people "and is enhanced and strengthened only through knowledge of that power" (p. 14).

The final characteristic of the epic, struggles, or a quest, is evident in Ged's search for knowledge for its own sake, and in his later quest to find the ring of Erreth-Akbe which will restore the king to his throne for the people of Earthsea. By accomplishing this feat, Ged is able to return home to a life of no longer having to prove himself through his actions.

Haselhuhn suggests that after the students are caught up in the exciting adventure, it is time to introduce the literary conventions of the epic: "extended similes, invocations to a muse, catalogues of characters, inspirational talks, descents into the underworld and *in medias res* (a Latin term meaning in the middle of things)" (p. 14).

She suggests that students first investigate these terms and then find examples of the conventions in the novels.

> The first, the extended simile, a device made famous by Homer, appears several times throughout the three LeGuin books. One such example is when Ged tries to explain the idea of natural balance to Arren, a young boy. He picks up the rock and in so doing proves to Arren that the earth is now lighter and his hand is heavier; thus the natural balance of things is altered. (p. 14)

Haselhuhn points out that the convention of invocations to a muse are present in all three LeGuin books. She suggests that students should be familiar with the muses of Greek mythology prior to reading the epics, and therefore should understand that they represent knowledge. If they understand this, it is easy for them to make the connection between the nine muses and the nine masters of the Roke school for wizards. These nine masters represent the knowledge of Earthsea, and, hence, Ged turns to them for advice, support, and knowledge. Catalogues, another convention of the epic, are used sparingly by LeGuin. She includes short lists of the nine masters of the Roke, the names of the stars in the constellation of Gobardon, and the nine people of Earthsea who know Ged's true name. These short lists can help prepare students for the long catalogues of the *Iliad*.

Inspirational talks abound in LeGuin's trilogy. Whenever Ged is in trouble he is given one by his superiors or friends. Ged, too, gives inspirational talks. In *The Tombs of Atuan* he gives several to Tenar, the young girl he is attempting to save from the Nameless Ones. Like most epic heroes, Ged descends into the underworld to save a dying soul and to save the dying belief in magic. *In medias res,* the convention of plunging the reader into the middle of the action, is also evident in the trilogy from the first page when readers learn that "this is the tale of Ged before he became a hero, before he became Archmage, before he became Dragonlord" (p. 15). LeGuin uses these hints about the future to entice her readers to find out how Ged accomplished these feats.

Haselhuhn suggests that after reading LeGuin's trilogy students will be comfortable moving on to a classical epic. During the study of the *Iliad* students and teachers will be able to continually refer back to the trilogy to note parallels that will enhance their understanding of the classical work.

Young Adult Literature in Historical Surveys

Reading young adult fiction in historical survey units may be more difficult than in thematic or generic units, but it is possible. One way to include young adult literature in a historical survey unit in American literature is to use parallel books. A good example of this approach is the combining of Howard Fast's *April Morning* with Stephen Crane's *The Red Badge of Courage*. Of course, *April Morning* was not written at the time of Stephen Crane's book, but it deals with a similar topic and can help students better understand the more complex work. Another example is the pairing of Elizabeth George Speare's *The Witch of Blackbird Pond* with Arthur Miller's *The Crucible*. Although each was written at a different time for a different audience, each deals with the topic of witches and witch trials. The approach here is not to combine two works that are written in the same period, but instead to make the classic book come to life by pairing it with a similar young adult book written by a contemporary author. Another way to help bring a historical period to life is by reading one or more young adult novels set in the period prior to reading works written in the period. For example, the literature of colonial New England is likely to make more sense to students after they have read a work such as *The Witch of Blackbird Pond.* Carefully chosen young adult books can often be referred to throughout the school year to help students understand historic periods, themes, literary elements, and the motivation of authors to write a particular work.

In units on British literature the task of introducing young adult fiction may seem especially difficult. One of the problems English teachers face in teaching British literature to high school students is their lack of understanding of British history, geography, and culture. In addition to introducing students to literary elements and themes, young adult books can fill in gaps in the students' knowledge that is necessary if they are to understand the classic works.

Ruth Cline and Elizabeth Poe suggest that teachers have students read one or more young adult books by contemporary British writers who write vividly about specific historical periods. British writer Rosemary Sutcliff, for example, could be read before introducing Arthurian legend.

> The Arthurian legend is important in British literature, and Rosemary Sutcliff has written several books that retell the tales associated with King Arthur. In *The Sword and the Circle: King Arthur and the Knights of the Round Table,* Sutcliff masterfully weaves stories from Sir Thomas Malory's *Le Morte d'Arthur,* Geoffrey of Monmouth's *British History,* Middle English poetry and ballads, and *The Mabinogion* to create a retelling remarkably suitable for adolescents. Sutcliff appropriately modernizes sentence structure and diction so the text reads easily but still suggests the formal language and technical terminology essential to tradition. She stresses the adventure in the tales, including violent battles, and delicately describes the sexual relationships intrinsic to the tales. In addition, she occasionally adds a bit of clarification designed to aid a reader unfamiliar with the legends.
>
> Sutcliff continues her Arthurian trilogy in *The Light beyond the Forest: The Quest for the Holy Grail* and *The Road to Camlann: The Death of King Arthur.* In *The Lantern Bearers* and *The Sword at Sunset,* she approaches Arthur as the war leader he actually was and not the legendary hero of high romance he became. All are retold with the creativity of a storyteller who embellishes or simplifies a beloved tale in response to her audience. The same is true in Sutcliff's retelling of *Beowulf,* which would also be an interesting addition in a British literature course. After reading Sutcliff's retellings, students might explore other versions of the tales. In any case, they will gain an understanding of the oral tradition and the Arthurian legend. (1987, p. 55)

Cline and Poe further suggest that teachers can use contemporary British young adult fiction in the British literature curriculum. They particularly suggest the following works: *Handles* by Jan Mark; *Watership Down* by Richard Adams; and James Herriot's *All Creatures Great and Small, All Things Bright and Beautiful,* and *All Things Wise and Wonderful.*

Epilogue: The Classics Brought to Life

Creative teachers can make classic books far more enjoyable, teachable, and enlightening by using young adult literature as a bridge to the literary conventions of the books, their themes, genres, and historic periods. Teachers who teach young adult books along with the classics often find that their students read the classic works with a greater depth of understanding. This should not be a surprise. In many other disciplines we first help students practice their new skills using less complex formulas, experiments, and models. Once the novices have developed their skills, they then move on to increasingly complex problems and concepts.

The world of young adult literature provides teachers with many outstanding books that allow us to teach sophisticated reading and literary skills. Likewise, these books provide students with the opportunity to respond to and experience the world of ideas through literature. There is no reason why every student cannot have access to the world's greatest literature, why they cannot share in our common literary heritage. If this is the goal of the English program, then the teacher's job is to foster the skills students need to understand complex works. When we pair excellent young adult books with classic books, students practice their skills while developing an understanding of the various reasons to read. At the same time, they move toward the ability to read, understand, and respond to classic works. Once students can think critically about books that are written for them, they can take their knowledge of literary conventions in these books and apply it to classic works. In this way they can begin to think critically about more complex works.

Suggested readings

Angelotti, M. "The Effect of Gamma Rays on Man-and-the Writer Zindel: *The Pigman* Plus Twenty and Counting." *ALAN Review,* Winter 1987, pp. 21–25, 43.

The California Literature Institute. *Literature for All Students: A Sourcebook for Teachers.* California State Department of Education, 1985.

Cline, R., and E. Poe. "Now That You Asked . . ." *ALAN Review,* Fall 1987, p. 55.

Haselhuhn, S. L. "YA Books in the Classroom: The Painless Epic." *ALAN Review,* Spring, 1985, pp. 14–15.

Kaywell, J. F., ed. *Adolescent Literature as a Complement to the Classics.* Christopher-Gordon Publishers, 1993.

McGee, T. "The Adolescent Novel in AP English: A Response to Patricia Spencer." *English Journal,* April 1992, pp. 57–58.

Paterson, K. *Gates of Excellence: On Reading and Writing Books for Children.* Elsevier/Nelson, 1981.

——— "Not for Children Only: *Absolute Zero.*" *Washington Post Book World,* 9 April 1978.

Samuels, B. G., R. O. Ingham, and H. Lowery-Moore. "Bridging the Basics: The Young Adult Novel in a Back-to-Basics Society." *ALAN Review,* Winter 1987, pp. 42–44.

Shattuck, M. L. "Parallels between Fox's *The Slave Dancer* and Melville's *Moby Dick* and *Billy Budd.*" *ALAN Review,* Winter 1987, pp. 9–10, 12.

Sheidy, M. "YA Books in the Classroom: From Odyssey to Dickens to Salinger to Zindel." *ALAN Review,* Spring 1988, pp. 24, 43–44.

PART FOUR

SELECTION AND THE CLASSROOM LIBRARY

14 Selecting and Obtaining Young Adult Books

Focus Questions

1. Why is it important for teachers to find books for *all* students?
2. How can teachers utilize lists of "best books" and award-winning books as a resource for selecting books for adolescents?
3. How can book reviews and indexes help in selecting books?
4. How can teachers utilize annotated bibliographies in helping students select their own books?
5. What are some good sources for finding information about authors?
6. How can teachers develop a classroom library without spending a lot of money?

PROLOGUE

I was lucky as a kid, although I didn't think so at the time. I was too fat for basketball or heavy petting. So I could read. Notice I wrote *could,* not *had to.* The point is, boys aren't really allowed to read, not good books, anyway, about relationships or feelings or how to treat girls. Boys are allowed to read books about conquering the world or gluing balsa plane models or scoring from second on a single, but nothing that might really help them or the planet in later life. Up front, let me say I don't know why this is so; maybe it's a conspiracy to keep us from making friends with girls and overthrowing the aliens who control Earth, or maybe it's something to do with publishers' overstock. In any case, it's my premise, and it's absolutely true. . . .

Many of the books boys read—those hard-core private eye vigilante texts, those international thrillers and techno-shootem-ups, and the dumber science fiction and fantasy—merely reinforce the existing condition in this society that encourages boys to grow into men who beat up smaller people, including women and children, to become men who are fearful of each other and will fight any attempt to socialize them out of their violence. Not that I'm suggesting any kind of censorship. It's time to market the positive as aggressively as we've been pushing the poison. . . .

Boys have to learn what girls already know: that a book is something you can make into a cave, and that you can crawl into the cave, roll around in it, explore it, find out what's in it, and what's in you. Someday, there will be books that boys really need—about how they can be friends with other boys by sharing emotions rather than scuffling, about how they can be friends with girls. That might even mean books on an issue rarely discussed that tortures thousands of boys, many of them macho athletes: dealing with sexual feelings toward other boys. What does it mean? As a journalist, I recently did a story on a young football player who had sexual longings for other men, tried to hide them in brawling and drinking, eventually tried to kill himself. He is a quadriplegic now, from that suicide attempt, and after my story came out, he and I were besieged with letters and phone calls from young men who wanted to talk. A book might have helped them, a book that told them they were not alone, that this was something they could share. A book is a secret place in which you can find your own secret places, where no one can see you laughing or crying. It is the El Dorado of this millennium—it is the intellectual and emotional equivalent of safe sex. ✦

From Robert Lipsyte, "Listening for the Footsteps: Books and Boys," *Horn Book Magazine,* May–June 1992, pp. 290–96. Reprinted with permission of *Horn Book Magazine.*

Finding Books for All Students

Ah, what a responsibility we have, we teachers who love books. It is a responsibility we treasure—introducing students to books, helping them find the books they will love, helping them locate books they can use as safe caves for self-exploration. We love books, all kinds of books. We can imagine a world without television, life without movies, but not a world without books. We hope our students will feel the same way. Earlier in this text, we talked about finding the right book for the right student, we discussed books from a variety of genres, and we examined how to utilize the books in the curriculum to teach concepts and skills and to encourage reading. Two major questions remain: How can we find the best books for our students? And how do we get those books into the hands of the students who need them?

Keeping up with young adult literature is a monumental task for the busy teacher. Every year thousands of books appropriate for adolescents are published. Add these to the thousands that make up the young adult backlists of dozens of publishers and you have an ever-growing field of literature. In addition to keeping up with new titles and new authors, teachers must be able to find the flowers in the garden of adolescent literature. Many of the books published each year may be appropriate for independent reading, but are probably not appropriate for classroom use. Because we want to attract our students to the best books available, books they are likely to enjoy and continue to remember after they have read them, it is essential that we find ways to locate and obtain these books. This chapter provides numerous helpful sources for locating good books and suggests ways you can collect books for your classroom library.

Teachers do not need to read every new young adult book. Instead, we can rely on reliable review and bibliographic sources. This chapter explains what each source offers and how it can be useful. You will want to select those sources that are the most useful in your situation.

"Best Book" Lists

Every year several library and educational organizations publish lists of what they consider to be the best books for young adults. The categories vary from books of great literary merit to books that are likely to be popular with young adult readers to books of political or social value (as defined by the organization compiling the list). Teachers can use these lists as one tool in selecting young adult books for the classroom. It is important to know the criteria used to prepare each list so you can recommend the right book to the right reader. Just because a book appears on a "best book" list does not mean it will be enjoyed by all young adults or that it has great value as a piece of young adult literature. Most "best book" lists use selection criteria established by adults. The criteria that adults use to select books may not match those of the adolescent seeking pleasure reading. A few of the lists, however, are designed to reflect the interests of adolescents.

Children's Book Council

Two excellent book lists for content area teachers are available from the Children's Book Council. Outstanding Science Trade Books for Children is a list of books selected by a joint committee of the Children's Book Council (CBC) and the National Science Teachers Association (NSTA). The list is printed each spring in *Science and*

Children, a journal for NSTA members. The list includes books appropriate for kindergarten through middle school students selected according to the following criteria: accuracy, readability, pleasing format, and illustrations. The committee seeks books without personal biases or values in which fact and theory are clearly distinguished and experiments are appropriate for the age of the readers. The books are listed by category and are annotated for teachers and parents.

Notable Children's Trade Books in the Field of Social Studies is a list compiled annually by a joint committee of the CBC and the National Council for the Social Studies (NCSS). The books are for readers from kindergarten through grade eight and are selected to represent a diversity of groups and emphasize human relations. They must present "an original theme or a fresh slant on a traditional topic," and they must have a pleasing format and illustrations. Titles on the list are grouped by historical period, genre, or subject area. Extensive annotations are provided for teachers and parents. This list is annually published in a spring issue of *Social Education,* a journal of NCSS.

If you are not a member of these organizations and do not have access to their journals, you may obtain free copies of the lists with a self-addressed 6-½-by-9-½-inch envelope with three ounces of first-class postage from the CBC Order Center. (Addresses of organizations that compile book lists are given on pages 440–441.)

International Reading Association

Some "best book" lists are based on judgments made by young adults and children. Each year the International Reading Association (IRA) publishes in their journals two lists selected by children and young adults. Author Jeannette Eyerly suggests that readers are often the best judges of good books, "I believe that children are better judges of what constitutes a good book than adults. Children care nothing about best seller lists, what book has won an award and which one has not. Children know what they like and they read it—not once, but a half dozen times or more" (1981).

The Journal of Reading, a journal for teachers who teach reading to adolescents, publishes the Young Adults' Choices list. This list is based on the votes of over 4,500 students. Each year publishers submit books for the project which selects approximately thirty titles. To be eligible the books must have received at least two positive reviews from adult review sources during the previous year. International Reading Association members are selected as team leaders. These team leaders, who serve as reading motivators, select the schools that will make up their team and distribute the books to students. The student ballots are mailed directly to IRA where they are tallied. The list gives a summary of each book along with bibliographic information. This list is particularly helpful to students seeking books of personal interest for independent reading or book reports. Because each book has also been positively reviewed by two professionals, it is also likely to be of high literary quality, making this yearly list an excellent resource.

A similar list for younger readers, Children's Choices, is published annually in the *Reading Teacher,* a journal of the IRA for elementary and middle school teachers. Many of the books on this list are appropriate for middle school and junior high school readers. Books for the current year are read by ten thousand children annually and their favorites make the list. The annotated list, grouped by age level, usually appears in the October issue of the *Reading Teacher.* Because this list is a joint project with the Children's Book Council, a reprint of the list is available by sending a 6-½-by-9½-inch, self-addressed, stamped envelope with first-class postage for two ounces to the CBC Order Center.

Each year the *Reading Teacher* also publishes Teachers' Choices, a list of children's books for prereaders through middle school students. These are books that teachers judge as "exceptional in curriculum use." Teachers try out between two and five hundred books annually in classrooms. Every book is read by a minimum of six teachers or librarians in each of seven regions of the country. Ratings are then collated by IRA to make up the national, annotated list.

New York Public Library

Each year the Office on Books for Young Adults of the New York Public Library publishes Books for the Teenage, an annotated list of over twelve hundred books recommended for young adults. The list is arranged by subject heading (e.g., "Vietnam Remembered," "AIDS," "The Universe") and is selected by adult librarians.

Young Adult Services Division of the American Library Association

Each year the Young Adult Services Division of the American Library Association (YASD) publishes the Best Books for Young Adults list. All the books have been published during the previous year. Although the selections are made by a committee of adults, mostly librarians, they select books that will both appeal to and be of value to readers between the ages of twelve and eighteen. The books must meet the following standards: "*Fiction* must have believable characters and dialogue and plausible plot development; *nonfiction* must have a readable text and an appealing format." If you are searching for a way to improve your students' independent reading selections, this list can be a wonderful resource.

If you are seeking good books for poor or reluctant readers, you may want to consult Quick Picks. This list is designed to help less able or unwilling readers find books they are likely to enjoy. According to the selectors, the books have "exciting stories and interesting characters"; they are "books about real-life heroes and fantastic adventures—books that tell you how to fix up your car and help you deal with day-to-day problems."

The YASD publishes numerous other lists that are helpful to teachers and students. One collection of five lists, Outstanding Books for the College Bound, is designed for college-bound adolescents. The lists cover the following areas: theater, fiction, nonfiction, biographies, and fine arts. Each list contains both contemporary and classic works that are selected by a committee of YASD to both entertain and stimulate students. Many of the titles on the lists are available in hardcover and paperback editions. The selectors try to choose books that are available in school and public libraries. These can make great summer reading lists for your most able students.

All of these lists are excellent resources for students and teachers. Departments, schools, or individual teachers can send for inexpensive multiple copies of these lists to share with students and parents. To order the lists or obtain more information, write to ALA Graphics.

Award Books

Every year some of the best young adult books and authors from around the world are selected to receive literary honors. The criteria for selection varies, but in each case the awards are based on the quality of the book for a particular audience.

The ALAN Award   The ALAN Award is given annually by the Assembly on Literature for Adolescents of the National Council of Teachers of English. The award honors authors, publishers, and teacher-scholars who have made significant contributions to the world of adolescent literature. Past award recipients include authors Robert Cormier, Sue Ellen Bridgers, and Gary Paulsen, and teacher-scholars Dwight Burton, Ken Donelson, Louise Rosenblatt, and M. Jerry Weiss.

Boston Globe–Horn Book Award   Awards for the best fiction and nonfiction books for children are given annually by the *Boston Globe* and *Horn Book Magazine*. Announcement of the awards and the acceptance speeches of the recipients appear annually in the *Horn Book Magazine*. Past award recipients include Andrew Davies for *Conrad's War,* Virginia Hamilton for *M. C. Higgins, the Great,* Zibby Oneal for *In Summer Light,* and Paula Fox for *The Village by the Sea.*

Carnegie Medal   The Carnegie Medal has been awarded annually since 1936 by the British Library Association to an outstanding book for children written in English and published initially in the United Kingdom during the preceding year. The award may be given in a variety of categories, including fiction and information books. The selection criteria for a work of fiction are plot, style, and characterization. Criteria for information books are accuracy, method of presentation, style, and format. The medal has been awarded to authors such as Leon Garfield and Edward Blishen for *The God beneath the Sea* and Alan Garner for *The Owl Service.*

Christopher Book Award   The Christopher medal is given to books that affirm "the highest values of human spirit." Winners are frequently young adult books, including Alicia Appleman-Jurman's *Alicia: My Story* and James Lincoln Collier and Christopher Collier's *Decision in Philadelphia: The Constitutional Convention of 1787.*

Coretta Scott King Award   The Coretta Scott King Award is presented annually by the Social Responsibilities Round Table of the American Library Association. The award, founded in 1969, is for African American authors or illustrators whose books "promote understanding and appreciation of the culture and contribution of all people to the realization of the 'American dream.'" Winners include Mildred Taylor for *The Road to Memphis* (1991), Patricia and Fredrick McKissack for *A Long Hard Journey: The Story of the Pullman Porter* (1990), and Walter Dean Myers for *Fallen Angels* (1989). A current list of these awards can be obtained from the American Library Association.

Edgar Allan Poe Award   The Edgar Award, established in 1961, is given each spring by the Mystery Writers of America in several categories, including the best children's mystery published during the previous year if one is considered worthy. Young adult authors such as Jay Bennett *(The Long Black Coat)*, Virginia Hamilton *(The House of Dies Drear),* and Patricia Windsor *(The Sandman's Eyes)* have won the award.

Hans Christian Andersen Medal   The Hans Christian Andersen International Medal is awarded every two years by the International Board on Books for Young People to a living author and a living artist for an outstanding body of work that has made a contribution to literature for young people. Several authors of young adult books, including Scott O'Dell and Virginia Hamilton, have won the award.

Hugo and Nebula Awards   The Hugo Award was established in 1953, and the winners are selected by participants to the annual World Science Fiction Convention. Because the awards, given for the best novel, short story, magazine, motion picture, fan letter, and dramatic presentation, are selected at a convention, they tend to emphasize popularity and the tastes of the audience. Although young adult writing is not specifically honored, the popular nature of the winning book often makes it appealing to teenagers. Young adult authors such as Ursula LeGuin have been honored by the convention.

Ursula LeGuin has also won a Nebula Award of the Science Fiction Writers of America. The awards, given for best novella, short story, and novel, consider style, characterization, plot structure, and imaginative style. The novella award is often presented to an author of young adult fiction.

Jane Addams Children's Book Award   The Jane Addams Award is given annually by the Jane Addams Peace Association and the Women's International League for Peace and Freedom to honor the book that most effectively promotes peace, social justice, and world community. Authors of adolescent literature are frequent recipients of this award. In 1977, for example, Milton Meltzer won the award for his nonfiction work for young adults *Never to Forget: The Jews of the Holocaust.* In 1991 the award recipient was Fredrick McKissack for *A Long Hard Journey: The Story of the Pullman Porter.*

Laura Ingalls Wilder Award   The Wilder Award is given by the Association for Library Service to Children of the American Library Association. It is given "in recognition of an author or illustrator whose books, published in the U.S., have made, over a period of years, a substantial and lasting contribution to literature for children." Although most award recipients have been authors of books for young children, some, like Beverly Cleary and Elizabeth George Speare, write books of interest to adolescents. A list of award winners is available from the American Library Association.

Lewis Carroll Shelf Award   The award named for the author of *Alice in Wonderland* has been given by the University of Wisconsin School of Education since 1958. Winners include Joan Aiken for *The Wolves of Willoughby Chase* and Norma Fox Mazer for *Saturday, the Twelfth of October.* The purpose of the award is to recognize annually "those books worthy enough to sit on the shelf with *Alice in Wonderland*."

A committee of five, representing librarians, teachers, parents, and writers, reviews the books submitted by publishers. They must agree unanimously on the winner.

Margaret A. Edwards Award   This award, named after a librarian who pioneered young adult services in public libraries, is given annually by the Young Adult Services Division of the American Library Association "to an author whose books are accepted by young adults as authentic expressions of their world, illuminating their experiences and emotions and giving insight into their lives." The award, established in 1987, has been given to S. E. Hinton, Richard Peck, Robert Cormier, and Lois Duncan. A list of award winners is available from the American Library Association.

Mildred L. Batchelder Award   The Batchelder Award is given annually to a publisher of children's books for a single book considered to be most outstanding of those originally published in a foreign language. It is given by the Association for Library Service to Children of the American Library Association. Often this award goes to a publisher of a young adult book. In 1972, for instance, it was presented to Holt, Rinehart and Winston for the publication of Hans Richter's *Friedrich.* Recent recipients include Dutton and Rafik Schami for *A Hand Full of Stars* (1991), Dutton and Bjarne Reuter for *Buster's World* (1990), and Lothrop and Peter Härtling for *Crutches* (1989). A copy of a list of recipients of this award, which is available from the American Library Association, is invaluable if you are teaching a course in world literature to adolescents.

The Newbery Medal   The most prestigious and best-known award for a non–picture book in literature for young readers is the John Newbery medal. First awarded in 1922, the medal is given annually to the author of the book that makes "the most distinguished contribution to American literature for children." It is presented by the Association for Library Service to Children, a division of the American Library Association. The award, named for an editor and author of children's books in mid-eighteenth-century England, is given to encourage original and creative work in literature for children. The criteria for selection of the medal book are the author's "interpretations of the theme or concept; presentation of information including accuracy, clarity and organization; development of plot; delineation of characters; delineation of setting; appropriateness of style." In addition to the medal book, honor books are designated each year. A pamphlet listing award recipients is available from the American Library Association.

In addition to the awards discussed above, many others are given for books appropriate to young adult audiences and the authors who write them. Teachers can gain current information about these award books by reading the "Hunt Breakfast" column in each issue of the *Horn Book Magazine.* This column lists many of the awards given in the previous two months, discusses the criteria used, and briefly examines the books and authors. Another excellent source for comprehensive but less up-to-date information about award books is *Children's Books: Awards and Prizes,* published annually by the Children's Book Council. Many libraries will have a copy of Dolores Blythe Jones's *Children's Literature Awards and Winners. Award-Winning*

Books for Children and Young Adults: An Annual Guide is another excellent source of information about books. The guide is published annually by Scarecrow Press and edited by Betty L. Criscoe. The directory is arranged in alphabetical order by award. Background of the award and biographical information about the winner is provided, along with a selected bibliography of the author's other books.

Book Review Sources

Book reviews, like "best book" lists, use a variety of criteria for evaluation. Teachers should consider the criteria used by the book review sources before recommending particular books to individual students. Some reviewing sources pride themselves on having strict standards for literary merit. Others favorably review books that they believe will be popular with the intended audience. Still other sources recommend books because they cover a particular social issue or concern. And some base their recommendations on a book's usefulness in the curriculum.

Primary Review Sources

There are numerous publications whose primary function is to review books. Some of these journals review only young adult books, others review children's books as well as young adult books, and others review a wide variety of books.

ALAN Review   The *ALAN Review,* published by the Assembly on Literature for Adolescents of the National Council of Teachers of English, is one of the few publications devoted entirely to adolescent literature. The journal is distributed three times per year (fall, winter, spring) to members of ALAN. It contains articles about and by authors, articles about using young adult books in the classroom, information useful to teachers interested in young adult literature, a column about connecting classrooms and libraries, and clip-out reviews of hardbound and paperback releases in the young adult category. The reviews are short enough to fit on a three-by-five-inch file card. Most reviews briefly summarize the book and even more briefly state the opinion of the reviewer, and they often discuss how the book can be used in the classroom. The genre or theme of the book is given along with bibliographic information. The conciseness of the reviews makes them valuable for the busy teacher who must learn as much as possible about young adult books in a short time.

Booklist   One of the most up-to-date review sources is the *Booklist,* published twice monthly from September through June and once in July and August by the American Library Association. The reviews range in size from brief annotations to long essays. A regular feature of the *Booklist* is "Books for Youth." This section includes adult books for young adults, books for older readers, and starred books for youth. Starred books are reviewed books that have high literary quality and popular appeal. Young adult books also appear in other regular features of the journal and are indicated in the index with the note "(youth)." *Booklist* also offers interviews with young adult authors, lists of paperback reprints, and information on videos. A semiannual index is issued in February and August. The ALA Best Books for Junior

High Readers and Best Books for Senior High Readers are published annually in *Booklist.*

Bulletin of the Center for Children's Books   Published by the University of Chicago Graduate Library School, the *Bulletin* is a primary review source of children's books and books for adolescents. The *Bulletin,* which is published monthly except in August, reviews approximately seventy recently published books per issue. The reviews include a shorthand evaluation of the quality of the books: * for books of special distinction, R for recommended books, and NR for not recommended books. Also included are special classifications of books:

SpC   subject matter or treatment will tend to limit the book to specialized collections

SpR   book will have appeal for the unusual reader only

C.U.   curriculum use (e.g., "U.S. History—Modern—Stories)

D.V.   developmental value (e.g., "Generosity," "Older-younger generations")

Another valuable aspect of the *Bulletin* is the grade-level recommendation that appears at the front of each review. The *Bulletin* also includes a list of recent book awards.

Horn Book Magazine   *Horn Book Magazine,* a bimonthly publication, is devoted to literary criticism of books for children and young adults. The reviews, which emphasize literary quality, are approximately 200 words in length. Numerous articles discuss books appropriate for young readers. Other regular features, including acceptance speeches for the Newbery, Laura Ingalls Wilder, and *Boston Globe–Horn Book* awards, lists of new professional publications, announcements of awards, and information about professional conferences for teachers and librarians, make this magazine a valuable resource.

Horn Book Guide   The *Horn Book Guide,* published twice a year in March and September, is a newcomer that is an important resource for both teachers and librarians. It annotates and evaluates several hundred books appropriate for young adults in each issue. A rating system for literary merit ranges from 1 (outstanding) to 6 (unacceptable). Books rated 1 and 2 are highlighted with a △. The guide includes general reviews of recent books in two sections: "Intermediate Fiction" and "Older Fiction." Books are also listed by subject area and genre. An index is included at the back of each guide. The *Guide* is one of the best resources on recent books. If your school library does not subscribe to this invaluable resource, request that they do so.

School Library Journal   *School Library Journal* is a comprehensive review journal covering both recommended and not recommended books. The highly recommended books are starred in each issue, and the reviewers provide teachers with information about books they considered to be exceptionally good. Titles of interest to young adults appear in the review listings by grade level (e.g., "Junior High Up") if they come from the juvenile division of publishing houses. If they come from the adult division, they are listed under the heading "Adult Books for Young Adults."

An index in each issue lists reviewed books by author and title. "In the YA Corner," a column by librarian Carolyn Caywood, provides information and opinions about young adult books, authors, and issues. The journal also reviews computer software by subject area and grade level.

Voice of Youth Advocates   *Voice of Youth Advocates* (VOYA), primarily of interest to librarians, has the goal of moving young adult literature out of the children's section of the library to its own section. To reach this goal the bimonthly journal, published from April through February, includes articles about young adults, library services for young adults, authors, thematic listings of young adult books, announcements of conferences and publications, reviews of books written for or of interest to young adults, reviews of pamphlets of interest to young adults and their parents, information about periodicals for teens, information about teachers' guides, and news about new paperback publications. The reviews are interesting for two reasons. They give good, brief summaries of the books, and they rate books on both quality and popularity. The highest-quality mark, 5Q, is given if the reviewer finds it "hard to imagine it being better written." The highest mark for popularity, 5P, is given if "every YA was dying to read it yesterday."

Secondary Review Sources

Many professional journals review books on a regular basis. These journals are frequently available in school libraries or from teachers who belong to the professional organizations.

English Journal   *English Journal,* a publication of the National Council of Teachers of English, regularly features reviews of and articles about young adult books. The column "Books for the Teenage Reader" is edited by well-known scholars Alleen Pace Nilsen and Ken Donelson. Their reviews are usually short (less than 200 words) and emphasize information about the book that is of interest to English teachers. Often the books reviewed are grouped thematically. *English Journal,* published monthly from September through April, also has many articles about teaching English in the junior and senior high school classroom which often discuss the use of young adult literature. Also included are announcements of conferences, book awards, reviews of professional publications, and other information of interest to English teachers.

Journal of Reading   *Journal of Reading,* published by the International Reading Association, is of particular interest to junior and senior high school teachers. In the past the only teacher likely to be interested in this journal was the reading teacher, but its appeal is broader now because of the emphasis on teaching reading in all subject areas, from social studies to physical education. *Journal of Reading,* published monthly from September through May, includes short reviews of adolescent books in every issue. Often the books selected for the column "Books for Adolescents" are related to a theme. The column focuses on the use of the literature in the classroom. Professional materials, classroom materials, and audiovisuals are also reviewed. A column reviewing high interest/low readability books for adults is also helpful to high school English teachers. Announcements of conferences, awards, articles about teaching reading in a variety of subjects, and reviews of recent research in reading make this an invaluable resource for all teachers.

Journal of Youth Services   Formerly *Top of the News,* the *Journal of Youth Services* is a quarterly of the Association for Library Service to Children and the Young Adult Services Division of the American Library Association, which is free to members of the two divisions. The publication is of interest because of its feature articles about using young adult literature in the library; it also lists major book award winners and the ALA Best Books for Young Adults and Quick Picks. Young adult books are reviewed in some but not all issues. Each review is designated M (middle school), J (junior high school) or S (senior high school), and reviews are grouped by genre. This journal, more than any other, is committed to reviewing nonfiction as well as fiction for adolescents. The journal also reviews professional books, indexes, and audiovisuals. Many school and public libraries subscribe to this source.

Indexes

Often the busy teacher, librarian, or parent wants to find information about a specific young adult book but does not have time to read it. Perhaps a young adult has asked about a particular title, an advertisement about the book looks intriguing, or the teacher has seen an interview with the author. To obtain information without reading the entire book, the teacher, librarian, or parent can read a review. The difficulty is in locating a review that supplies the necessary information about the book. Several excellent indexes of book reviews are available.

Book Review Digest   Published since 1905 by the H. W. Wilson Company, *Book Review Digest* indexes reviews published in approximately eighty-five American, Canadian, and British journals. Entries are arranged alphabetically by author, and each includes a brief descriptive note and excerpts from the reviews with references to the journals.

Book Review Index   Reviews of books of interest to older adolescents are likely to be listed in the comprehensive *Book Review Index* (Gale Research, 1965–present). This index lists books for adults and young adults. Reviews can be located by title or author. If the book has been reviewed during the time period covered by the index and the review appeared in one of the journals listed in the front of the index, the review will be listed. This index is available in most college or university libraries and many large public libraries. Some school libraries also have this index.

Children's Book Review Index   The *Children's Book Review Index* (Gale, 1975–present) lists current and past reviews of children's books. To find a review of a book, you need to know the title or the author. Review sources, from those listed in the front of the index, are given. This index is particularly valuable for adults working with younger adolescents and is highly recommended for school libraries.

Children's Literature Review   The *Children's Literature Review* (Gale, 1976–present) includes summaries of reviews of children's books and young adult books. Reviews are arranged alphabetically by author.

High-Interest Books for Teens: A Guide to Book Review and Biographical Sources   In this guide (Gale Research, 1988), edited by Joyce Nakamura, the review section is arranged by author. Each entry includes the review source as well as the subject of the book. A subject index is provided. This guide is particularly helpful for teachers searching for books for poor or reluctant readers.

Horn Book Index, 1924–1989   The *Horn Book Magazine* was one of the first journals devoted to children's books. The journal is filled with useful articles and reviews for teachers. The index, edited by Serenna F. Day and published by Oryx Press, lists over 80,000 titles discussed or mentioned in the journal between 1924 and 1989. If your library has back editions of the *Horn Book Magazine,* this index is worth ordering for your reference section.

Index to Literary Criticism for Young Adults   The *Index to Literary Criticism for Young Adults* (Scarecrow Press, 1988), edited by Nancy E. Shields, is an index covering over 4,000 authors who are included in standard reference books that are readily available in most libraries. The index, which is designed to help young adults become competent researchers, lists authors alphabetically and then lists reference book(s) containing information about the author and the author's works. For ease of use, authors are listed under all relevant names (e.g., Clare Boothe Luce and Clare Boothe) and each listing is complete. Many young adult authors are included in the index.

Masterplots II: Juvenile and Young Adult Literature   This useful four-volume work (Salem Press, 1991), edited by Frank N. Magill, presents essay-type reviews of numerous young adult books. Each entry includes the type of plot, time, setting, and themes of the novel, in addition to bibliographic notes. The "Context" section of each entry puts the novel in the context of the author's other works; the "Themes" and "Meaning" sections outline the issues presented in the work from the perspective of a young adult. Author, title, and subject indexes make this a particularly useful source for school libraries. Teachers who are searching for appropriate works on a particular theme can consult the subject index for such broad themes as "coming of age" and "job and work."

Olderr's Young Adult Fiction Index   Edited by Steven Olderr, this index (St. James Press, 1988) lists over 800 books for young adults reviewed in *Publisher's Weekly, Booklist, VOYA,* and *School Library Journal.* The index contains a main entry section and an index of authors, subjects, titles, and characters.

Young Adult Book Review Index   Edited by Barbara Beach, *Young Adult Book Review Index* (Gale Research, 1988) is arranged by author and includes an illustrator and title index. Reviews are from periodicals associated with young adult library services such as *VOYA* and *School Library Journal*. Each entry includes the title of the review source, date, volume, and page number.

Bibliographies

Compiling course bibliographies is a time-consuming task for the teacher. Because teachers of young adults are often unfamiliar with recent books written for teenagers, such books are often omitted from class bibliographies. Thus, bibliographic listings, particularly those that are annotated, carefully indexed with good cross-references, and thematically or generically grouped, are exceedingly useful to the busy teacher. Such listings can save hours of searching time.

The librarian is often faced with the task of ordering books that will be appealing to young readers as well as to teachers. At times, though, teachers do not have time to develop library order request lists for their classes. Therefore, the librarian must select books that are likely to be appropriate for the subjects being taught, the reading tastes of all the young readers, and the wide range of reading levels in the school. Bibliographies are particularly helpful in this situation.

Many bibliographies are also designed to help young adults find books that interest them. For the young adult who enjoyed a particular book, locating a similar book can be difficult. The card catalogue or computer catalogue may be of little or no help, searching the stacks may take too much time, and the student may be reluctant to ask for help. Such students can often find books of interest listed in annotated bibliographies designed for young readers.

General Bibliographies

In *Beacham's Guide to Literature for Young Adults* (1990), edited by Kirk H. Beetz and Suzanne Niemeyer, each entry offers a brief analysis of a major young adult book. Also included in each entry are an overview, sections on the author, setting, themes and characters, literary quality, and social sensitivity, plus topics for discussion, ideas for reports and papers, lists of other young adult books by the author, and an annotated bibliography of further readings. If students are taught how to use this reference for developing skills in literary criticism rather than for a quick way to do a book report, it can be an invaluable resource.

The Best Books for Junior High Readers (Bowker, 1991), edited by John T. Gillespie, is an excellent reference containing short annotations of several thousand books grouped by genre and nonfiction topic. Also edited by Gillespie is *Best Books for Senior High Readers*. These two books are excellent reference books for school libraries.

The Book Finder: A Guide to Children's Literature about the Needs and Problems of Youth Aged 2–15 (American Guidance Service, vol. 1, 1977; vol. 2, 1981; vol. 3, 1985; vol. 4, 1989), written by Sharon Spredemann Dreyer, is an extremely useful guide for teachers and guidance counselors. Each volume is actually two books in one: an index, cross-referenced by subject, author, and title, and a book of annotated entries with publication information (including hard- and softcover publishers, braille editions, cassette recordings of books, and other forms in which books are available), thematic headings, and ages for which the book is appropriate. This is a good source for recommending "a good book just like the other one," for suggesting books that relate to problems students are facing, and for developing thematic bibliographies. No school library should be without it.

Two dictionaries of children's fiction are useful resources for teachers and students. The *Dictionary of American Children's Fiction* (Greenwood, 1986) and *Dictionary of British Children's Fiction* (2 vols., Greenwood, 1989), both by Alethea K. Helbig and Agnes Regan Perkins, list children's and young adult fiction in alphabetical order by author and title. In these comprehensive and useful works, author entries give brief biographical and bibliographic information. Title entries give the author's name, a brief but thorough summary of the plot, brief critical comments, and awards the book has won.

Seniorplots: A Book Talk Guide for Use with Readers Ages 15–18 (Bowker, 1989), by John T. Gillespie and Corinne J. Naden, is an annotated list of works of fiction arranged by twelve subject and genre headings (e.g., "Growing Up," "The World around Us," "Suspense and Mystery"). Each entry includes sources of book reviews and biographical information on the author. This book is a good source for both teachers and students.

Bibliographies for Young Adults

Several bibliographic sources are specifically aimed at young adult readers. *Books for You: A Booklist for Senior High School Students* (1992) is a comprehensive, annotated guide to young adult and adult books appropriate for teen readers. The current edition of the book, which is updated semiannually by NCTE, is edited by Shirley Wurth. Entries are grouped by topic, such as drugs and alcohol, and dating and sexual awareness. It is designed to "stimulate senior high school students to read the best of the current books written for them." The index is cross-referenced by title and author.

Your Reading: A Booklist for Junior High and Middle School Students (1991), edited by Alleen Pace Nilsen and published by NCTE, annotates more than 1,000 books published between 1988 and 1990. It is organized to "capture student interest and to provide a base from which to discover reading as an active process." The guide includes an "Introduction to Readers," an appendix for teachers and librarians, and bibliographic information that allows students to locate each book in the library.

High Interest–Easy Reading (1990) is another excellent classroom reference for students and teachers. Edited by William G. McBride, the current edition contains over 400 annotations of best-selling books for hard-to-interest adolescent readers. Subject categories in the book include growing up, the supernatural, humor, and how-to. Author, title, and subject indexes make this a particularly helpful guide for students seeking "a book just like the other book." The book is written for students in grades seven through twelve. Published in paperback by the National Council of Teachers of English, this guide is an inexpensive reference for classroom libraries.

Special-Interest Bibliographies

Several useful bibliographic sources list multicultural literature. The following are recommended for school libraries:

- *Our Family, Our Friends, Our World: An Annotated Guide to Significant Multicultural Books for Children and Teenagers,* edited by Lyn Miller-Lachmann (Bowker, 1992)
- *Books by African-American Authors and Illustrators for Children and Young Adults,* edited by Helen E. Williams (ALA, 1991)
- *Literature by and about the American Indian: An Annotated Bibliography,* by Anna Less Stensland (NCTE, 1979)

The American Library Association regularly publishes pamphlets listing genre- or theme-related books for young adults, teachers, and librarians. These annotated lists are frequently updated and new ones appear periodically. Some current recommended lists are

- *1492–1992, The Columbian Experience: A Selected Bibliography*
- *100 Contemporary Classics: The Best of Adult Notable Books from 1944–1990*
- *Fictional Paths to Understanding: A Multicultural Reading List*

All of these are available in single or multiple copies from the American Library Association.

Other good special-interest bibliographies on world literature and cultures include the following:

- *The Indian Subcontinent in Literature for Children and Young Adults: An Annotated Bibliography of English-Language Books* by Meena Khorana (Bibliographies and Indexes in World Literature, no. 32; Greenwood Press, 1991)
- *The Soviet Union in Literature for Children and Young Adults: An Annotated Bibliography of English-Language Books* by Frances F. Povsic (see above; look for other reference works in this series)
- *Images: A Bibliography of Canadian Children's and Young Adult Literature* (Manitoba Instructional Resources Branch, 1990)
- *Books in Spanish for Children and Young Adults: An Annotated Guide* by Isabel Schon (1987)
- *Japan through Children's Literature: An Annotated Bibliography* by Yasuho Makino (Greenwood Press, 1985)

These bibliographies are especially useful for teachers of world history or world literature. With such sources available, there is no reason why young adult books cannot be included in these courses.

Other sources particularly helpful to social studies teaches and teachers teaching interdisciplinary units include

- *American History for Children and Young Adults: An Annotated Bibliographic Index* by Vandelia Van Meter (Libraries Unlimited, 1990)
- *A Reference Guide to Historical Fiction for Children and Young Adults* by Lynda G. Adamson (Greenwood Press, 1987)
- *Book Links: Connecting Books, Libraries and Classrooms* edited by Barbara Elleman

Book Links is not a book but a monthly resource journal published by *Booklist* and the American Library Association. It does not review new children's or young adult books, nor does it offer literary criticism. Rather, it provides information on bringing books on a variety of themes and in a variety of genres into the classroom. For example, one recent issue covered the following themes and genres: "Water and Waterways," "The Vote Is Yours!" "A World View—Children's Atlases," "The Former Yugoslavia," and "The Caribbean." Each article presents an annotated list of books with bibliographic information. The grade level for which each book is appropriate is indicated. Many of the articles also have sidebars on teaching ideas and activities. *Book Links* is a wonderful classroom or library reference available at reasonable subscription rates.

Several subject-oriented or genre bibliographic guides are available to teachers. *Supernatural Fiction for Teens* (Libraries Unlimited, 1990) by Cosette N. Kies annotates more than 1,300 paperbacks to read for wonderment, fear, and fun. This is a worthwhile source for students who become hooked on supernatural adult fiction but are unable to find good books in the genre. *Fantasy Literature for Children and Young Adults* (Bowker, 1989) by Ruth Nadelman Lynn is an excellent bibliographic source listing over 3,300 novels and short story collections. The books are arranged by type of fantasy and each entry includes a brief summary of the book and review sources. *Science and Technology in Fact and Fiction: A Guide to Young Adult Books* (Bowker, 1990) is a good reference for teachers in a variety of disciplines. Written by DayAnn M. Kennedy, Stella Spangler, and Mary Ann Vanderwerf, this bibliography contains annotated entries for titles related to physical and earth science. It is divided into two sections, science and technology, which are each divided into fiction and nonfiction.

Two resources are helpful for teachers and students looking for books with handicapped protagonists or dealing with disabilities. *Accept Me As I Am: Best Books of Juvenile Nonfiction on Impairment and Disabilities* (Bowker, 1985) by Joan B. Friedberg, June B. Mullins, and Adelaide W. Sukienik is arranged topically under such headings as deafness, speech impairments, and mental retardation. Excellent annotations and brief critical analyses of each book make this a valuable reference. *More Notes from a Different Drummer: A Guide to Juvenile Fiction Portraying the Disabled* (Bowker, 1984) by Barbara H. Baskin and Karen H. Harris is an updated guide of an earlier reference book. The extensive annotations describe books with disabled characters and themes related to disability. Look for new editions of both of these books in the near future.

Resources Especially for Teachers

A "too good to be missed" listing available to teachers is *CBC Features,* which is published twice a year by the Children's Book Council. This little pamphlet provides a wealth of information and is available for a small lifetime subscription fee. In addition to articles about writing and publishing books, the pamphlet includes information about free and reasonably priced resources and teaching aids from CBC and other sources. For current information on the subscription rate and materials available from CBC write to the Children's Book Council. If you happen to be in the neighborhood of the CBC offices in New York City, you might want to visit their new-book examination library which is open on most weekdays.

Other excellent professional resources provide both bibliographies, commentaries, criticism, and teaching ideas. *Beyond the Happy Ending: The Pedagogy and Promise of African American Literature for Youth* (Greenwood Press, 1990) by Dianne

Johnson looks at African American literature for young people since the 1920s. It particularly focuses on current themes and underlying philosophies.

Books for the Junior High Years (Southeastern Ohio Council of Teachers of English, Spring 1989) is a special publication of the journal *Focus: Teaching English Language Arts.* This excellent resource has articles about teaching specific young adult books, teaching the books of a single author, teaching thematic and genre units, and teaching cross-cultural books. Numerous annotated bibliographies are provided. Teachers should also check back issues of journals on adolescent literature published by professional organizations in their own state.

Nonfiction for Young Adults: From Delight to Wisdom (Oryz, 1990) by Betty Carter and Richard Abrahamson analyzes nonfiction for young adults in terms of interest, accuracy, content, style, organization, format, and uses. This guide can help teachers find specific nonfiction works as well as learn how to evaluate and select nonfiction. Also included are interviews with some of the best-known nonfiction authors writing for adolescents.

Autobiography and biography are useful in the classroom. A reprint of an issue of *Oregon English: Autobiography and Biography* (NCTE, 1990), edited by Ulrich H. Hardt, suggests that teachers use autobiography and biography "as a means for teaching students to tap their hidden impulses and memories." Specific teaching strategies are suggested in articles on subjects such as third world auto/biography, the civil rights movement, and teachers' lives.

Another unusual resource of bibliographic information is available from the Young Adult Services Division of the American Library Association. Genre Lists and Tip Kits contain excellent bibliographies printed on bookmarks, signs, and stickers. The kits are available for horror, sports, romance, science fiction, mystery, humor, and fantasy. The genre bookmarks can be ordered separately.

Publisher's catalogues are sometimes overlooked as a resource for selecting hardcover and paperback books for the classroom. Most catalogues contain annotated listings, often with comments from positive reviews. The awards received by the book or the author are usually listed in the annotation, as is the reading or interest level. Many catalogues are organized by topic, theme, genre, or subject area. Often each book is carefully cross-referenced and appears in all appropriate sections of the catalogue, and title and author indexes appear in the back. Well-qualified educational consultants frequently write brief articles for the catalogues. Some information about authors may also be given in catalogues. Many publishing companies prepare teacher guides to use when studying the books, the authors, or a particular topic covered by the publisher's books. Many of these materials are well done, written by educators, and available either free or for a minimal charge. Most paperback publishers have a single-copy review policy that allows teachers to obtain a review copy of a book at minimal cost.

Resources for Parents

Parents who ask about their children's reading will be interested in *From Comics to Classics: A Parent's Guide to Books for Teens and Preteens* (International Reading Association, 1985) by Arthea J. S. Reed. The annotated entries in this bibliography are divided by interest area and age level. In addition, it provides suggestions written specifically for parents about encouraging adolescents to read.

The American Library Association offers two excellent, inexpensive pamphlets that teachers, libraries, or schools can provide to parents: *Building a Home Library: Middle Grades* and *Building a Home Library: Young Adult.* Each makes suggestions for books to include.

A Bibliography of Bibliographies

A very special resource for obtaining information about additional bibliographies of young adult books is *Selecting Materials for Children and Young Adults: A Bibliography of Bibliographies and Review Sources* (1980). The guide is prepared by the Young Adult Services Division and Association for Library Service to Children of the American Library Association. Over 300 bibliographies and review sources useful in selecting books for children and young adults are listed in this annotated guide.

About Authors

One of the ways to bring books to life for students is to help them get to know the people behind the books. Knowing something about the authors is also very useful for teachers. Most of the following books are appropriate for both teacher reference and student use.

- *Authors and Articles for Young Adults* by Miriam Hoffman and Era Samuels (Gale Research, 1989). Entries are alphabetically arranged by author, and each entry is detailed and thorough. Extensive references appear at the end of each article.
- *Behind the Covers: Interviews with Authors and Illustrators for Children and Young Adults* by Jim Roginski, with bibliographies compiled by Murial Brown (Libraries Unlimited, 1985). This is an interesting collection of interviews with authors. Most deal with the creative process of writing; some discuss the publishing process.
- *Black Authors and Illustrators of Children's Books: A Biographical Dictionary* by Barbara Rollock (Garland, 1988). Now in its second edition, this book includes brief biographies of leading authors and illustrators, such as Virginia Hamilton, Walter Dean Myers, and Mildred Taylor, as well as lists of the authors' works.
- *Contemporary Authors* (Gale Research, 1962–present). This source, which is published in three, multi-volume sets, provides biographies of authors. Each entry also lists critical and bibliographical sources. The cumulative index for each of the sets helps users find the entries on each author. This resource includes more than young adult authors.
- *Dictionary of Literary Biography* (Gale Research, 1978–present). Another bio-bibliographical resource, this book offers essays about authors along with related references. The index in the final volume of each set can be used to locate author entries. Volumes of particular interest to teachers include *American Writers for Children, 1900–1960* (vol. 22), *American Writers for Children before 1900* (vol. 42), *American Writers for Children since 1960: Fiction* (vol. 52), and *American Writers for Children since 1960: Poets, Illustrators and Nonfiction Authors* (vol. 61).

- *Something about the Author: Autobiography Series* edited by Adele Sarkissian (Gale Research, 1986–present). This multi-volume set contains extensive autobiographies of important children's and young adult authors. Bibliographic information and additional references are included. This is an excellent source of interesting, readable autobiographies for students and teachers. It joins the equally successful and useful biography series *Something about the Author,* edited by Anne Commier since 1971. Both are highly recommended for school libraries.
- *Speaking for Ourselves: Autobiographical Sketches by Notable Authors of Books for Young Adults* edited by Donald R. Gallo (NCTE, 1990). This source includes one- to two-page autobiographical sketches of young adult authors. Each entry includes a photograph and bibliographic information about the author's books. This inexpensive book is excellent for classroom libraries.
- *Twayne's United States Author Series: Young Adult Books* edited by Patricia Campbell (G. K. Hall, hardcover; Dell, paperback). This series of biographies includes critical studies of the author's work as well as biographical information. Published since 1985, the series includes critical, literary biographies of Judy Blume, Sue Ellen Bridgers, Robert Cormier, Rosa Guy, S. E. Hinton, M. E. Kerr, Norma Klein, Norma Fox Mazer, Walter Dean Myers, and Richard Peck. The books are authored by some of the best-known scholars in the field of young adult literature.
- *Twentieth Century Children's Writers* edited by Tracy Chevalier (St. James, 1989). This major biographical resource has author biographies that include personal statements by authors regarding their writing. Bibliographic information and author addresses are also provided.

Obtaining Books for the Classroom

Once you have selected books to use in the curriculum and identified books you'd like to have in your classroom library, a major task still remains: obtaining the books. With educational budgets cut, teachers often ask, "How can I possibly use a variety of literature if I can't afford to buy the books?" Even without financial resources, however, the classroom teacher can begin a classroom paperback lending library of young adult books. The only thing needed is a little bit of time and the willingness to beg, borrow, and, in some cases, buy.

Begging

One of the problems with beginning a classroom young adult library is that one book leads to two books leads to twenty books. In other words, you never have enough. The books you purchase at full price, even in paperback, whet your appetite for more books. No teacher can be expected to buy all of these books from his or her budget or out of his or her own pocket. A better route is to become a book scavenger.

One day one of my students brought in a shopping bag of paperback books from her home library. I thanked her, but in skimming the books I found only three or four that were appropriate for the shelves in the classroom. However, I never throw one away. I stored the rest in a closet in my classroom. Sometime later it occurred to me that if fifty students were to bring in a bag full of books, and if each bag had four useful books, I would gain 200 new books for my classroom library. So I sent a notice home, and many students brought in paperback and hardback books from their home libraries. Several hundred titles were added to the classroom shelves, and several dozen shopping bags full of books were added to my closet. Thus began my home scavenger campaign, which eventually produced recent copies of dozens of magazines, many in multiple copies, day-old newspapers, and books, books, books. However, my search for additional materials continued.

Borrowing

The problem I faced was that I had hundreds of books and wanted to incorporate them into my curriculum. Since I was teaching English and much of my teaching was based on themes and genres, I developed classroom bibliographies that allowed students to select books on the topic or in the genre from the classroom library. At times, however, there were not enough books on a particular theme to allow each student to have one book. Similarly, the students who read more rapidly were not always able to find another book from the bibliography on the shelves after they returned a completed one. This problem led me first to the school library and later to the public library.

The School Library as a Resource for Classroom Books   The school librarian agreed to set aside several shelves in the library that related to the topic we were studying. On these shelves she placed books, journals, and pamphlets that addressed the theme. I have since discovered that most school librarians are more than willing to do this. In addition, many are happy to do book talks on these books. Unfortunately, I had several students who would not enter any library unless they were shackled and dragged there. Therefore, if I wanted them to read, I had to add more books to my classroom library.

The Public Library as a Resource for Classroom Books   I visited my friends in the public library and discovered that they had a long-term loan policy for teachers. Not only could I borrow fifty books on the same theme, but I could keep them in my classroom for up to eight weeks. And, to make my life even easier, the public library staff searched the stacks and put together a group of books for me on the topic at a variety of different reading levels. All I had to do was give them one week's notice and I could pick up the books to use in my classroom. Since that time I've discovered that many public libraries have a similar lending policy for teachers. The length of the checkout time usually varies from four to eight weeks. The number of books allowed may also have a ceiling, but the long-term of the library materials is invaluable. Of course, the teacher is responsible for returning all of the books on time, but in the twenty years I have been using books on long-term loan from public libraries, I have lost only three books. There have been a few other times when I thought a book was lost, but it turned up in the library book drop.

Today's public libraries not only lend books; many give teachers access to a free film and media lending library. Through many local public libraries teachers can borrow films of after-school television specials, for example, which include film presentations of many young adult books. Most public libraries also lend records and cassettes, many lend reproductions of famous paintings, and some even lend audiovisual equipment.

Buying

The overcrowded conditions in my classroom were becoming unbearable. I could not even fit my winter coat in my closet. I had to do something with all those books. In a class I was taking at the time one of the students suggested that I take the books to a used-book store and trade them for the books that I could use in my classroom. It would be a new way to get more books for my classroom library.

The Used-Book Store   One day I borrowed a van from the athletic department. In the van I piled all of the books and four of my strongest students. We drove approximately forty-five minutes to a used-book store with a large stock of young adult books that I had investigated the previous weekend. We deposited the home library books with the clerk, who told us we could have one book for each two "acceptable" books we brought in. The clerk was willing to accept over 300 books. The students, aware of the guidelines I had set, were allowed to select books from the bookstore shelves. The four of them, two young men and two young women, had a wonderful time grabbing books off the shelves. I sat down and looked over each book before leaving the store. The only problem we encountered was getting out of the store before it closed. The students were having so much fun reading the books that it was difficult to pry them out of the store. In that single afternoon, using books we had received free as barter, we obtained over 150 new titles for the classroom library.

Another way to get many books from a used-book store is to find one that sells books that have been on the shelves for a long period of time at a reduced rate, often as low as ten to twenty-five cents per copy. One teacher I know collected fifty cents from each of her students. Armed with over fifty dollars and one student representative from each of her classes, she went to a local used-book store. In two hours the teacher and five students collected more than 300 paperback books for the classroom library. The students understood when they made their fifty-cent contributions that at the end of the year they would each be allowed to select one paperback from the classroom library to keep. Even after each student received a favorite book, the classroom library had over 150 titles with which to begin the new year.

Used-book stores are good sources of paperbacks for the classroom. A Saturday tour of the used-book stores in your community can be very worthwhile. One rainy Saturday this spring I went into a shop about five miles from my home. The proprietor had a bin of books she was selling for ten cents each. Many of them were young adult titles. She said that her customers did not purchase these books and she was getting them off the shelves to make room for others. She told me that for five dollars I could have as many of the books in the bin as I wanted. I gave her five dollars, and after less than an hour I left with over seventy-five books for my classroom library.

Book Warehouses and Discount Bookstores   Another good source of reasonably priced books is book warehouses or discount bookstores that sell out-of-print books. Often you can purchase never-used paperbacks in these stores for a dollar or less.

Student Book Clubs   Several publishing companies have set up student book clubs. Each month the class receives a catalogue, geared to the appropriate age levels, containing approximately thirty offerings the students can buy at reduced rates. As in adult book clubs, dividend books are given after a certain number have been purchased. Not only do the students get dividend books, but so does each classroom. Book clubs can encourage students to read as well as provide additional dividend books for the classroom library each month. Many of the companies also provide posters and book promotional materials with each month's catalogue. Teachers should investigate several clubs to select the one that best fits the needs and interests of the students and the class. One word of caution is in order, though. If there are students in the class who cannot afford to purchase books from a club, the teacher should carefully weigh the frustrations these students will experience against the motivational advantages of the club. It is sometimes possible to find funds for these students to purchase books through such organizations as the school PTA.

Bookstores and Bookfairs   Another potential source for books is the book distributor. If you have a bookfair in your school, it is likely that the book distributor who conducts the fair will be willing to provide premium books for classrooms and school libraries. Likewise if you start a school bookstore (see Appendix C), you may be able to take some of your profits in books. Or you may be able to use your profits to purchase books for teachers who volunteer their time to help with the bookstore.

Textbook Budgets   In many school districts you can use your textbook budget to purchase classroom sets of paperbacks, or even books for the classroom library, instead of textbooks. In one school in my community, the English teachers decided that they liked the current textbook they were using as much as any that were up for adoption. They asked and were given permission to keep their current books, replacing only those that were torn and damaged. They agreed to use most of the allotted textbook budget to purchase classroom sets of several classic and young adult paperbacks and add reference books to each classroom library for the use of teachers and students. They also gave each teacher a budget of $250 to spend on books for the classroom library. One teacher, using many of the techniques suggested above, was able to purchase nearly 300 paperback books for that amount.

Publishers   Even today many free or inexpensive materials are available to the teacher. Publishers provide free and inexpensive materials about their books, authors, and the publishing industry. Teacher guides are often available to teachers who plan to use particular books in the classroom. The best source of information about these freebies (or near-freebies) is the publisher's catalogue. Usually the back pages of the catalogue list materials available to teachers. (About fifty publishers of young adult books, both hardbound and paperback, are listed in Appendix F.) Information about materials available from publishers for free or for a small charge appears in the *CBC Features*. Careful reading of this publication can help the teacher obtain free materials that relate to the young adult books and authors they introduce in their classrooms. Major national conferences, such as the annual convention of the National Council of Teachers of English the week prior to Thanksgiving and the International Reading Association Conference in late April or early May, provide access to many publishers and much free material. Most of the major publishers set up book stalls at these conferences. Many of them give out posters, biographical information about authors, teacher guides, bookmarks, and sometimes books. Even if books are not given away, they can often be purchased at convention rates. The teacher who stays until the end of the conference can buy many of the paperback display books at giveaway prices. Most of the paperback companies would rather sell the display books than ship them back to their warehouses.

Inexpensive Materials   Several guides that help direct teachers to free and inexpensive materials have been published. Most school libraries subscribe to at least one guide. If your library does not, request a subscription. Although expensive, subscriptions can help teachers find valuable materials that are often unavailable from any other source. For example, one of the best films I have ever used in the classroom is *Art Is*. Produced by the Sears Foundation, the film is available only by free loan. That means one cannot get it through any lending services that purchase or lease their films, even if the films are distributed free. Spending some time with this guide can save the school money and provide many teaching aids. Ask your school librarian if you can check the guide out for several weeks over the summer, and get your name on the many mailing lists by requesting free material. Some of it will be useless, but much will be valuable.

Local Businesses   Local businesses can be a great source of useful materials for the classroom. If it wasn't for the ends of the rolls of newsprint I collect from the local newspaper office (which I use as giant scratch paper), I might have quit teaching. Posters and travel brochures from travel agencies have been useful in units on foreign culture, particularly when used in conjunction with the many young adult books on the topic. The teacher's imagination is the only limit in finding useful free materials locally. Check your local resources. I have obtained free fabric to make costumes for plays from a local fabric company, carpet for the reading nook from a carpet manufacturer, strangely colored paper on which to print programs and creative writing journals from a paper company throwaway bin, and even a sound-slide show on dealing with death from a group of local funeral home directors.

EPILOGUE: A DIFFICULT SEARCH, REWARDING RESULTS

Selecting and locating good young adult literature to use in the classroom can be time-consuming and difficult. However, if you use the selection techniques discussed in previous chapters and the resources identified in this chapter, the process will be much easier and will yield rewarding results. Many of the bibliographic resources can help you develop bibliographies for units and reading lists for students. Excellent book lists can be purchased for reasonable prices. A program that includes a wide variety of books requires that students have access to the books.

A classroom library is critical to the success of an inclusive literature program. Far too many students live in environments devoid of books. If we truly want students to become readers, we must allow them to learn in an environment rich with reading materials. Likewise, many students are unwilling or unable to use the library. Teaching them to utilize both the school and the public library is important, but we must keep them reading while they are learning to locate books and gather information.

Obtaining books for your classroom library does not have to be expensive. Every classroom can have a good paperback lending library of young adult books. The teacher need not read every young adult book that is published but can become familiar with them by reading current reviews, keeping track of award books, and developing a professional library of bibliographic resources.

Once familiar with the market, the teacher can begin developing a classroom library of young adult titles and adult titles that are appropriate for young adult readers. Parents, used-book stores, libraries, book clubs, and students can all be helpful in developing a good lending library in the classroom.

As the library grows, the teacher can add to it information about the books and authors—posters, magazines, and other supplemental materials that help make reading an enjoyable experience. In my experience, students who learn in classrooms that are also libraries are far more likely to become readers than students who learn in classrooms with only textbooks and dictionaries.

IMPORTANT ADDRESSES

Before ordering materials from any of these sources, send for catalogues, price lists, and other information. Publishers of young adult books addresses appear in Appendix F.

Association for Library Service to Children and Young Adult Services Divisions
American Library Association
50 East Huron St.
Chicago, IL 60611

American Library Association Graphics
50 East Huron St.
Chicago, IL 60611

Children's Book Council, Inc.
568 Broadway
New York, NY 10012

CBC Order Center
350 Scotland Road
Orange, NJ 07050

International Reading Association
800 Barksdale Road
P.O. Box 8139
Newark, DE 19714-8139

National Council of Teachers of English
1111 Kenyon Road
Urbana, IL 61801

New York Public Library
Office of Branch Libraries
455 Fifth Ave.
New York, NY 10016

SUGGESTED READINGS

Eyerly, J. "Writing for Today's Youth." *ALAN Review,* Winter 1981, pp. 1–3.

Lipsyte, R. "Listening for the Footsteps: Books and Boys." *Horn Book Magazine,* May–June, pp. 290–96.

15 Censorship and the Young Adult Book

Focus Questions

1. What is censorship?
2. How has the court's view of censorship changed since the 1950s?
3. What position do the American Library Association and the National Council of Teachers of English take regarding censorship?
4. What is the difference between censorship and selection?
5. How can schools and teachers deal with censorship before and after it occurs?
6. What are some things teachers and schools can do to keep censorship from becoming an issue?

PROLOGUE

Imagine that you are sitting at your desk looking over some student portfolios when Chad, your high school's star three-sport athlete, walks in. Chad is in the tenth-grade English class to whom you have just assigned a book review list of adolescent literature available in the school library.

"Mr. Greenlee, I can't find anything I want to read on this list you gave us."

"There are some awfully good books on that list, Chad. How about one of the books we discussed in class like *The Chocolate War* or *The Outsiders* or maybe *Killing Mr. Griffin?*"

"They sound okay, but I sort of wanted to read something about sports, and I don't see any here. Do you know of one that I might like?"

After a quick review of the list you recognize one title that is sports oriented, *Halfback Tough* by Thomas Dygard (1986), but it is targeted for younger readers. So you look on your desk for a supplemental text that categorizes young-adult fiction. From several, you select *Reaching Adolescents: The Young Adult Book and the School* by Arthea J. S. Reed (1985). On page one hundred you find a list of titles under the category "Realistic Heroes in Sports." You make a copy of the list for Chad and send him off after school to the local public library, confident that you have helped a reluctant reader discover a genre of adolescent literature that will keep him happily engaged for weeks to come. Story over, right? Don't bet on it.

Having imagined just such a scenario, I decided to explore some of the novels recommended in *Reaching Adolescents,* to determine first-hand how appropriate they are as adolescent literature. I found *Vision Quest,* the third book on the list, in the adult books section of the local public library.

Vision Quest is a fun-filled narrative about a high-school wrestler's almost fanatical attempt to shed and keep off enough pounds to drop a weight class and wrestle Shute, the most feared competitor in the state. Though we don't actually see the match (the novel ends with the two wrestlers walking onto the mat), we witness the dedication to training and determination of spirit displayed by the protagonist, Louden Swain, and we never doubt for a moment that he will win. In fact, Louden is the quintessential role model for young male athletes.

Unfortunately, I could not in good conscience recommend this book to any of my students. My quarrel with Terry Davis's novel has nothing to do with structure or plot. Neither is the abundance of sexual material in *Vision Quest,* on its own, a cause for concern in this (or any other) novel. There are many young-adult books which deal with emerging sexuality in a way that gives young-adult readers an opportunity to examine their own sex/love relationships through fictional characters and situations (Reed 65). The notion that Louden sleeps with his girlfriend, Carla, in his father's house and has an active and creative sex life with her is no reason in and of itself to shy away from this book. Such stories, if handled gingerly, can and should prove enlightening to emerging adults.

The problem in *Vision Quest* is with the language Davis uses. I had to keep a dictionary handy in order to understand such passages as this one:

> I feel her lips on my abdomen. I curse the remaining adipose tissue lurking in the subcutaneous layers. There can't be much. I flex muscles of my rectus abdominous. "Narcissus," Carla whispers. (p. 37)

I also found the sexually explicit language to be stronger than any I have read since *Tropic of Capricorn* (Miller 1962). Witness this shock of imagery evoked by Louden during masturbation:

> I think of Belle's nipples all pumped up and brown, of Mrs. Brockington bending over her desk with a horse mounted behind, of Romaine Lewis about to introduce his cock to Carla's lips, of Lemon Pies' pictures of the dick-licking little boys, of Mom. Weird. (p. 29)

Truly! Granted I read *Tropic of Capricorn* when I was in high school, but I am sure it was urged upon me by one of my peers, not by an English teacher. The point here is that *Vision Quest* is not as totally consumed by graphic language as *Tropic,* the several places where this kind of rhetoric exists in the novel preclude my recommending Davis's book to my students, if for no other reason than pedagogical ethics.

To examine this opinion, I submitted these passages from *Vision Quest* to other English teachers and solicited their reactions. The responses ranged from concern over use of the book as a classroom assignment to apprehension about allowing a student to read it. . . . One teacher even suggested that the real "danger of *Vision Quest* lies in parental reaction." In a local case four or five years ago, the controversial book was *Of Mice and Men*. The problem was not brought to the attention of the teacher or administration. The first hint of a problem came from a letter to the editor of the local newspaper, then in a complaint to the superintendent of schools.

Regardless of the nature of the reaction, all of these teachers were in agreement that *Vision Quest* has no place in a high-school English classroom and were surprised to hear that it was recommended in an education textbook.   ❖

From Edwin D. Greenlee, "Recommended Adolescent Literature: Avoiding Those Hidden 'Secrets,'" *English Journal,* April 1992, pp. 23–24. Copyright 1992 by the National Council of Teachers of English. Reprinted with permission.

In Fear of Censorship

Censorship sends terror up and down the spine of teachers, librarians, and administrators. No educator has failed to reexamine the materials used in the classroom or library when well-publicized cases of censorship, book-banning, and book-burning have occurred. No creative teacher feels safe from the censor's wrath when he or she reads about teachers who were fired for using particular books in their classrooms. Note that one teacher's major concern about *Vision Quest* in Greenlee's article is how parents, the potential censors, will react to the book. Also note that if we base our selection of books on ones that are likely to avoid controversy, we will eliminate from our students' reading books like the masterful short novel by John Steinbeck *Of Mice and Men*.

Although it is difficult to find a book that has not been objected to by some individual or group, often the books that are censored from middle schools, junior high schools, and high schools fall into the category of young adult literature. Perhaps this is because adolescence is a difficult period in which many young people are experimenting and seeking their independence, often through means that are not compatible with family values. Many parents of adolescents comment on how difficult parenting is during these years. Most parents would like to protect their children from the trauma experienced by many adolescents. Therefore, it is not surprising that books with teenage protagonists, dealing with the concerns and problems of adolescents, are often the targets of censorship.

Censorship Defined

Censorship is commonly thought of as the attempt to limit access to a book or a work of art or a movie. But censorship is far more than that. As parents, we often limit our children's access to particular films, television shows, and books. Frequently, we do not do so consciously. We simply do not take them to the movie or we tell them that no television is to be watched after 8 P.M. on weeknights. Is this censorship? Of course not; it is good, sensible parenting. Whether or not you are a censor depends on your intent.

"Censorship is an act born of fear. Something is perceived to be dangerous, to pose a threat, and the censor moves to suppress it. The protesting parent may see the danger of moral corruption lurking in an 'obscene' book. The teacher may see no danger in the book but sense a very real threat from the parent. Both are acting out of fear, and the deeper the fear, the stronger the action each is likely to take" (LaConte, 1975). Parents who limit children's television viewing with the intent of giving them more time for other activities, including sleep, are not censors. Parents who take their children to the children's room of the public library are not censors. Parents who suggest one film for their children over another are not censors. Their intent is not to protect their children from evil, but instead to provide them with options appropriate to their age, maturity, and knowledge. Who, then, are the censors?

Who Are the Censors?

The more fearful parents are about the influence of others over their children, the less secure teachers are in what they are teaching, the less comfortable librarians are with their selections, and the less knowledge the principal has of the material used in the classrooms, the more likely each is to be a censor. Parents who are uncertain of the strength of the values they have inculcated in their children frequently fear the influence of other sources and often attempt to limit their children's access to these sources. Teachers and administrators who are unclear about why particular works have been selected and what the policy is for selecting curricular materials often react strongly to the pressure from a person or group criticizing the material.

To avoid overreacting to criticism of materials teachers must have extensive knowledge of the material used in their classrooms and must be able to carefully defend their selections. Librarians must know a great deal about the books they order and recommend. The principal must understand the selection policies of the classrooms and the library. Without knowledge of the material being used and the reasons for selecting it, the person whose choice is being criticized is likely to take the criticism personally and be unable to defend the material.

The person criticizing the material is not initially a censor, because he or she does not have the power to limit access to the material except to his or her own children. Rather, that person is exercising the right to question. Teachers or librarians or principals who act out of lack of knowledge of material and alternatives may become censors when, out of fear, they remove or force the removal of criticized material. Insecurity about one's own knowledge and fear of criticism may cause the professional to overreact and become the censor.

Censors not only fear the reactions of others to a work but often fear the work itself. The censor makes the assumption that his or her judgment about a work is superior to the judgment of others. Because the censor fears the effect of the work on the person or group he or she assumes is impressionable, the censor attempts to limit access to the feared work. Fear of the work itself is the cause of censorship by totalitarian governments, and, in this country, of censorship by groups on the political left, right, and in-between. Such a group might fear, for example, that what they see as a negative portrayal of African Americans or women will lead the young to develop prejudices or confirm incorrect assumptions. This kind of fear has led to the censorship of such books as *The Adventures of Huckleberry Finn* and *Little Women*. This kind of fear could lead teachers to limit students' access to *Vision Quest* if they object to the portrayal of women as sex objects. If the censor makes the assumption that he or she must protect others from ideas, opinions, or values to which he or she objects, numerous works, including many classics, will disappear from libraries and classrooms.

The Changing View of the Courts

Barbara G. Samuels (1992), in a response to Greenlee's article about the objectionable content of some books, quotes Louie Banks, a character in Chris Crutcher's young adult novel *Running Loose,* "The thing I hate about life, so far, is that nothing's ever clear." With censorship, too, things are seldom clear. As Samuels points out, all teachers face tough questions when selecting books as they sift through the 6,000-plus books that have been published for young people. The state and federal courts have struggled with the issue of censorship, and their views have changed over the past several decades. These court opinions represent important touchstones for teachers.

What is censorship? Who has the right to select books for the classroom? Who has the right to remove books from the classroom? What books are appropriate for classroom use? These questions have been argued in classrooms, in school board meetings, in legislatures, and in the courts. In legal cases related to censorship in the schools, the Supreme Court has interpreted the First Amendment, which guarantees freedom of speech and of the press, and specified how it applies to the selection and removal of classroom material.

In 1957 the Supreme Court, under Earl Warren, heard the case of *Roth v. United States*. The majority decision in *Roth* stated, in part, "All ideas having even the slightest redeeming social importance—unorthodox ideas, controversial ideas, even ideas hateful to the prevailing climate of opinion—have full protection of the First Amendment grantees unless excludable because they encroach upon the limited area of more important areas." This case set a precedent for censorship cases over the next decade and a half. Until the early 1970s any materials that were censored as obscene had to be shown to have no redeeming social value.

In 1973, however, the Supreme Court handed down a decision in *Miller v. California* that provided a new set of guidelines for determining obscenity. Under this ruling a work could be deemed obscene

1. if the "average person, applying contemporary community standards" would find that the work, taken as a whole, appeals to prurient interest
2. if the work depicts or describes, in a patently offensive way, sexual conduct specifically defined by the applicable state law
3. if the work, taken as a whole, lacks serious literary artistic, political, or scientific value

Richard Peck's *Are You in the House Alone?* has been criticized for being too realistic. On the basis of "community standards" it has been removed from the shelves of classrooms and libraries in many towns. In response to the censorship of his book Peck has said:

> [I owe my readers] entertainment and truth. Young people, in fact most people, won't read anything unless they are entertained on some level, and I can't write through a book without believing in its truth. This can be a very light truth or it can be a very heavy one. I have written a book called *Are You in the House Alone?* and I have written it because the typical victim of the crime of rape is a teenage girl in our country. That's a very hard truth. Yet, I wanted my readers to know some things about this crime, that our laws are stacked against the victim and in favor of the criminal. I wanted them to know what it's like to be a victim. I had to do a lot of research and interview a lot of people and go to a lot of places. I had to talk to doctors and lawyers and I couldn't put a happy ending on this story because we don't have any happy endings to this problem in our society. (in Weiss, 1979, pp. 79, 83)

Dozens of other young adult books have been removed from libraries and classrooms on the basis of community standards, including *The Chocolate War* (Cormier) and *Forever* (Blume).

The guidelines provided by the Supreme Court make it very difficult to determine whether a work is obscene. Who is the "average person"? How do we determine "community standards"? What does "contemporary" mean? Who decides? The ruling does, however, give increased control to the community in determining obscenity in censorship cases. Justice William O. Douglas, in a dissenting opinion, expressed concern about this increased control:

> What we do today is rather ominous as respects librarians. The anti-obscenity net now signed by the court is so finely meshed that taken literally it could result in raids on libraries. . . . Libraries, I had always assumed, were sacrosanct, representing every part of the spectrum. If what is offensive to the most influential person or group in the community can be purged from a library, the library system would be destroyed.

In a number of education-related cases before the 1973 Supreme Court ruling, the courts evaluated the content of a work in the context in which it was presented, frequently upholding the right of an individual or group to select a particular book. In *Keefe v. Geanokos* (1969) a teacher assigned to his students an article from the

Atlantic Monthly about student demonstrations in the 1960s in which the word *mother-fucker* was used several times. The case was ruled in favor of the teacher. The Massachusetts Supreme Court said that the article was acceptable since it was written in a scholarly manner and the word was an integral part of the thesis of the article. In a similar case a short autobiographical story containing the phrase "white-mother-fuckin' pig" was read to a class of tenth graders by Stanley Lindros. The California Supreme Court reversed a decision of a lower court saying that in reading the article Mr. Lindros was pursuing a "bona fide educational purpose" and no disruption was created by the reading of the story. Kurt Vonnegut's *Welcome to the Monkey House* was ruled appropriate for high school students by the U.S. District Court in Alabama in 1970. As in the California case, the court ruled that there was no disruption of the educational process or violation of any school policy for the selection of works. In this case the court upheld the teacher's right to "academic freedom."

In more recent cases, however, particularly since the 1973 *Miller* decision, the courts have ruled against teachers. The decisions have been based not on the appropriateness of the work in the context of instruction but rather on the board of education's right to select the material or remove it from use. Although there have been a few state court exceptions to this shift in opinions, the vast majority of decisions have not involved an appraisal of the material. In *Minarcini v. Strongsville (Ohio) City School District* (1976) the U.S. District Court found that the board of education had not violated First Amendment rights when it rejected faculty recommendations of books to be ordered for the library. The U.S. Court of Appeals upheld the decision, saying that the board's decision was neither "arbitrary" nor "capricious." As in most cases of the last two decades, the books were not on trial; obscenity was not the issue.

In a similar case, *Cary v. Board of Education of Adams-Arapahoe (Colo.) School District* (1979), the court ruled that the local school board had the right to rule on course content. The case involved a board-approved elective English course in contemporary literature for juniors and seniors. The books for the course were selected by the teacher and the students. The board objected to several of the selections. In its decision the court agreed that English teachers and students should be permitted to conduct an open discussion of free inquiry. "The student must be given an opportunity to participate openly if he is to become the kind of self-controlled individually motivated and independent thinking person who can function effectively as a contributing citizen." However, according to the court, free inquiry was not the issue at hand. The court decided in favor of the board, based on the question of who had the authority to select appropriate materials for the curriculum. It was claimed that when teachers submit to a collectively bargained contract they agree to allow the board to decide everything including the materials they use in the classroom.

The actual removal of books already in school libraries has been the issue in several court cases. One such case, first heard in 1972, appealed to the U.S. Court of Appeals, and argued before the Supreme Court in 1979, is *President's Council Dist. 25 v. Community School Board No. 25*. In this case Piri Thomas's *Down Mean Streets* was removed from all junior high school libraries in a New York school district. The appellate court upheld the lower court's ruling that the power to remove books is in the hands of the board. A similar question was argued in 1979 in Vermont in *Bicknell v. Vergennes Union High School Board of Directors*. In this instance the board of education ordered two books removed from the school library, calling them "obscene, vulgar, immoral, and perverted." The court ruled in favor of the board, not agreeing with the board's opinion of the books (again the books were not on trial), but affirming the authority of the elected board to control all curricular matters, including the removal of library books. Librarians, according to the court, do not have the right to control the library collection under the "rubric of academic freedom." The decision also stated that the board need not give any reason for refusing to purchase any book for the school library.

A third case dealing with the removal of books was first heard in 1979. In *Pico v. Board of Education of Island Trees Free School District* the court determined that "one of the principle functions of public education is indoctrinative, to transmit basic values of the community." For this reason the board has the right to remove any book from the school library that it believes is inconsistent with community values. The court again asserted the power of the school board to make decisions about the daily operation of the school. According to the decision the court should not intervene, even if, as in this case, the court believes the decision to remove the books "reflects a misguided educational philosophy." In 1980, however, a federal district court of appeals reversed the decision in the *Pico* case. The case was heard by the U.S. Supreme Court in March 1982. The Court upheld the opinion of the Court of Appeals, saying, "[the Board of Education's] reliance upon duty is misplaced where they attempt to extend their claim of absolute discretion beyond the compulsory environment of the classroom into the school library." Although this seems to be a shift from earlier decisions, the Court's ruling was based not on the books' content and appropriateness but on the board's authority. They contended that the board's authority was limited to the curriculum.

The Supreme Court again ruled in favor of the school board in a 7-to-2 decision in *Bethel School District No. 403 v. Fraser* (1986). School officials in Spanaway, Washington, had suspended a student for using sexual metaphors in describing candidates for a student government election. Chief Justice Warren Burger wrote in the majority opinion, "Surely it is a highly appropriate function of public school education to prohibit the use of vulgar and offensive terms in public discourse. . . . Schools must teach by example the shared values of a civilized social order." Although this case did not involve books, it did involve First Amendment rights and established the school board's right to limit them in the school environment.

In January 1988, the Supreme Court, in a five-to-three ruling, upheld a high school principal's right to censor a student newspaper. In the case *Hazelwood School District v. C. Kulmeir et Al.* Justice Byron White, writing for the majority, said that while the First Amendment prevented a school from silencing certain kinds of student expression, it did not require a school to promote such expression in plays and publications under the school's auspices. He said that educators may exert editorial control in such instances "so long as their actions are reasonably related to legitimate pedagogical concerns." The importance of this case to decisions about curricular matters is that it extended authority to administrators appointed by the board of education.

To summarize, court decisions related to the issue of censorship since the 1973 obscenity guidelines established in *Miller* have focused on the right of elected officials and officials appointed by elected officials, such as school superintendents and principals, to make decisions about the curriculum and materials used in the classrooms and school libraries. In obscenity cases from 1957 *(Roth)* until the early 1970s, the courts had focused on the inherent value of the material being questioned. This shift in emphasis was probably influenced by (1) the new conservative leaning toward autonomous decision making by local elected officials and (2) the difficulty of making decisions about the obscenity of a written work based on the three guidelines set forth in the *Miller* ruling. In almost all censorship cases, the higher federal courts have ruled in favor of the right of elected and appointed officials to make decisions about whether or not to limit access to a work, even when the judges did not agree with the officials' decisions. Thus, works used in the classroom are unlikely to be judged by the courts for their merit, and the teacher's autonomy in selecting classroom materials is limited to the level of support he or she has from administrators and the board of education. The court decisions, however, also point to ways in which teachers can protect themselves against censorship, as will be discussed later in the chapter.

Stands Taken by Major Professional Organizations

Almost all professional organizations in education have taken a stand against censorship. Many offer helpful publications, often free to members. The two that have taken the strongest stand and have the largest numbers of publications are the American Library Association and the National Council of Teachers of English.

The American Library Association

The American Library Association (ALA) has clearly voiced its opposition to any form of censorship since 1939, when it responded to attacks on John Steinbeck's *The Grapes of Wrath*. Its response to the criticism leveled against the book was the precursor to today's Library Bill of Rights.

The stand of the ALA regarding censorship is that all materials, no matter "the race or nationality or the social, political, or religious views of the authors," must be made available to all people. According to the Library Bill of Rights, all people, no matter their "origin, age, background, or views," should have free and open access to the library and all materials contained therein. The Library Bill of Rights further asserts that the library should cooperate with all groups or individuals who resist "abridgement of free expression and free access to ideas." In other words, the ALA believes that free access to ideas is essential in a democracy and that this freedom must be defended.

The detailed history of the ALA's fight against censorship is included in the second edition of the *Intellectual Freedom Manual* (1983). The manual also includes a helpful list of suggestions for librarians in resisting censorship of library materials.

In conjunction with the Association of American Publishers (AAP), the ALA further defines its stand in the Freedom to Read statement. The statement says, in part, that it is the responsibility of publishers and libraries to make available to the public a wide diversity of views and expressions, including those which appear unorthodox or unpopular. The statement further asserts that it is not in the public's interest for publishers, booksellers, and librarians to use their own personal political, moral, or aesthetic views as the standard for selecting materials to distribute, publish, or sell. No author should be discriminated against, no matter what his or her political affiliation or personal history. Further, the reading tastes of the reader and the artistic freedom of the author should never be challenged. According to the statement, the librarian and publisher should protest any encroachments on the individual's freedom to read. The library and the publisher must make available materials that express the diversity of life and thought. "The suppression of ideas is fatal to a democratic society. Freedom itself is a dangerous way of life, but it is ours." The joint statement by the American Library Association and Association of American Publishers has been endorsed by more than twenty other groups.

National Council of Teachers of English

The National Council of Teachers of English (NCTE), like the ALA, has fought a battle against censorship for many years. The major publication of NCTE that reflects its views on censorship is *The Students' Right to Read* (Donelson, 1982). This publication is divided into two sections: "The Right to Read" and "A Program of Action." The Right to Read statement upholds students' right to choose their own reading material: "Education is an effort to improve the quality of choices open to man. But to deny the freedom of choice in fear that it may be unwisely used is to destroy the freedom itself." The statement further claims that the right of individuals to read whatever they want is "basic to a democratic society" and that the "reading man possesses judgment and understanding and can be trusted with the determination of his own actions." The position of NCTE on censorship is spelled out more specifically in a book by Lee Burress and Edward B. Jenkinson, *The Students' Right to Know* (1982). The authors, both well-respected authorities on censorship, define intellectual and academic freedom, describe the rights of teachers, and help make clear the distinction between professional selection standards and censorship. (Single copies of *The Students' Right to Read* and *The Students' Right to Know* are available free of charge from National Council of Teachers of English.)

Selection versus Censorship

Selection . . . begins with a presumption in favor of liberty of thought, censorship, with a presumption in favor of thought control. Selection's approach to the book is positive, seeking its value in the book as a book and in the book as a whole. Censorship's approach is negative, seeking for vulnerable characteristics wherever they can be found—anywhere within the book, or even outside it. Selection seeks to protect the right of the reader to read; censorship seeks to protect—not the right—but the reader himself from the fancied effects of his reading. The selector has faith in the intelligence of the reader, the censor has faith only in his own.

In other words, selection is democratic while censorship is authoritarian, and in our democracy we have traditionally tended to put our trust in the selector rather than in the censor. (Asheim, 1953)

The line between selection and censorship is a very fine one. Selection attempts to introduce students to a wide variety of ideas that are inclusive of various historical periods and cultures. Some of the ideas may be misguided; others may be unpopular; still others may be objectionable to some students, and, perhaps, even the teacher. Lester Asheim suggests that the difference between selection and censorship lies in the intent of the selector. If the selector's intent is to look for value in the book, if it is to give the reader a choice and protect his or her right to read, if the selector believes that the reader is intelligent enough to detect biased, poorly written materials, the selector is merely a selector of materials. If, on the other hand, the selector crosses the fine line and tries to protect the reader from unpopular or unorthodox ideas, if the selector does not assume the reader has the intelligence to be a "trash detector," if the selector focuses only on the negative aspects of the book, then the selector has become the censor.

Both the ALA and the NCTE defend librarians' and teachers' right to select materials for a particular purpose or for a particular age group. Both organizations understand the difficulty of distinguishing between selection and censorship. The NCTE organized a group in December 1980 to examine the issue and formulate a definition of censorship. The group issued a position statement on the difference between censorship and professional selection guidelines in December 1982. The statement reaffirms the teacher's role as selector of classroom materials and defines professional guidelines in terms of their goal of providing criteria for selecting materials and methods. Inclusion of materials and methods rather than exclusion distinguishes professional selection guidelines from censorship, according to the statement. The American Library Association and the American Association of School Administrators have also published a very helpful book on this difficult issue. *Censorship and Selection: Issues and Answers for Schools* (1990), by Henry Reichman, explains major court decisions related to censorship, addresses current controversies concerning educational materials (e.g., sexuality, secular humanism, dirty words), and discusses how to plan ahead for potential censorship attacks.

In recent years threats to free choice and open access to materials have come in the form of guidelines from groups and individuals. Minority rights and women's rights groups who object to disparaging language or stereotypical images in classroom and library materials have been requesting that they be removed from the shelves. An NCTE news release, quoting young adult author John Donovan, noted:

> "Pressure groups are not only persuading school boards and librarians to remove certain children's books from circulation, but are attempting to control the content of children's books at the source. . . ." [Donovan] cited, in particular, the vigorous campaign against *The Cay* by Theodore Taylor and described a recent action by the Task Force on Gay Liberation of the American Library Association which has advised children's book editors that there must be more children's books with gay themes in which gay persons are presented positively and that, moreover, a person who is proudly identified as gay should review such books in manuscript form. (NCTE Convention news release, 28 November 1975)

The situation is complicated by the fact that most librarians and teachers are uncomfortable with the stereotypes presented in some books, which are often unattractive and unfair to the objecting group. Furthermore, the very groups that so vocally maintain the right of free access to and free choice of materials, such as ALA and NCTE, have member organizations that work for the fair portrayal of minorities and women in textbooks and other materials used in the classrooms.

At a 1980 NCTE convention educators expressed a variety of viewpoints on the guidelines-versus-censorship question. Edward B. Jenkinson, past chair of the NCTE Committee Against Censorship, believes that guidelines should be "voluntary, not mandatory," should "allow freedom of choice, not mandated selection," should make "sound attempts at consciousness raising," and should not "give the protectors of the young the license to go hunting through libraries and classrooms looking for the targets they can shoot down."

Robert Moore, director of the Racism and Sexism Resource Center for Educators, Council on Interracial Books for Children, expresses concern that "indiscriminate charges of censorship are having a chilling effect on the discussion of racism and sexism in children's books and textbooks, causing many to avoid active consideration of these issues." He cautions that if the cry of censorship is heard every time a person expresses a concern for educational materials, we will lose the "forum for alternative views that are not usually heard in the standard review media."

Lallie Coy, chair of the Women's Committee of NCTE, examined the common elements of all kinds of guidelines and determined that "those dealing with minority groups [seem] . . . to have a common theme: pluralism. It is the theme that saves such guidelines from being censorial." She describes censorship as the act of "exclusion," or removing books. Guidelines, on the other hand, "specifically those for minority groups, demand inclusion of different images" and "acknowledge the right of dissent. They are inclusive not exclusive in scope and philosophy." Therefore, Coy contends, "it is impossible for guidelines to act as censors."

The question of when guidelines restrict access to materials and the selectors of materials become censors remains a difficult one. It is the professional who ultimately removes the books from the classroom or the library. It is the professional who understands the reasons for selecting particular materials for the classroom. If materials are avoided because the teacher or librarian fears the complaints of parents or fears that students will be unable to handle them, than the professional may be acting as censor rather than selector. Similarly, if selection guidelines are written to be inclusive rather than exclusive and the professional follows these guidelines, then the professional is acting as a selector rather than a censor.

> Maybe the most important thing we [teachers] can do is to keep reminding ourselves that only we can censor, that parents have a right to complain if they don't like what's happening in the schools, and that protest, no matter how strident, is not censorship. If we keep asking what they are afraid of, we might all find out that the monster is nothing more than a little kitten with a big shadow. (LaConte, 1975)

───────────── ❖ **Between the Covers: *Authors at Work*** ❖ ─────────────

JULIAN THOMPSON:
IN DEFENSE OF CONTROVERSIAL BOOKS

Julian Thompson is the author of young adult books that have frequently been attacked by censors. Books like A Band of Angels, Simon Pure, Herb Seasoning, *and* Gypsyworld *are considered by most critics of young adult books to be unusual, entertaining, and well written. Most critics also acknowledge that they are likely to stir up controversy. In the following excerpt Thomas defends not only his own books, but all young adult books that may be thought of as controversial.*

Well, *is* it worth the trouble really?

Although I'm sure that there are people who would just say "Nah," or "No opinion," I am not among them. I imagine you are not surprised. It seems to me there are compelling reasons to defend this sort of writing [books for young adults], some of which apply to it uniquely.

But before I turn to them, I'd like to start by mentioning three different levels/kinds of literary censorship that I believe exist today.

The first and rarest of the three is front page stuff—such as the condemnation of *Satanic Verses.* The Ayatollah's additional insistence, though, that Salman Rushdie should be killed for having written it put him in a league that (thank God) even certain Senators and Congressmen do not aspire to.

The second level of censorship includes some cases that may also make the papers; but, if they do, on page 14. A recent example would be the banning of *The Catcher in the Rye* from the supplemental reading list of a high school in Boron, California. The case was also shocking, yes, but it was only one of 172 instances of this kind of censorship that took place in 42 different states last year (1990).

The third and final kind of censorship I want to mention is by far the commonest, although examples never make the newspapers at all. I call this third type "censorship by avoidance" and, sad to say, it's done by *friends* of YA literature as well as people hostile to some elements of it. This kind of censorship takes place whenever teachers decide they won't require (or suggest) a book, because they fear the consequences.

The common thread between all sorts of censorship, of course, is *grounds.* According to someone, or a lot of someones, there's something the matter with Rushdie's book, and Salinger's book, and all these other writers' books, including (I regret to say) my own sometimes. Why are they being burned, or banned, or just avoided?

It seems to me three main reasons for burning, banning, and avoiding are that they're alleged to promulgate (or just contain) one or more of the following:

1. Vulgar Language
2. Sexual Activity
3. Anti-establishment Attitudes

And even though numbers 1 and 2 are often cited as the reasons for the banning (or avoiding) of a YA book, I suspect it's number 3 that activates the censors fastest and most furiously. Holden Caulfield's sense that adults have sold out, become a bunch of phonies—well, that idea's completely unacceptable to members of the grown-ups' union. . . .

[The thing is, though,] *I* think it's *normal* and *appropriate* for kids to:

1. *Have a relationship of some sort with vulgarity.*

Why *do* they, after all?

First, I think, because it can be funny. "Respectable" western literature has been proving that since Aristophanes.

Secondly, because some adults make such a big deal out of it, for reasons that are not entirely clear to kids, at first. What *is* clear to them, however, is that vulgarity provides them with odd powers: first, that power to enrage and, second, the power to defy authority behind its back.

Most kids learn quite early on just how and when to use the vulgar words they know so that they're merely—useful words. By the time most kids are in their middle teens, they don't seem so "bad." Nor do they make them giggle anymore. Thoughtful adolescents wonder why their parents seem so shocked and horrified by *language,* when they choose, as TV "entertainment," movies based on "real-life" happenings: mutilation, rape, abuse, and murder.

It's also *normal* and *appropriate,* I feel for kids to be:

2. *Curious about sex—in terms of its mechanics and its context.*

Their bodies and the world around them see to that in equal measure; any list of youthful curiosities would certainly have sex up near the top of it.

No matter how much anyone may wish that it were otherwise, kids are going to decide for themselves about their own sexual behavior. Parents may opine, insist, even demand, and sons and daughters (depending on the nature of the relationship they have with them) will give their statements and their wishes more or less consideration. But almost every kid will want to understand the options, and think about the range of choices that are being made—and, certainly, their consequences. Books can sometimes offer insights and support that neither peers nor adults can provide. Books don't put pressure on a person; what they do, by offering believable analogies, is help young people to make wiser, more mature, decisions.

And, finally, I *also* do believe it's *normal* and *appropriate* for kids to:

3. *Question and, at times, resist the edicts of those elements of the "Establishment" they deal with, day by day—the authority of parents, or of teachers, or of any other adult in their lives.*

Horrifying? Possibly. But wait, think back a minute. Isn't what I'm calling "normal" and "appropriate" pretty much what *you* did, growing up?

When we were growing up, we all knew who had all the power, and it wasn't us. *They* had the money, and the houses that we lived in, and the food—and all the car keys, too. By reason of the love/respect we had for them (and threats and use of force, perhaps), we generally obeyed them. But as we moved into our teens, we got the feeling *we* were someone, too. Someone with ideas and, yes, *opinions!* Why *should* we do what *they* said, all the time? Especially when what they said was sometimes (clearly) *stupid.*

Luckily and usually, the feelings of hostility that adolescents have don't take them over. And parents—smart, exhausted ones—give their children more and more control of their own lives. In general, the "battles" that take place between the parent and the child don't lead to hatred or to violence. Kids are only totally turned off when authority is wielded thoughtlessly or inconsistently—unjustly. Kids *do* know who the "meanies" are, or those who look as if they just don't give a damn; the adults they rebel against the most are mostly undeserving of respect, in my opinion. Look around your neighborhood. How many *other* parents would you let bring up your child?

Don't misunderstand me here. I *do* believe that there are ways for kids to exercise their new-found and emerging sense of self. I'm not in favor of a world made up of bands of foul-mouthed, promiscuous kids running up to tell me, "I know what I can do." The pharisees and censors paint the issues that we're raising here in blackest blacks and whitest whites, as either-or. *My* point is: there *is* a golden mean, a middle ground. What I'm speaking for is moderation, understanding—yes, *appreciation* of the way that normal people grow into a genuine adulthood.

So, what I'm saying is that the first reason to defend YA literature from the pharisees and censors—the first thing that makes it "worth the trouble"—is that the normal, healthy development of young people, socially and intellectually, is best served by their having access to the kind of books that certain sorts of people want to ban. . . .   ❖

From Julian Thompson, "Defending YA Literature against the Pharisees and Censors: Is It Worth the Trouble?" *ALAN Review,* Winter 1991, pp. 2–5. Reprinted by permission of Julian Thompson.

Dealing with Censorship

No matter how careful librarians and teachers are in selecting reading material for the classroom and library, complaints are likely to occur. The ideal way to mitigate these complaints is for the school to work together with the community to answer these questions: What constitutes censorship? What is the difference between censorship and selection guidelines? What guidelines do we want for the selection of materials in our school? An open forum that encourages discussion of questions such as these is a positive step in developing an environment where the issue of censorship does not arise.

Opening Up the Selection Process

One school found that including a variety of people in the selection process helped solve the censorship issue.

> After a traumatic experience testifying before a Grand Jury to answer charges of misusing public funds in the purchase of "obscene" books (which resulted in no indictments), the English staff in a local junior high in an affluent neighborhood was understandably nervous the following year when it came time to compile new reading lists for literature classes. How were they to please everyone —themselves, students and patrons while avoiding a repetition of public criticism? The students did not want to read "dumb" stuff. . . . Parents wanted their children to read the "classics" and good stuff with "happy" endings. Teachers wanted their students to read and enjoy well-written literature; the principal wanted students to learn and everybody to be happy. (LaPota, 1976, p. 173)

To help reach an accord on the problem, the English staff decided to involve students and parents in creating the ninth-grade reading list. A committee of students and parents began reading books and book reviews that had been recommended by a variety of sources. The students selected fifty titles. These books were then read by the parents. The rest of the students voted on the books they would most like to read based on short summaries of each title. Twenty titles were selected. Finally, the students wrote a defense for each title selected and invited the parents to attend discussion sessions about the books. When a parent objected to a work, a student verbally defended the selection of students. "Often students were able to change parental opinion. One mother said, 'I read that book but I guess I was too busy looking for dirty words to understand what the story was saying. I just didn't see what a good message the book had for young people.' " As a result of the meetings, an approved reading list was developed. The efforts of these teachers, students, and parents resulted in far more than an approved reading list. LaPota reports that the PTA decided to purchase paperbacks for the school, students' attitude toward reading improved, and parents expressed a respect for the quality of the educational program in the school.

Setting a Schoolwide Policy

The best time to form a selection committee is before censorship becomes an issue. However, if it has already become an issue in your school, a joint committee to deal with future selections is very helpful and may even eliminate further problems with censorship. Forming a joint committee of parents, teachers, students, librarians, and administrators immediately is not always possible, although it should be a goal for all schools. When the development of such a committee is not feasible, there are several intermediate steps a school, department, or classroom teacher can take.

The school or the individual department should develop a policy for the selection of books. Even if censorship has already become an issue, it is not too late to develop a policy. The school board should be involved in the policy-writing as early as possible and should approve the policy as soon as it is completed. In addition, teachers, librarians, and administrators should do everything in their power to encourage the board of education to adopt a "students' right to read" policy.

The school or the individual department should work toward a consensus on what the policy should be. A consensus is not a majority opinion; it must be hammered out and agreed upon by all the members of the department. The following areas should be discussed in the process of developing a selection policy:

1. the student population of the school
2. the age and grade range of the school population
3. the philosophy and the goals of the school
4. the school's curricular focus
5. the process for selecting curricular materials and trade books for curricular use
6. the process for selecting library materials
7. the membership of the selection committee(s)
8. parents' involvement in the process (e.g., at selection time or when reviewing material used by their own children)
9. alternatives for students or parents who object to the use of particular materials
10. the process that will be followed if a complaint is filed

Establishing Book Selection Guidelines

Once a policy has been established regarding the selection process, professional book selection guidelines should be adopted. To help teachers select appropriate materials for the classroom that open the world to students, rather than materials that limit their access to ideas, organizations such as NCTE and ALA have developed selection guidelines (see Figure 15.1 for NCTE selection guidelines). These guidelines are helpful to teachers (and other committee members) when selecting books because they present an inclusive approach to selecting the best possible books for all students. Teachers should avoid guidelines that suggest the exclusion of particular types of works. Many organizations have developed such exclusive guidelines; they range from conservative organizations such as fundamentalist Christian groups to liberal organizations that wish to protect the rights of certain groups who have experienced discrimination. Book selection guidelines, unless they are written to be inclusive of a variety of ways of viewing the world, can actually promote censorship.

Each school should agree on a set of selection guidelines for the entire school or entire department. To protect teachers who use these guidelines against censors, they should be approved by appropriate administrative groups and ultimately the board of education. If the guidelines have been so approved and are then utilized by teachers as they select books, the courts (should a censorship case reach that level) are likely

Figure 15.1
NCTE Book Selection Guidelines for Trade Books

Literary Quality

- Literary quality relates to style of writing or the arrangement of words and sentences that best expresses the dominating theme. It includes sentence structure, dialogue and vocabulary. Literary quality is not affected by format or illustration.
- Characterization is an aspect of literary quality. An effectively realized character acts and speaks in a way that is believable for that character.
- Plot is another aspect of literary quality. The incidents of a story must be interrelated and carry the reading along to its climax.
- Still another aspect of literary quality is a story's theme, in which the philosophy of the author is expressed in the meaning of the story and often reflects developmental values in the growing-up process.

Appropriateness

- Factors to be considered in assessing the appropriateness of books are children's interests, the age level and/or maturity of children in relation to the book being considered, and the content, format and illustration. While the format and illustration are not directly related to the elements considered under literary quality, they should complement the text as well as be evaluated on the basis of artistic standards.

Usefulness

- An important aspect of usefulness is the purpose for using books in relation to curriculum objectives.
- Basic to the selection of any books is the suitability of the text but by no means is this to be construed to mean controversial materials will not be used.
- Accuracy is important in nonfiction and in fiction in regard to theme, setting, characters and incidents.
- Authenticity is important in fiction and biography, especially those books with a historical background.

Uniqueness

- All books are unique. Their uniqueness may be a result of their theme, plot, style of writing, characterization, format or illustration. Such books may have a special place and use in the classroom and library. Teachers must know what it is about a book that makes it unique, and must share this information with others.

Breadth of Coverage

- Books may present problems of stereotyping with respect to sex and to race. Religion, politics, and questions of morality or patriotism are issues about which there are considerable differences of opinion. The importance of such books may lie mainly, or only, in their historical viewpoint and should be presented as such to children who read them. Teachers and librarians should be aware of these considerations and should make every effort to provide materials which present alternate points of view. Historically there have always been those who have recognized the offensiveness of these materials. Children, like adults exposed to new ideas, can accept or reject them based on input from all viewpoints. All opinions require protection under the First Amendment.

Source: NCTE Committee on Bias and Censorship, "Censorship: Don't Let It Become an Issue in Your School," *Language Arts.* February 1978. Copyright 1978 by the National Council of Teachers of English. Reprinted with permission.

to support the right of the schools to establish these guidelines and the teachers' responsibility to follow them. Thus, establishing selection guidelines not only protects individual teachers but also the entire school district.

Avoiding Censorship

The suggestions above are designed to lessen the effects of censorship should it occur, and they may also have the effect of preventing formal complaints concerning censorship. The approaches discussed below are designed specifically to keep censorship from occurring.

Involving Parents with Books

One of the most creative approaches to avoiding censorship is to involve parents in reading the books their children read. In a Greenville, South Carolina, middle school, librarian Pat Scales has developed a program that actively involves parents with books. Parents participate in a program that encourages them not only to read the books their children are reading but to discuss the books with their children. The goals of the "Communicate through Young Adult Books" program are:

1. To introduce parents to a wide variety of young adult literature;
2. To relate the themes of young adult literature to teenagers' lives;
3. To invite parents to share personal concerns regarding adolescent behavior, young adult literature, and the communication process; and
4. To share with parents specific methods in using young adult literature to foster open and honest family discussions. (Scales, p. 4)

In this oversubscribed program parents meet with librarians in the library to discuss the books. The first book the parents read is one recommended by their children. Parents often want to discuss why their youngsters chose the books. At times they are distressed with the portrayal of parents in the books. During the discussion, parents and librarians spend time talking not only about the books but about what adolescents are like. After the initial sessions, the librarians, with the help of teachers, put together bibliographies of books on themes or topics suggested by the parents. Often each parent reads a different book and discussions revolve around a particular theme.

Through the "Communicate through Young Adult Books" program parents not only get to learn more about young adult books and authors, but they also learn more about how their children think and why they behave as they do. The program also provides the opportunity for parents to discuss with their children the books they are selecting to read. Although this particular program is conducted in the library by librarians, teachers could conduct a similar book discussion program with parents, perhaps encouraging them to read and discuss some of the books their children will be reading in class.

Using a Contract

Classroom teachers can also involve parents in their child's reading by making parents aware of the books a student has selected for reading and encouraging them to examine the books and discuss them with their child. One way to do this is by using a grade or work contract that both the student and the parent sign. In my own English classes every student was required to read a minimum of five books every quarter. The books were always available in the classroom or school library and were listed in an annotated bibliography based on the theme, genre, or historical period to be studied. Students selected the books they would read, and all titles were available for parental reading. At the beginning of each quarter students completed a contract in which they identified the books they planned to read during the next nine weeks (see Figure 15.2). On the contract the student also listed other materials he or she would be using as well as requirements for the awarding of the course grade. The contract was taken home with a copy of the annotated bibliography and returned with the signature of the student's parent or guardian. A completed copy of each contract was filed in the English office and could be renegotiated with the initialing of the parent/guardian and the student on the changed item. The percentage of the course grade represented by the contract varied depending on other course requirements. A contract could make up as little as 25 percent or as much as 100 percent of the course grade.

During the years that I used the contract system, I had several parental requests to examine books, not more than a handful of parents who asked their children to select a different book, and only one complaint about a book a student was reading. When the complaining parent entered my classroom for a scheduled conference, I expressed surprise at the complaint since she had signed the contract. "What contract?" she asked. I pulled the signed contract from the file. She said she had neither seen nor signed the contract. After explaining to her that all books were available for her to review, and a signed contract was an indication of her understanding of what her son was reading, the complaint was dropped. The issue was no longer the book her son was reading, but the fact that he had chosen to forge the contract rather than bring it home. After this incident the parent became a great supporter to the system, often asked for copies of the books her son would be reading, and reported to me that she and her son had gained a new appreciation for each other through their discussions of the books. In addition, the young man learned that the contract was not something he needed to fear.

Developing a Rationale

When a teacher plans to use a single book for reading by the entire class, the teacher *must* read the book. A teacher should never select a book based only on a review or a recommendation from a colleague. After selecting the book, the teacher should prepare a carefully written, educationally sound rationale for using the book. A dated copy of the rationale should be given to the department chair and principal, and the original should be filed in a safe place for the teacher's future reference. If the school district, school, or department has guidelines for selecting classroom materials, the teacher must be sure to examine the guidelines before making final selections and use these guidelines in the writing of the rationale. Likewise, if a selection committee has been formed, it may be necessary to have the committee review the book before incorporating it into the course plan. Although these steps are time-consuming, they ensure that a group of individuals agrees that a particular book meets the selection guidelines adopted by the school. This not only protects the teacher but also ensures that the best possible books are chosen (assuming, of course, the guidelines are carefully written and inclusive).

Whether or not the teacher presents the book to a selection committee for approval, developing a rationale as to why that book should be read by the entire class is important. An excellent source for preparing rationales is "Rationales for Commonly Challenged Taught Books" (1983), edited by Dianne P. Shugert. This issue of the *Connecticut English Journal* has twenty-five model rationales for commonly taught and commonly censored books. Of course, these models may need to be adapted for your particular situation. The issue also has information on how to prepare your own rationales. According to Shugert, rationales should explain

Figure 15.2
Grade Contract

I, _____, agree to meet the requirements for the grade of _____,[1] in the course of _____ for the quarter of _____, set forth in this grade contract. I further agree to fulfill the assignments set forth in this contract to the best of my ability.

I understand that if I am unable to meet or would like to change the manner in which I meet the requirements, I may renegotiate them with my teacher, _____, any time prior to the seventh week of the said quarter.

I further understand that if I do not meet the agreed-upon requirements and do not renegotiate my contract, I will receive an incomplete or an F for the contracted portion of my course grade.

The following requirements are those I agree to meet for the aforementioned course, grade, and quarter[2]:

The following books, articles, short stories, poems, etc. have been selected by me to fulfill the requirements[2]:

I understand that this contract is not valid unless it is complete (including a listing of requirements and reading material(s)), signed by all appropriate parties, and returned by _____ (date).

I further understand that this contract will be produced in duplicate. One copy will be kept in my file in the English office, and one copy each will be returned to me and my parent or guardian.

Signed:
Student _____   Teacher _____
Parent or Guardian _____   Date _____

[1]This contract will equal _____ percent of the course grade.
[2]Use the reverse side if additional space is needed.

1. How a chosen book fits the objectives of the schools and curriculum.
2. How a book qualifies as English material, including its literary value (see Figure 15.1) and professional acceptability. Here a rationale may draw upon critical reviews from articles in *English Journal,* the *ALAN Review,* and other review sources described in Chapter 14 of this text. Teachers might also refer to honors the book or author has received and the views of professional organizations in documents such as NCTE's *The Students' Right to Read, The Students' Right to Know,* and ALA's *Intellectual Freedom Manual.*
3. How a book meets the needs of the particular students who study it. Such explanations will include statements like, "Students at this age have access to drugs. They need to know the dangers involved so they can resist peer pressures to experiment with drugs."
4. How the teacher teaches the book. For example, "Although Holden Caulfield uses bad language, students see that his language is a pathetic attempt to be a big shot."
5. How the book relates to the democratic ideal of the educated citizen, prepared to make his or her own decisions. One democratic ideal, embodied in the First Amendment, requires respect for and knowledge of, though not necessarily agreement with, other people's ideas and opinions.

What to Do in Case of a Complaint

If a student or a parent complains about a particular book, the teacher should not take the complaint as a personal criticism but should be prepared to select an alternative book for the student. Students reading alternative books must not be penalized. One of the best ways to avoid criticism of the books being used in the classroom is to rarely require that any one title be read by every student. Allowing students to select from an annotated list of books and encouraging parental review and discussion of the selections should minimize criticism.

If someone complains about a book being used in the classroom, the teacher must be prepared to handle the complaint in a friendly, nondefensive manner. Keep in mind that it is the book that is the object of the criticism. Every parent has the right to complain about what is being taught in the classroom. Eliminating this right is as damaging as eliminating the diversity of books in the curriculum. If the teacher has alerted the principal and department chair to the books being used, has given them a written rationale for the selection of the books, and has followed the school selection policy and guidelines, the administrators are likely to feel as if they have a role in the selection and are therefore likely to support the teacher. The complaint can usually be handled during a conference with the parent. Often the objection is withdrawn when the parent discovers the child is not required to read a particular book, is free to select another, and will not be penalized for the change. Usually the parent is objecting to his or her child's reading the book, and when informed that the child need not read the book, in a friendly, nonthreatening way, will not take the objection further.

Sometimes a conference will not bring an end to the complaint and the parent may insist that the book be removed from the classroom or library. If this is the case, two excellent forms—the Statement of Concern about Library/Media Center

Resources (ALA) and the Citizen's Request for Reconsideration of a Work (NCTE)—can be given to the person requesting the removal to allow them to put their complaint in writing (see Figures 15.3 and 15.4). Often the simple acknowledgment that the citizen has the right to complain is enough to quell a complaint. At other times the questions asked on the form may convince the person that the complaint is not valid. On these forms the complainant must indicate whether he or she has read the book, what part of the book or resource is objectionable, whether he or she would recommend the book for another group, his or her awareness of critical comments about the book or resource, his or her understanding of the theme, suggestions of alternative courses of action, and recommendations of another book to be used in its place. These forms should be available in each classroom, office, and library. If the school is not currently using these forms, the teacher or librarian should suggest to the appropriate administrative officer that they be adopted. They can be incorporated in the school's policy statement.

Figure 15.3
Statement of Concern about Library/Media Center Resources

(This is where you identify who in your own structure has authorized use of this form—Director, Board of Trustees, Board of Education, etc.—and to whom to return the form.)

Name _____ Date _____

Address _____

City _____ State _____ Zip _____ Phone _____

1. Resource on which you are commenting:

  _____ Book   _____ Audiovisual Resource
  _____ Magazine   _____ Content of the Library Program
  _____ Newspaper   _____ Other

  Title _____
  Author/Producer _____

2. What brought this title to your attention?

3. Please comment on the resource as a whole as well as being specific on those matters which concern you. (Use other side if needed.) Comment:

Optional:
4. What resource(s) do you suggest to provide additional information on this topic?

Source: "Statement of Concern about Library/Media Center Resources," *Intellectual Freedom Manual.* Copyright 1983 by the American Library Association. Reprinted with permission.

Figure 15.4
Citizen's Request for Reconsideration of a Work

Hardcover _____

Author _____ Paperback _____

Title _____

Publisher (if known) _____

Request initiated by _____

Telephone _____ Address _____

City _____ State _____ Zip Code _____

Complainant represents

_____ Himself

_____ (Name organization) _____

_____ (Identify other group) _____

1. To what in the work do you object? Please be specific; cite pages.

2. What of value is there in this work?

3. What do you feel might be the result of reading this work?

4. For what age group would you recommend this work?

5. Did you read the entire work? _____ What pages or sections? _____

6. Are you aware of the judgment of this work by critics?

7. Are you aware of the teacher's purpose in using this work?

8. What do you believe is the theme or purpose of this work?

9. What would you prefer the school do about this work?
   _____ Do not assign or recommend it to my child.
   _____ Withdraw it from all students.
   _____ Send it back to the English department for reevaluation.

10. In its place, what work of equal value would you recommend that would convey as valuable a picture and perspective of society or a set of values?

_____   _____

(Date)   (Signature of complainant)

Source: Committee on the Right to Read of the National Council of Teachers of English, "Citizen's Request for Reconsideration of a Work." Copyright 1972 by the National Council of Teachers of English. Reprinted with permission.

Epilogue: censorship and its dangers

Some levels of censorship are more apparently dangerous than the others. Unfortunately, teachers and librarians have sometimes been the victims of violent examples of censorship (Moffett, 1988) and fear of this kind of censorship or simply of having to defend one's choice of reading materials often makes teachers and librarians decide to avoid a particular book. Although this kind of censorship may not be physically dangerous, it is dangerous nonetheless. As Thompson suggests, it may keep adolescents from reading important books that will help them to develop normally. It also keeps them from reading books that will keep them reading.

Censorship has the potential of forcing the school curriculum to be exclusive, to include only those few books that are not objectionable to anyone. Such a reading list will not help students reach all of the goals of English and language arts curriculum, nor will it reach out to the large percentage of our students who are from nonwhite, non-European cultures.

Censorship in any form violates one of the major protections provided to us in the Constitution. As Supreme Court Justice William O. Douglas has written, "Restriction of free thought and free speech is the most dangerous of all subversions. It is the one un-American act that can most easily defeat us."

Of course, there is no guarantee that parents will not object to the books we use in our curriculum. In fact, their right to object is a part of the same constitutional guarantee of free speech that permits all kinds of books to be published and distributed. However, if teachers, librarians, parents, administrators, and members of the board of education work together to establish educational policies and selection guidelines, and if teachers follow these guidelines and clearly understand and record why a book should be included in the curriculum, complaints about books are unlikely to go beyond the formal registering of an objection and a discussion and resolution of the objection. Legal precedent seems to indicate that the courts will respect the right of elected officials and appointed administrators to make decisions about the curriculum. Therefore, if these officials are involved in the formation of policy and selection guidelines and if these policies and guidelines are followed by professionals, the courts are likely to rule against the censors. If teachers and librarians do not work to prevent censorship in any form in our schools and libraries, who will? If individuals and groups of various political, social, and religious viewpoints are permitted to remove books and materials that do not reflect their viewpoints, it is up to teachers to protect students' right to freedom of thought and freedom of speech.

Suggested readings

American Library Association. *Intellectual Freedom and the Rights of Youth.* 1979.

American Library Association. *Intellectual Freedom Manual.* Rev. 2d ed. 1974.

American Library Association. *The Right to Read and the Nation's Libraries.* 1974.

Asheim, L. "Not Censorship but Selection." *Wilson Library Quarterly.* September 1953, pp. 63–67.

Bugniazet, J. "Librarians as Self-Censors." *ALAN Review,* Winter 1988, pp. 8–10.

Burress, L., and E. B. Jenkinson, eds. *The Students' Right to Know.* National Council of Teachers of English, 1982.

Davis, J. E. "Dare a Teacher Disturb the Universe? Or Even Eat a Peach? Closet Censorship: Its Prevention and Cure." *ALAN Review,* Fall 1986, pp. 66–73.

Davis, J. E., ed. *Dealing with Censorship.* National Council of Teachers of English, 1979.

Donelson, K., ed. *The Students' Right to Read.* National Council of Teachers of English, 1982.

Edwards, J. "A New Twist to an Old Problem: Recent Court Decisions on School Book Censorship." *English Journal,* March 1981, pp. 50–53.

Force, L., and J. Juska. "Working Together: English Teachers and Librarians Foster the Freedom to Read." *ALAN Review,* Spring 1988, pp. 14–16.

Greenlee, E. D. "Recommended Adolescent Literature: Avoiding Those Hidden Secrets." *English Journal,* April 1992, pp. 23–24.

Hentoff, N. *The First Freedom: The Tumultuous History of Free Speech in America.* Delacorte, 1980.

Jenkinson, E. B. *Censors in the Classroom: The Mind Benders.* Southern Illinois University Press, 1979.

Jenkinson, E. B., ed. "Organized Censors Never Rest." *Indiana English,* Fall 1977.

LaConte, R. T. "Censorship and the Teaching of English," *Arizona English Bulletin,* February 1975.

LaPota, M. "Censorship and Adolescent Literature: One Solution." *Arizona English Bulletin,* April 1976, pp. 173–75.

Luce, R., ed. "Free to Teach, Free to Learn." A special issue of Southeastern Ohio Council of Teachers of English *Focus,* Fall 1991.

Moffett, J. *Storm in the Mountains: A Case Study of Censorship, Conflict, and Consciousness.* Southern Illinois University Press, 1988.

NCTE Committee on Bias and Censorship. "Censorship: Don't Let It Become an Issue in Your School." *Language Arts,* February 1978.

Reed, A. J. S. "Selecting Adolescent Literature and Avoiding Censorship." *English Journal,* April 1992, pp. 26–27.

Reichman, H. *Censorship and Selection: Issues and Answers.* American Library Association and Association of School Administrators, 1990.

Samuels, B. G. "Our Objective: Thinking Lifetime Readers." *English Journal,* April 1992, pp. 28–29.

Scales, P. *Communicate through Young Adult Books: How Parents Can Understand More about Their Teenagers by Reading and Discussing Their Books.* Bantam, n.d.

Shugert, D. P., ed. "Rationales for Commonly Challenged Taught Books." A special issue of *Connecticut English Journal,* Fall 1983.

Simons, J. S. "Censorship in the Schools: No End in Sight." *ALAN Review,* Winter 1991, pp. 6–8.

———. "On Stemming the Tide." *ALAN Review,* Spring 1989, pp. 14–17.

Stanek, L. W. *Censorship: A Guide for Teachers, Librarians, and Others Concerned with Intellectual Freedom.* Dell, 1976.

Thompson, J. "Defending YA Literature against Pharisees and Censors: Is It Worth the Trouble?" *ALAN Review,* Winter 1991, pp. 2–5.

Weiss, M. J. "A Dangerous Subject: Censorship!" *ALAN Review.* Spring 1988, pp. 59–61.

———. *From Writers to Students: The Pleasures and Pains of Writing.* International Reading Association, 1979.

A HISTORY OF YOUNG ADULT LITERATURE AT A GLANCE

IMPORTANT BOOKS		KEY EVENTS
John Bunyan *The Pilgrim's Progress*	**1675**	
Jonathan Swift *Gulliver's Travels*	**1700**	Adventure stories with moral themes are popular.
Daniel Defoe *Robinson Crusoe*		
Thomas Day *The History of Sanford and Merton*	**1750**	
Hannah More *Repository Tracts*		
"Parson" Mason Locke Weems Books about George Washington	**1800**	
Samuel Goodrich (Peter Parley) The Peter Parley books	**1825**	
Jacob Abbott The Rollo books		
Susan Warner (Elizabeth Wetherell) More than 20 domestic novels	**1850**	
Augusta Jane Wilson *St. Elmo*		The first dime novel appears (June 7, 1860).

Books (by various authors) about the
dime novel characters: Seth Jones, Davy
Crockett, "Old Sleuth," Nick Carter,
Deadwood Dick

Louisa May Alcott
Little Women

Horatio Alger   **1870**
Ragged Dick books
Richard Hunter books

University entrance exams require specific
classic books for college-bound students.

Series books   **1875**
Harry Castlemon, Frank books
Oliver Optic, Boat Club books
Martha Farquharson, Elsie Dinsmore
books

Dime novels attacked for sentimentality
and ability to corrupt.

George Wilbur Peck
Peck's Bad Boy

Mark Twain
Tom Sawyer
Huckleberry Finn

Huckleberry Finn banned by Concord
Public Library.

Adventure writers
Howard Pyle, "Robin Hood"
Jules Verne
Robert Louis Stevenson

Arthur Conan Doyle, "Sherlock Holmes"   **1890**

Stratemeyer Syndicate (formula fiction) **1900**
Admiral Dewey books
Lakeport books
Rover boys
Hardy boys
Dana girls
Ruth Fielding
Tom Swift
Nancy Drew

Booth Tarkington
Seventeen

William Gilbert Patton
Frank Merriwell sports books

Books about the West
Owen Wister
The Virginian
Zane Grey

Kate Douglas Wiggin
Rebecca of Sunnybrook Farm

Lucy Maud Montgomery
Anne of Green Gables

John Fox, Jr.
  The Little Shepherd of Kingdom Come

The Reverend Harold Bell Wright
  The Winning of Barbara Worth

Eleanor Porter
  Pollyanna

Edgar Rice Burroughs
  Tarzan

John Buchan
  The Thirty-Nine Steps

Ralph Henry Barbour
  St. Marys series
  Fairview High series
  Lansing series
  School sports series

Joseph Gollomb
  Lincoln High Series
Charles Nordholl and James Norman Hall
  Mutiny trilogy

"Big-Little Books"
  Dick Tracy
  Flash Gordon
  Moon Mullins
  Our Gang
  Donald Duck

John Tunis
  Iron Duke

Janet Lambert
  Star Spangled Summer

Maureen Daly
  Seventeenth Summer

Henry Gregor Felsen
  Navy Diver (1942) and other World
  War II books until 1947

John Tunis
  All American (1942) and other sports
  books until 1964

Esther Forbes
  Johnny Tremain (1943)

1910 National Council of Teachers of English is formed to protest use of college entrance exams.

1915

Reorganization of English in the Secondary Schools, prepared by U.S. Bureau of Education, adds modern works to English curriculum.

1920

First Newbery Medal awarded to *The Story of Mankind* by Hendrik Van Loon.

Comic Monthly and *Funnies on Parade* founded.

1930

Detective Comics and *Marvel Comics* introduced.

Career books gain popularity and continue through the 1950s.

1935

First paperback published by Pocket Books. *The Good Earth* by Pearl Buck.

1940 Rise of paperback industry increases availability of popular books.

A touch of realism appears in young adult fiction.

War books popular throughout the 1940s.

Florence Crannell Means
The Moved-Outers

Books about the high school years   **1945**

    Rosamond DuJardin
    Wait for Marcy
    Boy Trouble

    Betty Cavanna
    Going on Sixteen

    Anne Emory
    Going Steady

Books of the 1940s and 1950s usually avoided sex, smoking, profanity, social or racial injustice, and anything that might be considered controversial.

James Summers   **1950**
    Girl Trouble

Paul Annixter
    Swift Water (1950)

Henry Gregor Felsen
    Hot Rod (1938) and other car books through 1958

William Gault
    Thunder Road (1952)

Philip Harkin
    Road Race (1953)

C. H. Frick
    Five against the Odds (1955) and other sports books through 1961

John F. Carson
    Floorburns (1957) and other sports books through 1961

J. D. Salinger
    The Catcher in the Rye (1951)

Elizabeth Yates
    Amos Fortune, Free Man (1950)

Anne Frank
    Diary of a Young Girl (1952)

Robert Havighurst outlines the developmental tasks of the adolescent.

Car and sports books popular throughout the 1950s and early 1960s.

Formula romances also popular during the 1950s and 1960s.

Nonfiction emerges as popular reading fare for young adults.

Shirley Graham   **1955**
    Booker T. Washington

Lorenz Graham
    South Town

Christine Arnothy
    I Am Fifteen and I Do Not Want to Die

Ian Fleming
    James Bond series from 1954 through the 1960s

Realistic African American characters emerge in fiction for young adults.

Reviews of and articles about young adult literature begin to appear in professional journals by scholars such as G. Robert Carlsen, Dwight Burton, Emma Patterson, and Margaret Edwards.

Clifton Fadiman
Fantasia Mathematica

Harper Lee
To Kill a Mockingbird

John Knowles
A Separate Peace

Scott O'Dell
Island of the Blue Dolphins

John Howard Griffin
Black Like Me

Joan Aiken
The Wolves of Willoughby Chase

Madeleine L'Engle
A Wrinkle in Time

Irene Hunt
Across Five Aprils

Hannah Green
I Never Promised You a Rose Garden

Frank Bonham
Durango Street

Nat Hentoff
Jazz Country

Ann Head
Mr. and Mrs. Bo Jo Jones

Virginia Hamilton
Zeely

S. E. Hinton
The Outsiders

Robert Lipsyte
The Contender

James Forman
My Enemy, My Brother

Paul Zindel
The Pigman

John Donovan
I'll Get There. It Better Be Worth the Trip

John Neufeld
Lisa Bright and Dark

Vera Cleaver and Bill Cleaver
Where the Lilies Bloom

Judy Blume
Are You There God? It's Me, Margaret

Maya Angelou
I Know Why the Caged Bird Sings

1960

1965

1970

Dwight Burton *Literature Study in the High Schools* (1959) is published.

Magaret Early publishes study on developmental reading stages.

A new realism in young adult literature emerges.

Dan Fader writes *Hooked on Books: Program and Proof* (1966).

First book marketed as a young adult book is published (1967).

Young adult problem novels become popular.

Anonymous
  Go Ask Alice

Robert Newton Peck
  A Day No Pigs Would Die

Jean Craighead George
  Julie of the Wolves

Isabelle Holland
  Man without a Face

Norma Klein
  Mom, the Wolfman, and Me

Alice Childress
  A Hero Ain't Nothin' but a Sandwich

Rosa Guy
  The Friends

Jeanne W. Houston and James D. Houston
  Farewell to Manzanar

Sandra Scoppettone
  Trying Hard to Hear You

Robert Cormier
  The Chocolate War

Paula Danziger
  The Cat Ate My Gymsuit

G. Robert Carlsen publishes *Books and the Teenage Reader* (1971).

ALAN Review first published (1973).

Supreme Court ruling on censorship (1973) placed decision-making power on boards of education.

Richard Peck   **1975**
  Are You in the House Alone?

Judy Blume
  Forever

Linda Bird Franke
  The Ambivalence of Abortion

Robin Brancato
  Blinded by the Light

Formula romances are reintroduced and become very popular.

Fewer problem novels are published as censorship becomes an issue.

Ellen Raskin   **1980**
  The Westing Game

Zibby Oneal
  The Language of Goldfish

Katherine Paterson
  Jacob Have I Loved

Milton Meltzer
  Never to Forget: The Jews of the Holocaust

Educational reformers urge excellence rather than equality of opportunity; a move back to the classics (e.g., William Bennett, *James Madison High School: A Curriculum for American Students*).

Censorship attacks limit use of young adult books in schools.

More young adult genres are introduced by publishers.

Nancy Willard
*A Visit to William Blake's Inn
Poems for Innocent and Experienced
Travelers*

Bruce Brooks
The Moves Make the Man

Maureen Daly   **1985**
Acts of Love
                                                            Formula books, classics and nonfiction
                                                            dominate publishers' backlists.

Jerry Spinelli   **1990**
Maniac Magee
                                                            New interest in multiculturalism.

Walter Dean Myers   Educators take stand against censorship.
Scorpions

Julian Thompson
A Band of Angels

Bette Greene
The Drowning of Stephan Jones

HOW TO ORGANIZE AND PREPARE FOR AUTHOR INTERVIEWS

How to Organize an Author Interview

1. Begin this process at least two months prior to the interview.
2. Call the publicity department or education department of the author's publisher (see Appendix F for a list of young adult book publishers and their addresses). Ask if the author is available to do school visits or telephone interviews with students. A school visit may involve paying an honorarium and travel expenses to the author.
3. If the author is visiting the school, involve as many of the students, teachers, staff, and parents as possible.
4. Contact the author or the author's representative to make travel and living arrangements (note: many authors prefer not to stay in private homes).
5. As a team of teachers discuss how you will prepare the students for the visit or telephone hookup (see Figure 11.1 for ideas for preparing students).
6. Invite teachers from a variety of subject areas to be involved in the planning. Develop an interdisciplinary unit using the author's books.
7. Be sure that each group of students who will participate in the interview is prepared for the interview.

8. Be sure the school library has multiple copies of the author's books. Make the books available in classroom libraries. Inform the local public library and local bookstores of the author's visit so they can have available extra copies of the author's books.
9. If the author is visiting the school, plan the day carefully:
   a. Have the students do bulletin boards in the hallways about the author and his or her books.
   b. Put out a welcome sign for the author.
   c. Arrange some media coverage of the day; call your local papers, radio stations, or television stations.
   d. Have students from the school newspaper interview the author for a special story, or videotape or record an interview with the author for future use.
   e. Have one class write and produce a play based on one of the author's books; invite the author to see the play.
   f. Make arrangements with the publisher or a book distributor to sell paperback copies of the author's books to students at discount prices (parents or other adult volunteers can help organize the sale).

g. Invite parents and other adults to prepare and attend a reception for the author.

h. Have an autographing party.

i. Show a film based on one of the author's books to the students during the day of the visit.

j. Arrange a special lunch party with students and dinner with adults.

k. Have one or more students serve as the author's hosts during the school day.

l. Be sure to give the author some "downtime" throughout the school day.

10. Phone-conference equipment can be purchased for a limited amount of money (or you may be able to rent or borrow equipment from your local phone company). Before using the equipment be sure that speakers are attached to it so that all students can hear.

11. With phone conversations, allow as many students to participate as possible (individual student questions and comments may need to be briefer than with a class visit).

12. Be sure to test the equipment with the students prior to the phone hookup.

13. Call the author prior to the visit or the phone hookup to see if he or she has any special requests or dos and don'ts.

Preparing Students for an Author Interview

1. Whenever possible allow students to be involved in the process of selecting an author.

2. Provide students with access to information about the author and the author's books.

3. Read aloud one of the author's books to all students who will participate in the interview.

4. Do book talks on the author's books (or ask the librarian to do them).

5. Require each student to select at least one of the author's books to read individually.

6. Send home annotated bibliographies of the author's books to parents with lists of where they are available (libraries and bookstores).

7. Assign students to literature groups to discuss the books (use some of the response techniques discussed in Chapter 11).

8. If a film or video based on one of the author's books is available, show it to the class and compare it to the book.

9. Allow students to select from a variety of projects designed to help them get to know the author and his or her books:

a. Do a bulletin board about the author.

b. Do a display about the author and his or her books.

c. Write a play from a section of the author's book.

d. Write a new ending for one or more of the author's books.

e. Do illustrations for the author's books.

f. Use one of the author's books as a model for an original story.

g. Prepare reviews of the author's books and publish them in the school newspaper or read them over the school "radio."

h. Prepare and write publicity about the interview and submit it to local media.

i. Prepare an author display for a local bookstore, the school library, or the public library.

j. Write a sequel to one of the author's books.

k. Write a screenplay from one of the author's books.

l. Do research on the author and write a report or present it orally.

10. Assign biographical information about the author to be read and discussed by the students. Suggested sources include

a. Twayne United States Author Series: Young Adult Author, published in paperback by Dell

b. *Something about the Author: Autobiography Series*

c. *Speaking for Ourselves*

d. *Contemporary Authors*

e. *ALAN Review*

f. *CBC Features* of the Children's Book Council

g. *Voice of Youth Advocates*

h. publicity about the author from the publisher
Using these sources can help students develop or review library research skills (see Chapter 14 for information about these works).

11. If available, watch a video interview with the author or listen to a cassette tape of the author speaking about his or her work (the author's publisher will be able to help you locate these).

12. Use book-sharing techniques (see Appendix D) to share all of the author's books with as many students as possible.

13. Prior to the interview, discuss the author's life and how it has influenced his or her writing.

14. Write questions to ask the author.

HOW TO ORGANIZE AND RUN A SCHOOL BOOKSTORE

1. The entire school community should support the idea and be involved in the store.
2. The store should be a part of the entire school's policy toward books and reading.
3. Once the school community is committed to the idea, a committee of interested people should be established. If possible, the committee should include teachers, parents or other adult volunteers, administrators, school librarians or media personnel, other school staff, and students. If students are going to be involved in the operation of the bookstore, it is helpful to have a school staff member, perhaps a business teacher, organize their involvement.
4. Members of the committee can read a helpful pamphlet available from the American Reading Council called *How to Set Up and Run a School Paperback Bookstore.*
5. The location for the bookstore must be accessible and attractive, but it need not be large. An easily locked, large closet off a main lobby or corridor can make an excellent small bookstore.
6. Security is important. Either the bookstore or the cabinets holding the books must be able to be locked and reopened easily, with minimum setup and dismantling. Responsible and easily accessible persons should hold the keys.

7. A local retailer, jobber, or distributor must be contacted to supply the bookstore. Discounts, return or exchange privileges, credit arrangements, and payment schedules must be organized before the bookstore is opened.
8. The committee, or a subcommittee, can select books from catalogs, reviews, and reference books (see Chapter 14). The stock should appeal to a cross section of interests, reading levels, and age levels. Nonfiction and fiction should be available. Puzzle and joke books are often good sellers. TV and movie tie-ins also sell well. Whatever you do, don't stock the bookstore with books that teachers think the students *should* be reading. Be sure a representative group of students participates in the selection process. Follow sales trends and tailor the stock to students' interests.
9. Aim to turn over the stock three times per year (sell an average of 25 percent of the stock each month). Exchange slower-selling titles as frequently as possible to keep stock looking fresh. Try to offer new books frequently so that the students will keep coming.
10. Involve students as much as possible in staffing the bookstore. Be sure an adult is on hand whenever the store is open.

11. Keep the bookstore hours regular so that students know when it will be open. The best hours to be open are before school, during lunch, after school, and during special events when parents are likely to be in the school.
12. Discount cards often encourage students to buy books. Layaway plans are helpful. A book exchange and second-hand section can help keep prices down.
13. Keep an up-to-date inventory on a card index or computer. Record all sales. Reorder when necessary. Keep track of profit or loss.
14. Publicize the store. Have an elaborate opening ceremony to which students and parents are invited. Keep thinking of new and fresh ideas for promoting the store to maximize student involvement:
    a. posters, stickers, and buttons
    b. announcements over the PA system
    c. seasonal displays
    d. fund-raising schemes such as sponsored spelling bees or readathons
    e. competitions related to books in the bookstore
    f. book talks of bookstore books in classes
    g. showing films or videos related to bookstore books in class
    h. class trips to the bookstore
    i. student book reviews of bookstore books in the student newspaper or over the PA system
    j. a newsletter for parents about the bookstore, special events, and new books
    k. storytelling events
    l. author visits

Adapted from John Mason, "Promote Reading for Pleasure: Start a School Bookstore." *ALAN Review,* Spring 1985, pp. 43–46. Reprinted with permission of John Mason.

SIXTY WAYS TO TELL ABOUT BOOKS

1. Hold a panel discussion among several students who have read the same book or a group of similar books.
2. Organize a pro-and-con panel made up of some students who liked a book and some who did not. Let one person represent the author. Try to have an impartial chairman.
3. Dramatize an incident or an important character. The student may relate an incident in the first person.
4. Prepare and deliver radio announcements to advertise books.
5. Have individual conferences in which students talk about favorite books with the teacher.
6. Appoint a committee of pupils who are avid readers to conduct peer discussions and seminars about books.
7. Hold a mock trial permitting the defendant to tell the story of a book of his or her choosing. The class renders a decision on its merits.
8. Reproduce illustrators' interpretations of important scenes for the whole class to enjoy.
9. Give brief oral talks of not more than five minutes each.
10. Summarize the plot in one succinct paragraph (this takes practice).
11. Hold dialogues between several students to reveal the style and story of the book.
12. Design book jackets that convey the genre of the book as well as the story.
13. Write a precis, or summary of essential points or facts (use this activity sparingly).
14. Compose a telegram that captures the essence of a book in fifteen words. Then expand it into a hundred-word message.
15. Compose a publisher's blurb to sell the book.
16. Read aloud an interesting part of the book, stopping at a strategic point.
17. Give a sales talk, pretending your audience is composed of clerks in a bookstore and you want to promote a new book.
18. Have students question the readers of the book, or let three students challenge the reader with difficult questions.
19. Make comparisons with the movie and television versions of the same book.
20. Create a poster advertising the book.
21. Build a miniature stage setting for part of the story.
22. Design costumes for characters, in miniature or life-size.
23. Make a rebus of a short story and try it out on friends.
24. Write a book review for a newspaper or magazine and send it in for possible publication.
25. Write a movie script to sell to Hollywood.

26. For a how-to book, bring in something you made according to the directions.
27. Prepare a travel lecture based on a travel book.
28. Write an original poem after studying a book of poetry for both style and choice of subjects.
29. After reading a book of poems, learn a verse to recite to the class or read one aloud.
30. Tell a friend why you did or did not like a book.
31. Explain how the book could be used in social studies or science classes.
32. Make sketches of some of the action sequences.
33. Describe an interesting character, trying to make him or her come alive to your audience.
34. Write or tell a different ending to the story.
35. Write or tell about the most humorous, most exciting, or most interesting incident in the book, or the part you liked best.
36. Select a descriptive passage and read it aloud to the class.
37. List interesting new words and expressions to add to your vocabulary.
38. Describe a scene to orient your audience; then show it in pantomime.
39. Write a letter recommending the book to a friend.
40. Deliver an oral synopsis of the story, but don't give away the climax.
41. Make a scrapbook suggested by information in the book.
42. Construct puppets and present a show of an interesting part of the story.
43. Make a map that shows information gathered from a geographical book.
44. Have a friend who has read the story try to stump you with questions.

45. Make a list of facts you learned from reading a factual story.
46. Write questions you think everyone should be able to answer after reading the book; then try them on other readers.
47. Dress as one of the characters and act out the part you play.
48. Broadcast a book review on your school public address system.
49. Write a note to the school librarian explaining why the library ought to recommend the book to other students.
50. Review the book you read for another class.
51. Research the author's career and tell about his or her other books.
52. Make a clay, soap, or wood model to illustrate a phase of the story.
53. Construct a diorama or table exhibit to illustrate a phase of the story.
54. Make a bulletin-board exhibit.
55. Give a talk using the chalkboard or an overhead projector.
56. Paint or draw an illustration of the story.
57. Make a mural to illustrate the book; get others who have read it to help.
58. Rewrite an incident in the book, simplifying vocabulary for a lower grade.
59. For a science book, plan a demonstration of what you learned.
60. For a historical book, make a time line of events.

Based on a list of book-telling techniques distributed at a 1972 conference (author unknown).

YOUNG ADULT NOVELS RELATED TO THEMES IN CLASSIC WORKS

The Scarlet Letter by Nathaniel Hawthorne

Alienation

Cormier, Robert. *The Chocolate War*. Pantheon, 1974. Dell, 1986.

Hall, Lynn. *Sticks and Stones*. Follett, 1972. Dell, 1972.

Miklowitz, Gloria D. *Good-Bye Tomorrow*. Delacorte, 1987. Dell, 1988.

Sebestyen, Ouida. *Words by Heart*. Little, Brown, 1979. Bantam, 1981, 1983.

Breaking Society's Rules about Sexual Relationships

Crutcher, Chris. *Chinese Handcuffs*. Greenwillow, 1989.

Irwin, Hadley. *Abby, My Love*. Atheneum, 1985. Macmillan, 1985.

Luger, Harriet. *Lauren*. Viking, 1979. Dell, 1981.

Paton, Alan. *Too Late the Phalarope*. Scribner's, 1953.

Rylant, Cynthia. *A Kindness*. Orchard Books, 1988. Dell, 1990.

Appearance Versus Reality

Brooks, Bruce. *The Moves Make the Man*. Harper & Row, 1984. HarperCollins, 1987.

Duncan, Lois. *Killing Mr. Griffin*. Little, Brown, 1978. Dell, 1979.

Hawthorne, Nathaniel. "The minister's black veil." From *The Celestial Railroad and Other Stories*. NAL/Signet Classic, 1963.

Kerr, M. E. *Gentlehands*. Harper & Row, 1978.

Knowles, John. *A Separate Peace*. Dell, 1959. Macmillan, 1959. Bantam, 1975.

Stoker, Bram. *Dracula*. NAL/Signet Classic, 1978.

Wilde, Oscar. *The Picture of Dorian Gray*. NAL/Signet Classic, 1962.

Love Triangles

Brontë, Charolette. *Jane Eyre*. Puffin Books, 1992.

Pasternak, Boris. *Doctor Zhivago*. Pantheon, 1958. Knopf, 1991.

Shakespeare, William. *Othello: The Moor of Venice*. NAL/Signet Classic, 1962.

Religious Communities

Kerr, M. E. *What I Really Think of You*. Harper Junior, 1982. Harper, 1991.

Miller, Arthur. *The Crucible*. Viking, 1973. Penguin, 1976.

Speare, Elizabeth. *The Witch of Blackbird Pond*. Houghton Mifflin, 1958. Dell, 1975; Dell, 1978.

Single Parenthood

Koertge, Ron. *Where the Kissing Never Stops*. Little, Brown, 1987. Dell, 1988.

Lowry, Lois. *Rabble Starkey.* Houghton Mifflin, 1987. Dell, 1988.

Mazer, Norma Fox. *Silver.* Morrow, 1988. Avon, 1989.

Voigt, Cynthia. *A Solitary Blue.* Atheneum, 1983.

Puritan New England

Fleischman, Paul. *Saturnalia.* HarperCollins, 1990.

Miller, Arthur. *The Crucible.* Viking, 1973. Penguin, 1976.

Speare, Elizabeth. *The Witch of Blackbird Pond.* Houghton Mifflin, 1958. Dell, 1975; Dell, 1978.

From Elizabeth Poe, "A Teacher's Guide to the Signet Classic Edition of Nathaniel Hawthorne's *The Scarlet Letter*" (Penguin, 1991).

1984 by George Orwell

Repression by Government

Cridle, Joan, and Teeda Butt Mann. *To Destroy You Is No Loss.* Atlantic Monthly Press, 1987.

Hoobler, Dorothy and Thomas. *Nelson and Winnie Mandela.* Franklin Watts, 1987.

Houston, Jeanne Wakatsuki and James. *Farewell to Manzanar.* Houghton Mifflin, 1973. Bantam, 1974.

Kheridan, David. *The Road from Home.* Greenwillow, 1979.

Mathabane, Mark. *Kaffir Boy.* Macmillan, 1986. New American Library, 1990.

Solzhenitsyn, Alexander. *One Day in the Life of Ivan Denisovich.* E. P. Dutton, 1963. NAL/Signet Classic.

Behavioral Conditioning/Isolation

Cormier, Robert. *The Bumblebee Flies Anyway.* Pantheon, 1983. Dell, 1984.

———. *I Am the Cheese.: A Novel.* Pantheon, 1977. Dell, 1978.

George, Jean Craighead. *Julie of the Wolves.* Harper & Row, 1972.

Sleator, William. *House of Stairs.* Dutton, 1974. Avon, 1975.

Utopias and Dystopias

Bradbury, Ray. *Fahrenheit 451.* Ballantine, 1987.

Golding, William. *Lord of the Flies.* Wideview/Perigee Books, 1954.

Huxley, Aldous. *Brave New World.* Harper & Row, 1932.

More, Thomas. *Utopia.* AHM Publishing, 1949. NAL/Signet Classic.

Nolan, William F., and George Clayton Johnson. *Logan's Run.* Dial, 1967. Dell, 1969.

Orwell, George. *Animal Farm.* New American Library, 1974.

Wells, H. G. *The Island of Doctor Moreau.* NAL/Signet Classic, 1977.

From Lisa Session, "A Teacher's guide to the Signet Classic Edition of George Orwell's *1984*" (Penguin/Signet Classic, 1991).

Ethan Frome by Edith Wharton

Personal Inclinations Versus Group Obligations

Arrick, Fran. *God's Radar.* Bradbury, 1983. Dell, 1986.

Cormier, Robert. *Beyond the Chocolate War.* Knopf, 1985.

———. *The Chocolate War.* Pantheon, 1974.

Duncan, Lois. *Killing Mr. Griffin.* Little, Brown, 1978. Dell, 1979.

Golding, William. *Lord of the Flies.* Wideview/Perigee Books, 1954.

Hentoff, Nat. *The Day They Came to Arrest the Book.* Delacorte, 1982.

Kerr, M. E. *Is That You, Miss Blue?* Harper & Row, 1975. Dell, 1976.

Pfeffer, Susan Beth. *A Matter of Principle.* Delacorte, 1982.

Personal Control over Choice

Asher, Sandy. *Everything Is Not Enough.* Delacorte, 1987. Dell, 1988.

Brooks, Bruce. *The Moves Make the Man.* Harper & Row, 1984. HarperCollins, 1987.

Cleaver, Vera and Bill Cleaver. *Where the Lilies Bloom.* Lippincott, 1969. New American Library, 1974.

Lipsyte, Robert. *The Contender.* Harper & Row, 1967. HarperCollins, 1987.

Major, Kevin. *Far from Shore.* Delacorte, 1981. Dell, 1983.

Mazer, Norma Fox. *Downtown.* Morrow, 1984. Avon, 1984.

Newton, Suzanne. *I Will Call It Georgie's Blues.* Viking, 1983. Dell, 1986.

Paterson, Katherine. *Jacob Have I Loved.* Crowell, 1980. Avon, 1981.

Oneal, Zibby. *In Summer Light.* Viking, 1985. Bantam, 1986.

Voigt, Cynthia. *Homecoming.* Atheneum, 1981. Fawcett Juniper, 1982.

Zindel, Paul. *The Pigman.* Harper & Row, 1968. Bantam, 1978.

Suicide

Anonymous. *Go Ask Alice.* Prentice-Hall, 1971. Avon, 1976.

Bridgers, Sue Ellen. *Notes for Another Life.* Knopf, 1981. Bantam, 1985.

Bunting, Eve. *If I Asked, Would You Stay?* Lippincott, 1984. HarperCollins, 1987.

Guest, Judith. *Ordinary People.* Viking, 1976. Ballantine, 1980.

Irwin, Hadley. *So Long at the Fair.* Macmillan/McElderry, 1988.

Oneal, Zibby. *The Language of Goldfish.* Viking, 1980.

Peck, Richard. *Remembering the Good Times.* Delacorte, 1985.

Pfeffer, Susan Beth. *About David.* Delacorte, 1980. Dell, 1982.

From Wendy H. Bell, "A Teacher's Guide to the Signet Classic Edition of Edith Wharton's *Ethan Frome*" (NAL/Signet Classic, 1989).

Beloved by Toni Morrison

End of Slavery and Beginning of Reconstruction

NONFICTION

Meltzer, Milton. *The Black Americans: A History in Their Own Words, 1619–1983.* Crowell, 1984. Harper & Row, 1987.

FICTION

Hurmence, Belinda. *Tancy.* Clarion, 1984.

First Taste of Freedom

NONFICTION

Lester, Julius. *This Strange New Feeling.* Dial, 1982. Scholastic, 1985.

FICTION

Fast, Howard. *Freedom Road.* Crown, 1969.

Hurmence, Belinda. *Tancy.* Clarion, 1984.

Rinaldi, Ann. *Wolf by the Ears.* Scholastic, 1991.

Fugitive Slaves

NONFICTION

Douglass, Frederick. *Narrative of the Life of Frederick Douglass an American Slave: Written by Himself.* 1845. Harvard University Press, 1960. NAL/Signet Classic, 1968.

Hamilton, Virginia. *Anthony Burns: The Defeat of Triumph of a Fugitive Slave.* Knopf, 1988.

Sterling, Dorothy. *Black Foremothers.* Feminist Press, 1979, 1988.

FICTION

Hurmence, Belinda. *A Girl Called Boy.* Clarion, 1982.

Smucker, Barbara. *Runaway to Freedom: A Story of the Underground Railroad.* Harper & Row, 1977. Harper Junior, 1979.

Stowe, Harriet Beecher. *Uncle Tom's Cabin.* NAL/Signet Classic, 1852.

Searching for Family Members

FICTION

Hurmence, Belinda. *Tancy.* Clarion, 1984.

Slave Narratives

NONFICTION

Bontemps, Arna. *Great Slave Narratives.* Beacon Press, 1969.

Davis, Charles T., and Henry Louis Gates, Jr., eds. *The Slave's Narrative.* Oxford University Press, 1985.

Five Slave Narratives: A Compendium. Arno Press and the *New York Times,* 1968.

Gates, Henry Louis, Jr., ed. *The Classic Slave Narratives.* New American Library, 1987.

Lester, Julius. *To Be a Slave.* Dial, 1968. Scholastic, 1986.

Meltzer, Milton. *The Black Americans: A History in Their Own Words, 1619–1983.* Crowell, 1984. Harper & Row, 1987.

Still, William. *The Underground Railroad.* Porter & Coats, 1872. Arno Press and the *New York Times,* 1968.

Weld, Theodore. *American Slavery As It Is: Testimony of a Thousand Witnesses.* American Anti-Slavery Society, 1839.

FICTION

Hurmence, Belinda. *A Girl Called Boy.* Clarion, 1982.

———. *Tancy.* Clarion, 1984.

Slave Ships from Africa

NONFICTION

Cable, Mary. *Black Odyssey: The Case of the Slave Ship Amistad.* Viking, 1971. Penguin, 1977.

FICTION

Fox, Paula. *The Slave Dancer.* Bradbury, 1973. Dell, 1975.

Johnson, Charles. *Middle Passage.* Atheneum, 1990. Plume, 1991.

Underground Railroad

NONFICTION

Blockson, Charles L. *The Underground Railroad: First Person Narratives of Escapes to Freedom in the North.* Prentice-Hall, 1987. Berkley, 1989.

Douglass, Frederick. *Narrative of the Life of Frederick Douglass an American Slave: Written by Himself.* 1845. Harvard University Press, 1960. NAL/Signet Classic, 1968.

Petry, Ann. *Harriet Tubman: Conductor on the Un-*

derground Railroad. Crowell, 1955. Archway, 1971.

Quarles, Benjamin. *Black Abolitionists.* Oxford University Press, 1969.

Siebert, Wilbur H. *The Underground Railway from Slavery to Freedom.* Macmillan, 1898. Arno Press and the *New York Times,* 1968.

FICTION

Gaines, Ernest J. *The Autobiography of Miss Jane Pittman.* Dial, 1971. Bantam, 1982.

Smucker, Barbara. *Runaway to Freedom: A Story of the Underground Railroad.* Harper & Row, 1977. Harper Junior, 1979.

Stowe, Harriet Beecher. *Uncle Tom's Cabin,* 1852. NAL/Signet Classic.

Black Female Writers

Angelou, Maya. *I Know Why the Caged Bird Sings.* Random House, 1969. Bantam, 1983.

Hansberry, Lorraine. *A Raisin in the Sun.* Random House, 1959. NAL/Signet Classic, 1961.

Taylor, Mildred. *Roll of Thunder, Hear My Cry.* Dial, 1976. Bantam, 1978.

Walker, Alice. *The Color Purple.* Harcourt Brace Jovanovich, 1982. Washington Square Press, 1982.

From Elizabeth Ann Poe, "A Teacher's Guide to the Signet and Plume editions of Toni Morrison's *Beloved* " (Penguin/Signet Classic, 1991).

Romeo and Juliet by William Shakespeare

Hostility and Its Effect on the Innocent

Houston, Jeanne W., and James Houston, *Farewell to Manzanar.* Houghton Mifflin, 1973. Bantam, 1974.

Lee, Harper. *To Kill a Mockingbird.* Lippincott, 1960. Warner, 1988.

Lingard, J. *Across the Barricades.* Nelson, 1973. Penguin, 1973.

Speare, Elizabeth. *The Witch of Blackbird Pond.* Houghton Mifflin, 1958. Dell, 1975; Dell, 1978.

Sebestyen, Ouida. *Words by Heart.* Little, Brown, 1979. Bantam, 1981, 1983.

Teenage Suicide

Anonymous. *Go Ask Alice.* Prentice-Hall, 1971. Avon, 1976.

Guest, Judith. *Ordinary People.* Viking, 1976. Ballantine, 1980.

Jacobs, J. *Adolescent Suicide.* Wiley Press, 1971.

Mack, John, and Holly Hickler. *Vivienne: The Life and Suicide of an Adolescent Girl.* New American Library, 1982.

Peck, Richard. *Remembering the Good Times.* Delacorte, 1985.

Pfeffer, Susan Beth. *About David.* Delacorte, 1980. Dell, 1982.

Decision Making

Hinton, S. E. *The Outsiders.* Viking, 1967. Dell, 1980.

Lipsyte, Robert. *The Contender.* Harper & Row, 1967. HarperCollins, 1987.

The Generation Gap

Bridgers, Sue Ellen. *Home before Dark.* Knopf, 1976. Bantam, 1985.

Frank, Anne. *Anne Frank: The Diary of a Young Girl.* Doubleday, 1952. Pocketbook, 1978.

Kerr, M. E. *Dinky Hocker Shoots Smack!* Harper & Row, 1972.

The Role of Friendship and Peer Pressure

Brooks, Bruce. *The Moves Make the Man.* Harper & Row, 1984.

Golding, William. *Lord of the Flies.* Wideview/Perigee Books, 1954. Putnam, 1954.

Guy, Rosa. *The Friends.* Holt, 1973.

The Use of Deception and Its Consequences

Cormier, Robert. *I Am the Cheese.* Pantheon, 1977.

Duncan, Lois. *Killing Mr. Griffin.* Little, Brown, 1978.

Kerr, M. E. *Gentlehands.* Harper & Row, 1978.

Shreve, Susan. *The Masquerade.* Knopf, 1980. Dell, 1981.

Teenage Love

Greene, Bette. *Summer of My German Soldier.* Dial, 1973. Bantam, 1974.

Guy, Rosa. *My Love, My Love; or, The Peasant Girl.* Holt, Rinehart & Winston, 1985.

Lee, Mildred. *The People Therein.* Houghton Mifflin, 1980.

Lyle, Katie Letcher. *Fair Day, and Another Step Begun.* Lippincott, 1974.

Mazer, Norma Fox. *When We First Met.* Scholastic, 1991.

Isolation of the Tragic Hero

Cormier, Robert. *The Chocolate War.* Pantheon, 1974. Dell, 1986.

Miller, Arthur. *Death of a Salesman.* Viking, 1981.

From Arthea J. S. Reed, "A Teacher's Guide to the Signet Classic Edition of William Shakespeare's *Romeo and Juliet*" (NAL/Signet Classic, 1988).

Macbeth by William Shakespeare

Things Are Not What They Seem

Bograd, Larry. *Travelers*. Lippincott, 1986.

Bridgers, Sue Ellen. *Permanent Connections*. Harper & Row, 1987.

Brooks, Bruce. *Midnight Hour Encores*. Harper & Row, 1986. HarperCollins, 1988.

Cormier, Robert. *The Bumblebee Flies Anyway*. Pantheon, 1983. Dell, 1984.

————. *I Am the Cheese: A Novel*. Pantheon, 1977. Dell, 1978.

Duncan, Lois. *Killing Mr. Griffin*. Little, Brown, 1978. Dell, 1979.

Hamilton, Virginia. *M. C. Higgins, the Great*. Macmillan, 1974. Dell, 1976.

Irwin, Hadley. *Abby, My Love*. Atheneum, 1985. Macmillan, 1985.

Kerr, M. E. *Gentlehands*. Harper & Row, 1978.

Lasky, Kathryn. *Prank*. Macmillan, 1984. Dell, 1986.

Major, Kevin. *Far from Shore*. Delacorte, 1981. Dell, 1983.

Paterson, Katherine. *Jacob Have I Loved*. Harper & Row, 1980. Avon, 1981.

Peck, Richard. *Remembering the Good Times*. Delacorte, 1985.

Voigt, Cynthia. *A Solitary Blue*. Atheneum, 1983.

The Corruption of Power

Cormier, Robert. *The Chocolate War*. Pantheon, 1974. Dell, 1986.

————. *Beyond the Chocolate War*. Knopf, 1985.

Duncan, Lois. *Down a Dark Hall*. Little, Brown, 1974. New American Library, 1975.

Golding, William. *The Lord of the Flies*. Wideview Pedigree Books, 1954.

Huxley, Aldous. *Brave New World*. Harper & Row, 1932.

L'Engle, Madeleine. *The Young Unicorns*. Farrar, Straus & Giroux, 1968. Dell, 1989.

Rhue, Morton. *The Wave*. Dell, 1981. Delacorte, 1981.

Sleater, William. *House of Stairs*. Dutton, 1974. Avon, 1975.

Tolkien, J. R. R. *The Lord of the Rings*. Allen, 1954.

Blind Ambition

Dean, John. *Blind Ambition: The White House Years*. Simon and Schuster, 1976.

Warren, Robert Penn. *All the King's Men*. Harcourt, Brace and World, 1946.

Superstition and Its Effects on Human Behavior

Clemens, S. L. (Twain, Mark). *The Adventures of Huckleberry Finn*. 1884.

Hamilton, Virginia. *Sweet Whispers, Brother Rush*. Philomel, 1983.

Miller, Arthur. *The Crucible*. Viking, 1973. Penguin, 1976.

Myers, Walter Dean. *Mojo and the Russians*. Viking, 1977. Avon, 1977.

Peck, Richard. *Ghosts I Have Been*. Viking, 1977. Dell, 1979.

Speare, Elizabeth George. *The Witch of Blackbird Pond*. Houghton Mifflin, 1958. Dell, 1975; Dell, 1978.

From Linda N. Underwood, "A Teacher's Guide to the Signet Classic Edition of William Shakespeare's *Macbeth*" (NAL/Signet Classic, 1989).

PUBLISHERS OF YOUNG ADULT BOOKS

Aladdin Books
(an imprint of the Macmillan Children's Book
Group)
866 Third Avenue
New York, NY 10022
(212) 702-2000

Arcade Publishing
(a subsidiary of Little, Brown & Co.)
141 Fifth Avenue
New York, NY 10010
(212) 475-2633

Atheneum Publishers
(an imprint of the Macmillan Children's Book
Group)
866 Third Avenue
New York, NY 10022
(212) 702-2000

Avon Books
1350 Avenue of the Americas
New York, NY 10019
(212) 261-6800

Barron's Educational Series, Inc.
250 Wireless Blvd.
PO Box 8040
Hauppauge, NY 11788
(516) 434-3311

Boyds Mills Press
4 Hubbell Mountain Rd.
Sherman, CT 06784
(203) 355-9498

Bradbury Press
(an affiliate of Macmillan, Inc.)
866 Third Avenue
New York, NY 10022
(212) 702-9809

Clarion Books
215 Park Avenue South
New York, NY 10003
(212) 420-5800

Cobblehill Books
(an affiliate of Dutton Children's Books/Penguin
USA)
375 Hudson Street
New York, NY 10014
(212) 366-2328

Crown Publishers
225 Park Avenue South
New York, NY 10003
(212) 254-1600

Delacorte/Doubleday Books for Young Readers
666 Fifth Avenue
New York, NY 10103
(212) 765-6500

Dell Publishing
666 Fifth Avenue
New York, NY 10103
(212) 765-6500

Dial Books for Young Readers
(a division of Penguin USA)
375 Hudson Street
New York, NY 10014
(212) 366-2800

Dorling Kindersley, Inc.
232 Madison Avenue
New York, NY 10016
(212) 684-0404

Dutton Children's Books
(a division of Penguin USA)
375 Hudson Street
New York, NY 10014
(212) 366-2600

Enslow Publishers, Inc.
Bloy Street & Ramsey Avenue
Box 777
Hillside, NJ 07205
(201) 964-4116

Farrar, Straus & Giroux, Inc.
19 Union Square West
New York, NY 10003
(212) 741-6900

Four Winds Press
(an imprint of the Macmillan Children's Book
Group)
866 Third Avenue
New York, NY 10022
(212) 702-2000

Greenwillow Books
1350 Avenue of the Americas
New York, NY 10019
(212) 261-6500

Grosset & Dunlap, Inc.
(the Putnam & Grosset Book Group)
200 Madison Avenue
New York, NY 10016
(212) 951-8700

Gulliver Books
(an imprint of Harcourt Brace Jovanovich, Inc.)
1250 Sixth Avenue
San Diego, CA 92101
(619) 699-6810

Harcourt Brace Jovanovich, Inc.
1250 Sixth Ave.
San Diego, CA 92101
(619) 699-6810

Harper Trophy Paperbacks
(HarperCollins Children's Books)
10 East 53rd Street
New York, NY 10022
(212) 207-7044

HarperCollins Children's Books
10 East 53rd Street
New York, NY 10022
(212) 207-7044

Holiday House
425 Madison Avenue
New York, NY 10017
(212) 688-0085

Henry Holt and Company, Inc.
115 West 18th Street
New York, NY 10011
(212) 886-9200

Houghton Mifflin Co.
2 Park Avenue South
New York, NY 10003
(617) 725-5000

Hyperion Books for Children
114 Fifth Avenue
New York, NY 10011
(212) 633-4400

The Jewish Publication Society
2112 Broadway
New York, NY 10023
(212) 873-8399

Joy Street Books
(an imprint of Little, Brown & Co.)
34 Beacon Street
Boston, MA 01208
(617) 227-0730

Alfred A. Knopf, Inc.
225 Park Avenue South
New York, NY 10003
(212) 254-1600

Lerner Publications Company
241 First Avenue North
Minneapolis, MN 55401
(612) 332-3344

Little, Brown & Co.
34 Beacon Street
Boston, MA 02108
(617) 227-0730

Lodestar Books
(an affiliate of Dutton's Children Books/Penguin USA)
375 Hudson Street
New York, NY 10014
(212) 366-2627

Lothrop, Lee & Shepard Books
1350 Avenue of the Americas
New York, NY 10019
(212) 261-6641

Margaret K. McElderry Books
(an imprint of the Macmillan Children's Book Group)
866 Third Avenue
New York, NY 10022
(212) 702-7855

Macmillan Publishing Co.
866 Third Avenue
New York, NY 10022
(212) 702-2000

Millbrook Press, Inc.
2 Old New Milford Road
Brookfield, CT 06804
(203) 740-2220

Morrow Junior Books
1350 Avenue of the Americas
New York, NY 10019
(212) 261-6691

Orchard Books
387 Park Avenue South
New York, NY 10016
(212) 686-7070

Pelican Publishing Company, Inc.
1101 Monroe Street
PO Box 189
Gretna, LA 70054
(504) 368-1175

Philomel Books
(the Putnam & Grosset Book Group)
200 Madison Avenue
New York, NY 10016
(212) 951-8700

Puffin Books
(a division of Penguin USA)
375 Hudson Street
New York, NY 10014
(212) 366-2000

Scholastic Hardcover
730 Broadway
New York, NY 10003
(212) 505-3000

Scholastic Inc.
730 Broadway
New York, NY 10003
(212) 505-3000

Charles Scribner's Sons
(an imprint of the Macmillan Children's Book Group)
866 Third Avenue
New York, NY 10022
(212) 702-7885

Simon and Schuster Books for Young Readers
15 Columbus Circle
New York, NY 10023
(212) 373-8424

Stemmer House Publishers, Inc.
2627 Caves Road
Owings Mills, MD 21117
(301) 363-3690

Stewart, Tabori & Chang
575 Broadway
New York, NY 10012
(212) 941-2955

Tambourine Books
1350 Avenue of the Americas
New York, NY 10019
(212) 261-6500

Viking Press
(a division of Penguin USA)
375 Hudson Street
New York, NY 10014
(212) 366-2000

Walker and Company
720 Fifth Avenue
New York, NY 10019
(212) 265-3632

Franklin Watts, Inc.
95 Madison Avenue
New York, NY 10016
(212) 447-7788

BIBLIOGRAPHY

Aaron, C. *Better Than Laughter*. Harcourt Brace Jovanovich, 1972. Dell, 1973.

———. *Lackawanna*. Lippincott, 1986.

———. *Out of Sight, Out of Mind*. Lippincott, 1985.

Abbey, E. *The Brave Cowboy*. University of New Mexico Press, 1980. Avon, 1992.

Adams, A. *The Log of a Cowboy: A Narrative of the Old Trail Days*. 1903. Leisure Books, 1976. University of Nebraska Press, 1964.

Adams, D. *The Restaurant at the End of the Universe*. Crown, 1982.

Adams, J. *We Dare You to Solve This!* Berkley, 1957.

Adams, L. *Art Cop: Robert Volpe, Art Crime Detective*. Dodd, Mead, 1974.

Adams, R. *Watership Down*. Macmillan, 1974. Avon, 1976.

Adamson, J. *Born Free: A Lioness of Two Worlds*. Random House, 1974. Pantheon Books, 1987.

———. *The Searching Spirit: Joy Adamson's Autobiography*. Harcourt Brace Jovanovich, 1979.

Adoff, A., ed. *Black Out Loud: Anthology of Modern Poems by Black Americans*. Macmillan, 1970. Dell, 1975.

———. *Celebrations, the Poetry of Black America: Anthology of the Twentieth Century*. Follett, 1977.

———. *I Am the Darker Brother: An Anthology of Modern Poems by Negro Americans*. Macmillan, 1970.

———. *It Is the Poem Singing into Your Eyes*. Harper & Row, 1972.

———. *My Black Me: A Beginning Book of Black Poetry*. Dutton, 1974.

———. *The Poetry of Black America: An Anthology of the Twentieth Century*. HarperCollins, 1973.

———. *Under the Early Morning Trees*. Dutton, 1978.

Agee, J. *A Death in the Family*. Bantam, 1983.

Aiken, J. *Black Hearts in Battersea*. Doubleday, 1964. Dell, 1981.

———. *Died on a Rainy Sunday*. Holt, Rinehart & Winston, 1972. Dell, 1988.

———. *Nightfall*. Holt, Rinehart & Winston, 1969. Dell, 1988.

———. *The Shadow Guests*. Delacorte, 1980. Dell, 1986.

———. *A Touch of Chill*. Dell, 1989.

———. *A Whisper in the Night: Tales of Terror and Suspense*. Delacorte, 1985. Dell, 1988.

———. *The Wolves of Willoughby Chase*. Doubleday, 1989.

Aiken, J., ed. *Authors' Choice 2*. Crowell, 1974.

Albert, L. *But I'm Ready to Go*. Bradbury, 1976. Dell, 1978.

Alcott, L. M. *Little Women*. Dell, 1987.

Alexander, L. *The Beggar Queen*. Dutton, 1984. Dell, 1985.

———. *The Black Cauldron.* Holt, Rinehart & Winston, 1965. Dell, 1980.

———. *The Book of Three.* Holt, Rinehart & Winston, 1964. Dell, 1980.

———. *The Castle of Llyr.* Holt, Rinehart & Winston, 1966. Dell, 1980.

———. *The El Dorado Adventure.* E. P. Dutton, 1987. Dell, 1990.

———. *The High King.* Holt, Rinehart & Winston, 1968. Dell, 1980.

———. *The Kestrel.* Dutton, 1981. Dell, 1983.

———. *Taran Wanderer.* Holt, Rinehart & Winston, 1967. Dell, 1980.

———. *Westmark.* Dutton, 1981. Dell, 1982.

———. *The Wizard in the Tree.* Dutton, 1975. Dell, 1981.

Alexander, R. P., and J. Lester, eds. *Young and Black in America.* Random House, 1970.

Alexander, S. *Anyone's Daughter: The Times and Trials of Patty Hearst.* Viking, 1979. Bantam Books, 1980.

———. *Small Plays for You and a Friend.* Houghton Mifflin, 1973.

Allen, D. M., ed. *The New American Poetry, 1945–1968.* Grove Press, 1960.

Allen, T. D., ed. *Arrows Four: Prose and Poetry by Young American Indians.* Washington Square Press, 1974.

———. *The Whispering Wind: Poetry by Young American Indians.* Doubleday, 1972.

Alvin, V. and R. Silverstein, *Saving Endangered Animals.* Enslow, 1993.

Ames, M. *Is There Life on a Plastic Planet?* Dutton, 1975.

Amory, C. *Mankind? Our Incredible War on Wildlife.* Harper & Row, 1974. Dell, 1974.

Anaya, R. *Bless Me, Ultima.* Tonatiuh International, 1972. TQS Publishers, 1976.

Anderson, C. *The Butterfly Kid.* Gregg, 1967. Pyramid, 1967.

Anderson, C. C. *John F. Kennedy: Young People's President.* Lerner, 1991.

Anderson, J. *1787.* Harcourt Brace Jovanovich, 1987.

Anderson, M. *In the Keep of Time.* Knopf, 1977. Scholastic, 1978.

Anderson, P. *The Broken Sword.* Abelard-Shumen, 1954. Baen Books, 1988.

Anderson, P., and G. Dickson. *Star Prince Charlie.* Putnam's, 1975. Berkley, 1975.

Angell, J. *Dear Lola; or, How to Build Your Own Family.* Bradbury, 1980. Dell, 1986.

———. *Ronnie and Rosey.* Bradbury, 1977. Dell, 1979.

———. *Secret Selves.* Bradbury, 1979. Dell, 1981.

———. *A Word from Our Sponsor; or, My Friend Alfred.* Bradbury, 1979. Dell, 1981.

Angelou, M. *And Still I Rise.* Random House, 1978. Bantam, 1980.

———. *Gather Together in My Name.* Random House, 1974. Bantam, 1985.

———. *The Heart of a Woman.* Random House, 1981. Bantam, 1984.

———. *I Know Why the Caged Bird Sings.* Random House, 1969. Bantam, 1983.

———. *Just Give Me a Cool Drink of Water 'fore I Diiie.* Random House, 1971. Bantam, 1977.

———. *Oh Pray My Wings Are Gonna Fit Me Well.* Random House, 1975. Bantam, 1977.

———. *Singin' and Swingin' and Gettin' Merry Like Christmas.* Random House, 1976. Bantam, 1977. Bantam, 1985.

Annixter, J., and P. Annixter. *The Last Monster.* Harcourt Brace Jovanovich, 1980.

Annixter, P. *Swift Water.* A. A. Wyn, 1950. Paperback Library, 1965.

Anonymous. *Go Ask Alice.* Prentice-Hall. 1971. Avon, 1976.

Ansell, R., and R. Percy. *To Fight the Wild.* Harcourt Brace Jovanovich, 1986.

Anson, R. S. *Best Intentions.* Random House, 1988. Vintage, 1988.

Appleman-Jurman, A. *Alicia: My Story.* Bantam, 1990.

Armer, L. A. *Waterless Mountain.* David McKay, 1931. Knopf, 1993.

Armstrong, J. M. *Women in Mathematics.* Education Commission of the States, 1980.

Armstrong, W. *Sounder.* Harper, 1969. HarperCollins, 1989.

Arnold, C. *Too Fat? Too Thin? Do You Have a Choice?* Morrow, 1984.

Arnold-Forster, M. *The World at War.* New American Library, 1973. Madison Books, 1986.

Arrick, F. *Chernowitz!.* Bradbury, 1981. Dutton, 1983.

———. *God's Radar.* Bradbury, 1983. Dell, 1986.

———. *Nice Girl from Good Home.* Bradbury, 1984. Dell, 1986.

———. *Steffie Can't Come Out to Play.* Bradbury, 1979.

———. *Where'd You Get the Gun, Billy?* Bantam, 1991.

Arundel, H. *The Blanket Word.* T. Nelson, 1973. Dell, 1975.

———. *A Family Failing.* T. Nelson, 1972. Scholastic, 1972.

Ashbranner, B. *A Greatful Nation: The Story of Arlington National Cemetery.* Putnam's, 1990.

Asher, S. *Daughters of the Law.* Beaufort Books, Dell, 1980.

———. *Everything Is Not Enough.* Delacorte, 1987. Dell, 1988.

———. *Missing Pieces.* Delacorte, 1984.

———. *Summer Begins.* Elsevier/Nelson, 1980. Bantam, 1982.

Asimov, I. *Asimov on Astronomy.* Doubleday, 1977. Crown, 1982.

———. *Asimov on Numbers.* Doubleday, 1977. Pocket Books, 1978.

———. *The Collapsing Universe.* Walker, 1977. Pocket Books, 1978.

———. *Foundation.* Gnome, 1951. Bantam, 1991.

———. *Foundation and Empire.* Gnome, 1952. Bantam, 1991.

———. *From Earth to Heaven.* Doubleday, 1966. Avon, 1972.

———. *The Left Hand of the Electron.* Doubleday, 1972. Dell, 1976.

———. *Life and Energy.* Doubleday, 1962. Avon, 1972.

———. *The Nearest Star.* Lothrop, Lee & Shepard 1976.

———. *The Neutrino: Ghost Particles of the Atom.* Doubleday, 1966. Avon, 1975.

———. *Of Time and Space and Other Things.* Doubleday, 1965. Avon, 1975.

———. *The Planet That Wasn't.* Doubleday, 1976. Avon, 1977.

———. *The Second Foundation.* Gnome, 1953. Bantam, 1991.

———. *The Solar System and Back.* Doubleday, 1970. Avon, 1972.

———. *Tomorrow's Children.* Doubleday, 1966.

———. *The Tragedy of the Moon.* Doubleday, 1973. Dell, 1978.

———. *The Universe: From Flat Earth to Quasar.* Walker, 1966. Avon, 1968.

Asimov, J., and I. Asimov. *Norby and the Oldest Dragon.* Walker, 1990.

Atkinson, L. *In Kindling Flame: The Story of Hannah Senesh, 1921–1944.* Lothrop, Lee & Shepard, 1985. Morrow, 1992.

Atwood, A., ed. *Fly with the Wind, Flow with the Water.* Scribner's, 1979.

———. *Haiku-Vision in Poetry and Photography.* Scribner's, 1977.

Auel, J. *The Clan of the Cave Bear.* Crown, 1980. Bantam, 1984.

Avery, G. *The Elephant War.* Dell, 1988.

Avi. *The Fighting Ground.* Lippincott, 1985. Harper, 1987.

———. *Nothing but the Truth: A Documentary Novel.* Orchard/Richard Jackson, 1991.

———. *The True Confessions of Charlotte Doyle.* Orchard, 1990.

Bacon, M. H. *I Speak for My Slave Sister: The Life of Abbey Kelley Foster.* Crowell, 1974.

Baer, E. *A Frost in the Night.* Pantheon, 1980. Schocken, 1988.

Baird, T. *Smart Rats.* HarperCollins, 1990.

Baker, B. *The Dunderhead War.* Harper & Row, 1967.

———. *The Spirit Is Willing.* Macmillan, 1974.

Baker, C. *Ernest Hemingway: A Life Story.* Collins, 1969. Macmillan, 1988.

Baklanov, G. I. Translated by A. W. Bouis. *Forever Nineteen.* Lippincott, 1989.

Baldwin, N. *To All Gentleness: William Carlos Williams, The Doctor Poet.* Atheneum, 1984.

Banfield, S. *The Rights of Man, the Reign of Terror: The Story of the French Revolution.* Lippincott, 1989. Harper, 1990.

Bankier, J., et al., eds. *The Other Voice.* Norton, 1976.

Banks, L. R. *One More River.* Simon & Schuster, 1973. Morrow, 1992.

Barlow, J., ed. *Plays by American Women, 1990–1930.* Applause, 1985.

Barnett, L. *The Universe and Dr. Einstein.* Harper & Row, 1948. Bantam, 1974.

Barrett, P. A., ed. *To Break the Silence.* Dell, 1986.

Bates, B. *Ask Me Tomorrow.* Holiday House, 1987.

———. *Bugs in Your Ears.* Holiday House, 1977. Pocket Books, 1979.

———. *Love Is Like Peanuts.* Holiday House, 1980. Pocket Books, 1981.

———. *The Ups and Downs of Jorie Jenkins.* Holiday House, 1978. Pocket Books, 1981.

Bauer, Y. *Flight and Rescue: Brichah.* Random House, 1970.

Baum, L. F. *Ozma of Oz.* Reilly & Britton, 1907. Ballantine, 1986.

Baylor, B. *The Other Way to Listen.* Scribner's, 1978.

———. *Yes Is Better Than No.* Scribner's 1977. Treasure Chest, 1991.

Bayly, J. *The View from a Hearse.* Cook, 1973.

Beagle, P. *The Last Unicorn.* Viking, 1968. Dutton, 1991.

Beatty, P. *Be Ever Hopeful, Hannalee.* Morrow, 1988.

———. *Behave Yourself, Bethany Brant.* Morrow, 1986.

————. *Wait for Me, Watch for Me, Eula Bee.* Morrow, 1990.

Beatty, P., and P. Robbins. *Eben Tyne, Powdermonkey.* Morrow, 1990.

Beckman, G. *Mia Alone.* Viking, 1975. Dell, 1978.

Beddall, B. G., ed. *Wallace and Bates in the Tropics: An Introduction to the Theory of Natural Selection.* Macmillan, 1969.

Bell, C. *Ratha and Thistle Chaser.* Macmillan/McElderry, 1990.

Bell, E. *Men of Mathematics.* Simon & Schuster, 1962, 1986.

Bell, R., et al. *Changing Bodies, Changing Lives: Revised and Updated.* Random House, 1988.

Bell, W. *Forbidden City: A Novel of Modern China.* Bantam, 1990.

Bellow, S., ed. *Great Jewish Short Stories.* Dell, 1985.

Benard, R. *A Catholic Education.* Holt, 1982. Dell, 1987.

————. *Do You Like It Here?* Dell, 1989.

Benchley, N. *Beyond the Mists.* Harper & Row, 1975.

————. *Bright Candles: A Novel of the Danish Resistance.* Harper & Row, 1974.

————. *Only Earth and Sky Last Forever.* Harper & Row, 1974.

Benedict, H. *Safe, Strong, and Streetwise.* Atlantic Monthly Press, 1986. Little, Brown, 1987.

Benford, G. *Jupiter Project.* Nelson, 1975. Berkley, 1980. Bantam, 1990.

Bennett, G., ed. *Great Tales of Action and Adventure.* Dell, 1978.

Bennett, J. *The Birthday Murderer.* Delacorte, 1977. Dell, 1979.

————. *The Dark Corridor.* Franklin Watts, 1988.

————. *Deathman, Do Not Follow Me.* Meredith Press, 1968. Scholastic, 1968.

————. *The Executioner.* Avon, 1982.

————. *The Haunted One.* Fawcett, 1987. Ballantine, 1989.

————. *The Killing Tree.* Franklin Watts, 1972. Avon, 1979.

————. *The Long Black Coat.* Delacorte, 1973.

————. *Masks: A Love Story.* Franklin Watts, 1971.

————. *The Pigeon.* Methuen, 1980. Avon, 1981.

————. *Say Hello to the Hit Man.* Delacorte, 1976. Dell, 1977.

————. *Slowly, Slowly I Raise the Gun.* Avon, 1983.

————. *To Be a Killer.* Scholastic, 1985.

Bentley, P. E. *The Brontës and Their World.* Scribner's, 1969, 1979.

Bentley, T. *Winter Season: A Dancer's Journal.* Random House, 1984.

Berloquin, P. *100 Geometric Games.* Scribner's, 1977.

Bernstein, J. E. *Fiddle with a Riddle: Write Your Own Riddles.* Dutton, 1979.

Berry, J. *When I Dance.* Harcourt Brace Jovanovich, 1991.

Berry, L. *Mel.* Viking, 1991.

Betancourt, J. *More Than Meets the Eye.* Bantam, 1990.

Bethancourt, E. T. *The Dog Days of Arthur Cane.* Holiday House, 1976. Bantam, 1981.

————. *Doris Fein: Deadly Aphrodite.* Holiday House, 1982.

————. *Doris Fein: The Mad Samurai.* Holiday House, 1981.

————. *Doris Fein: Phantom of the Casino.* Holiday House, 1981.

————. *Doris Fein: Quartz Boyar.* Holiday House, 1980.

————. *Doris Fein: Superspy.* Holiday House, 1980.

————. *Tune in Yesterday.* Holiday House, 1978. Bantam, 1978.

Biemiller, C. *The Hydronauts.* Doubleday, 1970.

Bird, C. *Born Female: The High Cost of Keeping Women Down.* McKay, 1978.

Blackwood, G. L. *The Dying Sun.* Atheneum, 1989.

Blankfort, M. *Take the A Train.* Dutton, 1978.

Blanton, C. *Hold Fast to Your Dreams.* Messner, 1955. Archway, 1968.

Blish, J. *Cities in Flight.* Doubleday, 1970. Baen Books, 1991.

————. *Star Trek 1–12.* Bantam, 1967–1977.

————. *Star Trek Reader 1–10.* Dutton, 1976–1978.

Blockson, Charles L. *The Underground Railroad: First-Person Narratives of Escapes to Freedom in the North.* Prentice-Hall, 1987. Berkley, 1989.

Blos, J. *Brothers of the Heart.* Scribner's, 1985. Macmillan, 1989.

————. *A Gathering of Days: A New England Girl's Journal.* Scribner's, 1979.

Blumberg, R. *The Great American Gold Rush.* Bradbury, 1989.

Blume, J. *Are You There God? It's Me, Margaret.* Bradbury, 1970. Dell, 1991.

————. *Blubber.* Bradbury, 1982. Dell, 1978.

————. *Deenie.* Bradbury, 1982. Dell, 1979.

————. *Forever.* Bradbury, 1975. Pocket Books, 1975.

————. *Freckle Juice.* Four Winds Press, 1971. Dell, 1979.

————. *Iggie's House.* Bradbury, 1970. Dell, 1986.

———. *It's Not the End of the World*. Bradbury, 1982. Dell, 1986.

———. *Starring Sally J. Freeman as Herself*. Bradbury, 1977. Dell, 1986.

———. *Superfudge*. Dutton, 1980. Dell, 1981.

———. *Tales of a Fourth Grade Nothing*. Dutton, 1972. Dell, 1976.

———. *Then Again, Maybe I Won't*. Bradbury, 1971. Dell, 1986.

Blumenthal, S., and J. S. Ozer. *Coming to America: Immigrants from the British Isles*. Dell, 1981.

Bode, J. *Kids Having Kids: The Unwed Teenage Parent*. Franklin Watts, 1980.

———. *New Kids on the Block: Oral Histories of Immigrant Teens*. Franklin Watts, 1989.

Bodecker, N. M. *Hurry, Hurry, Mary Dear*. McElderry, 1976.

Boesan, V. *William P. Lear: From High School Dropout to Space Age Inventor*. Hawthorn, 1974.

Bogle, D. *Brown Sugar: Eighty Years of America's Black Female Superstars*. Harmony Books, 1980. Quality Paperback, 1990.

Bograd, L. *The Better Angel*. Lippincott, 1985.

———. *The Kolokol Papers*. Farrar, Straus & Giroux, 1981. Dell, 1983.

———. *Los Alamos Light*. Farrar, Straus & Giroux, 1983.

———. *Travelers*. Lippincott, 1986.

Boissard, J. *Cecile*. Little, Brown, 1988. Fawcett, 1989.

———. *A Matter of Feeling*. Translated by E. Walter. Little, Brown, 1979. Fawcett, 1981.

Bolton, C. *Never Jam Today*. Atheneum, 1971.

Bonham, F., ed. *Cool Cat*. Dutton, 1971. Dell, 1972.

Bonham, F.. *Durango Street*. Dutton, 1965. Dell, 1972.

———. *Viva Chicano*. Dutton, 1970. Dell, 1971.

Bonnell, D. *Passport to Freedom*. Messner, 1967.

Bontemps, A. W., ed. *American Negro Poetry*. Hill & Wang, 1963. 1974.

———. *Black Thunder* (1935). Beacon Press, 1982.

———. *Great Slave Narratives*. Beacon Press, 1969.

Boorstin, D. J. *The Americans: The Colonial Experience*. Random House, 1985.

———. *The Americans: The Democratic Experience*. Random House, 1984.

———. *The Americans: The National Experience*. Random House, 1985.

Bor, J. *The Terezin Requiem*. Translated by E. Pargeter. Knopf, 1963.

Borland, H. *When the Legends Die*. Lippincott, 1963. Bantam, 1984.

Borland, K., and H. Speicher. *Goodbye to Stony Crick*. McGraw-Hill, 1976.

Bosse, M. *Captives of Time*. Delacorte, 1987. Dell, 1989.

———. *Ganesh*. Crowell, 1981. HarperCollins, 1981.

Bosworth, J. A. *White Water, Still Water*. Doubleday, 1966. Pocket Books, 1969.

Bova, B. *City of Darkness*. Scribner's, 1976. Berkley, 1982.

Bowe-Gutman, S. *Teen Pregnancy*. Lerner, 1987.

Boyer, R. H., and K. J. Zahorski, eds. *Dark Imaginings*. Dell, 1978.

Brackett, L. *The Long Tomorrow*. Doubleday, 1955. Ballantine, 1974.

Bradbury, B. *The Blue Year*. Ives Washburn, 1967.

———. *The Loner*. McKay, 1963.

Bradbury, R. *Dandelion Wine*. Doubleday, 1957. Bantam, 1990.

———. *Fahrenheit 451*. Ballantine, 1987.

———. *I Sing the Body Electric*. Knopf, 1978. Bantam, 1971.

———. *The Martian Chronicles*. Doubleday, 1990. Bantam, 1984.

Bradford, R. *Red Sky at Morning*. Lippincott, 1968. Pocket Books, 1969.

Bradley, W. *Life on the Run*. Quadrangle, 1976.

Braithwaite, E. R. *Choice of Straws*. Bobbs-Merrill, 1967. Pyramid. 1972.

Brancato, R. *Blinded by the Light*. Knopf, 1978. Bantam, 1979.

———. *Facing Up*. Knopf, 1984. Scholastic, 1985.

———. *Something Left to Lose*. Knopf, 1976. Bantam, 1979.

———. *Winning*. Knopf, 1977. Bantam, 1979.

Brandon, W., ed. *The Magic World: American Indian Songs and Poems*. Morrow, 1971. Ohio University Press, 1992.

Branscum, R. *Cheater and Flitter Dick*. Viking, 1983.

———. *The Girl*. Harper & Row, 1986.

———. *Johnny May*. Doubleday, 1975. Avon, 1976.

———. *Me and Jim Luke*. Doubleday, 1971. Avon, 1975.

———. *The Murder of Hounddog Bates*. Viking, 1982.

———. *To the Tune of the Hickory Stick*. Doubleday, 1978.

———. *Toby Alone*. Doubleday, 1979. Avon, 1980.

———. *Toby and Johnny Joe*. Doubleday, 1979. Avon, 1981.

———. *Toby, Granny, and George*. Doubleday, 1976. Avon, 1977.

Brashler, W. *Josh Gibson: A Life in the Negro League.* Harper & Row, 1978.

Brautigan, R. *A Confederate General from Big Sur.* Grove, 1968. Houghton Mifflin, 1991.

Bredes, D. *Hard Feelings.* Atheneum, 1977.

Brewton, J., and S. Brewton, eds. *Of Quarts, Quasars, and Other Quirks: Quizzical Poems for the Supersonic Age.* Crowell, 1977. HarperCollins, 1990.

——. *Shrieks at Midnight: Macabre Poems, Eerie and Humorous.* Crowell, 1969.

Bridgers, S. E. *All Together Now.* Knopf, 1979. Bantam, 1990.

——. "The Beginning of Something." In *Visions: Nineteen Short Stories by Outstanding Writers for Young Adults,* ed. D. Gallo. Delacorte, 1987. Dell, 1988.

——. *Home before Dark.* Knopf, 1976. Bantam, 1985.

——. *Notes for Another Life.* Knopf, 1981. Bantam, 1989.

——. *Permanent Connections.* Harper & Row, 1987.

——. *Sara Will.* Harper, 1986.

Brittain, B. *The Fantastic Freshman.* Harper & Row, 1988. HarperCollins.

Brittain, V. *Testament of Youth.* Macmillan, 1933. Wideview, 1980.

Britton, A. *Fike's Point.* Coward, McCann & Geoghegan, 1979.

Brodie, F. *Thomas Jefferson: An Intimate History.* Norton, 1974. Bantam, 1981.

Brontë, C. *Jane Eyre.* Puffin Books, 1992.

Brontë, E. *Wuthering Heights.* Pocket Books, 1992.

Brooke, M. *Coin Games and Puzzles.* Dover, 1963, 1973.

——. *Paradise Cafe and Other Stories.* Joy Street Books, 1990.

Brooks, B. *Midnight Hour Encores.* Harper & Row, 1986. HarperCollins, 1988.

——. *The Moves Make the Man.* Harper & Row, 1984. HarperCollins, 1987.

——. *No Kidding.* Harper & Row, 1989.

Brooks, G. *The World of Gwendolyn Brooks.* Harper & Row, 1971.

Brooks, J. *Uncle Mike's Boy.* Harper & Row, 1973.

Brooks, P. *The Pursuit of Wilderness.* Houghton Mifflin, 1971.

Brooks, P. S. *Beyond Myth: The Story of Joan of Arc.* Lippincott, 1990.

Broughton, T. A. *A Family Gathering.* Dutton, 1977. Fawcett, 1977.

Brown, C. *Manchild in the Promised Land.* Macmillan, 1965. New American Library, 1965.

Brown, D., ed. *Bury My Heart at Wounded Knee: An Indian History of the American West.* Holt, Rinehart & Winston, 1971. Pocket Books, 1981.

——. *Creek Mary's Blood.* Holt, Rinehart & Winston, 1980. Pocket Books, 1981.

——. *Lonesome Whistle: The Story of the First Transcontinental Railroad.* Adapted by L. Proctor from *Hear the Lonesome Whistle Blow.* Holt, Rinehart & Winston, 1980.

——. *Wounded Knee: An Indian History of the American West.* Adapted by A. Ehrlich from *Bury My Heart at Wounded Knee.* Holt, Rinehart & Winston, 1974. Dell, 1975.

Brown, H. *Yesterday's Child.* Evans, 1976. New American Library, 1977.

Brown, M. H. *Laying Waste: The Poisoning of America by Toxic Chemicals.* Pantheon, 1980. Pocket Books, 1981.

Brown, M. M., and R. Crone. *The Silent Storm.* Abingdon Press, 1968.

Brown, M. W. *The Second Stone.* Putnam, 1974.

Brown, P. *Uncle Whiskers.* Little, Brown, 1974.

Brunner, J. *The Sheep Look Up.* Harper & Row, 1972. Ballantine, 1981.

Bryan, C. *Friendly Fire.* Putnam, 1976. Bantam, 1982.

Bunting, E. *The Haunting of Safekeep.* Lippincott, 1985.

——. *If I Asked You, Would You Stay?* Lippincott, 1984. HarperCollins, 1987.

Burchard, P. *Digger: A Novel.* Putnam, 1980.

Burnette, F. H. *The Secret Garden.* New American Library, 1989.

Burt, O. W. *First Woman Editor: Sarah J. Hale.* Messner, 1960.

Bushnaq, I. *Arab Folk Tales.* Pantheon, 1987.

Buss, F. *Journey of the Sparrows.* Dutton, 1991.

Butler, B. *A Girl Named Wendy.* Dodd, Meade, 1976.

Butterworth, E. M. *As the Waltz Was Ending.* Macmillan, 1982. Scholastic, 1991.

Butterworth, W. E. *Leroy and the Old Man.* Four Winds Press, 1980.

Byars, B. *The Night Swimmers.* Delacorte, 1980. Dell, 1983.

——. *Summer of the Swans.* Viking, 1970. Avon, 1974.

Cable, M. *Black Odyssey: The Case of the Slave Ship Amistad.* Viking, 1971. Penguin, 1977.

Cahill, S. *Mothers: Memories, Dreams and Reflections.* New American Library, 1988.

Caidin, M. *Cyborg*. Arbor House, 1972. Ballantine, 1978.

———. *The God Machine*. Dutton, 1968. Baen Books, 1989.

Callahan, S. *Adrift: Seventy-Six Days Lost at Sea*. Houghton Mifflin, 1986. Ballantine, 1987.

Calvert, P. *The Snowbird*. Scribner's, 1980. Macmillan, 1989.

———. *Yesterday's Daughter*. Scribner's, 1986. Avon, 1988.

Calvocoressi, Peter, and Guy Wint. *Total War: The Story of World War II*. Pantheon, 1972.

Cameron, E. *Beyond Silence*. Dutton, 1980. Dell, 1985.

Cameron, I. *The Lost Ones*. Morrow, 1968. Avon, 1974.

———. *The Mountains at the Bottom of the World: A Novel of Adventure*. Morrow, 1972. Avon, 1974.

Canning, J., ed. *Fifty Great Ghost Stories*. Bantam, 1978. Outlet Book, 1988.

———. *Fifty Great Horror Stories*. Bantam, 1978. Outlet Book, 1991.

Cannon, A. E. *The Shadow Brothers*. Delacorte, 1990.

Capek, K. *The War with the Newts*. Translated by M. Weatherall and R. Weatherall. Berkley, 1976. Catbird Press, 1990.

Capps, B. *A Woman of the People*. Fawcett, 1966. University of New Mexico Press, 1985.

Capps, M. J. *Yellow Leaf*. Concordia, 1974.

Caras, R. *The Forest*. Holt, Rinehart & Winston, 1979. University of Nebraska Press, 1991.

Carr, T., ed. *Dream's Edge*. Sierra Club, 1980.

Carroll, D. *Wonders of the World*. Bantam, 1977.

Carroll, L. *Jabberwocky*. Warne, 1977.

———. *Poems of Lewis Carroll*. Crowell, 1973.

Carruth, H., ed. *The Voice That Is Great Within Us*. Bantam, 1983.

Carson, J. *Silent Voices: The Southern Negro Woman Today*. Delacorte, 1969. Dell, 1971.

Carter, A. R. *Growning Season*. Berkley/Pacer, 1985.

———. *RoboDad*. Putnam, 1990.

———. *Sheila's Dying*. Putnam, 1987.

———. *Up Country*. Putnam, 1989. Scholastic, 1991.

Carter, F. *The Education of Little Tree*. Delacorte, 1976. University of New Mexico Press, 1986.

Carter J. *Why Not the Best?* Broadman, 1975. Bantam, 1976.

Carter, P. *Borderlands*. Farrar, Straus & Giroux, 1990.

Carver, J. *Star Rigger's Way*. Doubleday, 1978. Dell, 1978.

Cary, L. *Black Ice*. Knopf, 1991.

Cassedy, S. *In Your Own Words: A Beginner's Guide to Writing*. Doubleday, 1979. HarperCollins, 1990.

Castaneda, O. S. *Among the Volcanoes*. Lodestar, 1991.

Cather, W. *My Antonia*. Houghton Mifflin, 1961.

Catling, P. S. *The Chocolate Touch*. Morrow, 1952. Bantam, 1981.

Chamberlin, H. *A Minority of Members: Women in the U.S. Congress*. Praeger, 1973. Mentor, 1974.

Chambers, A. *N-I-K—Now I Know*. Harper & Row, 1988.

———. *These Other People*. Putnam, 1989.

Chaneles, S. *Three Children of the Holocaust*. Avon, 1974.

Chapman, A., ed. *Black Voices: An Anthology of Afro-American Literature*. New American Library, 1968. St. Martin's, 1970.

Charnas, S. M. *The Bronze King*. Houghton Mifflin, 1985. Bantam, 1988.

———. *The Golden Thread*. Bantam, 1990.

———. *The Silver Glove*. Bantam, 1988.

Chetwin, G. *The Crystal Stair*. Bradbury, 1988. Dell, 1990.

Childress, A. *A Hero Ain't Nothin' but a Sandwich*. Coward, McCann & Geoghegan, 1973. Avon, 1974.

———. *The Other People*. Putnam, 1989.

———. *Rainbow Jordan*. Coward, McCann & Geoghegan, 1981.

Christopher, J. *The City of Gold and Lead*. Macmillan, 1967. Collier, 1970.

———. *The Pool of Fire*. Macmillan, 1968. Collier, 1970.

———. *The White Mountains*. Macmillan, 1967. Collier, 1970.

Christopher, M. *Takedown*. Little, Brown, 1990.

Ciardi, J. *Fast and Slow: Poems for Advanced Children and Beginning Parents*. Houghton Mifflin, 1975.

Clapp, P. *Constance: A Story of Early Plymouth*. Lothrop, Lee & Shepard, 1968. Dell, 1975.

———. *I'm Deborah Sampson: A Soldier in the War of the Revolution*. Lothrop, Lee & Shepard, 1977.

———. *Jane-Emily*. Lothrop, Lee & Shepard, 1969. Dell, 1978.

Clarke, A. C. *Childhood's End*. Harcourt, Brace & World, 1953. Ballantine, 1981.

———. *2001: A Space Odyssey*. New American Library, 1968.

Clark, A. N. *Year Walk*. Viking, 1975.

Clark, K. *Another Part of the Wood: A Self Portrait*. Harper & Row, 1975.

Clark, M. T. *The Min-Min*. Macmillan, 1978.

———. *Wildfire*. Macmillan, 1974.

Clark, S. *Fight against Time: Five Athletes—A Legacy of Courage*. Atheneum, 1979.

Clarke, J. *The Heroic Life of Al Capsella*. Holt, Rinehart & Winston, 1990.

Clarke, J. M. *The Life and Adventures of John Muir*. Sierra Club, 1980.

Clarke, M. S. *Bloomers and Ballots: Elizabeth Cady Stanton and Women's Rights*. Viking, 1972.

Cleary, B. *Beezus and Ramona*. Morrow, 1955. Dell, 1980.

———. *A Girl from Yamhill: A Memoir*. Morrow, 1988.

———. *Henry and the Clubhouse*. Morrow, 1962. Dell, 1979.

———. *Henry and the Paper Route*. Morrow, 1957. Dell, 1980.

———. *Jean and Johnny*. Morrow, 1959. Dell, 1981.

———. *Ramona, the Pest*. Morrow, 1968. Scholastic, 1968.

Cleaver, E. *Soul on Ice*. McGraw-Hill, 1967. Dell, 1978.

Cleaver, V. *Sugar Blue*. Lothrop, Lee & Shepard, 1984.

———. *Sweetly Sings the Donkey*. Lippincott, 1985.

Cleaver, V., and B. Cleaver. *Dust of the Earth*. Lippincott, 1975.

———. *Ellen Grae*. Lippincott, 1967. New American Library, 1978.

———. *Grover*. Lippincott, 1970. New American Library, 1975.

———. *I Would Rather Be a Turnip*. Lippincott, 1971. New American Library, 1976.

———. *Lady Ellen Grae*. Lippincott, 1968. New American Library, 1978.

———. *Trial Valley*. Lippincott, 1977. Bantam, 1978.

———. *Where the Lillies Bloom*. Lippincott, 1969. New American Library, 1974.

Clemens, S. L. [Mark Twain]. *The Adventures of Huckleberry Finn*. Bantam, 1981.

———. *The Adventures of Tom Sawyer*. Bantam, 1981.

———. *The Complete Short Stories of Mark Twain*. Bantam, 1981.

———. *Pudd'nhead Wilson*. Bantam, 1981.

Clements, B. *Anywhere Else but Here*. Dell, 1982.

———. *Tom Loves Anna Loves Tom*. Farrar, Straus & Giroux, 1990.

Clifford, E. R. *The Year of the Three-Legged Deer*. Houghton Mifflin, 1972. Dell, 1973.

Coe, C. *Young Man in Vietnam*. Scholastic, 1990.

Coffey, W. *Straight Talk about Drinking: Teenagers Speak Out about Alcohol*. New American Library, 1988.

Cohen, B.. *Roses*. Lothrop, Lee & Shepard, 1984.

———. *Seven Daughters and Seven Sons*. Atheneum, 1982.

———. *Unicorns in the Rain*. Atheneum, 1980.

Cohen, B., and B. Lovejoy. *The Carp in the Bathtub*. Lothrop, Lee & Shephard, 1972. Dell, 1975.

Cohen, S. *Taking Gary Feldman*. Putnam, 1970.

Cole, B. *Celine*. Farrar, Straus & Giroux, 1989.

Cole, S. *Working Kids on Working*. Lothrop, Lee & Shepard, 1980.

Cole, W., ed. *The Book of Giggles*. World, 1970. Dell, 1980.

———. *A Book of Love Poems*. Viking, 1965.

———. *Fireside Book of Humorous Poetry*. Simon & Schuster, 1959.

Coles, R., and J. H. Coles. *Women in Crisis: Lives of Struggle and Hope*. Delacorte, 1978. Dell, 1979.

———. *Women in Crisis II: Lives of Work and Dreams*. Delacorte, 1980. Dell, 1980.

Collier, J. L. *When the Stars Begin to Fall*. Delacorte, 1986.

———. *The Winchesters*. Macmillan, 1988. Avon, 1989.

Collier, J. L., and C. Collier. *The Bloody Country*. Scholastic, 1974. Four Winds, 1985.

———. *Decision in Philadelphia: The Constitutional Convention of 1787*. Random House, 1986.

———. *Jump Ship to Freedom*. Delacorte, 1981.

———. *My Brother Sam Is Dead*. Four Winds, 1974. Scholastic, 1974.

———. *War Comes to Willy Freeman*. Delacorte, 1983.

———. *Who Is Carrie?* Delacorte, 1984.

———. *The Winter Hero*. Macmillan, 1978. Scholastic, 1985.

Collin, M. *Maiden Crown*. Houghton Mifflin, 1979.

Collins, M., ed. *The Last Rain Forest: A World Conservation Atlas*. Oxford University Press, 1990.

Colman, H. *Just the Two of Us*. Scholastic, 1984.

———. *Nobody Told Me What I Need to Know*. Morrow, 1984. Fawcett, 1987.

———. *Suddenly*. Fawcett, 1987.

———. *Tell Me No Lies*. Crown, 1978. Pocket Books, 1980.

———. *Weekend Sisters*. Morrow, 1985.

Compton, D. G. *The Unsleeping Eye*. DAW Books, 1974. Pocket Books, 1980.

Conford, E. *The Alfred G. Graebner Memorial High School Handbook of Rules and Regulations*. Little, Brown, 1976. Pocket Books, 1977.

Conot, R. *A Streak of Luck: The Life and Legend of Thomas Alva Edison*. Seaview Books, 1979. Bantam, 1980.

Conover, T. *Coyotes*. Random House, 1987.

Conrad, B., and N. Mortensen. *Endangered*. Putnam, 1978. Berkley, 1980.

Conrad, P. *My Daniel.* Harper & Row, 1989.

———. *Prairie Songs.* Harper & Row, 1985.

———. *Prairie Visions: The Life and Times of Soloman Butcher.* HarperCollins, 1991.

Conroy, F. *Stop-Time.* Viking, 1967. Penguin, 1977.

Constant, A. W. *Paintbox on the Frontier: The Life and Times of George Caleb Bingham.* Crowell, 1975.

Cook, P. D. *The Ages of Mathematics: The Modern Ages.* Doubleday, 1977.

Cooney, C. B. *Among Friends.* Bantam, 1987.

———. *The Face on the Milk Carton.* Bantam, 1991.

———. *Flight #116 Is Down.* Scholastic, 1992.

———. *When the Party's Over.* Scholastic, 1991.

Cooper, H. S., Jr. *A House in Space.* Holt, Rinehart & Winston, 1976. Bantam, 1978.

Cooper, S. *The Dark Is Rising.* Atheneum, 1973. Macmillan, 1973.

———. *Greenwitch.* Atheneum, 1974. Puffin Books, 1980.

———. *The Grey King.* Atheneum, 1975.

———. *Over Sea, Under Stone.* Harcourt, 1965. Penguin, 1978.

———. *Silver on the Tree.* Atheneum, 1977.

Corcoran, B. *The Clown.* Atheneum, 1975.

———. *Hey, That's My Soul You're Stomping On.* Atheneum, 1978.

———. *Me and You and a Dog Named Blue.* Atheneum, 1979.

———. *Stay Tuned.* Atheneum, 1991.

———. *This Is a Recording.* Atheneum, 1971.

Cormier, R. *After the First Death.* Pantheon, 1979. Avon, 1980.

———. *Beyond the Chocolate War.* Knopf, 1985.

———. *The Bumblebee Flies Anyway.* Pantheon, 1983. Dell, 1984.

———. *The Chocolate War.* Pantheon, 1974. Dell, 1986.

———. *Eight Plus One: Stories by Robert Cormier.* Pantheon, 1980.

———. *Fade.* Delacorte, 1988.

———. *I Am the Cheese: A Novel.* Pantheon, 1977. Dell, 1978.

———. *I Have Words to Spend: Reflections of a Small-Town Editor.* Delacorte, 1991.

———. *Other Bells for Us to Ring.* Delacorte, 1990.

———. *We All Fall Down.* Delacorte, 1991.

Cossi, O. *The Magic Box.* Pelican, 1990.

Court, N. A. *Mathematics in Fun and Earnest.* Dial, 1958. New American Library, 1964.

Cousteau, J., and P. Diole. *Life and Death in a Coral Sea.* Doubleday, 1971.

Covert, P. *Cages.* Liveright, 1971.

Craig, E. *If We Could Hear the Grass Grow.* Simon & Schuster, 1983. New American Library, 1985.

Craig, M. M. *It Could Happen to Anyone.* Crowell, 1961. Berkley, 1973.

Crane, S. *The Red Badge of Courage.* Vintage Books, 1990.

Crane, W. B. *Oompah.* Atheneum, 1981.

Crawford, C. *Mommie Dearest.* Morrow, 1978. Berkley, 1981.

Crawford, C. P. *Bad Fall.* Harper & Row, 1972. Bantam, 1973.

———. *Split Time.* Harper, 1987.

———. *Three-Legged Race.* Harper & Row, 1974. Dell, 1977.

Crawford, T. E. *The West of the Texas Kid, 1881–1910.* University of Oklahoma Press, 1962.

Cresswell, Helen. *Absolute Zero.* Puffin Books, 1987.

———. *Ordinary Jack.* Macmillan, 1977.

Crew, L. *Children of the River.* Delacorte, 1989.

———. *Someday I'll Laugh about This.* Delacorte, 1990.

Cridle, J., and T. B. Mann. *To Destroy You Is No Loss.* Atlantic Monthly Press, 1987.

Crompton, E. *A Woman's Place.* Little, Brown, 1978. Ballantine, 1980.

Cross, G. *Born of the Sun.* Holiday House, 1983. Dell, 1987.

———. *The Dark behind the Curtain.* Oxford, 1982. Dell, 1988.

———. *A Map of Nowhere.* Holiday House, 1989.

———. *On the Edge.* Holiday House, 1985.

———. *Roscoe's Leap.* Holiday House, 1987.

———. *Wolf.* Holiday House, 1991.

Crutcher, C. *Athletic Shorts.* Greenwillow, 1991.

———. *Chinese Handcuffs.* Greenwillow, 1989.

———. *The Crazy Horse Electric Game.* Greenwillow, 1987.

———. *Running Loose.* Greenwillow, 1983.

———. *Stotan.* Bantam, 1986.

Crypton, Dr. *Timid Virgins Make Dull Company and Other Puzzles, Pitfalls, and Paradoxes.* Viking, 1984.

Cullinan, T. *The Bedeviled.* Putnam, 1978. Avon, 1979.

Cummings, B. S. *Let a River Be.* Atheneum, 1978.

cummings, e. e. *Ninety-Five Poems.* Harcourt Brace Jovanovich, 1970.

Cunningham, A. M., and R. White. *Ryan White: My Own Story.* Dial Books, 1991.

Cunningham, J. *Come to the Edge.* Pantheon, 1977.

———. *Far in the Day.* Pantheon, 1972. Dell, 1980.

Currie, R. *Yarrow: Prairie Poems*. Oberon Books, 1980.

Curtis, M., ed. *The Nature of Politics*. Avon, 1962.

Curtis, P. *Animal Rights: Stories of People Who Defend the Rights of Animals*. Four Winds, 1980.

Dahl, R. *Charlie and the Chocolate Factory*. Knopf, 1964. Bantam, 1979.

———. *The Wonderful Story of Henry Sugar and Six More*. Knopf, 1977. Bantam.

Daly, M. *Acts of Love*. Scholastic, 1986.

———. *First a Dream*. Scholastic, 1990.

———. *Seventeenth Summer*. Dodd, Mead, 1942.

Dana, B. *Young Joan*. HarperCollins, 1991.

Dank, M. *The Dangerous Game*. Lippincott, 1977.

———. *Khaki Wings*. Delacorte, 1980.

Danziger, P. *Can You Sue Your Parents for Malpractice?* Delacorte, 1979. Dell, 1980.

———. *The Cat Ate My Gymsuit*. Delacorte, 1974. Dell, 1978.

———. *Earth to Matthew*. Delacorte, 1991.

———. *Make Like a Tree and Leave*. Delacorte, 1990.

———. *The Pistachio Prescription*. Delacorte, 1978. Dell, 1978.

———. *There's a Bat in Bunk Five*. Delacorte, 1980. Dell, 1982.

———. *This Place Has No Atmosphere*. Dell, 1989.

Darby, J. *Martin Luther King, Jr*. Lerner, 1990.

Darke, M. *First of Midnight*. Seabury, 1977.

David, J., ed. *Growing Up Black*. Morrow, 1968. Pocket Books, 1969.

———. *Growing Up Jewish*. Morrow, 1969. Pocket Books, 1970.

Davidowicz, L. S. *The War against the Jews, 1933– 1945*. Holt, Rinehart & Winston, 1975.

Davies, A. *Conrad's War*. Crown, 1980.

Davies, L. P. *The Paper Dolls*. New American Library, 1965.

Davis, C. T., and H. L. Gates, Jr., eds. *The Slave's Narrative*. Oxford University Press, 1985.

Davis, J. *Sex Education*. Dell, 1989.

Davis, J. A. *Samaki: The Story of an Otter in Africa*. Dutton, 1979.

Davis, M. *Sports Shorts*. Grosset & Dunlap, 1959. Bantam, 1963.

Davis, T. *Vision Quest*. Viking, 1979. Bantam, 1981.

Dean, J. *Blind Ambition: The White House Years*. Simon & Schuster, 1976.

Dear, W. *The Dungeon Master: The Disappearance of James Dallas Egbert, III*. Houghton Mifflin, 1984. Ballantine, 1985.

Deaver, J. R. *First Wedding, Once Removed*. Harper & Row, 1990.

———. *Say Goodnight, Gracie*. Harper & Row, 1989.

Decker, W. *To Be a Man*. Little, Brown, 1967. Pocket Books, 1975.

DeClements, B. *Seventeen and In-Between*. Viking, 1984.

Defoe, D. *Robinson Crusoe* (1719). Bantam, 1981.

DeFord, D. H., and H. S. Stout. *An Enemy among Them*. Houghton Mifflin, 1987.

Degens, T. *Transport 7-41-R*. Viking, 1974.

de Jenkins, L. B. *The Honorable Prison*. Dutton, 1988.

deJongh, J., and C. Cleveland. *City Cool*. Random House, 1978.

de Lint, C. *The Dreaming Place*. Atheneum, 1990.

Deloria, V. *Behind the Trail of Broken Treaties: An Indian Declaration of Independence*. Delacorte, 1974. Dell, 1974.

del Rey, L. *Prisoners of Space*. Westminster, 1966. Scholastic, 1966.

———. *Tunnel through Time*. Westminster, 1966. Scholastic, 1966.

Deming, R. *Man and the World: International Law at Work*. Hawthorn, 1974. Dell, 1975.

———. *Women: The New Criminals*. Nelson, 1977. Dell, 1979.

deRopp, R. S. *Drugs and the Mind*. Delacorte, 1976. Dell, 1976.

DeVaux, A. *Don't Explain: A Song of Billie Holiday*. Harper & Row, 1980.

Devi, S. *Figuring: The Joy of Numbers*. Barnes & Noble, 1977, 1981.

The Diagram Group. *Child's Body*. Paddington, 1976. Bantam, 1977.

———. *Man's Body: An Owner's Manual*. Paddington, 1977. Bantam, 1978.

———. *Woman's Body: An Owner's Manual*. Paddington, 1977. Bantam, 1978.

Dickens, C. *Great Expectations*. Macmillan, 1962.

———. *A Tale of Two Cities*. New American Library, 1980.

Dickinson, E. *Emily Dickinson*. Dell, 1960.

Dickinson, P. *The Dancing Bear*. Little, Brown, 1972.

———. *The Flight of Dragons*. Harper & Row, 1979.

Dickson, G. R. *Dorsail!* DAW Books, 1960. Ace, 1980.

———. *The Dragon and the George*. Doubleday, 1976. Ballantine, 1980.

———. *The Far Call*. Dial, 1978. Dell, 1978.

Diggin, J. *String, Straight Edge and Shadow: The Story of Geometry*. Viking, 1965.

Diggs, L. *Moon in the Water*. Atheneum, 1988.

Diole, P. *The Errant Ark*. Translated by J. F. Bernard. Putnam, 1974.

Dizenzo, P. *An American Girl*. Holt, Rinehart & Winston, 1971. Avon, 1976.

————. *Phoebe*. McGraw-Hill, 1970. Bantam, 1975.

————. *Why Me? The Story of Jenny*. Avon, 1977.

Domalaim, J. Y. *The Animal Connection*. Translated by M. Barnett. Morrow, 1977.

Donovan, J. *Family*. Harper & Row, 1976. Dell, 1978.

————. *I'll Get There. It Better Be Worth the Trip*. Harper & Row, 1969. Dell, 1973.

————. *Remove the Protective Coating a Little at a Time*. Harper & Row, 1973. Dell, 1975.

————. *Wild in the World*. Harper & Row, 1971. Avon, 1971.

Douglas, G. *Hard to Tackle*. Crowell, 1956. Dell, 1967.

Douglass, F. *Narrative of the Life of Frederick Douglass an American Slave: Written by Himself*. 1845. Harvard University Press, 1960. NAL/Signet Classic, 1968.

Doyle, A. C. *The Adventures of Sherlock Holmes*. 4 vols. Adapted by C. E. Sadler. Avon, 1981.

Doyle, B. *Angel Square*. Bradbury, 1986.

Duder, T. *In Lane Three, Alex Archer*. Bantam, 1991.

Due, L. A. *High and Outside*. Harper & Row, 1980.

Duncan, L. *Chapters: My Growth as a Writer*. Little, Brown, 1982.

————. *Down a Dark Hall*. Little, Brown, 1974. New American Library, 1975.

————. *Five Were Missing*. Signet, 1966. New American Library, 1972.

————. *A Gift of Magic*. Little, Brown, 1971. Pocket Books, 1972.

————. *I Know What You Did Last Summer*. Little, Brown, 1973. Pocket Books, 1975.

————. *Killing Mr. Griffin*. Little, Brown, 1978. Dell, 1979.

————. *Locked in Time*. Little Brown, 1985.

————. *Ransom*. Dell, 1984.

————. *Stranger with My Face*. Little, Brown, 1981. Dell, 1982.

————. *The Third Eye*. Dell, 1984. Little, Brown, 1984.

Dunning, S., ed. *Reflection on a Gift of Watermelon Pickle*. Lothrop, Lee & Shepard, 1966. Scholastic, 1967.

————. *Some Haystacks Don't Even Have Any Needles*. Lothrop, Lee & Shepard, 1969.

Durham, P., and E. L. Jones. *The Adventures of the Negro Cowboys*. Dodd, Mead, 1966. Bantam, 1969.

Dusky, L. *Birthmark*. Evans, 1979.

Dygard, T. J. *Halfback Tough*. Morrow, 1986.

————. *Quarterback Walk-on*. Morrow, 1982.

————. *Wilderness Peril*. Morrow, 1985.

Eareckson, J., and J. Musser. *Joni*. Zondervan, 1976. Bantam, 1978.

East, B. *The Last Eagle*. Crown, 1974.

Easton, P. H. *Rebel's Choice*. Harcourt Brace Jovanovich, 1989.

————. *Summer's Chance*. Gulliver's Books, 1988.

Eckert, A. *Incident at Hawk's Hill*. Little, Brown, 1971. Dell, 1978.

Eddison, E. R. *Mistress of Mistresses: A Vision of Zirmiamvia*. Dutton, 1935. Ballantine, 1967.

Edel, L. *Henry James*. Lippincott, 1953.

Edelman, B., ed. *Dear America: Letters Home from Vietnam*. Norton, 1985. Pocket Books, 1985.

Edmond, W. D. *Wolf Hunt*. Little, Brown, 1970.

Edwards, C. *Crazy for God: The Nightmare of Cult Life*. Prentice-Hall, 1979.

Egan, F. *The Taste of Time*. McGraw-Hill, 1977.

Ehrhart, W. D., ed. *Carrying the Darkness: The Poetry of the Vietnam War*. Texas Tech University, 1985.

Ehrlich, A. *The Dark Card*. Viking, 1991.

————. *Where It Stops, Nobody Knows*. Dial, 1988.

Ehrlich, P. *Extinction*. Random House, 1981.

Eisenstadt, J. *From Rockaway*. Knopf, 1987.

Elfman, B. *The Girls of Huntington House*. Houghton Mifflin, 1972. Bantam, 1973.

————. *A House for Jonnie O*. Houghton Mifflin, 1976. Bantam, 1978.

————. *The Sister Act*. Houghton Mifflin, 1978. Bantam, 1979.

Elwood, R., ed. *Children of Infinity: Original Science Fiction Stories for Young Readers*. Franklin Watts, 1973.

Emerson, Z. *#1 Echo Company Welcome to Vietnam*. Scholastic, 1991.

————. *Echo Company #2 Hill*. Scholastic, 1987.

————. *Echo Company #3 'Tis the Season*. Scholastic, 1991.

Emery, A. *Mountain Laurel*. Putnam, 1948. Scholastic, 1961.

Engdahl, S. *Beyond the Tomorrow Mountains*. Atheneum, 1973.

————. *Enchantress from the Stars*. Atheneum, 1970.

————. *The Far Side of Evil*. Atheneum, 1972.

————. *This Star Shall Abide*. Atheneum, 1972.

Englebrekston, S. *Stars, Planets, and Galaxies*. Ridge Press, 1975. Bantam, 1975.

Ephron, D. *Teenage Romance, or, How to Die of Embarrassment*. Viking, 1981.

Esterow, M. *The Art Stealers*. Macmillan, 1966.

Evans, P. *Ourselves and Other Animals.* Pantheon, 1987.

Evarts, H. *Bigfoot.* Scribner's, 1973. Atheneum, 1981.

Eyerly, J. *Bonnie Jo, Go Home.* Lippincott, 1972. Bantam, 1978.

———. *He's My Baby Now.* Lippincott, 1977. Pocket Books, 1978.

Fadiman, C., ed. *Fantasia Mathematica.* Simon & Schuster, 1961.

———. *The Mathematical Magpie.* Simon & Schuster, 1981.

Fahrmann, W. *The Long Journey of Lukas B.* Bradbury, 1985.

Fair, R. L. *Cornbread, Earl, and Me.* Bantam, 1975.

Fairbairn, A. *Five Smooth Stones.* Crown, 1966. Bantam, 1968.

Farago, L. *Patton: Ordeal and Triumph.* Astor-Honor, 1964. Dell, 1971.

Farish, T. *Shelter for a Seabird.* Greenwillow, 1990.

Fast, H. *April Morning.* Crown, 1961. Bantam, 1970.

———. *Freedom Road.* Crown, 1969.

———. *The Hessian.* Morrow, 1972. Dell, 1980.

Fast, J. *The Beast.* Random House, 1981.

Felsen, H. G. *Can You Do It Until You Need Glasses? The Different Drug Book.* Dodd, Mead, 1977.

Fenton, E. *Duffy's Rocks.* Dutton, 1974.

———. *The Morning of the Gods.* Delacorte, 1987.

Field, E., ed. *A Geography of Poets: An Anthology of New Poetry.* Bantam, 1979.

Fielding, H. *The History of Tom Jones, a Foundling.* Wesleyan University Press, 1975. Harper & Row, 1983.

Fine, J. *Afraid to Ask: A Book for Families to Share about Cancer.* Lothrop, Lee & Shepherd, 1986.

Finney, J. *Time and Again.* Simon & Schuster, 1970. Warner, 1974.

Fisher, L. E. *The Oregon Trail.* Holiday House, 1990.

Fitzgerald, F. S. *The Great Gatsby.* Scribner's, 1980.

Fitzhugh, L. *The Long Secret.* Harper & Row, 1965.

Five Slave Narratives: A Compendium. Arno Press and the *New York Times,* 1968.

Fleischman, P. *The Borning Room.* HarperCollins, 1991.

———. *Coming-and-Going Men: Four Tales.* Harper & Row, 1985.

———. *I Am Phoenix: Poems for Two Voices.* Harper & Row, 1985.

———. *Saturnalia.* HarperCollins, 1990.

Fleming, A. *Alcohol: The Delightful Poison.* Delacorte, 1975.

———. *Ida Tarbell: First of the Muckrakers.* Crowell, 1971. Dell, 1976.

———. *The Senator from Maine: Margaret Chase Smith.* Crowell, 1969. Dell, 1976.

——— ed. *Hosannah, the Home Run! Poems about Sports.* Little, Brown, 1972.

Flender, H. *Rescue in Denmark.* Macfadden, 1964.

Fletcher, C. *The Thousand Mile Summer.* Howell-North Books, 1964. Vintage, 1987.

Flexner, J. *The Double Adventure of John Singleton Copley.* Little, Brown, 1969.

Flinker, Moshe. *Young Moshe's Diary: The Spiritual Torment of a Jewish Boy in Nazi Europe.* New York Board of Jewish Education, 1965.

Fluek, T. K. *Memories of My Life in a Polish Village, 1930–1949.* Knopf, 1990.

Fonstad, K. W. *The Atlas of Middle-Earth.* Houghton Mifflin, 1981.

Forbes, E. *Johnny Tremain.* Houghton Mifflin, 1945. Dell, 1969.

———. *A Mirror for Witches.* Dell, 1956, 1971.

Forfreedom, A., ed. *Women Out of History: A Herstory Anthology.* Ann Forfreedom, 1975.

Forman, J. *Anarchism: Political Innocence or Social Violence?* Franklin Watts, 1975. Dell, 1976.

———. *Capitalism: Economic Individualism to Today's Welfare State.* Franklin Watts, 1972. Dell, 1976.

———. *A Ceremony of Innocence.* Hawthorn, 1969. Scholastic, 1979.

———. *Communism: From Marx's Manifesto to Twentieth-Century Reality.* Franklin Watts, 1972. Dell, 1976.

———. *Cry Havoc.* Scribner's, 1988.

———. *Fascism: The Meaning and Experience of Reactionary Revolution.* Watts, 1974. Dell, 1976.

———. *A Fine, Soft Day.* Farrar, Straus & Giroux, 1978.

———. *Horses of Anger.* Farrar, Straus & Giroux, 1967.

———. *The Life and Death of Yellow Bird.* Farrar, Straus & Giroux, 1973.

———. *The Mad Game.* Scribner's, 1980.

———. *My Enemy, My Brother.* Hawthorn, 1969. Scholastic, 1979.

———. *Nazism.* Franklin Watts, 1978. Dell, 1980.

———. *People of the Dream.* Farrar, Straus & Giroux, 1972. Dell, 1974.

———. *Ring the Judas Bell.* Farrar, Straus & Giroux, 1965. Dell, 1977.

———. *So Ends This Day.* Farrar, Straus & Giroux, 1970.

———. *Socialism: Its Theoretical Roots and Present-Day Development.* Franklin Watts, 1972. Dell, 1976.

———. *The Traitors.* Farrar, Straus & Giroux, 1968.

Forrester, V. *A Latch against the Wind.* Atheneum, 1985.

Fosburgh, L. *Summer Lion.* William Morrow, 1987.

Foster, A. D. *Splinter of the Mind's Eye.* Ballantine, 1978.

Foster, R. C. *Dr. Wildlife: The Crusade of a Northwoods Veterinarian.* Franklin Watts, 1985. Ballantine, 1986.

Fox, P. *Blowfish Live in the Sea.* Bradbury, 1970. Dell, 1975.

———. *Monkey Island.* Orchard/Richard Jackson, 1991.

———. *The Moonlight Man.* Bradbury, 1986. Dell, 1988.

———. *One-Eyed Cat.* Dell, 1985.

———. *The Slave Dancer.* Bradbury, 1973. Dell, 1975.

———. *The Village by the Sea.* Orchard, 1988.

Francis, D. B. *Golden Girl.* Scholastic, 1974.

———. *Mystery of the Forgotten Map.* Follett, 1968.

Francke, L. B. *The Ambivalence of Abortion.* Random House, 1978. Dell, 1979.

Frank, A. *Anne Frank: The Diary of a Young Girl.* Doubleday, 1952. Pocketbook, 1978.

Frank, P. *Alas, Babylon.* Lippincott, 1959. Bantam, 1979.

Frank, R. *No Hero for the Kaiser.* Lothrop, Lee & Shepard, 1986.

Frankel, M. E., with E. Saideman. *Out of the Shadows of Night: The Struggle for International Human Rights.* Delacorte, 1989.

Frazier, N. L. *Stout-Hearted Seven.* Harcourt Brace Jovanovich, 1973.

Freedman, B., and N. Freedman. *Mrs. Mike.* Coward, McCann & Geoghegan, 1947. Berkley, 1968.

Freedman, R. *An Indian Winter.* Holiday House, 1992.

———. *Lincoln: A Photobiography.* Clarion, 1987.

Freedman, S. G. *Small Victories: The Real World of a Teacher, Her Students, and Their High School.* Harper & Row, 1990.

French, M. *Circle of Revenge.* Bantam, 1988.

———. *Pursuit.* Delacorte, 1982. Dell, 1983.

French, S. *All We Know.* Macmillan, 1989.

Friedman, I. R. *The Other Victims: First-Person Stories of non-Jews Persecuted by the Nazis.* Houghton Mifflin, 1990.

Friedman, M. *Buried Alive: The Biography of Janis Joplin.* Morrow, 1973. Bantam, 1974.

———. *The Story of Josh.* Praeger, 1974. Ballantine, 1974.

Fritz, J. *And Then What Happened, Paul Revere?* Coward, McCann & Geoghegan, 1973. Scholastic, 1974.

———. *Bully for You, Teddy Roosevelt!* Putnam's, 1991.

———. *The Great Little Madison.* Putnam's, 1989.

———. *What's the Big Idea, Ben Franklin?* Coward, McCann & Geoghegan, 1976, 1982.

———. *Where Was Patrick Henry on the Twenty-Ninth of May?* Coward, McCann & Geoghegan, 1975, 1982.

———. *Why Don't You Get a Horse, Sam Adams?* Coward, McCann & Geoghegan, 1982.

———. *Will You Sign Here, John Hancock?* Coward, McCann & Geoghegan, 1976.

Froman, R., ed. *Street Poems.* McCall, 1971.

Fujimura, K. *The Tokyo Puzzles.* Scribner's, 1978.

Furlong, M. *Juniper.* Knopf, 1991.

Gackenbach, B. *Do You Love Me?* Seabury, 1975. Dell, 1978.

Gaines, Ernest J. *The Autobiography of Miss Jane Pittman.* Dial, 1971. Bantam, 1982.

———. *A Gathering of Old Men.* Knopf, 1983.

Galbraith, J. K. *Money: Whence It Came from and Where It Went.* Houghton Mifflin, 1975. Bantam, 1976.

Galbraith, J. K., and N. Salinger. *Almost Everyone's Guide to Economics.* Houghton Mifflin, 1978. Bantam, 1979.

Galgut, D. *A Sinless Season.* Jonathan Ball, 1982. Penguin, 1984.

Gallo, D. R. *Center Stage: One-Act Plays for Teenage Readers and Actors.* HarperCollins, 1990.

———. *Connections.* Delacorte, 1989. Dell, 1990.

———. *Sixteen Short Stories.* Delacorte, 1984.

———. *Visions: Nineteen Short Stories by Outstanding Writers for Young Adults.* Delacorte, 1987.

Gard, W. *The Chisholm Trail.* University of Oklahoma Press, 1969.

Garden, N. *The Loners.* Viking, 1972. Avon, 1974.

Gardner, M. *Mathematical Carnival.* Knopf, 1975. Viking, 1977.

———. *Mathematical Circus.* Knopf, 1979. Vintage, 1981.

———. *Perplexing Puzzles and Tantalizing Teasers.* Simon & Schuster, 1969. Pocket Books, 1971.

Gardner, R. *The Boys' and Girls' Books about Divorce.* Aronson, 1970. Bantam, 1971.

Garfield, B. *The Paladin.* Simon & Schuster, 1979. Bantam, 1981.

Garfield, L. *Devil-in-the-Fog.* Constable, 1966. Dell, 1988.

———. *Footsteps.* Delacorte, 1980.

———. *Jack Holborn.* Pantheon, 1965.

———. *The Sound of the Coaches.* Viking, 1974.

Garfield, L., and E. Blishen. *The God beneath the Sea.* Pantheon, 1971.

Garner, A. *The Owl Service.* Philomel, 1967. Ballantine, 1981.

Gates, H. L., Jr., ed. *The Classic Slave Narratives.* New American Library, 1987.

Gauch, P. *The Green of Me.* Putnam, 1978. Berkley/Pacer, 1985.

———. *The Year the Summer Died.* Putnam's, 1985.

Gault, F., and C. Gault. *The Home Run Kings: Babe Ruth/Hank Aaron.* Walker, 1974. Scholastic, 1974.

George, J. C. *Gull Number 737.* Crowell, 1964.

———. *Hold Zero!* Crowell, 1966.

———. *Julie of the Wolves.* Harper & Row, 1972.

———. *My Side of the Mountain.* Dutton, 1969. Grosset & Dunlap, 1969.

———. *One Day in the Tropical Rain Forest.* HarperCollins, 1990.

———. *River Rats, Inc.* Dutton, 1979.

———. *Spring Comes to the Ocean.* Crowell, 1965.

———. *Who Really Killed Cock Robin?* Dutton, 1971. Young Readers Press, 1973.

Geras, A. *Pictures of the Night.* Harcourt, Brace, Jovanovich, 1993.

———. *The Tower Room.* Hamish Hamilton, 1990. Harcourt Brace Jovanovich, 1992.

———. *Watching the Roses.* Hamish Hamilton, 1991. Harcourt Brace Jovanovich, 1992.

Gerber, M. J. *Handsome as Anything.* Scholastic, 1990.

Gerrold, D. *When Harlie Was One.* Doubleday, 1972. Ballantine, 1972.

Gerson, C. *Passing Through.* Dial, 1978. Dell, 1978.

Gibbons, F. *Mighty Close to Heaven.* Morrow, 1985.

Giff, P. R. *The War Began at Supper: Letters to Miss Loria.* Delacorte, 1991.

Gilbert, N. *Champions Don't Cry.* Harper & Row, 1960. Scholastic, 1979.

Gildner, G. *Blue Like the Heavens: New and Selected Poems.* University of Pittsburgh Press, 1984. Distributed by Harper & Row.

Gioia, D. *Daily Horoscope.* Graywolf, 1986.

Giovanni, N. *Those Who Ride the Night Winds.* Morrow, 1983.

Girion, B. *A Tangle of Roots.* Scribner's, 1979. Dell, 1981.

———. *A Very Brief Season.* Scribner's, 1984.

Glass, F. *Marvin and Tige.* St. Martin's, 1977. Fawcett, 1977.

Glasser, R. J. *The Body Is the Hero.* Random House, 1976. Bantam, 1979.

Gleeson, L. *Eleanor, Elizabeth.* Holiday House, 1990.

Glemser, B. *Radar Commandos.* Pocket Books, 1953.

Glenn, M. *Back to Class.* Clarion, 1988.

———. *Class Dismissed! High School Poems.* Clarion, 1982.

———. *My Friend's Got This Problem, Mr. Chandler: High School Poems.* Clarion, 1991.

Glidden, M. *Outer Space and All That Junk.* Lippincott, 1989.

Godden, R. *Thursday's Children.* Viking, 1984. Dell, 1987.

Godey, J. *The Snake.* Putnam, 1978. Berkley, 1979.

Godfrey, M. *Can You Teach Me to Pick My Nose?* Avon, 1990.

Gold, R., ed. *Point of Departure: Nineteen Stories of Youth and Discovery.* Dell, 1981.

———. *Stepping Stones: Seventeen Powerful Stories of Growing Up.* Dell, 1981.

Golding, W. *Lord of the Flies.* Wideview/Perigee Books, 1954.

Goodrich, F., and A. Hackett. *The Diary of Anne Frank. Dramatization of the Book* Anne Frank: The Diary of a Young Girl. Random House, 1956.

Gordan, S. *Waiting for the Rain.* Franklin Watts, 1987. Bantam, 1989.

———. *You Would If You Loved Me.* Bantam, 1978.

Gordon, J. *Give Me One Wish.* Norton, 1988.

Gordon, R., ed. *Under All Silences: Shades of Love.* Harper & Row, 1987.

Gotlieb, P. *O Master Caliban!* Harper & Row, 1976.

Goulart, R. *What's Become of Screwloose?* Scribner's, 1971. DAW Books, 1973.

Graham, L. *South Town.* Follett, 1958. New American Library, 1958.

Graham, W. *Demelza: A Novel of Cornwall, 1788–1790.* Ballantine, 1978.

———. *Ross Poldark: A Novel of Cornwall, 1783–1787.* Ballantine, 1978.

Grahame, K. *The Wind in the Willows.* Scribner's, 1908.

Green, C. J. *The War at Home.* Macmillan/McElderry, 1989.

Green, M. *Defender of the Constitution: Andrew Johnson.* Messner, 1962.

Green, R. J. *The Throttlepenny Murder.* Oxford University Press, 1989.

Greenberg, J. [Hannah Green]. *I Never Promised You a Rose Garden*. Holt, Rinehart, & Winston, 1964. New American Library, 1964.

——. *In This Sign*. Holt, Rinehart & Winston, 1970. Avon 1972.

——. *Of Such Small Differences*. Henry Holt, 1988.

——. *A Season In-Between*. Farrar, Straus & Giroux, 1979. Dell, 1981.

Greene, B. *The Drowning of Stephan Jones*. Bantam, 1991.

——. *Morning Is a Long Time Coming*. Dial, 1978. Pocket Books, 1979.

——. *Summer of My German Soldier*. Dial, 1973. Bantam, 1974.

Greene, C. *Beat the Turtle Drum*. Viking, 1976. Dell, 1979.

——. *Monday I Love You*. Harper & Row, 1988.

Greene, S. *The Boy Who Drank Too Much*. Viking, 1979. Dell, 1980.

Greenfeld, H. *Gypsies*. Crown, 1977.

Gregorian, J. B. *The Broken Citadel*. Atheneum, 1975.

——. *Castledown*. Atheneum, 1977.

Grey, Z. *To the Last Man*. Harper & Brothers, 1921. Pocket Books, 1976.

Grossman, M. *The Summer Ends Too Soon*. Westminster, 1975.

Grove, V. *The Fastest Friend in the West*. Putnam, 1990.

Grunberger, R. *Hitler's SS*. Dell, 1972.

——. *Twelve-Year Reich: A Social History of Nazi Germany, 1933–1945*. Holt, Rinehart & Winston, 1969.

Grunfeld, F. V. *The Hitler File: A Social History of Germany and the Nazis, 1918–1945*. Random House, 1974.

Guest, E. *Over the Moon*. Morrow, 1986.

Guest, J. *Ordinary People*. Viking, 1976. Ballantine, 1980.

Gunter, J. *The Gunter Papers*. Avon, 1975.

Gunther, J. *Death Be Not Proud: A Memoir*. Harper & Row, 1949. Pyramid, 1979.

Gurko, M. *The Ladies of Seneca Falls*. Macmillan, 1974.

Guthrie, A. B., Jr. *The Way West*. Houghton Mifflin, 1949. Bantam, 1979.

Guy, D. *Football Dreams*. Seaview, 1980. New American Library, 1982.

Guy, R. *And I Heard a Bird Sing*. Delacorte, 1987.

——. *The Disappearance*. Delacorte, 1979. Dell, 1979.

——. *Edith Jackson*. Viking, 1978. Bantam, 1978.

——. *The Friends*. Holt, Rinehart & Winston, 1973. Bantam, 1974.

——. *My Love, My Love; or, The Peasant Girl*. Holt, Rinehart & Winston, 1985.

——. *Ruby*. Viking, 1976. Bantam, 1979.

Haar. J. *The World of Ben Lighthart*. Delacorte, 1977.

Hahn, M. D. *December Stillness*. Clarion, 1988. Avon, 1988.

Haines, G. K. *The Great Nuclear Power Debate*. Dodd, Mead, 1985.

Halacy, D. C. *Charles Babbage: Father of the Computer*. Crowell-Collier, 1970.

——. *Return from Luna*. Norton, 1969.

Hale, J. C. *The Owl's Song*. Bantam, 1991.

Haley, A. *Roots*. Doubleday, 1976. Dell, 1977.

Hall, L. *Fair Maiden*. Scribner's, 1990.

——. *Gently Touch the Milkweed*. Follett, 1970. Avon, 1970.

——. *The Giver*. Scribner's, 1985.

——. *Halsey's Pride*. Macmillan, 1990.

——. *Just One Friend*. Scribner's 1985.

——. *The Leaving*. Collier, 1980.

——. *Murder in a Pig's Eye*. Harcourt Brace Jovanovich, 1989.

——. *Ride a Dark Horse*. Morrow, 1987. Avon, 1988.

——. *The Secret of Stone House*. Follett, 1968.

——. *Sticks and Stones*. Follett, 1972. Dell, 1972.

——. *Up Hill All the Way*. Scribner's, 1984.

Halpern, D. E., ed. *The American Poetry Anthology*. Avon, 1976.

Halvorson, M. *Hold On, Geronimo*. Delacorte, 1988. Dell, 1989.

Hamilton, E. *Sex with Love: A Guide for Young People*. Beacon, 1978.

Hamilton, M. *Effie's House*. Greenwillow, 1990.

Hamilton, V. *Anthony Burns: The Defeat and Triumph of a Fugitive Slave*. Knopf, 1988.

——. *Arilla Sun Down*. Greenwillow, 1976. Dell, 1979.

——. *The House of Dies Drear*. Macmillan, 1968. Dell, 1978.

——. *Junius Over Far*. Harper & Row, 1985; HarperCollins, 1985.

——. *Justice and Her Brothers*. Greenwillow, 1978. Avon, 1981.

——. *A Little Love*. Philomel, 1984. Berkley, 1985.

——. *The Magical Adventures of Pretty Pearl*. Harper & Row, 1983. Harper Trophy, 1983.

——. *M. C. Higgins, the Great*. Macmillan, 1974. Dell, 1976.

——. *The Mystery of Drear House*. Greenwillow, 1987.

———. *Paul Robeson: The Life and Times of a Free Black Man*. Harper & Row, 1974. Dell, 1979.

———. *The Planet of Junior Brown*. Macmillan, 1971. Dell, 1978.

———. *Sweet Whispers, Brother Rush*. Philomel, 1983.

———. *A White Romance*. Philomel, 1987.

———. *Zeely*. Macmillan, 1967. Dell, 1978.

Hamlin, G. *Beneath the Surface*. New American Library, 1985.

Hammond, A. L., ed. *A Passion to Know: 20 Profiles in Science*. Scribner's, 1984.

Haney, L. *The Lady Is a Jock*. Dodd, Mead, 1973.

Hanlon, E. *It's Too Late for Sorry*. Bradbury, 1978. Dell, 1981.

Hansberry, L. *A Raisin in the Sun*. Random House, 1959. NAL/Signet Classic, 1961.

Hansen, J. *Which Way Freedom?* Walker, 1986.

Hard, T. W. *Sum VII*. Harper & Row, 1979. Ballantine, 1980.

Harris, J. *Come the Morning*. Bradbury, 1989.

Harris, Marilyn. *The Runaway's Diary*. Four Winds, 1971. Pocket Books, 1974.

Harris, Mark. *Bang the Drum Slowly*. Knopf, 1956. Dell, 1974.

Harrison, M., and C. Stuart-Clark. *Peace and War: A Collection of Poems*. Oxford University Press, 1989.

Hartley, A. B. *Unexploded Bomb*. Norton, 1958.

Hartling, P. *Crutches*. Lothrop, Lee & Shepard, 1989.

Haskins, J. *Black Dance in America: A History through Its People*. Crowell, 1990.

———. *Black Music in America: A History through Its People*. Crowell, 1987.

———. *One More River to Cross*. Scholastic, 1992.

———. *The Story of Stevie Wonder*. Lothrop, Lee & Shepard, 1976. Dell, 1979.

———. *Winnie Mandela: Life of Struggle*. Putnam, 1988.

———. *Witchcraft, Mysticism and Magic in the Black World*. Doubleday, 1974. Dell, 1976.

Haugaard, E. C. *Chase Me, Catch Nobody!* Houghton Mifflin, 1980.

———. *Cromwell's Boy*. Houghton Mifflin, 1978.

———. *A Messenger for Parliament*. Houghton Mifflin, 1976.

———. *The Samurai's Tale*. Houghton Mifflin, 1984.

Hautzig, D. *Hey, Dollface*. Greenwillow, 1978. Bantam, 1980.

———. *Second Star to the Right*. Greenwillow, 1981.

Haven, S. *Is It Them or Is It Me?* Putnam's, 1990.

Haverstock, M. S. *Indian Gallery: The Story of George Catlin*. Four Winds Press, 1973.

Havrevold, F. *Undertow*. Translated by C. B. Curry. Atheneum, 1968.

Hawthorne, N. *The Celestial Railroad and Other Stories*. NAL/Signet Classic, 1963.

———. *The Scarlet Letter*. Vintage, 1990.

Haydon, T. L. *One Child*. Avon, 1980.

Hayes, E. K., and A. Lazzarino. *Broken Promise*. Putnam, 1978. Fawcett, 1978.

Hays, J. D. *Our Changing Climate*. Atheneum, 1977.

Head, A. *Mr. and Mrs. Bo Jo Jones*. Putnam's, 1967. New American Library, 1968.

Heaven, C. *The Wildcliffe Bird*. Coward-McCann, 1983.

Heinlein, R. *Rocketship Galileo*. Scribner's, 1947. Ballantine, 1977.

———. *Stranger in a Strange Land*. Putnam, 1961. Berkley, 1971.

Hellman, L. *Scoundrel Time*. Little, Brown, 1976.

Hemingway, E. *A Farewell to Arms*. Collier, 1986.

———. *For Whom the Bell Tolls*. Dell, 1979.

———. *The Old Man and the Sea*. Scribner's, 1968.

Hendry, F. M. *Quest for a Maid*. Farrar, Straus & Giroux, 1990.

Hensler, P. G., with J. W. Houston. *Don't Cry, It's Only Thunder*. Doubleday, 1984. New American Library, 1985.

Hentoff, N. *American Heroes: In and Out of School*. Delacorte, 1987.

———. *Boston Boy*. Knopf, 1986.

———. *The Day They Came to Arrest the Book*. Delacorte, 1982.

———. *Does This School Have Capital Punishment?* Delacorte, 1981.

———. *The First Freedom: The Tumultuous History of Free Speech in America*. Delacorte, 1980. Dell, 1981.

———. *I'm Really Dragged but Nothing Gets Me Down*. Simon & Schuster, 1968. Dell, 1974.

———. *Jazz Country*. Harper & Row, 1965. Dell, 1967.

Herbert, F. *Soul Catcher*. Putnam's, 1972. Bantam, 1973.

Herbert, K. *Queen of the Lightning*. St. Martin's, 1984.

Hermes, P. *Be Still My Heart*. Putnam's, 1989.

———. *I Hate Being Gifted*. Putnam's, 1990.

———. *Mama, Let's Dance*. Little, Brown, 1991.

———. *A Small Pleasure*. Macmillan, 1988.

Herriot, J. *All Creatures Great and Small*. St. Martin's, 1972. Bantam, 1978.

———. *All Things Bright and Beautiful*. St. Martin's, 1974. Bantam, 1978.

———. *All Things Wise and Wonderful*. St. Martin's, 1977, Bantam, 1978.

Hersey, J. *Hiroshima*. Knopf, 1978. Bantam, 1975.

Heslewood, J., ed. *Earth, Air, Fire and Water*. Charlotte Zolotow/Harper & Row, 1989.

Hesse, H. *Siddhartha*. Translated by H. Rosner. New Directions, 1951.

Heyerdahl, T. *Aku-Aku*. International Collector's Library, 1958. Ballantine, 1974.

————. *Kon Tiki: Across the Pacific by Raft*. Rand McNally, 1950.

————. *The Ra Expeditions*. Doubleday, 1971. New American Library, 1972.

Heyman, A. *Final Grades*. Dodd, Mead, 1983.

Hickman, J. *The Valley of the Shadow*. Macmillan, 1974.

Hieatt, C. *The Minstrel Knight*. Crowell, 1974.

Highwater, J. *The Ceremony of Innocence*. Harper & Row, 1985.

————. *Eyes of Darkness*. Lothrop, Lee & Shepard, 1985.

————. *I Wear the Morning Star*. Harper & Row, 1986.

————. *Legend Days*. Harper & Row, 1984.

Hilgartner, B. *Colors in the Dreamweaver's Loom*. Houghton Mifflin, 1989.

Hill, H., A. Perkins, and A. Helbig, eds. *Straight on Till Morning: Poems of the Imaginary World*. Crowell, 1977.

Hilton, S. *Faster Than a Horse: Moving West with Engine Power*. Westminster, 1983.

Hinton, S. E. *The Outsiders*. Viking, 1967. Dell, 1980.

————. *Rumble Fish*. Delacorte, 1975. Dell, 1976.

————. *Tex*. Delacorte, 1979. Dell, 1980.

————. *That Was Then, This Is Now*. Viking, 1971. Dell, 1980.

Ho, M. *Rice without Rain*. Lothrop, Lee & Shepard, 1990.

Hoban, R. *The Mouse and His Child*. Harper & Row, 1967. Avon, 1974.

Hobbs, W. *Bearstone*. Atheneum, 1989.

————. *Changes in Latitudes*. Atheneum, 1988.

————. *Downriver*. Atheneum, 1991.

Hodges, E. J. *A Song for Gilgamesh*. Atheneum, 1971.

Hogben, L. *Mathematics in the Making*. Doubleday, 1960.

————. *The Wonderful World of Mathematics*. Doubleday, 1955, 1968.

Holland, I. *After the First Love*. Fawcett, 1983.

————. *Alan and the Animal Kingdom*. Lippincott, 1977. Dell, 1979.

————. *Heads You Win, Tails I Lose*. Lippincott, 1973. Dell, 1979.

————. *Hitchhike*. Lippincott, 1977. Dell, 1979.

————. *Man without a Face*. Lippincott, 1979. Dell, 1980.

————. *Of Love and Death and Other Journeys*. Lippincott, 1975. Dell, 1977.

————. *Summer of My First Love*. Fawcett, 1981.

————. *The Unfrightened Dark*. Little, Brown, 1989.

Holliday, L., ed. *Heart Songs: The Intimate Diaries of Young Girls*. Bluestocking, 1978. Avon, 1981.

Holman, F. *Secret City USA*. Scribner, 1990.

————. *Slake's Limbo*. Scribner's, 1974. Aladdin, 1986.

Homer. *The Iliad*. Many editions available.

————. *Odyssey*. Many editions available.

Hoobler, D. and T. Hoobler. *Nelson and Winnie Mandela*. Franklin Watts, 1987.

————. *Vietnam: Why We Fought; an Illustrated History*. Knopf, 1990.

Hooke, R., et al. *Math and Aftermath*. Walker, 1965.

Hooker, R. *Kennaquhair*. Abingdon, 1976.

Hoover, H. M. *Another Heaven, Another Earth*. Viking, 1981.

————. *The Bell Tree*. Viking, 1982.

————. *The Delikon*. Viking, 1977. Avon, 1978.

————. *The Lost Star*. Viking, 1979. Avon, 1980.

————. *The Rains of Eridan*. Viking, 1977. Avon, 1979.

————. *Return to Earth*. Viking, 1980.

————. *Treasures of Morrow*. Four Winds, 1976.

Hopkins, L. B. *Mama: A Novel*. Knopf, 1977. Dell, 1978.

————. *Mama and Her Boys: A Novel*. Harper & Row, 1981.

Hopkins, L. B., ed. *Books Are by People*. Scholastic/Citation, 1969.

————. *I Am the Cat*. Harcourt Brace Jovanovich, 1982.

————. *Moments: Poems about the Seasons*. Harcourt Brace Jovanovich, 1980.

————. *More Books by More People*. Scholastic/Citation, 1974.

————. *Munching: Poems about Eating*. Little, Brown, 1985.

————. *My Mane Catches the Wind: Poems about Horses*. Harcourt Brace Jovanovich, 1979.

————. *On Our Way: Poems of Pride and Love*. Knopf, 1974.

————. *Rainbows Are Made: Poems by Carl Sandburg*. Harcourt Brace Jovanovich, 1952.

————. *To Look at Any Thing*. Harcourt Brace Jovanovich, 1978.

Hopkins, L. B., and M. Arenstein, eds. *Faces and Places: Poems for You*. Scholastic, 1971.

Hopkins, L. B., and S. Rasch, eds. *I Really Want to Feel Good about Myself: Poems by Former Drug Addicts.* Nelson, 1974.

Horgan, D. *Then the Zeppelins Came.* Oxford University Press, 1989.

Horgan, P. *Whitewater.* Farrar, Straus & Giroux 1970. Paperback Library, 1973.

Horowitz, A. *The Devil's Door-Bell.* Holt, Rinehart & Winston, 1983.

———. *The Night of the Scorpion.* Putnam, 1984. Berkley, 1986.

Horwitz, S. *Toulouse-Lautrec: His World.* Harper & Row, 1973.

Hosford, J. *You Bet Your Boots I Can.* Nelson, 1971.

Houghton, E. *Gates of Glass.* Oxford University Press, 1987.

Houston, J. *Ghost Fox.* Harcourt Brace Jovanovich, 1977. Avon, 1978.

———. *The White Dawn: An Eskimo Saga.* Harcourt Brace Jovanovich, 1983.

Houston, J. W., and J. D. Houston. *Farewell to Manzanar.* Houghton Mifflin, 1973. Bantam, 1974.

Howard, E. *Edith, Herself.* Macmillan, 1987.

———. *Her Own Song.* Atheneum, 1988.

———. *We Are Mesquakie, We Are One.* Feminist Press, 1980.

Howe, F., and E. Bass. eds. *No More Masks: An Anthology of Poems by Women.* Doubleday, 1973.

Howe, I., and K. Libo, eds. *How We Lived: A Documentary History of Immigrant Jews in America, 1880–1930.* Marek, 1979. New American Library, 1981.

Hoyt, E. *Extinction A–Z.* Enslow, 1991.

Hubmann, F. *The Jewish Family Album.* Little, Brown, 1975.

Hughes, L. *Selected Poems of Langston Hughes.* Knopf, 1981. Vintage, 1990.

Hughes, L., M. Meltzer, and C. E. Lincoln, eds. *A Pictorial History of Black Americans.* Crown, 1973.

Hughes, M. *Beyond the Dark River.* Atheneum, 1981.

———. *Crisis on Cornshelf Ten.* Atheneum, 1975.

———. *Devil on My Back.* Atheneum, 1985. Bantam, 1987.

———. *Invitation to the Game.* Simon & Schuster, 1990.

———. *The Keeper of the Isis Light.* Atheneum, 1981.

Hughey, R. *The Question Box.* Delacorte, 1984.

Huie, W. B. *A New Life to Live: Jimmy Putman's Story.* Nelson, 1977. Bantam, 1980.

Humphrey, W. *My Moby Dick.* Doubleday, 1978. Penguin, 1979.

Hunt, I. *Across Five Aprils.* Follett, 1964. Grossett & Dunlap, 1964.

———. *Claws of a Young Century.* Scribner's, 1980.

———. *Up a Road Slowly.* Follett, 1966.

Hunter, J. A. *Fun with Figures.* Dover, 1965.

Hunter, K. *Guests in the Promised Land.* Scribner's, 1973. Avon, 1976.

———. *The Soul Brothers and Sister Lou.* Scribner's, 1968. Avon, 1970.

Hunter, M. *Hold On to Love.* Harper & Row, 1983.

———. *A Sound of Chariots.* Harper & Row, 1972. Avon, 1972.

Hurmence, B. *A Girl Called Boy.* Clarion, 1982.

———. *Tancy.* Clarion, 1984.

Hurston, Z. N. *Their Eyes Were Watching God.* Harper & Row, 1990.

Huthmacher, J. J. *A Nation of Newcomers: Ethnic Minority Groups in American History.* Delacorte, 1967. Dell, 1967.

Huxley, Aldous. *Brave New World.* Harper & Row, 1932.

Hyde, M. O. *Drug Wars.* Walker, 1990.

———. *Your Brain: Master Computer.* McGraw-Hill, 1964.

Hyde, M. O., and L. E. Hyde. *Meeting Death.* Walker, 1989.

Hymowitz, C., and M. Weissman. *A History of Women in America.* Bantam, 1978.

Ibsen, H. A Doll's House. *Four Major Plays, 1.* Signet, 1965.

———. *An Enemy of the People.* Heinemann, 1957. Oxford University Press, 1988.

Irwin, H. *Abby, My Love.* Atheneum, 1985. Macmillan, 1985.

———. *Bring to a Boil and Separate.* Atheneum, 1980.

———. *Can't Hear You Listening.* McElderry, 1990. Macmillan, 1990.

———. *I Be Somebody.* Atheneum, 1984.

———. *Kim/Kimi.* McElderry, 1987.

———. *Lilith Summer.* Feminist Press, 1979.

———. *Moon and Me.* Atheneum, 1981.

———. *So Long at the Fair.* Macmillan/McElderry, 1988.

———. *We Are Mesquakie, We Are One.* Feminist Press, 1980.

———. *What about Grandma?* Atheneum, 1982.

Ish-kishor, S. *Our Eddie.* Pantheon, 1969.

Ives, J. *Fear in a Handful of Dust.* Dutton, 1978. Jove, 1979.

Jackson, J. *Call Me Charley*. Harper & Row, 1945. Dell, 1970.

Jackson, T. *Guerrilla Tactics in the Job Market*. Bantam, 1978.

Jacobs, H. *Mathematics, a Human Endeavor: A Textbook for Those Who Think They Don't Like the Subject*. Freeman, 1982.

Jacobs, J. *Adolescent Suicide*. Wiley Press, 1971.

Jacobs, K. F. *GirlSports!* Bantam, 1978.

Jacobs, P. S. *Born into Light*. Scholastic, 1988.

Jacot, M. *The Last Butterfly*. McClelland & Stewart, 1973. Ballantine, 1975.

Jacques, B. *Mattimeo*. Philomel, 1990.

———. *Redwall*. Philomel, 1987.

Jaffe, D. T., and T. Clark, eds. *Worlds Apart: Young People and Drug Programs*. Vintage, 1974.

Janeczko, P. B. *Going Over to Your Place: Poems for Each Other*. Bradbury, 1987.

———. *The Music of What Happens: Poems That Tell Stories*. Orchard, 1985.

Janeczko, P. B. ed. *Bridges to Cross*. Macmillan, 1986.

———. *The Crystal Image*. Dell, 1977.

———. *Don't Forget to Fly: A Cycle of Modern Poems*. Bradbury, 1981.

———. *The Place My Words Are Looking For: What Poets Say about and through Their Work*. Bradbury, 1990.

———. *Pocket Poems*. Bradbury, 1985.

———. *Poetspeak: In Their Work, about Their Work*. Bradbury, 1983.

———. *Postcard Poems: A Collection of Poetry for Sharing*. Bradbury, 1979.

———. *String: A Gathering of Family Poems*. Bradbury, 1984.

Jarunkova, K. *Don't Cry for Me*. Four Winds, 1968. Scholastic, 1969.

Jaspersohn, W. *The Ballpark: A Behind-the-Scenes View of Fenway Park*. Little, Brown, 1980.

———. *A Day in the Life of a Marine Biologist*. Little, Brown, 1982.

———. *A Day in the Life of a Veterinarian*. Little, Brown, 1978.

———. *Grounded: A Novel*. Bantam, 1988.

Jenkins, A. *Wildlife in Danger*. St. Martin's, 1973.

Jensen, K. *Pocket Change*. Macmillan, 1989.

Joffo, J. *A Bag of Marbles*. Houghton Mifflin, 1974.

Johannesson, O. *The Tale of the Big Computer*. Coward, McCann & Geoghegan, 1968.

John, T., ed. *The Great Song Book*. Doubleday, 1978.

Johnson, A. *Count Me Gone*. Simon & Schuster, 1968.

Johnson, C. *Middle Passage*. Atheneum, 1990. Plume, 1991.

Johnson, D. *Fiskadoro*. Knopf, 1985.

Johnson, E. W. *Love and Sex in Plain Language*. Lippincott, 1985. Bantam, 1988.

Johnson, J. *How Many Miles to Babylon?* Doubleday, 1974. Avon, 1975.

Johnston, N. *The Days of the Dragon's Seed*. Atheneum, 1982.

———. *The Delphic Choice*. Macmillan, 1989.

———. *Whisper of the Cat*. Bantam, 1988.

Jonathan, M. *Come the Morning*. Harris Bradbury, 1989.

Jones, A. *So Nothing Is Forever*. Houghton Mifflin, 1974.

———. *Street Family*. HarperCollins, 1987.

Jones, D. W. *Dogsbody*. Greenwillow, 1975. Dell, 1979.

Jones, D. W., ed. *Hidden Turnings: A Collection of Stories through Time and Space*. Greenwillow, 1990.

Jones, H. *Big Star Fallin' Mama: Five Women in Black Music*. Viking, 1974. Dell, 1974.

Jones, R. *The Acorn People*. Bantam, 1976.

Jordan, G. *Home Below Hell's Canyon*. Crowell, 1954. University of Nebraska Press, 1962.

Jordan, J. *Dry Victories*. Holt, Rinehart & Winston, 1972. Avon, 1975.

———. *His Own Where*. Crowell, 1971. Dell, 1973.

———. *Naming Our Destiny: New and Selected Poems*. Thunder's Mouth, 1989.

Josephson, H. *Jeanette Rankin: First Lady in Congress*. Bobbs-Merrill, 1974.

Josephy, A. M. *The Indian Heritage of America*. Knopf, 1968. Bantam, 1976.

Judson, W. *Cold River*. Mason & Lipscomb, 1974. New American, 1976.

Juster, N. *The Phantom Tollbooth*. Random House, 1961.

Kahn, J., ed. *Some Things Strange and Sinister*. Harper & Row, 1973. Avon, 1974.

———. *Handle with Care: Frightening Stories*. Greenwillow, 1985.

Kahn, K. *Hillbilly Women*. Doubleday, 1973. Avon, 1980.

Kane, J. N. *Facts about the Presidents*. 3d ed. Ace, 1976.

Kantor, A. *The Book of Alfred Kantor*. McGraw-Hill, 1971. Schocken, 1987.

Kaplan, B. *The Empty Chair*. Harper & Row, 1975.

Kaplan, P. *More Posers*. Harper & Row, 1964.

Karl, J. *Beloved Benjamin Is Waiting*. Dutton, 1978. Dell, 1980.

Karr, K. *It Ain't Always Easy.* Farrar, 1991.

Katz, W. *Black People Who Made the Old West.* HarperCollins, 1977.

Kaye, M. *The Incredible Umbrella.* Doubleday, 1979.

Keith, H. *Rifles for Watie.* Crowell, 1957.

Kellogg, M. *Tell Me That You Love Me, Junie Moon.* Farrar, Straus & Giroux, 1968. Popular Library, 1968.

Kelly, E. P. *The Trumpeter of Krakow.* Macmillan, 1966.

Kelly, G. F. *Learning about Sex: The Contemporary Guide for Young Adults.* Barron, 1976.

Kennedy, J. F. *Profiles in Courage.* Harper & Row, 1964. Scholastic, 1964.

Kennedy, X. J. *Cross Ties: Selected Poems.* University of Georgia Press, 1985.

Kerr, J. *The Other Way Round.* Coward, 1975.

Kerr, M. E. *Dinky Hocker Shoots Smack!* Harper & Row, 1972. Dell, 1978.

———. *Fell.* Harper, 1987.

———. *Fell Back.* Harper & Row, 1989.

———. *Fell Down.* HarperCollins, 1991.

———. *Gentlehands.* Harper & Row, 1978.

———. *If I Love You, Am I Trapped Forever?* Harper & Row, 1973. Dell, 1975.

———. *I'll Love You When You're More Like Me.* Harper & Row, 1977. Dell, 1979.

———. *I Stay Near You.* Harper & Row, 1985.

———. *Is That You, Miss Blue?* Harper & Row, 1975. Dell, 1976.

———. *Little, Little.* Harper & Row, 1981.

———. *Me Me Me Me Me.* Harper & Row, 1983.

———. *Night Kites.* Harper & Row, 1986.

———. *Son of Someone Famous.* Harper & Row, 1974. Ballantine, 1975.

———. *What I Really Think of You.* Harper Junior, 1982. Harper, 1991.

Kesey, K. *One Flew Over the Cuckoo's Nest.* Viking, 1962. New American Library, 1975.

Kettlecamp, L. *Modern Sports Science.* Morrow, 1986.

Kevles, B. *Thinking Gorillas: Testing and Teaching the Greatest Ape.* Dutton, 1980.

Key, A. *The Forgotten Door.* Westminster, 1965. Scholastic, 1968.

Keyes, D. *Flowers for Algernon.* Harcourt Brace Jovanovich, 1966. Bantam, 1978.

Kheridan, D. *The Road from Home.* Greenwillow, 1979.

Kiesel, Stanley. *Skinny Malinky Leads the War for Kidness.* Lodestar, 1984.

———. *The War between the Pitiful Teachers and the Splendid Kids.* Dutton, 1980.

Kililea, M. *Karen.* Prentice-Hall, 1962. Dell, 1983.

———. *With Love from Karen.* Prentice-Hall, 1963. Dell, 1963.

Killien, C. *Rusty Fertlanger, Lady's Man.* Dell, 1989.

Kingman, L. *Break a Leg, Betsy Maybe!* Houghton Mifflin, 1976. Dell, 1979.

———. *Head over Wheels.* Houghton Mifflin, 1978. Dell, 1981.

Kirkwood, J. *Good Times/Bad Times.* Fawcett, 1968. Penguin, 1975.

Klass, P. *A Not Entirely Benign Procedure.* Putnam, 1987. Signet, 1987.

Klass, S. *Page Four.* Bantam, 1988. Scribner's, 1986.

Klein, N. *It's Not What You Expect.* Random House, 1973. Avon, 1974.

———. *Love Is One of the Choices.* Dial, 1978. Fawcett, 1979.

———. *Mom, the Wolfman, and Me.* Pantheon, 1972. Avon, 1982.

———. *Sunshine.* Avon, 1974.

———. *Taking Sides.* Pantheon, 1974. Avon, 1982.

———. *That's My Baby.* Viking, 1988.

Knowles, J. *A Separate Peace.* Dell, 1959. Macmillan, 1959. Bantam, 1975.

Knudson, R. R. *Just Another Love Story.* Farrar, Straus & Giroux, 1983. Avon, 1984.

———. *Zanballer.* Delacorte, 1972. Dell, 1979.

———. *Zanbanger.* Harper & Row, 1977. Dell, 1979.

———. *Zanboomer.* Harper & Row, 1978. Dell, 1978.

———. *Zan Hagen's Marathon.* Farrar, Straus & Giroux, 1983. Signet, 1985.

Knudson, R. R., and P. K. Elbert. eds. *Sports Poems.* Dell, 1971.

Knudson, R. R., and M. Swenson. eds. *American Sports Poems.* Franklin Watts/Orchard, 1988.

Koch, K. *Sleeping on the Wing: An Anthology of Modern Poetry with Essays on Reading and Writing.* Random House, 1981.

Koch, K., and K. Farrell. eds. *Talking to the Sun: An Illustrated Anthology of Poems for Young People.* Holt, Rinehart & Winston, 1985.

Koehn, I. *Mischling, Second Degree.* William Morrow, 1977.

Koertge, R. *Where the Kissing Never Stops.* Little, Brown, 1987. Dell, 1988.

———. *Mariposa Blues.* Joy Street/Little, Brown, 1991.

Kohl, J., and H. Kohl. *The View from the Oak.* Sierra Club, 1977.

Konigsburg, E. L. *From the Mixed-Up Files of Mrs. Basil E. Frankweiler.* Atheneum, 1967. Dell, 1977.

———. *A Proud Taste for Scarlet and Miniver.* Atheneum, 1973. Dell, 1985.

————. *The Second Mrs. Giaconda.* Atheneum, 1980.

Korczak, J. *Ghetto Diary.* Schocken, 1978.

Kordemsky, B. A. *The Moscow Puzzles: 359 Mathematical Recreations.* Scribner's, 1972.

Korman, G. *Losing Joe's Place.* Scholastic, 1990.

————. *A Semester in the Life of a Garbage Bag.* Scholastic, 1987.

————. *The Zucchini Warriors.* Scholastic, 1988.

Kornfeld, A. *In a Bluebird's Eye.* Holt, Rinehart & Winston, 1975. Avon, 1976.

Krentel, M. *Melissa Comes Home.* Moody Press, 1972. Popular Library, 1972.

Kresh, P. *Isaac Bashevis Singer: The Story of a Storyteller.* Dutton, 1984.

Kroeber, T. *Ishi, Last of His Tribe.* Parnassus, 1964.

Krumgold, J. *. . . And Now Miguel.* Crowell, 1953.

Kübler-Ross, E. *Questions and Answers on Death and Dying.* Macmillan, 1974.

Kuchler-Silberman, L. *My Hundred Children.* Dell, 1987.

Kuklin, S. *What Do I Do Now? Talking about Teenage Pregnancy.* Putnam's, 1991.

Kunitz, S. J., and H. Haycraft. *The Junior Book of Authors.* H. W. Wilson, 1951.

Kytle, R. *Fire and Ice.* McKay, 1975.

La Bastille, A. *Woods Woman.* Dutton, 1978. Viking, 1991.

Lader, L., and M. Meltzer. *Margaret Sanger: Pioneer of Birth Control.* Doubleday, 1955. Dell, 1974.

LaFarge, O. *Laughing Boy.* New American Library, 1971.

Laird, C. *Shadow of the Wall.* Greenwillow, 1989.

L'Amour, L. *Down the Long Hills.* Bantam, 1968, 1975.

————. *The Quick and the Dead.* Bantam, 1973, 1979.

Lamp, W. *Hey Little Walker and Other Prize-Winning Plays from the 1989 and 1990 Young Playwright's Festival.* Dell, 1991.

Lampman, E. S. *Go Up the Road.* Atheneum 1972.

Langone, J. *Like, Love, Lust: A View of Sex and Sexuality.* Little, Brown, 1980. Avon, 1981.

Larrick, N., ed. *Bring Me All Your Dreams.* Evans, 1988.

————. *I Heard a Scream in the Street: Poetry by Young People in the City.* Evans, 1970. Dell, 1974.

————. *On City Streets.* Evans, 1968. Bantam, 1969.

————. *Room for Me and a Mountain Lion.* Evans, 1979. Bantam, 1975.

————. *Somebody Turned on a Tap in These Kids: Poetry and Young People Today.* Delacorte, 1971. Dell, 1971.

Larsen, R. *Paul Robeson: Hero before His Time.* Franklin Watts, 1989.

Lash, J. P. *Eleanor and Franklin.* Norton, 1971. New American Library, 1973.

Lasky, K. *Beyond the Divide.* Macmillan, 1983. Dell, 1986.

————. *The Bone Wars.* Morrow, 1988. Puffin, 1989.

————. *Pageant.* Macmillan, 1984. Dell, 1986.

————. *Prank.* Macmillan, 1984. Dell, 1986.

Laurents, A. *West Side Story: A Musical.* Random House, 1958.

Lawrence, L. *Andra.* HarperCollins, 1991.

————. *The Warriors of Taan.* HarperCollins, 1988.

Lawrence, R. D. *Secret Go the Wolves.* Holt, Rinehart & Winston, 1980. Ballantine, 1985.

————. *The Zoo That Never Was.* Holt, Rinehart & Winston, 1981. HarperCollins, 1992.

Lawson, D. *The Eagle and the Dragon: The History of U.S.–China Relations.* Crowell, 1985.

————. *The United States in the Indian Wars.* HarperCollins, 1988.

Lawson, R. *Mr. Revere and I.* Little, Brown, 1988. Dell, 1976.

Leahy, S. R. *Circle of Love.* Putnam, 1980.

Lear, E. *The Complete Nonsense Book.* Dodd, Mead, 1943.

————. *The Nonsense Book of Edward Lear.* New American Library, 1964.

Lee, G. *China Boy.* New American Library, 1991.

Lee, H. *To Kill a Mockingbird.* Lippincott, 1960. Warner, 1988.

Lee, M. *Fog.* Houghton Mifflin, 1972. Dell, 1974.

————. *The People Therein.* Houghton Mifflin, 1980.

————. *The Rock and the Willow.* Lothrop, Lee & Shepard, 1963. Washington Square Press, 1970.

————. *The Skating Rink.* Seabury, 1969. Dell, 1972.

Lee, V. *The Magic Moth.* Seabury, 1972.

LeFlore, R., with J. Hawkins. *Breakout: From Prison to the Big Leagues.* Harper & Row, 1978.

LeGuin, U. K. *The Beginning Place.* Harper & Row, 1980. Bantam, 1981.

————. *The Dispossessed: An Ambiguous Utopia.* Harper & Row, 1974. HarperCollins, 1991.

————. *The Farthest Shore.* Atheneum, 1972. Bantam, 1984.

————. *The Left Hand of Darkness.* Walker, 1969. Ace Books, 1983.

————. *Tehanu: The Last Book of Earthsea.* Atheneum, 1990.

————. *The Tombs of Atuan.* Atheneum, 1971. Bantam, 1984.

————. *Very Far Away from Anywhere Else.* Atheneum, 1976. Bantam, 1982.

———. *The Wizard of Earthsea*. Parnassus, 1968. HarperCollins, 1990.

———. *The Word for World Is Forest*. Berkley, 1976.

L'Engle, M. *An Acceptable Time*. Farrar, Straus & Giroux, 1989. Dell, 1990.

———. *And Both Were Young*. Delacorte, 1983. Dell, 1986.

———. *The Arm of the Starfish*. Farrar, Straus & Giroux, 1965. Dell, 1980.

———. *Camilla*. Dell, 1982.

———. *Dragons in the Water*. Farrar, Straus & Giroux, 1976. Dell, 1982.

———. *A House Like a Lotus*. Farrar, Straus & Giroux, 1984. Dell, 1985.

———. *Many Waters*. Farrar, Straus & Giroux, 1986. Dell, 1987.

———. *Meet the Austins*. Vanguard, 1960. Dell, 1981.

———. *The Moon by Night*. Farrar, Straus & Giroux, 1963. Dell, 1981.

———. *A Ring of Endless Light*. Farrar, Straus & Giroux, 1980. Dell, 1981.

———. *The Summer of the Great-Grandmother*. Farrar, Straus & Giroux, 1974. Harper, 1980.

———. *A Swiftly Tilting Planet*. Farrar, Straus & Giroux, 1978. Dell, 1979.

———. *Two-Part Invention: The Story of a Marriage*. Farrar, Straus & Giroux, 1988. Harper, 1989.

———. *Walking on Water: Reflections on Faith and Art*. Harold Shaw, 1980.

———. *A Wind in the Door*. Farrar, Straus & Giroux, 1973. Dell, 1981.

———. *A Wrinkle in Time*. Farrar, Straus & Giroux, 1962. Dell, 1976.

———. *The Young Unicorns*. Farrar, Straus & Giroux, 1968. Dell, 1989.

Lerman, R. *Eleanor*. Holt, Rinehart & Winston, 1979.

Lester, J. *Black Folktales*. R. W. Baron, 1969. Grove, 1991.

———. *Long Journey Home: Stories from Black History and Black Folktales*. Dial, 1972. Scholastic, 1988.

———. *This Strange New Feeling*. Dial, 1982. Scholastic, 1985.

———. *To Be a Slave*. Dial, 1968. Scholastic, 1986.

Lester, J., and D. Gahr, eds. *Who I Am*. Dial, 1974.

Levenkron, S. *The Best Little Girl in the World*. Contemporary Books, 1978. Warner, 1989.

LeVert, J. *The Flight of the Cassowary*. Atlantic Monthly Press, 1986. Bantam, 1988.

Levi, B. *Survival in Auschwitz: The Nazi Assault on Humanity*. Macmillan, 1987.

Levin, I. *The Boys from Brazil*. Random House, 1976. Bantam, 1991.

———. *This Perfect Day*. Random House, 1970. Bantam, 1991.

Levin, J. W. *Star of Danger*. Harcourt, Brace & World, 1966.

Levine, I. E. *Young Man in the White House: John Fitzgerald Kennedy*. Messner, 1964. Folkstone, 1970.

Levitin, S. *Journey to America*. Atheneum, 1970. Aladdin, 1987.

———. *The Return*. Atheneum, 1987. Ballantine, 1987.

———. *Roanoke: A Novel of the Lost Colony*. Atheneum, 1973.

Levoy, M. *Three Friends*. Harper & Row, 1984.

Levy, E. *Came a Spider*. Arbor House, 1978. Berkley, 1980.

Levy, E., and M. Miller. *Doctors for the People: Profiles of Six Who Serve*. Knopf, 1977. Dell, 1979.

Levy, M. *No Way Home*. Fawcett Juniper, 1990. Peter Smith, 1992.

———. *Putting Heather Together Again*. Fawcett Juniper, 1989.

———. *Rumors and Whispers*. Fawcett Juniper, 1990.

———. *Touching*. Fawcett, 1988.

Lewis, C. S. *The Horse and His Boy*. Collier, 1970, 1988.

———. *The Last Battle*. Bodley Head/Penguin, 1969. Macmillan, 1988.

———. *The Lion, the Witch and the Wardrobe*. Collier, 1970. Macmillan, 1988.

———. *The Magician's Nephew*. Collier, 1970. Macmillan, 1988.

———. *Out of the Silent Planet*. Macmillan, 1943, 1990.

———. *Prince Caspian*. Collier, 1970. Macmillan, 1988.

———. *The Silver Chair*. Collier, 1970. Macmillan, 1988.

———. *The Voyage of the "Dawn Treader."* Collier, 1970. Macmillan, 1988.

Lewis, E. *Young Fu of the Upper Yangtze*. Winston, 1932. Dell, 1990.

Lewis, P., and D. Rubenstein. *The Human Body*. Grosset & Dunlap, 1971. Bantam, 1972.

Lewis, S. *Main Street*. New American Library, 1980. Buccaneer, 1989.

Lightfood, S. *Balm in Gilead: Journey of a Healer*. Addison-Wesley, 1988.

Likhanov, A. *Shadows across the Sun*. Harper & Row, 1983.

Lind, J. *Counting My Steps.* Macmillan, 1969.

Lindwer, W. *The Last Seven Months of Anne Frank.* Pantheon, 1991. Doubleday, 1992.

Lingard, J. *Across the Barricades.* Nelson, 1973. Penguin, 1973.

Linn, C. F. ed. *The Ages of Mathematics.* 4 vols. Doubleday, 1977.

Linnaeus, Carl. *Travels.* Edited by D. Black. Scribner's, 1979.

Lipsyte, R. *The Brave.* HarperCollins, 1991.

———. *The Contender.* Harper & Row, 1967. HarperCollins, 1987.

———. *Free to Be Muhammad Ali.* Harper & Row, 1978. Bantam, 1980.

———. *One Fat Summer.* Harper & Row, 1977. HarperCollins, 1991.

———. *Summerboy.* Harper & Row, 1982.

———. *Summer Rules.* Harper & Row, 1981. HarperCollins, 1992.

Liston, R. *Politics from Precinct to Presidency.* Delacorte, 1968. Dell, 1970.

Livingston, M. C., ed. *The Malibu and Other Poems.* Atheneum, 1972.

———. *Monkey Puzzle and Other Poems.* Atheneum, 1984.

———. *O Frabjous Day: Poetry for Holidays and Special Occasions.* Atheneum, 1977.

———. *Speak Roughly to Your Little Boy: A Collection of Parodies and Burlesques.* Harcourt Brace Jovanovich, 1971.

———. *What a Wonderful Bird the Frog Are.* Harcourt Brace Jovanovich, 1973.

———. *Why Am I Grown So Cold? Poems of the Unknowable.* Atheneum, 1982.

Llewellyn, R. *How Green Was My Valley.* Macmillan, 1940.

Lofts, N. *Madselin.* Doubleday, 1983.

———. *The Maude Reed Tale.* Nelson, 1972. Dell, 1974.

London, J. *Call of the Wild.* Vintage Books, 1990.

Longfellow, H. W. *Paul Revere's Ride.* Crowell, 1963.

Lopez, B. H. *Giving Birth to Thunder, Sleeping with His Daughter.* Andrews & McMeel, 1977. Avon, 1981.

———. *Of Wolves and Men.* Scribner's, 1978. Macmillan, 1979.

Lord, N. *Survival.* Coffee House Press, 1991.

Lowry, L. *Find a Stranger, Say Goodbye.* Dell, 1990.

———. *Rabble Starkey.* Houghton Mifflin, 1987. Dell, 1988.

Lueders, E., and P. St. John, eds. *Zero Makes Me Hungry.* Lothrop, Lee & Shephard, 1976.

Luger, H. *Lauren.* Viking, 1979. Dell, 1981.

Lund, D. *Eric.* Lippincott, 1974. Dell, 1979.

Lustig, A. *Darkness Casts No Shadow.* Avon, 1978.

———. *Night and Hope.* Hutchinson, 1962. Avon, 1978.

———. *A Prayer for Katerina Horovitzova.* Harper & Row, 1973. Avon, 1975.

Lyle, K. L. *Dark but Full of Diamonds.* Bantam, 1983. Coward, McCann & Geoghegan, 1981.

———. *Fair Day, and Another Step Begun.* Lippincott, 1974.

———. *I Will Go Barefoot All Summer for You.* Lippincott, 1973. Dell, 1974.

———. *The Man Who Wanted Seven Wives.* Algonquin Books, 1986. Dell, 1975.

———. *Scalded to Death by Steam.* Algonquin, 1983.

Lyons, M. E. *Sorrow's Kitchen: The Life and Folklore of Zora Neale Hurston.* Scribner's, 1990.

Macaulay, D. *Castle.* Houghton Mifflin, 1982.

———. *Cathedral: The Story of Its Construction.* Houghton Mifflin, 1981.

———. *City: A Story of Roman Planning and Construction.* Houghton Mifflin, 1983.

———. *Great Moments in Architecture.* Houghton Mifflin, 1978.

———. *Pyramid.* Houghton Mifflin, 1982.

———. *The Way Things Work.* Houghton Mifflin, 1988.

McCaffrey, A. *Crystal Singer.* Ballantine, 1985.

———. *Dragondrums.* Atheneum, 1979. Bantam, 1980.

———. *Dragonsinger.* Atheneum, 1977. Bantam, 1983.

———. *Dragonsong.* Atheneum, 1976. Bantam, 1986.

———. *Killashandra.* Ballantine, 1986.

———. *Moreta: Dragon Lady of Pern.* Ballantine, 1984.

McCarthy, M. *Birds of America.* Harcourt Brace Jovanovich, 1992. Avon, 1981.

McCaughrean, G. *A Little Lower Than the Angels.* Oxford, 1987.

McClung, R. M. *America's Endangered Birds: Programs and People Working to Save Them.* Morrow, 1979.

McCracken, M. *A Circle of Children.* Lippincott, 1973. New American Library, 1975.

McCuaig, S. *Blindfold.* Holiday House, 1990.

McCullers, C. *The Heart Is a Lonely Hunter.* Houghton Mifflin, 1940. Bantam, 1983.

McCullough, C. *The Thorn Birds.* Harper & Row, 1977. Avon, 1978.

McCullough, F., ed. *Earth, Air, Fire and Water*. Charlotte Zolotow/Harper & Row, 1989.

———. *Love Is Like the Lion's Tooth: An Anthology of Love Poems*. Harper & Row, 1984.

McFarlane, M. C. *Cudjoe of Jamaica: Pioneer for Black Freedom in the New World*. Enslow, 1977.

Macguire, J. *Just Friends*. Ivy, 1990.

McGuire, P. *Putting It Together: Teenagers Talk about Family Breakup*. Delacorte, 1987.

McHargue, G. *Funny Bananas: The Mystery in the Museum*. Holt, Rinehart & Winston, 1975. Dell, 1976.

———. *Little Victories, Big Defeats: War as the Ultimate Pollution*. Delacorte, 1974. Dell, 1978.

Mack, J., and H. Hickler. *Vivienne: The Life and Suicide of an Adolescent Girl*. New American Library, 1982.

McKay, R. *The Running Back*. Harcourt Brace Jovanovich, 1979.

———. *The Troublemaker*. Nelson, 1971. Dell, 1972.

McKillip, P. A. *Fool's Run*. Warner, 1988.

———. *The Forgotten Beast of Eld*. Atheneum, 1974. Avon, 1975.

———. *Heir of Sea and Fire*. Atheneum, 1977. Ballantine, 1978, 1987.

———. *Moon-Flash*. Atheneum, 1984.

———. *The Night Gift*. Atheneum, 1976, 1980.

———. *The Riddle-Master of Hed*. Atheneum, 1976. Ballantine, 1985.

McKinley, R. *Beauty: A Retelling of the Story of Beauty and the Beast*. Harper, 1978.

———. *The Blue Sword*. Greenwillow, 1982.

———. *The Dark Is Rising*. Macmillan, 1973.

———. *The Hero and the Crown*. Greenwillow, 1985.

———, ed. *Imaginary Lands*. Greenwillow, 1986.

MacKinnon, B. *Song for a Shadow*. Houghton Mifflin, 1991.

McKissack, P., and F. McKissack. *A Long Hard Journey: The Story of the Pullman-Porter*. Walker, 1989.

McKown, R. *Patriot of the Underground*. Putnam's, 1964.

———. *The World of Mary Cassatt*. Crowell, 1972. Dell, 1976.

McLaughlin, F. *Yukon Journey*. Scholastic, 1991.

Maclean, N. *A River Runs Through It*. University of Chicago Press, 1983.

McLuhan, T. C. *Touch the Earth: A Self-Portrait of Indian Existence*. Dutton, 1971.

McMutry, L. *The Last Picture Show*. Penguin, 1979.

McNab, O. *Horror Story*. Houghton Mifflin, 1979.

McPhee, J. *Encounters with the Archdruid*. Farrar, Straus & Giroux, 1971. Ballantine, 1972.

Madison, W. *Growing Up in a Hurry*. Little, Brown, 1973. Pocket Books, 1975.

———. *Max's Wonderful Delicatessen*. Little, Brown, 1972.

Mahy, M. *Aliens in the Family*. Scholastic, 1985. Dial, 1987.

———. *The Changeover: A Supernatural Romance*. Atheneum, 1984. Scholastic, 1984.

———. *The Door in the Air and Other Stories*. Delacorte, 1991.

———. *Memory*. McElderry, 1986. Macmillan, 1987.

———. *The Tricksters*. Scholastic, 1988.

Maiorano, R. *Worlds Apart: The Autobiography of a Dancer from Brooklyn*. Coward, McCann & Geoghegan, 1980.

Major, K. *Blood Red Ochre*. Delacorte, 1989. Dell, 1990.

———. *Doryloads*. Breakwater, 1974.

———. *Far from Shore*. Delacorte, 1981. Dell, 1983.

———. *Hold Fast*. Delacorte, 1979. Dell, 1981.

———. *Thirty-Six Exposures*. Delacorte, 1984.

Malamud, B. *The Assistant*. Modern Library, 1952. Avon, 1980.

Malcolm X, with A. Haley. *The Autobiography of Malcolm X*. Grove Press, 1965.

Malmgren, D. *The Ninth Issue*. Delacorte, 1989.

———. *The Whole Nine Yards*. Dell, 1987. Delacorte, 1986.

Malory, T. *Le Morte D'Arthur*. 1485. University of California, 1983.

Mandel, D. *Uncommon Eloquence: A Biography of Angna Enters*. Arden Press, 1986.

Mandel, S. *Change of Heart*. Delacorte, 1979. Dell, 1981.

Mango, K. N. *Just for the Summer*. HarperCollins/Zolotow, 1990.

Manley, S., and G. Lewis. *Masters of Macabre*. Doubleday, 1975.

———. *Mistresses of Mystery: Two Centuries of Suspense. Stories by the Gentle Sex*. Lothrop, Lee & Shepard, 1973.

Mansfield, S., and M. B. Hall. *Reasons for War*. Crowell, 1988.

Manvell, Roger. *Films and the Second World War*. Barnes, 1974. Dell, 1976.

March, W. *Company K*. Hill & Wang, 1957. University of Alabama Press, 1989.

Marek, M. *Matt's Crusade*. Knopf, 1989.

Mark, J. *Handles*. Atheneum, 1985. Puffin, 1987.

Marquis, D. M., and R. Sachs. *I Am a Teacher: A Tribute to America's Teachers*. Simon & Schuster, 1990.

Martin, R. G. *President from Missouri: Harry S. Truman.* Messner, 1973.

Martinez, A., ed. *Rising Voices.* New American Library, 1974.

Massler, J. *Jemmy.* Atheneum, 1980.

Matas, C. *Lisa's War.* Macmillan, 1989. Scholastic, 1991.

Mathabane, M. *Kaffir Boy.* Macmillan, 1986. New American Library, 1990.

Mather, M. *One Summer in Between.* Harper & Row, 1967. Avon, 1968.

Mathis, S. B. *Listen for the Fig Tree.* Viking, 1974. Puffin, 1990.

———. *Teacup Full of Roses.* Viking, 1972. Puffin, 1987.

Mayer, M. *They Thought They Were Free: The Germans, 1933–1945.* University of Chicago Press, 1966.

Mayer, M., ed. *A Poison Tree and Other Poems.* Scribner's, 1977.

Mazer, H. *Cave under the City.* Crowell, 1986. HarperCollines, 1989.

———. *City Light.* Scholastic, 1988.

———. *The Girl of His Dreams.* Crowell, 1987. Avon, 1988.

———. *Guy Lenny.* Delacorte, 1971. Dell, 1977.

———. *Hey Kid! Does She Love Me?* Crowell, 1984.

———. *The Island Keeper.* Delacorte, 1981. Dell, 1989.

———. *The Last Mission.* Delacorte, 1979. Dell, 1981.

———. *Snow Bound.* Delacorte, 1973. Dell, 1975.

———. *Someone's Mother Is Missing.* Delacorte, 1990.

———. *The War on Villa Street.* Delacorte, 1978. Dell, 1979.

———. *When the Phone Rang.* Scholastic, 1985.

Mazer, N. F. *After the Rain.* Morrow, 1987. Avon, 1987.

———. *Babyface.* Morrow, 1990. Avon, 1991.

———. *B, My Name Is Bunny.* Scholastic, 1987.

———. *Dear Bill, Remember Me? And Other Stories.* Delacorte, 1976. Dell, 1978.

———. *Downtown.* Morrow, 1984. Avon, 1984.

———. *A Figure of Speech.* Delacorte, 1973. Dell, 1975.

———. *Saturday, the Twelfth of October.* Delacorte, 1975. Dell, 1976.

———. *Silver.* Morrow, 1988. Avon, 1989.

———. *Someone to Love.* Delacorte, 1983. Dell, 1985.

———. *Summer Girls, Love Boys.* Delacorte, 1982.

———. *Taking Terri Mueller.* Avon, 1981.

———. *Three Sisters.* Scholastic, 1986, 1991.

———. *Up in Seth's Room.* Delacorte, 1979.

———. *When We First Met.* Scholastic, 1991.

Mazer, N. F., and M. Lewis, eds. *Waltzing on Water: Poetry by Women.* Dell, 1989.

Mazer, N. F., and H. Mazer. *Heartbeat.* Bantam, 1989.

Means, F. C. *The Moved-Outers.* Houghton Mifflin, 1972.

Medearis, M. *Big Doc's Girl.* Lippincott, 1974. Pyramid, 1974.

Meigs, C. *Jane Addams: Pioneer for Social Justice.* Little, Brown, 1970.

Melton, D. *A Boy Called Hopeless.* Independence Press, 1976. Scholastic, 1977.

Meltzer, M. *The American Promise: Voices of a Changing Nation, 1945–Present.* Bantam, 1990.

———. *The Bill of Rights: How We Got It and What It Means.* Crowell, 1990.

———. *Brother Can You Spare a Dime? The Great Depression, 1929–1933.* New American Library, 1977.

———. *Columbus and the World around Him.* Franklin Watts, 1990.

———. *Never to Forget: The Jews of the Holocaust.* Harper & Row, 1976. Dell, 1977.

———. *Poverty in America.* Morrow, 1986.

———. *Rescue: The Story of How Gentiles Saved Jews in the Holocaust.* Harper & Row, 1988.

———. *Taking Root: Jewish Immigrants in America.* Farrar, Staus & Giroux, 1976. Dell, 1977.

———. *Underground Man.* Bradbury, 1972. Dell, 1974.

———. *Violins and Shovels: The WPA Arts Projects.* Delacorte, 1976.

———. *World of Our Fathers: The Jews of Eastern Europe.* Farrar, Straus & Giroux, 1974. Dell, 1976.

——— ed. *The American Revolutionaries: A History in Their Own Words.* Crowell, 1987.

———. *The Black Americans: A History in Their Own Words, 1619–1983.* Crowell, 1984. Harper & Row, 1987.

———. *Bound for the Rio Grande: The Mexican Struggle, 1845–1850.* Knopf, 1974.

———. *The Chinese Americans: A History in Their Own Words.* HarperCollins, 1980.

———. *In Their Own Words: A History of the American Negro, 1619–1965.* 3 vols. Crowell, 1964–1967.

Melville, H. *Billy Budd.* Penguin, 1986.

———. *Moby Dick.* Vintage, 1991.

Meriwether, L. *Daddy Was a Number Runner.* Prentice-Hall, 1970. Pyramid, 1974.

Merriam, E., ed. *Growing Up Female in America: Ten Lives.* Doubleday, 1971. Dell, 1973.

———. *If Only I Could Tell You: Poems for Young Lovers and Dreamers.* Knopf, 1983.

Merrill, J., and R. Solbert, eds. *A Few Flies and I.* Pantheon, 1969.

Mersand, J., ed. *Great Modern American Short Biographies.* Dell, 1966.

Meyer, C. *C. C. Poindexter.* Atheneum, 1978.

———. *Voices of South Africa.* Harcourt Brace Jovanovich, 1986.

Michaels, B. *Wait for What Will Come.* Fawcett, 1978.

———. *Witch.* Dodd, Mead, 1973. Fawcett, 1989.

Michener, J. A. *Chesapeake.* Fawcett, 1978.

———. *Hawaii.* Random House, 1959. Fawcett, 1973.

———. *Kent State: What Happened and Why.* Fawcett, 1978.

Miklowitz, G. D. *After the Bomb.* Scholastic, 1985.

———. *The Day the Senior Class Got Married.* Delacorte, 1983.

———. *Did You Hear What Happened to Andrea?* Delacorte/Dell, 1979.

———. *Good-Bye Tomorrow.* Delacorte, 1987. Dell, 1988.

———. *The Love Bombers.* Delacorte, 1981. Dell, 1980.

———. *Love Story, Take Three.* Delacorte, 1986.

———. *Standing Tall, Looking Good.* Delacorte, 1991.

———. *The War between the Classes.* Delacorte, 1985. Dell, 1986.

Miles, B. *The Trouble with Thirteen.* Knopf, 1979. Avon, 1980.

Millay, E. S. V. *Poems Selected for Young People.* Harper & Row, 1979.

Miller, A. *The Crucible.* Viking, 1973. Penguin, 1976.

———. *Death of a Salesman.* Viking, 1981.

———. *Tropic of Capricorn.* Obelisk Press, 1939. Grove, 1965.

Miller, F. A. *Aren't You the One Who . . .?* Atheneum, 1983.

———. *Cutting Loose.* Fawcett Juniper, 1991.

———. *Losers and Winners.* Ballantine, 1986.

———. *The Truth Trap.* Dutton, 1980. Fawcett Juniper, 1984.

Miller, J. W. *Newfound.* Orchard, 1989.

Miller, R. *Robyn's Book, a True Diary.* Scholastic, 1990.

Miller, R. H. *Cowboys.* Silver Burdett, 1991.

Miller, W. M. *A Canticle for Leibowitz.* Lippincott, 1959. Bantam, 1980.

Millhiser, M. *The Mirror.* Putnam, 1978.

Mills, J. F. *Treasure Keepers.* Doubleday, 1973.

Mirer, M., ed. *Modern Black Stories.* Barron, 1971.

Mitchell, A. *Wildlife of the Rainforest.* Mallard Press, 1989.

Mitchell, J. S. *I Can Be Anything: Careers and Colleges for Young Women.* Bantam, 1978. College Examination Board, 1978.

———. *The Men's Career Book: Work and Life Planning for a New Age.* Bantam, 1979.

———. *Other Choices for Becoming a Woman.* Know, 1974. Dell, 1975.

———. *The Work Book: A Guide to Skilled Jobs.* Sterling, 1978. Bantam.

Mitchell, M. *Gone with the Wind.* Macmillan, 1936. Avon, 1976.

Moeri, L. *Downwind.* Dutton, 1984.

———. *The Forty-Third War.* Houghton Mifflin, 1989.

———. *Save Queen of Sheba.* Dutton, 1981. Avon, 1982.

Mohr, N. *In Nueva York.* Delacorte, 1977. Dell, 1979.

Momaday, N. S. *House Made of Dawn.* Harper & Row, 1977.

Monroe, J. G., and R. A. Williamson. *They Dance in the Sky: Native American Star Myths.* Houghton Mifflin, 1987.

Montgomery, R. A. *Traitors from Within.* Bantam, 1990.

Moody, A. *Coming of Age in Mississippi.* Dial, 1968. Dell, 1980.

Moore, Y. *Freedom Songs.* Orchard, 1991.

More, T. *Utopia.* AHM Publishing, 1949. NAL/Signet Classic.

Morey, W. *Canyon Winter.* Dutton, 1972.

Morgan, A. *The Eyes of the Blind.* Oxford University Press, 1986.

Morgan, R. *At the Edge of the Orchard Country.* Wesleyan University Press, 1987. Distributed by Harper & Row.

Morrell, D. *First Blood.* Evans, 1972.

———. *The Totem.* Evans, 1979. Ballantine, 1985.

Morris, D. *The Naked Ape.* McGraw-Hill, 1967. Dell, 1984.

Morris, J. *Brian Piccolo: A Short Season.* Rand McNally, 1971. Dell, 1972.

Morrison, L. *The Break Dance Kids: Poems of Sports, Motion and Locomotion.* Lothrop, Lee & Shepard, 1984.

———. *Overheard in a Bubble Chamber and Other Science Poems.* Lothrop, Lee & Shepard, 1981.

———. *The Sidewalk Racer and Other Poems of Sports and Motion.* Lothrop, Lee & Shepard, 1977.

————. *Sprints and Distances: Sports in Poetry and the Poetry in Sports.* Crowell, 1965.

Morrison, L., ed. *Best Wishes, Amen: A New Collection of Autograph Verses.* Crowell, 1974.

Morrison, T. *Beloved.* Knopf, 1987. Signet Classic, 1991.

Morse, D., ed. *Grandfather Rock.* Delacorte, 1972. Dell, 1974.

Moser, D. *A Heart to the Hawks.* Atheneum, 1975.

Moskin, M. D. *I Am Rosemarie.* John Day, 1972. Dell, 1987.

Mosse, G. L., ed. *Nazi Culture: Intellectual, Cultural, and Social Life in the Third Reich.* Grosset & Dunlap, 1966.

Mowat, F. *The Boat Who Wouldn't Float.* Little, Brown, 1970. Bantam, 1981.

————. *The Dog Who Wouldn't Be.* Little, Brown, 1957. Bantam, 1981.

————. *Never Cry Wolf.* Little, Brown, 1963. Bantam, 1979.

————. *A Whale for the Killing.* Little, Brown, 1972. Bantam, 1981.

Murphy, J. *The Boys' War: Confederate and Union Soldiers Talk about the Civil War.* Clarion, 1990.

Murphy, S. R. *The Dragonbards.* Harper & Row, 1989.

Murray, M. *The Crystal Nights.* Seabury, 1973.

Myers, W. D. *Crystal.* Viking, 1987.

————. *Fallen Angels.* Scholastic, 1988.

————. *Fast Sam, Cool Clyde, and Stuff.* Viking, 1975. Avon, 1978.

————. *Hoops.* Delacorte, 1981.

————. *It Ain't All for Nothin'.* Viking, 1978. Avon, 1979.

————. *The Legend of Tarik.* Viking, 1981.

————. *Malcolm X: By Any Means Necessary.* Scholastic, 1993.

————. *Me, Mop and the Moondance Kid.* Delacorte, 1988.

————. *Mojo and the Russians.* Viking, 1977. Avon, 1977.

————. *Mop, Moondance, and the Nagasaki Knights.* Delacorte, 1992.

————. *Motown and Didi: A Love Story.* Viking, 1984.

————. *The Mouse Rap.* Harper & Row, 1990.

————. *Now Is Your Time! The African-American Struggle for Freedom.* HarperCollins, 1991.

————. *Scorpions.* Harper, 1990.

————. *Somewhere in the Darkness.* Scholastic, 1992.

————. *Tales of a Dead King.* Morrow, 1983.

————. *The Young Landlords.* Viking, 1979.

Nabokov, P., ed. *Native American Testimony: An Anthology of Indian and White Relations, First Encounter to Dispossession.* HarperCollins, 1972.

Naidoo, B. *Chain of Fire.* Lippincott, 1990.

Nash, O. *Pocket Book of Ogden Nash.* Pocket Books, 1963.

Nash, R. *From These Beginnings.* Harper & Row, 1973.

Naughton, J. *My Brother Stealing Second.* Harper & Row, 1991.

Naylor, P. R. *The Keeper.* Macmillan, 1986. Bantam, 1987.

————. *Night Cry.* Atheneum, 1984.

————. *Send No Blessings.* Atheneum, 1990.

Nelson, T. *And One for All.* Dell, 1991.

Neufeld, J. *Edgar Allan.* Phillips, 1968. New American Library, 1969.

————. *Sleep Two, Three, Four!.* Harper & Row, 1971. Avon, 1972.

————. *Sunday Father.* New American Library, 1976.

Newell, H. *A Cap for Mary Ellis.* Harper & Row, 1953. Berkley, 1969.

————. *Mary Ellis, Student Nurse.* Harper & Row, 1958. Berkley, 1966.

Newton, S. *I Will Call It Georgie's Blues.* Viking, 1983. Dell, 1986.

Ney, J. *Ox: The Story of a Kid at the Top.* Little, Brown, 1970. Bantam, 1971.

Niatum, D., ed. *Harper's Anthology of Twentieth-Century Native American Poetry.* Harper & Row, 1988.

Nixon, J. L. *A Candidate for Murder.* Delacorte, 1991.

————. *Caught in the Act.* Bantam, 1988, 1989.

————. *A Family Apart.* Bantam, 1987, 1988.

————. *The Ghosts of Now.* Dell, 1984.

————. *High Trail to Danger.* Bantam Starfire, 1991.

————. *In the Face of Danger.* Bantam, 1988, 1989.

————. *The Kidnapping of Christina Lattimore.* Harcourt Brace Jovanovich, 1979. Dell, 1980.

————. *A Place to Belong.* Bantam, 1990.

————. *The Seance.* Harcourt Brace Jovanovich, 1980. Dell, 1981.

————. *The Weekend Was Murder.* Delacorte, 1992.

Nolan, W. F., and G. C. Johnson. *Logan's Run.* Dial, 1967. Dell, 1969.

Nolen, W. *The Making of a Surgeon.* Random House, 1970. Dell, 1980.

Norton, A. *Here Abide Monsters.* Atheneum, 1973. Daw, 1974.

————. *Huon of the Horn.* Harcourt Brace, 1951. Fawcett Crest, 1980.

Norton, A., and M. H. Greenberg, eds. *Catfantastic.* DAW Books, 1989.

Nye, N. S. *Hugging the Jukebox.* 2d ed. Breitenbush, 1984.

Nye, R. *Beowulf: A New Telling.* Hill & Wang, 1968. Dell, 1982.

O'Brien, R. *Z for Zachariah.* Atheneum, 1975. Dell, 1977.

O'Brien, T. *If I Die in a Combat Zone, Box Me Up and Ship Me Home.* Delacorte, 1973. Dell, 1979.

O'Dell, Scott. *The Amethyst Ring.* Houghton Mifflin, 1983.

———. *The Black Pearl.* Houghton Mifflin, 1967.

———. *Black Star, Bright Dawn.* Fawcett, 1990.

———. *The Captive.* Houghton Mifflin, 1979.

———. *Carlota.* Houghton Mifflin, 1977.

———. *The Castle in the Sea.* Houghton Mifflin, 1983.

———. *The Feathered Serpent.* Houghton Mifflin, 1981.

———. *The Hawk That Dare Not Hunt by Day.* Houghton Mifflin, 1975.

———. *Island of the Blue Dolphins.* Houghton Mifflin, 1960. Dell, 1978.

———. *Kathleen, Please Come Home.* Houghton Mifflin, 1978. Dell, 1980.

———. *The King's Fifth.* Houghton Mifflin, 1966. Dell, 1978.

———. *My Name Is Not Angelica.* Houghton Mifflin, 1989.

———. *The Road to Damietta.* Houghton Mifflin, 1985.

———. *Sarah Bishop.* Houghton Mifflin, 1980.

———. *The Serpent Never Sleeps.* Houghton Mifflin, 1987. Fawcett, 1989.

———. *Sing Down the Moon.* Houghton Mifflin, 1970. Dell, 1970.

———. *The Spanish Smile.* Houghton Mifflin, Mifflin, 1966.

———. *Streams to the River; River to the Sea.* Houghton Mifflin, 1986. Ballantine, 1988.

———. *The 290.* Houghton Mifflin, 1976. Dell, 1979.

Ogilvie, E. *The Pigeon Pair.* McGraw-Hill, 1967.

Okada, J. *No-No Boy.* University of Washington Press, 1981.

Okimoto, J. D. *Molly by Any Other Name.* Scholastic, 1990.

Olsen, T. *Silences.* Delacorte, 1978.

Oneal, Z. *A Formal Feeling.* Ballantine, 1982.

———. *In Summer Light.* Viking, 1985. Bantam, 1986.

———. *The Language of Goldfish.* Viking, 1980.

Orgel, Doris. *Crack in the Heart.* Juniper, 1989.

———. *The Devil in Vienna.* Dial, 1978.

———. *Risking Love.* Dial, 1985.

Orwell, G. *Animal Farm.* New American Library, 1974.

———. *1984.* New American Library, 1981.

Osen, L. *Women in Mathematics.* MIT Press, 1974.

Overton, J. *The Ship from Simnel Street.* Faber & Faber, 1986. Greenwillow, 1986.

Oz, A. *Elsewhere, Perhaps.* Translated by N. DeLange. Harcourt Brace Jovanovich, 1973. Penguin, 1979.

Park, R. *My Sister Sif.* Viking, 1991.

Parker, R. *A Time to Choose.* Harper & Row, 1974.

Parks, G. *The Learning Tree.* Harper & Row, 1963. Fawcett World, 1970.

Parlin, John. *Amelia Earhart.* Dell, 1976.

Pascal, F. *Hangin' Out with Cici.* Viking, 1977. Pocket Books, 1978.

Pasternak, B. L. *Doctor Zhivago.* Pantheon, 1958. Knopf, 1991.

Patent, D. H. *The Challenge of Extinction.* Enslow, 1991.

———. *Evolution Goes on Every Day.* Holiday, 1977.

———. *The Quest for Artificial Intelligence.* Harcourt Brace Jovanovich, 1986.

Paterson, K. *Bridge to Terabithia.* Crowell, 1977. Avon, 1979.

———. *Come Sing, Jimmy Jo.* Dutton, 1985. Avon, 1985.

———. *The Great Gilly Hopkins.* Crowell, 1978. Avon, 1979.

———. *Jacob Have I Loved.* Harper & Row, 1980. Avon, 1981.

———. *Lyddie.* Dutton, 1991.

———. *The Master Puppeteer.* Crowell, 1975. Avon, 1981.

———. *Of Nightingales That Weep.* Crowell, 1974. Avon, 1980.

———. *Park's Quest.* Puffin, 1988.

Paton, A. *Cry, the Beloved Country.* Scribner's, 1948.

———. *The Land and People of South Africa.* Lippincott, 1955, 1964.

———. *Too Late the Phalarope.* Scribner's, 1953.

Paton, J. *The Land and People of South Africa.* Lippincott, 1990.

Patterson, S. *The Distant Swimmer.* Simon & Schuster, 1976.

Paul, C. *A Child Is Missing.* Putnam, 1970. Berkley, 1978.

Paulsen, G. *Canyons.* Delacorte, 1990.

———. *The Cookcamp.* Orchard, 1991.

———. *The Crossing.* Orchard Books, 1987. Dell, 1990.

———. *Dancing Carl.* Puffin, 1987.

———. *The Foxman.* Scholastic, 1991.

————. *Hatchet.* Bradbury, 1987. Penguin, 1988.

————. *The Haymeadow.* Doubleday, 1992.

————. *The Island.* Orchard, 1988.

————. *The Monument.* Delacorte, 1991.

————. *The Night the White Deer Died.* Delacorte, 1990.

————. *The River.* Delacorte, 1991.

————. *Sentries.* Bradbury, 1986.

————. *Tracker.* Macmillan, 1984.

————. *The Winter Room.* Orchard, 1989. Dell, 1989.

————. *Woodsong.* Bradbury, 1990.

Peck, R. *Are You in the House Alone?* Viking, 1976. Dell, 1978.

————. *Blossom Culp and the Sleep of Death.* Delacorte, 1986.

————. *Don't Look and It Won't Hurt.* Holt, Rinehart & Winston, 1972.

————. *The Dreadful Future of Blossom Culp.* Delacorte, 1983; Dell, 1984.

————. *Dreamland Lake.* Holt, Rinehart & Winston, 1973. Avon, 1973.

————. *Father Figure.* Viking, 1978. New American Library, 1979.

————. *The Ghost Belonged to Me.* Viking, 1975. Dell, 1978.

————. *Ghosts I Have Been.* Viking, 1977. Dell, 1979.

————. *Remembering the Good Times.* Delacorte, 1985.

————. *Secrets of the Shopping Mall.* Delacorte, 1979. Dell, 1980.

————. *Those Summer Girls I Never Met.* Delacorte, 1988.

————. *Through a Brief Darkness.* Viking, 1973.

————. *Unfinished Portrait of Jessica.* Delacorte, 1991.

————. *Voices after Midnight.* Delacorte, 1989.

Peck, R., ed. *Mindscapes.* Dell, 1971.

————. *Pictures That Storm Inside My Head.* Avon, 1976.

————. *Sounds and Silences.* Delacorte, 1970. Dell, 1970.

Peck, R. N. *A Day No Pigs Would Die.* Knopf, 1972. Dell, 1978.

————. *Eagle Fur.* Knopf, 1978. Avon, 1979.

————. *Fawn: A Novel.* Little, Brown, 1975. Dell, 1979.

————. *Soup.* Knopf, 1974. Dell, 1979.

————. *Soup and Me.* Knopf, 1975. Dell, 1979.

Perl, L. *That Crazy April.* Seabury, 1974. Houghton Mifflin, 1980.

Perrin, L. *Coming to America: Immigrants from the Far East.* Delacorte, 1980. Dell, 1981.

Petersen, P. J. *The Boll Weevil Express.* Dell, 1984.

————. *Corky and the Brothers Cool.* Delacorte, 1985.

————. *The Freshman Detective Blues.* Dell, 1989.

————. *Would You Settle for Improbable?* Delacorte, 1981. Dell, 1985.

Petry, A. *Harriett Tubman, Conductor on the Underground Railroad.* Crowell, 1955. Archway, 1971.

Pettepiece, T., and A. Aleksin, eds. *Face to Face: A Collection of Stories by Celebrated Soviet and American Writers.* Philomel, 1990.

Pevsner, S. *And You Give Me a Pain, Elaine.* Seabury, 1978. Pocket Books, 1981.

————. *How Could You Do It, Diane?* Clarion, 1989.

Peyton, K. M. *The Beethoven Medal.* Crowell, 1971. Scholastic, 1974.

————. *Darkling.* Delacorte, 1990.

————. *A Midsummer Night's Death.* Philomel, 1979. Dell, 1981.

Pfeffer, S. B. *About David.* Delacorte, 1980. Dell, 1982.

————. *A Matter of Principle.* Delacorte, 1982.

————. *Turning Thirteen.* Scholastic, 1988.

Phelan, M. D. *Probing the Unknown: The Story of Dr. Florence Sabin.* Crowell, 1969. Dell, 1976.

Phleger, M. *Pilot Down, Presumed Dead.* Harper & Row, 1963.

Pierce, M. A. *The Darkangel.* Little, Brown, 1982.

————. *A Gathering of Gargoyles.* Little, Brown, 1984.

————. *The Woman Who Loved Reindeer.* Atlantic, 1985.

Piers, A. *A Spell for Chameleon.* Ballantine, 1977.

Pinkwater, D. M. *Alan Mendelson, the Boy from Mars.* Dalton, 1979. Bantam, 1981.

————. *Lizard Music.* Dodd, Mead, 1976. Dell, 1979.

————. *The Snarkout Boys and the Avocado of Death.* Lothrop, Lee & Shepard, 1982.

————. *The Snarkout Boys and the Baconburg Horror.* Lothrop, Lee & Shepard, 1984.

Pizer, V. *Glorious Triumphs: Athletes Who Conquered Adversity.* Dodd, Mead, 1980.

Place, M. T. *The Resident Witch.* Washburn, 1970. Avon, 1973.

Plath, S. *Colossus and Other Poems.* Knopf, 1962. Vintage, 1968.

Platt, K. *The Boy Who Could Make Himself Disappear.* Chilton, 1968. Dell, 1972.

————. *Brogg's Brain.* Lippincott, 1981.

————. *Chloris and the Creeps.* Chilton, 1973. Dell, 1974.

————. *Chloris and the Freaks.* Bradbury, 1975. Bantam, 1976.

———. *Chloris and the Wierdos.* Bradbury, 1978. Bantam, 1980.

———. *Hey, Dummy.* Chilton, 1971. Dell, 1973.

———. *The Terrible Love Life of Dudley Cornflower.* Bradbury, 1976.

Plotz, H., ed. *Eye's Delight: Poems of Art and Architecture.* Greenwillow, 1983.

———. *Gladly Learn and Gladly Teach: Poems of the School Experience.* Greenwillow, 1981.

———. *Imagination's Other Place: Poems of Science and Mathematics.* Crowell, 1955.

———. *Saturday's Children: Poems of Work.* Greenwillow, 1982.

Poe, E. A. *Eighteen Best Stories by Edgar Allan Poe.* Edited by R. Wilbur. Dell, 1974.

Polk, D. *The Linnet Estate.* McKay, 1974.

Pomeroy, W. B. *Girls and Sex.* Delacorte, 1970. Dell, 1981.

Pople, M. *A Nugget of Gold.* Knopf, 1990.

Potok, C. *The Chosen.* Simon & Schuster, 1967. Fawcett, 1968. Ballantine, 1982.

———. *Davita's Harp.* Knopf, 1985. Fawcett, 1986.

———. *My Name Is Asher Lev.* Knopf, 1972. Fawcett, 1972.

Powell, P. *Edisto.* Farrar, Straus & Grioux, 1984.

Powers, J. R. *Do Black Patent Leather Shoes Really Reflect Up?* Regnery, 1975. Popular Library, 1976.

Poynter, M. *A Time Too Swift.* Atheneum, 1990.

Prago, A. *Strangers in Their Own Land: A History of Mexican Americans.* Four Winds, 1973.

Presley, P., et al., as told to Martin Torgoff. *Elvis, We Love You Tender.* Delacorte, 1980. Dell, 1981.

Preussler, O. *The Satanic Mill.* Translated by A. Bell. Macmillan, 1973.

Price, C. *Made in Ancient Egypt.* Dutton, 1970.

———. *Made in Ancient Greece.* Dutton, 1967.

———. *Made in the Middle Ages.* Dutton, 1961.

———. *Made in the Renaissance: Arts and Crafts of the Age of Exploration.* Dutton, 1963.

———. *Made in West Africa.* Dutton, 1975.

———. *The Story of Moslem Art.* Dutton, 1964.

Pringle, L. *Lives at Stake.* Macmillan, 1980.

———. *What Shall We Do with the Land? Choices for America.* Crowell, 1981.

Pullman, P. *The Ruby in the Smoke.* Knopf, 1987.

———. *The Shadow in the North.* Knopf, 1988.

———. *The Tiger in the Well.* Knopf, 1990.

Pyke, M. *Butter Side Up! The Delights of Science.* Sterling, 1977.

Quarles, B. *Black Abolitionists.* Oxford University Press, 1969.

Quimby, M. *White Crow.* Criterion, 1970.

Quinn, J. B. *Everyone's Money Book.* Delacorte, 1979. Dell, 1980.

Rabe, B. *The Girl Who Had No Name.* Dutton, 1977. Bantam, 1979.

Rabin, G. *The Changes.* Harper & Row, 1973.

Rabinowitz, A. *Bethie.* Macmillan, 1989.

Rabinowitz, D. *New Lives: Survivors of the Holocaust Living in America.* Knopf, 1976.

Randall, D., ed. *The Black Poets.* Bantam, 1976.

Rappaport, D., ed. *American Women: Their Lives in Their Words.* Crowell, 1990.

———. *Escape from Slavery: Five Journeys to Freedom.* HarperCollins, 1991.

Raskin, E. *The Westing Game.* Dutton, 1978. Avon, 1980.

Raucher, H. *Summer of '42.* Putnam's, 1971.

Rawls, W. *Summer of the Monkeys.* Doubleday, 1976. Dell, 1979.

———. *Where the Red Fern Grows.* Macmillan, 1961. Bantam, 1981.

Ray, D. *Behind the Blue and Gray: The Soldier's Life in the Civil War.* Lodestar, 1991.

———. *A Nation Torn: The Story of How the Civil War Began.* Lodestar, 1990.

Ray, M. *The Ideas of April.* Farrar, Straus & Giroux, 1975. Lodestar, 1990.

Reid, R. W. *Marie Curie.* Saturday Review Press, 1974.

Reiss, J. *The Upstairs Room.* Crowell, 1972. Bantam, 1973.

Reit, A. *Alone Amid All This Noise: A Collection of Women's Poetry.* Four Winds, 1976.

Reuter, B. *Buster's World.* Dutton, 1990.

Rhodes, R. H., ed. *All for the Union: The Civil War Diary and Letters of Elisha Hunt Rhodes.* Crown, 1991.

Rhue, M. [T. Strasser]. *The Wave.* Dell, 1981. Delacorte, 1981.

Richard, A. *Pistol.* Little, Brown, 1969. Dell, 1970.

Richards, A., and I. Willis. *How to Get Together When Your Parents Are Coming Apart.* Bantam, 1977.

Richter, C. *A Country of Strangers.* Knopf, 1972.

———. *Light in the Forest.* Knopf, 1953. Bantam, 1971.

Richter, E. *Losing Someone You Love: When a Brother or Sister Dies.* Putnam, 1986.

Richter, H. P. *Friedrich.* Holt, Rinehart & Winston, 1970.

———. *I Was There.* Dell, 1973.

Rinaldi, A. *But in the Fall I'm Leaving.* Holiday House, 1985.

————. *Ride into Morning: The Story of Tempe Wick.* Harcourt Brace Jovanovich, 1991.

————. *Time Enough for Drums.* Holiday House, 1986.

————. *Wolf by the Ears.* Scholastic, 1991.

Roberts, D. *Deborah: A Wilderness Narrative.* Vanguard, 1970.

————. *The Mountain of My Fear.* Vanguard, 1968.

Roberts, N. *These Are the Best Years?* Fawcett, 1989.

————. *With Love, from Sam and Me.* Fawcett Juniper, 1990.

Robertson, D. *The Sum and Total of Now.* Putnam's, 1966.

Robinson, B. *The Best Christmas Pageant Ever.* Harper & Row, 1972. Avon, 1979.

Robinson, M. A. *A Woman of Her Tribe.* Scribner's, 1990.

Robinson, S., and J. Robinson. *Stardance.* Dial, 1979. Dell, 1980.

Rockwell, T. *How to Eat Fried Worms.* Franklin Watts, 1973. Dell, 1980.

Rockwood, J. *Long Man's Song.* Holt, Rinehart & Winston, 1975. Dell, 1978.

————. *To Spoil the Sun.* Holt, Rinehart & Winston, 1976. Dell, 1979.

Rofes, E. E. *Socrates, Plato, and Guys Like Me: Confessions of a Gay Schoolteacher.* Alyson, 1985.

Rogasky, B. *Smoke and Ashes: The Story of the Holocaust.* Holiday House, 1988.

Rogers, T. *At the Shores.* Simon & Schuster, 1980.

Rose, M. *Lives on the Boundary: The Struggles and Achievements of America's Underprepared.* Collier Macmillan, 1989.

Rosen, W. *Cruisin' for a Bruisin'.* Knopf, 1976. Dell, 1977.

Rosenthal, T. *How Could I Not Be Among You?* Avon, 1973.

Roth, A. *The Iceberg Hermit.* Four Winds, 1974. Scholastic, 1974.

Ruby, L. *Arriving at a Place You've Never Left.* Dial, 1977. Dell, 1980.

————. *This Old Man.* Houghton Mifflin, 1984. Ballantine, 1987.

Ruckman, I. *No Way Out.* Harper, 1989.

Ruesch, H. *Back to the Top of the World.* Scribner's, 1973. Ballantine, 1974.

Russ, L. *The April Age.* Atheneum, 1975.

Russell, T., and R. Russell. *On the Loose.* Sierra Club, 1969.

Ryden, H. *America's Last Wild Horses.* Dutton, 1978.

————. *God's Dog.* Coward, McCann & Geoghegan, 1975. Viking, 1979.

————. *Mustangs: A Return to the Wild.* Viking, 1972.

Rylant, C. *A Kindness.* Orchard Books, 1988. Dell, 1990.

Sachar, L. *Dogs Don't Tell Jokes.* Knopf, 1991.

————. *There's a Boy in the Girl's Bathroom.* Knopf, 1988.

Sachs, M. *The Fat Girl.* Dutton, 1984.

————. *A Pocket Full of Seeds.* Doubleday, 1973.

Sagan, C. *Cosmos.* Random House, 1980.

Sahandi, L. *All-Time Basketball Stars.* Scholastic.

St. George, J. *Haunted.* Putnam's 1980. Bantam, 1982.

Salassi, O. R. *Jimmy D., Sidewinder, and Me.* Greenwillow, 1987.

————. *And Nobody Knew They Were There.* Greenwillow, 1984.

Salinger, J. D. *The Catcher in the Rye.* Little, Brown, 1951. New American Library, 1962.

Salisbury, G. *Blue Skin of the Sea: A Novel in Stories.* Doubleday, 1972.

Sallis, S. *Only Love.* Harper & Row, 1980.

Salzman, M. *Iron and Silk.* Random House, 1986.

Samson, J. G. *The Pond.* Knopf, 1979.

Sandburg, C. *Abraham Lincoln.* 6 vols. Scribner's, 1926–1939.

Sanders, M. K. *Dorothy Thompson: A Legend in Her Time.* Houghton Mifflin, 1973.

Sandoz, M. *These Were the Sioux.* Hastings, 1961. Dell, 1971.

Sargent, P. *Alien Child.* Harper & Row, 1988.

Saroyan, W. *The Human Comedy.* Harcourt, Brace, 1943, 1971.

Savage, D. *A Rumor of Otters.* Houghton Mifflin, 1986.

Savitz, H. M. *On the Move.* Day, 1973. Avon, 1979.

Sayers, G., with A. Silverman. *I Am Third.* Viking, 1970. Bantam, 1972.

Schaeffer, S. F. *Anya.* Macmillan, 1974.

Schami, R. *A Hand Full of Stars.* Dutton, 1990.

Schell, J. *The Fate of the Earth.* Knopf, 1982.

Schlossberg, E., and J. Brockman. *Pocket Calculator Game Book.* Morrow, 1975. Bantam, 1976.

————. *Pocket Calculator Game Book 2.* Morrow, 1977. Bantam, 1977.

Schoenberner, G. *The Yellow Star: The Persecution of the Jews in Europe, 1933–1945.* Bantam, 1973.

Schotter. *A Matter of Time.* Collins, 1979. Grossett & Dunlap, 1981.

Schulman, J., A. Shatter, and R. Ehrlich. *Pride and Protest: Ethnic Roots in America.* Dell, 1977.

Schulman, L. M. ed. *The Random House Book of Sport Stories.* Random House, 1990.

Schwartz, A. *Cross Your Fingers, Spit in Your Hat: Superstitions and Other Beliefs.* Lippincott, 1974.

————. *Scary Stories to Tell in the Dark.* Lippincott, 1981.

————. *Tomfoolery: Trickery and Foolery with Words.* Lippincott, 1973. Bantam, 1976.

————. *A Twister of Twists, a Tangler of Tongues: Tongue Twisters.* Lippincott, 1972. Bantam, 1977.

————. *Whoppers: Tall Tales and Other Lies.* Lippincott, 1975.

————. *Witcracks: Jokes and Jests from American Folklore.* Lippincott, 1973. Bantam, 1977.

Schwartz, J. L., A. MacFarlane, and A. McPherson. *Will the Nurse Make Me Take My Underwear Off?* Dell, 1990.

Schwartz, S. *Growing Up Guilty.* Pantheon, 1978.

Schwartz-Bart, A. *The Last of the Just.* Atheneum, 1960.

Scoppettone, S. *Happy Endings Are All Alike.* Harper & Row, 1978. Dell, 1979.

————. *The Late Great Me.* Putnam's 1976. Bantam, 1977.

————. *Playing Murder.* Harper & Row, 1985.

————. *Trying Hard to Hear You.* Harper & Row, 1974. Bantam, 1976.

Scott, J. A. *Fanny Kemble's America.* Crowell, 1973. Dell, 1975.

Scott, W., Sir. *Ivanhoe.* Many editions available.

Sebestyen, O. *Far from Home.* Little, Brown, 1980.

————. *On Fire.* Atlantic Monthly Press, 1985.

————. *Words by Heart.* Little, Brown, 1979. Bantam, 1981, 1983.

Segal, E. *Love Story.* Harper & Row, 1970. Avon, 1977.

Seidman, L. *Once in the Saddle: The Cowboy's Frontier, 1866–1896.* Knopf, 1973. New American Library, 1977.

Seilig, B. *The Last Legal Spitball and Other Little-Known Facts about Sports.* Doubleday, 1975.

Sendak, M. *Where the Wild Things Are.* Harper & Row, 1963.

Sender, R. M. *The Cage.* Macmillan, 1986. Bantam, 1988.

Service, P. F. *The Reluctant God.* Atheneum, 1988. Fawcett, 1990.

————. *Vision Quest.* Atheneum, 1989.

Sevela, E. translated by A. Bouis. *We Were Not Like Other People.* Harper & Row, 1989.

Severn, B. *Impromptu Magic.* Scribner's, 1984.

Shakespeare, W. *The Comedy of Errors.* NAL/Signet Classic.

————. *Macbeth.* NAL/Signet Classic.

————. *Othello: The Moor of Venice.* NAL/Signet Classic.

————. *Romeo and Juliet.* New American Library/Signet Classic.

————. *The Tempest.* NAL/Signet Classic.

Shange, N. *Nappy Edges.* St. Martin's, 1978. Bantam, 1980.

Shannon, G. *Unlived Affections.* Harper & Row, 1989.

Shelley, M. *Frankenstein: Cartoons and Caricatures.* Bantam, 1978.

Shelley, N. *Family at the Lookout.* Oxford University Press, 1972.

Sherburne, Z. *Too Bad about the Haines Girl.* Morrow, 1967.

Sherman, D. R. *The Lion's Paw.* Doubleday, 1974.

Shettle, A. *Flute Song Magic.* Avon, 1990.

Shirer, W. L. *The Rise and Fall of Adolf Hitler.* Random House, 1884.

Shreve, S. *Loveletters.* Knopf, 1978. Bantam, 1981.

————. *The Masquerade.* Knopf, 1980. Dell, 1981.

Shura, M. F. *Gentle Annie: The True Story of a Civil War Nurse.* Scholastic, 1991.

Shusterman, N. *What Daddy Did.* Little, Brown, 1991.

Siebert, W. H. *The Underground Railway from Slavery to Freedom.* Macmillan, 1898. Arno Press and the *New York Times,* 1968.

Siegal, A. *Grace in the Wilderness.* Farrar, Straus & Giroux, 1985. Signet, 1987.

————. *Upon the Head of the Goat.* Farrar, Straus & Giroux, 1981.

Silsbee, P. *The Big Way Out.* Bradbury, 1984. Dell, 1987.

Silverberg, R. *Letters from Atlantis.* Atheneum/Dragonflight, 1990.

————. *Lord Valentine's Castle.* Harper & Row, 1980. Bantam, 1981.

Silverberg, R., ed. *The Auk, the Dodo and the Oryz: Vanished and Vanishing Creatures.* Crowell, 1967.

————. *Men and Machines.* Hawthorne, 1968.

Silverman, D. L. *Your Move.* McGraw-Hill, 1971.

Silverstein, S. *A Light in the Attic.* Harper & Row, 1981.

————. *Where the Sidewalk Ends.* Harper & Row, 1974.

Simak, C. D. *Mastodonia.* Ballantine, 1978.

Simon, W. *Mathematical Magic.* Scribner's, 1964.

Six Great Modern Plays. Dell, 1967.

Skarmeta, A. *Burning Patience.* Pantheon, 1987.

Sleator, W. *The Boy Who Reversed Himself.* Dutton, 1986.

———. *The Duplicate*. Bantam, 1990.

———. *House of Stairs*. Dutton, 1974. Avon, 1975.

———. *Interstellar Pig*. Dutton, 1984.

———. *Singularity*. Dutton, 1985.

———. *The Spirit House*. Dutton, 1991.

———. *Strange Attractors*. Dutton, 1990.

Slepian, J. *Something beyond Paradise*. Philomel, 1987.

Smith, G. *The Horns of the Moon: A Short Biography of Adolf Hitler*. Charterhouse, 1973. Dell, 1975.

Smith, G. O. *The Fourth "R."* Ballantine, 1959. Dell, 1979.

Smith, P. *Forever Island*. Norton, 1973. Dell, 1974.

Smith, S. *The Boy Who Was Thrown Away*. Atheneum, 1987.

Smith, W. J., ed. *A Green Place*. Delacorte, 1982.

Smucker, B. *Runaway to Freedom: A Story of the Underground Railroad*. Harper & Row, 1977. Harper Junior, 1979.

Sneve, V. D. H. *Betrayed*. Holiday House, 1974.

Snyder, H. *The Hall of the Mountain King*. Scribner's, 1973.

Snyder, Z. K. *Libby on Wednesday*. Delacorte, 1990.

Solzhenitsyn, A. *One Day in the Life of Ivan Denisovich*. E. P. Dutton, 1963. NAL/Signet Classic.

Sonnenmark, L. A. *Something's Rotten in the State of Maryland*. Scholastic, 1990.

Soto, G. *Baseball in April and Other Stories*. Harcourt Brace Jovanovich, 1990.

———. *Black Hair*. University of Pittsburgh Press, 1985. Distributed by Harper & Row.

———. *Taking Sides*. Harcourt Brace Jovanovich, 1991.

Southall, I. *Josh*. Macmillan, 1971.

Speare, E. *The Bronze Bow*. Houghton Mifflin, 1961.

———. *The Witch of Blackbird Pond*. Houghton Mifflin, 1958. Dell, 1975; Dell, 1978.

Spielberg, S. *Close Encounters of the Third Kind*. Delacorte, 1977. Dell, 1977.

Spinelli, J. *Maniac Magee*. Little, Brown, 1990. HarperCollins, 1990.

———. *Night of the Whale*. Little, Brown, 1985. Dell, 1986.

———. *Space Station Seventh Grade*. Dell, 1984.

———. *There's a Girl in My Hammerlock*. Simon & Schuster, 1991.

———. *Who Put That Hair in My Toothbrush?* Little, Brown, 1984.

Spolin, V. *Improvisation for the Theatre*. Northwestern University Press, 1963.

Stadler, B. *Holocaust: A History of Courage and Resistance*. Behrman House, 1974.

Staples, S. F. *Shabanu: Daughter of the Wind*. Knopf, 1989.

Stark, N. *The Formula Book*. Andrews & McMell, 1975, 1979. Avon, 1977.

Steinbeck, J. *Grapes of Wrath*. Viking, 1986.

———. *Of Mice and Men*. Viking, 1986.

———. *The Pearl*. Penguin, 1992.

Steptoe, J. *Marcia*. Viking, 1976.

Sterling, D. *Black Foremothers*. Feminist Press, 1979, 1988.

Sterling, P. *Sea and Earth: The Life of Rachel Carson*. Crowell, 1970. Dell, 1970.

Sternberg, P. *Speak to Me*. Lothrop, Lee & Shepherd, 1984.

Stewart, G. *Fire*. Ballantine, 1974.

Still, W. *The Underground Railroad*. Porter & Coats, 1872. Arno Press and the *New York Times,* 1968.

Stirling, N. *You Would If You Loved Me*. Evans, 1969. Avon, 1982.

Stoker, B. *Dracula*. NAL/Signet Classic, 1978.

Stolz, M. *The Edge of Next Year*. Harper & Row, 1974. Dell, 1979.

———. *Leap Before You Look*. Harper & Row, 1972. Dell, 1973.

———. *A Love, or a Season*. Harper & Row, 1964.

———. *Pray Love, Remember*. Harper & Row, 1954.

Stone, B. *Been Clever Forever*. Harper & Row, 1988.

———. *Half Nelson, Full Nelson*. Harper & Row, 1985.

Stone, I. *They Also Ran*. Pyramid, 1964. New American Library, 1968.

———. *Those Who Love*. Doubleday, 1965. New American Library, 1968.

Stoutenburg, A. *Out There*. Viking, 1971. Dell, 1971.

Stowe, H. B. *Uncle Tom's Cabin*. 1852. NAL/Signet Classic.

Strasser, T. *The Accident*. Delacorte, 1988.

———. *The Angel Dust Blues*. Coward, McCann & Geoghegan, 1979. Dell, 1981.

———. *Rock 'n' Roll Nights*. Delacorte, 1982.

———. *Turn It Up*. Dell, 1984.

———. *Wildlife*. Delacorte, 1987. Dell, 1987.

Stren, P. *I Was a Fifteen Year Old Blimp*. Harper & Row, 1985.

Strom, Y. *A Tree Still Stands: Jewish Youth in Eastern Europe Today*. Putnam, 1990.

Suhl, Y. *The Merrymaker*. Four Winds, 1975.

———. *On the Other Side of the Gate*. Franklin Watts, 1975. Schocken, 1975.

Suhl, Y., ed. *They Fought Back: The Story of the Jewish Resistance in Nazi Europe*. Schocken, 1975.

Sun Through Small Leaves: Poems of Spring. Illustrated by S. Ichikawa. Collins, 1980.

Sussman, A. *The Rights of Young People: An American Civil Liberties Union Handbook.* Avon, 1977.

Sutcliff, R. *Beowulf.* Dutton, 1962.

———. *Blood Feud.* Dutton, 1977.

———. *Blue Remembered Hills: A Collection.* Bodley Head, 1983.

———. *The Capricorn Bracelet.* Walck, 1973.

———. *The Eagle of the Ninth.* Walck, 1961.

———. *Knight's Fee.* Walck, 1961.

———. *The Lantern Bearers.* Walck, 1959.

———. *The Light Beyond the Forest: The Quest for the Holy Grail.* Dutton, 1979.

———. *The Mark of the Horse Lord.* Walck, 1965.

———. *Rider on a White Horse.* Conward, McCann & Geoghegan, 1959.

———. *The Road to Camlann: The Death of King Arthur.* Dutton, 1982.

———. *The Shining Company.* Farrar, Straus & Giroux, 1990.

———. *The Silver Branch.* Walck, 1958. Dell, 1966.

———. *Simon.* Oxford University Press, 1953.

———. *Song for a Dark Queen.* Crowell, 1979.

———. *The Sword and the Circle: King Arthur and the Knights of the Round Table.* (1981). Dutton, 1981.

———. *Sword at Sunset.* Coward, McCann & Geoghegan, 1963.

———. *Warrior Scarlet.* Walck, 1958.

Swarthout, G. *Bless the Beasts and the Children.* Doubleday, 1970. Pocket Books, 1973.

Sweeney, J. *Center Line.* Delacorte, 1984.

Swenson, M. *Poems to Solve.* Scribner's, 1966.

Swindells, R. *Brother in the Land.* Holiday House, 1985.

Swortzell, L., ed. *All the World's a Stage.* Delacorte, 1972.

Szabo, J., and A. Ziegler, eds. *Almost Grown: A Book of Photographs and Poems.* Harmony, 1978.

Talbert, M. *Dead Birds Singing.* Little, Brown, 1985. 1978.

———. *Pillow of Clouds.* Dial, 1991.

Tanenhaus, S. *Literature Unbound.* Doubleday, 1984. Ballantine, 1986.

Tapert, A. *Lines of Battle: Letters from American Servicemen.* Times Books, 1987.

Tarpert, A., ed. *The Brothers War: Civil War Letters to Their Loved Ones from the Blue and Gray.* Times Books, 1988.

Tate, E. *The Secret of Gumbo Grove.* Bantam, 1987.

Taylor, M. *Let the Circle Be Unbroken.* Dial, 1981.

———. *The Road to Memphis.* Dial, 1990.

———. *Roll of Thunder, Hear My Cry.* Dial, 1976. Bantam, 1978.

———. *Song of the Trees.* Dial, 1975. Bantam, 1978.

Taylor, T. *Battle in the Arctic Seas.* Crowell, 1976.

———. *The Cay.* Doubleday, 1969. Avon, 1970.

———. *The Friendship.* Dial, 1987.

———. *Timothy of the Cay.* Harcourt Brace Jovanovich, 1993.

———. *Walking Up a Rainbow.* Delacorte, 1986. Dell, 1988.

———. *The Weirdo.* Harcourt Brace Jovanovich, 1992.

Taylor, W. *Agnes the Sheep.* Scholastic, 1991.

Tchudi, S., and S. Tchudi. *The Young Writer's Handbook.* Scribner's, 1984.

Telemaque, E. W. *It's Crazy to Stay Chinese in Minnesota.* Nelson, 1978.

Ten Boom, C. with J. Sherrill and E. Sherrill. *The Hiding Place.* Bantam, 1984.

Terada, A. M. *Under the Starfruit Tree: Folktales from Vietnam.* University of Hawaii Press, 1989.

Terkel, S. *American Dreams: Lost and Found.* Pantheon, 1980.

———. *Working: People Talk about What They Do All Day and How They Feel about What They Do.* Pantheon, 1974. Penguin, 1985.

Terkel, S. N. *Should Drugs Be Legalized?* Franklin Watts, 1990.

Terrell, J. U., and D. M. Terrell. *Indian Women of the Western Morning: Their Life in Early America.* Dial, 1974. Anchor, 1976.

Terris, S. *Author! Author!* Farrar, 1990.

———. *Nell's Quilt.* Farrar, 1987.

Tevis, W. *Mockingbird.* Doubleday, 1980. Bantam, 1981.

Thomas, J. C. *The Golden Pasture.* Scholastic, 1988.

———. *Journey.* Scholastic, 1988.

———. *Marked by Fire.* Avon/Flare, 1982.

———. *Water Girl.* Avon, 1986.

Thomas, J. C., ed. *A Gathering of Flowers: Stories about Being Young in America.* Harper & Row, 1990.

Thomas, L. *The Lives of a Cell: Notes of a Biology Watcher.* Viking, 1974. Penguin, 1978.

———. *The Medusa and the Snail: More Notes of a Biology Watcher.* Viking, 1979. Bantam, 1980.

Thompson, J. E. *A Band of Angels.* Scholastic, 1986.

———. *Discontinued.* Scholastic, 1985.

———. *Gypsyworld.* Holt, 1992.

———. *Herb Seasoning.* Scholastic, 1990.

———. *Simon Pure.* Scholastic, 1987.

Thompson, T. *Richie*. Saturday Review Press, 1973. Dell, 1981.

Thurman, J., ed. *I Became Alone*. Atheneum, 1975.

Toffler, A. *Future Shock*. Random House, 1970. Bantam, 1971.

———. *The Third Wave*. Morrow, 1980. Bantam, 1981.

Tolan, S. S. *A Good Courage*. Morrow, 1988. Fawcett, 1989.

———. *The Plague Year*. Morrow, 1990.

———. *Pride of the Peacock*. Scribner's, 1986. Ballantine, 1987.

Tolkien, J. R. R. *The Fellowship of the Ring*. Allen & Unwin, 1954. Ballantine, 1965.

———. *The Lord of the Rings*. Allen, 1954.

———. *The Return of the King*. Allen & Unwin, 1954. Ballantine, 1965.

———. *The Two Towers*. Allen & Unwin, 1954. Ballantine, 1965.

Torchia, J. *The Kryptonite Kid*. Holt, Rinehart & Winston, 1980.

Townsend, J. R. *Good Night, Prof. Dear*. Lippincott, 1971.

———. *The Intruder*. Lippincott, 1970. Dell, 1977.

———. *Noah's Castle*. Lippincott, 1976. Dell, 1978.

———. *The Visitors*. Lippincott, 1977.

Townsend, S. *The Secret Diary of Adrian Mole, Aged 13-3/4*. Avon, 1987.

Trivers, J., and A. Davis. *I Can Stop Anytime I Want*. Prentice-Hall, 1974. Dell, 1977.

Trumbo, D. *Johnny Got His Gun*. Bantam, 1970.

Tunis, J. R. *His Enemy, His Friend*. Morrow, 1967. Avon, 1967.

Tunnel, M. O. *The Prydain Companion*. Greenwood Press, 1989.

Turner, A. *A Hunter Comes Home*. Crown, 1980.

———. *The Way Home*. Crown, 1982.

Ure, J. *What If They Saw Me Now?* Dell, 1985.

Uris, L. *Mila 18*. Bantam, 1970.

Valens, E. G. *The Other Side of the Mountain*. Warner Books, 1975.

Van Leeuwen, J. *I Was a Ninety-Eight Pound Duckling*. Dial, 1972. Dell, 1979.

Van Raven, P. *The Great Man's Secret*. Scribner's, 1989.

Verne, J. *Journey to the Center of the Earth*. Scholastic, 1973.

Vestal, S. *Jim Bridger, Mountain Man*. Morrow, 1946. University of Nebraska Press, 1970.

———. *The Missouri (1945)*. University of Nebraska Press, 1964.

Vogt, H. *The Burden of Guilt: A Short History of Germany, 1914–1945*. Oxford University Press, 1964.

Voigt, C. *Building Blocks*. Atheneum, 1984.

———. *The Callender Papers*. Atheneum, 1983. Ballantine, 1984.

———. *Dicey's Song*. Atheneum, 1982.

———. *Homecoming*. Atheneum, 1981. Fawcett Juniper, 1982.

———. *Izzy, Willy-Nilly*. Atheneum, 1986. Ballantine, 1987.

———. *On Fortune's Wheel*. Atheneum, 1990.

———. *The Runner*. Atheneum, 1985.

———. *Seventeen against the Dealer*. Atheneum, 1989.

———. *A Solitary Blue*. Atheneum, 1983.

———. *Sons from Afar*. Atheneum, 1987.

———. *Tree by Leaf*. Atheneum, 1988.

Volavkova, H., ed. *I Never Saw Another Butterfly*. McGraw-Hill, 1964.

Von Canon, C. *The Moonclock*. Houghton Mifflin, 1979.

Vonnegut, K. *Cat's Cradle*. Holt, Rinehart & Winston, 1963. Dell, 1979.

———. *Player Piano*. Scribner's, 1952. Avon, 1966.

———. *Welcome to the Monkey House*. Delacorte, 1974. Dell, 1970.

Wagner, R. *Sarah T.—Portrait of a Teenage Alcoholic*. Ballantine, 1975.

Walker, A. *The Color Purple*. Harcourt Brace Jovanovich, 1982. Washington Square Press, 1982.

Walker, M. P. *Because We Are*. Lothrop, Lee & Shepard, 1983.

Walker, P. R. *Pride of Puerto Rico: The Life of Roberto Clemente*. Harbrace, 1991.

Wallace, B. *Shadow on the Snow*. Holiday House, 1985.

Wallace, D. R. *The Dark Range: A Naturalist's Night Notebook*. Sierra Club, 1978.

———. *Idle Weeds: The Life of a Sandstone Ridge*. Sierra Club, 1980.

Walsh, J. P. *A Parcel of Patterns*. Farrar, Straus & Giroux, 1983.

Walton, B. *Harpoon Gunner*. Crowell, 1968.

Walton, D. *A Rockwell Portrait: An Intimate Biography*. Andrews & McMell, 1978. Bantam, 1979.

Wangerin, W. *The Book of the Dun Cow*. Harper & Row, 1978. Pocket Books, 1979.

Warburton, L. *Rainforests*. Lucent, 1991.

Ward, H. M., ed. *Poems for Pleasure*. Hill & Wang, 1978.

Wardlaw, L. *Corey's Fire*. Avon, 1990.

Warner, W. W. *Beautiful Swimmers*. Little, Brown, 1976. Avon, 1981.

Warren, R. P. *All the King's Men*. Harcourt, Brace & World, 1946.

Waters, F. *The Man Who Killed the Deer*. Farrar & Rinehart, 1942. Pocket Books, 1971.

Watson, J. *Talking in Whispers*. Knopf, 1983.

Waugh, E. *The Loved One*. Dell, 1948, 1966.

Webb, S., and R. W. Nelson. *Selma, Lord, Selma: Girlhood Memories of the Civil Rights Days*. University of Alabama Press, 1980. Morrow, 1980.

Weingast, D. E. *We Elect a President*. Messner, 1977.

Weiss, H. S., and M. J. Weiss, eds. *The American Way of Laughing*. Bantam, 1977.

Weld, T. *American Slavery As It Is: Testimony of a Thousand Witnesses*. 1839. Ayer, 1991.

Wells, H. G. *The Island of Doctor Moreau*. NAL/Signet Classic, 1977.

Wells, R. *The Man in the Woods*. Dial, 1984.

———. *Through the Hidden Door*. Dial, 1987. Scholastic, 1987.

———. *When No One Was Looking*. Dial, 1980. Fawcett, 1981.

Wersba, B. *The Farewell Kid*. Harper & Row, 1990.

———. *Run Softly, Go Fast*. Atheneum, 1970. Bantam, 1972.

———. *Tunes for a Small Harmonica*. Harper & Row, 1976. Dell, 1976.

———. *Wonderful Me*. Harper & Row, 1989.

West, J. *Except for Thee and Me*. Harcourt, Brace & World, 1969. Avon, 1969.

———. *The Massacre at Fall Creek*. Harcourt Brace Jovanovich, 1975. Fawcett, 1976.

Westall, R. *Blitzcat*. Scholastic, 1989.

———. *Break of Dark*. Greenwillow, 1982.

———. *The Cats of Seroster*. Greenwillow, 1984.

———. *Echoes of War*. Farrar, Straus & Giroux, 1991.

———. *Fathom Five*. Greenwillow, 1979. Knopf, 1990.

———. *Futuretrack 5*. Greenwillow, 1983.

———. *The Machine Gunners*. Greenwillow, 1976.

———. *Urn Burial*. Greenwillow, 1987.

Wetanson, B., and T. Hoobler. *The Hunters*. Doubleday, 1978.

Wetherby, T., ed. *Conversations: Working Women Talk about Doing a "Man's Job"*. Les Femmes, 1977.

Wharton, E. *Ethan Frome*. Scribner's, 1911. Penguin, 1987.

Wheeler, M. *Lies, Damn Lies, and Statistics: The Manipulation of Public Opinion in America*. Liveright, 1976. Dell, 1977.

White, E. E. *Life without Friends*. Scholastic, 1987.

White, R. *Deathwatch*. Doubleday, 1972. Dell, 1973.

White, T. *Breach of Faith: The Fall of Richard Nixon*. Atheneum, 1975. Dell, 1976.

White, T. H. *The Sword in the Stone*. Collins, 1938. Berkley, 1966.

Wibberley, L. *Encounter near Venus*. Farrar, Straus & Giroux, 1967.

Wier, E. *The Loner*. McKay, 1963. Scholastic, 1973.

Wiesel, E. *The Gates of the Forest*. Holt, Rinehart & Winston, 1966. Schocken, 1982.

———. *Night, Dawn, the Accident: Three Tales*. Hill & Wang, 1972. Avon, 1972.

Wigginton, E., ed. *Foxfire*. Doubleday, 1972.

———. *Sometimes a Shining Moment: The Foxfire Experience*. Anchor Press, Doubleday, 1985.

Wilde, O. *The Picture of Dorian Gray*. NAL/Signet Classic, 1962.

Wilder, L. I. The Little House Books. 9 vols. Harper & Row, 1971.

Wilhelm, M. *For the Glory of France: The Story of the French Resistance*. Messner, 1968.

Wilkinson, Brenda. *Ludell*. Harper & Row, 1975. Bantam, 1980.

———. *Ludell and Willie*. Harper & Row, 1977. Bantam, 1981.

———. *Ludell's New York Time*. Harper & Row, 1980.

Wilkinson, Burke, ed. *Cry Sabotage! True Stories of Twentieth-Century Saboteurs*. Bradbury, 1972. Dell, 1975.

Willard, N. *A Visit to William Blake's Inn: Poems for Innocent and Experienced Travelers*. Harcourt Brace Jovanovich, 1981.

Willey, M. *The Bigger Book of Lydia*. Harper & Row, 1983.

———. *Finding David Delores*. Harper & Row, 1986.

———. *If Not for You*. Harper & Row, 1988.

Williams, Jay. *The Hero from Otherwhere*. Walck, 1972. Dell, 1973.

Williams, Juan. *Eyes on the Prize: America's Civil Rights Years, 1954–1965*. Viking, 1987.

Williams-Garcia R. *Blue Tights*. Bantam, 1989.

Williamson, J. *The Humanoids*. Lancer, 1949. Avon, 1975.

Wilson, E. *American Painter in Paris: The Life of Mary Cassatt*. Farrar, Straus & Giroux, 1971.

Windsor, P. *The Christmas Killer*. Scholastic, 1991.

———. *Diving for Roses*. Harper & Row, 1974.

———. *Something's Waiting for You, Baker D*. Harper & Row, 1974.

————. *The Summer Before*. Harper & Row, 1973. Dell, 1973.

Winthrop, E. *A Little Demonstration of Affection*. Harper & Row, 1975. Dell, 1977.

Wirths, C. G., and M. Bowman-Kruhm. *I Hate School: How to Hang in and When to Drop Out*. Crowell, 1986.

Wister, O. *The Virginian: A Horseman of the Plains*. New American Library, 1979.

Wojciechowska, M. *Don't Play Dead before You Have To*. Harper & Row, 1970.

————. *Shadow of a Bull*. Atheneum, 1964.

————. *A Single Light*. Harper & Row, 1968. Bantam, 1971.

————. *Till the Break of Day*. Harcourt Brace/Jovanovich, 1972.

————. *Tuned Out*. Harper & Row, 1969. Bantam, 1971.

Wolfe, T. *The Right Stuff*. Farrar, Straus & Giroux, 1979. Bantam, 1980.

Wolitzer, H. *Toby Lived Here*. Farrar, Straus & Giroux, 1978. Bantam, 1980.

Wolverton, L. *Running before the Wind*. Houghton Mifflin, 1987.

Wong, J. S. *Fifth Chinese Daughter*. Harper & Row, 1950.

Wood, G. A. *Catch a Killer*. Harper & Row, 1972. Dell, 1973.

Woodson, J. *The Dear One*. Delacorte, 1991.

Woolger, D., ed. *Who Do You Think You Are? Poems about People*. Oxford University Press, 1990.

Wouk, H. *The Caine Mutiny*. Doubleday, 1951. Dell, 1965.

Wright, J. W. *The American Almanac of Jobs and Salaries*. Avon, 1982.

Wrightson, P. *Down to Earth*. Harcourt Brace Jovanovich, 1965.

————. *The Ice Is Coming*. Atheneum, 1977.

————. *A Little Fear*. Atheneum, 1983.

Yates, E. *Amos Fortune, Free Man*. Dutton, 1950, 1968.

Yee, P. *Tales from Gold Mountain: Stories of the Chinese in the New World*. Macmillan, 1989.

Yep, L. *Child of the Owl*. Harper & Row, 1977.

————. *Dragon Cauldron*. HarperCollins, 1991.

————. *Dragon of the Lost Sea*. Harper & Row, 1982.

————. *Dragon Steel*. Harper & Row, 1985.

————. *Dragonwings*. Harper & Row, 1975.

————. *Liar, Liar*. Morrow, 1983.

————. *The Lost Garden*. Messner, 1991.

————. *Monster Makers, Inc.* Arbor House, 1986. New American Library, 1987.

————. *Mountain Light*. Harper & Row, 1985.

————. *The Rainbow People*. HarperCollins, 1989.

————. *The Serpent's Children*. Harper & Row, 1984.

————. *The Star Fisher*. Morrow, 1991.

Yglesias, R. *The Game Player*. Doubleday, 1978.

Yolen, J. *Dragon's Blood*. Delacorte, 1982. Dell, 1984.

————. *Heart's Blood*. Delacorte, 1984. Dell, 1986.

————. *A Sending of Dragons*. Delacorte, 1987. Dell, 1989.

Yolen, J., ed. *2041: Twelve Stories about the Future by Top Science Fiction Writers*. Delacorte, 1991.

Yolen, J., and M. H. Greenberg, eds. *Things That Go Bump in the Night: A Collection of Original Stories*. Harper & Row,   .

York, C. B. *Nothing Ever Happens Here*. Hawthorn, 1970. New American Library, 1975.

Zassenhaus, H. *Walls: Resisting the Third Reich—One Woman's Story*. Beacon Press, 1974.

Zelazny, R. *The Guns of Avalon*. Doubleday, 1972. Avon, 1974.

————. *The Hand of Oberon*. Doubleday, 1976. Avon, 1977.

————. *Nine Princes in Amber*. Doubleday, 1970. Avon, 1973.

————. *Sign of the Unicorn*. Doubleday, 1975. Avon, 1976.

Ziemian, Joseph. *The Cigarette Sellers of Three Crosses Square*. Lerner, 1975.

Zimmer, P. *Family Reunion: Selected and New Poems*. University of Pittsburgh Press, 1983. Distributed by Harper & Row.

Zindel, P. *The Amazing and Death-Defying Diary of Eugene Dingman*. Harper, 1987.

————. *A Begonia for Miss Applebaum*. Harper & Row, 1989.

————. *Confessions of a Teenage Baboon*. Harper & Row, 1977.

————. *My Darling, My Hamburger*. Harper & Row, 1969. Bantam, 1971.

————. *The Effect of Gamma Rays on Man-in-the-Moon Marigolds*. Harper & Row, 1971.

————. *Harry and Hortense at Hormone High*. Harper & Row, 1984.

————. *Pardon Me, You're Stepping on My Eyeball*. Harper & Row, 1976. Bantam, 1977.

————. *The Pigman*. Harper & Row, 1968. Bantam, 1978.

————. *The Pigman's Legacy*. Harper & Row, 1980. Bantam, 1981.

————. *The Undertaker's Gone Bananas*. Harper & Row, 1978. Bantam, 1979.

Zindel, B., and P. Zindel. *A Star for the Latecomer*. Harper & Row, 1988.

Zolotow, C. *Early Sorrow*. Harper & Row, 1986.

CREDITS

Chapter 1   p. 12—Reprinted by permission of Nancie Atwell: *In the Middle: Writing, Reading, and Learning with Adolescents* (Boynton/Cook Publishers, Portsmouth, NH, 1987). p. 13—Dan Jackson, "Books in the Bronx: A Personal Look at How Literature Shapes Our Lives," *Media and Methods,* March 1980. Copyright 1980 by the American Library Association. Reprinted with permission. p. 14—Margaret Early, "Stages of Growth in Literary Appreciation," *English Journal,* March 1960. Copyright 1960 by the National Council of Teachers of English. Reprinted with permission. p. 15—Daniel Fader and Elton McNeil, *Hooked on Books: Program and Proof.* Reprinted with permission. p. 19—Lance M. Gentile and Merna M. McMillan, "Why Won't Teenagers Read?" *Journal of Reading,* May 1977. Copyright 1977 by the International Reading Association. Reprinted with permission.

Chapter 2   p. 30—Reprinted by permission of Nancie Atwell: *In the Middle: Writing, Reading, and Learning with Adolescents* (Boynton/Cook Publishers, Portsmouth, NH, 1987). p. 38—J. W. Halsted, *Guiding Gifted Readers: From Preschool to High School.* Copyright 1988 by Ohio Psychology Press. Reprinted with permission. p. 35—Katherine Paterson, *Gates of Excellence: On Reading and Writing Books for Children.* Copyright 1981 by Elsevier/Nelson. Reprinted with permission of Penguin USA.

Chapter 3   p. 50—Sandy Asher, "The Problem with Realism," *ALAN Review,* Spring 1985. Reprinted with permission of the author. pp. 62–63—Michael Angelotti, "Zindel on Writing and the Writing Process," *ALAN Review,* Fall 1991. Reprinted with permission of the author. p. 76—Norma Fox Mazer, "After the Rain" *ALAN Review,* Fall 1991. Reprinted with permission of the author.

Chapter 4   p. 97—"Robert Newton Peck: Soup's Best Pal," in *Something about the Author,* ed. A. Sarkissian. Copyright 1986. Reprinted with permission of the author. pp. 101–102—Robert Lipsyte, *The Contender.* Reprinted with permission. pp. 107–108—Susan P. Bloom and Cathryn M. Mercier, *Presenting Zibby Oneal.* Copyright 1991 © by G. K. Hall & Co. Reprinted with permission of Macmillan Publishing Company.

Chapter 5   pp. 120–121—Christopher Collier, "Fact, Fiction and History: The Role of Historian, Writer and Teacher," *ALAN Review,* Winter 1987. Reprinted with permission of the author. p. 135—Patricia Ann Romero and Don Zancanella, "Expanding the Circle: Hispanic Voices in American Literature," *English Journal,* January 1990. Copyright 1990 by the National Council of Teachers of English. Reprinted with permission. p. 137—Virginia Hamilton, "The Spirit Spins: A Writer's Resolution," *ALAN Review,* Fall 1987. Reprinted with permission. pp. 145–146—Sue Ellen Bridgers, "Stories My Grandmother Told Me: Part One," *ALAN Review,* Fall 1985. Reprinted with permission of the author.

Chapter 6   p. 156—Marijane Meaker, "Getting All Kids to Read My Books," *ALAN review,* Fall 1989. Reprinted with permission of the author. pp. 161–163—From *Killing Mr. Griffin* by Lois Duncan. Copyright © 1978 by Lois Duncan. By permission of Little, Brown, and Company.

Chapter 7   pp. 179–180—Madeleine L'Engle, "Understanding the Universe," *ALAN Review,* Winter 1988. Reprinted with permission. pp. 194–195—excerpts from *Two-Part Invention* by Madeleine L'Engle. Copyright © 1988 by Crosswicks Ltd. Reprinted by permission of Farrar, Straus & Giroux, Inc.

Chapter 8   pp. 208–209—From Frank Sloan, "Publishing Nonfiction for the Classroom," *CBC Features,* July–December, 1991, © The Children's Book Council. Reprinted with

Author and Title Index

Subject Index

About the Author

Arthea J. S. Reed is called Charlie by her students, family, and friends. She lives in Asheville, North Carolina, in the beautiful Blue Ridge Mountains with Donald, her husband, and two dogs. She has traveled widely and is most recently pursuing research on a comparative study of literature-based curriculum in New Zealand and the United States.

Charlie has taught at the University of North Carolina at Asheville for fifteen years. She is currently a professor and the chair of the Education Department in this public liberal arts university. She is the author of two books in the field of young adult literature: *Reaching Adolescents: The Young Adult Book and the School* and *Comics to Classics: A Parents' Guide to Books for Teens and Preteens.* She was editor of *The ALAN Review,* one of the most highly regarded and recognized journals in the field of young adult literature, for six years. She is the co-editor of the Penguin/Signet Classic teachers' guide series in which authors include young adult books to use as bridges to the classical works. She has taught courses in adolescent literature to pre-service teachers, in-service teachers, librarians, and parents for more than fifteen years. She lectures widely in the field of young adult literature and on the topic of censorship.

With her co-author Verna E. Bergemann, Charlie has recently published two textbooks designed for foundations or introduction to education courses. *In the Classroom: An Introduction to Education* and *Observation and Participation in the Classroom* were both published in 1992.

Charlie is also the current chair of the National Council of Teachers of English eighth grade Promising Young Writers competition. She has served on numerous local and state commissions dealing with issues related to children and to education and has published articles in a variety of journals.

Personal Remarks

As many of you know, *Reaching Adolescents: The Young Adult Book and the School* is now in its second edition. I have been teaching adolescent literature classes to pre-service and in-service teachers, librarians, and parents for more than fifteen years. More than ever I am convinced of the importance of young adult literature in the classroom. The low level of literacy of many students suggests that using what is known about how reading appreciation and ability develop is critical if we hope to convince teenagers to continue reading and become literate adults. The vast amount of research done in recent decades by such scholars as Louise Rosenblatt and teachers such as Nancie Atwell proves that in order to hook students on reading and writing we must provide them with reading materials to which they can respond.

In the first edition of this text, I included a brief autobiographical sketch of how I discovered young adult literature. I'd like to include this confession in the second edition as well.

The book (the title of which has gone through many mutations; my favorite still remains "Are You There, God? It's Me, Margaret's Teacher") was first conceived in 1968, when I was an ill-prepared first-year English teacher of high school sophomores. The young adults I was assigned to teach did not fit my middle-class image of fifteen-year-olds. They appeared to me to be undisciplined, unmotivated, uninterested (and uninteresting), and altogether illiterate. I suffered through six months of attempting to force into their heads the material in the literature anthology. At every turn they outwitted me. They lost their books or left them in their lockers. They became deathly ill during class and had to flee to the restroom. They argued with their classmates and with me. They slept through my oral readings. They flung spitwads at classmates who attempted to answer questions. The coup de grace was one of my all-time favorite literary works, Shakespeare's *Romeo and Juliet*. They mocked me, my love of literature, and the Bard; they stole my class notes.

I went home to my husband in tears. I needed a new plan of attack, as I perceived it. I spent the evening inventing "appropriate" punishments: ten points off the final grade for uttering an unsolicited remark, detention for an incomplete paper, a phone call to parents each time a grade lower than 75 was recorded on a quiz, and other similar acts of retribution. Donald, by partner of six months of wedded less-than-bliss (these unthankful teenagers were destroying my marriage), wiped my tears and listened to me as I prepared my onslaught.

By 10:00 P.M. I had prepared by purple encyclical, to be duplicated and given unceremoniously to my students the next day. I read it aloud with great expression. When I had finished, I asked my husband, "Well, what do you think of that? That should work, shouldn't it?" (I really didn't want him to answer.).

Donald walked over to me, put his arm around my shoulder, and said, "Yes, no doubt it will have some effect. It will do two things for sure: make them hate you and hate to read. You're too kind and care too much about kids and about books to carry that off, Charlie."

I started to cry. But through my tears and a night without sleep came a new birth. I threw away my purple prose and decided to go into the classroom with my defenses down and, for the first time, really listen to my students. The next day, as the students entered the room—expecting to find a raving maniac, no doubt—they found instead the real me, perched on top of my desk. Without a lesson plan, I began, "Well, you've convinced me; you hate English. I'm a slow learner, but now I'm convinced. I don't understand why and I'd like to find out."

And find out I did. At first the students were hesitant to talk, as they had every right to be. But when they opened up, they talked nonstop for a week. I learned how books, school, and teachers had become their enemies. Together we began to plan a new approach. Through my students I learned about books written for young adults. One of the students, who worked in a book distribution center, brought me a copy of a new book by S. E. Hinton, *The Outsiders*. (I think he stole it, but I didn't dare ask.) I read the book with great enthusiasm. The next day he queried, "Did you like it? Did you know that S. E. Hinton's person's only sixteen? Could we read it in class?"

I didn't have any other copies of the book, but there was no reason I could not read it aloud. And so began my love of young adult literature. Those kids in my class did have sparkling eyes—I glimpsed them as I read. The depth of their understanding was remarkable. I was having a wonderful time; this was the way teaching was supposed to be. My students were so enthusiastic, in fact, that they were asking for more books.

But alas, my euphoria did not last, because I realized that I was not teaching what I was expected to teach. I decided not to scrap my new English program, but to seek ways to add the skills and concepts of the English classroom to the motivational reading program. I posed the problem to the students, explaining that their parents, the school, and the community expected them to learn certain things in the English class. They protested that they had not learned anything before. "What are we supposed to learn, anyway?" I decided to give each one a copy of the state's guidelines for sophomore English. With the help of these students I began to develop a curriculum that included all aspects of English required in secondary school classrooms, and much more. The curriculum included books, books, and more books.

That summer I made a commitment to read two young adult books per week, a commitment I have kept through the years. Since 1968 I have taught in two public school systems, one urban and one rural. I have taught English, journalism, history, and a year-long course in the humanities. I have acted as a director of instruction for a county school system and a supervisor of student teachers. In these positions I have observed thousands of teachers of young adults. This book is a compilation of what I have observed and discovered through experience and observation. My first class of students taught me to teach. They taught me the value of beginning instruction with the student. Since that time I have gained significant data to support what a group of incredibly intelligent fifteen-year-olds already knew.

ISBN 0-02-398861-4

90000>